Human Rights in Western Civilization:
1600 to the Present

Second Edition

Editors

John A. Maxwell
Department of History
West Virginia University

James J. Friedberg
College of Law
West Virginia University

Associate Editor

Deirdre A. DeGolia

Copyright © 1994 by Kendall/Hunt Publishing Company

ISBN 0-8403-9243-5

All rights reserved. No part of this publication may be reproduced, stored in a retrieval system, or transmitted, in any form or by any means, electronic, mechanical, photocopying, recording, or otherwise, without the written permission of the copyright owner.

Printed in the United States of America
10 9 8 7 6 5 4 3 2 1

Table of Contents

Preface vii

Introduction ix

Historical Introduction 1

Section 1—1600–1815 15

Chapter 1—Power: Its Origin and Use 17

Document 1: Address to Parliament (1609), James I 17
Document 2: Second Treatise of Civil Government (1690), John Locke 17
Document 3: The Social Contract (1762), Jean-Jacques Rousseau 20
Document 4: The American Declaration of Independence (1776), Thomas Jefferson 22
Document 5: Reflections on the Revolution in France (1790), Edmund Burke 23

Chapter 2—Individual Rights: Declarations of Rights in England, America, France 25

Document 6: Magna Carta (1215) 25
Document 7: The Rights of Man (1792), Thomas Paine 27
Document 8: The English Bill of Rights (1689) 28
Document 9: The United States Bill of Rights (1791) 28
Document 10: The Declaration of the Rights of Man and the Citizen (1789) 29

Chapter 3—Forgotten Individuals 33

Document 11: On the Indians (1696 edition), Franciscus de Vittoria 33
Document 12: Letter from Abigail Adams to Her Husband, John Adams (1776) 33
Document 13: Declaration of the Rights of Woman and the Female Citizen (1791),
    Olympe de Gouges 34
Document 14: A Dialogue Concerning the Slavery of the African (1776), Samuel Hopkins 36

Chapter 4—Intellectual and Religious Freedom 39

Document 15: The Sentence of Galileo by the Inquisitors General (1633) and his Recantation 39
Document 16: Aeropagitica (1644), John Milton 40
Document 17: What Is Enlightenment? (1784), Immanuel Kant 42
Document 18: A Bill For Establishing Religious Freedom (1785), Thomas Jefferson 44

Section II—1815–1900 47

Chapter 5—Political Participation and Individual Rights 49

Document 19: An Introduction to the Principles of Morals and Legislation (1796)
    Jeremy Bentham 49
Document 20: Rights, Liberty and Social Reform (1847), Louis Blanc 51
Document 21: Of The Limits of the Authority of Society Over the Individual (1859),
    John Stuart Mill 52
Document 22: Concerning Universal Suffrage and Concerning Proportional Representation of
Minorities (1873), Louis Blanc 52
Document 23: The Great Reform (1831), Lord John Russell 53
Document 24: The People's Charter (1838), William Lovett 54
Document 25: The Emancipation of Women (1851), Harriet Taylor Mill 55
Document 26: Married Women and the Law (1854), Barbara Leigh Smith Bodichon 57
Document 27: Reminiscences of the Akron Convention (1848), Frances D. Gage 58
Document 28: The Emancipation Proclamation (1862), Abraham Lincoln 59

Document 29: The Abolition of Russian Serfdom (1861), Alexander II	60
Document 30: I Accuse (1898), Émile Zola	63
Document 31: The Jewish State (1896), Theodore Herzl	64
Document 32: Blood and Iron, Otto von Bismarck	67
Document 33: On Administering the Oath to the Recruits (1897), Wilhelm II	68
Document 34: Letter Sent to Alexander III By the Executive Committee (1881)	69

Chapter 6—Economic Development and Individual Rights 73

Document 35: The Wealth of Nations (1776), Adam Smith	73
Document 36: Rules for Workers in the Factory of Benck and Company in Bühl (Alsace) (1842)	76
Document 37: Social Statics (1850), Herbert Spencer	77
Document 38: Manifesto of the Equals (1796), Francois Babeuf	78
Document 39: The Communist Manifesto (1848), Karl Marx and Friedrich Engels	80
Document 40: What Is Property? (1840), Pierre Joseph Proudhon	82
Document 41: Socialism and the Worker (1907), Kier Hardie	82
Document 42: Woman in Socialism (1910), August Bebel	86

Chapter 7—Nationalism, Empires and Individualism 93

Document 43: What Is the Fatherland?, Voltaire	93
Document 44: Emancipate Your Colonies! (1793), Jeremy Bentham	94
Document 45: The Monroe Doctrine (1823), James Monroe	97
Document 46: The Expansion of England (1888), J.R. Seeley	98
Document 47: How German East Africa Was Created (1890), Carl Peters	99
Document 48: The Meaning of Race (1904), Houston Stewart Chamberlain	100
Document 49: The White Man's Burden (1899), Rudyard Kipling	101
Document 50: The Chinese Situation and the Mailed Fist (1897), Wilhelm II	101
Document 51: The Great Famine (1845–1855), Kerby A. Miller	102
Document 52: The Demand for Catholic Emancipation (1830), Daniel O'Connell	105
Document 53: Do Not Ask Us to Give Up the Buffalo for the Sheep (1867), Ten Bears.	106
Document 54: The Balfour Declaration (1917), Arthur J. Balfour	107
Document 55: On the Duties of Man (1848), Giuseppe Mazzini	107

Section III—1900–1945 111

Chapter 8—International Affairs, World War and Individual Rights 115

Document 56: Hague Convention with Respect to the Laws and Customs of War on Land (1899)	115
Document 57: Thoughts for the Times on War and Death (1915), Sigmund Freud	117
Document 58: Defense of the Realm Act (DORA)(1915)	120
Document 59: The Fourteen Points (1918), Woodrow Wilson	120
Document 60: The Covenant of the League of Nations (1919)	122
Document 61: Rumanian Minority Treaty	125
Document 62: The Geneva Protocol	127
Document 63: Kellogg-Briand Pact (1929)	128
Document 64: The Anti-French Resistance (1921–1926), Ho Chi Minh	128
Document 65: Appeal to America (1931), Mahatma Gandhi	129
Document 66: The Atlantic Conference (1941), Franklin D. Roosevelt	130

Chapter 9—Human Rights and Human Needs 133

Document 67: The Fight for the Vote, Militant Suffragism in England (1914)	133
Document 68: Birth Control: A Parents' Problem or a Woman's? (1920), Margaret Sanger	133
Document 69: Children's Work (1922)	135
Document 70: Report on the Sharecropper Demonstrations (1939), Aubrey Williams	136

Document 71: Why Should We March? (1942), A. Philip Randolph	138
Document 72: "Four Freedoms" Speech (1941), Franklin D. Roosevelt	140
Chapter 10—The Soviet Challenge	143
Document 73: Petition to the Tsar (1905), Father Gapon	143
Document 74: Imperialism: The Highest Stage of Capitalism (1916), V.I. Lenin	144
Document 75: Declaration of the Rights of the Russian Peoples (1917), Pravda	145
Document 76: The Five-Year Plan (1933), Joseph Stalin	146
Document 77: Article 58 of the Criminal Code of the R.S.F.S.R.(1934)	148
Document 78: The Great Purge Trial (1938), The Trial of N.I. Bukharin	149
Chapter 11—The Fascist Assault on Human Rights	153
Document 79: Mein Kampf (1925), Adolf Hitler	153
Document 80: The Political and Social Doctrine of Fascism (1935), Benito Mussolini	154
Document 81: The Common Interest Before Self Interest: Nazi Values	156
Document 82: The Nuremberg Laws (1935)	158
Document 83: The Poisonous Mushroom (1938), Ernst Heimer	158
Document 84: Unnecessary Sentiment (1943), Heinrich Himmler	159
Document 85: First Night in Auschwitz (1943), Elie Wiesel	160
Section IV—1945 to the Present	163
Chapter 12—Post-War Internationalization of Human Rights	165
Document 86: Crimes Coming Within the Jurisdiction of the International Military Tribunal (Nuremberg) (1945)	165
Document 87: Charter of the United Nations (1945)	165
Document 88: Convention on the Prevention and Punishment of the Crime of Genocide (1948)	167
Document 89: Universal Declaration of Human Rights (1948)	168
Document 90: The Geneva Conventions of 1949	171
Document 91: United Nations Covenant on Civil and Political Rights (1966)	180
Document 92: Optional Protocol to the U.N. Covenant on Civil and Political Rights (1966)	186
Document 93: United Nations Covenant on Economic, Social and Cultural Rights (1966)	186
Document 94: European Convention on Human Rights (1953)	190
Document 95: International Convention on the Elimination of All Forms of Racial Discrimination (1965)	193
Document 96: Convention Against Torture and Other Cruel, Inhuman or Degrading Treatment or Punishment (1984)	196
Chapter 13—National Challenges and Challenges to Nationalism	199
Document 97: For All Mankind (1945), Leon Blum	199
Document 98: Ideas That Have Harmed Mankind (1950), Bertrand Russell	199
Document 99: Report on the Tripartite Conference of Berlin (The Potsdam Protocol) (1945)	200
Document 100: Civil Rights Act of 1964	203
Document 101: Pastoral Letter on War and Peace (1983), U.S. Catholic Bishops	206
Document 102: Israel's Proclamation of Independence (1948)	210
Document 103: Declaration of the Palestinian State (1988)	211
Document 104: Statement on Israel and Terrorism (1988), Yasir Arafat	213
Document 105: Declaration of Independence of the Democratic Republic of Vietnam (1945), Ho Chi Minh	214
Chapter 14—Contemporary Problems of Human Rights	217
Document 106: Myth and Reality (1952), Simone de Beauvoir	217
Document 107: Equal Rights Amendment (1972)	218

Document 108: Roe v. Wade (1973)	218
Document 109: Torturing Children (1976), Alicia B. Morales de Galamba	224
Document 110: Torture and Kidnapping (1978), Norberto Liwsky	225
Document 111: The Last Sermon (1980), Bishop Oscar Romero	227
Document 112: Salvador's Grievous Loss (1993), Mark O. Hatfield	229
Document 113: I Have a Dream (1963), Martin Luther King, Jr.	231
Document 114: Letter From Birmingham Jail (1963), Martin Luther King, Jr.	233
Document 115: Nobel Lecture on Acceptance of the Nobel Peace Prize (1984), Bishop Desmond Mpilo Tutu	239
Document 116: Apartheid Has No Future, Africa is Ours (1990), Nelson Mandela	243
Document 117: Independence Day Address (1963), Jomo Kenyatta	245
Document 118: Multi-Party Debate: Kenya Needs A Strong Opposition (1990)	246
Document 119: Famine in Somalia (1992), Jane Perlez	248
Document 120: African Charter on Human and People's Rights (1981)	249
Document 121: Khrushchev's Secret Speech (1956), Nikita Khrushchev	253
Document 122: Peace, Progress, and Human Rights: The Nobel Prize Lecture (1975), Andrei Sakharov	259
Document 123: A Free Press in the Soviet Union (1988), Mikhail S. Gorbachev	267
Document 124: A State of Emergency: All Power Transferred to the State Committee (1991), Gennadi Yanayev	268
Document 125: The Gravest Crisis: To Restore Law and Order (1991), Gennadi Yanayev	268
Document 126: A Bold Faced and Unprecedented Coup D'État (1991), Boris Yeltsin	270
Chapter 15—New Problems and New Rights	273
Document 127: Keeping Our Balance in the 90s: Women at Work, Women at Home (1990), Rosalyn Wiggins Berne	273
Document 128: The Recommendations of the National Commission on Children (1991), John D. Rockefeller IV	278
Document 129: The Second Epidemic—Violence Against Lesbians and Gay Men (1990)	282
Document 130: God is not a Homophobe (1993), James A. Michener	283
Document 131: The Rights of the Environment (1976–1991)	284
Document 132: Americans With Disabilities Act (1990)	286
Document 133: Manifesto of Charter 77 (1977)	289
Document 134: Intellectual Dissent (1985), Fang Lizhi	292
Document 135: Poland—Solidarity and Freedom (1989), Lech Walesa	293
Document 136: How the Wall was Cracked (1989), Whitney, Binder, and Schmemann	295
Document 137: Social Reforms in Russia: A Plea to Pass the Freedom Support Act (1992) Boris Yeltsin	299
Document 138: Haiti: Human Rights Violations in the Month of February 1992	303
Document 139: A Wound to the Soul (1993), Amnesty International	304
Document 140: Women Under the Gun (1993), Amnesty International	305
Document 141: Ethnic Cleansing (1992), Watson, Waller, Warner, Nordland, and Breslau	306

Preface

This volume resulted from efforts to improve the teaching of History at the introductory college level. It originated in a search for documents which students could use to come to grips with some of the great human problems in the past four centuries that contribute to our modern concern for human rights.

West Virginia University's education reform project, funded by the Claude Worthington Benedum Foundation, helped to support the research for this volume. The project addresses goals of the Holmes group Consortium for improving the preparation of teachers, goals which this volume is intended to further in the study of Western Civilization. Professor Perry Phillips and Assistant to the Dean Dr. Kathy Lovell of the College of Human Resources and Education at West Virginia University supported this work at every stage.

This selection of documents expanded into a multi-disciplinary effort as it was realized that good documentary collections were not available for the use of Political Science and Law classes that deal with human rights. The West Virginia College of Law assisted with support for Professor Friedberg's introductory essay and his collaboration in selecting and editing international documents concerning human rights.

This volume was a group effort of the editors and associate editor. Michael Slaven assisted in the first edition of this book with vital help in selecting, translating, editing and introducing many documents. Technical assistance was rendered for the first edition by Kristina Slaven Olson and Stella Schultz. Mary Heironimus did much proofreading for the second edition. Sherry Fox was a great help in formatting and printing the text.

Profits from the sale of this book accrue to the West Virginia Department of History's Rebecca Donnally and Henry Everett Thornburg Scholarship for graduate students.

Introduction

The editors of this volume have designed it to complement the general study of Western Civilization or Modern European History by furnishing students the opportunity to make a more detailed inquiry into one of the most critical areas of modern life, human rights. In addition, it has been developed for the needs of students of political science and law who wish to study international law and human rights within a solid historical framework.

The introductory essay, "An Historical and Critical Introduction to Human Rights" provides a background to Western thought that underlies our concepts of human rights in different historical periods. The student can thus follow this major theme through time and understand it more fully within political, social and economic contexts. The closely related development of international law is also traced as people have tried to limit the consequences of the unchecked sovereignty of modern nation-states. The enormous abuses of human rights in the Twentieth Century led to the post-World War II internationalization of human rights through the United Nations, regional understandings, and the developing consensus around the world for the expansion of these rights. Human rights are thus well articulated in international agreements since 1945. The violation of these rights, however, remains a matter of grave concern. Around the world, public and private organizations monitor and investigate, report and condemn those practices that fly in the face of our emerging global concern for human rights.

The text is divided into four parts, based upon historical periods, and these were chosen to parallel the most common chronological divisions employed in presenting modern history. Documents were chosen to illustrate some of the major developments and ideas and they are organized into chapters according to broad themes. Short introductions are provided for each part and brief identification notes for each document. Part I deals with the period from 1600 (and before) until the end of the French Revolution and Napoleon. It traces the great debates on changing governance from divine right monarchy to parliamentary monarchy. It looks at the philosophical bases for participation in government and in ensuring the rights of citizens. The second part covers the Nineteenth Century. It considers the great changes caused by the Industrial Revolution and follows the continued efforts to expand political participation and to come to grips with the problems of the new national states. It looks at the rise of social and economic demands that go beyond the political demands of the previous century. Part III, 1900–1945, is dominated by world wars, the revolution in Russia and the advent of Fascism that led to World War II and the loss of forty million lives. Part IV traces the new era after World War II when the internationalization of human rights occurred and precedents were established to limit the rights of national states.

This volume resulted from efforts to improve the teaching of History by applying critical reasoning skills to study documents illustrating the development of human rights in Western civilization during the past four centuries. The Benedum Foundation helped to fund the research for this volume as a part of its support for the improvement of education for our public school teachers, one of the major goals of the Holmes Group Consortium, in which West Virginia University has been active. When the volume grew into a multi-disciplinary effort, the West Virginia College of Law assisted with support for Professor Friedberg's introductory essay.

This volume is a group effort of the four editors, who shared in the selection and analysis of documents and spent many hours discussing the project from differing perspectives. Throughout the enterprise, technical support was rendered by Christina Olson and Stella Schultz. Deirdre DeGolia's contribution exceeded that of associate editor when she assumed the laborious management of the physical and electronic assembling of documents and text.

An Historical and Critical Introduction to Human Rights

James Friedberg

1. Roots

The firestorms and ovens of World World II forged the structure for modern human rights doctrine. However, its "Western"* precursors date back thousands of years. Hebrew scriptures, first in the Mosaic law and later in the books of the Prophets, contain numerous prescriptions and proscriptions concerning behavior between human beings. The Prophets in fact may represent the first example of social critics as moral leaders of the people. Of course compared to our present expectations regarding human rights, Biblical society was usually lacking, with phenomena such as slavery, tribalism, and arbitrary and cruel punishments being common. However, it is undeniable that these teachings represented progress in the respect for human beings and limitations on government power. Such respect and limitation was usually couched in the theology of monotheism. The law-like orientation of many of the Hebrew scriptures makes it easier to understand these religious commands as rights.

Christian scripture continued the theme of social justice. As a proselytizing creed, it put even more emphasis on the universality of God's mandate, although the Hebrew scriptures did have elements of a universal morality. The Christian scriptures are to some extent more other worldly than the Hebrew ones, with emphasis somewhat less on rights and obligations in this life and more on rewards for faith waiting in the next one. The shift in emphasis may partly be explained by the church's desire to expand without provoking unnecessary resistance by the worldly Roman Empire. In any event, the tradition of the Gospels helps lay a strong foundation for the universalism of justice if not for its earthly application.

Greece and Rome also contributed to the foundation in which modern human rights have been constructed. Greek and Roman philosophers and statesmen provided early notions of certain civil and political rights and obligations to the Western tradition. However, while civil rights (i.e. the rights of *citizens*) were highly developed by ancient standards, significant defects existed by modern standards. The definition of citizen was narrowly restricted excluding most colonialized peoples, women, and, of course, slaves. Nonetheless, the seminal contribution of the ideas of rational morality and democratic institutions was immensely valuable. The Romans were also responsible for articulating the idea of natural law—norms that were not created by human lawmakers, but were deducible from the immutable order of the world.[1]

2. Theology and Natural Law

Philosophical theologians of the Middle Ages were a major bridge between Biblical/classical times and modern precursors to human rights. While Muslim and Jewish Aristotelian philosophers such as Averroes and Maimonnides were significant contributors to medieval notions of rational morality, Christian natural law theorists, especially Thomas Aquinas, probably constituted the most influential link between the ancient and the modern in the development of philosophy underlying human rights. Aquinas believed that natural law reflected God's perfection and natural order and that human law was subservient to it and ideally should reflect it. Christian natural philosophy, as it developed in the last few centuries of the Middle Ages, would prove to be a forerunner to the more secular natural rights theory of the Enlightenment.

Jurists and scholars consider international human rights to be a category of international law.[2] The historical sense of this can be seen by considering the Spanish School of International Law, represented most notably by Vittoria and Suarez. These men compete with the Dutch scholar Grotius who succeeded them by a century or so for claim as founders of modern international law. These Spanish theologians/

1

lawyers/philosophers wrote during the height of Spanish Hapsburg power in the fifteenth and sixteenth centuries. Significantly, one of the most crucial of Vittoria's tracts from the international law perspective is his essay on the Indians in America, a tract which has a strong human rights flavor. Rather courageously, considering his imperial and inquisitorial rulers, Vittoria advocated restraint in the manner in which the Spanish dealt with the New World "Indians". His argument was couched in the language of international law. Finding the Indians to have certain rights as a nation, his work is seen as providing the philosophical basis for the future development of the Law of Nations. Given his concern for the humane treatment of such Amerindians, it is apparent that the roots of international human rights law share the common ground with the roots of international law.

3. The Modern State and the Law of Nations

In many ways, the Thirty Years War (1618–1648) in central Europe was a watershed event in Western history. It marked the end of any serious threat of modern Western Europe being dominated by a single imperial dynasty, the Hapsburgs. Conversely, it marked emergence of the nation state as the predominant form of political organization in the modern world. At the beginning of the war, the Spanish and Austrian Hapsburgs together sought to dominate all of Europe and (implicitly in this age of European expansion) all of the world. By the conclusion of Peace of Westphalia in 1648, it was clear that a number of strong European nation states had permanently emerged and would not be dominated by the declining Hapsburgs.

France, England, Spain, Austria and the Netherlands were major powers of sufficiently equal strength such that none could dominate the others. A number of other European states remained independent minor powers. The significance of these events for the advance of human rights norms lay chiefly in the horrors of that war and the efforts of one brilliant diplomat scholar to mitigate the brutality of future warfare. Hugo Grotius wrote his master work, *The Law of War and Peace* in 1625 in the midst of the first decade of carnage of the Thirty Years War. Grotius was a Dutch Protestant citizen who served outside the academy as ambassador to France as well as being an accomplished scholar. He saw in the Thirty Years War the horrors of unlimited combat. For future human rights law the greatest significance of *The Law of War and Peace* were the limits that the Law of Nations, as articulated by Grotius, placed on combat. His was the first compendium of rules prohibiting mistreatment of prisoners, mistreatment of wounded, mistreatment of civilians, and the use of excessive brutality against combatants. These particular prohibitions form the core of what later came to be called "humanitarian law." Such humanitarian law was codified centuries later in the Hague and Geneva conventions and today forms one major branch of international human rights law.

Beyond being a substantive precursor to a particular present-day branch of human rights law, these norms propounded by Grotius established the fundamental principle that individuals have certain core rights to humane treatment under the Law of Nations. Grotius' Law of Nations was the earliest comprehensively described body of what was to grow into today's International Law.

Grotius is important to modern-day human rights theory for another reason. Like Vittoria and Suarez of the Spanish school, he was a proponent of natural law. Unlike them, however, he was a northern European Protestant from a small emerging nation rather than a Catholic churchman from an imperial Hapsburg land. Thus it is not surprising that his view of natural law was less dependent on theocratic universality. While not denying God's existence or supremacy (as might have been unwise even in liberal Holland) Grotius asserted that natural law was derivable purely from human reason. He found that the Law of Nations and its humanitarian norms were derivable from human reason via natural law. The significance of this insight by Grotius should not be lost for our times, over three and a half centuries later. *Human rights norms must exist today in a diverse world of immensely varied ideologies and beliefs*. Grotius's step away from a theological to a humanistic natural law was a major step on the path to pluralistic modern universal human rights.

Grotius has received from some scholars partial credit for the two and a half centuries of relative peace that prevailed in Europe until World War I. This period is sometimes referred to, in fact, as the Grotian peace. It is a tribute to Grotius and to his Law of Nations for their role in limiting the scope and barbarity of warfare on the European continent. It is also unfortunately an oversimplified image. First of all, even in Europe, the so called Grotian peace had significant interruptions, the most notable being the Wars of the French Revolution and Napoleon. Furthermore, while the recently emerged nations of Europe behaved relatively well in their own back yards, the Grotian peace was marked by colonial expansion during which these same nations plundered the rest of the world, sometimes with a disregard for human well-beings that matched the brutality of the Thirty Years War.

4. Revolution and Natural Rights

Shortly after the Peace of Westphalia in 1648, the Enlightenment began in northern Europe adding another source to the current of human rights development. Where monarchs attempted to rule the newly emerged nation states with pretensions of divine absolute prerogative, thoughtful and brave men quickly challenged such hubris. Philosophers such as Locke in England and Voltaire and Montesquieu in France asserted the natural rights of man and from these rights inferred limits on governmental powers. The political expression of this philosophy is found in such documents as the *English Bill of Rights* adopted by Parliament in 1689 upon the overthrow of the Stuarts in the Glorious Revolution[3] and a century later in the American *Bill of Rights* and in the French *Declaration of the Rights of Man and the Citizen* promulgated by new revolutionary governments in the United States and France.

The major political documents of this era reflected a natural rights philosophy. Men *by their nature* were entitled to life, liberty and property. This view assumes that there is a moral authority higher than a state: perhaps God or perhaps natural reason. This notion implies that the sovereignty of a state is inherently limited by certain higher moral imperatives. It also implies erroneous overstatement by those international law scholars who have maintained that from Grotius' time on, positivism with its doctrine of absolute state sovereignty was a consensus viewpoint in International Law. In fact, there was always a significant strain of naturalism, especially natural rights theory, co-existing with the legal positivism that was really dominant only during the nineteenth century. This natural rights philosophy carried the seeds of today's international human rights doctrine.

5. The Nineteenth Century

The French Revolution was the political culmination of the philosophical revolution of the Enlightenment that had been proceeding for a century. The emergence of revolutionary France dominated the political scene at the dawn of the nineteenth century. At first this revolution had seemed a triumph of reason over superstition and old forms of unjust domination. To this degree the revolution still has a major place in the chronology of human rights development. Its creed, the *Declaration of the Rights of Man and the Citizen*, still provides a laudable catalog of political and civil liberties. However, Robespierre, the Terror, and Napoleon followed quickly on the heels of the democratic revolution. Even the post-revolutionary Napoleonic years, despite their predominantly dictatorial tenor, were of some value in spreading the ideals of 1789.

Napoleon did much to shake the foundations of the old European monarchies. While as an alternative he offered only a new tyranny, the process at least delegitimated the old order. Ironically, he may also have given impetus to the development of the modern collective right of *self-determination* by his unwelcome conquests of non-French peoples as initial liberation turned to oppressive imperialism. On the other hand, he continued the spirit of 1789 and served human rights by continuing the reform and rationalization of public governance within France, e.g. in law and education. This process often gave the common citizen certain rights previously only held by the aristocrats.

In 1815, Europe's old guard tried to turn the clock back. Upon Napoleon's final defeat, Metternich, the Holy Alliance and the Congress of Vienna did what they could to promote the reentrenchment of old monarchial and aristocratic power. However, much had already transpired. The promises of 1776 and 1789 could not be forgotten.

Nor could the Industrial Revolution be stopped. This latter event, a change in the basic economic nature of society, propelled the successful entrepreneurial segments of the middle class to join or surpass the old landed aristocracies in economic and, eventually, political power. It also created a new group of oppressed: industrial workers. This group labored under miserable conditions little ameliorated by the civil and political liberties being won by the middle classes.

The revolutions of 1848 punctuated the failed attempt of the old pre-Napoleonic order to re-establish itself—even where revolt was squelched, the seeds of democracy and human rights remained. Monarchs not eliminated were giving up their powers to constitutionalism. Land-holding was disappearing as a requirement for political participation. By mid-century, although the plight of the industrial poor was often worsening, at least the catalog of political and civil rights was growing.

Across the Atlantic another major issue of human rights festered: slavery was still being practiced in the United States, the most rapidly growing country in the world. Half a century after Americans and Frenchmen had based their revolutions on liberty, a large proportion of the United States population was absolutely denied that most basic right. The movement for abolition must be regarded as one of the major precursors to the modern human rights movement. Its recognition that a higher law must, on occasion, supercede national legislation is an essential premise of present day international human rights law.

Various international assurances to protect Christian minorities in the Ottoman Empire during the nineteenth century exemplify early attempts at human rights type norm setting. There is a problem, however, in uncritically presenting these international agreements as early examples of the growth of respect for universal human rights. They were not really that. They were in fact fraternal protection demanded by the increasingly stronger Christian West for brethren found within the confines of the weakening Turkish realm. No similar international guarantees were sought or won, for instance, on behalf of Indians within the United States or Jews within the Russian Empire. These and other groups were certainly under threats comparable to those faced by Christian communities under Ottoman rule. Nonetheless, despite these moral limitations, the concept of international protection of minorities was an important step forward in the eventual human rights norms. It was another signal (like abolitionism) that state sovereignty was not absolute and could be forced to yield to demands of decency.

6. Humanitarian Law

The Industrial Revolution, in addition to creating issues of economic and social rights for a downtrodden working class, impacted human rights in another way. This significance harkened back to Grotius's original and highly successful attempt to limit the brutality of warfare. The ability to follow the Grotian limits on treatment of civilians, combatants, wounded, and prisoners was substantially affected by the invention of new means of destruction with the advent of industrialism. New weapons could do more damage more quickly to more people than was the case in the past. Furthermore, the weapons themselves and the tactics used to employ them were often indiscriminate. The distinction between combatant and non-combatant so central to the Grotian scheme was threatened.

In the late nineteenth and early twentieth centuries, conferences were held at the Hague, in St. Petersburg[4] and in Geneva in an effort to reassert the principles of Grotius in a way that would limit the new industrial capacity for destruction of human life. These conferences gave birth to the modern version of humanitarian law. As mentioned earlier in the essay, humanitarian law is one of the principle sources for present day international human rights law.

The efforts at St. Petersburg and the Hague while successful in enunciating new norms, did not prevent the carnage of World War I. The industrial age had brought aerial bombardment and gas warfare to the international arena. Both of these methods of destruction showed less regard for the distinction between combatant and non-combatant than previous means of warfare. Furthermore, even the weapons used only against the combatants had become more efficient in their ability to maim and kill on a large scale. The limitations sought by Grotius thereby suffered a grievous setback in the early twentieth century.

After the First World War, the Geneva conventions again attempted to limit some of this, especially insofar as the wounded, civilians, and prisoners were concerned. An ironic contrast exists here. These emerging norms really do seem to have been taken seriously and become accepted values by most peoples of the civilized world. But in World War II, shortly after their adoption, they were ignored on a gross scale, most horrendously by the Nazis, frequently by the Japanese, and even to some degree by the allied powers.

For the evolution of human rights law the significance of early twentieth century humanitarian law seems to be this: new industrial capacity spawned new weapons which spawned new humanitarian limits on warfare. Although the limits were ignored in both world wars, the norms survived to be reinstated in the virtually universally-accepted new Geneva Conventions of the late 1940s, concurrent with the birth of the modern human rights movement.

7. Colonialism

Colonialism was another phenomenon that gave impetus to the evolution toward modern human rights norms. Just as abolitionists reacted against slavery, nationalists reacted against colonialism spurring development of the concept of self-determination. This concept is probably the earliest articulation of a collective or group right. Colonialism generally represented the domination by Europeans of non-European peoples.[5] This domination by Europeans has had significance on more than one level. First, it evidences the close link between colonialism and racial domination, thus it provides a theoretical link between the individual right of equal treatment under law and the collective right of self-determination. Second, it qualifies notions of a Grotian peace. Whatever general peace existed in Europe after the treaty of Westphalia in 1648, it did not extend to non-white subjects of the Europeans in far off lands.

Decolonization was one of a number of critical movements that accelerated at the conclusion of World War II promoting rise of an international human rights law. (Other such events include the founding of the United Nations, the Nuremburg trials, the drafting of international and regional human rights declarations and conventions and the reenactment of the Geneva conventions.) Decolonization is significant to the modern human rights movement both for its timing and its substance. Occurring concurrently with the other phenomena just mentioned, it gave credence to the claim that the new international human rights norms were truly universal: no longer were Asians, Africans, and indigenous peoples in lands settled by Europeans to be excluded from the promises of 1776 and 1789. Rather they were to be included—man, woman, and child—with the white male Europeans who had been the prime beneficiaries of the rights proclaimed in the English, French and American revolutions a few centuries earlier.

At least in the theory of the new human rights law, no longer would excluded peoples be forced to experience the yoke of servitude while hearing the rhetoric of democracy from their masters.[6] Decolonization did not occur in a single swift and painless stroke. Obviously, it is more difficult to change numerous geopolitical arrangements than it is to draft a charter or administer a court proceeding; nor has the movement itself been free from tyrants and charlatans. However, the important point is that decolonization as an idea took hold with other great human rights ideas at the end of World War II. And that idea has formed part of a theoretical foundation and moral consensus which underlie present-day human rights law.

8. A Right to Peace?

Some human rights theorists have propounded a "right to peace" as a collective right of all peoples. While such a particular articulation of this concept is quite recent, its modern roots are implanted in the reaction against the First World War and its older roots arguably are imbedded in the medieval Christian concept of "just war". A right to peace is partly the product of that body of international law traditionally referred to as *jus ad bellum*. This body of doctrine deals with questions concerning when it is appropriate to use armed force in the international arena.[7] In the nineteenth century when legal positivism dominated the viewpoints of most international lawyers, it also generally asserted that states were free to choose when to go to war as a matter of national policy. The statesmen and lawyers who held this nineteenth century view saw the discretion to wage war as an incident of state sovereignty.[8] Since they were only willing to conceive of such sovereignty as indivisible and absolute, they could envision no permissible legal limit on a state's ability to choose warfare as a tool of national policy. Interestingly, there does not seem to have been a similar positivist consensus against Grotian rules moderating behavior *within* warfare (*jus in bellum*), even though such humanitarian rules necessarily also cut into state sovereignty.

In any event, the mass slaughter of World War I made it clear that the positivist position was untenable. In the industrial age, the world community could not permit individual states to wage war at their whim without condoning and inviting mass destruction and suffering. The attempts of League of Nations' procedures to delegitimize warfare as a tool of national policy demonstrated the rejection of nineteenth century notions of absolute state sovereignty. The League of Nations thus planted the seeds from which sprang a modern human right to peace. The Kellogg-Briand Pact of 1929 (a multilateral treaty signed by most major powers at the time) more explicitly enunciated the principle that war is not a legitimate tool of national policy. Notwithstanding the emergence of this principle limiting state claims to a sovereign right of aggression, the Axis powers ignored their obligations both under the League of Nations and the Kellogg-Briand Pact, choosing aggressive warfare and precipitating World War II.

The period between the world wars marked the decline of the positivist consensus that states were free to commit war. The conclusion of World War II marked the emergence of a new neo-naturalist[9] consensus that aggressive warfare was illegal. Both the Nuremburg principles and the United Nations *Charter* clearly outlawed aggressive warfare. A logical corollary to this doctrine is that human societies collectively possess a right to peace. This right is reciprocal of the duty of states not to wage war.

The modern human rights movement was born traumatically in the agonizing labor of the Second World War. Concurrent historic events monumentally changed not only the international political scene but world moral norms in the aftermath of that horrendous war.[10] The latter half of the 1940s saw, among other events, the founding of the United Nations, the Nuremburg trials and the freeing of India, the start or acceleration of other decolonization movements, and the adoption of the *Universal Declaration of Human Rights* and of other major human rights documents. These major historic events reflected a new vision of humanity. This vision saw a world governed by moral order, not by the whims of national sovereignty. In the wake of the Holocaust, the Nuremburg trials proclaimed that it was contrary to international law for any state to slaughter with impunity, whether outside or *inside* its borders.

The concept of a "crime against humanity" implies that certain activity is always illegal under international law regardless of whether such activity is condoned by domestic legislation. Furthermore, individuals who violate the legal norms of humanity will be held directly accountable within the international legal system. Essentially, the Nuremburg principles of 1945 mean that the racist laws passed by the Nazis in the 1930s must be considered *void ab initio*. What all this signifies is a waning of positivist sovereignty doctrine and the emergence of a new neo-naturalist world order in which ideals (if not practice) centered on basic human rights.

The founding of the United Nations at the same moment in history as the Nuremburg trials similarly evidences the death of one international moral viewpoint (absolute sovereignty) and the birth of another (neo-naturalist international human rights). The United Nations' *Charter* lists the promotion of human rights as a principal purpose of the organization in Article 1 and in Articles 55 and 56 obligates all members to take action necessary for this goal.

The *Universal Declaration of Human Rights* was passed by the United Nations General Assembly in 1948. It followed the spirit of Nuremburg and the United Nations' *Charter*, particularizing the general promise of human rights made in the latter. It was to be the first part of a triad of human rights documents which would constitute an international bill of rights, the other parts being an international covenant on civil and political rights and one on economic, social, and cultural rights. These other parts of the triad would take the better part of two decades to negotiate, complete and ratify. However, the *Universal Declaration* successfully articulated the principle items which have come to reflect a consensus within the world community as to the core of international human rights. (Related regional events, particularly the adoption of an American *Declaration of Human Rights* and a European *Convention for Human Rights*, reiterated the dominance of this growing international moral consensus in the late 1940s.)

The drafters of the *Universal Declaration* included economic and social rights such as minimum expectations for conditions of health, education and work in this document. This inclusion reflected the fact that modern human rights had progressed beyond eighteenth century ideas of personal liberty. Of course, the liberties proclaimed by the English and American *Bills of Rights* and the French *Declaration of the Rights of Man and the Citizen* were included in the *Universal Declaration*. However, the *Universal Declaration* significantly stepped beyond its seventeenth and eighteenth century predecessors in asserting rights to a basic decent human existence. Immunity against the arbitrary exercise of power was still a central theme, but the theme of human welfare had been added.

9. Second and Third Generations

The economic and social deprivation born of the Industrial Revolution gave rise to reformist beliefs that were to form the basis of the social and economic branch of human rights. "[T]he majestic equality of the laws...forbid rich and poor alike to sleep under bridges, to beg in the streets, and to steal their bread." This ironic remark by Anatole France embodied the realization that political liberty and equality alone are not enough to assure a decent existence. Various liberal, progressive and socialist philosophers from the early nineteenth century onward attacked the conditions created for the poor by the new industrial age. By the late nineteenth century and early twentieth century such phenomena as child labor laws, compulsory public education, unionization, and health standards in the workplace demonstrated the partial success of such a new consciousness. During the same period of time judicial obstructionism, police repression on behalf of business interests and other forms of reaction demonstrated that the battle for such rights was far from won. However, by the 1930s most industrialized countries had accepted social welfare rights[11] in varying degrees. These rights were embodied after World War II in general form in the *Universal Declaration of Human Rights* and eventually in more particular form in the United Nations *Covenant on Economic, Social and Cultural Rights*.

In recent years some human rights theorists have referred to the economic and social rights discussed above as "second generation rights." This description presumably implies a quantum leap beyond the political and civil rights enunciated in the eighteenth and nineteenth centuries. The same theorists often imply a further leap by speaking of "third generation rights." These would include collective or people's rights, not held solely by individuals but held by groups. Examples might be the rights to self-determination, language, culture, a livable natural environment, and peace. At present, the status of these items as "rights" is debated. More traditional rights theorists argue that such concepts tend to expand the idea of rights so broadly that the idea loses its power. Some of them would allow that peace, a clean environment and cultural pluralism are worthwhile goals, but not that they are rights. An even more conservative (and smaller) group of theorists challenges the so-called second generation of rights, arguing that social welfare is a matter of public policy, not a matter of human rights, and that only those eighteenth century prohibitions against arbitrary government interference should be considered true human rights. The intellectual case for such a restrictive approach is weak and the political case is even weaker.

The United States has not played a helpful role in the drama surrounding the adoption of an international bill of rights. In the post-Roosevelt reaction of late 1940s and 1950s in America, the notion of social and economic rights was fought by those who viewed them as threateningly "socialistic." In the Cold War era, this was sufficient to throttle discussion of reforms.

Pressure by the United States and other western governments probably resulted in the need separately to negotiate and draft two *Covenants* to elucidate the rights guaranteed by the *Universal Declaration*. The separation of economic, social and cultural rights in their own covenant to distinguish them from political and civil rights certainly reflected Western, and especially the United States', discomfort with economic, social and cultural rights. Even after that separation, the United States long refused, to ratify either *Covenant*, although both were open for signature by the late 1960s. All other Western major democracies have signed them. President Carter sent the covenants to the Senate for its approval during his term, but they lingered there without action throughout the conservative 1980s. Finally, toward the end of his term George Bush declared support for the civil and political treaty only, whereupon it was approved by the Senate and ratified by the U.S. in 1992.

There are probably numerous explanations for why the United States resisted accepting of the *Covenants*. Especially as to economic and social rights, one can easily guess the motives for resistance by dominant elements in our society who fear a redistribution of wealth and power to the less powerful. However, it is not as obvious why there had been resistance to ratifying the *Covenant on Civil and Political Rights*. Looking to recent history provides one explanation and also introduces another significant step in the path of human rights development. The civil rights movement in America is that step.[12] Resistance to domestic civil rights undoubtedly caused certain conservatives to also resist international human rights affirmations like the *Covenant on Civil and Political Rights*.

10. Civil Rights in America

The early resistance in the 1950s and 1960s to an international civil rights document (i.e., the proposed United Nations *Covenant on Civil and Political Rights*) at least partly reflected the power of segregationists in this country in their general resistance to human rights progress during those decades. By the time civil rights had become firmly entrenched as U.S. national policy in the 1970s, we had begun a string of presidential administrations not prone to push the ratification of human rights documents (with the exception of the Carter administration, which did seek ratification prior to its ouster from office.)

In any event, civil rights in America was significant not just for our domestic social order but also for international human rights generally. It marked demands being made by the largest racial minority in the world's most powerful democracy for that democracy to finally live up to its ideals. It marked a demand that the *Declaration of Independence* and the *Bill of Rights* be taken seriously. It marked a demand that the residual injustice of slavery at last be rectified. A significant interplay between the growth of human rights consciousness and civil rights consciousness existed in the 1950s. It was no coincidence that *Brown v. Board of Education* (the Supreme Court case declaring segregated schools unconstitutional) was decided in an era of worldwide decolonization and emerging U.S. world leadership. How could the United States seriously claim the mantle of leadership in the free world if a tenth of its population at home was legally unequal? Just as international events may have thus affected the speed of civil rights change in America, so American civil rights change has affected much of the rest of the world. Events in Birmingham, Selma and Washington, D.C. were disseminated by news media throughout the world. In the main stream, Nobel prize winner Martin Luther King, Jr. became a national hero carrying the legacy of Gandhi—even today felt back in Gandhi's early home of South Africa. Somewhat out of the main stream, ideals of black liberation nurtured each other across the Atlantic.

In less than half a century, the world has progressed from a situation in which notions of racial superiority were accepted as valid, to a situation in which they are hardly ever uttered in public discourse in civilized society. This is not to say that all prejudice has left people's hearts of course. But it is real progress that such prejudice is no longer accepted as public policy. It is not too much to hope that through education and socialization, public values can shape private values. The American civil rights movement deserves major credit for changing these public values not just in this country, but worldwide.

11. International Organizations

The growth of international organizations is one of the most significant phenomena of the post-war years. Both intergovernmental and nongovernmental organizations deal with almost every kind of problem facing the world today. Human rights is no exception. In fact, the significance of these forms of organization to the human rights movement is perhaps larger than to other areas of international concern. This is because the existence of such organizations reflects structurally the same phenomenon that the normative advent of human rights reflects substantively, namely the diminishing centrality of state sovereignty in world affairs. The strength of international organization means that fewer decisions affecting world society are taken solely at the national government level. The progress of human rights norms means that humankind is accepting the moral assertion that there is law superior to national law. Both these phenomena—one structural, the other normative—reflect the demise of nineteenth century notions of exclusive state preeminence on the world stage.

12. United Nations Institutions

United Nations human rights institutions provide mechanisms for monitoring the behavior of member states toward their own populations. A number of institutions associated with the United Nations have become responsible for enforcing human rights. The Commission on Human Rights, the Commission on Prevention of Discrimination and Protection of Minorities and the Commission on the Status of Women are the three principal human rights organizations based on the United Nations *Charter*. Other United Nations-related bodies exist as enforcement arms of both the two general human rights covenants and of certain specific human rights treaties (e.g. conventions outlawing genocide, racial discrimination and torture).

The Commission on Human Rights exists under mandate from Article 68 of the United Nations *Charter* directing the Economic and Social Council (ECOSOC) to establish commissions for the promotion of human rights. It is composed of representatives of a cross section of United Nations member states. The commission periodically submits proposals and reports dealing with human rights matters. It also has established various United Nations programs for dealing with human rights violations, such as special investigators (rapporteurs) and working groups.

The Subcommission on the Prevention of Discrimination and Protection of Minorities is a subsidiary organ of the Commission on Human Rights. Unlike the members of the Commission, the Subcommission members serve in their personal capacities rather than as representatives of their states. Therefore the Subcommission's actions are less prone to be affected by political considerations. The Subcommission spends much of its time examining particular charges of human rights violations. As with the Commission, it has no direct enforcement powers. But the publicity that it can throw on human rights violators can be most unwelcome and may have deterrent or abative effects. Powers conferred on the Commission and Subcommission by resolutions 1235 and 1503 of the Economic and Social Council provide for detailed examination of alleged human rights violations committed by individual states.

The practice of the Commission and Subcommission and of the numerous other agencies related to human rights has gone far to establish a highly important principle.[13] The principle is this: a state which significantly violates human rights norms is subject to international investigation and sanctions (and this occurs, notwithstanding even Article 2(7) of the United Nations *Charter* which bars intervention made within a member state's domestic jurisdiction.) That principle is the essence of the triumph of world morality over nineteenth century notions of absolute state sovereignty. The profound point here is that with the internationalization of human rights, especially through United Nations' practices, such state action may no longer be considered solely a matter of domestic concern.

Activity such as torture, genocide, and racial discrimination provoke such international moral consensus that their legal condemnation may be regarded as *jus cogens* (mandatory, non-derogable international norms) and as the basis of universal jurisdiction over certain international crimes. Humanity has reached a point where it can make certain legal statements about phenomena such as torture and genocide. They not only are unlawful, but they cannot be made legal by otherwise procedurally legitimate acts of any government or governments. They are most exemplary of human rights as world law above state law, a core of behavioral taboos about which there can be no reasonable debate in civilized society.

On the day of the last editing of this edition, Dec. 20, 1993, the United Nations took what turned out to be a monumental step. It created the office of High Commissioner for Human Rights. Critical opposition from less than democratic regimes had to be overcome to accomplish this creation. The resulting compromise leaves the mandate of the office vague, but its mere existence gives the human rights movement a prestigious and hopefully influential global voice.

13. Non-Governmental Organizations

Non-governmental organizations (NGO's) have come to play a significant role in the promotion of human rights since the end of World War II. This is another example of players other than nation-states taking principal roles on the world stage. Organizations like the International Red Cross, Amnesty International, the Watch Committees, and similar groups have used information and moral pressure as effective tools in fighting human rights abuse. Where governments are often deterred from criticism of other governments because of political or economic considerations, non-governmental organizations have often been willing to speak out. Many of these bodies have achieved observer status in the United Nations and other international organizations, effectively interacting with government representatives.

14. A Daunting Challenge: Diversity and Disenfranchisement

The issue of *universal* human rights in a *diverse* world is probably the most profound philosophical and practical issue facing the human rights movement today. This work has focused on human rights development within the West and related it to non-Western areas at times. A principal significance of the internationalization of human rights after World War II is that human rights are no longer the exclusive domain of Western civilization. In fact, the notion of rights held by all humans supercedes pre-1945 conceptions of distinctly "Western" values. While allowing for diversity, modern human rights doctrine envisions a post-Western civilization where European notions of civil liberty combine with traditional ideals of community and mutual responsibility from other cultures as well.

There are dangers when writers in the West attempt to judge critically the human rights records of non-Western cultures. There is the challenge of viewing another society through lenses not distorted by ethnocentric bias. This requires caution in making judgments and humility in defending them. It does not condemn us to silence, however. If human rights are to be truly universal, we must, with due deference to cultural autonomy, be willing to identify shortcomings in other societies *almost* as readily as we condemn them in our own.

At the time of this writing, great changes are occurring around the globe. Western Europe is seeking a more complete economic union and a place for a united Germany. Most Eastern European nations are in the process of changing to pluralistic democracies, while some are faced with ethnic fragmentation. Europeans, East and West, are speaking of a future single Europe. It has been a short time since Iraqi troops invaded Kuwait and an American-led coalition forced them out. It has also been a short time since Chinese leaders killed the peaceful human rights demonstrators in Tiananmen Square. Initial elation over the dismantling of the Iron Curtain has melted into an almost despairing concern when viewing new prejudice and bloodletting in the former Soviet empire. An attempt to see these events in a broad global picture reveals a rapidly changing international mosaic, into some portions of which it may be difficult to fit consensus values of human rights.

Prior to the Iraqi invasion, a period of naive euphoria had been engulfing Western media, scholars and government officials. Rhetoric about victory in the Cold War often included too sanguine an outlook concerning human rights. Such an outlook ignored phenomena, both East and West, which belied such optimism, including the rise of ethnic hatred in former Marxist lands and the bitter impoverishment of the underclass in the United States and elsewhere. But more than this, it misgauged the power of ideological alternatives both to democratic and to Marxist values that had emerged within developing nations. If most of Eastern Europe has apparently embraced democratic pluralism, most of the Third World has not. Patterns of government in many developing nations have not been consistent with universal human rights norms that have developed since World War II.

Iraq under Saddam Hussein is but an example of a direction disdainful of modern notions of human rights, as well as other international norms of behavior. The invasion of Kuwait and the treatment of hostages were evidence of the continued rejection of international norms, particularly of human rights perceived as Western. The popular support Saddam Hussein seemed to generate among some people in the Middle East should be cause for concern to human rights advocates. This conflict between Saddam Hussein and the West reflects the clash of historic forces that make solutions to crises difficult. It underscores the difficulty in establishing standards that are accepted by all. However, the "cure" to the Iraqi aggression—political decision-making dominated by the United States and military enforcement executed by the United States—is not viewed by all as auguring well for human rights. The concentration of power does not foster respect for human rights and the rule of law. In the Kuwait crisis, as in others, there have been failures on both sides.

Western states have failed to make amends fully for the harm done by colonialism and related international ills. While for most North Americans, Europeans and Japanese, modernism has meant increased liberty and prosperity (at least since the conclusion of World War II), for Third World peoples it has often meant economic deprivation, resource depletion, Western supported authoritarian elites and a torn social fabric. Until recently, the West has failed to break the deadlock in the Arab-Israeli conflict, leaving the Palestinians disenfranciased refugees in their own land and outside of it and undercutting Western claims to leadership in the area of human rights. Hopefully, the recent Israeli-Palestinian agreement will be implemented with the needed Western support and further the human rights of all involved. Finally and most recently, the West has failed the poorest of the poor by turning its emotional and economic attention to the needs of the (white) Eastern European states, while in Africa and elsewhere, living conditions much worse than anything in Poland or Czechoslovakia are left unattended.

There also have been failures on the part of the governments of the developing nations. Demagogic strongmen too often have manipulated their people by cynical calls to channel religious and ethnic feelings into *jihad* (holy war) or similar adventures. Such manipulation has often led to further suffering for the people. Leaders in some of the Middle Eastern states preside over regimes that have opposed (and cultures that have resisted) the kind of intellectual and political Enlightenment that Europe experienced in the seventeenth and eighteenth centuries.[14] The fervor of the fundamentalist Movement in Iran under Khomeni left no room for opposition, for the free play of differing ideas, for the toleration of different values, for other visions in religion. How can the broad range of human rights be established without a minimal acceptance of conditions that respect other differences in our complex world? Cultural differences cannot justify Saddam Hussein who imposed a dictatorship that did not permit a free press or political opposition, conducted savage wars against the Kurds and Shiites where poison gases were used and embarked on a long and costly war with his neighbors in Iran, before the invasion of Kuwait. Human rights advocates must resist being silenced by tyrants who cynically wrap themselves in the mantle of cultural autonomy and anticolonialism. All nations East, West, North and South are subject to the measure of decency.

As we have noted in this collection of documents, many of the present problems in various parts of the world, including the Middle East, stem from the problems left by the West in those areas. These unsettled national, ethnic, territorial and other historical problems must somehow be settled before the realization of stable governance and the expansion of human rights in this region as in other ones. The roles to be played by the United Nations and other forms of international cooperation are still uncertain. The new found ability of the Security Council to act, unhampered by Cold War vetoes is somewhat encouraging, but perceived U.S. domination of that body limits its moral credibility.

15. Cautious Hope: Social Liberalism

Respect for the rights guaranteed by either of the United Nations human rights covenants is impossible without respect for the rights guaranteed by both. One cannot accept civil and political rights in the first and reject the economic, social and cultural rights of the other. This should be a fundamental truth recognizable at the end of the twentieth century.

One of the insights to be drawn from recent events is that it is difficult for tyrants to maintain indefinitely the gap between public pronouncement and public reality. The Soviet and Eastern European dictatorships espoused the interest of the people, but gave them little; finally the people demanded more than words. South Africa's pretense of democratic forms has been shaken by the reality of her unresolved problems. In sub-Saharan Africa, one-party regimes are being challenged. Military regimes practicing torture in Latin America in the name of protecting Western values against communism have been exposed for what they are and in most cases replaced by more democratic regimes (although military elites still threaten human rights gains.) Some of these gains reflect the removal of Western support for dictatorships no longer convenient now that the Cold War has ended, as much as they reflect the promotion of human rights.

It is simplistic to view the "failure of Communism" as the "triumph of capitalism." The extreme versions of the latter, as were practiced in Thatcherite Britain and Reaganite America failed in important areas. By stressing the "liberty" of property with little regard for economic or social justice, these societies have spawned permanent underclasses, drug epidemics, homelessness, endemic urban crime and environmental degradation. And it is unclear how heavily the truly greedy have mortgaged the moderate prosperity of the middle classes with Savings and Loan crises, immense public debt and yet-to-be internalized environmental costs.

Human beings often prefer simple answers to complex ones. This is the essence of fundamentalism, whether Islamic, Christian, Jewish, Marxist or capitalist. But simple answers are often wrong. (And simple fundamentalism is the enemy of human rights.) It is simple to say that society will flourish by promoting liberty above all else. It is also simple to say that society will flourish by an equitable distribution of material wealth above all else. One simplification reflects the core ideals of liberal capitalism, the other of Marxian socialism. Both fail because they disregard the complexity of modern industrial society. A tension—not a contradiction—exists between personal liberty and social regulation. It is a tension best resolved not by choosing liberty or equality, but by seeking a dynamic equilibrium where economic rights and individual liberties balance each other. It is only through such a social liberalism that the rights promised in both United Nations human rights covenants can be fulfilled.

The major world events since 1989 have resonated strongly with human rights concerns. Perhaps the gap between professed ideals and practiced reality might be narrowing at last. Apartheid is crumbling finally in South Africa. Democratic governments rule most of the nations of Latin America, though democracy is still fragile because of economic injustice and threats from repressive military elites. The Soviet satellites have spun out of orbit. The former Soviet Union itself is a place of greater freedom, although suffering from ethnic tension, instability and lack of prosperity. Even sad episodes have held a glimmer of hope. The massacre in Tiananmen Square, while tragic in itself, was a chapter in a larger democratic struggle in the world's most populous country, from which one senses an irrepressible ground swell for human freedom. In sub-Saharan Africa, one-party regimes, justified by the rhetoric of nationalism, are finally being challenged. Dictatorship is clearly not the trend of the day.

The great task for many nations in the field of human rights is to reconcile the promises and goals of the *Covenant on Civil and Political Rights* and those of the *Covenant on Economic, Social and Cultural Rights*. They complement each other; they are entwined. They are inseparable for a stable, fair and mature society. A society that promises economic justice but disrespects individual liberty will deliver neither. The Soviets have shown this. A more subtle truth for Westerners is a difficult one: a society that values only political liberty but ignores the need for that economic and social well-being which permits the exercise of political liberty, faces grave problems.

There is a need in many places to recognize that the best legacy of Western liberalism must be combined with the promises of social reform, socialism or the tradition of communal responsibility from other cultures. Liberalism's free expression, freedom of religion, political participation and due process must combine with equal access to education, health care, housing and work. A socially-minded liberal society could take many forms. Such a synthesis of liberty and fairness could best realize the full range of human rights proclaimed in the *Universal Declaration*.

HISTORICAL INTRODUCTION—NOTES

*The term "Western" is obviously problematic in many ways, partly addressed by our sections on empire, decolonization and forgotten peoples.

[1] Natural law, whether flowing from physical nature, God, or human reason is contrasted to "positive" law which is decreed by a ruler (King, Congress, judge, etc.).

[2] For the purposes of this essay, "international law" and "the law of nations" are interchangeable terms.

[3] Not all those people under English rule in the British Isles saw this revolution as "glorious," nor enjoyed these newly declared rights. The Irish saw the imperious James II as their champion against their Protestant English masters—a lesson for other times that the dispossessed may find national pride and self-determination of more immediate concern than liberal individual rights. See section 14 of this essay.

[4] There were also pressures to slow down the arms race in which the Russians were having difficulty participating, probably feeling threatened by both the Germans and the British in this regard. Such Russian concern provides an interesting parallel to the recent movement toward relaxing of world tensions, prompted in part by the Soviet need to turn its limited resources toward domestic needs and away from military ones.

[5] There were some exceptions to this general trend. The Irish and certain Balkan nationalities were colonialized Europeans and the Japanese were non-European colonizers in East Asia and the Pacific. Also from the Middle Ages there had been Arab colonization in Africa, e.g., Zanzibar.

[6] Complications do attend this otherwise positive development. The eighteenth century vintage civil liberties that form the core of Western democracy were articulated by men of similar background, products of the liberal European Enlightenment. The chjallenge of making human rights norms truly universal in a diverse world is a daunting task. How does one react, for instance, to claims that those eighteenth century liberties are merely products of European cultural preferences? Are non-Western practices that strike us as authoritarian, intolerant or even cruel subject to defense on the grounds that they represent valid cultural preferences not our own?

[7] Traditionally, this arena of doctrine is distinctly from *jus in bellum*, which deals with standards for behavior during warfare such as treatment of combatants, treatment of noncombatants, permissible weapons, etc.

[8] After the overthrow of Napoleon, European states attempted to maintain the peace by collective action of the "congress" system of great power conferences. But the system often simply opposed change, particularly demands for reform of the existing monarchies. The congress system failed and was succeeded by the unification movements that produced Italy, the German Empire and a larger Rumania and Bulgaria. During the last of the nineteenth century opposing alliances consolidated the blocs of individual national states that would fight in World War I.

[9] Naturalism had been dominant in late medieval philosophy and also important in Enlightenment natural rights theory. It fell prey to positivist international lawyers in the sovereignty oriented nineteenth century. The neo-naturalism of the twentieth century is probably more secular than its antecedents.

[10] Perhaps 40 million were killed in World War II. Six million Jews were exterminated in the concentration camps because they did not fit in to the stark racial ideals of Nazism.

[11] The very word "welfare" has negative connotations in the United States not shared in the rest of the world. In most of the industrialized world the right to social welfare is viewed as a positive good, and the term "welfare" is not used by politicians as a rhetorical hammer to beat out votes on the anvil of racial and class antagonisms.

[12] Human Rights are those held by a person simply as a function of his or her being a human being. There is a naturalist tone to the concept. Civil rights are held by a person as a function of his or her being a member of a particular society whose laws guarantee such rights. They have a positivist tone. Of course, the areas protected by many civil rights overlap those protected by human rights.

[13] See Burgenthal, *International Human Rights Law*, 77, St. Paul: West Publishing, 1989.

[14] Of course, this is no claim that Enlightenment prevents atrocities on the part of Europeans. Slavery, colonialism, war and genocide clearly belie any such assertion. The West often has not been true to its own values. The point here is that an intellectual and political Enlightenment is *necessary* for the cultural acceptance of human rights values, not that it *guarantees* the achievement of a humane society. So, for instance, one of the great intellectual and cultural challenges of our age is the reconciliation of some Islamic social orders with modern human rights norms.

SECTION I 1600–1815

The beginning of the modern period in Europe saw profound changes in Western Civilization; indeed it may be said to have been marked by three revolutionary breaks with tradition: the Scientific Revolution, the Enlightenment, and the French Revolution. Increasingly centralized national power, nearly constant international conflict, invasion and exploitation of non-European cultures, population growth, urbanization, and expanding trade and commerce were distinguishing features of modern Europe.

Governments responded to the pressures of new European conditions by attempting to increase their powers. The national states required more complex and sophisticated administrative machinery in order to cope with the difficulties of handling large budgets, conducting and regulating international trade, maintaining standing armies, running efficient postal systems, keeping public records, and providing better transportation to growing populations.

The early seventeenth century witnessed a rising tide of absolutism, sanctioned by divine right. As national power increased, it became obvious that the Old Regime was no longer able to function efficiently. The "society of orders," in which birth and privilege mattered more than talent, was fast becoming anachronistic. "Natural rights" presented a challenge to the divine right theory and eventually led to the demise of the Old Regime in the latter part of the eighteenth century. By the time of the French Revolution in 1789, realms inhabited by subjects were gradually evolving into nations of citizens.

The period of transition to the more modern era was a time of tremendous contradictions. Witch-burnings, symbols of persecution, and the Edict of Nantes, a shining example of tolerance, co-existed in its early years, and later calls for tolerance and reason were counterpoised by irrational behavior, such as the persecution of the Jewish inhabitants of Lisbon after the 1755 earthquake. It was a time of dynamism and flux, when memories of the executions of heretics by both Church and State remained in the minds of the thinkers who made the Scientific Revolution; when the Enlightenment, with its cries for freedom of thought and conscience, competed with state and religious censorship.

Although the great majority of Europeans remained poor and were long unaware of the changing intellectual climate, the great social, political, cultural, and demographic changes of the period nonetheless affected them deeply.

The rights of individuals became a focus of attention during these two tumultuous centuries, for as the power of government increased, so too did its ability to repress its subjects; as the nations of Europe exploited the New World, the *philosophes* of the Enlightenment began to view other cultures as different, not inferior. As permanent armies were created, attempts were also made to create international laws regarding warfare. Womens' rights, prison reform, educational opportunity, rationalization of government, critiques of religious intolerance, and the rights of individuals within the state were all topics of debate in the fashionable salons of Europe.

What is the human rights legacy of the period? Needless to say, no final answers to the questions of rights that were raised from the late-sixteenth to the late-eighteenth century have been reached to the present day, but it remains important that these questions of basic human rights were even considered.

The Renaissance had earlier focused upon humanity and individuality, and the Reformation undermined one of the great institutional supports for the Old Regime, the Church; but it remained for the modern period to redefine the relationship between individuals and government, and to systematically begin to articulate and then protect individual rights.

CHAPTER 1 — Power: Its Origin and Use

Document 1:
ADDRESS TO PARLIAMENT (1609)
James I

James I, King of England from 1603–1625, was once called "the wisest fool in Christendom" by Henri IV of France. James was unable to work effectively with Parliament due to his belief that kings drew their authority directly from God. He asserts his Divine Right powers in an address to Parliament in 1609. Absolutism was the essence of kingship for James, who built a case for monarchical authority upon a base of medieval contract theory. This attempt to impose increased central authority underscores the growing power of nations in Modern Europe. This was an era of change that was producing new problems in government requiring new definitions of government. James I's assertion of absolute monarchy added to over a century of debate and counter-definitions on the origin and use of power. The following excerpt, taken from a speech that James made to Parliament in 1609, contains the King's theories on the proper relationship between a king and his subjects. Editors' note: the spellings and grammar of this document have been rendered in standard 20th century English for the convenience of the reader.

The monarchical state is the most supreme on earth, for kings are not only God's lieutenants on earth and sit upon God's throne, but are called gods even by God himself. There are three principal similarities [to God] that illustrate the monarchical state; one taken from the word of God, the other two grounded in policy and philosophy. In the Scriptures kings are called gods, and their power is compared in relationship to divine power. Kings are also compared to the fathers of families, for a king is truly *parens patriae,* [father of the family] the political father of his people. Lastly, kings are compared to the head of this microcosm of the body of man.

Kings are justly called gods, because they exercise a manner or resemblance of divine power on earth, for if you consider the attributes of God, you will see how they are found in the person of a king. God has the power to create or destroy, to make or unmake at His pleasure, to give life or send death, to judge all and be accountable to nobody. He has the power to raise low things and to make high things low at his pleasure, and to God both body and soul are due. And kings have like power: they make and unmake their subjects, they have the power of raising them up or casting them down, they have the power of life and death. They are judges over all of their subjects in all causes, and yet are themselves accountable to no one but God. They have the power to exalt low things and to abase high things, and to treat their subjects as if they were chessmen; a pawn to take a bishop or a knight....

Now a father of a family may dispose of his inheritance to his children at his pleasure; yea, he may even disinherit the eldest on just grounds and give preference to the youngest. He may make them beggars or rich at his pleasure. He can restrain them, or banish them from his presence if he finds them offensive, or he may restore them to favor again like penitent sinners: so may the King deal with his subjects....

Reprinted by permission of the publishers from *The Political Works of James I* edited by Charles Howard McIlwain, Cambridge: Harvard University Press, 1918.

Document 2:
SECOND TREATISE OF CIVIL GOVERNMENT (1690)
John Locke

The Second Treatise of Civil Government, which appeared in 1690, was one of John Locke's most influential works. A Whig opponent of absolute monarchy, Locke wrote this alternative theory on the origin of government after the English Civil War and the Glorious Revolution had destroyed the basis of divine right monarchy. As many other theorists of his age and the Enlightenment, Locke describes a "state of nature" that supposedly preceded organized societies and governments. Locke gives his theory of the contractual nature of government, the goals of government, and a justification of revolution should governments fail. Many of these ideas inspired Americans in the next century.

...2. To This purpose, I Think it may not be amiss to set down what I take to be political power. That the power of a magistrate over a subject may be distinguished from that of a father over his children, a master over his servant, a husband over his wife, and a lord over his slave. All which distinct powers happening sometimes together in the same man, if he be considered under these different relations, it may help us to distinguish these powers from one another, and show the difference betwixt a ruler of a commonwealth, a father of a family, and a captain of a galley.

3. Political power, then, I take to be a right of making laws, with penalties of death, and consequently all less penalties for the regulating and preserving of property, and of employing the force of the community in the execution of such laws, and in the defence of the commonwealth from foreign injury, and all this only for the public good.

Chapter II
Of the State of Nature

4. To understand political power right, and derive it from its original, we must consider what state all men are naturally in, and that is, a state of perfect freedom to order their actions and dispose of their possessions and persons as they think fit, within the bounds of the law of Nature; without asking leave or depending upon the will of any other man.

A state also of equality, wherein all the power and jurisdiction is reciprocal, no one having more than another, there being nothing more evident, than that creatures of the same species and rank, promiscuously born to all the same advantages of Nature, and the use of the same faculties, should also be equal one amongst another without subordination or subjection, unless the lord and master of them all should, by any manifest declaration of his will, set one above another, and confer on him, by an evident and clear appointment, an undoubted right to dominion and sovereignty....

6. But though this be a state of liberty, yet it is not a state of license; though man in that state have [sic] an uncontrollable liberty to dispose of his person or possessions, yet he has not liberty to destroy himself, or so much as any creature in his possession, but where some nobler use than its bare preservation call for it. The state of Nature has a law of Nature to govern it, which obliges every one, and reason, which is that law, teaches all mankind who will but consult it, that being all equal and independent, no one ought to harm another in his life, health, liberty, or possessions; for men being all the workmanship of one omnipotent and infinitely wise Maker; all the servants of one sovereign Master, sent into the world by His order and about His business; they are His property, whose workmanship they are made to last during His, not one another's pleasure. And, being furnished with like faculties, sharing all in one community of Nature, there cannot be supposed any such subordination among us that may authorize us to destroy another, as if we were made for one another's uses, as the inferior ranks of creatures are for ours. Every one as he is bound to preserve himself, and not to quit his station wilfully, so by the like reason, when his own preservation comes not in competition, ought he as much as he can to preserve the rest of mankind, and not unless it be to do justice to an offender, take away, or impair the life, or what tends to the preservation of life, the liberty, health, limb, or goods of another.

7. And that all men may be restrained from invading others' rights, and from doing hurt to one another, and the law of Nature be observed, which willeth the peace and preservation of all mankind, the execution of the law of Nature is in that state put into every man's hands, whereby every one has a right to punish the transgressors of that law to such a degree as may hinder its violation. For the law of nature would, as all other laws that concern men in this world, be in vain, if there were nobody that in the state of Nature had a power to execute the law, and thereby preserve the innocent and restrain offenders; and if any one in the state of nature may punish another for any evil he has done, every one may do so. For in that state of perfect equality, where naturally there is no superiority or jurisdiction of one over another, what any may do in prosecution of that law, every one must needs have a right to do.

8. And thus, in the state of nature, one man comes by a power over another, but yet this is not an absolute or arbitrary power to use a criminal, when he has got him in his hands, according to the passionate heats, or boundless extravagancy of his own will, but only to retrib-

ute to him so far as calm reason and conscience dictate, what is proportionate to his transgression, which is so much as may serve for reparation and restraint. For these two are the only reasons why one may lawfully do harm to another, which is what we call punishment. In transgressing the law of Nature, the offender declares himself to live by another rule than that of reason and common equity, which is that measure God has set to the actions of men for their mutual security, and so he becomes dangerous to mankind; the tie which is to secure them from injury and violence being slighted and broken by him, which being a trespass against the whole species, and the peace and safety of it, provided for by the law of Nature, every man upon this score, by the right he hath to preserve mankind in general, may restrain, or where it is necessary, destroy things noxious to them, and so may bring such evil on any one who hath transgressed that law, as may make him repent the doing of it, and thereby deter him, and by his example, others from doing the like mischief. And in this case, and upon this ground, every man hath a right to punish the offender, and be executioner of the law of Nature....

Chapter IV
Of Slavery

22. The natural liberty of man is to be free from any superior power on earth, and not to be under the will or legislative authority of man, but to have only the law of Nature for his rule. The liberty of man, in society, is to be under no other legislative power but that established by consent in the commonwealth, nor under the dominion of any will, or restraint of any law, but what that legislative shall enact according to the trust put in it. Freedom then is not..."a liberty for every one to do what he lists, to live as he pleases, and not to be tied by any laws;" but freedom of men under government is to have a standing rule to live by, common to every one of that society, and made by the legislative power erected in it. A liberty to follow my own will in all things where that rule prescribes not, not to be subject to the inconstant, uncertain, unknown, arbitrary will of another man, as freedom of nature is, to be under any other restraint but the law of Nature.

23. This freedom from absolute, arbitrary power, is so necessary to, and closely joined with, a man's preservation, that he cannot part with it, but by what forfeits his preservation and life together....

Chapter VIII
Of the Beginning of Political Societies

95. Men being, as has been said by Nature all free, equal, and independent, no one can be put out of this estate and subjected to the political power of another without his own consent, which is done by agreeing with other men to join and unite into a community for their comfortable, safe, and peaceable living, one amongst another, in a secure enjoyment of their properties, and a greater security against any, that are not of it. This any number of men may do, because it injures not the freedom of the rest; they are left as they were in the liberty of the state of Nature. When any number of men have so consented to make one community or government, they are thereby presently incorporated, and make one body politic, wherein the majority have a right to act and conclude the rest.

96. For, when any number of men have, by the consent of every individual, with a power to act as one body, which is only by the will and determination of the majority....

97. And thus every man, by consenting with others to make one body politic under one government, puts himself under an obligation, to every one of that society, to submit to the determination of the majority, and to be concluded by it; or else this original compact, whereby he with others incorporates into one society, would signify nothing, and be no compact if he be left free, and under no other ties than he was in before in the state of Nature....

Chapter IX
Of The Ends of Political Society and Government

123. If man in the state of Nature be so free as has been said, if he be absolute lord of his own person and possessions, equal to the greatest and subject to nobody, why will he part with his freedom, this empire, and subject himself to the dominion and control of any other power? To which it is obvious to answer, that though in the state of Nature he hath such a right,

yet the enjoyment of it is very uncertain, and constantly exposed to the invasion of others; for all being kings as much as he, every man his equal, and the greater part no strict observers of equity and justice, the enjoyment of the property he has in this state is very unsafe, very insecure. This makes him willing to quit a condition which, however free, is full of fears and continual dangers; and it is not without reason, that he seeks out and is willing to join in society with others who are already united, or have a mind to unite for the mutual preservation of their lives, liberties, and estates, which I call by the general name—property.

124. The great and chief end, therefore, of men uniting into commonwealths, and putting themselves under government, is the preservation of their property; to which in the state of nature there are many things wanting.

Firstly, there wants an established, settled, known law, received and allowed by common consent to be the standard of right and wrong, and the common measure to decide controversies between them....

Chapter XIX
Of the Dissolution of Government

222. The reason why men enter into society is the preservation of their property; and the end why they choose and authorize a legislative, is that there may be laws made, and rules set, as guards and fences to the properties of all the members of the society, to limit the power, and moderate the dominion of every part and member of the society. For since it can never be supposed to be the will of the society that the legislative should have a power to destroy that which every one designs to secure by entering into society, and for which the people submitted themselves to legislators of their own making; whenever the legislators endeavour to take away and destroy the property of the people, or to reduce them to slavery under arbitrary power, they put themselves into a state of war with the people, who are thereupon absolved from any farther obedience, and are left to the common refuge, which God hath provided for all men, against force and violence. Whensoever, therefore, the legislative shall transgress this fundamental rule of society, and either by ambition, fear, folly, or corruption, endeavour to grasp themselves, or put into the hands of any other, an absolute power over the lives, liberties, and estates of the people; by this breach of trust they forfeit the power the people had put into their hands for quite contrary ends, and it devolves to the people, who have a right to resume their original liberty, and, by the establishment of a new legislative, (such as they shall think fit) provide for their own safety and security, which is the end for which they are in society. What I have said here concerning the legislative in general holds true also concerning the supreme executor, who having a double trust put in him, both to have a part in the legislative and the supreme execution of the law, acts against both, when he goes about to set up his own arbitrary will as the law of the society....

From John Locke, *Two Treatises on Government*, in *Locke on Civil Government*, London: George Routledge and Sons, 1889, 240–307.

Document 3:
DU CONTRAT SOCIAL, OU PRINCIPES DU DROIT POLITIQUE
[The Social Contract] (1762)
Jean-Jacques Rousseau

Jean-Jacques Rousseau wrote his famous The Social Contract in 1762. In this work, he breaks with many of the figures of the Enlightenment who believed in social progress. Rousseau thought that mankind had been corrupted by society. "Man was born free, and everywhere he is in chains," asserts The Social Contract. Rousseau helped to usher in the next intellectual movement in Europe, Romanticism, which stressed the "natural" over the "artificial," feelings over reason, distinctiveness of individuals over similarities of all. These could be used by some to buttress individual freedoms. But he also wrote of a "general will" to which he demanded that individuals subsume their individual rights. Thus his writings on the one hand advocate great personal freedom, but on the other hand they seem to justify the suppression of individuality and minority rights. Even the French Revolution's Reign of Terror has been viewed as a working out of Rousseau's thoughts on the "general will." Another contradiction in his writings and life was his relegation of women to merely domestic roles. Nevertheless, he is important for his theories about the origin of states and societies in contracts and his tremendous influence on social, educational, and political theory.

Book I, Chapter 1
Subject of the First Book

Man is born free, and everywhere he is in chains. A person who believes himself to be the master of others, does not escape being a slave any more than them. How is this change made? I will ignore that. What can make it legitimate? I believe I can resolve this question.

If I would consider only that power, and the effect which derives from it, I would say: So long as a people is constrained to obey, and does obey, it does well; as soon as it can shake off the yoke, and does shake it off, it does better still; because, recovering its liberty by the same right that stole it away, either it is justified to reestablish it, or those who took it were not justified in their deeds. But the social order, which is a sacred right, is the foundation for all the others. However, this right does not come from nature....

Book I, Chapter 6
Concerning the Social Compact

I suppose that men in a state of nature have come to a point where the obstacles that threaten the safety of each individual in a state of nature are weightier than the strength that he can employ to maintain himself in this state. Then this primitive state can exist no longer; and the human race should perish if they do not change their manner of living.

However, since men cannot engender new forces, but merely unite and direct those which exist, the only other means they can employ for preservation is to form by aggregation an adding together of forces that might be able to carry on resistance, to be able to take the field in a single movement, and act in concert.

This adding together of forces must be born of the agreement of many; but since the strength and the freedom of each man are the chief instruments of his preservation, how can he engage them without threat and without neglecting the cares which he owes to himself?

This difficulty, leading to my subject, may be expressed in these terms:

"To find a form of association which defends and protects with the whole communal force the person and the goods of each person, and by which each person, united to all, shall obey only himself, and also remain as free as he had been?" Such is the fundamental problem, to which the social contract gives the solution.

The clauses of this contract are so determined by the nature of the act, that the least modification renders them null and void; and that, although they have perhaps never been formally enunciated, they are everywhere the same, everywhere tacitly accepted and recognized, so that once the social compact is violated each person regains his first freedom, and retakes his natural freedom, while losing the conventional freedom for which he had renounced it.

These clauses, well-understood, are reducible to a single point: the total alienation of each member, with all of his rights to the whole community; because first of all, each person gives himself wholly entire, the condition is equal for everyone; and the condition being equal for all, no one has an interest in rendering it onerous to the others.

Moreover, the alienation is made without any reserve; the union is as perfect as it can be, and no member has a claim to anything; because if he was to retain rights in particular, there would be no common superior who could decide between him and the public, each person being in some points his own proper judge, would soon pretend he were so in everything; and the state of nature would be revived, and the association necessarily would become tyrannical or vanquished.

Finally, each person gives himself to everyone, but not to any individual person; and as there is not a member over whom the same right is not acquired which is lost to him by others, each gains an equivalent for what he loses, and gains more strength for preserving that which he has.

If, therefore, we pare down from the social compact all that is not of the essence, one finds that it reduces to the following terms:

"Each of us takes in common and puts his person and all of his power under the supreme direction of the general will; and we shall accept each member as an indivisible part of the whole."

At this moment, instead of so many separate persons as there are contracting parties, this act of association produces a moral collective body, composed of such members as there are voices in the assembly; which from this act receives its unity, its common self, its life, and its will. This public person, who thus is formed by the union of all the others, took formerly the name of "city," and now takes that of "republic" or "body politic," and which is called by its members "state" when it is passive, and "sovereign" when it is active, and "power" when comparing it with similar bodies. Regarding its members, they take collectively the name of the "people," and separately that of "citizens," while participating in the sovereign authority, and "subjects" when they are put under the law of the state. But these terms are frequently confounded, and taken for one another; it suffices to know and to distinguish them when they are employed in all their precision....

Chapter 8
Concerning the Civil State

This passage from a state of nature to a civil state produces in man a very remarkable change, by substituting in his conduct justice for instinct, and giving to his actions a morality which had been lacking previously. It is only then when the voice of duty replaces physical impulse, and right replaces appetite, that man, who had until then looked only to himself, seems forced to act on other principles, and to consult his reason before listening to his penchants. Although he deprives himself in this state of several advantages that he owns in a state of nature, he regains several great ones, his faculties are used and developed, his ideas are broadened, his sentiments ennobled, his whole soul elevated to such an extent that, if the abuse of this new condition did not often degrade him to below the status that he had left, he should bless constantly the happy moment that detached him forever from it, and which changed him forever from a stupid, narrow-minded animal into being intelligent and a man.

Let us reduce this entire balance to easily-compared terms: that which natural man loses by the social contract, which is his natural freedom and an unlimited right to possess all that appeals to him and that he can acquire; and that which he gains, that is civil liberty and the ownership of all that he possesses. In order not to be mistaken about these compensations, it is necessary to distinguish between natural liberty, that which is limited only by the strength of the individual; and civil liberty, which is limited by the general will; and between possession, which is merely the effect of force or the right of first occupancy, and property, which can only be based upon positive title.

One can add to that which precedes that the acquisition of the civil state of moral liberty is alone what renders man truly master of himself; because to be impelled by appetite alone is slavery, and obedience to the law one has given to oneself is liberty. But I have already said too much on this topic, and the philosophical sense of the word "liberty" is not my topic here.

From Jean-Jacques Rousseau, *Du Contrat social, ou principes du droit politique* in *Oeuvres complètes de J.J. Rousseau*, volume V, Paris: P. Dupont, 1823, 64–84, translation by Michael Slaven.

Document 4:
THE AMERICAN DECLARATION OF INDEPENDENCE (1776)
Thomas Jefferson

This document, like the English Bill of Rights, *was an assertion of rights. But it was also a unique moment in Western history before the twentieth century when a group of colonies declared and successfully defended their independence from one of the most powerful states in the world. The authors of the* Declaration *justified their break with England in terms of the philosophy of the Enlightenment. The "natural rights of man" gave the colonists the right, according to the logic of the framers of the* Declaration, *"to dissolve the political bonds which have long connected them" to Great Britain. The philosophe Rousseau had said that government and individuals have made a "social contract," trading a portion of their liberty for the benefits that government could provide. He further stated that government must express the "general will" of the people, and that when it does not, it could rightfully be overthrown. Note that the right to abolish a tyranny, given in the declaration, had been discussed in many works dating back at least to the* Vindiciae Contra Tyrannos, *or even earlier, to the early Protestant doctrine of the rightful rebellion of the "lesser magistrate." Many vital ideas of the West are reflected in this document. Revolution is justified; unalienable rights are asserted. The goals of government are stated and the rights of people to take part in their own governance are asserted.*

The Declaration of Independence (1776)
In Congress, July 4, 1776
The Unanimous Declaration of the Thirteen
United States of America

When in the course of human events, it becomes necessary for one people to dissolve the political bonds which have long connected them with another, and to assume among the powers of the earth, the separate and equal station to which the Laws of Nature and of Nature's God require them, a decent respect to the opinions of mankind requires that they should declare the causes which impel them to the separation.

We hold these truths to be self-evident, that all men are created equal, that they are endowed by their Creator with certain unalienable rights, that among these are Life, Liberty, and the pursuit of Happiness; That to secure these rights, Governments are instituted among Men, deriving their just powers from the consent of the governed; That whenever any Form of Government becomes destructive of these ends, it is the Right of the People to alter or to abolish it, and to institute new Government, laying its foundation on such principles, and organizing its powers in such form, as to them shall seem most likely to effect their Safety and Happiness. Prudence, indeed, will dictate that Governments long established should not be changed for light and transient causes; and accordingly all experience hath shown, that mankind are more disposed to suffer, while evils are sufferable, than to right themselves by abolishing the forms to which they are accustomed. But when a long train of abuses and usurpations, pursuing invariably the same Object, evinces a design to reduce them under absolute despotism, it is their right, it is their duty, to throw off such Government, and to provide new Guards for their future security. Such has been the patient sufferance of these colonies; and such is now the necessity which constrains them to alter their former systems of government.

Document 5:
REFLECTIONS ON THE REVOLUTION IN FRANCE (1790)
Edmund Burke

Edmund Burke's Reflections on the Revolution in France *is considered a classic defense of conservatism. Burke thought that the French Revolution was a terrible mistake because it broke with traditions and existing institutions and invited unknown evils. Burke called for slow, evolutionary changes made within the existing system. Government, he argued, was on the one hand a contract, but it was one between the living, the dead, and those yet to be born. On the other hand, Burke believed that a system that could not change could not continue to exist. He was not opposed to all change; indeed, he spoke out for the Irish and the Americans during this era when he felt that government policies were wrong towards those peoples.*

To avoid...the evils of inconstancy and versatility, ten thousand times worse than those of obstinacy and the blindest prejudice, we have consecrated the state, that no man should approach to look into its defects or corruptions but with due caution; that he should never dream of beginning its reformation by its subversion; that he should approach to the faults of the state as to the wounds of a father, with pious awe and trembling solicitude. By this wise prejudice we are taught to look with horror on those children of their country who are prompted rashly to hack that aged parent in pieces and put him into the kettle of magicians, in hopes that by their poisonous weeds and wild incantations they may regenerate the paternal constitution and renovate their father's life.

Society is, indeed, a contract. Subordinate contracts for objects of mere occasional interest may be dissolved at pleasure; but the state ought not to be considered as nothing better than a partnership agreement in a trade in pepper and coffee, calico, or tobacco, or some other such low concern, to be taken up for a little temporary interest, and to be dissolved by the fancy of the parties. It is to be looked on with other reverence; because it is not a partnership in things subservient only to the gross animal existence of a temporary and perishable nature. It is a partnership in all science, a partnership in all art, a partnership in every virtue and in all perfection. As the end of such a partnership cannot be obtained in many generations, it becomes a partnership not only between those who are living, but between those who are living, those who are dead, and those who are to be born. Each contract of each particular state is but a clause in the great primeval contract of eternal society, linking the lower with the higher natures, connecting the visible and the invisible, according to a fixed compact sanctioned by the inviolable oath which holds all physical and all moral natures each in their appointed place. This law is not subject to the will of those who, by an obligation above them, and infinitely superior, are bound to submit their will to that law. The municipal corporations of that universal kingdom are not morally at liberty, at their pleasure, and on their speculations of a contingent improvement, wholly to separate and tear asunder the bands of their subordinate community, and to dissolve it into an unsocial, uncivil, unconnected chaos of elementary principles. It is the first and supreme necessity only, a necessity that is not chosen but chooses, a necessity paramount to deliberation, that admits no discussion and demands no evidence, which alone can justify a resort to anarchy. This necessity is no exception to the rule; because this necessity is a part, too, of that moral and physical disposition of things to which man must be obedient by consent or by force: but if that which is only submission to necessity should be made the object of choice, the law is broken, Nature is disobeyed, and the rebellious are outlawed, cast forth, and exiled, from this world of reason, and order, and peace, and virtue, and fruitful penitence, into the antagonist world of madness, discord, vice, confusion, and unavailing sorrow.

From *Reflections on the Revolution in France* in *The Writings and Speeches of the Right Honorable Edmund Burke* [Beaconsfield Edition], volume 3, Boston: Little, Brown, 1901, 358–360.

CHAPTER 2

Individual Rights: Declarations of Rights in England, America and France, 1689–1789

Document 6:
MAGNA CARTA (1215)

The Magna Carta (1215) is often cited as a foundation stone of human rights in the English tradition and is included here because of its obvious importance, in spite of its date which otherwise is outside the scope of this work. King John was forced by his great nobles to agree to follow the traditions and respect the rights of people of his realm. An important principle was thus enunciated: even the king was subject to the law. The specific grievances listed merely reveal the complaints of the era (note also the anti-semitic content of paragraph 10, an ironic blemish in a seminal human rights document); but the articulation of grievances and the demand to remedy them has become a critical vehicle for change in the West. Many of the terms used in this document are specialized and need not concern the general reader.

John, by the Grace of God, King of England, Lord of Ireland, Duke of Normandy, Aquitaine, and Count of Anjou, to his Archbishops, Bishops, Abbots, Earls, Barons, Justiciaries, Foresters, Sheriffs, Governors, Officers, and to all Bailiffs, and his faithful subjects greeting. Know ye, that we, in the presence of God, and for the salvation of our soul, and the souls of all our ancestors and heirs, and unto the honour of God and the advancement of Holy Church, and the amendment of our Realm, by advice of our venerable Fathers, Stephen, Archbishop of Canterbury, Primate of all England and Cardinal of the Holy Roman Church...;and others, our liegemen, have, in the first place granted to God, and by this our present Charter confirmed, for us and our heirs for ever:—

1. That the Church of England shall be free, and have her whole rights, and her liberties inviolable; and we will have them so observed that it may appear thence that the freedom of elections, which is reckoned chief and indispensable to the English Church, and which we granted and confirmed by our Charter, and obtained the confirmation of the same from our Lord the Pope Innocent III, before the discord between us and our barons, was granted of mere free will; which Charter shall observe, and we do will it to be faithfully observed by our heirs forever.

2. We also have granted to all the freemen of our kingdom, for us and for our heirs for ever, all the underwritten liberties, to be had and holden by them and their heirs, of us and our heirs for ever....

3. But if the heir of any such shall be under age, and shall be in ward, when he comes of age he shall have his inheritance without relief and without fine.

4. The keeper of the land of such an heir being under age, shall take of the land of the heir none but reasonable issues, reasonable customs, and reasonable services, and that without destruction and waste of his men and his goods....

6. Heirs shall be married without disparagement, and so that before matrimony shall be contracted, those who are near in blood to the heir shall have notice.

7. A widow, after the death of her husband, shall forthwith and without difficulty have her marriage and inheritance; nor shall she give anything for her dower, or her marriage, or her inheritance, which her husband and she held at the day of his death; and she may remain in the mansion house of her husband forty days after his death, within which time her dower shall be assigned....

8. Neither we nor our bailiffs shall seize any land or rent for any debt as long as the chattels of the debtor are sufficient to pay the debt....

9. No widow shall be distrained to marry herself, so long as she has a mind to live without a husband; but yet she shall give security that she will not marry without our assent....

10. If any one have borrowed anything of the Jews, more or less, and die before the debt be satisfied, there shall be no interest paid for that debt, so long as the heir is under age, of whomsoever he may hold; and if the debt falls into our hands, we will only take the chattel mentioned in the deed....

12. No scutage or aid shall be imposed in our kingdom, unless by the general council of our kingdom; except for ransoming our person, making our eldest son a knight and once for marrying our eldest daughter; and for these there shall be paid no more than a reasonable aid. In like manner it shall be concerning the aids of the City of London.

13. And the City of London shall have all its ancient liberties and free customs, as well by land as by water; furthermore, we will grant that all other cities and boroughs, and towns and ports, shall have all their liberties and free customs.

14. And for holding the general council of the kingdom concerning the assessment of aids, except in the three cases aforesaid, and for the assessing or scutages, we shall cause to be summoned the archbishops, bishops, abotts, earls, and greater barons of the realm, singly by our letters. And furthermore, we shall cause to be summoned generally, by our sheriffs and bailiffs, all others who hold of us in chief, for a certain day, that is to say, forty days before their meeting at least, and to a certain place; and in all letters of such summons we will declare the cause of such summons. And summons being thus made, the business shall proceed on the day appointed, according the advice of such as shall be present, although all that were summoned come not....

23. Neither a town nor any tenant shall be distrained to make bridges or embankments, unless that anciently and of right they are bound to do it....

29. No constable shall distrain any knight to give money for castle-guard, if he himself will do it in his person, or by another able man, in case he cannot do it through any reasonable cause. And if we have carried or sent him into the army, he shall be free from such guard for the time he shall be in the army by our command.

30. No sheriff or bailiff of ours, or any other, shall take horses or carts of any freeman for carriage, without the assent of the said freeman....

36. Nothing from henceforth shall be given or taken for a writ of inquisition of life or limb, but it shall be granted freely, and not denied....

38. No bailiff from henceforth shall put any man to his law upon his own bare saying, without credible witnesses to prove it.

39. No freeman shall be taken or imprisoned or disseised, or outlawed, or banished, or in any way destroyed, nor will we pass upon him, nor will we send upon him, unless by the lawful judgment of his peers or by the law of the land.

40. We will sell to no man, we will not deny to any man, either justice or right....

45. We will not make any justices, constables, sheriffs, or bailiffs, but of such as know the law of the realm and mean duly to observe it....

56. If we have disseised or dispossessed the Welsh of any lands, liberties, or other things, without the legal judgment of their peers, either in England or in Wales, they shall be immediately restored to them....

59. We will treat with Alexander, King of Scots, concerning the restoring of his sister and hostages, and his right and liberties, in the same form and manner as we shall do to the rest of our barons of England....

61. And whereas, for the honour of God and the amendment of our kingdom, and for the better quieting the discord that has arisen between us and our barons, we have granted all these things aforesaid; willing to render them firm and lasting, we do give and grant our subjects the underwritten security, namely that the barons may choose five-and-twenty barons of the kingdom, whom they think convenient; who shall take care, with all their amight, to hold and observe, and cause to be observed, the peace and liberties we have granted them, and by this our present Charter confirmed in this manner....

63. Wherefore we will and firmly enjoin, that the Church of England be free, and that all men in our kingdom have and hold all the aforesaid liberties, rights, and concessions, truly and peaceably, freely and quietly, fully and wholly to themselves and their heirs, of us and our heirs, in all things and places, for ever, as is aforesaid. It is also sworn, as well on our part as on the part of the barons, that all the things aforesaid shall be observed in good faith, and without evil subtilty. Given under our hand, in the presence of the witnesses above named, and many others, in the meadow called Runingmede, between Windsor and Staines, the 15th day of June, in the 17th year of our reign.

From *Old South Leaflets No. 5*, Volume I, Boston: Directors of the Old South Work, 1896, 1–13.

Document 7:
THE RIGHTS OF MAN (1792)
Thomas Paine

In this famous work, Paine justifies revolution and answers Burke's criticism of revolution in France. Paine was one of the more radical thinkers who early on advocated American independence from Britain, and established a classic defense of natural rights.

Every generation is equal in rights to the generation which preceded it, by the same rule that every individual is born equal in rights with his contemporary.

Every history of the creation, and every traditionary account, whether from the lettered or the unlettered world, however they may vary in their opinion or belief of certain particulars, all agree in establishing one point, *the unity of man*; by which I mean that men are all of *one degree*, and consequently that all men are born equal, and with equal natural right, in the same manner as if posterity had been continued by *creation* instead of *generation*, the latter being only the mode by which the former is carried forward; and consequently every child born into the world must be considered as deriving its existence from God. The world is as new to him as it was to the first man that existed, and his natural right in it is of the same kind....

The duty of man is not a wilderness of turnpike gates through which he is to pass by tickets from one to the other. It is plain and simple, and consists but of two points: his duty to God, which every man must feel; and with respect to his neighbor, to do as he would be done by. If those to whom power is delegated do well, they will be respected; if not, they will be despised; and with regard to those to whom no power is delegated, but who assume it, the rational world can know nothing of them....

Natural rights are those which appertain to man in right of his existence. Of this kind are all the intellectual rights, or rights of the mind, and also all those rights of acting as an individual for his own comfort and happiness which are not injurious to the natural rights of others. Civil rights are those which appertain to man in right of his being a member of society. Every civil right has for its foundation some natural right pre-existing in the individual, but to the enjoyment of which his individual power is not, in all cases, sufficiently competent. Of this kind are all those which relate to security and protection.

From this short review, it will be easy to distinguish between that class of natural rights which man retains after entering into society, and those which he throws into the common stock as a member of society....

From these premises two or three certain conclusions follow:

First, that every civil right grows out of a natural right; or, in other words, is a natural right exchanged.

Secondly, that civil power properly considered as such is made up of the aggregate of that class of the natural rights of man which becomes defective in the individual in point of power, and answers not his purpose, but when collected to a focus, becomes competent to the purpose of every one.

Thirdly, that the power produced from the aggregate of natural rights, imperfect in power in the individual, cannot be applied to invade the natural rights which are retained in the individual, and in which the power to execute is as perfect as the right itself.

We have now, in a few words, traced man from a natural individual to a member of society, and shown the quality of the natural rights retained, and of those which are exchanged for civil rights. Let us now apply these principles to governments.

It has been thought a considerable advance towards establishing the principle of freedom to say that government is a compact between those who govern and those who are governed; but this cannot be true, because it is putting the effect before the cause; for a man must have existed before governments existed, there necessarily was a time when governments did not exist....

A constitution is not a thing in name only, but in fact. It has not an ideal, but a real existence; and wherever it cannot be produced in a visible form, there is none. A constitution is a thing *antecedent* to a government, and a government is only the creature of a constitution. The constitution of a country is not the act of its government, but of the people constituting its government. It is the body of elements to which you can refer and quote article by article; and which contains the principles on which the government shall be established, the manner in which it shall be organized, the powers it shall have, the mode of elections, the duration of parliaments, or by what other name such bodies may be called; the powers which the executive part of the government shall have; and, in fine, everything that relates to the complete organization of a civil government, and the principles on which it shall act, and by which it shall be bound. A constitution, therefore, is to a government what the laws made afterward by that government are to a court of judicature. The court of judicature does not make the laws, neither can it alter them; it only acts in conformity to the laws made: and the government is in like manner governed by the constitution.

From Thomas Paine, *The Rights of Man: Being an Answer to Mr. Burke's Attack on the French Revolution, Part I*, London: H.D. Symonds, 1792, 21–24.

Document 8:
THE ENGLISH BILL OF RIGHTS (1689)

As a part of the settlement that changed the British throne and instituted a new balance based upon the crown and Parliament, it was felt necessary to assert again the traditional rights that had been violated during the long period of strife in the seventeenth century. Many of these rights will appear in later bills of rights in various other countries until the present time. They represent fundamental protections against arbitrary government.

And whereas the said late King James II having abdicated the government, and the throne being thereby vacant, his Highness the Prince of Orange...did...cause letters to be written to the other Lords Spiritual and Temporal being Protestants, and other letters to the several counties, cities, universities, boroughs, and cinque ports for the choosing of such persons to represent them as were of right to be sent to Parliament to meet and sit at Westminster upon the two-and-twentieth day of January in the year...[1689] in order to such an establishment as that their religion, laws, and liberties might not again be in danger of being subverted; upon which letters elections have been accordingly made.

And thereupon the said Lords Spiritual and Temporal and Commons...declare:—

1. That the pretended power of suspending of laws or the execution of laws by regal authority without consent of Parliament is illegal.

2. That the pretended power of dispensing with laws or the execution of laws by regal authority, as it hath been assumed and exercised of late, is illegal.

3. That the commission for erecting the late Court of Commissioners for Ecclesiastical Causes and all other Commissions and Courts of like nature, are illegal and pernicious.

4. That levying money for or to the use of the Crown by pretence of prerogative without consent of Parliament for longer time or in other manner than the same is or shall be granted, is illegal.

5. That it is the right of the subjects to petition the King, and all commitments and prosecutions for such petitioning, are illegal.

6. That the raising or keeping a standing army within the kingdom in time of peace unless it be with consent of Parliament, is against law.

7. That the subjects which are Protestants may have arms for their defence suitable to their conditions and as allowed by law.

8. That election of members of Parliament ought to be free.

9. That the freedom of speech and debates or proceedings in Parliament ought not to be impeached or questioned in any court or place out of Parliament.

10. That excessive bail ought not to be required, nor excessive fines imposed, nor cruel and unusual punishments inflicted.

11. That jurors ought to be duly impanelled and returned, and jurors which pass upon men in trials for high treason, ought to be freeholders.

12. That all grants and promises of fines and forfeitures of particular persons before conviction, are illegal and void.

Document 9:
THE UNITED STATES BILL OF RIGHTS (1791)

These are the first ten amendments to the Constitution of the United States. Note the similarities to the English Bill of Rights. *Again, these represent some of the most essential human rights and remain the subject of discussion and interpretation until the present. The implications of the* Bill of Rights *seem to justify a wide latitude of legislative action to some legal scholars, while the same ten articles are viewed by others as fixed limits in law not to be tampered with without extreme cause.*

Article I

Congress shall make no law respecting an establishment of religion, or prohibiting the free exercise thereof; or abridging the freedom of speech, or of the press; or the right of the people peaceably to assemble, and to petition the Government for a redress of grievances.

Article II

A well regulated Militia, being necessary to the security of a free State, the right of the people to keep and bear Arms, shall not be infringed.

Article III

No Soldier shall, in time of peace be quartered in any house, without the consent of the Owner, nor in time of war, but in manner to be prescribed by law.

Article IV

The rights of the people to be secure in their persons, houses, papers, and effects against unreasonable searches and seizures, shall not be violated, and no Warrants shall issue, but upon probable cause, supported by Oath or affirmation, and particularly describing the place to be searched, and the persons or things to be seized.

Article V

No person shall be held to answer for a capital, or otherwise infamous crime, unless on a presentment or indictment of a Grand Jury, except in cases arising in the land or naval forces, or in the Militia, when in actual service in time of War or public danger; nor shall any person be subject for the same offence to be twice put in jeopardy of life or limb; nor shall be compelled in any Criminal Case to be a witness against himself, nor be deprived of life, liberty, or property, without due process of law; nor shall private property be taken for public use, without just compensation.

Article VI

In all criminal prosecutions, the accused shall enjoy the right to a speedy and public trial, by an impartial jury of the State and district wherein the crime shall have been committed, which district shall have been previously ascertained by law, and to be informed of the nature and cause of the accusation; to be confronted with the witnesses against him; to have compulsory process for obtaining witnesses in his favor, and to have the Assistance of Counsel for his defense.

Article VII

In Suits at common law, where the value in controversy shall exceed twenty dollars, the right of trial by jury shall be preserved, and no fact tried by a jury, shall be otherwise reexamined in any Court of the United States than according to the rules of the common law.

Article VIII

Excessive bail shall not be required, nor excessive fines imposed, nor cruel and unusual punishments inflicted.

Article IX

The enumeration in the Constitution, of certain rights, shall not be construed to deny or disparage others retained by the people.

Article X

The powers not delegated to the United States by the Constitution, nor prohibited by it to the States, are reserved to the States respectively, or to the people.

Document 10:
THE DECLARATION OF THE RIGHTS OF MAN AND THE CITIZEN (1789)

France's Declaration of the Rights of Man and the Citizen *has been one of the most widely admired documents in European history. The French Revolution called for "Liberty, Equality, and Fraternity," and this detailed articulation of that call has inspired generations of revolutionaries, reformers, and philosophers.*

In 1789 the Declaration *was a radical break with the French tradition of absolutism. No longer were distinctions of class to be used to distinguish men under the laws of the country. The document declared that "All citizens being equal in its eyes are equally admissible to all public dignities, offices and employments, according to their capacity, and with no other distinction than that of their virtues and talents." This statement sounds quite impressive, but several inconsistencies are discernable to the critical reader. The right to hold property is guaranteed, and yet the property of the nobility and the church was confiscated and sold during the revolution. Women are not given full rights as citizens. Nowhere does the* Declaration *give rights to a decent standard of living, or freedom from hunger, or the right to an education. Still, given the limits of the document, the* Declaration *rightfully has remained a symbol of enlightened political theory.*

The representatives of the French people, organized as a National Assembly, believing that the ignorance, neglect, or contempt of the rights of man are the sole causes of public calamities and of corruption of governments, have determined to set forth in a solemn declaration of the natural, inalienable and sacred rights of man, in order that this declaration, being constantly before all the members of the social body, shall remind them continually of their rights and duties; in order that the acts of the legislative power, as well as those of the executive power, may be compared at any moment with the ends of all political institutions and may be thus more respected; and, lastly, in order that grievances of the citizens, based hereafter upon simple and incontestable principles, shall tend to the maintenance of the constitution and redound to the happiness of all. Therefore the National Assembly recognizes and proclaims, in the presence and under the auspices of the Supreme Being, the following rights of man and citizen:—

1. Men are born free and remain free and equal in rights. Social distinctions may only be founded upon the general good.

2. The aim of all political association is the preservation of the natural and imprescriptible rights of man. These rights are liberty, property, security, and resistance to oppression.

3. The principle of sovereignty resides essentially in the nation. No body nor individual may exercise any authority which does not proceed directly from the nation.

4. Liberty consists in the freedom to do everything which injures no one else; hence the exercise of the natural rights of each man has no limits except those which assure to other members of the society the enjoyment of the same rights. These limits can only be determined by law.

5. Law can only prohibit those actions as are hurtful to society. Nothing may be prevented which is not forbidden by law, and no one may be forced to do anything not provided for by law.

6. Law is the expression of the general will. Every citizen has a right to take part personally or through his representative in its formation. It must be the same for all, whether it protects or punishes. All citizens, being equal in the eyes of the law, are equally eligible to all public positions and occupations, according to their abilities, and without distinction except that of their virtues and talents.

7. No person shall be accused, arrested or imprisoned except in the cases and according to the forms prescribed by law. Any one soliciting, transmitting, executing or causing to be executed any arbitrary order shall be punished. But any citizen summoned or arrested in virtue of the law shall submit without delay, as resistance constitutes an offence.

8. The law shall provide for such punishments only as are strictly and obviously necessary, and no one shall suffer punishment except it be legally inflicted in virtue of a law passed and promulgated before the commission of the offense.

9. As all persons are held innocent until they shall have been declared guilty, if arrest shall be deemed indispensable, all harshness not essential to the securing of the prisoner's person shall be severely repressed by law.

10. No one shall be disquieted on account of his opinions, including his religious views, provided their manifestation does not disturb the public order established by law.

11. The free communication of ideas and opinions is one of the most precious of the rights of man. Every citizen may, accordingly, speak, write, and print with freedom, but shall be responsible for such abuses of this freedom as shall be defined by law.

12. The security of the rights of man and the citizen requires public military force. These forces are, therefore, established for the good of all, and not for the personal advantage of those to whom they shall be entrusted.

13. A common contribution is essential for the maintenance of the public forces and for the cost of administration. This should be equitably distributed among all the citizens in proportion to their means.

14. All citizens have a right to decide either personally or by their representatives, as to the necessity of the public contribution; to grant this freely; to know to what uses it is put; and to fix the proportion, the mode of assessment, and of collection, and the duration of the taxes.

15. Society has the right to require of every public agent an account of his administration.

16. A society in which the observance of the law is not assured, nor the separation of powers defined, has no constitution at all.

17. Since property is an inviolable and sacred right, no one shall be deprived thereof except where public necessity, legally determined, shall clearly demand it, and then only on the condition that the owner shall have been previously and equitably indemnified.

From *Translations and Reprints from the Original Sources in European History*, edited by Dept. of History of the University of Pennsylvania, Philadelphia, 1897, I, no. 5, 6–8.

CHAPTER 3

Forgotten Individuals

Document 11:
ON THE INDIANS (1696 Edition)
Franciscus de Vittoria

Franciscus de Vittoria [also known as Victoria] (1480?-1546) was a contemporary of Erasmus, and a Dominican friar. He studied Spanish law and lectured on the rights of the "Indians" of the Americas. Vittoria's was a rare voice raised for tolerance, even for those whom good Catholics condemned as heretics.

...The Pope has no temporal power over the Indian aborigines or over other unbelievers....For he has no temporal power save such as subserves spiritual matters. But he has no spiritual power over them (I Corinth., ch. 5, v. 12). Therefore he has no temporal power either.

The corollary follows that even if the barbarians refuse to recognize any lordship of the Pope, that furnishes no ground for making war on them and seizing their property. This is clear, because he has no such lordship. And it receives manifest confirmation from the fact that, even if the barbarians refuse to accept Christ as their lord, this does not justify making war on them or doing them any hurt. Now, it is utterly absurd for our opponents [in the legal debate over the rights of Indians] to say that, while the barbarians go scatheless for rejecting Christ, they should be bound to accept His vicar under penalty of war and confiscation of their property, aye, and penal chastisement. And a second confirmation is furnished by the fact that the ground, according to the persons in question, for disallowing compulsion, even if they refuse to accept Christ or His faith, is that it can not be evidently proved to them by natural reasoning. But the lordship of the Pope admits of this proof still less. Therefore they can not be compelled to recognize this lordship....

Accordingly, there is another title which can be set up, namely, by right of discovery; and no other title was originally set up, and it was in virtue of this title alone that Columbus the Genoan first set sail. And this seems to be an adequate title because those regions which are deserted become, by the law of nations and the natural law, the property of the first occupant. Therefore, as the Spaniards were the first to discover and occupy the provinces in question, they are in lawful possession thereof, just as if they had discovered some lonely and thitherto uninhabited region.

Not much, however, need be said about this...title of ours, because, as proved above, the barbarians were true owners, both from the public and from the private standpoint. Now the rule of the law of nations is that what belongs to nobody is granted to the first occupant, as is expressly laid down in the aforementioned passage....And so, as the object in question was not without an owner, it does not fall under the title which we are discussing. Although, then, this title, when conjoined with another, can produce some effect here, yet in and by itself it gives no support to a seizure of the aborigines any more than if it had been they who had discovered us....

From Franciscus de Victoria, *De Indis et de Iure Belli Relectiones* reprinted in *The Classics of International Law, De Indis Et De Iure Belli Relectiones, Being Parts of Relectiones Theologicae*, translated by John Bawley Pate, Washington, D.C.: Carnegie Institute, 1917, 137–139.

Document 12:
LETTER FROM ABIGAIL ADAMS TO HER HUSBAND, JOHN ADAMS (1776)

Abigail Adams raises an obvious question: Why were women omitted during the important debates concerning American rights and governance? She questioned one of the basic assumptions of patriarchal society: that husbands have a legal priority over their wives. The original language and grammar are kept in this selection in order that the modern reader can better appreciate Adams's folksy, witty style.

B[raintre]e May 7, 1776

How many are the solitary hours I spend, ruminating upon the past, and anticipating the future, whilst you overwhelmd with the cares of State, have but few moments you can devote to any individual. All domestick pleasures and injoyments are absorbed in the great and important duty you owe your Country "for our Country is as it were a secondary God, and the

First and greatest parent. It is to be preferred to Parents, Wives, Children, Friends and all things the Gods only excepted. For if our Country perishes it is as imposible to save an Individual, as to preserve one of the fingers of a Mortified Hand." Thus do I supress every wish, and silence every Murmer, acquiesceing in a painfull Seperation from the companion of my youth, and the Friend of my Heart.

I believe tis near ten days since I wrote you a line. I have not felt in a humour to entertain you. If I had taken up my pen perhaps some unbecomeing invective might have fallen from it; the Eyes of our Rulers have been closed and a Lethargy has seazd almost every Member. I fear a fatal Security has taken possession of them. Whilst the Building is on flame they tremble at the expence of water to quench it, in short two months has elapsed since the evacuation of Boston, and very little has been done in that time to secure it, or the Harbour from future invasion till the people are all in a flame; and no one among us that I have heard of even mentions expence, they think universally that there has been an amaizing neglect some where. Many have turnd out as volunteers to work upon Nodles Island, and many more would go upon Nantaskit if it was once set on foot. "Tis a Maxim of state That power and Liberty are like Heat and moisture; where they are well mixt every thing prospers, where they are single, they are destructive."

A Government of more Stability is much wanted in this colony, and they are ready to receive it from the Hands of the Congress, and since I have begun with Maxims of State I will add an other viz. that a people may let a king fall, yet still remain a people, but if a king let his people slip from him, he is no longer a king. And as this is most certainly our case, why not proclaim to the World in decisive terms your own importance?

Shall we not be dispiced by foreign powers for hesitateing so long at a word?

I can not say that I think you very generous to the Ladies, for whilst you are proclaiming peace and good will to Men, Emancipating all Nations, you insist upon retaining an absolute power over Wives. But you must remember that Arbitary power is like most other things which are very hard, very liable to be broken—and notwithstanding all your wise Laws and Maxims we have it in our power not only to free ourselves but to subdue our Masters, and without violence throw both your natural and legal authority at our feet—

"Charm by accepting, by submitting sway
Yet have our Humour most when we obey."

I thank you for several Letters which I have received since I wrote Last. They alleviate a tedious absence, and I long earnestly for a Saturday Evening, and experience a similar pleasure to that which I used to find in the return of my Friend upon that day after a weeks absence. The Idea of a year dissolves all my Phylosophy.

Our Little ones whom you so often recommend to my care and instruction shall not be deficient in virture or probity if the precepts of a Mother have their desired Effect, but they would be doubly inforced could they be indulged with the example of a Father constantly before them; I often point them to their Sire

"engaged in a corrupted State
Wrestling with vice and faction."

From L.H. Butterfield, Marc Friedlander and Mary-Jo Kline, eds., *The Book of Abigail and John, Selected Letters of the Adams Family, 1762–1784*, Cambridge, Massachussetts: Harvard University Press, 1975, 126–127.

Document 13:
DECLARATION OF THE RIGHTS OF WOMAN AND THE FEMALE CITIZEN (1791)
Olympe De Gouges

Olympe de Gouges's Declaration of the Rights of Woman and the Female Citizen *was presented to the Queen of France, Marie Antoinette, in an attempt to get her support for the rights of women in revolutionary France. The* Declaration of the Rights of Man and Citizen *had been adopted two years previously, and had blamed all governmental abuse on the disregard of the rights of man. Olympe de Gouges wrote her own version of the declaration, this time based on the rights of* women, *not men. Her preamble is a direct parody of the earlier document. The attempt by Gouges to rectify the exclusion of women from political and social equality was unsuccessful in spite of the important role that women played in the*

Revolution. Two years later, her opposition to the Jacobin Terror caused her to be brought to trial and beheaded by the Revolutionary Tribunal.

For the National Assembly to decree in its last sessions, or in those of the next legislature:
Preamble

Mothers, daughters, sisters [and] representatives of the nation demand to be constituted into a national assembly. Believing that ignorance, omission, or scorn for the rights of woman are the only causes of public misfortunes and of the corruption of governments, [the women] have resolved to set forth in a solemn declaration the natural, inalienable, and sacred rights of woman in order that this declaration, constantly exposed before all the members of the society, will ceaselessly remind them of their rights and duties; in order that the authoritative acts of women and the authoritative acts of men may be at any moment compared with and respectful of the purpose of all political institutions; and in order that citizens' demands, henceforth based on simple and incontestable principles, will always support the constitution, good morals, and the happiness of all.

Consequently, the sex that is as superior in beauty as it is in courage during the sufferings of maternity recognizes and declares in the presence and under the auspices of the Supreme Being, the following Rights of Women and of Female Citizens.

Article I. Woman is born free and lives equal to man in her rights. Social distinctions can be based only on the common utility.

Article II. The purpose of any political association is the conservation of the natural and imprescriptible rights of woman and man; these rights are liberty, property, security, and especially resistance to oppression.

Article III. The principle of all sovereignty rests essentially with the nation, which is nothing but the union of woman and man; no body and no individual can exercise any authority which does not come expressly from it [the nation].

Article IV. Liberty and justice consist of restoring all that belongs to others; thus, the only limits on the exercise of the natural rights of woman are perpetual male tyranny; these limits are to be reformed by the laws of nature and reason.

Article V. Laws of nature and reason proscribe all acts harmful to society; everything which is not prohibited by these wise and divine laws cannot be prevented, and no one can be constrained to do what they do not command.

Article VI. The law must be the expression of the general will; all female and male citizens must contribute either personally or through their representatives to its formation; it must be the same for all: male and female citizens, being equal in the eyes of the law, must be equally admitted to all honors, positions, and public employment according to their capacity and without other distinctions besides those of their virtues and talents.

Article VII. No woman is an exception; she is accused, arrested and detained in cases determined by law. Women, like men, obey this rigorous law.

Article VIII. The law must establish only those penalties that are strictly and obviously necessary, and no one can be punished except by virtue of a law established and promulgated prior to the crime and legally applicable to women.

Article IX. Once any woman is declared guilty, complete rigor is [to be] exercised by the law.

Article X. No one is to be disquieted for his very basic opinions; woman has the right to mount the scaffold; she must equally have the right to mount the rostrum, provided that her demonstrations do not disturb the legally established public order.

Article XI. The free communication of thoughts and opinions is one of the most precious rights of woman, since that liberty assures the recognition of children by their fathers. Any female citizen thus may say freely, I am the mother of a child which belongs to you, without being forced by a barbarous prejudice to hide the truth; [an exception may be made] to respond to the abuse of this liberty in cases determined by the law.

Article XII. The guarantee of the rights of woman and the female citizen implies a major benefit; this guarantee must be instituted for the advantage of all, and not for the particular benefit of those to whom it is entrusted.

Article XIII. For the support of the public force and the expenses of administration, the contributions of woman and man are equal; she shares all the duties [*corvées*] and all the painful tasks; therefore, she must have the same share in the distribution of positions, employment, offices, honors, and jobs [*industrie*].

Article XIV. Female and male citizens have the right to verify, either by themselves or through their representatives, the necessity of the public contribution. This can only apply to women if they are granted an equal share, not only of wealth, but also of public administration, and in the determination of the proportion, the base, the collection, and the duration of the tax.

Article XV. The collectivity of women, joined for tax purposes to the aggregate of men, has the right to demand an accounting of his administration from any public agent.

Article XVI. No society has a constitution without the guarantee of rights and the separation of powers; the constitution is null if the majority of individuals comprising the nation have not cooperated in drafting it.

Article XVII. Property belongs to both sexes whether united or separate; for each it is an inviolable and sacred right; no one can be deprived of it, since it is the true patrimony of nature, unless the legally determined public need obviously dictates it, and then only with a just and prior indemnity.

From *Women in Revolutionary Paris, 1789–1795*, selected and translated by Darline Gay Levy, Harriet Branson Applewhite, Mary Durham Johnson, Urbana: University of Illinois Press, 1979, 89–92.

Document 14:
A DIALOGUE CONCERNING THE SLAVERY OF THE AFRICAN (1776)
Samuel Hopkins

Hopkins was a New England Congregational minister who addressed his fellow Americans in the moment of the revolution about their concern for ending British tyranny and seeking liberty, while owning slaves at the same time. He chided his contemporaries for making demands based upon principles which they did not extend to others.

The present situation of our public affairs, and our struggle for liberty, and the abundant conversation this occasions in all companies; while the poor negroes look on and hear, what aversion we have to slavery, and how much liberty is prized; they are often hearing it declared publickly and in private, as the voice of all, that slavery is more to be dreaded than death, and we are resolved to live free or die, &c. &c. This I say, necessarily leads them to attend to their own wretched situation, more than otherwise they could. They see themselves deprived of all liberty and property, and their children after them, to the latest posterity, subjected to the will of those who appear to have no feeling for their misery, and are guilty of many instances of hard heartedness and cruelty towards them, while they think themselves very kind; and therefore to make the least complaint, would be deemed the height of arrogance and abuse: And often, if they have a comparatively good master now, with constant dread they see a young one growing up, who bids fair to rule over them, or their children with rigour.

They see the slavery the *Americans* dread as worse than death, is lighter than a feather, compared to their heavy doom; and may be called liberty and happiness when contrasted with the most abject slavery and unutterable wretchedness to which they are subjected. And in the dark and dreadful situation, they look round, and find none to help—no pity—no hope! And when they observe all this cry and struggle for liberty for ourselves and children; and see themselves and their children wholly overlooked by us, and behold the *sons of liberty*, oppressing and tyrannizing over many thousands of poor blacks, who have as good a claim to liberty as themselves, they are shocked with the glaring inconsistence and wonder they themselves do not see it....

A state of slavery has a mighty tendency to sink and contract the minds of men, and prevent their making improvements in useful knowledge of every kind: It sinks the mind down in darkness and dispair; it takes off encouragements to activity, and to make improvements, and naturally tends to lead the enslaved to abandon themselves to a stupid carelessness, and to vices of all kinds. No wonder then the blacks among us are, many of them, so destitute of prudence and sagacity to act for themselves, and some are given to vice. It is rather a wonder there are so many instances of virtue, prudence, knowledge and industry among them. And shall we, because we have reduced them to this abject, helpless, miserable state, by our oppression of them, make this an argument for continuing them and their children in this wretched condition? God forbid! This ought rather to excite our pity, and arouse us to take some effectual method without delay, to deliver them and their children from this most unhappy state. If your own children were in this situation, would you offer this as a good reason why they and their posterity should be made slaves forever? Were some of your children unable to provide for themselves through infirmity of body, or want of mental capacity; and others of them were very vicious, would you have them sold into a state of slavery for this? Or would you make slaves of them yourself? Would you not be willing to take the best care of them in your power, and give them all possible encouragement to behave well, and direct and assist them in proper methods to get a living? I know you would. And why will you not go and do likewise to your slaves? Why will you not take off the galling yoke from their necks, and restore them to that liberty, to which they have as good a claim as you yourself and your children and which has been violently taken from them, and unjustly withheld by you to this day? If any of them are disposed to behave ill, and make a bad use of their freedom, let them have all the motives to behave well that can be laid before them. Let them be subject to the same restraints and laws with other freemen; and have the same care taken of them by the public. And be as ready to direct and assist those who want discretion and assistance to get a living, as if they were your own children; and as willing to support the helpless, the infirm and aged. And give all proper encouragement and assistance to those who have served you well, and are like to get a good living, if not put under peculiar disadvantages, as freed negroes most commonly are; by giving them reasonable wages for their labour, if they still continue with you, or liberally furnishing them with what is necessary in order to their living comfortably, and being in a way to provide for themselves. This was the divine command to the people of *Israel*; and does it not appear, at least, equally reasonable, in the case before us?

From Winthrop D. Jordan, *The Negro Versus Equality, 1762–1826*, the *Berkeley Series in American History*, edited by Charles Sellers, Chicago: Rand-McNally Corp., 1969.

CHAPTER 4

Intellectual and Religious Freedom

Document 15:
THE SENTENCE OF GALILEO BY THE INQUISITORS GENERAL IN 1633 AND HIS RECANTATION

Galileo's recantation was a dramatic moment in intellectual history and the development of science when the elderly scientist was forced to renounce his ideas about the sun being the center of the universe (heliocentrism), because it differed with established and religiously sanctioned theory about the earth being the center of the universe (geocentrism). Although some recent scholarship points to heliocentric theory itself actually being a convenient excuse to condemn Galileo when the real issues were much more obscure philosophical positions, this case nonetheless highlights the human problem when new knowledge conflicts with received truth. Galileo probably was keenly aware of Giordano Bruno's death at the stake for intellectual heterodoxy in 1600, and yet, after he was forced to recant, he supposedly muttered "Nevertheless it [the earth] moves."

Whereas you, Galileo, son of the late Vincenzo Galilei, Florentine, aged seventy years, were in the 1615 denounced to this Holy Office for holding as true the false doctrine taught by some that the sun is the centre of the world and immovable, and that the earth moves, and also with a diurnal motion; for having disciples to whom you taught the same doctrine; for holding correspondence with certain mathematicians of Germany concerning the same; for having printed certain letters, entitled "On the Sunspots," wherein you developed the same doctrine as true; and for replying to the objections from the Holy Scriptures, which from time to time were urged against it, by glossing the said Scriptures according to your own meaning: and whereas there was thereupon produced the copy of a document in the form of a letter, purporting to be written by you to one formerly your disciple,....

And whereas a book appeared here recently, printed last year at Florence, the title of which shows that you were the author, this title being: *Dialogues of Galileo Galilei on the Great World Systems*; and whereas the Holy Congregation was afterward informed that through the publication of the said book the false opinion of the motion of the Earth and the stability of the Sun was daily gaining ground; the said book was taken into careful consideration, and in it there was discovered a patent violation of the aforesaid injunction that had been imposed upon you, for in this book you have defended the said opinion previously condemned and to your face declared to be so, although in the said book you strive by various devises to produce the impression that you leave it undecided, and in express terms as probable: which, however, is a most grievous error, as an opinion can in no wise be probable which has been declared and defined to be contrary to Divine Scripture....

We say, pronounce, sentence, and declare, that you, the said Galileo, by reasons of the matters adduced in trial, and by you confessed as above, have rendered yourself in the judgment of this Holy Office vehemently suspected of heresy, namely, of having believed and held the doctrine—which is false and contrary to the sacred and divine Scripture—that the Sun is the center of the world and does not move from east to west and that the Earth moves and is not the center of the world; and that an opinion may be held and defended as probable after it has been declared and defined to be contrary to the Holy Scriptures; and that consequently you have incurred all the censures and penalties imposed and promulgated in the sacred canons and other constitutions, general and particular, against such delinquents. From which we are content that you be absolved, provided that, first, with a sincere heart, and unfeigned faith, you abjure, curse, and detest before us the aforesaid errors and heresies and every other errors and heresy contrary to the Apostolic Roman Church in the form prescribed by us for you.

And, in order that this your grave and pernicious error and transgression may not remain altogether unpunished and that you may be more cautious for the future and an example to others that they may abstain from similar delinquencies, we ordain that the book of the "*Dialogues of Galileo Galilei*" be prohibited, by public edict.

We condemn you to the formal prison of this Holy Office during our pleasure, and by way of salutary penance, we enjoin that for three years to come you repeat once a week the seven penitential Psalms....

Recantation (1633)
Galileo Galilei

I, Galileo, desiring to remove from the minds of your Eminences, and of all faithful Christians, this vehement suspicion, justly conceived against me, with sincere heart and unfeigned faith I abjure, curse, and detest the aforesaid errors and heresies and generally every other error, heresy, and sect whatsoever contrary to the Holy Church, and I swear that in future I will never again say or assert, verbally or in writing anything that might furnish occasion for a similar suspicion regarding me; but should I know any heretic or person suspected of heresy, I will denounce him to this Holy Office or to the Inquisitor or Ordinary of the place where I may be. Furthermore, I swear and promise to fulfill and observe in their integrity all penances that have been, or that shall be, imposed upon me by this Holy Office. And in the event of my contravening (which God forbid!) any of these promises and oaths, I submit myself to all the pains imposed and promulgated in the sacred canons and other constitutions, general and particular, against such delinquents. So help me God and these His Holy Gospels which I touch with my hands.

From Giorgio de Santillana, *The Crime of Galileo*, Chicago,: University of Chicago Press, 1955, 306–308.

Document 16:
AEROPAGITICA (1644)
John Milton

Milton published this oration which was addressed to the English Parliament. The name comes from ancient Greece and a famous court of enlightened judges in Athens. Milton criticizes Parliament for passing an ordinance for licensing the press in 1643. It is a powerful statement for a free press. A reading of the full text would reveal Milton's hostility to his religious enemies but this important part of his demand for freedom was omitted.

A Speech For The Liberty Of
Unlicensed Printing,
To The Parliament Of England

This is true liberty, when free-born men,
Having to advise the public, may speak free,
Which he who can will, deserves high praise;
Who neither can nor will, may hold his peace;
What can be juster in a State than this?
—Euripides, *The Supplicants*

...I deny not but that it is of greatest concernment in the church and commonwealth to have a vigilant eye how books demean themselves as well as men; and thereafter to confine, imprison, and do sharpest justice on them as malefactors. For books are not absolutely dead things, but do contain a potency of life in them to be as active as that soul was whose progeny they are; nay, they do preserve as in a vial the purest efficacy and extraction of that living intellect that bred them. I know they are as lively and as vigorously productive as those fabulous dragon's teeth; and being sown up and down, may chance to spring up armed men. And yet, on the other hand, unless wariness be used, as good almost kill a man as kill a good book: who kills a man kills a reasonable creature, God's image; but he who destroys a good book kills reason itself, kills the image of God, as it were, in the eye. Many a man lives a burden to the earth; but a good book is the precious lifeblood of a master spirit, embalmed and treasured up on purpose to a life beyond life. 'Tis true, no age can restore a life, whereof perhaps there is no great loss; and revolutions of ages do not oft recover the loss of a rejected truth, for the want of which whole nations fare the worse. We should be wary, therefore, what persecution we raise against the living labors of public men, how we spill that seasoned life of man preserved and store up in books; since we see a kind of homicide may be thus committed, sometimes a martyrdom; and if it extend to the whole impression, a kind of massacre, whereof the execution ends not in the slaying of an elemental life, but strikes at that ethereal and fifth essence, the breath of reason itself, slays an immortality rather than a life. But lest

I should be condemned of introducing license, while I oppose licensing, I refuse not the pains to be so much historical as will serve to show what hath been done by ancient and famous commonwealths against this disorder, till the very time that this project of licensing crept out of the Inquisition, was caught up by our prelates, and hath caught some of our presbyters...

For if they fell upon one kind of strictness, unless their care were equal to regulate all other things of like aptness to corrupt the mind, that single endeavor they knew would be but a fond labor; to shut and fortify one gate against corruption, and be necessitated to leave others round about wide open. If we think to regulate printing, thereby to rectify manners, we must regulate all recreations and pastimes, all that is delightful to man. No music must be heard, no song be set or sung, but what is grave and Doric. There must be licensing dancers, that no gesture, motion, or deportment be taught our youth, but what by their allowance shall be thought honest; for such Plato was provided of. It will ask more than the work of twenty licensers to examine all the lutes, the violins, and the guitars in every house; they must not be suffered to prattle as they do, but must be licensed what they may say. And who shall silence all the airs and madrigals that whisper softness in chambers? The windows also, and the balconies must be thought on; there are shrewd books, with dangerous frontispieces, set to sale; who shall prohibit them? Shall twenty licensers? The villages also must have their visitors inquire what lectures the bagpipe and the rebeck reads even to the balladry and the gamut of every municipal fiddler, for these are the countryman's Arcadias, and his Monte Mayors...

Many there be that complain of divine providence for suffering Adam to transgress. Foolish tongues! when God gave him reason, he gave him freedom to choose, for reason is but choosing, he had been else a mere artificial Adam, such an Adam as he is in the motions. We ourselves esteem not of that obedience, or love, or gift, which is of force. God therefore left him free, set before him a provoking object, ever almost in his eyes; herein consisted his merit, herein the right of his reward, the praise of his abstinence. Wherefore did he create passions within us, pleasures round about us, but that these rightly tempered are the very ingredients of virtue? They are not skillful considerers of human things who imagine to remove sin by removing the matter of sin. For, besides that it is a huge heap increasing under the very act of diminishing, though some part of it may for a time be withdrawn from some persons, it cannot from all, in such a universal thing as books are; and when this is done, yet the sin remains entire. Though ye take from a covetous man all his treasure, he has yet one jewel left—ye cannot bereave him of his covetousness. Banish all objects of lust, shut up all youth into the severest discipline that can be exercised in any hermitage, ye cannot make them chaste that came not thither so: such great care and wisdom is required to the right managing of this point.

Suppose we could expel sin by this means; look how much we thus expel of sin, so much we expel of virtue: for the matter of them both is the same; remove that, and ye remove them both alike. This justifies the high providence of God, who, though he command us temperance, justice, continence, yet pours out before us, even to a profuseness, all desirable things, and gives us minds that can wander beyond all limit and satiety. Why should we then affect a rigor contrary to the manner of God and of nature, by abridging or scanting those means which books freely permitted are, both to the trial of virtue and the exercise of truth?...

And how can a man teach with authority, which is the life of teaching, how can he be a doctor in his book as he ought to be, or else had better be silent, whenas all he teaches, all he delivers, is but under the tuition, under the correction of his patriarchal licenser to blot or alter what precisely accords not with the hidebound humor which he calls his judgment? When every acute reader upon the first sight of a pedantic license, will be ready with these like words to ding the book a quoit's distance from him: "I hate a pupil teacher, I endure not an instructor that comes to me under the wardship of an overseeing fist. I know nothing of the licenser, but that I have his own hand here for his arrogance; who shall warrant me his judgment?"...

Whence, to include the whole nation, and those that never yet thus offended, under such a diffident and suspectful prohibition, may plainly be understood what a disparagement it is. So much the more, whenas debtors and delinquents may walk abroad without a keeper, but unoffensive books must not stir forth without a visible jailor in their title. Nor is it to the common people less than a reproach; for if we be so jealous over them as that we dare not trust them with an English pamphlet, what do we but censure them for a giddy, vicious, and ungrounded people, in such a sick and weak estate of faith and discretion, as to be able to take nothing down but through the pipe of a licenser. That this is care or love of them, we cannot pretend, whenas in those popish places where the laity are most hated and despised, the same strictness is used over them. Wisdom we cannot call it, because it stops but breach of license, nor that neither; whenas those corruptions which it seeks to prevent break in faster at other doors which cannot be shut....

That this is not, therefore, the disburdening of a particular fancy, but the common grievance of all those who had prepared their minds and studies above the vulgar pitch to advance truth in others, and from others to entertain it, thus much may satisfy. And in their name I shall for neither friend nor foe conceal what the general murmur is; that if it come to inquisitioning again and licensing, and that we are timorous of ourselves and so suspicious of all men as to fear each book and the shaking of every leaf, before we know what the contents are; if some who but of late were little better than silenced from preaching, shall come now to silence us from reading except what they please, it cannot be guessed what is intended by some but a second tyranny over learning; and will soon put it out of controversy that bishops and presbyters are the same to us both name and thing....

Well knows he who uses to consider, that our faith and knowledge thrives by exercise, as well as our limbs and complexion. Truth is compared in scripture to a streaming fountain; if her waters flow not in a perpetual progression, they sicken into a muddy pool of conformity and tradition. A man may be a heretic in the truth; and if he believe things only because his pastor says so, or the Assembly so determines, without knowing other reason, though his belief be true, yet the very truth he holds becomes his heresy. There is not any burden that some would gladlier post off to another than the charge and care of their religion. There be, who knows not that there be, of protestants and professors who live and die in as arrant an implicit faith as any lay papist of Loreto....

If it be desired to know the immediate cause of all this free writing and free speaking, there cannot be assigned a truer than your own mild and free and humane government. It is the liberty, Lords and Commons, which your own valorous and happy counsels have purchased us, liberty which is the nurse of all great wits. This is that which hath rarefied and enlightened our spirits like the influence of heaven; this is that which hath enfranchised, enlarged, and lifted up our apprehensions degrees above themselves. Ye cannot make us now less capable, less knowing, less eagerly pursuing of the truth, unless ye first make yourselves, that made us so, less the lovers, less the founders of our true liberty. We can grow ignorant again, brutish, formal, and slavish, as ye found us; but you then must first become that which ye cannot be, oppressive, arbitrary, and tyrannous, as they were from whom ye have freed us. That our hearts are now more capacious, our thoughts more erected to the search and expectation of greatest and exactest things, is the issue of your own virtue propagated in us. Ye cannot suppress that unless ye reinforce an abrogated and merciless law, that fathers may despatch at will their own children. And who shall then stick closest to ye, and excite others? not he who takes up arms for coat and conduct, and his four nobles of Danegelt. Although I dispraise not the defense of just immunities, yet love my peace better, if that were all. Give me the liberty to know, to utter, and to argue freely according to conscience, above all liberties.

From John Milton, *Complete Poems and Major Prose*, edited by Merritt Y. Hughes, Indianapolis: Odyssey Press, 1957, 716–749.

Document 17:
WAS IST AUFKLÄRUNG? (1784) [WHAT IS ENLIGHTENMENT?]
Immanuel Kant

Immanuel Kant, the great philosopher, presents a clear argument for the value of education and the life of the mind and the necessity of freedom for Enlightenment. Kant gave this stirring defense of reason late in the Enlightenment, at about the same time that feeling and emotion were making great inroads in intellectual circles, and what may be termed an "anti-Enlightenment," the Romantic movement, was starting to exert a profound effect on intellectual and artistic life in the late eighteenth and early nineteenth centuries.

Enlightenment is release of human beings from their self-imposed childish dependency. Childish dependency is mankind's inability to make use of understanding without guidance from another. This dependency is self-imposed when its cause lies not in absence of reason but rather in the decision and fortitude to use it without decision from another. *Sapere aude!* "Have fortitude to use your own reason!"—that is the motto of the Enlightenment.

Idleness and cowardice are the causes of why such a great part of mankind, after nature has long bespoke to them their freedom from external guidance nevertheless remain under lifelong dependency (*naturaliter majorennes*), and why it is so simple for others to remain as their guides. It is so simple to be dependent. I have a book that has understanding for me, a minister who has scruples for me, a doctor who chooses my diet, and so forth; and so I do not need to trouble myself. I have nothing to think about, if I can only pay; others will undertake the disagreeable work for me. Among the greater part of mankind (and by all of the fair sex) that competence is thought to be dangerous, in addition to being inconvenient. This concern is borne for them by those very guides whose superintendence over the greater part of mankind they have so graciously given to themselves. After they have first of all made their cattle dumb and have made sure that these tranquil beasts will not dare to take a single step without being confined to the harness of the coach, the guides then show them the danger which threatens if they try to go alone. Now, however, this danger is not so great, for by falling a few times they would eventually learn to walk alone; but an example of this kind makes them timid and usually frightens them away from all further experiments.

It is hard for each individual to work out of the life under childish dependency which has become well-nigh human nature. The individual comes to like this condition, and is for the present truly unable to use reason, for no one has ever allowed this person to experiment with it. Dogma and formulas, those mechanical tools of the rational usages or rather mis-usages of the individual's natural gifts, are the leg-irons of an eternal childish dependency. Whoever throws them off makes an uncertain jump over the thinnest trench because this person is not used to that sort of free movement. Thus there are only a few who have done well and through their efforts have succeeded in freeing themselves from dependency and keeping a steady course.

But that the public should enlighten itself is more feasible; in fact, if one is only granted freedom, enlightenment almost certainly will follow. Then there will always be some who think for themselves, even among the constituted guides of the great herds, who, after throwing off the yoke of dependency from themselves, will spread the spirit of rational appraisal of both their own worth and of every person's vocation for independent thinking. It must be added, however, that the public, which has first of all been put under the yoke by their guides, compels the guides themselves to remain bound when it is excited into doing this by some of the guides who are themselves incapable of any enlightenment—so detrimental it is to implant biases, because they take their revenge later on their cultivators or on their descendants. Therefore the public can only attain enlightenment over a long period. Perhaps a fall of personal despotism and rapacious or tyrannical oppression may be accomplished by a revolution, but never a true reform in thinking methods; because new biases would be as useful as old ones to harness the great majority.

For this enlightenment, however, nothing is required but *freedom*; and truly the most benign among all of the things, to which freedom can rightly be applied; namely these: the freedom to use publicly one's reason at every point. Now I hear on all sides, "Do not argue!" The officer says: "Do not argue but drill!" The tax-collector: "Do not argue but pay!" The holy man: "Do not argue but believe!" (Not a single person in the world says: "Argue, as often as you wish, and over whatever you want, but obey!") Everywhere there is this check on freedom.

From Immanuel Kant, "Was ist Aufklärung?", *Immanuel Kant's Sämmtliche Werke*, Leipzig: Leopold Voss, 1867, volume 4, 161–163, translation by Michael Slaven.

Document 18:
A BILL FOR ESTABLISHING RELIGIOUS FREEDOM (1785)
Thomas Jefferson

Thomas Jefferson wrote the Bill for Establishing Religious Freedom *for his state of Virginia. From a long and noteworthy career, Jefferson chose this as one of the outstanding accomplishments of his life to be noted on his grave marker. The bill stands as a model for religious toleration, still admired and quoted until the present day.*

Well aware that the opinions and belief of men depend not on their own will, but follow involuntarily the evidence proposed to their minds; that Almighty God hath created the mind free, *and manifested his supreme will that free it shall remain by making it altogether insusceptible of restraint*; that all attempts to influence it by temporal punishments, or burthens, or by civil incapacitations, tend only to beget habits of hypocrisy and meanness, and are a departure from the plan of the holy author of our religion, who being lord both of body and mind, yet chose not to propagate it by coercions on either, as was in his Almighty power to do, *but to extend it by its influence on reason alone*; that the impious presumption of legislators and rulers, civil as well as ecclesiastical, who, being themselves but fallible and uninspired men, have assumed dominion over the faith of others, setting up their own opinions and modes of thinking as the only true and infallible, and as such endeavoring to impose them on others, hath established and maintained false religions over the greatest part of the world and through all time: That to compel a man to furnish contributions of money for the propagation of opinions which he disbelieves *and abhors*, is sinful and tyrannical; that even the forcing him to support this or that teacher of his own religious persuasion, is depriving him of the comfortable liberty of giving his contributions to the particular pastor whose morals he would make his pattern, and whose powers he feels most persuasive to righteousness; and is withdrawing from the ministry those temporary rewards, which proceeding from an approbation of their personal conduct, are an additional incitement to earnest and unremitting labours for the instruction of mankind; that our civil rights have no dependance on our religious opinions, any more than our opinions in physics or geometry; that therefore the proscribing any citizen as unworthy the public confidence by laying upon him an incapacity of being called to offices of trust and emolument, unless he profess or renounce this or that religious opinion, is depriving him injuriously of those privileges and advantages to which, in common with his fellow citizens, he has a natural right; that it tends also to corrupt the principles of that *very* religion it is meant to encourage, by bribing, with a monopoly of worldly honours and emoluments, those who will externally profess and conform to it; that though indeed these are criminal who do not withstand such temptation, yet neither are those innocent who lay the bait in their way; *that the opinions of men are not the object of civil government, nor under its jurisdiction*; that to suffer the civil magistrate to intrude his powers into the field of opinion and to restrain the profession or propagation of principles on supposition of their ill tendency is a dangerous fallacy, which at once destroys all religious liberty, because he being of course judge of that tendency will make his opinions the rule of judgment, and approve or condemn the sentiments of others only as they shall square with or differ from his own; that it is time enough for the rightful purposes of civil government for its officers to interfere when principles break out into overt acts against peace and good order; and finally, that truth is great and will prevail if left to herself; that she is the proper and sufficient antagonist to error, and has nothing to fear from the conflict unless by human interposition disarmed of her natural weapons, free argument and debate; errors ceasing to be dangerous when it is permitted freely to contradict them.

We, the General Assembly of Virginia do enact that no man shall be compelled to frequent or support any religious worship, place, or ministry whatsoever, nor shall be enforced, restrained, molested, or burthened in his body or goods, nor shall otherwise suffer, on account of his religious opinions or belief; but that all men shall be free to profess, and by argument to maintain, their opinions in matters of religion, and that the same shall in no wise diminish, enlarge, or affect their civil capacities.

And though we well know that this Assembly, elected by the people for the ordinary purposes of legislation only, have no power to restrain the acts of succeeding Assemblies, constituted with powers equal to our own, and that therefore to declare this act irrevocable would be of no effect in law; yet we are free to declare, and do declare, that the rights hereby asserted are of the natural rights of mankind, and that if any act shall be hereafter passed to repeal the present or to narrow its operation, such act will be an infringement of natural right.

From Thomas Jefferson, *The Papers of Thomas Jefferson, Volume 2, 1777 to 18 June 1779, Including the Revisal of the Laws, 1776–1786*, edited by Julian P. Boyd, Princeton, New Jersey: Princeton University Press, 1950, 545–547.

SECTION II 1815–1900

After the French Revolution and Napoleon, the West continued the great debates about individuals' rights within the political system. It mattered greatly who had the vote when legislatures decided upon taxes, the price of bread, or the right to form a trade union. It was not surprising that a system controlled by landlords in Britain or beholden to aristocrats in Austria or the German states kept food prices high, despite the impact upon workers or the new manufacturing middle classes. The Irish probably lost over a million people because they had no power to affect food policies when a potato blight hit in the 1840s. They watched as food was exported to England while hundreds of thousands starved in Ireland. When the Industrial Revolution increased the numbers of the middle classes, they challenged the existing orders for political participation, and learned to exploit the power which they gained to help themselves in important respects.

The middle classes used the powerful ideas of the eighteenth century to expand their rights in all areas of life in the nineteenth century. Freedom for the individual particularly meant freedom for middle class interests. As Adam Smith had taught, all would profit from the liberation of every other economic enterprise in a free marketplace. At its worst, the demand for unregulated economic activity adapted the ideas of Darwin for a harsh, jungle-like scenario where mercy was banished and the fittest survived. However popular this doctrine, in practice compromises were made throughout the century. At the core of moderate demands was the issue of the democratic franchise.

Reformers in different countries argued in much the same way for a democratic right to vote. Whether in Britain, France, or in the United States, the right to vote flowed from the demand for equality and the ability of men—and later women—to participate in government. The vote was followed by demands for equal electoral districts, secret elections, salaries for representatives, testing for civil service and a host of subsequent reforms. The natural rights of the eighteenth century had liberated many middle class people in Western nations; but once they had power they were not anxious to share it with others. Thus the nation which had declared its independence in the stirring document of July 4, 1776, did not emancipate any of its slaves until 1862, a year after the Russians liberated their serfs. Abigail Adams' female offspring waited until 1920 to vote in the United States.

A different foundation was sought for rights. Jeremy Bentham attacked the idea of a conservative natural law that limited the rights of others. In its place he advocated a rather complicated "calculus of pain and pleasure" that would be used to determine policy: What action brings the greatest happiness to the greatest number, he asked. In the process, Bentham gave a rather practical test for policies that should benefit the majority—an approach quite compatible with growing democracy. From the bench, jurists would argue for a more expansive view of rights.

The new ideology of socialism challenged *laissez faire* by asserting that the economy should be managed collectively for the good of all. Democratic socialists had a profound impact upon politics as competition for the expanding working class voters made it urgent to address working class needs. Democratic socialists sought the eventual replacement of capitalism, but in the short term they worked for greater democracy and considerable reform of the existing system. Others, such as Karl Marx, were less patient and prescribed revolutions to make the necessary changes. Trade unions rose to demand higher wages, better hours and protection from unsafe conditions.

The nineteenth century was a time when many peaceful reforms occurred. Motives were mixed. Some thought slavery or war immoral because of their religious or philosophical views. Change often occurred to prevent the new socialists from gaining support or the revolutionaries from growing in number. The concept of who should benefit from government was expanded throughout the century: workers, women, children, slaves or peasants and even colonial peoples soon were the subjects of debate over rights. Those whose economic interests were tied to the old ways—in Ireland, on the plantations, in the factories—were reluctant to see new rights legislated. Great lags occurred between the various phases of reform: the middle class got the vote in England in 1832; workers only in the 1860s and 1870s; women only in 1929. The emancipation of slaves in America did not permit African Americans to enter fully into public life. Rather, African Americans were discriminated against and often terrorized until the Civil Rights movement after World War II brought them access to civil and political rights. The demand for national self-determination was considered understandable for Europeans, but in the colonies its advocates were treated harshly. The legacy would be bitter for the next century.

The movement toward greater participation and more responsive governments did not occur everywhere in the West. Germany remained a half-way house with a democratically-elected parliament after the unification in 1870–71. But real power was held by a chancellor beholden to the emperor, who ruled through a bureaucracy, the military, and special interest groups. Russia remained an autocracy, tolerating a weak legislature and partial reforms only after defeat in its 1905 war with Japan triggered revolution.

The nation-state continued to be a foundation stone of the international order, and it grew ever more complex and active at home and abroad. The weariness that was felt by many Europeans after the long wars with the French and Napoleon receded after 1815 as an attempt was made by the more conservative powers to enforce the peace settlement and ensure against revolution, or much change at all, by periodic summit meetings that were called "congresses." Time and again in the decade after 1815, troops were called in to quell rebellions for domestic change, for a constitution in Spain, or demands for national self-determination in Italy or Austria. A series of revolutions in 1848 indicated that many forces for change were underway in Europe. Although defeated in the streets, those who demanded national unity and change in economic and social conditions were often accomodated in the next several decades.

International tensions increased in the late nineteenth century. Strong national states appeared where none had been before in Central Europe. The intensive era of imperial expansion which occurred during the last thirty years of the century resulted in one-tenth of the world's population being claimed by Europeans. By 1900, approximately half of Asia, nearly all of Micronesia and more than 90% of Africa were in European hands. With these changes came the desire to avoid the increasingly destructive warfare made possible by professional mass armies equipped by the industrial economies. National self-determination became an explosive issue and when dependent people within colonies raised it, they were suppressed. Military alliances were constructed that required automatic responses to the moves of others. An ultra-nationalism spread throughout the West which praised one's own nation over others, glorified its achievements in the past and sanctioned its present and future actions. Everywhere popular culture exhibited an increasingly fanatical tone about one's own nation and one's enemies. The spread of literacy and the beginning of advertising, mass newspapers, and cynical government use of nationalistic feelings provided bases for the international violence ahead.

There were attempts at international efforts to advance human rights. The anti-slavery movement had great impact in stopping the trade in human beings in the British Empire and around the world. Agendas for political rights, access to education, women's rights within society and the family, all brought great hope toward the end of the nineteenth century. The international tensions led many in the West to seek a limit to war and especially offer protection for non-combatants. The start of the twentieth century seemed to auger well for an expansion of human rights.

CHAPTER 5: Political Participation And Individual Rights

Document 19:
AN INTRODUCTION TO THE PRINCIPLES OF MORALS AND LEGISLATION (1796)
Jeremy Bentham

Jeremy Bentham's complicated idea "calculus of pain and pleasure" might seem a bit silly. However, it offered an alternative to the conservative interpretations of natural law which were used to defend entrenched interests and institutions. Bentham suggested that legislation—or governmental actions—be based upon a calculation of how many could benefit. This practical approach could facilitate a more democratic trend in politics.

Value of a Lot of Pleasure or Pain, How to be Measured

I. Pleasures then, and the avoidance of pains are the *ends* which the legislator has in view: it behoves him therefore to understand their *value*. Pleasures and pains are the *instruments* he has to work with: it behoves him therefore to understand their force, which is again, in another point of view, their value.

II. To a person considered by *himself*, the value of a pleasure or pain considered *by itself*, will be greater or less according to the four following circumstances:

1. Its *intensity*.
2. Its *duration*.
3. Its *certainty* or *uncertainty*.
4. Its *propinquity* or *remoteness*.

III. These are the circumstances which are to be considered in estimating a pleasure or a pain considered each of them by itself. But when the value of any pleasure or pain is considered for the purpose of estimating the tendency of any *act* by which it is produced, there are two other circumstances to be taken into account; these are,

5. Its *fecundity*, or the chance it has of being followed by sensations of the *same* kind: that is, pleasures, if it be a pleasure: pains, if it be a pain.

6. Its *purity*, or the chance it has of not being followed by sensations of the *opposite* kind: that is, pains, if it be a pleasure: pleasures, if it be a pain.

These two last, however, are in strictness scarcely to be deemed properties of the pleasure or the pain itself; they are not, therefore, in strictness to be taken into the account of the value of that pleasure or that pain. They are in strictness to be deemed properties only of the act, or other event, by which such pleasure or pain has been produced; and accordingly are only to taken into the account of the tendency of such act or such event.

IV. To a *number* of persons, with reference to each of whom the value of a pleasure or a pain is considered, it will be greater or less, according to seven circumstances: to wit, the six preceding ones; *viz.*

1. Its *intensity*.
2. Its *duration*.
3. Its *certainty* or *uncertainty*.
4. Its *propinquity* or *remoteness*.
5. Its *fecundity*.
6. Its *purity*.

And one other, to wit:

7. Its *extent*; that is, the number of persons to whom it *extends*; or (in other words) who are affected by it.

V. To take an exact account, then, of the general tendency of any act, by which the interests of a community are affected, proceed as follows. Begin with any one person of those whose interests seem most immediately to be affected by it: and take an account,

1. Of the value of each distinguishable *pleasure* which appears to be produced by it in the *first* instance.

2. Of the value of each *pain* which appears to be produced by it in the *first* instance.

3. Of the value of each pleasure which appears to be produced by it *after* the first. This constitutes the *fecundity* of the first *pleasure* and the *impurity* of the first *pain*.

4. Of the value of each *pain* which appears to be produced by it after the first. This constitutes the *fecundity* of the first *pain*, and *impurity* of the first pleasure.

5. Sum up all the values of all the *pleasures* on the one side, and those of all the pains on the other. The balance, if it be on the side of pleasure, will give the *good* tendency of the act upon the whole, with respect to the interests of that *individual* person; if on the side of pain, the *bad* tendency of it upon the whole.

6. Take an account of the *number* of persons whose interests appear to be concerned; and repeat the above process with respect to each. *Sum up* the numbers expressive of the degrees of *good* tendency, which the act has, with respect to each individual in regard to whom the tendency of it is *good* upon the whole: do this again with respect to each individual, in regard to whom the tendency of it is *bad* upon the whole. Take the *balance*; which, if on the side of *pleasure*, will give the general *good* tendency of the act, with respect to the total number or community of individuals concerned; if on the side of pain, the general *evil tendency*, with respect to the same community.

VI. It is not to be expected that this process should be strictly pursued previously to every moral judgment, or to every legislative or judicial operation. It may, however, be always kept in view: and as near as the process actually pursued on these occasions approaches to it, so near will such process approach to the character of an exact one.

VII. The same process is alike applicable to pleasure and pain, in whatever shape they appear; and by whatever denomination they are distinguished: to pleasure, whether it be called *good* (which is properly the cause or instrument of pleasure), or *profit* (which is distant pleasure, or the cause or instrument of distant pleasure), or *convenience*, or *advantage*, *benefit*, *emolument*, *happiness*, and so forth: to pain, whether it be called *evil* (which corresponds to *good*), or *mischief*, or *inconvenience*, or *disadvantage*, or *loss*, or *unhappiness*, and so forth.

VIII. Nor is this a novel and unwarranted, any more than it is a useless theory. In all this there is nothing but what the practice of mankind, wheresoever they have a clear view of their own interest, is perfectly conformable to. An article of property, an estate in land, for instance, is valuable: on what account? On account of the pleasures of all kinds which it enable a man to produce, and, what comes to the same thing, the pains of all kinds which it enables him to avert. But the value of such an article of property is universally understood to rise or fall according to the length or shortness of the time which a man has in it: the certainty or uncertainty of its coming into possession: and the nearness or remoteness of the time at which, if at all, it is to come into possession. As to the *intensity* of the pleasures which a man may derive from it, this is never thought of, because it depends upon the use which each particular person may come to make of it; which cannot be estimated till the particular pleasures he may come to derive from it, or the particular pains he may come to exclude by means of it, are brought to view. For the same reason, neither does he think of the *fecundity* or *purity* of those pleasures.

Thus much for pleasure and pain, happiness and unhappiness, in *general*. We come now to consider the several particular kinds of pain and pleasure.

Pleasures and Pains, Their Kinds

I. Having represented what belongs to all sorts of pleasures and pains alike, we come now to exhibit, each by itself, the several sorts of pains and pleasures. Pains and pleasures may be called by one general word, interesting perceptions. Interesting perceptions are either simple or complex. The simple ones are those which cannot any one of them be resolved into more: complex are those which are resolvable into divers simple ones.

1. Of pleasures alone: 2. Of pains alone: or, 3. Of a pleasure or pleasures, and a pain or pains together. What determines a lot of pleasures, for example, to be regarded as one complex pleasure, rather than as divers simple ones, is the nature of the exciting cause. Whatever pleasures are excited all at once by the action of the same cause, are apt to be looked upon as constituting all together but one pleasure.

II. The several simple pleasures of which human nature is susceptible, seem to be as follows: 1. The pleasures of sense. 2. The pleasures of wealth. 3. The pleasures of skill. 4. The pleasures of amity. 5. The pleasures of a good name. 6. The pleasures of power. 7. The pleasures of piety. 8. The pleasures of benevolence. 9. The pleasures of malevolence. 10. The pleasures of imagination. 11. The pleasures of memory. 12. The pleasures of expectations. 13. The pleasures dependent on association. 14. The pleasures of relief.

III. The several simple pains seem to be as follows: 1. The pains of privation. 2. The pains of the senses. 3. The pains of awkwardness. 4. The pains of enmity. 5. The pains of an ill name.

6. The pains of piety. 7. The pains of benevolence. 8. The pains of malevolence. 9. The pains of the memory. 10. The pains of the imagination. 11. The pains of expectation. 12. The pains dependent on association....

XXXIII. Of all these several sorts of pleasures and pains, there is scarce any one which is not liable, on more accounts than one, to come under the consideration of the law. Is an offence committed? It is the tendency which it has to destroy, in such or such person, some of these pleasures, or to produce some of these pains, that constitutes the mischief of it, and the ground for punishing it. It is the prospect of some of these pleasures, or of security from some of these pains, that constitutes the motive or temptation: it is the attainment of them that constitutes the profit of the offence. Is the offender to be punished? It can be only by the production of one or more of these pains, that the punishment can be inflicted.

From Jeremy Bentham, *The Works of Jeremy Bentham*, published under the superintendence of his executor, John Bowring, Vol. I, Edinburgh: William Tait, 1843, 17–21.

Document 20:
RIGHTS, LIBERTY, AND SOCIAL REFORM (1847)
Louis Blanc

After members of the sturdy middle classes received political benefits from reforms and great economic power from industrialization, they were slow to continue reforms that benefitted the lower classes. In his writing, Louis Blanc of France points out the need for power and action to help improve the lives of those in the poorer classes.

...But does not the poor man have a *right* to better himself? Yet what does it matter, if he lacks the *power*? What good is the *right* to be cured to the invalid whom no one cures?

Rights, considered in an abstract manner, are the mirage which, since 1789, has deluded the people. Rights are a dead, metaphysical protection which has replaced, for the people, the living protection owed to them. Rights, pompously and with no results proclaimed in charters, have served only to mask the injustice of a regime of individualism and the barbarism of the abandonment of the poor. It is because liberty has been defined with the word *right* that men have been called free who were slaves to hunger, slaves to cold, slaves to ignorance, slaves to chance. Let us then say once and for all: liberty consists not only in a RIGHT granted but in the POWER given to a man to exercise, to develop his faculties under the empire of justice and under the safeguards of the law.

And note well, this is not a futile distinction: its meaning is profound; its consequences are immense. For as soon as one admits that man needs, to be truly free, the *power* to exercise and develop his faculties, it follows that society owes to each of its members both the education, without which the human understanding *cannot* develop, and the instruments of labor, without which human *activity* cannot be given free scope. Now by whose intervention other than the state's can society give to each of its members suitable instruction and the tools necessary for work? Thus it is in the name, and for the sake, of liberty that we demand the rehabilitation of the principle of authority. We want a strong government because, in the regime of inequality in which we are still vegetating there are feeble persons who need a social force to protect them. We want a government which intervenes in industry because in a situation where loans are made only to the rich there is need of a social banker who will lend to the poor. In a word, we invoke the idea of the state because the liberty of the future must be real liberty.

Let there be no mistake, moreover; this need for government intervention is a relative matter; it stems only from the condition of weakness, poverty, and ignorance into which past tyrannies have plunged the people. There will come a day, if our dearest hopes are not disappointed, when there will no longer be any need for a strong and active government, because there will no longer be in society any inferior class in a state of minority. Until then, the establishment of a tutelary authority is indispensable. Socialism can be fertilized only by politics.

Oh rich people, you are being deceived when you are turned against those who are devoting themselves to the calm and pacific solution of social problems. Yes, this holy cause of the poor is your cause. A solidarity of heavenly origin binds you to their poverty by fear, and links you by your very self-interest to their future deliverance....

From Paul H. Beik, *Louis Philippe and the July Monarchy*, Princeton: D. Van Nostrand Company, Inc., 1965, 173–174. Reprinted by permission of Paul H. Beik.

Document 21:
OF THE LIMITS TO THE AUTHORITY OF SOCIETY OVER THE INDIVIDUAL (1859)
John Stuart Mill

British philosopher John Stuart Mill was a nineteenth-century liberal who wrote about the relationship between the individual and the state. The following reading is from Mill's work On Liberty, *published in 1859. Particularly important for him was the moral question of personal liberty versus the legal power of the state. Mill argued that the individual has rights over his or her body that cannot be denied by the state.*

What, then, is the rightful limit to the sovereignty of the individual over himself? Where does the authority of society begin? How much of human life should be assigned to individuality, and how much to society?

Each will receive its proper share, if each has that which more particularly concerns it. To individuality should belong the part of life in which it is chiefly the individual that is interested; to society, the part which chiefly interests society.

Though society is not founded on a contract, and though no good purpose is answered by inventing a contract in order to deduce social obligations from it, every one who receives the protection of society owes a return for the benefit, and the fact of living in society renders it indispensable that each should be bound to observe a certain line of conduct towards the rest. This conduct consists, first, in not injuring the interests of one another; or rather certain interest, which either by express legal provision or by tacit understanding, ought to be considered as rights; and secondly, in each person's bearing his share (to be fixed on some equitable principle) of the labors and sacrifices incurred for defending the society or its members from injury and molestation. These conditions society is justified in enforcing at all costs to those who endeavor to withhold fulfillment. Nor is this all that society may do. The acts of an individual may be hurtful to others, or wanting in due consideration for their welfare, without going the length of violating any of their constituted rights. The offender may then be justly punished by opinion, though not by law. As soon as any part of a person's conduct affects prejudicially the interests of others, society has jurisdiction over it, and the question whether the general welfare will or will not be promoted by interfering with it, becomes open to discussion. But there is no room for entertaining any such question when a person's conduct affects the interests of no persons besides himself, or needs not affect them unless they like (all the persons concerned being of full age, and the ordinary amount of understanding). In all such cases there should be perfect freedom, legal and social, to do the action and stand the consequences.

From John Stuart Mill, *On Liberty*, New York: Appleton-Century-Crofts, 1947, 75–76.

Document 22:
CONCERNING UNIVERSAL SUFFRAGE AND CONCERNING PROPORTIONAL REPRESENTATION OF MINORITIES (1873)
Louis Blanc

Louis Blanc makes the argument for the right of all men to vote in France. Not until 1946 would French women receive the right to vote. His demand for the right to vote echoes through all democratic reform movements through the present day.

The people is sovereign. It expresses its will by direct universal suffrage. Its will formulated is the law. Obedience to law has as a necessary condition the right to discuss the law, in order that it can be changed if it is harmful.

Freedom of the press, freedom of conscience, freedom of association, the right of assembly, the right to subsist by working, shall not depend on a vote of the majority.

The sovereignty of the people, within its limits, is unassailable and sacred.

It is inalienable, and excludes all idea of monarchy. It exercises itself by means of revocable mandates.

The people acknowledges no power other than that which it holds itself: so that the State, that is it.

If it adopts universal suffrage that is sufficient, there are no longer any insurrections possible.

If one takes up arms against universal suffrage, one risks unleashing civil war.

If civil war explodes and universal suffrage succumbs momentarily, one returns, up until the definitive triumph, to the course of deadly troubles, bloody agitation, and revolts.

We must choose.

Universal suffrage is the first condition of order, because it is the first guarantee of freedom.

Without the sovereignty of the people exercised by universal suffrage, there will be nothing but violence and anarchy, unpunished oppression or bloody revolutions.

We are thus resolutely for this system. Only there is right, only there is justice, only there is the security for all and reason.

The result of this is that submission is owed to the vote of the majority, but not in every case, not in defiance of the *evidence*, not in the *defiance* of conscience.

Not only is it possible that at a given moment that the majority could become oppressive, but sometimes this does happen. And thus is rendered necessary the existence of a *Constitution*, that is to say, a pact that is permanent, fundamental, superior to simple laws, and that the majority is bound to accept....

From Louis Blanc, *Questions d'Aujourd'hui et de Demain*, Paris: E. Dentu, 1873, 237–240, translated by Michael Slaven.

Document 23:
THE GREAT REFORM (1831)
Lord John Russell

Britain was often the model for European systems that sought change and stability in the nineteenth century. John Russell was a leading parliamentary advocate of democratic change that involved expanding the number of people who could vote. In 1832, after a great crisis, the Great Reform Bill was passed. It doubled the number of middle class men who could vote and it took seats from villages in order to create seats in Parliament for the rapidly growing cities. Thereafter, each year, the voting rolls grew. Voting reforms in the second half of the century gave urban and rural male laborers the vote; not until 1929 would women get the vote.

...Let us now look at the question as one of reason. Allow me to imagine for a moment, a stranger from some distant country, who should arrive in England to examine our institutions. All the information he had collected would have told him that this country was singular for the degree which it had attained in wealth, in science, and in civilization. He would have learned that in no country have the arts of life been carried further, no where the inventions of mechanical skill been rendered more conducive to the comfort and prosperity of mankind. He would have made himself acquainted with its fame in history, and above all, he would have been told, that the proudest boast of this celebrated country was its political freedom. If, in addition to this, he had heard that once in six years this country, so wise, so renowned, so free, chose its Representatives to sit in the great Council, where all the ministerial affairs were discussed and determined; he would not be a little curious to see the process by which so important and solemn an operation was effected. What then would be his surprise, if he were taken by his guide, whom he had asked to conduct him to one of the places of election, to a green mound and told, that this green mound sent two Members to Parliament—or, to be taken to a stone wall, with three niches in it, and told that these three niches sent two Members to Parliament—, or if he were shown a green park, with many signs of flourishing vegetable life, but none of human habitation, and told that this green park sent two Members to Parliament? But his surprise would increase to astonishment if he were carried into the North of England, where he would see large flourishing towns, full of trade and activity, containing vast magazines of wealth and manufactures, and were told that these places had no Representatives in the Assembly which was said to represent the people. Suppose him, after all, for I will not disguise any part of the case, suppose him to ask for a specimen of popular election, and to be carried, for that purpose, to Liverpool; his surprise would be turned into disgust at the gross venality and corruption which he would find to pervade the electors. After seeing all this, would he not wonder that a nation which had made such progress in every kind of knowledge, and which valued itself for its freedom, should permit so absurd and defective a system of representation any longer to prevail?....

From *Readings in European History Since 1814*, edited by Jonathan F. Scott and Alexander Baltzley, New York: F.S. Crofts & Co., 1931, 74–75.

Document 24:
THE PEOPLE'S CHARTER (1838)
William Lovett

The Great Reform Bill of 1832 gave middle class males the right to vote, but not laborers in the towns and countryside. Those who wanted more change presented a People's Charter to Parliament with six demands. Before World War I, all but one of these demands would be realized. The Chartists had great confidence in the British system and wanted it reformed to meet the needs of more people.

THE PEOPLE'S CHARTER
Being the Outline of an Act
To Provide for the
Just Representation of the People of
Great Britain and Ireland
IN THE COMMONS' HOUSE OF PARLIAMENT
Embracing the Principles of
UNIVERSAL SUFFRAGE, NO PROPERTY QUALIFICATION,
ANNUAL PARLIAMENTS, EQUAL REPRESENTATION,
PAYMENT OF MEMBERS, AND VOTE BY BALLOT

Prepared by a Committee of Twelve Persons, Six Members of Parliament and Six Members of the London Working Men's Association, and addressed to the People of the United Kingdom.

WHEREAS, to insure, in as far as it is possible by human forethought and wisdom, the just government of the people, it is necessary to subject those who have the power of making the laws to a wholesome and strict responsibility to those whose duty it is to obey them when made;

And whereas, this responsibility is best enforced through the instrumentality of a body which emanates directly from, and is itself immediately subject to, the whole people, and which completely represents their feelings and their interests;

And, whereas, as the Commons' House of Parliament now exercises, in the name, and on the supposed behalf of the people, the power of making the laws, it ought, in order to fulfill with wisdom and with honesty the great duties imposed on it, to be made the most faithful and accurate representation of the people's wishes, feelings, and interests;

Be it therefore enacted, That from and after the passing of this Act, every male inhabitant of these realms be entitled to vote for the election of a Member of Parliament; subject, however, to the following conditions:—

1. That he be a native of these realms, or a foreigner who has lived in this country upwards of two years, and been naturalized.
2. That he be twenty-one years of age.
3. That he be not proved insane when the lists of voters are revised.
4. That he be not undergoing the sentence of the law at the time when called upon to exercise the electoral right.
5. That his electoral rights be not suspended for bribery at elections, or for personation, or for forgery of election certificates, according to the penalties of this Act.

ELECTORAL DISTRICTS

Be it enacted, I. That for the purpose of obtaining an equal representation of the people in the Commons' House of Parliament, the united kingdom be divided into three hundred electoral districts.

II. That each such district contain, as nearly as may be, an equal number of inhabitants....

V. That each electoral district return one representative to sit in the Commons' House of Parliament.

ARRANGEMENT FOR NOMINATIONS

XI. That no other qualification shall be required than the choice of electors, according to the provisions of this Act, providing that no persons, (excepting the Cabinet Ministers), be eligible to serve in the Commons' House of Parliament, who are in the receipt of any emolument derivable from any place or places held under government, or of retired allowances arising therefrom.

ARRANGEMENTS FOR ELECTIONS

XIII. That when any voter's certificate is examined by the registration clerk and found to be correct, he shall be allowed to pass on to the next barrier, where a balloting ball shall be given him by the person appointed for that purpose; he shall then pass on to the balloting box, and with all due despatch, shall put the balloting ball into the aperture opposite the name of the candidate he wishes to vote for, after which he shall without delay, leave the room by the door assigned for the purpose.

DURATION OF PARLIAMENT

Be it enacted, I. That the Members of the House of Commons chosen as aforesaid, shall meet on the first Monday in June in each year, and continue their sittings from time to time as they may deem it convenient, till the first Monday in June following, when the next new Parliament *shall* be chosen; they shall be eligible to be re-elected.

PAYMENT OF MEMBERS

Be it enacted, I. That every member of the House of Commons be entitled, at the close of the session, to a writ of expenses on the Treasury, for his legislative duties in the public service; and shall be paid per annum.

From *Readings in European History Since 1814*, edited by Jonathan F. Scott and Alexander Baltzley, New York: F.S. Crofts & Co., 1931, 107–109.

Document 25:
THE EMANCIPATION OF WOMEN (1851)
Harriet Taylor Mill

Harriet Taylor Mill presents a modern argument for the emancipation of women. Mill was a leading feminist thinker in Victorian England. One by one she counters the common arguments used to exclude women from the political franchise.

When...we ask why the existence of one-half the species should be merely ancillary to that of the other—why each woman should be a mere appendage to a man, allowed to have no interests of her own that there may be nothing to compete in her mind with his interests and his pleasure; the only reason which can be given is, that men like it. It is agreeable to them that men should live for their own sake, women for the sake of men: and the qualities and conduct in subjects which are agreeable to rulers, they succeed for a long time in making the subjects themselves consider as their appropriate virtues.... [H]ow wonderfully the ideas of virtue set afloat by the powerful, are caught and imbibed by those under their dominion, is exemplified by the manner in which the world were once persuaded that the supreme virtue of subjects was loyalty to kings, and are still persuaded that the paramount virtue of womanhood is loyalty to men. Under a nominal recognition of a moral code common to both, in practice self-will and self-assertion form the type of what are designated as manly virtues, while abnegation of self, patience, resignation, and submission to power, unless when resistance is commanded by other interests than their own, have been stamped by general consent as pre-eminently the duties and graces required of women. The meaning being merely, that power makes itself the centre of moral obligation, and that a man likes to have his own will, but does not like that his domestic companion should have a will different from his.

The common opinion is, that whatever may be the case with the intellectual, the moral influence of women over men is almost salutary. It is, we are often told, the great counteractive of selfishness. However the case may be as to personal influence, the influence of the position tends eminently to promote selfishness. The most insignificant of men, the man who can obtain influence or consideration nowhere else, finds one place where he is chief and head. There is one person, often greatly his superior in understanding, who is obligated to consult him, and whom he is not obliged to consult. He is judge, magistrate, ruler, over their joint concerns; arbiter of all differences between them....If there is any self-will in the man, he becomes either the conscious or unconscious despot of his household. The wife, indeed, often succeeds in gaining her objects, but it is by some of the many various forms of indirectness and management.

Thus the position is corrupting equally to both; in the one it produces the vices of power, in the other those of artifice....

We are not now speaking of cases in which there is anything deserving the name of strong affection on both sides....That, where it exists, is too powerful a principle not to modify greatly the bad influences of the situation; it seldom, however, destroys them entirely. Much oftener the bad influences are too strong for the affection, and destroy. The highest order of durable and happy attachments would be a hundred times more frequent than they are, if the affection which the two sexes sought from one another were that genuine friendship, which only exists between equals in privileges as in faculties. But with regard to what is commonly called affection in married life—the habitual and almost mechanical feeling of kindliness, and pleasure in each other's society, which generally grows up between persons who constantly live together, unless there is actual dislike—there is nothing in this to contradict or qualify the mischievous influence of the unequal relation. Such feelings often exist between a sultan and his favourites, between a master and his servants; they are merely examples of the pliability of human nature, which accommodates itself in some degree even to the worst circumstances, and the commonest natures always the most easily....

[T]he assertion, that the wife's influence renders the man less selfish, contains, as things now are, fully as much error as truth. Selfishness towards the wife herself, and the children, the wife's influence, no doubt, tends to counteract. But the general effect on him of her character, so long as her interests are concentrated in the family, tends but to substitute for individual selfishness a family selfishness, wearing an amiable guise, and putting on the mask of duty. How rarely is the wife's influence on the side of the public virtue; how rarely does it do otherwise than discourage any effort of principle by which the private interests or worldly vanities of the family can be expected to suffer. Public spirit, sense of duty towards the public good, is of all virtues, as women are now educated and situated, the most rarely to be found among them; they have seldom even, what in men is often a partial substitute for public spirit, a sense of personal honour connected with any public duty....In England, the wife's influence is usually the illiberal and anti-popular side: this is generally the gaining side for personal interest and vanity; and what to her is the democracy of liberalism in which she has no part—which leaves her the Pariah it found her? The man himself, when he marries, usually declines into Conservatism; begins to sympathize with the holders of power, more than with its victims, and thinks it his part to be on the side of authority....

Custom hardens human beings to any kind of degradation, by deadening the part of their nature which would resist it. And the case of women is, in this respect, even a peculiar one, for no other inferior caste that we have heard of have been taught to regard their degradation as their honour....They are taught to think, that to repel actively even an admitted injustice done to themselves, is somewhat unfeminine, and had better be left to some male friend or protector. To be accused of rebelling against anything which admits of being called an ordinance of society, they are taught to regard as an imputation of a serious offence, to say the least, against the proprieties of their sex. It requires unusual moral courage as well as disinterestedness in a woman, to express opinions favourable to women's enfranchisement, until, at least, there is some prospect of obtaining it. The comfort of her individual life, and her social consideration, usually depend on the good-will of those who hold the undue power; and to possessors of power any complaint, however bitter, of the misuse of it, is a less flagrant act of insubordination than to protest against the power itself. The professions of women in this matter remind us of the State offenders of old, who on the point of execution, used to protest their love and devotion to the sovereign by whose unjust mandate they suffered. Griselda herself might be matched from the speeches put by Shakespeare into the mouths of male victims of kingly caprice and tyranny....

The literary class of women, especially in England, are ostentatious in disclaiming the desire for equality or citizenship, and proclaiming their complete satisfaction with the place which society assigns to them; exercising in this, as in many other respects, a most noxious influence over the feelings and opinions of men, who unsuspectingly accept the servilities of toadyism as concessions to the force of truth, not considering that it is in the personal interest of these women to profess whatever opinions they expect will be agreeable to men....They depend on men's opinion for their literary as well as for their feminine successes; and such is their bad opinion of men, that they believe there is not more than one in ten thousand who does not dislike and fear strength, sincerity, or high spirit in a woman. They are therefore anxious to earn pardon and toleration for whatever of these qualities their writing may exhibit on other subjects, by a studied display of submission on this: that they may give no occasion for vulgar men to say (what nothing will prevent vulgar men from saying), that learning makes women unfeminine, and that literary ladies are likely to be bad wives.

From *Strong-Minded Women*, edited by Janet Horowitz Murray, New York: Pantheon Books, 1982, 32–35.

Document 26:
MARRIED WOMEN AND THE LAW (1854)
Barbara Leigh Smith Bodichon

Barbara Leigh Smith Bodichon was the first female lawyer in Great Britain. This document illustrates the status of women in the West at the mid-point of the nineteenth century. It describes the contemporary position of women in legal terms, as the property of their husbands and not persons in their own right.

A man and wife are one person in law; the wife loses all her rights as a single woman, and her existence is entirely absorbed in that of her husband. He is civilly responsible for her acts; she lives under his protection or cover, and her condition is called coverture.

A woman's body belongs to her husband; she is in his custody, and he can enforce his right by a writ of *habeas corpus*.

What was her personal property before marriage, such as money in hand, money at the bank, jewels, household goods, clothes, &c., becomes absolutely her husband's, and he may assign or dispose of them at his pleasure whether he and his wife live together or not.

A wife's *chattels real* (i.e., estates held during a term of years, or the next presentation to a church living, &c.) become her husband's....

Neither the Courts of Common Law nor Equity have any direct power to oblige a man to support his wife....

Money earned by a married woman belongs absolutely to her husband; that and all sources of income, excepting those mentioned above, are included in the term personal property.

By the particular permission of her husband she can make a will of her personal property, for by such a permission he gives up his right. But he may revoke his permission at any time before *probate*....

The legal custody of children belongs to the father. During the life-time of a sane father, the mother has no rights over her children, except a limited power over infants, and the father may take them from her and dispose of them as he thinks fit.

If there be a legal separation of the parents, and there be neither agreement nor order of Court, giving the custody of the children to either parent, then the *right to the custody of the children* (except for the nutriment of infants) belongs legally to the father.

A married woman cannot sue or be sued for contracts—nor can she enter into contracts except as the agent of her husband; that is to say, her word alone is not binding in law, and persons giving a wife credit have no remedy against her....

A wife cannot bring actions unless the husband's name is joined.

As the wife acts under the command and control of her husband, she is excused from punishment for certain offenses, such as theft, burglary, housebreaking, &c., if committed in his presence and under his influence. A wife cannot be found guilty of concealing her felon husband or of concealing a felon jointly with her husband. She cannot be found guilty of stealing from her husband or of setting his house on fire, as they are one person in law. A husband and wife cannot be found guilty of conspiracy, as that offence cannot be committed unless there are two persons.

From *Strong-Minded Women*, edited by Janet Horowitz Murray, New York: Pantheon Books, 1982, 119–120.

Document 27:
REMINISCENCES OF THE AKRON CONVENTION (1848)
Frances D. Gage

Sojourner Truth (1797–1882), whose legal name was Isabella van Wagener, was one of the truly fascinating persons of her age. She was born a slave in Massachusetts, was finally freed, recovered her son from his kidnapping and illegal sale into slavery in the South, and eventually ended up as an evangelist in New York. She claimed to hear voices that gave her divine inspiration, and was "called upon" by these supernatural voices to travel the country and preach. She took the name Sojourner Truth, and became an ardent abolitionist. In the 1850s, she became an important advocate of women's rights, and continued her activist position in numerous causes until her death. The following passage attempts to capture her powerful presence as a public speaker. This account of the convention, written by one of its speakers, Frances D. Gage, is an attempt to accurately record Truth's moving speech.

Sojourner Truth. The leaders of the movement trembled on seeing a tall, gaunt black woman in a gray dress and white turban, surmounted with an uncouth sun-bonnet, march deliberately into the church, walk with the air of a queen up the aisle, and take her seat upon the pulpit steps. A buzz of disapprobation was heard all over the house, and there fell on the listening ear, "An abolition affair!" "Woman's rights and niggers!" "I told you so!" "Go it, darkey!"

I chanced on that occasion to wear my first laurels in public life as president of the meeting. At my request order was restored, and the business of the Convention went on. Morning, afternoon, and evening exercises came and went. Through all these sessions old Sojourner, quiet and reticent as the "Lybian Statue," sat crouched against the wall on the corner of the pulpit stairs, her sun-bonnet shading her eyes, her elbows on her knees, her chin resting upon her broad, hard palms. At intermission she was busy selling the "Life of Sojourner Truth," a narrative of her own strange and adventurous life. Again and again, timorous and trembling ones came to me and said, with earnestness, "Don't let her speak, Mrs. Gage, it will ruin us. Every newspaper in the land will have our cause mixed up with abolition and niggers, and we shall be utterly denounced." My only answer was, "We shall see when the time comes."

The second day the work waxed warm. Methodist, Baptist, Episcopal, Presbyterian, and Universalist ministers came in to hear and discuss the resolutions presented. One claimed superior rights and privileges for man, on the ground of "superior intellect"; another, because of the "manhood of Christ; if God had desired the equality of woman, He would have given some token of His will through birth, life, and death of the Saviour." Another gave us a theological view of the "sin of our first mother."

There were very few women in those days who dared to "speak in meeting"; and the august teachers of the people were seemingly getting the better of us, while the boys in the galleries, and the sneerers among the pews, were hugely enjoying the discomfiture, as they supposed, of the "strong-minded." Some of the tender-skinned friends were on the point of losing dignity, and the atmosphere betokened a storm. When, slowly from her seat in the corner rose Sojourner Truth, who, till now, had scarcely lifted her head. "Don't let her speak!" gasped half a dozen in my ear. She moved slowly and solemnly to the front, laid her old bonnet at her feet, and turned her great speaking eyes to me. The was a hissing sound of disapprobation above and below. I rose and announced "Sojourner Truth," and begged the audience to keep silence for a few moments.

The tumult subsided at once, and every eye was fixed on this almost Amazon form, which stood nearly six feet high, head erect, and eyes piercing the upper air like one in a dream. At her first word there was a profound hush. She spoke in deep tones, which, though not loud, reached every ear in the house, and away through the throng at the doors and windows.

"Wall, chilern, whar dar is so much racket dar must be somethin' out o' kilter. I tink dat 'twixt de niggers of de Souf and womin at de Norf, all talkin' 'bout rights, de white men will be in a fix pretty soon. But what's all dis here talkin' 'bout?

"Dat man ober dar say dat womin needs to be helped into carriages, and lifted ober ditches, and to hab de best place everywhar. Nobody eber helps me into carriages, or ober mud-puddles, or gibs me any best place!" And raising herself to her full height, and her voice to a pitch like rolling thunder, she asked, "And a'n't I a woman? Look at me! Look at my arm! (and she bared her right arm to the shoulder, showing her tremendous muscular power). I have ploughed, and planted, and gathered into barns, and no man could head me! And a'n't I a woman? I could work as much and eat as much as a man—when I could get it—and bear de lash as well! and a'n't I a woman? I have borne thirteen chilern, and seen 'em mos' all sold off to slavery, and when I cried out with my mother's grief, none but Jesus heard me! And a'n't I a woman?

"Den dey talks 'bout dis ting in de head; what dis dey call it?" ("Intellect," whispered some one near). "Dat's it, honey. What's dat got to do wid womin's rights or nigger's rights? If my cup won't hold but a pint, and yours holds a quart, wouldn't ye be mean not to let me have my little half-measure full?" And she pointed her significant finger, and sent a keen glance at the minister who had made the argument. The cheering was long and loud.

"Den dat little man in black dar, he say women can't have as much rights as men, 'cause Christ wan't a woman! Whar did your Christ come from?" Rolling thunder couldn't have stilled that crowd, as did those deep, wonderful tones, as she stood there with outstretched arms and eyes of fire. Raising her voice still louder, she repeated, "Whar did your Christ come from? From God and a woman! Man had nothin' to do wid Him." Oh, what a rebuke that was to that little man.

Turning again to another objector, she took up the defense of Mother Eve. I can not follow her through it all. It was pointed, and witty, and solemn; eliciting at almost every sentence deafening applause; and she ended by asserting: "If de fust woman God ever made was strong enough to turn the world upside down all alone, dese women togedder (and she glanced her eye over the platform) ought to be able to turn it back, and get it right side up again! And now dey is asking to do it, de men better let 'em." Long-continued cheering greeted this. "'Bleeged to ye for hearin' on me, and now ole Sojourner han't got nothin' more to say."

Amid roars of applause, she returned to her corner, leaving more than one of us with streaming eyes, and hearts beating with gratitude. She had taken us up in her strong arms and carried us safely over the slough of difficulty turning the whole tide in our favor. I have never in my life seen anything like the magical influence that subdued the mobbish spirit of the day, and turned the sneers and jeers of an excited crowd into notes of respect and admiration. Hundreds rushed up to shake hands with her, and congratulate the glorious old mother, and bid her God-speed on her mission of "testifyin' agin concerning the wickedness of this 'ere people."

From *History of Woman Suffrage*, edited by Elizabeth Cady Stanton, Susan B. Anthony and Matilda Joslyn Gage, Volume I, 1848–1861, New York: Fowler and Wells Publisher, 1881, 115–117.

Document 28:
THE EMANCIPATION PROCLAMATION (1862)
Abraham Lincoln

The President of the United States emancipated slaves in the Confederate States. This proclamation put the differences between North and South on a new plane. It also made European intervention in the Civil War unlikely. The Emancipation Proclamation was intended more as a weapon against the South than as a humanitarian gesture, but it did clearly state abolition of slavery as an aim of the Civil War. It also hurt the slave economy of the South and gave a powerful moral dimension to the North's cause.

Whereas on the twenty-second day of September, in the year of our Lord 1862, a proclamation was issued by the President of the United States, containing, among other things, the following, to wit:

"That on the first day of January,...1863, all persons held as slaves within any state or designated part of a state, the people whereof shall then be in rebellion against the United States, shall be then, thenceforward, and forever, free; and the Executive Government of the United States, including the military and naval authority thereof, will recognize and maintain the freedom of such persons, and will do no act or acts to repress such persons, or any of them, in any efforts they may make for their actual freedom."

"That the Executive will on the first day of January aforesaid, by proclamation, designate the states and parts of states, if any, in which the people thereof, respectively, shall then be in rebellion against the United States; and the fact that any state or the people thereof, shall on that day be in good faith represented in the Congress of the United States, by members chosen thereto at elections wherein a majority of the qualified voters of such states shall have participated, shall, in the absence of strong countervailing testimony, be deemed conclusive evidence that such state, and the people thereof, are not then in rebellion against the United States."

Now, therefore, I, Abraham Lincoln, President of the United States, by virtue of the power in me vested as Commander-in-Chief of the Army and Navy of the United States, in time of actual armed rebellion against the authority and government of the United States, and as a fit and necessary war measure for suppressing said rebellion, do, on this first day of January...1863, and in accordance with my purpose so to do, publicly proclaimed for the full period of one hundred days from the day first above mentioned, order and designate as the states and parts of states wherein the people thereof, respectively, are this day in rebellion against the United States the following, to wit:

Arkansas, Texas, Louisiana (except the parishes of St. Bernard, Plaquemines, Jefferson, St. John, St. Charles, St. James, Ascension, Assumption, Terre Bonne, Lafourche, St. Mary, St. Martin, and Orleans, including the city of New Orleans), Mississippi, Alabama, Florida, Georgia, South Carolina, North Carolina, and Virginia (except the forty-eight counties designated as West Virginia, and also the counties of Berkeley, Accomac, Northhampton, Elizabeth City, York, Princess Anne, and Norfolk, including the cities of Norfolk and Portsmouth), and which excepted parts are for the present left precisely as if this proclamation were not issued.

And by virtue of the power and for the purpose aforesaid, I do order and declare that all persons held as slaves within said designated states and parts of states are, and henceforward shall be, free; and that the Executive Government of the United States, including the military and naval authorities thereof, will recognize and maintain the freedom of said persons.

And I hereby enjoin upon the people so declared to be free to abstain from all violence, unless in necessary self-defense; and I recommend to them that, in all cases when allowed, they labor faithfully for reasonable wages.

And I further declare and make known that such persons of suitable condition, will be received into the armed service of the United States to garrison forts, positions, stations, and other places, and to man vessels of all sorts in said service.

And upon this act of justice, warranted by the Constitution upon military necessity, I invoke the considerate judgment of mankind and the gracious favor of Almighty God.

From *United States Statutes at Large*, XII (1859–63), 1268–1269.

Document 29:
THE ABOLITION OF RUSSIAN SERFDOM (1861)
Czar Alexander II

This declaration ending serfdom in Russia indicates the vast differences between the West of Europe and the Russian Empire. Note the references to divine right rule and the obvious power of the nobility in a nation without a parliamentary government.

By the grace of God, we, Alexander II., Emperor and Autocrat of all the Russias, King of Poland, Grand Duke of Finland, etc., to all our faithful subjects make known:—

Called by Divine Providence and by the sacred right of inheritance to the throne of our ancestors, we took a vow in our innermost heart so to respond to the mission which is intrusted to us as to surround with our affection and our Imperial solicitude all our faithful subjects of every rank and of every condition, from the warrior who nobly bears arms for the defence of the country to the humble artisan devoted to the works of industry; from the official in the career of the high offices of the State to the labourer whose plough furrows the soil.

In considering the various classes and conditions of which the State is composed we came to the conviction that the legislation of the empire having wisely provided for the organization of the upper and middle classes and having defined with precision their obligations, their rights, and their privileges, has not attained the same degree of efficiency as regards the peasants attached to the soil, thus designated because either from ancient laws or from custom they have been hereditarily subjected to the authority of the proprietors, on whom it was incumbent at the same time to provide for their welfare. The rights of the proprietors have been hitherto very extended and very imperfectly defined by the law, which has been supplied by tradition, custom, and the good pleasure of the proprietors. In the most favourable cases this state of things has established patriarchal relations founded upon a solicitude sincerely equitable and benevolent on the part of the proprietors, and on an affectionate submission on the part of the peasants; but in proportion as the simplicity of morals diminished, as the diversity of the mutual relations became complicated, as the paternal character of the relations between the proprietors and the peasants became weakened, and, moreover, as the seigneurial authority fell sometimes into hands exclusively occupied with their personal interests, those bonds of mutual good-will slackened, and a wide opening was made for an arbitrary sway, which weighed upon the peasants, was unfavourable to their welfare, and made them indifferent to all progress under the conditions of their existence.

These facts had already attracted the notice of our predecessors of glorious memory, and they had taken measures for improving the conditions of the peasants; but among those measures some were not stringent enough, insomuch that they remained subordinate to the spontaneous initiative of such proprietors who showed themselves animated with liberal intentions; and others, called forth by peculiar circumstances, have been restricted to certain localities or simply adopted as an experiment. It was thus that Alexander I. published the regulation for the free cultivators, and that the late Emperor Nicholas, our beloved father, promulgated that one which concerns the peasants bound by contract. In the Western Governments regulations called "inventaires" had fixed the territorial allotments due to the peasants, as well as the amount of their rent dues; but all these reforms have only been applied in a very restricted manner.

We thus came to the conviction that the work of a serious improvement of the condition of the peasants was a sacred inheritance bequeathed to us by our ancestors, a mission which, in the course of events, Divine Providence called upon us to fulfil.

We have commenced this work by an expression of our Imperial confidence towards the nobility of Russia, which has given us so many proofs of its devotion to the Throne, and of its constant readiness to make sacrifices for the welfare of the country.

It is to the nobles themselves, conformable to their own wishes, that we have reserved the task of drawing up the propositions for the new organization of the peasants—propositions which make it incumbent upon them to limit their rights over the peasants, and to accept the onus of a reform which could not be accomplished without some material losses. Our confidence has not been deceived. We have seen the nobles assembled in committees in the districts, through the medium of their confidential agents, making the voluntary sacrifice of their rights as regards the personal servitude of the peasants. These committees, after having collected the necessary data, have formulated their propositions concerning the new organization of the peasants attached to the soil in their relations with the proprietors.

These propositions having been found very diverse, as was to be expected from the nature of the question, they have been compared, collated, and reduced to a regular system, then rectified and completed in the superior committee instituted for that purpose; and these new dispositions thus formulated relative to the peasants and domestics of the proprietors have been examined in the Council of the Empire....

In virtue of the new dispositions above mentioned, the peasants attached to the soil will be invested within a term fixed by the law with all the rights of free cultivators.

The proprietors retaining their rights of property on all the land belonging to them, grant to the peasants for a fixed regulated rental the full enjoyment of their close; and, moreover, to assure their livelihood and to guarantee the fulfilment of their obligations towards the Government, the quantity of arable land is fixed by the said dispositions, as well as other rural appurtenances.

But, in the enjoyment of these territorial allotments, the peasants are obliged, in return, to acquit the rentals fixed by the same dispositions to the profit of the proprietors. In this state, which must be a transitory one, the peasants shall be designated as "temporarily bound."

At the same time, they are granted the right of purchasing their close, and, with the consent of the proprietors, they may acquire in full property the arable lands and other appurtenances which are allotted to them as a permanent holding. By the acquisition in full property of the quantity of land fixed, the peasants are free from their obligations towards the proprietors for land thus purchased, and they enter definitely into the condition of free peasants—landholders.

By a special disposition concerning the domestics, a transitory state is fixed for them, adapted to their occupations and the exigencies of their position. On the expiration of a term of two years, dating from the day of the promulgation of these dispositions, they shall receive their full enfranchisement and some temporary immunities....

Aware of all the difficulties of the reform we have undertaken, we place above all things our confidence in the goodness of Divine Providence, who watches over the destinies of Russia.

We also count upon the generous devotion of our faithful nobility, and we are happy to testify to that body the gratitude it has deserved from us, as well as from the country, for the disinterested support it has given to the accomplishment of our designs. Russia will not forget that the nobility, acting solely upon its respect for the dignity of man and its love for its neighbour, has spontaneously renounced rights given to it by serfdom actually abolished, and laid the foundation of a new future, which is thrown open to the peasants.

To render the transactions between the proprietors and the peasants more easy, in virtue of which the latter may acquire in full property their close (homestead) and the land they occupy, the Government will advance assistance, according to a special regulation, by means of loans or a transfer of debts encumbering an estate....

When the first news of this great reform meditated by the Government became diffused among the rural populations, who were scarcely prepared for it, it gave rise, in some instances, to misunderstandings among individuals more intent upon liberty than mindful of the duties which it imposes. But, generally, the good sense of the country has not been wanting. It has not misunderstood either the inspirations of natural reason, which says that every man who accepts freely the benefits of society owes it in return the fulfilment of certain positive obligations; nor the teachings of the Christian law, which enjoins that "every one be subject unto the higher powers" (St. Paul to the Romans, xiii. 1); and to "render to all their dues," and, above all, to whomsoever it belongs, tribute, custom, respect, and honour (Ibid., xiii. 7). It has understood that the proprietors would not be deprived of rights legally acquired, except for a fit and sufficient indemnity, or by a voluntary concession on their part; that it would be contrary to all equity to accept this enjoyment of the lands conceded by the proprietors without accepting also towards them equivalent charges.

And now we hope with confidence that the freed serfs, in the presence of the new future which is opened before them, will appreciate and recognize the considerable sacrifices which the nobility have made on their behalf. They will undertand that the blessing of an existence supported upon the base of guaranteed property, as well as a greater liberty in the administration of their goods, entails upon them, with new duties towards society and themselves, the obligation of justifying the protecting designs of the law by a loyal and judicious use of the rights which are now accorded to them. For if men do not labour themselves to insure their own well-being under the shield of the laws, the best of those laws cannot guarantee it to them.

It is only by assiduous labour, a rational employment of their strength and their resources, a strict economy, and, above all, by an honest life, a life constantly inspired by the fear of the Lord, that they can arrive at prosperity and insure its development.

The authorities entrusted with the duty of preparing by preliminary measures the execution of the new organization, and of presiding at its inauguration, will have to see that this work is accomplished with calmness and regularity, taking into account the requirements of the seasons, in order that the cultivator may not be drawn away from his agricultural labours. Let him apply himself with zeal to those labours, that he may be able to draw from an abundant granary the seed which he has to confide to that land which will be given him for permanent enjoyment, or which he has acquired for himself as his own property.

And now, pious and faithful people, make upon the forehead the sacred sign of the cross, and join thy prayers to ours to call down the blessing of the Most High upon thy first free labours, the sure pledge of thy personal well-being and of the public prosperity.

Given at St. Petersburg, the 19th day of February (March 3), of the year of Grace 1861, and the seventh of our reign.

Alexander

From *Readings in European History since 1814*, edited by Jonathan F. Scott and Alexander Baltzley, New York: F.S. Crofts & Co., 1931, 289–293.

Document 30:
I ACCUSE (1898)
Émile Zola

A theft of French military secrets led the army and government to accuse Dreyfus, a Jewish captain in the French army, of treason. Despite great problems with the case, Dreyfus was convicted, retried and again convicted. France was bitterly divided and a great deal of anti-semitism colored the attitudes of government, military and church officials in this case. Only after elections changed the government was Dreyfus pardoned. In the midst of the crisis, Zola published this famous attack on those who were opposed to Dreyfus.

I accuse Lieutenant-Colonel du Payd de Clam of having been the diabolical author, unwittingly, I would believe, of a miscarriage of justice, and of having afterwards, for three years, defended his ill-omened work by the most absurd and culpable tricks.

I accuse General Mercier of having made himself an accomplice, at least by weakness of will, in one of the greatest acts of injustice of the century.

I accuse General Billot of having had in his hands the sure proofs of the innocence of Dreyfus and of having suppressed them, thus rendering himself guilty of the crime of outraging humanity and outraging justice, for a political purpose and to save the face of the General Staff, which had been compromised.

I accuse General Boisdeffre and General Gonse of having made themselves accomplices of the same crime, the first without doubt affected by his passion for the Church, the other affected perhaps by that *esprit de corps* which would transform the War Office into a Holy Place, that must not be attacked.

I accuse General de Pellieux and Commandant Ravary of having carried on a villainous investigation characterized by the most monstrous partiality, of which we have in the report of the second an imperishable monument of naive audacity.

I accuse the three handwriting experts, Messrs. Belhomme, Varinard and Couard, of having made false and fraudulent reports, unless a medical examination should prove that they are affected with infirmity of eyesight and of judgment.

I accuse the departments of the War Office of having conducted in the Press, particularly in the clair and in the Echo de Paris, an abominable campaign, to mislead public opinion and to cover up their errors.

Finally I accuse the first Council of War of having violated justice in condemning an accused man on the basis of a document which has remained secret and I accuse the second Council of War of having officially concealed this illegality, thus in its turn committing the crime against justice of knowingly acquitting the guilty.

From a letter from Émile Zola to the President of the French Republic, January 13, 1898, in *Readings in European History Since 1814*, edited by Jonathan F. Scott and Alexander Baltzley, New York: F.S. Crofts and Co., 1931, 314–15.

Document 31:
THE JEWISH STATE (1896)
Theodor Herzl

Theodor Herzl, the father of modern Zionism—the movement for a Jewish state in the Middle East—describes the kinds of discrimination and persecution Jews faced in Europe. His experiences were mostly in Central Europe. The solution? He advocated the creation of a Jewish state.

The Jewish Question still exists. It would be foolish to deny it. It is a remnant of the Middle Ages, which civilized nations do not even yet seem able to shake off, try as they will. They certainly showed a generous desire to do so when they emancipated us. The Jewish question exists wherever Jews live in perceptible numbers. Where it does not exist, it is carried by Jews in the course of their migrations. We naturally move to those places where we are not persecuted, and there our presence produces persecution. This is the case in every country, and will remain so, even in those highly civilized—for instance, France—until the Jewish question finds a solution on a political basis. The unfortunate Jews are now carrying the seeds of Anti-Semitism into England; they have already introduced it into America.

I believe that I understand Anti-Semitism, which is really a highly complex movement. I consider it from a Jewish standpoint, yet without fear or hatred. I believe that I can see what elements there are in it of vulgar sport, of common trade jealousy, of inherited prejudice, of religious intolerance, and also of pretended self-defence. I think the Jewish question is no more a social than a religious one, notwithstanding that it sometimes takes these and other forms. It is a national question, which can only be solved by making it a political world-question to be dicussed and settled by the civilized nations of the world in council.

We are a people—one people.

We have honestly endeavored everywhere to merge ourselves in the social life of surrounding communities and to preserve the faith of our fathers. We are not permitted to do so. In vain are we loyal patriots, our loyalty in some places running to extremes; in vain do we make the same sacrifices of life and property as our fellow-citizens; in vain do we strive to increase the fame of our native land in science and art, or her wealth by trade and commerce. In countries where we have lived for centuries we are still cried down as strangers, and often by those whose ancestors were not yet domiciled in the land where Jews had already had experience of suffering. The majority may decide which are the strangers; for between nations, is a question of might. I do not here surrender any portion of our prescriptive right, when I make this statement merely in my own name as an individual. In the world as it now is and for an indefinite period will probably remain, might precedes right. It is useless, therefore, for us to be loyal patriots, as were the Huguenots who were forced to emigrate. If we could only be left in peace....

But I think we shall not be left in peace.

Oppression and persecution cannot exterminate us. No nation on earth has survived such struggles and sufferings as we have gone through. Jew-baiting has merely stripped off our weaklings; the strong among us were invariably true to their race when persecution broke out against them. This attitude was most clearly apparent in the period immediately following the emancipation of the Jews. Those Jews who were advanced intellectually and materially entirely lost the feeling of belonging to their race. Wherever our political well-being has lasted for any length of time, we have assimilated with our surroundings. I think this is not discreditable. Hence, the statesman who would wish to see a Jewish strain in his nation would have to provide for the duration of our political well-being; and even a Bismarck could not do that.

For old prejudices against us still lie deep in the hearts of the people. He who would have proofs of this need only listen to the people where they speak with frankness and simplicity; proverb and fairy-tale are both Anti-Semitic. A nation is everywhere a great child, which can certainly be educated; but its education would, even in most favorable circumstances, occupy such a vast amount of time that we could, as already mentioned, remove our own difficulties by other means long before the process was accomplished.

Assimilation, by which I understood not only external conformity in dress, habits, customs, and language, but also identity of feeling and manner—assimilation of Jews could be effected only by intermarriage. But the need for mixed marriages would have to be felt by the majority; their mere recognition by law would certainly not suffice....

No one can deny the gravity of situation of the Jews. Whenever they live in perceptible numbers, they are more or less persecuted. Their equality before the law, granted by statute, has become practically a dead letter. They are debarred from filling even moderately high positions, either in the army, or in any public or private capacity. And attempts are made to thrust them out of business also: "Don't buy from Jews!"

Attacks in Parliaments, in assemblies, in the press, in the pulpit, in the street, on journeys—for example, their exclusion from certain hotels—even in places of recreation, become daily more numerous. The forms of persecutions varying according to the countries and social circles in which they occur. In Russia, imposts are levied on Jewish villages; in Rumania, a few persons are put to death; in Germany, they get a good beating occasionally; in Austria, Anti-Semites exercise terrorism over all public life; in Algeria, there are travelling agitators; in Paris, the Jews are shut out of the so-called best social circles and excluded from clubs. Shades of anti-Jewish feeling are innumerable. But this is not to be an attempt to make out a doleful category of Jewish hardships.

I do not intend to arouse sympathetic emotions on our behalf. That would be foolish, futile, and undignified proceeding. I shall content myself with putting the following questions to the Jews: Is it not true that, in countries where we live in perceptible numbers, the position of Jewish lawyers, doctors, technicians, teachers, and employees of all descriptions becomes daily more intolerable? Is it not true, that the Jewish middle classes are seriously threatened? Is it not true, that the passions of the mob are incited against our wealthy people? Is it not true, that our poor endure greater sufferings than any other proletariat? I think that this external pressure makes itself felt everywhere. In our economically upper classes it causes discomfort, in our middle classes continual and grave anxieties, in our lower classes absolute despair.

Everything tends, in fact, to one and the same conclusion, which is clearly enunciated in that classic Berlin phrase: "*Juden Raus!*" (Out with the Jews!)

I shall now put the Question in the briefest possible form: Are we to "get out" and where to?

Or, may we yet remain? And, how long?

Let us first settle the point of staying where we are. Can we hope for better days, can we possess our souls in patience, can we wait in pious resignation till the princes and peoples of this earth are more mercifully disposed towards us? I say that we cannot hope for a change in the current of feeling. And why not? Even if we were as near to the hearts of princes as are their other subjects, they could not protect us. They would only feel popular hatred by showing us too much favor. By "too much," I really mean less than is claimed as a right by every ordinary citizen, or by every race. The nations in whose midst Jews live are all either covertly or openly Anti-Semitic.

The common people have not, and indeed cannot have, any historic comprehension. They do not know that the sins of the Middle Ages are now being visited on the nations of Europe. We are what the Ghetto made us. We have attained pre-eminence in finance, because medieval conditions drove us to it. The same process is now being repeated. We are again being forced into finance, now it is the stock exchange, by being kept out of other branches of economic activity. Being on the stock exchange, we continue to produce an abundance of mediocre intellects who find no outlet, and this endangers our social position as much as does our increasing wealth. Educated Jews without means are now rapidly becoming Socialists. Hence we are certain to suffer very severely in the struggle between classes, because we stand in the most exposed position in the camps of both Socialists and Capitalists....

THE PLAN

The whole plan is in its essence perfectly simple, as it must necessarily be if it is to come within the comprehension of all.

Let the sovereignty be granted us over a portion of the globe large enough to satisfy the rightful requirements of a nation; the rest we shall manage for ourselves.

The creation of a new State is neither ridiculous nor impossible. We have in our day witnessed the process in connection with nations which were not largely members of the middle class, but poorer, less educated, and consequently weaker than ourselves. The Governments of all countries scourged by Anti-Semitism will be keenly interested in assisting us to obtain the sovereignty we want.

The plan, simple in design, but complicated in execution, will be carried out by two agencies: The Society of Jews and the Jewish Company.

The Society of Jews will do the preparatory work in the domains of science and politics, which the Jewish Company will afterwards apply practically.

The Jewish Company will be the liquidating agent of the business interests of departing Jews, and will organize commerce and trade in the new country.

We must not imagine the departure of the Jews to be a sudden one. It will be gradual, continuous, and will cover many decades. The poorest will go first to cultivate the soil. In accordance with a preconceived plan, they will construct roads, bridges, railways and telegraph installations; regulate rivers; and build their own dwellings; their labor will create trade, trade will create markets and markets will attract new settlers, for every man will go voluntarily, at his own expense and his own risk. The labor expended on the land will enhance its value, and the Jews will soon perceive that a new and permanent sphere of operation is opening here for that spirit of enterprise which has heretofore met only with hatred and obloquy.

If we wish to found a State today, we shall not do it in the way which would have been the only possible one a thousand years ago. It is foolish to revert to old stages of civilization, as many Zionists would like to do. Supposing, for example, we were obliged to clear a country of wild beasts, we should not set about the task in the fashion of Europeans of the fifth century. We should not take spear and lance and go out singly in pursuit of bears; we would organize a large and active hunting party, drive the animals together, and throw a melinite bomb into their midst.

If we wish to conduct building operations, we shall not plant a mass of stakes and piles on the shore of a lake, but we shall build as men build now. Indeed, we shall build in a bolder and more stately style than was ever adopted before, for we now possess means which men never yet possessed.

The emigrants standing lowest in the economic scale will be slowly followed by those of a higher grade. Those who at this moment are living in despair will go first. They will be led by the mediocre intellects which we produce so superabundantly and which are persecuted everywhere.

This pamphlet will open a general discussion on the Jewish Question, but that does not mean that there will be any voting on it. Such a result would ruin the cause from the outset, and dissidents must remember that allegiance or opposition is entirely voluntary. He who will not come with us should remain behind.

Let all who are willing to join us, fall in behind our banner and fight for our cause with voice and pen and deed.

Those Jews who agree with our idea of a State will attach themselves to the Society, which will thereby be authorized to confer and treat with Governments in the name of our people. The Society will thus be acknowledged in its relations with Governments as a State-creating power. This acknowledgement will practically create the State.

Should the Powers declare themselves willing to admit our sovereignty over a neutral piece of land, then the Society will enter into negotiations for the possession of this land. Here two territories come under consideration, Palestine and Argentine. In both countries important experiments in colonization have been made, though on the mistaken principle of a gradual infiltration of Jews. An infiltration is bound to end badly. It continues till the inevitable moment when the native population feels itself threatened, and forces the Government to stop a further influx of Jews. Immigration is consequently futile unless we have sovereign right to continue such immigration.

The Society of Jews will treat with the present masters of the land, putting itself under the protectorate of the European Powers, if they prove friendly to the plan. We could offer the present possessors of the land enormous advantages, assume part of the public debt, build new roads for traffic, which our presence in the country would render necessary, and do many other things. The creation of our State would be beneficial to adjacent countries, because the cultivation of a strip of land increases the value of its surrounding districts in innumerable ways.

From *The Israel-Arab Reader* edited by Walter Laqueur, New York: The Citadel Press, 1968, 6–11.

Document 32:
BLOOD AND IRON
Otto von Bismarck

Otto von Bismarck became Minister-President of Prussia, the large, northern German state that united Germany into an empire after a series of wars in the 1860s and 1870s. Bismarck became chancellor of the empire until his ouster in 1890. He represented a strong, authoritarian trend in European politics which downplayed political participation of the middle and working classes and exalted the "natural" leaders from the past. Of the failed revolutions of 1848–1849 which tried to reform the German states and create a united Germany, he wrote that "Not to Prussia's liberalism but to her power is Germany looking. . .not by speeches and majority votes are the great questions of the day decided—that was the great mistake of 1848 and 1849—but by iron and blood." The following extract from his Memoirs reveals his hostility to the revolution of 1848 and his desire to crush it and expand Prussia.

The softness of Frederick William IV, under the pressure of uninvited and perhaps treacherous advisers and the stress of women's tears, in attempting to terminate the bloody event in Berlin, after it had been victoriously carried through, by commanding his troops to renounce the victory they had won, exercised on the further development of our policy in the first instance all the mischief of a neglected opportunity. Whether the progress would have been lasting if the King had maintained the victory of his troops, and made the most of it, is another question. At any rate the King would not have been in the crushed mood in which I found him during the second United Diet, but in that soaring flight of eloquence, invigorated by victory, which he had displayed on the occasion of the homage in 1840, at Cologne in 1842, and elsewhere. I venture upon no conjecture as to what effect upon the King's attitude, upon his romantic medieval reminiscences of the Empire as regarded Austria and the Princes, and upon the previous and subsequent strong royalist sentiment in the country, would have been produced by a consciousness that he had definitely overcome the insurrection which elsewhere on the continent outside of Russia remained face to face with him as the sole victor. A victory won on the pavement would have been of a different sort and of less range than that afterwards won on the battlefield. It has, perhaps, proved better for our future that we had to stray plodding through the wilderness of intestine conflicts from 1848 to 1866, like the Jews before they entered the Promised Land. We should hardly have been spared the wars of 1866 and 1870 even if our neighbours, who collapsed in 1848, had regained strength and courage by means of support from Paris, Vienna, and other quarters. It is a question whether the operation of historical events upon the Germans by the shorter and quicker path of a victory in March 1848 would have been the same as that which we see to-day, and which gives the impression that the dynasties, and more especially those which were formerly prominently 'particularistic,' are more friendly disposed towards the Empire than are the political groups and parties.

My first visit to Sans-Souci took place under unfavourable conditions. In the early part of June, a few days before the retirement of the Minister-President Rudolf Camphausen, I was at Potsdam, when a court messenger sought me out at the inn to tell me that the King wanted to speak to me. I said, being still under the impression of my critical mood, that I regretted I could not comply with his Majesty's commands as I was about to go home, and my wife, whose health was in a very delicate state, would be anxious if I stayed away longer than had been arranged. After some time Edwin von Manteuffel, aide-de-camp in waiting, appeared, repeated the command, in the form of an invitation to dinner, and added that the King put a special messenger at my disposal to inform my wife. I had no choice but to repair to Sans-Souci. The party at table was very small, comprising, if I remember aright, besides the ladies and gentlemen in attendance, only Camphausen and myself. After dinner the King took me on to the terrace, and asked me in a friendly sort of way: 'How are you getting on?' In the irritable state I had been in ever since the March days I replied: 'Badly.' The King said: 'I think the feeling is good in your parts.' Thereupon, under the impression made by some regulations, the contents of which I do not remember, I replied: 'The feeling was very good, but since we have been inoculated with the revolution by the King's officials under the royal sign-manual, it has become bad. What we lack is confidence in the support of the King.' At that moment the Queen stepped out from a shrubbery and said: 'How can you speak so to the King!' 'Let me alone, Elise,' replied the King, 'I shall soon settle his business;' and turning to me, he said: 'What do you really reproach me with, then?' 'The evacuation of Berlin.' 'I did not want it done,' replied the King; and the Queen, who had remained within hearing, added: 'Of that the King is quite innocent. He had not slept for three days.' 'A King ought to be able to stop sleep,' I replied. Unmoved by this blunt remark the King said: 'It is always easier to prophesy when you know. What would be gained if I admitted that I had behaved like a donkey? Something more than reproaches is wanted to set an overturned throne up again. To do that I need assistance and active devotion, not criticism.' The kindness with which he said all this, and much more to the same effect, overpowered me. I had come in the spirit of a *frondeur* [rebellious French nobles during the minority of Louis XIV], who would not have cared if he had been dismissed ungraciously; I went away completely disarmed and won over.

Upon my representing that he was master in the country parts, and possessed the power to restore the threatened order everywhere, he said he must be careful not to forsake the strictly legal path; if he must break with the Berlin Assembly—the 'day-labourer parliament,' as it was called in certain circles—he must have strict law on his side, otherwise his case would have a weak footing and the whole monarchy be in danger, not only of internal disturbances, but also from without. He possibly meant by that a French war, in partnership with insurrections in Germany. It seems to me more probable, however, that at the moment when he wanted my services he specially avoided expressing to me his fear of damaging his views for Prussia in Germany. I replied that strict legality and its limitations appeared to me obliterated in the actual situation, and would be as little respected by his opponents, when once they had the power, as on March 18; and that I saw the situation more in the light of war and self-defence than in that of legal argumentation. The King persisted, however, that his situation would be too weak if he quitted the legal footing, and I took away with me the impression that he was for the moment subordinating the possibility of the restoration of order in Prussia to the ideas that Radowitz used to instil into him, the 'black, red and gold theories,' as they were called at the time.

Among the numerous conversations that ensued upon this one, I remember these words of the King: 'I want to carry out the struggle against the tendencies of the National Assembly, but in the present state of the matter, while I may be fully convinced of my right, it is uncertain whether others, and ultimately the great masses of the people, will be also convinced. In order that I may be sure of this, the Assembly must put itself still farther in the wrong, especially in questions where my right to defend myself by force is plain not only to myself but to every one.'

I could not induce the King to share my conviction that his doubts as to his power were without foundation, and that therefore it only came to the question whether he could believe in his rights when he proposed to defend himself against the usurpations of the Assembly....

From Otto von Bismarck, *Memoirs*, Volume 1, edited by Horst Kohl, New York: Howard Fertig, 1966, 56–60.

Document 33:
ON ADMINISTERING THE OATH TO THE RECRUITS (1897)
Kaiser Wilhelm II

These words of Wilhelm II of Germany illustrate how obedience to the will of those in power came to characterize nationalism in the late nineteenth century. Note how religion is used to buttress Wilhelm's policies. Again, you see leaders appealing to patriotism and religion and threatening those who disagree.

After the administering of the oath to the recruits of the garrisons of Berlin, Charlottenburg, and Spandau by the representatives of the Evangelical and the Catholic churches, the Emperor took the occasion to deliver the following admonition:

To-day I greet you as soldiers of my army, as grenadiers of my guard. With the oath to the flag you have sworn allegiance as German men, and even before the altar of God, under the open skies, and upon His crucifix, as good Christians must. He who is not a good Christian is not a brave man and no Prussian soldier; and he cannot fulfill under any circumstances what is demanded of a soldier in the Prussian army.

Your duty is not easy; it demands of you self-control and self-abnegation, the two highest qualities of a Christian, and in addition unconditional obedience and subordination to the will of those who are appointed above you.

But you have examples before you out of the history of the German army. Thousands before your time have sworn their oath and kept it. And because they did keep it our Fatherland has become great and our army victorious and unconquerable. Because they kept their oath, their flags stand before you, garlanded with honor and covered with the tokens of glory, and wherever they are shown, heads are uncovered and regiments present arms.

In the time of your service temptation will surely draw near to many of you. If it does approach, either with regard to your personal conduct or with regard to your relationship as a soldier, turn it from you with the thought of the past of your regiments; turn it from you with the thought of your uniform, which is the uniform of your King. Whoever offends against the uniform of the King lays himself open to the most grievous punishments. Wear your uniform in such wise that you will compel respect from the world and from those who oppose you.

My glorious ancestors look down upon you from the vaulted heavens. The monuments of the Kings look down upon you and, above all, the statue of the great Emperor. When you are discharging your service remember the grievous times through which our Fatherland had to pass; remember them when your labor seems heavy and bitter. Stand firm in your inviolable faith and trust in God who never forsakes us. Then will my army and especially my guard be equal to its task in all times, whether in peace or war.

It is now your task to stand faithfully by me and to defend our highest possessions, whether against enemies from without or from within, and to obey when I command and never to forsake me.

From *The German Emperor as Shown in his Public Utterances*, edited by Christian Gauss, New York: Charles Scribner's Sons, 1915, 113–115.

Document 34:
LETTER SENT TO ALEXANDER III BY THE EXECUTIVE COMMITTEE (1881)

In the Russian Empire, there were no constructive channels for political expression to take. Thus, revolutionary groups developed. In this document, the Executive Committee of one such group, the People's Will, addressed their thoughts to Alexander III.

March 10, 1881

Your Majesty: Although the Executive Committee understands fully the grievous oppression that you must experience at this moment, it believes that it has no right to yield to the feeling of natural delicacy which would perhaps dictate the postponement of the following explanation to another time. There is something higher than the most legitimate human feeling, and that is duty to one's country—the duty for which a citizen must sacrifice himself and his own feelings, and even the feelings of others. In obedience to this all-powerful duty we have decided to address you at once, waiting for nothing, as will wait for nothing the historical process that threatens us with rivers of blood and the most terrible convulsions.

The tragedy enacted on the Ekaterinski canal was not a mere casualty, nor was it unexpected.

After all that had happened in the course of the previous decade it was absolutely inevitable; and in that fact consists its deep significance for a man who has been placed by fate at the head of governmental authority....

You are aware, your Majesty, that the Government of the late Emperor could not be accused of a lack of energy. It hanged the innocent and the guilty, and filled prisons and remote provinces with exiles. Tens of so-called "leaders" were captured and hanged, and died with the courage and tranquility of martyrs; but the movement did not cease — on the contrary it grew and strengthened. The revolutionary movement, your Majesty, is not dependent upon any particular individuals; it is a process of the social organism; and the scaffold raised for its more energetic exponents are as powerless to save the out-grown order of things as the cross that was erected for the Redeemer was powerless to save the ancient world from the triumph of Christianity. The Government, of course, may yet capture and hang an immense number of separate individuals, it may break up a great number of separate revolutionary groups, it may even destroy the most important of existing revolutionary organizations; but all this will not change, in the slightest degree, the condition of affairs. Revolutionists are the creation of circumstances; of the general discontent of the people; of the striving of Russia after a new social framework. It is impossible to exterminate the whole people; it is impossible, by means of repression, to stifle its discontent. Discontent only grows the more when it is repressed....This we actually see from the history of the last ten years. Of what use was it to destroy the Dolgushintsi, the Chaikoftsi, and the workers of 1874? Their places were taken by much more resolute democrats. Then the awful repressive measures of the Government called upon the stage the terrorists of 1878–9....In vain it destroyed tens of revolutionary circles. From among those incomplete organizations, by virtue of natural selection, arose only stronger forms, until, at last, there has appeared an Executive Committee with which the Government has not yet been able successfully to deal.

A dispassionate glance at the grievous decade through which we have just passed will enable us to forecast accurately the future progress of the revolutionary movement, provided the policy of the Government does not change. The movement will continue to grow and extend; deeds of a terroristic nature will increase in frequency and intensity, and the revolutionary organization will constantly set forth, in the places of destroyed groups, stronger and more perfect forms. Meanwhile the number of the discontented in the country will grow larger and larger; confidence in the Government on the part of the people, will decline; and the idea of revolution — of its possibility and inevitability — will establish itself in Russia more and more firmly. A terrible explosion, a bloody hurly-burly, a revolutionary earthquake throughout Russia will complete the destruction of the old order of things.... Whence proceeds this lamentable necessity for bloody conflict? It arises, your Majesty, from the lack in Russia of a real government in the true sense of that word. A government, in the very nature of things, should only give outward form to the aspirations of the people and effect to the people's will. But with us — excuse the expression — the Government has degenerated into a mere camarilla, and deserves the name of a usurping "gang" much more than does the Executive Committee.

Whatever may be the *intentions* of the Tsar, the *actions* of the Government have nothing in common with the popular welfare, or popular aspirations. The Imperial Government subjected the people to serfdom, put the masses into the power of the nobility, and is now openly creating the most injurious class of speculators and jobbers. All of its reforms result merely in a more perfect enslavement and a more complete exploitation of the people. It has brought Russia to such a pass that, at the present time, the masses of the people are in a state of pauperism and ruin; are subjected to the most humiliating surveillance, even at their own domestic hearths; and are powerless even to regulate their own communal and social affairs. The protection of the law and of the Government is enjoyed only by the extortionist and the exploiter, and the most exasperating robbery goes unpunished. But, on the other hand, what a terrible fate awaits the man who sincerely considers the general good! You know very well, you Majesty, that it is not only socialists who are exiled and prosecuted....

These are the reasons why the Russian Government exerts no moral influence, and has no support among the people. These are the reasons why Russia brings forth so many revolutionists. These are the reasons why even such a deed as Tsaricide excites in the minds of a majority of the people only gladness and sympathy. Yes, your Majesty! Do not be deceived by the reports of flatterers and sycophants—saricide, in Russia, is popular.

From such a state of affairs there can be only two exits: either a revolution, absolutely inevitable and not to be averted by any punishments, or a voluntary turning of the Supreme Power to the people. In the interest of our native land, in the hope of preventing the useless waste of energy, in the hope of averting the terrible miseries that always accompany revolution, the Executive Committee approaches your Majesty with the advice to take the second course. Be assured, so soon as the Supreme Power ceases to rule arbitrarily, so soon as it firmly resolves to accede to the demands of the people's conscience and consciousness, you may, without fear, discharge the spies that disgrace the administration, send your guards back to their barracks, and burn the scaffolds that are demoralizing the people. The Executive Committee will voluntarily terminate its own existence, and the organizations formed about it will disperse, in order that their members may devote themselves to the work of culture among the people of their native land.

We address your Majesty as those who have discarded all prejudices, and who have suppressed the distrust created by the actions of the Government throughout the century. We forget that you are the representative of the authority that has so often deceived and that has so injured the people. We address you as a citizen and as an honest man. We hope that the feeling of personal exasperation will not extinguish in your mind your consciousness of your duties and your desire to know the truth. *We* also might feel exasperation. You have lost your father. We have lost not only our fathers, but our brothers, our wives, our children and our dearest friends. But we are ready to suppress personal feeling if it be demanded by the welfare of Russia. We expect the same from you.

We set no conditions for you—do not let our proposition irritate you. The conditions that are prerequisite to a change from revolutionary activity to peaceful labor are created, not by us, but by history. These conditions, in our opinion, are two.

1. A general amnesty to cover all past political crimes; for the reason that they were not crimes but fulfillments of civil duty.

2. The summoning of representatives of the whole Russian people to examine the existing framework of social and governmental life, and to remodel it in accordance with the people's wishes.

We regard it as necessary, however, to remind you that the legalization of the Supreme Power, by the representatives of the people, can be valid only in case the elections are perfectly free....

We declare solemnly, before the people of our native land and before the whole world, that our party will submit unconditionally to the decisions of a National Assembly elected in the manner above indicated, and that we will not allow ourselves, in future, to offer violent resistance to any Government that the National Assembly may sanction.

And now, your Majesty, decide! Before you are two courses, and you are to make your choice between them. We can only trust that your intelligence and conscience may suggest to you the only decision that is compatible with the welfare of Russia, with your own dignity, and with your duty to your native land.

The Executive Committee

From *Readings in European History since 1814*, edited by Jonathan F. Scott and Alexander Baltzley, New York: F.S. Crofts, 1931, 330–333.

CHAPTER 6

Economic Development and Individual Rights

Document 35:
THE WEALTH OF NATIONS (1776)
Adam Smith

Adam Smith published The Wealth of Nations *in 1776 and crystalized thinking about a free market replacing the many government regulations that characterized mercantilism. Free enterprise, laissez faire [leave alone] doctrines seemed the appropriate ones for the growth of economies during the Industrial Revolution. Economic liberalism and the "Manchester School" became famous for the next two centuries after Smith's work appeared. It remains a force in economic thinking today.*

There is in every society or neighborhood an ordinary or average rate both of wages and profit in every different employment of labour and stock. This rate is naturally regulated, as I shall show hereafter, partly by the general circumstances of the society, their riches or poverty, their advancing, stationary, or declining condition; and partly, by the particular nature of each employment.

There is likewise in every society or neighbourhood an ordinary or average rate of rent, which is regulated, too, as I shall show hereafter, partly by the general circumstances of the society or neighbourhood in which the land is situated, and partly by the natural or improved fertility of the land.

These ordinary or average rates may be called the natural rates of wages, profit, and rent, at the time and place in which they commonly prevail.

When the price of any commodity is neither more nor less than what is sufficient to pay the rent of the land, the wages of the labour, and the profits of the stock employed in raising, preparing, and bringing it to market, according to their natural rates, the commodity is then sold for what may be called its natural price.

The commodity is then sold precisely for what it is worth, or for what it really costs the person who brings it to market; for though in common language what is called the prime cost of any commodity does not comprehend the profit of the person who is to sell it again, yet if he sells it at a price which does not allow him the ordinary rate of profit in his neighbourhood, he is evidently a loser by the trade; since by employing his stock in some other way he might have made that profit. His profit, besides, is his revenue, the proper fund of his subsistence. As, while he is preparing and bringing the goods to market, he advances to his workmen their wages, or their subsistence; so he advances to himself, in the same manner, his own subsistence, which is generally suitable to the profit which he may reasonably expect from the sale of his goods. Unless they yield him this profit, therefore, they do not repay him what they may very properly be said to have really cost him.

Though the price, therefore, which leaves him this profit, is not always the lowest at which a dealer may sometimes sell his goods, it is the lowest at which he is likely to sell them for any considerable time; at least where there is perfect liberty, or where he may change his trade as often as he pleases.

The actual price at which any commodity is commonly sold is called its market price. It may either be above, or below, or exactly the same with its natural price.

The market price of every particular commodity is regulated by the proportion between the quantity which is actually brought to market, and the demand of those who are willing to pay the natural price of the commodity, or the whole value of the rent, labour, and profit, which must be paid in order to bring it thither. Such people may be called the effectual demanders, and their demand the effectual demand; since it may be sufficient to effectuate the bringing of the commodity to market. It is different from the absolute demand. A very poor man may be said in some sense to have a demand for a coach and six; he might like to have it; but his demand is not an effectual demand, as the commodity can never be brought to market in order to satisfy it.

When the quantity of any commodity which is brought to market falls short of the effectual demand, all those who are willing to pay the whole value of the rent, wages, and profit, which must be paid in order to bring it thither, cannot be supplied with the quantity which they want. Rather than want it altogether, some of them will be willing to give more. A competition will immediately begin among them, and the market price will rise more or less above the natural price, according as either the greatness of the deficiency, or the wealth and wanton luxury of the competitors, happen to animate more or less the eagerness of the competition. Among competitors of equal wealth and luxury the same deficiency will generally occasion a more or less eager competition, according as the acquisition of the commodity happens to be of more or less importance to them. Hence the exorbitant price of the necessaries of life during the blockade of a town or in a famine.

When the quantity brought to market exceeds the effectual demand, it cannot be all sold to those who are willing to pay the whole value of the rent, wages and profit, which must be paid in order to bring it thither. Some part must be sold to those who are willing to pay less, and the low price which they give for it must reduce the price of the whole. The market price will sink more or less below the natural price, according as the greatness of the excess increases more or less the competition of the sellers, or according as it happens to be more or less important to them to get immediately rid of the commodity. The same excess in the importation of perishable, will occasion a much greater competition than in that of durable commodities; in the importation of oranges, for example, than in that of old iron.

When the quantity brought to market is just sufficient to supply the effectual demand and no more, the market price naturally comes to be either exactly, or as nearly as can be judged of, the same with the natural price. The whole quantity upon hand can be disposed of for this price, and cannot be disposed of for more. The competition of the different dealers obliges them all to accept of this price, but does not oblige them to accept of less.

The quantity of every commodity brought to market naturally suits itself to the effectual demand. It is the interest of all those who employ their land, labour, or stock, in bringing any commodity to market, that the quantity should never exceed the effectual demand; and it is the interest of all other people that it never should fall short of that demand.

If at any time it exceeds the effectual demand, some of the component parts of its price must be paid below their natural rate. If it is rent, the interest of the landlords will immediately prompt them to withdraw a part of their land; and if it is wages or profit, the interest of the labourers in the one case, and of their employers in the other, will prompt them to withdraw a part of their labour or stock from this employment. The quantity brought to market will soon be no more than sufficient to supply the effectual demand. All the different parts of its price will rise to their natural rate, and the whole price to its natural price.

If, on the contrary, the quantity brought to market should at any time, fall short of the effectual demand, some of the component parts of its price must rise above their natural rate. If it is rent, the interest of all other landlords will naturally prompt them to prepare more land for the raising of this commodity; if it is wages or profit, the interest of all other labourers, and dealers will soon prompt them to employ more labour and stock in preparing and bringing it to market. The quantity brought thither will soon be sufficient to supply the effectual demand. All the different parts of its price will soon sink to their natural rate, and the whole price to its natural price.

The natural price, therefore, is, as it were, the central price, to which the prices of all commodities are continually gravitating. Different accidents may sometimes keep them suspended a good deal above it, and sometimes force them down even somewhat below it. But whatever may be the obstacles which hinder them from settling in this center of repose and continuance, they are constantly tending towards it.

The whole quantity of industry annually employed in order to bring any commodity to market, naturally suits itself in this manner to the effectual demand. It naturally aims at bringing always that precise quantity thither which may be sufficient to supply, and no more than supply, that demand....

It is the maxim of every prudent master of a family, never to attempt to make at home what it will cost him more to make than to buy. The tailor does not attempt to make his own shoes, but buys them of the shoemaker. The shoemaker does not attempt to make his own clothes, but employs a tailor. The farmer attempts to make neither the one nor the other, but employs these different artificers. All of them find it for their interest to employ their whole industry in a way in which they have some advantage over their neighbours, and to purchase with a part of its produce, or what is the same thing, with the price of a part of it, whatever else they have occasion for.

What is prudence in the conduct of every private family, can scarce be folly in that of a great kingdom. If a foreign country can supply us with a commodity cheaper than we ourselves can make it, better buy it of them with some part of the produce of our own industry, employed in a way in which we have some advantage. The general industry of the country, being always in proportion to the capital which employs it, will not thereby be diminished, no more than that of the above mentioned artificers; but only left to find out the way in which it can be employed with the greatest advantage, when it is thus directed towards an object which it can buy cheaper than it can make. The value of its annual produce is certainly more or less diminished, when it is thus turned away from producing commodities evidently of more value than the commodity which it is directed to produce. According to the supposition, that commodity could be purchased from foreign countries cheaper than it can be made at home. It could, therefore, have been purchased with a part only of the commodities, or, what is the same thing, with a part only of the price of the commodities, which the industry employed by an equal capital would have produced at home, had it been left to follow its natural course. The industry of the country, therefore, is thus turned away from a more to a less advantageous employment, and the exchangeable value of its annual produce, instead of being increased, according to the intention of the lawgiver, must necessarily be diminished by every such regulation.

By means of such regulations, indeed, a particular manufacture may sometimes be acquired sooner than it could have been otherwise, and after a certain time may be made at home as cheap or cheaper than in the foreign country. But though the industry of the society may be thus carried with advantage into a particular channel sooner than it could have been otherwise, it will by no means follow that the sum total, either of its industry, or of its revenue, can ever be augmented by any such regulation. The industry of the society can augment only in proportion as its capital augments, and its capital can augment only in proportion to what can be gradually saved out of its revenue. But the immediate effect of every such regulation is to diminish its revenue, and what diminishes its revenue is certainly not very likely to augment its capital faster than it would have augmented of its own accord, had both capital and industry been left to find out their natural employments.

Though for want of such regulations the society should never acquire the proposed manufacture, it would not, upon that account, necessarily be the poorer in any one period of its duration. In every period of its duration its whole capital and industry might still have been employed, though upon different objects, in the manner that was most advantageous at the time. In every period its revenue might have been the greatest which its capital could afford, and both capital and revenue might have been augmented with the greatest possible rapidity.

The natural advantages which one country has over another in producing particular commodities are sometimes so great, that it is acknowledged by all the world to be in vain to struggle with them. By means of glasses, hotbeds, and hotwalls, very good grapes can be raised in Scotland, and very good wine too can be made of them at about thirty times the expence for which at least equally good can be brought from foreign countries. Would it be a reasonable law to prohibit the importation of all foreign wines, merely to encourage the making of claret and burgundy in Scotland? But if there would be a manifest absurdity in turning towards any employment, thirty times more of the capital and industry of the country than would be necessary to purchase from foreign countries an equal quantity of the commodities wanted, there must be an absurdity, though not altogether so glaring, yet exactly of the same kind, in turning towards any such employment a thirtieth, or even a three hundredth part more of either. Whether the advantages which one country has over another, be natural or acquired, is in this respect of no consequence. As long as the one country has those advantages, and the other wants them, it will always be more advantageous for the latter, rather to buy of the former than to make. It is an acquired advantage only, which one artificer has over his neighbour, who exercises another trade; and yet they both find it more advantageous to buy of one another, than to make what does not belong to their particular trades....

From Adam Smith, *The Wealth of Nations*, Hartford: Cooke & Hale, 1818, 38–40, 320–321.

Document 36:
RULES FOR WORKERS IN THE FACTORY OF BENCK AND COMPANY IN BÜHL (ALSACE) (1842)

These factory rules reflect an extreme of individual power over an economic enterprise, which could lead to the most arbitrary expression of control over workers. Note the wide range of regulations imposed upon the workers.

Article 1. Every worker who accepts employment in any work-site is obligated to read these rules and to submit to them. No one should be unfamiliar with them. If the rules are violated in any work-site, the offenders must pay fines according to the disorder or damage they have caused.

Article 2. All workers without exception are obligated, after they have worked in the factory for fourteen days, to give a month's notice when they wish to quit. This provision can be waived only for important reasons.

Article 3. The work day will consist of twelve hours, without counting rest periods. Children under twelve are excepted; they have to work only eight hours a day.

Article 4. The bell denotes the hours of entry and departure in the factory when it first rings. At the second ring every worker should be at his work. At quitting time the bell will also be sounded when each worker should clean his workplace and his machine (if he has one). It is forbidden under penalty of fines to abandon the workplace before the bell indicates that the work-site is closed.

Article 5. It is forbidden to smoke tobacco inside the factory. Whoever violates this prohibition is subjected to a heavy fine and can be dismissed. It is also forbidden under penalty of fines to bring beer or brandy into the factory. Any worker who comes to the factory drunk will be sent away and fined.

Article 6. The porter, whoever he may be, is forbidden to admit anyone after the workday begins. If someone asks for a worker he will make him wait and have the worker called. All workers are forbidden to bring anyone into the factory and the porter is forbidden to admit anyone. The porter is also forbidden to let any workers in or out without the foreman's permission during the hours of work.

Article 7. Any worker who misses a day without the Director's permission must pay a fine of two francs. The fine is doubled for a second offense. Any worker who is absent several times is dismissed, and if he is a weaver he is not paid for any piece he may have begun unless he can prove he missed work because of illness and should therefore be paid for work he has already done.

Article 8. All workers in the factory are obligated to be members of the Sickness Fund, to pay their dues, and conduct themselves according to its statutes.

Article 9. The foreman and the porter are empowered to retain any worker leaving the factory and to search him, as often as the interests of the Director may require. It is also recommended to the foreman to close the work-site himself, give the key to the porter, and to allow no worker inside during meal periods.

Article 10. Workers should only go in and out of doors where a porter resides, else they will be fined, brought under suspicion, and dismissed. They cannot refuse to surrender any of their belongings at work, for which they will be reimbursed according to the valuation of the Director and the foreman. Workers are also ordered to be obedient to the foreman, who is fully empowered by the Director. Any disobedience will be punished by fines according to the importance of the case. Any offender is responsible for the consequences of his action. It is also forbidden for any worker to seek work in any of the company's work-sites other than the one in which he is employed; anyone encountered in another work-site will be punished.

Article 11. Every worker is personally responsible for the objects entrusted to him. Any object that cannot be produced at the first request must be paid for. Weavers are obligated to pay careful attention to their cloth when they dry it. They will be fined and held responsible for any damage.

Article 12. In return for the protection and care which all workers can expect from the Director, they pledge to him loyalty and attachment. They promise immediately to call to his attention anything that threatens good order or the Director's interests. Workers are also put on notice that any unfortunate who commits a theft, however small it may be, will be taken to court and abandoned to his fate.

From *Documents in World History, Vol. I*, translated by Peter N. Stearns. © 1988 by Peter N. Stearns, Stephen S. Gosch, Erwin P. Grieshaber and Jay Pascal Anglin. Reprint by permission of Harper Collins Publishers.

Document 37:
SOCIAL STATICS (1850)
Herbert Spencer

Herbert Spencer was perhaps the most famous proponent of "social Darwinism." By using Darwin's theory of natural selection in ways that Darwin himself never intended, and, in fact, disagreed with, Spencer argued that the weak and helpless should not be helped in their struggle to survive. In his work Social Statics, *Spencer argued that allowing the weak to perish was a method for improving the whole of mankind. As you can see, these arguments could be used to justify racism, to justify the rule over others in the colonies, or to oppose government policies seeking to improve social and economic conditions.*

Pervading all Nature we may see at work a stern discipline which is a little cruel that it may be very kind. The state of universal warfare maintained throughout the lower creation, to the great perplexity of many worthy people, is at bottom the most merciful provision which the circumstances admit of. It is much better that the ruminant animal, when deprived by age of the vigour which made its existence a pleasure, should be killed by some beast of prey, than it should linger out a life made painful by infirmities, and eventually die of starvation. By the destruction of all such, not only is existence ended before it becomes burdensome, but room is made for a younger generation capable of the fullest enjoyment; and, moreover, out of the very act of substitution happiness is derived for a tribe of predatory creatures. Note, further, that their carnivorous enemies not only remove from herbivorous herds individuals past their prime, but also weed out the sickly, the malformed, and the least fleet or powerful. By the aid of which purifying process, as well as by the fighting so universal in the pairing season, all vitiation of the race through the multiplication of its inferior samples is prevented; and the maintenance of a constitution completely adapted to surrounding conditions, and therefore most productive of happiness, is ensured.

The development of the higher creation is a progress towards a form of being, capable of a happiness undiminished by these drawbacks. It is in the human race that the consummation is to be accomplished. Civilization is the last stage of its accomplishment. And the ideal man is the man in whom all the conditions to that accomplishment are fulfilled. Meanwhile, the well-being of existing humanity and the unfolding of it into this ultimate perfection, are both secured by that same beneficial though severe discipline, to which the animate creation at large is subject. It seems hard that an unskillfulness which with all his efforts he cannot overcome, should entail hunger upon the artisan. It seems hard that a labourer incapacitated by sickness from competing with his stronger fellows, should have to bear the resulting privations. It seems hard that widows and orphans should be left to struggle for life or death. Nevertheless, when regarded not separately but in connexion with the interests of universal humanity, these harsh fatalities are seen to be full of beneficence—the same beneficence which brings to early graves the children of diseased parents, and singles out the intemperate and the debilitated as the victims of an epidemic.

There are many very amiable people who have not the nerve to look this matter fairly in the face. Disabled as they are by their sympathies with present suffering, from duly regarding ultimate consequences, they pursue a course which is injudicious, and in the end even cruel. We do not consider it true kindness in a mother to gratify her child with sweetmeats that are likely to make it ill. We should think it a very foolish sort of benevolence which led a surgeon to let his patient's disease progress to a fatal issue, rather than inflict pain by an operation. Similarly, we must call those spurious philanthropists who, to prevent present misery, would entail greater misery on future generations. That rigorous necessity which, when allowed to operate, becomes so sharp a spur to the lazy and so strong a bridle to the random, these pauper's friends would repeal, because of the wailings it here and there produces. Blind to the fact that under the natural order of things society is constantly excreting its unhealthy, imbecile, slow, vacillating, faithless members, these unthinking, though well-meaning, men advocate an interference which not only stops the purifying process, but even increases the vitiation—absolutely encourages the multiplication of the reckless and incompetent by offering them an unfailing provision, and *dis*courages the multiplication of the competent and provident by heightening the difficulty of maintaining a family. And thus, in their eagerness to prevent the salutary sufferings that surround us, these sigh-wise and groan foolish-people bequeath to posterity a continually increasing curse....

From Herbert Spencer, *Social Statics*, New York: D. Appleton and Company, 1897, 149–151.

Document 38:
MANIFESTO OF THE EQUALS (1796)
François Babeuf

Babeuf was one of the earliest social revolutionaries of modern Europe. The demands for equality raised by the French Revolution led him to sweeping demands for equality in this "Manifesto of the Equals." He was one of the first to argue for a radical redistribution of wealth, and he predicted this would occur through a great revolution.

"REAL EQUALITY—THE LAST END OF THE SOCIAL ART"—Condorcet, "Picture of the Human Mind"

PEOPLE OF FRANCE!—During fifteen ages you have lived slaves, and consequently unhappy. During six years you breathe with difficulty in the expectation of independence, of prosperity, and of equality.

EQUALITY!—first vow of nature, first want of man, and chief bond of all legitimate association! People of France! you have not been more favoured than the other nations which vegetate on this ill-fated globe! Always and everywhere does the unfortunate human species, delivered over to cannibals more or less artful, serve for a plaything to all ambitions—for pasture to all tyrannies. Always and everywhere have men been fooled by fine words; never and nowhere have they obtained the *thing* with the word. From time immemorial we have been hypocritically told—*men are equal*; and from time immemorial does the most degrading and monstrous inequality insolently oppress the human race. Ever since the first existence of civil societies has the finest apanage of man been uncontradictedly *acknowledged*; but never, up to this moment, has it been once *realized*. Equality has never been other than a beautiful and barren fiction of law. Even now, when it is claimed with a stronger voice, we are answered, "Be silent, miserables!—absolute equality is but a chimaera; be content with conditional equality; you are all equal before the law. Rabble! what more do you want?" What more do we want? Legislators, governors, rich proprietors—listen in your turn.

We are all equal, are we not? This principle remains uncontested, because, without being self-convicted of folly, one cannot seriously say that it is night when it is day. "Well! we pretend henceforward to live and die equal, as we are born so. We desire real equality or death; behold what we want. And we shall have this real equality, no matter at what price. Woe to them who will interpose themselves between it and us! Woe to him who will offer resistance to so determined a resolve!" The French Revolution is but the forerunner of another revolution far more grand, far more solemn, and which will be the last. The people has marched over dead bodies against the kings and priests coalesced against it; it will do the same against the new tyrants—against the new political Tartuffes who have usurped the places of the old.

"What do we want," you ask, "more than equality of rights?" We want that equality not merely written in the "Declaration of the Rights of Man and of the Citizens;" we want it in the midst of us—under the roofs of our houses. We consent to everything for it—to become as *pliable wax, in order to have its characters engraven upon us.* Perish, if needs be, all the arts, provided real equality abides with us!

Legislators and governors, who are as destitute of genius as of honesty—you rich proprietors, without bowels of pity—in vain do you essay to neutralize our holy enterprize, by saying "They are only re-producing the old Agrarian law, so often demanded already before them."

Calumniators! be silent in your turn; and in the silence of confusion hearken to our pretensions, dictated by nature herself, and based upon eternal justice. The Agrarian law, or partition of lands, was only the instantaneous wish of certain soldiers without principles—of certain small tribes, moved by instinct rather than by reason. We aim at something more sublime, and more equitable; we look to *common property*, or to the *community of goods*! No more individual property in lands. *The earth belongs to no one.* We claim—we demand—we *will* the communal enjoyment of the fruits of the earth; *the fruits belong to all.*

We declare that we can no longer suffer that the great majority of men shall labour and sweat to serve and pamper the extreme minority. Long enough, and too long, have less than a million of individuals disposed of what belongs to more than twenty millions of men like themselves—of men in every respect their equals. Let there be at length an end to this enormous scandal, which posterity will scarcely credit. Away for ever with the revolting distinctions of rich and poor, of great and little, of masters and servants, of *governors* and *governed.*

Let there be no longer any other differences in mankind than those of age and sex. Since all have the same wants, and the same faculties, let all have accordingly the same education—the same nourishment. They are content with one sun, and the same air for all; why should not the like portion, and the same quality of food, suffice for each according to his wants?

But already do the enemies of an order of things, the most natural that can be imagined, declaim against us,—"Disorganizers, and seditionists," they exclaim, "you want but massacres and plunder."

PEOPLE OF FRANCE!—We will not waste our time to answer them; but we will tell you,— the holy enterprise we are organizing has no other object in view than to put an end to civil dissensions and to public disorder. Never was a more vast design conceived and put in execution. At distant intervals in the history of the world it has been talked of by some men of genius—by a few philosophers—but they spoke it with a low and trembling voice. Not one of them has had the courage to speak the entire truth.

The moment for great measures has arrived. Evil is at its height; it has reached its *maximum*, and covers the face of the earth. Chaos, under the name of politics, has too long reigned over it. Let everything revert to order, and resume its proper place. At the voice of equality, let the elements of justice and felicity be organized. The moment is come to found the REPUBLIC OF EQUALS—that grand asylum open to all human kind. The days of general restitution are come. Weeping families, come and seat yourselves at the common table provided by nature for all her children.

PEOPLE OF FRANCE!—The purest of all earthly glories has been reserved for you—yes, 'tis you who are first destined to present the world with this touching spectacle.

Old habits, old prejudices, will again seek to oppose obstacles to the establishment of the REPUBLIC OF EQUALS. The organization of real equality —the only one which satisfies all wants, without making victims, without costing sacrifices—will not, perhaps, at first please everybody. The egotist, the ambitious, will yell with rage. Those who possess unjustly, will raise the cry of injustice. Exclusive enjoyments, solitary pleasures, personal ease and privileges, will cause poignant regrets to some few individuals who are dead or callous to the pangs of others. The lovers of absolute power, the vile instruments of arbitrary authority, will feel it hard that their haughty chiefs should bend to the level of equality. Their short-sightedness will, with difficulty, penetrate into the future of public happiness, however near; but what can avail a few thousand malcontents against such a mass of human beings, all happy, and astonished at having been so long in quest of a felicity which they had within hands' reach. On the day that follows this real revolution, they will say to one another in amazement—"What—universal happiness depended on so little! We had but to will it. Ah, why had we not willed it sooner? Was it then necessary to have it told to us so often?" Yes, no doubt, a single man on the earth, more rich, more powerful, than his fellow men, than his equals, destroys the equilibrium, and crime and misfortune come on the world.

PEOPLE OF FRANCE!—By what sign then need you henceforward to recognise the excellence of a constitution?...That which altogether reposes on actual, absolute equality is the only one that can be suitable to you, and satisfy all your desires.

The aristocratic charters of 1791 and 1795 riveted your chains, instead of breaking them. That of 1793 was a great practical step towards real equality; never before was equality so nearly approached; but that Constitution did not yet touch the end, nor was it fully competent to attain general happiness, of which, however, it has solemnly consecrated the great principle. [ed. note: the 1793 Constitution, never implemented, would have made education universally available, and work and subsistence guaranteed by law]

PEOPLE OF FRANCE!—Open your eyes and hearts to the fulness of felicity; recognize and proclaim with us the REPUBLIC OF EQUALS!

From Philippe Buonarroti, *History of Babeuf's Conspiracy for Equality*, London: H. Hetherington, translated by Bronterre O'Brien.

Document 39:
THE COMMUNIST MANIFESTO (1848)
Karl Marx and Friedrich Engels

The Communist Manifesto was published in 1848, just in time to appear during the most tumultuous year since the Napoleonic era. Marx thought that society was based on a hierarchy of classes, controlled by those who held the means of production and controlled the distribution of goods. Marx declared that capitalism, because it tends to concentrate capital in the hands of fewer and fewer people, would eventually cause the proletariat to revolt and inaugurate socialism where society, instead of individuals, owned the means of production and used these for the good of all. Then a truly classless civilization would emerge.

The history of all hitherto existing society is the history of class struggles.

Freeman and slave, patrician and plebian, lord and serf, guild-master and journeyman, in a word: oppressor and oppressed, stood in constant opposition to one another, carried on an uninterrupted, now hidden, now open fight, a fight that each time ended, either in a revolutionary re-construction of society at large, or in the common ruin of the contending classes....

The modern bourgeois society that has sprouted from the ruins of feudal society, has not done away with class antagonisms. It has but established new classes, new conditions of oppression, new forms of struggle in place of the old ones.

Our epoch, the epoch of the bourgeoisie, possesses, however, this distinctive feature; it has simplified the class antagonisms. Society as a whole is more and more splitting up into two great hostile camps, into two great classes directly facing each other: Bourgeoisie and Proletariat....

The feudal system of industry, under which industrial production was monopolized by closed guilds, now no longer sufficed for the growing wants of the new markets. The manufacturing system took its place. The guild-masters were pushed on one side by the manufacturing middle-class; division of labor between the different corporate guilds vanished in the face of division of labor in each single workshop.

Meantime the markets kept ever growing, the demand, ever rising. Even manufacturing no longer sufficed. Thereupon steam and machinery revolutionized industrial production. The place of manufacture was taken by the giant, Modern Industry, the place of the industrial middle-class, by industrial millionaires, the leaders of whole industrial armies, the modern bourgeoisie....

We see, therefore, how the modern bourgeoisie is itself the product of a long course of development, of a series of revolutions in the modes of production and of exchange.

Each step in the development of the bourgeoisie was accompanied by a corresponding political advance of that class....The executive of the modern State is but a committee for managing the common affairs of the whole bourgeoisie....

The bourgeoisie has stripped off its halo every occupation hitherto honored and looked up to with reverent awe. It has converted the physician, the lawyer, the priest, the poet, the man of science, into its paid wage-laborers.

The bourgeoisie has torn away from the family its sentimental veil, and has reduced the family relation to a mere money relation....

The bourgeoisie cannot exist without constantly revolutionizing the instruments of production, and thereby the relations of society. Conservation of the old modes of production in unaltered form, was, on the contrary, the first condition of existence for all earlier industrial classes. Constant revolutionizing of production, uninterrupted disturbance of all social conditions, everlasting uncertainty and agitation distinguish the bourgeois epoch from all earlier ones. All fixed, fast-frozen relations, with their refrain of ancient and venerable prejudices and opinions, are swept away, all newly-formed ones become antiquated before they can ossify. All that is solid melts into air, all that is holy is profaned, and man is at last compelled to face with sober senses, his real conditions of life, and his relations with his kind.

The need of a constantly expanding market for its products chases the bourgeoisie over the whole surface of the globe. It must nestle everywhere, settle everywhere, establish connections everywhere....

A similar movement is going on before our own eyes. Modern bourgeois society with its relations of production, of exchange and of property, a society that had conjured up such gigantic means of production and of exchange, is like the sorcerer, who is no longer able to control the powers of the nether world whom he has called up by his spells. For many a decade past the history of industry and commerce is but the history of the revolt of modern productive forces against modern conditions of production, against the property relations that are the condition for the existence of the bourgeoisie and of its rule. It is enough to mention the commercial crises that by their periodical return put on trial, each time more threateningly, the existence of the entire bourgeois society. In these crises a great part not only of the existing products, but also of the previously created productive forces, are periodically destroyed. In these crises there breaks out an epidemic that, in all earlier epochs, would have seemed an absurdity—the epidemic of overproduction. Society suddenly finds itself put back into a state of momentary barbarism; it appears as if a famine, a universal war of devastation had cut off the supply of every means of subsistence; industry and commerce seem to be destroyed; and why? Because there is too much civilization, too much means of subsistence, too much industry, too much commerce. The productive forces at the disposal of society no longer tend to further the development of the conditions of bourgeois property; on the contrary, they have become too powerful for these conditions, by which they are fettered, and so soon as they overcome these fetters, they bring disorder into the whole of bourgeois society, endangering the existence of bourgeois property. The conditions of bourgeois society are too narrow to comprise the wealth created by them. And how does the bourgeoisie get over these crises? On the one hand by enforced destruction of a mass of productive forces; on the other, by the conquest of new markets, and by the more thorough exploitation of the old ones. That is to say, by paving the way for more extensive and more destructive crises, and by diminishing the means whereby crises are prevented.

The weapons which the bourgeoisie forged are the weapons that bring death to itself; it has also called into existence the men who are to wield those weapons—the modern working-class—the proletarians.

In proportion as the bourgeoisie, i.e., capital, is developed, in the same proportion is the proletariat, the modern working-class, developed, a class of laborers, who live only so long as they find work, and who find work only so long as their labor increases capital. These laborers, who must sell themselves piecemeal, are a commodity, like every other article of commerce, and are consequently exposed to all the vicissitudes of competition, to all the fluctuations of the market....

Of all the classes that stand face to face with the bourgeoisie today, the proletariat alone is a really revolutionary class. The other classes decay and finally disappear in the face of modern industry; the proletariat is its special and essential product....

The modern laborer, on the contrary, instead of rising with the progress of industry, sinks deeper and deeper below the conditions of existence of his own class. He becomes a pauper, and pauperism develops more rapidly than population and wealth. And here it becomes evident that the bourgeoisie is unfit any longer to be the ruling class in society, and to impose its conditions of existence upon society as an over-riding law. It is unfit to rule, because it is incompetent to assure an existence to its slave within his slavery, because it cannot help letting him sink into such a state that it has to feed him, instead of being fed by him. Society can no longer live under the bourgeoisie, in other words, its existence is no longer compatible with society.

The essential condition for the existence, and for the sway of the bourgeois class, is the formation and augmentation of capital; the condition for capital is wage-labor. Wage-labor rests exclusively on competition between the laborers. The advance of industry, whose involuntary promoter is the bourgeoisie, replaces the isolation of the laborers, due to competition, by their revolutionary combination, due to association. The development of Modern Industry, therefore, cuts from under its feet the very foundation on which the bourgeoisie produces and appropriates products. What the bourgeoisie therefore produces, above all, are its own gravediggers. Its fall and the victory of the proletariat are equally inevitable....

© 1954 by H. Regnery Company. All rights reserved. Reprinted by special permission from Regnery Gateway, Inc., Washington, D.C.

Document 40:
WHAT IS PROPERTY? (1840)
Pierre Joseph Proudhon

Pierre Joseph Proudhon (1809–1865) was a self-described anarchist who believed that employers should be condemned for making profit at the expense of their workers. Proudhon also saw private ownership of land as another social evil. He was a curious mixture of utopian thinker and skeptic. A member of the Constituent Assembly, he was unwilling to sacrifice his political idealism in the face of practical problems. His most famous work is undoubtedly What is Property? *In the portion excerpted below, Proudhon claims that property is theft, and that the private ownership of property is destined to come to an end.*

If I were to answer the following question: *What is slavery?* and I should answer in one word, *It is murder*, my meaning would be understood at once. No extended argument would be required to show that the power to take from a man his thought, his will, his personality, is a power of life and death; and that to enslave a man is to kill him. Why, then, to this other question: *What is property?* may I not likewise answer, *It is robbery*, without the certainty of being misunderstood; the second proposition being no other than a transformation of the first?

I shall undertake to discuss the vital principle of our government and our institutions, property....I contend that neither labor, nor occupation, nor law, can create property, that it is an effect without a cause: am I censurable?

But murmurs arise!

Property is robbery! That is the war-cry of '93! [1793 was the most radical year of the French Revolution.] That is the signal of revolutions!

Reader, calm yourself: I am no agent of discord, no firebrand of sedition. I anticipate history by a few days; I disclose a truth whose development we may try in vain to arrest; I write the preamble of our future constitution. This proposition which seems to you blasphemous—*property is robbery*—would, if our prejudices allowed us to consider it, be recognized as the lightening-rod to shield us from the coming thunderbolt; but too many interests stand in the way! ... Alas! philosophy will not change the course of events: destiny will fulfill itself regardless of prophecy. Besides, must not justice be done and our education be finished?

From P.J. Proudhon, *What is Property?* New York: Howard Fertig, 1966, 11–12.

Document 41:
SOCIALISM AND THE WORKER (1907)
Keir Hardie

Keir Hardie organized mineworkers in Britain and was elected to Parliament. He helped to organize the Labour Party. In this document he points out the needs of labor and calls for change to give laborers a better life.

In England it took the State two hundred years to reduce the worker, town and country alike, from independent affluence to a poverty stricken condition. Legislation for regulating wages and for chaining the worker to one parish, to fix the kind of cloth he should dress in, the number of hours he should work, and other like regulations intended to weaken the power of the working-class, had all been tried; but it was only when the land was taken from the peasants, the commons confiscated, and the Guilds broken up, and, finally, when the price of food had been doubled and quadrupled through the operations of a debased coinage, that success attended these maleficent acts. The Protestant Reformation, by despoiling the monasteries of their lands, the one refuge to which the needy worker could fly for succour, also told heavily against the poor, whilst the new gospel of individual salvation lent the sanction of religion to the selfish creed of each for himself which was then just beginning to assert itself as the dominant principle in business. Under its baneful influence old customs and habits and the old communal traditional life of the people in town and country were ruthlessly broken and destroyed, and that era of desolation and barren inhumanity entered upon from which we are now only just beginning to emerge. For,...the prosperity of the worker was coincident with, and its continuance in no small measure attributable to, a period chiefly remarkable for the strong element of Communism which characterised town and village life. If the Anabaptists and the various other sects who had sought to make Communism and Christianity synonymous terms had been washed out in a tempest of blood and flame, much of their spirit remained. It was not for nothing that John Ball and Wat Tyler had taught the peasantry of England the doctrine of the dignity of manhood and the emptiness of titles.

John Stuart Mill expressed a doubt whether all the mechanical inventions of the nineteenth century had lightened the labour of one human being. The social investigator of the twentieth century is prepared to affirm positively that the lot of the poor in normal times under Capitalism is worse than it ever could have been in normal times in any previous period in British history. Production, say the Fawcetts in their lectures on Social and Political subjects, has been stimulated beyond the expectations of the most sanguine; still, however, so far as the labourer is concerned, the age of golden plenty seems as remote as ever, and in the humble homes of the poor a no less constant war has to be waged against penury and want. This, however, is but half the truth. The conditions attendant upon poverty in these latter days are more demoralising than ever before. In the less complex life of former days the poor were more akin to other classes, and better able to help themselves. In the great vortex of modern life they are almost completely shut off from human fellowship. The stress and strain are so great, the organisation of Society so anarchic, that once a man gets down into the depths his chances of rising again are exceedingly remote.

I know that it is a commonplace of the Jeremiahs of every age to hold that the men of former ages were better than those of their own. In certain respects I confess that I rank with those who believe that we have deteriorated, especially in the sphere of intellect, since the days of our great-grandparents. The stage, the press, and the pulpit could easily be cited as evidence in support of this. The plays of Shakespeare were performed, even in his own day, to crowded audiences without the scenic effects and curtailments which are now necessary to make them acceptable to the modern playgoer. Any one familiar with the popular literature of the Radical and Chartist movements of the opening and middle years of the last century will see how far its modern successor falls below the standard of those days. The solid sermon and newspaper articles of even half-a-hundred years ago would not now be tolerated; not because of their dullness, but because of the mental effort needed to follow and understand them. A snippety press and a sensational pulpit are outstanding marks of modern times. Nor are the reasons far to seek. Previous to the introduction of machinery and the factory system every workman was an individual. They were not herded together in masses, regimented, numbered, and specialised. The blacksmith, the weaver, the carpenter, the shoemaker, and the tailor either worked direct for their own customers or for masters only a very small degree removed from themselves. A master was in those days more of a master workman than an employer. Each journeyman could confidently look forward to the time when he too would be a master. The master's income rarely exceeded by more than 20 per cent. the wage of his workmen, with whom he freely mingled both in work and play. It was only when machinery and the factory system were introduced that great fortunes began to be accumulated and masters and workmen separated into distinct classes with an ever-widening breach between them. When working for themselves, as a very large proportion of the old-time craftsmen did, they started work in the morning when it pleased them, broke off during the day as it suited them, and left off in the evening according to the necessities of the moment or their own whim or convenience. Each such man was his own master; he owned the tools wherewith he worked, and the product was his own property when completed. A man had some pride in the labour of his hands, some incentive to do his best, since his good name was at stake in every job he turned out. Under those conditions the tendency was to develop individuality. The free exchange of opinion which resulted from men of this type meeting together for a social glass or pipe developed an intellectuality which we look for in vain in the modern factory hand. Nor is this all. The uncertainty and irresponsibility of the modern workman's lot in life must produce evil effects upon his character.

We are all more or less the products of our environment, and modern workshop conditions are not conducive to the production of either intellect or individuality. The workman is called into the workshop when capital can profitably employ him, and turned adrift again the moment capital finds it can no longer turn his services to profitable account. He is not consulted as to when he shall be employed or when cast adrift. His necessities and those of his dependents are no concern of any one save himself. He has no right to employment, no one is under obligation to find him work, nor is he free to work for himself since he has neither the use of land nor the command of the necessary capital. He must be more or less of a nomad, ready to go at a moment's notice to where a job is vacant. He may be starving, but may not grow food; naked, but may not weave cloth; homeless, but may not build a house. When in work he has little if any say in the regulations which govern the factory, and none in deciding what work is to be done or how it is to be done. His duty begins and ends in doing as he is bid. To talk to a neighbour workman at the bench is an offence punishable by a fine; so, too, in some cases is whistling while at work. At a given hour in the morning the factory bell warns him that it is time to be inside the gate ready for the machines to start; at a set hour the bell or hooter calls him out to dinner and again recalls him to his task one hour later. He does not own the machines he manipulates, nor does he own the product of his labour. He is a hireling, and glad to be any man's hireling who will find him work. During one period when trade is good he is not only fully employed but has to work overtime; at another when trade is slack he is only partially employed, if employed at all. The result of all this is to produce demoralisation of the most fatal kind. There is no sense of unity between the man and his work. He can have no pride in it since there is nothing personal to him which will attach to it after it is finished. It will be sold he knows not by whom nor to whom. All day long he works under the eye of a taskmaster set over him to see that he does not shirk his duties. At the end of the week he is paid so many shillings for what he has done, and, naturally enough, his one concern is with the number of shillings he will receive. This is the cash nexus which binds him to his employer, who, by the way, is very likely a huge impersonal soulless concern known as a company. Of the individuals composing it he knows nothing, nor they of him.

There is no sense of honour or of Chivalry in business. A big wealthy concern will cheat its workpeople of their wages, or spend thousands in resisting the claim to compensation of some poor widow or orphan whose husband or father has been killed in their service. It is not that employers are inhuman; but their connection with their workpeople is a business one, from which every trace of human feeling has been carefully excluded.

Time has no birthday gifts for such as these
A human herd of starved and stunted growth,
That knows not how to walk, to whom the speech
Of England, of the land that gave them birth,
Comes twisted, harsh and scarce articulate,
Whose minds lie fallow, while they chew the cud
Of hunger, darkness, impotence, disease.

As old age approaches—and for the workman this may mean anything over forty —a cold grey terror begins to take possession of his heart. Fight against it as he may, he cannot get away from the fact that within the circle of his acquaintance there are men just turned forty, as good workmen as himself, for whom the ordinary labour market no longer has any use. He knows his turn will also come some day. A slackness of trade, some petty offence which in a younger man would pass unnoticed, and out he goes to return no more. Then begins life's tragedy in grim earnest. From place to place he goes in search of a job. He knows himself to be still capable of much good work. To the business man forty-five is the period of life at which he is at his best; it is also the age at which a rising statesman enters upon his career, when the powers of the artist and the man of letters are at their fullest. But all this only adds bitterness to the cup of humiliation which the aged workman has now to drain to the dregs. Most large establishments have a standing order that no one over forty-five is to be given employment; with many the age limit is forty; whilst in one case to which publicity was recently given it is as low as thirty-five. And so the aged workman who has too much honour left to lie about his age and too much honesty to use hair dye, at last wearies of his vain quest for what will never again be his, a steady job at his own trade, and resorts to any odd job which turns up. As for savings to meet a case of this kind, that is usually quite out of the question. The thrifty, steady workman who is a member of a trade union and a benefit society is entitled to certain old age benefits, but these do not accrue until he is fifty-five or sixty; and although it is common to stretch the rules of these organisations to meet the more deserving cases, obviously the funds would not stand the strain of meeting all of them. Besides, not more than one half of the working people are in a position to make any such provision for old age. The earnings of the working-class only average about 21s.6d. a week. That figure, be it remembered, is got by taking the total income of all who are not paid more then £160 a year and dividing it by the number of wage-workers. But low as this figure must appear to the comfortable classes, it does not reveal the whole truth. Knowing the facts both from personal experience and a thorough familiarity with the circumstances, I assert fearlessly that one half of the adult workers of Great Britain earn less than one pound per week, year in and year out, when in work. This leaves no margin for saving, nor does it provide even that subsistence wage which the economists are so fond of telling us competition will not fail to provide for the worker. Perhaps this can best be brought out by a reference to a work the conclusions of which have never been seriously challenged. In his painstaking and exhaustive inquiry into the condition of the people of York, a typical industrial town, Mr. Seebohm Rowntree arrived at pretty much the same conclusion as was reached by Mr. Charles Booth when he made a similar inquiry concerning the life of the people of London. Mr. Rowntree says that in York the minimum upon which bare physical efficiency can be maintained is 21s.8d. a week, and that in a year of abounding trade and prosperity he found that forty-five percent. of the working-class, taking their income from every source and treating the family earning as a unit for the purpose of calculation were receiving less than this sum, and consequently were in poverty. Here is his definition of poverty:—

It is thus seen that *the wages paid for unskilled labour in York are insufficient to provide food, shelter, and clothing adequate to maintain a family of moderate size in a state of bare physical efficiency*. It will be remembered that the above estimates of necessary minimum expenditure are based upon the assumption that the diet is even less generous than that allowed to able-bodied paupers in the York Workhouse, and that *no allowance is made for any expenditure other than that absolutely required for the maintenance of merely physical efficiency*.

And let us clearly understand what "merely physical efficiency" means. A family living upon the scale allowed for in this estimate must never spend a penny on railway fare or omnibus. They must never go into the country unless they walk. They must never purchase a halfpenny newspaper or spend a penny to buy a ticket for a popular concert. They must write no letters to absent children, for they cannot afford to pay the postage. They must never contribute anything to their church or chapel, or give any help to a neighbour which costs them money. They cannot save, nor can they join sick club or trade union, because they cannot pay the necessary subscriptions. The children must have no pocket money for dolls, marbles, or sweets. The father must smoke no tobacco, and must drink no beer. The mother must never buy any pretty clothes for herself or for her children, the character of the family wardrobe as for the family diet being governed by the regulation. Nothing must be bought but that which is absolutely necessary for the maintenance of physical health, and what is bought must be of the plainest and most economical description. Should a child fall ill, it must be attended by the parish doctor; should it die it must be buried by the parish. Finally the wage-earner must never be absent from his work for a single day. If any of these conditions are broken, the extra expenditure is met, *and can only be met*, by limiting the diet, or, in other words, by sacrificing physical efficiency.... It cannot, therefore, be too clearly understood, nor too emphatically repeated, *that whenever a worker having three children dependent on him, and receiving not more than 21s. per week, indulges in any expenditure beyond that required for the barest physical needs, he can do so only at the cost of his own physical efficiency, or of that of some members of his family.*

The italics are the author's. These, then, are the causes which have led to the intellectual and moral deterioration of the working-class. Under all these circumstances the workman would have been different from every other created being had he not deteriorated physically and mentally. True, we have got over the worst in this respect, and already a very decided change is noticeable among the younger men. From 1780 to 1850 was a transition period, and then the process of demoralisation was doing its worst. The generation following inherited all the bad effects of the conditions which had been prevailing, but the young generation of to-day, thoroughly in touch with their environment and intelligently conscious of the causes which make them the slaves of the machine, are in full revolt; and just as the awakened serfs of the thirteenth century carved their way to comparative freedom and prosperity, so too shall the awakening proletariat of the twentieth century. But the foundation on which they shall build their industrial freedom shall be more abiding than any which has gone before. When the modern industrial movement reaches fruition, land, capital, and the State itself shall all be owned and controlled by the useful classes. There shall be no longer an exploiting class left to reduce the workers again to penury and want by the methods which, as we have seen, were so successful in the Middle Ages. Socialism, by taking away the power to exploit, ensures permanent freedom for all.

From J. Keir Hardie, *From Serfdom to Socialism*, Edinburgh: Ballantyne, Hanson & Co., 1907, 47–60.

Document 42:
WOMAN AND SOCIALISM (1910)
August Bebel

August Bebel (1840–1913) was the leader of the German Social Democratic Party, the largest party in the German Empire before World War I. He did not believe that simply giving the vote to women would solve all of the economic and social problems that women faced. Bebel believed that the economy and society must be changed and that then women would be fully liberated—in socialism. His party had explicitly endorsed the vote for women in 1891 in its Erfurt Program. The following excerpt shows that Bebel and many European socialists believed that middle class reformers were overstating the changes that would come with suffrage for women. Bebel criticized the institution of marriage and called for sexual freedom for women; for this he and other socialists were called enemies of the family and advocates of "free love."

Introduction

We are living in an age of great social transformations that are steadily progressing. In all strata of society we perceive an unsettled state of mind and an increasing restlessness, denoting a marked tendency toward profound and radical changes. Many questions have arisen and are being discussed with growing interest in ever widening circles. One of the most important of these questions and one that is constantly coming into greater prominence, is the *woman question.*

The woman question deals with the position that woman should hold in our social organism, and seeks to determine how she can best develop her powers and her abilities, in order to become a useful member of human society, endowed with equal rights and serving society according to her best capacity. From our point of view this question coincides with that other question: In what manner should society be organized to abolish oppression, exploitation, misery and need, and to bring about the physical and mental welfare of individuals and of society as a whole? To us then, the woman question is only one phase of the general social question that at present occupies all intelligent minds; its final solution can only be attained by removing social extremes and the evils which are a result of such extremes.

Nevertheless, the woman question demands our special consideration. What the position of woman has been in ancient society, what her position is to-day and what it will be in the coming social order, are questions that deeply concern at least one half of humanity. Indeed, in Europe they concern a majority of organized society, because women constitute a majority of the population. Moreover, the prevailing conceptions concerning the development of woman's social position during successive stages of history are so faulty, that enlightenment on this subject has become a necessity. Ignorance concerning the position of woman, chiefly accounts for the prejudice that the woman's movement has to contend with among all classes of people, by no means least among the women themselves. Many even venture to assert that there is no woman question at all, since woman's position has always been the same and will remain the same in the future, because nature has destined her to be a wife and a mother and to confine her activities to the home. Everything that is beyond the four narrow walls of her home and is not closely connected with her domestic duties, is not supposed to concern her.

In the woman question then we find two contending parties, just as in the labor question, which relates to the position of the workingman in human society. Those who wish to maintain everything as it is, are quick to relegate woman to her so-called "natural profession," believing that they have thereby settled the whole matter. They do not recognize that millions of women are not placed in a position enabling them to fulfill their natural function of wifehood and motherhood.... They furthermore do not recognize that to millions of other women their "natural profession" is a failure, because to them marriage has become a yoke and a condition of slavery, and they are obliged to drag on their lives in misery and despair. But these wiseacres are no more concerned by these facts than by the fact that in various trades and professions millions of women are exploited far beyond their strength, and must slave away their lives for a meagre subsistence. They remain deaf and blind to these disagreeable truths, as they remain deaf and blind to the misery of the proletariat, consoling themselves and others by the false assertion that it has always been thus and will always continue to be so. That woman is entitled, as well as man, to enjoy all the achievements of civilization, to lighten her burdens, to improve her condition, and to develop all her physical and mental qualities, they refuse to admit. When, furthermore, told that woman—to enjoy full physical and mental freedom—should also be economically independent, should no longer depend for subsistence upon the good will and favor of the other sex, the limit of their patience will be reached. Indignantly they will pour forth a bitter indictment of the "madness of the age" and its "crazy attempts at emancipation." These are the old ladies of both sexes who cannot overcome the narrow circle of their prejudices. They are the human owls that dwell wherever darkness prevails, and cry out in terror whenever a ray of light is cast into their agreeable gloom.

Others do not remain quite as blind to the eloquent facts. They confess that at no time has woman's position been so unsatisfactory in comparison to general social progress, as it is at present. They recognize that it is necessary to investigate how the condition of the self-supporting woman can be improved; but in the case of married women they believe the social problem to be solved. They favor the admission of unmarried women only into a limited number of trades and professions. Others again are more advanced and insist that competition between the sexes should not be limited to the inferior trades and professions, but should be extended to all higher branches of learning and the arts and sciences as well. They demand equal educational opportunities and that women should be admitted to all institutions of learning, including the universities. They also favor the appointment of women to government positions, pointing out the results already achieved by women in such positions, especially in the United States. A few are even coming forward to demand equal political rights for women. Woman, they argue, is a human being and a member of organized society as well as man, and the very fact that men have until now framed and administered the laws to suit their own purposes and to hold woman in subjugation, proves the necessity of woman's participation in public affairs.

It is noteworthy that all these various endeavors do not go beyond the scope of the present social order. The question is not propounded whether any of these proposed reforms will accomplish a decisive and essential improvement in the condition of women. According to the conceptions of bourgeois, or capitalistic society, the civic equality of men and women is deemed an ultimate solution of the woman question. People are either unconscious of the fact, or deceive themselves in regard to it, that the admission of women to trades and industries is already practically accomplished and is being strongly favored by the ruling classes in their own interest. But under prevailing conditions woman's invasion of industry has the detrimental effect of increasing competition on the labor market, and the result is a reduction in wages for both male and female workers. It is clear then, that this cannot be a satisfactory solution.

Men who favor these endeavors of women within the scope of present society, as well as the bourgeois women who are active in the movement, consider complete civic equality of women the ultimate goal. These men and women then differ radically from those who, in their narrow-mindedness, oppose the movement. They differ radically from those men who are actuated by petty motives of selfishness and fear of competition, and therefore try to prevent women from obtaining higher education and from gaining admission to the better paid professions. But there is no difference of class between them, such as exists between the worker and the capitalist.

If the bourgeois suffragists would achieve their aim and would bring about equal rights for men and women, they would still fail to abolish the sex slavery which marriage, in its present form, is to countless numbers of women; they would fail to abolish prostitution; they would fail to abolish the economic dependence of wives. To the great majority of women it also remains a matter of indifference whether a few thousand members of their sex, belonging to the more favored classes of society, obtain higher learning and enter some learned profession, or hold a public office. The general condition of the sex as a whole is not altered thereby.

The female sex as such has a double yoke to bear. Firstly, women suffer as a result of their social dependence upon men, and the inferior position allotted to them in society; formal equality before the law alleviates this condition, but does not remedy it. Secondly, women suffer as a result of their economic dependence, which is the lot of women in general, and especially of the proletarian women, as it is of the proletarian men.

We see, then, that all women, regardless of their social position, represent that sex which during the evolution of society has been oppressed and wronged by the other sex, and therefore it is to the common interest of all women to remove their disabilities by changing the laws and institutions of the present state and social order. But a great majority of women is furthermore deeply and personally concerned in a complete reorganization of the present state and social order which has for its purpose the abolition of wage-slavery, which at present weighs most heavily upon the women of the proletariat, as also the abolition of sex-slavery, which is closely connected with our industrial conditions and our system of private ownership.

The women who are active in the bourgeois suffrage movement, do not recognize the necessity of so complete a transformation. Influenced by their privileged social position, they consider the more radical aims of the proletarian woman's movement dangerous doctrines that must be opposed. The class antagonism that exists between the capitalist and working class and that is increasing with the growth of industrial problems, also clearly manifests itself then within the woman's movement. Still these sister-women, though antagonistic to each other on class lines, have a great many more points in common than the men engaged in the class struggle, and though they march in separate armies they may strike a united blow. This is true in regard to all endeavors pertaining to equal rights of woman under the present social order; that is, her right to enter any trade or profession adapted to her strength and ability, and her right to civic and political equality. These are, as we shall see, very important and very far-reaching aims. Besides striving for these aims, it is in the particular interest of proletarian women to work hand in hand with proletarian men for such measures and institutions that tend to protect the working woman from physical and mental degeneration, and to preserve her health and strength for a normal fulfillment of her maternal functions. Furthermore, it is the duty of the proletarian woman to join the men of her class in the struggle for a thorough-going transformation of society, to bring about an order that by its social institutions will enable both sexes to enjoy complete economic and intellectual independence.

Our goal then is, not only to achieve equality of men and women under the present social order, which constitutes the sole aim of the bourgeois woman's movement, but to go far beyond this, and to remove all barriers that make one human being dependent upon another, which includes the dependence of one sex upon the other. *This* solution of the woman question is identical with the solution of the social question. They who seek a complete solution of the woman question must, therefore, join hands with those who have inscribed upon their banner the solution of the social question in the interest of all mankind—the Socialists.

The Socialist Party is the only one that has made the full equality of women, their liberation from every form of dependence and oppression, an integral part of its program; not for reasons of propaganda, but from necessity. *For there can be no liberation of mankind without social independence and equality of the sexes.*

Woman in the Future

In the new society woman will be entirely independent, both socially and economically. She will not be subjected to even a trace of domination and exploitation, but will be free and man's equal, and mistress of her own lot. Her education will be the same as man's, with the exception of those deviations that are necessitated by the differences of sex and sexual functions. Living under normal conditions of life, she may fully develop and employ her physical and mental faculties. She chooses an occupation suited to her wishes, inclinations and abilities, and works under the same conditions as man. Engaged as a practical working woman in some field of industrial activity, she may, during a second part of the day, be educator, teacher or nurse, during a third she may practice a science or an art, and during a fourth she may perform some administrative function. She studies, works, enjoys pleasures and recreation with other women or with men, as she may choose or as occasions may present themselves.

In the choice of love she is as free and unhampered as man. She woos or is wooed, and enters into a union prompted by no other considerations but her own feelings. This union is a private agreement, without the interference of a functionary, just as marriage had been a private agreement until far into the middle ages. Here Socialism will create nothing new, it will merely reinstate, on a higher level of civilization and under a different social form, what generally prevailed before private property dominated society.

Man shall dispose of his own person, provided that the gratification of his impulses is not harmful or detrimental to others. The satisfaction of the sexual impulse is as much the private concern of each individual, as the satisfaction of any other natural impulse. No one is accountable to any one else, and no third person has a right to interfere. What I eat and drink, how I sleep and dress is my private affair, and my private affair also is my intercourse with a person of the opposite sex. Intelligence and culture, personal independence,—qualities that will become natural, owing to the education and conditions prevailing in the new society,—will prevent persons from committing actions that will prove detrimental to themselves. Men and women of future society will possess far more self-control and a better knowledge of their own natures, than men and women of to-day. The one fact alone, that the foolish prudery and secrecy connected with sexual matters will disappear, will make the relation of the sexes a far more natural and healthful one. If between a man and woman, who have entered into a union, incompatibility, disappointment or revulsion should appear, morality commands a dissolution of the union which has become unnatural, and therefore immoral. As all those circumstances will have vanished that have so far compelled a great many women either to choose celibacy or prostitution, men can no longer dominate over women. On the other hand, the completely changed social conditions will have removed the many hindrances and harmful influences that affect married life to-day and frequently prevent its full development or make it quite impossible.

The impediments, contradictions and unnatural features in the present position of woman are being recognized by ever wider circles, and find expression in our modern literature on social questions, as well as in modern fiction; only the form in which it is expressed sometimes fails to answer the purpose. That present day marriage is not suited to its purpose, is no longer denied by any thinking person. So it is not surprising that even such persons favor a free choice of love and a free dissolution of the marriage relation, who are not inclined to draw the resulting conclusions that point to a change of the entire social system. They believe that freedom in sexual intercourse is justifiable among members of the privileged classes only....

Compulsory marriage is the normal marriage to bourgeois society. It is the only "moral" union of the sexes; any other sexual union is "immoral." Bourgeois marriage is,—this we have irrefutably proved,—the result of bourgeois relations. Closely connected with private property and the right of inheritance, it is contracted to obtain "legitimate" children. Under the pressure of social conditions it is forced also upon those who have nothing to bequeath. It becomes a social law, the violation of which is punished by the state, by imprisonment of the men or women who have committed adultery and have become divorced.

But in Socialistic society there will be nothing to bequeath, unless house furnishings and personal belongings should be regarded as hereditary portions; so the modern form of marriage becomes untenable from this point of view also. This also settles the question of inheritance, which Socialism will not need to abolish. Where there is no private property, there can be no right of inheritance. So woman will be *free*, and the children she may have will not impair her freedom, they will only increase her pleasure in life. Nurses, teachers, women friends, the rising female generation, all these will stand by her when she is in need of assistance....

For thousands of years human society has passed through all phases of development, only to return to its starting point: communistic property and complete liberty and fraternity; but no longer only for the members of the gens, but for all human beings. That is what the great progress consists of. What bourgeois society has striven for in vain, in what it failed and was bound to fail,—to establish liberty, equality and fraternity for all,—will be realized by Socialism. Bourgeois society could merely advance the theory, but here, as in many other things, practice was contrary to the theories. Socialism will unite theory and practice.

But as mankind returns to the starting point of its development, it will do so on an infinitely higher level of civilization. If primitive society had common ownership in the gens and the clan, it was but in a coarse form and an undeveloped stage. The course of development that man has since undergone, has reduced common property to small and insignificant remnants, has shattered the gens and has finally atomized society; but in its various phases it has also greatly heightened the productive forces of society and the extensiveness of its demands; it has transformed the gentes and the tribes into nations, and has thereby again created a condition that is in glaring contradiction to the requirements of society. It is the task of the future to remove this contradiction by re-establishing the common ownership of property and the means of production on the broadest basis.

Society takes back what it has at one time possessed and has itself created, but it enables all to live in accordance with the newly created conditions of life on the highest level of civilization. In other words, it grants to all what under more primitive conditions has been the privilege of single individuals or classes. Now woman, too, is restored to the active position maintained by her in primitive society; only she no longer is mistress, but man's equal.

From August Bebel, *Woman: Past, Present and Future*, New York: Boni and Liveright, 1918, 4–7, 466–473, translated by Meta L. Stern.

CHAPTER 7: Nationalism, Empires and Individualism

Document 43:
WHAT IS THE FATHERLAND?
Voltaire

Perhaps the most famous of the philosophers of the Enlightenment, Voltaire often parted company with many of his colleagues in the Age of Reason. In this writing, he ridicules the extent to which nationalism is taken. He reminds his generation about the real concerns of people far removed from the concerns of ultra-nationalism.

Thus what is the fatherland? Is it not perhaps a good field, of which the possessor, lodged comfortably in a well-maintained house, is able to say, this field that I cultivate, this house that I have built, are mine. I live under the protection of laws that no tyrant can infringe upon? When those who possess, as I do, fields and houses, assemble for their common interests, I have my voice in this assembly. I am a part of the whole, a part of the community, a part of the sovereignty: that is my fatherland. Are not all those who are not included in this assembly like a stable of horses under a groom who whips them according to his pleasure? One has a fatherland under a good king, one never has one under a scoundrel.

Section II

A young lad, a pastry-cook who had been to college, and who still knew some phrases from Cicero, was one day putting on airs about loving his fatherland. "What do you mean by your fatherland," asked a neighbor, "is it your oven? Is it the village where you were born, and that you have never returned to? Is it the street that your father and mother inhabited, where they were ruined, and which has reduced you to selling little pastries in order to live? Is it the town hall where you will never be the clerk of a policeman? Is it the church of Our Lady where you have not been able to succeed in becoming a choirboy, whereas a foolish man is archbishop and duke and receives an income of twenty thousand gold *louis* income?"

The pastry-cook lad did not know how to answer that, and a thinker, who was listening to this conversation, concluded that in a fatherland of any size, there were frequently millions of men who have no fatherland at all.

You pleasure-loving Parisians, who have made no greater voyage than to Dieppe to eat fresh seafood, who are only acquainted with your magnificent townhouse, your pretty country villa, and your box at the Opera where the rest of Europe persists in boring itself, you who speak your own language well enough because you do not know any other, you love all these things. And you love still more the the girls that you keep, the champagne that arrives from Rheims, your income that is paid to you every six months from the town hall, and you say that you love your fatherland!

In good conscience, does a financier cordially love his fatherland? The officer and the soldier who lay waste to their winter quarters, if they are allowed to, have they a very tender love for the countryside that they ruin?

Where was the country of the scarred Duke of Guise? Was it in Nancy, Paris, or Rome?

What fatherland had you, cardinals Balue, Duprat, Lorraine, and Mazarin?

Where was the fatherland of Attila and a hundred other heros of this kind who were always on the move and never off track?

I would truly like someone to tell me the homeland of Abraham.

The first person who wrote that the fatherland was wherever one feels at home was Euripides, in his *Phaeton*.... but the first man who left his birthplace in order to search elsewhere for his happiness said it before him.

Section III

A fatherland is composed of many families, and as a family is commonly supported by self-respect, when there is no interest to the contrary, one supports by this same self-respect his town or his village; that is called his fatherland.

The larger this fatherland becomes, the less it is loved, because this love is weakened by extension. It is impossible to love tenderly a family so numerous that one scarcely knows it.

He who burns with ambition to be mayor, tribune, moneylender, consul, or dictator, cries out that he loves his fatherland, but he only loves himself. Each man wishes to be sure of the power to sleep at home without any other man claiming the power to send him off to sleep elsewhere. Every man wants to be sure of his fortune and his life. With everyone forming thus the same wishes, it is found that particular interest becomes the general interest. Vows are made to the republic, when they are truly made only for self interest.

It is impossible that a state was ever formed on earth that was not governed by a republic at the first; that is the natural progression of human nature. Some families gathered together in the first place against bears and wolves. Those who had some grain traded with those who had wood.

When we discovered America, we found all the tribes divided into republics; there were only two kingdoms in this part of the world. Of a thousand nations, we only discovered two that were subjugated.

It was once this way in the Old World. Everything was republican in Europe before the petty kings of Etruria and Rome. One still sees today some republics in Africa, Tripoli, Tunis, and Algiers. To our north are some republics of brigands. The Hottentots, in the south, still live, it is said, as people are supposed to have lived in the first ages of the world: free, equal among each other, without masters, without subjects, without money, and nearly without wants. The meat of their sheep feeds them, their skins clothe them, huts of mud and wood are their shelters. They are the foulest-smelling of men, but they do not notice it; they live and die more sweetly than we do.

There remain eight republics without monarchs in our Europe: Venice, Holland, Switzerland, Genoa, Lucca, Ragusa, and San Marino. One can regard Poland, Sweden, and England as republics under a king, but Poland is the only one that takes the name.

But now, which of them is better as a fatherland, a monarchical or a republican state? Four thousand years of debate stirs this question. Ask this question to the rich and they all answer that they better love an aristocracy. Ask the people, and they want democracy; it is only the kings who prefer monarchy. How is it then possible that nearly all of the earth is governed by monarchs? Ask the rats, who proposed hanging a bell around the cat's neck. But in truth, the real reason is, as has been said before, that men rarely are worthy of governing themselves.

It is sad that in order to be a good patriot one frequently must be an enemy to the rest of mankind. The ancient Cato, that good citizen, always said while giving his opinion to the Senate, "Such is my advice, and Carthage must be destroyed." To be a good patriot is to wish your country to be enriched by trade and powerful in arms. It is clear that one nation is not able to profit except by loss to another, and that it is not able to conquer except by doing evil.

Such is the human condition, that to wish for the greatness of one's own country is to wish harm to one's neighbors. He who wishes that his fatherland never be greater nor smaller, richer nor poorer, would be a citizen of the world.

From *Oeuvres Complètes de Voltaire*, edited by Louis Moland, Paris: Garnier Frères, 1877–1885, volume 20, 1879, 182–186, translated by Michael Slaven.

Document 44:
EMANCIPATE YOUR COLONIES! (1793)
Addressed to the National Convention of France
Jeremy Bentham

Jeremy Bentham presented his arguments against French colonies in the midst of the French Revolution. He pointed out the contradictions of workers' demands for greater equality and participation in government within their own nations, while denying it to others in their colonies.

Your predecessors made me a French Citizen: hear me speak like one. War thickens round you: I will show you a vast resource:— EMANCIPATE YOUR COLONIES. You start: Hear and you will be reconciled. I say again, EMANCIPATE YOUR COLONIES. Justice, consistency, policy, economy, honour, generosity, all demand it of you: all this you shall see. Conquer, you are still but running the race of vulgar ambition: emancipate, you strike out a new path to glory. Conquer, it is by your armies: emancipate, the conquest is your own, and made over yourselves. To give freedom at the expense of others, is but conquest in disguise: to rise superior to conquerors, the sacrifice must be your own. Reasons you will not find wanting, if you will hear them; some more pressing than you might wish. What is least pleasant among them may pay you best for hearing it. Were it ever so unpleasant, better hear it while it is yet time, than when it is too late, and from one friend, than from a host of enemies. If you are kings, you will hear nothing but flattery; if you are republicans, you will bear rugged truths.

I begin with *justice*: it stands foremost in your thoughts. And are you yet to learn, that on this ground the question is already judged?—that you at least have judged it, and given judgment against yourselves?—You abhor tyranny: you abhor it in the lump not less than in detail: you abhor the subjection of one nation to another: you call it slavery. You gave sentence in the case of Britain against her colonies: have you so soon forgot that sentence?—have you so soon forgot the school in which you served your apprenticeship to freedom?

You choose your own government: why are not other people to choose theirs? Do you seriously mean to govern the world, and do you call that *liberty*? What is become of the rights of men? Are you the only men who have rights? Alas! my fellow citizens, have you two measures?

"Oh! but they are but a part of the empire, and a part must be governed by the whole."—Part of the empire, say you? Yes, in point of fact, they certainly are, or at least were. Yes: so was New York a part of the British empire, while the British army garrisoned it: so were Longwy and Verdun parts of the Prussian or the Austrian empire t'other day. That you have, or at least had *possession* of them, is out of dispute: the question is, whether you now ought to have it?

Yes you have, or had it: but whence came it to you? Whence, but from the hand of despotism. Think how you have dealt by them. One common Bastile enclosed them and you. You knock down the jailor, you let yourselves out, you keep them in, and put yourselves into his place. You destroy the criminal, and you reap the profit, I mean always what seems to you profit, of the crime.

"Oh, but they will send deputies; and those deputies will govern us, as much as we govern them." Illusion! What is that but doubling the mischief, instead of lessening it? To give yourselves a pretence for governing a million or two of strangers, you admit half a dozen. To govern a million or two of people you don't care about, you admit half a dozen people who don't care about you. To govern a set of people whose business you know nothing about, you encumber yourselves with half a dozen starers who know nothing about yours. Is this fraternity?—is this liberty and equality? Open domination would be a less grievance. Were I an American, I had rather not be represented at all, than represented thus. If tyranny must come, let it come without a mask. "Oh, but information." True, it must be had; but to give information, must a man possess a vote?

Frenchmen, how would you like a parliament of ours to govern you, you sending six members to it? London is not a third part so far from Paris as London from the Orkneys, or Paris from Perpignan. You start—think then, what may be the feelings of the colonists. Are they Frenchmen? —they will feel like Frenchmen. Are they not Frenchmen? —Then where is your right to govern them?

Is equality what you want? I will tell you how to make it. As often as France sends commissaries with fleets and armies to govern the colonies, let the colonies send commissaries with equal fleets and armies to govern France.

What are a thousand such pleas to the purpose? Let us leave imagination, and consult feelings. Is it for their advantage to be governed by you rather than by themselves? Is it for your advantage to govern them rather than leave them to themselves.

Is it then for their advantage to be governed by a people who never know, nor ever can know, either their inclinations or their wants? What is it you ever can know about them? The wishes they entertain? The wants they labour under? No such thing; but the wishes they entertained, the wants they laboured under, two months ago: wishes that may have changed, and for the best reasons: wants that may have been relieved, or become unrelievable. Do they apply to you for justice: You get not a tenth part, perhaps, of the witnesses you ought to have, and those perhaps only on one side. Do they ask succours of you? You put yourselves to immense expense: You fit out an armament, and when it arrives, it finds nothing to be done; the party to whom you send it are either conquerors or conquered—Do they want subsistence? Before your supply reaches them, they are starved. No negligence could put them in a situation so helpless as that in which, so long as they continue dependent on you, the nature of things has fixed them, in spite of all your solicitude.

Solicitude, did I say? How can they expect any such thing? What care you, or what can you care, about them? What do you know about them? What picture can you so much as form to yourselves of the country? What conception can you frame to yourselves of manners and modes of life so different from your own? When will you ever see them? When will they ever see you? If they suffer, will their cries ever wound your ears? Will their wretchedness ever meet your eyes? What time have you to think about them? Pressed by so many important objects that are at your door, how uninteresting will be the tale that comes from St. Domingo or Martinique?

What is it you want to govern them for? What, but to monopolize and cramp their trade? What is it they can want you to govern them for? Defence? Their only danger is from you.

Do they like to be governed by you? Ask them, and you will know. Yet why ask them, as if you did not know? They may be better pleased to be governed by you than by anybody else; but is it possible they should not be still better pleased to be governed by themselves? A minority among them might choose rather to be governed by you than by their antagonists, the majority: but is it for you to protect minorities? A majority, which did not feel itself so strong as it could wish, might wish to borrow a little strength of you:—but for the loan of a moment, would you exact a perpetual annuity of servitude?

"Oh, but they are aristocrats." Are they so? Then I am sure you have no right to govern them: then I am sure it is not their interest to be governed by you: then I am sure it is not your interest to govern them. Are they aristocrats? They hate you. Are they aristocrats? You hate them. For what would you wish to govern a people who hate you? Will they hate you the less for governing them? Are a people the happier for being governed by those they hate? If so, send for the Duke of Brunswick, and seat him on your throne. For what can you wish to govern a people whom you hate? Is it for the pleasure of making them miserable? Is not this copying the Fredericks and the Francises?—is not this being aristocrats, and aristocrats with a vengeance?

But why deal in suppositions and put cases? Two colonies, Martinico and Guadalupe, have already pronounced the separation. Has that satisfied you? I am afraid rather it has irritated you. They have shaken off the yoke; and you have decreed an armament to fasten it on again. You are playing over again our old game. Democrats in Europe, you are aristocrats in America. What is this to end in? If you will not be good citizens and good Frenchmen, be good neighbours and good allies. When you have conquered Martinico and Guadalupe, conquer the United States, and give them back to Britain.

"Oh, but the Capets will get hold of them." [ed. note: "Capet" was the royal name of the first French monarchs. Louix XVI, "citizen Capet," was executed on January 21, 1793.] So much the better. Why not let the Capets go to America? Europe would then be rid of them. Are they bad neighbours? Rejoice that they are at a distance. Why should not the Capets even reign, since there are those that choose to be governed by them? Why should not even the Capets reign, while it is in another hemisphere? Such aristocrats as you do not kill, you yourselves talk of transporting. What do you mean to make of them when transported? Slaves? If you must have slaves, keep them rather at home, where they will be more out-numbered by freeman, and kept in better order. If you mean they should be transported without being enslaved, why not let them transport themselves?

Does your delicacy forbid your communicating with the degraded despots? You need not communicate with them. Your communication is with the people. You take the people as you find them: you give them to themselves: and if afterwards they choose to give themselves to anybody else, it is their doing: you neither need, nor ought to have any concern in it.

"Oh, but the good citizens! what will become of the good citizens?" What will become of them? Their fate depends upon yourselves. Give up your dominion, you may save them: fight for it, you destroy them. Secure, if you can do it without force, a fair emission of the wishes of all the citizens: if what you call the good citizens are the majority, they will govern; if a minority, they neither will nor ought to govern: but you may give them safety if you please. This you may do for them at any rate, whether those in whose hands you find them submit to collect the sense of the majority or refuse it. Conclude not, that if you cease to maintain tyranny, you have no power to insure justice. Think not, that those who resist oppression must be deaf to kindness. Set the example of justice: you who, if you preferred destruction, might use force, set the example of justice: the most perverse will be ashamed not to follow it. How different are the same words from a tyrant and from a benefactor! Abhorrence and suspicion poison them in the one case: love and confidence sweeten them in the other....

From Jeremy Bentham, *The Works of Jeremy Bentham*, published under the superintendence of his executor, John Bowring, Volume IV. Edinburgh: William Tait, 1843, 408–410.

Document 45:
THE MONROE DOCTRINE (1823)
James Monroe

This statement by the American President James Monroe in 1823 asserted as American policy that European powers should not try to interfere with the Americas. Of course, it opened Latin America to American trade and influence. The British Empire enforced the doctrine because it also opened the area to British Trade.

...the occasion has been judged proper for asserting, as a principle in which the rights and interests of the United States are involved, that the American continents, by the free and independent condition which they have assumed and maintain are henceforth not to be considered as subjects for future colonization by any European powers.

It was stated at the commencement of the last session that a great effort was then making in Spain and Portugal to improve the condition of the people of those countries, and that it appeared to be conducted with extraordinary moderation. It need scarcely be remarked that the result has been so far very different from what was then anticipated. Of events in that quarter of the globe, with which we have so much intercourse and from which we derive our origin, we have always been anxious and interested spectators. The citizens of the United States cherish sentiments the most friendly in favor of the liberty and happiness of their fellow-men on that side of the Atlantic. In the wars of the European powers, in matters relating to themselves, we have never taken any part, nor does it comport with our policy so to do. It is only when our rights are invaded or seriously menaced, that we resent injuries or make preparation for our defense. With the movements in this hemisphere we are, of necessity, more immediately connected and by causes which must be obvious to all enlightened and impartial observers. The political system of the allied powers is essentially different in this respect from that of America. This difference proceeds from that which exists in their respective governments. And to the defense of our own, which has been achieved by the loss of so much blood and treasure, and matured by the wisdom of their most enlightened citizens, and under which we have enjoyed unexampled felicity, this whole nation is devoted. We owe it, therefore, to candor and to the amicable relations existing between the United States and those powers, to declare that *we should consider any attempt on their part to extend their system to any portion of this hemisphere as dangerous to our peace and safety*. With the existing colonies or dependencies of any European power we have not interfered, and shall not interfere. But with the governments who have declared their independence and maintained it, and whose independence we have, on great consideration and on just principles, acknowledged, we could not view any interposition for the purpose of oppressing them, or controlling in any other manner their destiny, by any European power, in any other light than as *the manifestation of an unfriendly disposition toward the United States*. In the war between those new governments and Spain we declared our neutrality at the time of their recognition, and to this we have adhered and shall continue to adhere, provided no change shall occur which, in the judgment of the competent authorities of this government, shall make a corresponding change on the part of the United States indispensable to their security.

The late events in Spain and Portugal show that Europe is still unsettled. Of this important fact no stronger proof can be adduced than that the allied powers should have thought it proper, on a principle satisfactory to themselves, to have interposed by force in the internal concerns of Spain. To what extent such interposition may be carried on the same principle, is a question to which all independent powers, whose governments differ from theirs, are interested; even those most remote, and surely none more so than the United States. Our policy in regard to Europe, which was adopted at an early stage of the wars which have so long agitated that quarter of the globe, nevertheless remains the same, which is, not to interfere in the internal concerns of any of its powers; to consider the government *de facto* as the legitimate government for us; to cultivate friendly relations with it, and to preserve those relations by a frank, firm, and manly policy; meeting, in all instances, the just claims of every power; submitting to injuries from none. But in regard to these continents, circumstances are eminently and conspicuously different. It is impossible that the allied powers should extend their political system to any portion of either continent without endangering our peace and happiness; nor can any one believe that our southern brethren, if left to themselves, would adopt it of their own accord. It is equally impossible, therefore, that we should behold such interposition, in any form, with indifference. If we look to the comparative strength and resources of Spain and those new governments, and their distance from each other, it must be obvious that she can never subdue them. It is still the true policy of the United States to leave the parties to themselves, in hope that other powers will pursue the same course.

From *Readings in American History*, edited by Oscar Handlin, New York: Alfred A. Knopf, 1963, 270–271.

Document 46:
THE EXPANSION OF ENGLAND (1888)
J.R. Seeley

The well-known historian, J.R. Seeley, reflects a late nineteenth century Briton's attitude toward the rights of Britain to empire and the necessity of empire for the British.

I remarked before that Greater Britain is an extension of the English State and not merely that of the English nationality. But it is an equally striking characteristic of Greater Britain that nevertheless it *is* an extension of the English nationality. When a nationality is extended without any extension of the State, as in the case of the Greek colonies, there may be an increase of political power. On the other hand when the State advances beyond the limits of the nationality, its power becomes precarious and artificial. This is the condition of most empires; it is the condition for example of our own empire in India. The English State is powerful there, but the English nation is but an imperceptible drop in the ocean of an Asiatic population. And when a nation extends itself into other territories the chances are that it will there meet with other nationalities which it cannot destroy or completely drive out, even if it succeeds in conquering them. When this happens, it has a great and permanent cause of weakness and danger. It has been the fortune of England in extending itself to evade on the whole this danger. For it has occupied parts of the globe which were so empty that they offered an unbounded scope for new settlement. There was land for every emigrant who chose to come, and the native races were not in a condition sufficiently advanced to withstand even the peaceful competition, much less the power, of the immigrants.

This statement is true on the whole. The English Empire is on the whole free from that weakness which has brought down most empires, the weakness of being a mere mechanical forced union of alien nationalities. It is sometimes described as an essentially feeble union which could not bear the slightest shock, with what reason I may examine later, but it has the fundamental strength which most empires and some commonwealths want. Austria for instance is divided by the nationality-rivalry of German, Slav, and Magyar; the Swiss Confederation unites three languages, but the English Empire in the main and broadly may be said to be English throughout....

Now we have this conception more or less distinctly in our minds whenever we ask the question, What is the good of colonies? That question implies that we think of a colony, not as part of our State, but as a possession belonging to it. For we should think it absurd to raise such a question about a recognised part of the body politic. Who ever thought of inquiring whether Cornwall or Kent rendered any sufficient return for the money which we lay out upon them, whether those countries were worth keeping? The tie that holds together the parts of a nation-state is of another kind; it is not composed of considerations of profit and loss, but is analogous to the family bond. The same tie would hold a nation to its colonies, if colonies were regarded as an extension of the nation. If Greater Britain in the full sense of the phrase really existed, Canada and Australia would be to us as Kent and Cornwall. But if once we cease to regard a colony in this way, if we consider that the emigrants who have gone forth from us have ceased to belong to our community, then we must form some other conception of their relation to us. And this must either be the old Greek conception which treats them as grown-up children who have married and settled at a distance, so that the family bond has dissolved away by the mere necessity of circumstances, or if the connexion is maintained, as the modern States insisted on maintaining it, it must change its character. It must rest on interest. The question must be asked, What is the good of the colony? and it must be answered by some proof that the colony considered as a piece of property, or an an investment of public money, pays....

England is now preeminently a maritime, colonising and industrial country. It seems to be the prevalent opinion that England always was so, and from the nature of her people can never be otherwise. In Ruckert's poem the deity that visited the same spot of earth at intervals of five hundred years, and found there now a forest, now a city, now a sea, whenever he asked after the origin of what he saw, received for answer, "It has always been so, and always will be." This unhistorical way of thinking, this disposition to ascribe an inherent necessity to whatever we are accustomed to, betrays itself in much that is said about the genius of the Anglo-Saxon race. That we might have been other than we are, nay that we once were other, is to us so inconceivable that we try to explain *why* we were always the same before ascertaining by an inquiry whether the fact is so. It seems to us clear that we are the great wandering, working, colonizing race, descended from sea-overs and Vikings. The sea, we think, is ours by nature's decree, and on this highway we travel to subdue the earth and to people it....

From J.R. Seeley, *The Expansion of England*, edited by John Gross, Chicago: University of Chicago Press, 1971, 40–41, 53–54, 66.

Document 47:
HOW GERMAN EAST AFRICA WAS CREATED (1890)
A Personal Report of the Founder Carl Peters

Carl Peters led the Germans into exploring and claiming East Africa. His personal account indicates the attitudes of Europeans to their superior claims to others' land. The envy of Germans for the British Empire is obvious as is the hostility that imperial countries created.

Chapter 1

How did it actually happen that a German colony was founded in East Africa? How often this question is directed to me!

When I myself look back at my career, I wonder even more, not that I founded German East Africa, but rather, that I could not obtain much greater land masses for the German Empire, and that I was not successful in winning a personal empire according to my own tastes. From childhood on it was my dream and I was occupied with such plans. My models and heroes were Pericles, Hannibal, the Gracchi, Cortez, Sir Walter Raleigh, Nelson and others. The subjective reason for such decisions was thus within myself. The motive lay in the development of Germany for the foundation of the Reich. My generation experienced the War of 1870–71 at the height of its manhood. [ed. note: This was the Franco-Prussian War that resulted in the creation of the German Empire.] The powerful impressions of Sedan and Versailles could not be without effect on our hearts. For us, the Germans were militarily the most powerful people on the earth. And when we looked at the maps we found, that of all European nations, this powerful land alone did not possess a colony: when we went abroad we found that the Germans were the least respected of all the peoples of Europe, that even the Dutch, the Danes and Norwegians looked down upon us with contempt. Thus our hearts had to be filled with great shame and our reaction was to increase our national pride.

I had such feelings during the years 1880–1883, when I spent several years of financial independence in England [studying]. At the end of my studies and completing my examinations, I suffered most passionately and out of this suffering I came to the firm decision to use all of my power to help my people out of this desolute condition.

In all of England I observed the positive effects of a good colonial policy. I recognized what the exchange between mother country and colonies meant for commercial and economic policies and what Germany loses each year by buying its coffee, its tea, rice, tobacco, its spices, in short all of its colonial products from foreign peoples. What value it must have for each person in England; each can find an opportunity in the colonies to earn his keep, to create an independent fortune in service to the state or outside it. This appeared to me to be the vital point in the free and proud development of a country in contrast to the narrow-mindedness and the niche-seeking one runs into everywhere in Germany.

In fact, the comparison favored the foreigners, and I confess that this is the factor that drove me to a German colonial policy.

I wish to mention here that it was my instinct and my patriotism that warned me to return to my home and to my people and that it was exclusively my patriotism that overcame this instinct. My uncle, Carl Engel, who had a respected position in England and had no children, asked if he could adopt me and leave his fortune to me if I could decide to become an Englishman like he was and could satisfy my ambition within the bounds of the British Empire. His nephew by marriage, Joseph Chamberlain, was at that time President of the Board of Trade and would have easily assisted my entry into the British-Indian Service. I said "no," and with this decision I brought all the misfortune and suffering of my life upon myself. I decided then to narrow my entire existence and career in an undertaking for my fatherland and knew that it could have two outcomes—either failure or complete success. I could not think of the possibility of failure....

From Carl Peters, *Wie Deutsch-Ostafrika Entstand! Personlicher Bericht des Grunders*, Leipzig: Koehler & Voistlander Verlag, 1940, 7–9, translated by John A. Maxwell.

Document 48:
THE MEANING OF RACE (1904)
Houston Stewart Chamberlain

H.S. Chamberlain was a racial theorist who believed in the superiority of the so-called "Aryan" race. Chamberlain was a British-born philosopher who was deeply influenced by the work of Joseph Arthur, comte de Gobineau. Chamberlain's The Foundations of the Nineteenth Century *(1911) was a major influence on German nationalist thought and pan-Germanism. The Nazi party in Germany was also highly influenced by Chamberlain's theories that the Aryans were the bringers of culture to Europe.*

Nothing is so immediately convincing as the possession of "Race" in one's consciousness. A man who belongs outright to a pure race is aware of it everyday. The guardian angel of his family tree is always at his side and guides him. When his foot slips, he warns him. Like the Socratic Demon; when he is on the verge of a mistaken idea, he demands obedience, and often forces him to undertakings, which, the man thinking impossible, he would not have (otherwise) dared to attempt. Weak and flawed as is all that is human, such a man knows himself (and others know him), to be trustworthy in his character, and performs deeds that are marked by a simple greatness, and which are to be explained by his consistently altruistic qualities.

Race raises a man up above himself; it gives him extraordinary, almost supernatural abilities, so completely does it separate him from the chaotic mishmash of other sorts of peoples. And if this noble breed of man by chance is unusually gifted, and becomes a genius standing far above the rest of humanity, it is not because he is a flaming meteor thrown down to earth as a caprice of nature, but because he rises towards the heavens like a strong, slender tree, nurtured by thousands and thousands of roots—not an isolated individual, but rather the living summation of similarly minded souls.

From H.S. Chamberlain, *Die Grundlagen des Neuntzehn Jahrhunderts, Volume 1*, Munich: Verlagsanstalt F. Bruckmann, 1904, 271–272, translated by Michael Slaven.

Document 49:
THE WHITE MAN'S BURDEN (1899)
Rudyard Kipling

Rudyard Kipling's poem captures the feeling of superiority and obligation that many Westerners felt towards the peoples of the Third World. This poem was one of the most popular in the English language. Kipling gradually changed his mind about imperialism. Early in his life he supported it, later he became a critic.

> Take up the White Man's burden-
> Send forth the best ye breed-
> Go bind your sons to exile
> To serve your captives' need;
> To wait in heavy harness
> On fluttered fold and wild-
> Your new-caught, sullen peoples,
> Half devil and half child.
>
> Take up the White Man's burden-
> In patience to abide,
> To veil the threat of terror
> And check the show of pride;
> By open speech and simple,
> An hundred times made plain.
> To seek another's profit,
> And work another's gain.
>
> Take up the White Man's burden-
> The savage wars of peace-
> Fill full the mouth of Famine
> And bid the sickness cease;
> And when your goal is nearest
> The end for others sought,
> Watch Sloth and heathen Folly
> Bring all your hope to nought.
>
> Take up the White Man's burden-
> No tawdry rule of kings,
> But toil of serf and sweeper-
> The tale of common things.
> The ports ye shall not enter,
> The roads ye shall not tread,
> Go make them with your living,
> And mark them with your dead!
>
> Take up the White Man's burden-
> And reap his old reward:
> The blame of those ye better,
> The hate of those ye guard-
> The cry of hosts ye humour
> (Ah, slowly!) toward the light:-
> "Why brought ye us from bondage,
> "Our loved Egyptian night?"
>
> Take up the White Man's burden-
> Ye dare not stoop to less-
> Nor call too loud on Freedom
> To cloak your weariness;
> By all ye cry or whisper,
> By all ye leave or do,
> The silent, sullen peoples
> Shall weigh your Gods and you.
>
> Take up the White Man's Burden-
> Have done with childish days-
> The lightly proffered laurel,
> The easy, ungrudged praise.
> Comes now, to search your manhood
> Through all the thankless years,
> Cold-edged with dear-bought wisdom,
> The judgement of your peers!

From *Kipling, A Selection of His Stories and Poems*, edited by John Beecroft, New York: Doubleday & Co., 1956, 444–445.

Document 50:
THE CHINESE SITUATION AND THE MAILED FIST (1897)
Kaiser Wilhelm II

In December 1897, the German Emperor, Wilhelm II, addressed Prince Henry as he took command of the German East Asia Squadron before it set sail to China to assert German imperial claims. In Wilhelm's speech are found the chief ingredients that led to European expansion in the age of imperialism.

As I rode into Kiel to-day I thought of the many times on which I had visited this city joyfully at your side and on my ships, either to be present at the sports or at some one of our military undertakings. On my arrival in the city to-day an earnest and deep feeling moved me, for I am perfectly conscious of the task which I have set before you and of the responsibility which I bear. But I am likewise conscious of the fact that it is my duty to build up and carry farther what my predecessors have bequeathed me.

The journey which you are to undertake and the task which you are to accomplish indicate nothing new in themselves; it is merely the logical consequence of what my departed grandfather and his great Chancellor inaugurated politically and what our glorious father won with his sword on the field of battle. It is nothing more than the first expression of the newly united and newly arisen German Empire in its tasks beyond the seas. The empire has developed so astonishingly through the extension of its commercial interest that it is my duty to follow up the new German Hansa and to give it the protection which it has a right to expect from the empire and the Emperor.

Our German brothers of the church who have gone out to their quiet work and have not spared risking their lives in order to spread and make a home for our religion on foreign soil have placed themselves under my protection, and it is now a question of providing support and safety for these brothers who have been so often insulted and oppressed. For that reason the undertaking which I entrust to you and which you must fulfil in company with your comrades and the ships which are already out there is really one of protection and not one of defiance. Under the protecting banner of our German flag of war we expect that the rights which we are justified in demanding will be guaranteed to our commerce, to the German merchant, and to German ships—the same right which is vouchsafed by strangers to all other nations.

Our commerce is not new; in old times the Hanseatic League was one of the most powerful enterprises which the world has ever seen, and the German cities were able to build a fleet such as the sea's broad back had never carried in earlier days, but finally it came to naught because the one condition was lacking, namely that of an Emperor's protection. Now things have changed; the first condition, the German Empire, has been created; the second condition, German commerce, flourishes and develops, and it can only develop properly and securely if it feels itself safe under the power of the empire. Imperial power means sea power, and sea power and imperial power are so interdependent that the one cannot exist without the other.

As a token of this imperial sea power the squadron which has been strengthened by your division must now take its place, with all the comrades of the foreign fleet out there in close relationship and on good terms of friendship, but for the purpose of protecting our particular interests against every one who might be tempted to intrude upon the right of the Germans. That is your task and your mission.

Make it clear to every European there, to the German merchant, and, above all things, to the foreigner in whose country we are or with whom we have to deal, that the German Michel [ed. note: *Michel* was the proverbial representative of the German character, as Uncle Sam is of the American or John Bull of the English. He is usually pictured as a simple good-natured fellow.] has set his shield, decorated with the imperial eagle, firmly upon the ground. Whoever asks him for protection will always receive it. And may our countrymen out there cherish the firm conviction, whether they are priests or merchants or whatever profession they follow, that the protection of the German Empire as exemplified in the Emperor's ships will continuously be granted them! But if any one should undertake to insult us in our rights or to wish to harm us, then drive in with the mailed fist and, as God wills, bind about your young brow the laurels which no one in the entire German Empire will begrudge you!

In the firm conviction that you, following good examples—and, God be praised, examples are not wanting in our house—will carry out my thoughts and wishes, I raise my glass and drink it to your health, with the wish for a good voyage, for a happy issue to your task, and for a joyous return. Long live his Royal Highness, Prince Henry! Hurrah! Hurrah! Hurrah!

From *The German Emperor as Shown in His Public Utterances*, edited by Christian Gauss, New York: Charles Scribner's Sons, 1915, 116–121.

Document 51:
THE GREAT FAMINE 1845–1855
Kerby A. Miller

This reader consists of primary sources that are used for the study of history. This selection, however, is different. It is an excerpt from a secondary source—a work written from other documents. It was chosen for its treatment of a great Western problem that has within it similarities to other areas which are often ignored in classroom texts. Note the comments from people suffering from the famine.

Between 1845 and 1855 the prophesied "Distruction" of Ireland became a reality. From the summer of 1845 through the early 1850s, every harvest of potatoes—practically the only food for most of the island's inhabitants—failed totally or partially, resulting in perhaps a million deaths and precipitating the exodus of another 1.8 million people to North America. Although Irish emigration had increased steadily in the preceding decades, it is unlikely that more than a third that number would have departed in 1845–55 had the social catastrophe caused by the potato blight not occurred. As starvation and disease devastated Ireland, thousands of panic-stricken people embraced emigration as their only escape from destitution and death. A large proportion were poor smallholders, cottiers, and laborers, often Irish-speakers or their children—fugitives from a Gaelic-peasant culture which they might not have abandoned under ordinary circumstances; indeed, many were literally driven from the land as proprietors and strong farmers seized the opportunity to evict thousands of demoralized paupers....

Despite every relief effort, the potato blight brought horrible distress to Ireland: "not all the exertions of man," wrote one woman, "have been able to stay the progress of *desolation*." One historian estimates that between 1.1 and 1.5 million persons died of starvation or famine-related disease, and contemporary observers were horrified by scenes of suffering unparalleled in recent European experience. For example, in 1846 the absentee landlord Nicholas Cummins found the cabins on his west Cork estate near Skibbereen inhabited by "famished and ghastly skeletons...such frightful spectres as no words can describe." "Their demonic yells are still ringing in my ears," Cummins later wrote, "and their horrible images are fixed upon my brain." In the north midlands another visitor "saw sights that will never wholly leave the eyes that beheld them, cowering wretches almost naked in the savage weather, prowling in turnip fields, and endeavouring to grub up roots...little children...their limbs fleshless...their faces bloated yet wrinkled and of a pale greenish hue,...who would never, it was too plain, grow up to be men and women." In 1847 and 1848 the Quaker philanthropists Jonathan Pim, William Bennett, and Richard Webb reported similar horrors in west Connaught: in northwest Mayo, wrote Bennett, "[t]he scene was one and invariable, differing in little but the number of the suffers....It was my impression that *one-fourth* of those we saw were in a *dying state*, beyond the reach of any relief that could now be afforded; and many more would follow." In Queen's County as elsewhere, "many familyes...liv[ed] on the wild caribs of the fields"; others fed on grass, seaweed and shellfish, rotten potatoes, dead animals, even human corpses. Weakened by malnutrition, thousands fell victim to typhus or "black fever," scurvy, "famine dropsy," cholera, relapsing fever, and dysentery or the "bloody flux." Many simply barricaded themselves in their hovels and waited for death; others wandered about searching for food, spreading disease throughout the island. In towns such as Kenmare, wrote Bennett, "the poor people came in from the rural districts in such numbers, in the hopes of getting some relief, that it was utterly impossible to meet their most urgent exigencies, and therefore they came in literally *to die*...in the open streets, actually dying of starvation and fever within a stone's throw of the inn." "I cant let you know how we are suffering," wrote one desperate woman to her emigrant son, "unless you were in Starvation and want without friend or fellow to give you a Shilling But on my too bended Neese fresh and fasting I pray to god that you Nor one of yers may [n]ever know Nor ever Suffer what we are Suffering At the present." Truly, one priest declared, "the Angel of death and desolation reigns triumphant in Ireland."...

The potato blight was unavoidable, but the Great Famine was largely the result of Ireland's colonial status and grossly inequitable social system. Underrepresented and outnumbered at Westminster, Irish MPs could only beg relief from English ministers who often knew little and cared less about Ireland's condition;

although an autonomous Irish parliament would not have been O'Connell's promised panacea of Irish ills, a native legislature would surely have been more responsive to its constituents' distress. The continued exportation of Ireland's grain, cattle, and other foodstuffs to feed British markets while the Irish perished from hunger was an especially poignant example of Ireland's political and economic subservience to British interests; although the exported food could not have compensated for more than a small proportion of the destroyed potato crop, its retention for home consumption might have saved several hundred thousand lives in the dreadful winter of 1846–47, between the exhaustion of the last potatoes and the arrival of new shipments of American meal. Another example of a colonial society's weakness in dealing with crisis was the distracting and debilitating controversy between Irish Protestant philanthropists who charged that some priests, especially in western dioceses, were "plundering avaricious Wretch[es]" who misappropriated relief funds or ran away from their stricken parishioners. Catholics countered that Protestant missionaries were proselytizing the starving poor, giving free soup only in return for recantations of "popery." In fact, most clergymen of all denominations labored nobly and disinterestedly in the face of appalling difficulties. Although some conversions did occur, as might be expected in a time of profound social trauma, the virulent controversy over proselytism or "souperism" largely reflected the ongoing contest for religious and political supremacy over a famished people who could scarcely afford such diversionary strife.

Irish colonialism's most lethal legacy was a predominantly alien landlord class which, despite individual instances of benevolence, did little to alleviate and much to exacerbate the crisis. For thirty years prior to the Famine, Irish landlords had striven against popular opposition to rationalize their estates by consolidating farms and evicting insolvent or "superfluous" tenants; the potato blight now provided unique opportunities and added incentives to carry out their designs. By mid-1846, thousands of tenants were in arrears: middling and small farmers could stave off hunger by consuming grain and livestock formerly sent to market, but then they had no money to pay their rents; even large farmers and middlemen frequently fell into arrears as subtenants defaulted, taxes increased, and grain and cattle prices plummeted after the repeal of the Corn Laws. In general, landlords refused to grant abatements, responding instead with distraining orders and eviction notices. Moreover, since proprietors were liable for poor rates on all holdings valued at 4 pounds or less, the Famine gave them an additional compelling reason to clear their estates of pauper tenants and cottiers; consequently, as poor rates soared after 1847—sometimes exceeding the annual rental of entire baronies—so did the numbers of evictions. In mid-1847 Parliament further stimulated clearances by adding the infamous "Gregory clause" to the amended Poor Law. The clause, named for the Irish landlord who proposed it, forbade public relief to any household head who held a quarter-acre or more of land and refused to relinquish possession to his proprietor. Although many peasants tried to evade the law, and some chose to die rather than forfeit their holdings, thousands acquiesced to prevent starvation; after all, evasion was nearly impossible when local Poor Law boards, dominated by landlords or their agents, applied the clause even more ruthlessly than Parliament had intended, often denying relief to wives and children of farmers who refused to give up their land. In all, between 1846 and 1855 perhaps half a million or more persons suffered eviction from their homes, often under especially heartless and brutal circumstances: "All Haggard, half-naked, houseless, hungry, and Clamorous for help" was Richard Webb's description of those evicted "in the depths of Winter" from the Bingham estates in County Mayo; "they crowded into the neighbouring Villages, and filled them with fever and dysentery." Clearances were most common in Munster, Connaught, and north Leinster, but even in County Wexford, one priest reported, "though we are...partially exempt from the calamitous suffering of the West of Ireland, we every day behold the cottages of the Poor levelled in the ground, & their inmates sent adrift on the World." Some evicted tenants found new holdings elsewhere; others lingered in the ruins of their leveled cabins until driven away by force; many squatted by the roadsides, burrowing in ditches or erecting rude huts or "sheelings" made of turf and branches; some gave up and entered the workhouses; thousands died of hunger, fever, and exposure. "[W]e are all without a place to lea our head," wrote one of the more fortunate, "And this day we are without a Bit to eat and I wood be Dead long go only for two Nebours that ofen gives me a Bit for god Sake But little ever I thought that it wood come to my turn to Beg Nomore."

From Kerby A. Miller, *Emigrants and Exiles, Ireland and the Irish Exodus to North America*, New York: Oxford University Press, 1985, 280–288.

Document 52:
THE DEMAND FOR CATHOLIC EMANCIPATION (1830)
Daniel O'Connell

Roman Catholics in Ireland paid taxes for the Anglican Church and were denied religious, educational and political rights. British and Protestant Irish owned most of the economic assets of Ireland and, in the 1840s allowed millions to starve or immigrate during the Great Potato Famine.

(In a letter to Richard Newton Bennett, member of Parliament)
My dear Bennett,

You ask me (for your friend) what *I want*. The question is easily answered.

For myself *nothing*—for Ireland much.

For Ireland I place my wants in numerical order, not according to their importance but as they chance to come uppermost:

1. The total repeal of the Subletting Act. [ed. note: passed in 1826, the Subletting act subjected tenants who sublet without their landlords' consent to severe legal penalties.]

2. The repeal of the grand jury laws and a new system to be introduced for county taxation on the principle of a parochial election. I have matured a plan for this purpose.

3. The repeal of the Vestry Acts and placing the expense of building etc. churches on those who want or use them. [ed. note: Vestry cess (tax) was levied on all property holders to defray the expenses of performing divine service and maintaining and repairing the buildings of the established (i.e., Protestant) church. In 1826, the various vestry acts had been consolidated into one act.]

4. The total abolition of all tolls and customs except where the public get value for them, as for example, I would leave the toll of stallage in a market house built by individuals or by corporations.

5. A total abolition of corporate monopoly, by abolishing fictitious rights of freedom, by taking away non-resident voters and by giving the freedom to all householders of a certain value in the corporate cities and towns.

6. There should be a strict inquiry into the disposal of corporate property and a public accounting in future.

7. Speedy means should be taken to terminate the existence of the horrid Charter schools. [ed. note: These were schools conducted under the direction of the Incorporated Society for Promoting English Protestant Schools in Ireland. They had been founded about a century previously and from their early years had enjoyed an annual state subsidy.]

8. The education grants should be distributed according to the numbers of each persuasion, and the Kildare Place Society should have no control over public money.

9. The Orangemen and Ribbonmen in the North should be equally disarmed, and the yeomanry in the North reduced to the number in such one of the three other provinces as contains most yeomen.

10. The constabulary should not carry deadly weapons save in case of being attacked, and that force should be put on a scale of gradual reduction with a view to their total abolition. [ed. note: In England the constabulary were only allowed to carry staves, but in Ireland were permitted to carry firearms.]

11. Pecuniary grants should be made for public works in Ireland.

12. The temporalities of the Established Church should be at once taken into the hands of the government so that on the death of each incumbent the revenue should cease except according to the number of Protestants, that is, every Protestant clergyman should be well paid for doing duty, no clergyman to be paid but according to the duty he actually performs. The object is to exonerate the Protestant Dissenters and Catholics from the burden of the Estab-

lished Church. There are Church lands in abundance to form an ample fund for these purposes.

I must add that the temporalities of the Protestant church *must* be reformed or *nothing* is in my judgment done for Ireland. All the rest are trifles compared with this. This is the giant oppression to be prostrated in the first instance.

You will perhaps smile at the extent of my views but recollect that the people of Ireland are the most miserable on the face of the earth and that palliatives will not assuage the daily accumulating evil.

The Repeal of the Union [ed. note: Irish Independence] would *produce* the only radical cure but you ask me to omit that and I only throw it in to show that I have not forgotten or mistaken the cause of all our misery.

From *The Correspondence of Daniel O'Connell, Volume IV (1829–1832)*, edited by Maurice R. O'Connell, Dublin: Blackwater (For the Irish Manuscripts Division), 1977, 244–245.

Document 53:
DO NOT ASK US TO GIVE UP THE BUFFALO FOR THE SHEEP (1867)
Ten Bears

Native Americans suffered the fate of many other indigenous peoples who experienced the forces unleashed by colonization of hunting and living territory. Relentlessly, new settlers took the lands of the Amerindians. Treaties were made and broken over the years. Amerindians were given "reservations" that did not have enough land to support the continuation of a traditional lifestyle. Ten Bears was a Comanche chieftain who pondered peace and acceptance of the dominant white men's ways. Born around 1792, he visited the President in 1872, just before his death. On 20 October 1867, he gave the following speech at the Medicine Lodge Council, at which were gathered the greatest number of warriors and chiefs ever assembled in one place.

My heart is filled with joy, when I see you here, as the brooks fill with water, when the snows melt in the spring, and I feel glad, as the ponies do when the fresh grass starts in the beginning of the year. I heard of your coming, when I was many sleeps away, and I made but few camps before I met you. I knew that you had come to do good to me and to my people. I looked for the benefits, which would last forever, and so my face shines with joy, as I look upon you. My people have never first drawn a bow or fired a gun against the whites. There has been trouble on the line between us, and my young men have danced the war dance. But it was not begun by us.

It was you who sent out the first soldier, and it was we who sent out the second. Two years ago, I came up upon this road, following the buffalo, that my wives and children might have their cheeks plumb, and their bodies warm. But the soldiers fired on us, and since that time there has been a noise, like that of a thunderstorm, and we have not known which way to go. So it was upon the Canadian. Nor have we been made to cry once alone. The blue-dressed soldiers and the Utes came from out of the night, when it was dark and still, and for campfires, they lit our lodges. Instead of hunting game, they killed my braves and the warriors of the tribe cut short their hair for the dead. So it was in Texas. They made sorrow come into our camps, and we went out like the buffalo bulls, when the cows are attacked. When we found them we killed them, and their scalps hang in our lodges.

The Comanches are not weak and blind, like the pups of a dog when seven sleeps old. They are strong and farsighted, like grown horses. We took their road and we went on it. The white women cried, and our women laughed. But there are things which you have said to me which I do not like. They were not sweet like sugar, but bitter like gourds. You said that you wanted to put us upon a reservation, to build us houses and to make us Medicine lodges. I do not want them.

I was born upon the prairie, where the wind blew free, and there was nothing to break the light of the sun. I was born where there were no enclosures, and where everything drew a free breath. I want to die there, and not within walls. I know every stream and every wood between the Rio Grande and the Arkansas. I have hunted and lived over that country. I lived like my fathers before me, and like them, I lived happily.

When I was at Washington, the Great Father told me that all the Comanche land was ours, and that no one should hinder us in living upon it. So why do you ask us to leave the rivers, and the sun, and the wind, and live in houses? Do not ask us to give up the buffalo for the sheep. The young men have heard talk of this, and it has made them sad and angry. Do not speak of it more. I love to carry out the talk I get from the Great Father. When I get goods and presents, I and my people feel glad since it shows that he holds us in his eye. If the Texans had kept out of my country, there might have been peace. But that which you now say we must live on is too small.

The Texans have taken away the places where the grass grew the thickest and the timber was the best. Had we kept that, we might have done the thing you ask. But it is too late. The white man has the country which we loved and we only wish to wander on the prairie until we die. Any good thing you say to me shall not be forgotten. I shall carry it as near to my heart as my children, and it shall be as often on my tongue as the name of the Great Spirit. I want no blood upon my land to stain the grass. I want it all clear and pure, and I wish it so, that all who go through among my people may find peace when they come in, and leave it when they go out.

From W.C. Vanderwerth, *Indian Oratory*, New York: Ballantine Books, 1971, 131–133.

Document 54:
THE BALFOUR DECLARATION (1917)
Arthur J. Balfour

This famous declaration called for a Jewish state in Arab Palestine in the midst of World War I. At the time of this declaration, Lord Rothschild was one of the leaders of the English Jewish community and Lord Balfour was the British Foreign Secretary.

Dear Lord Rothschild:

I have much pleasure in conveying to you, on behalf of His Majesty's Government, the following declaration of sympathy with the Jewish Zionist aspirations which has been submitted to, and approved by, the Cabinet.

"His Majesty's Government view with favour the establishment in Palestine of a national home for the Jewish people, and will use their best endeavours to facilitate the achievement of this object, it being clearly understood that nothing shall be done which may prejudice the civil and religious rights of existing non-Jewish communities in Palestine, or the rights and political status enjoyed by Jews in any other country."

I should be grateful if you would bring this declaration to the knowledge of the Zionist Federation.
Signed: Arthur James Balfour

From *The Israel-Arab Reader, A Documentary History of the Middle East Crisis*, edited by Walter Laqueur, New York: The Citadel Press, 1968, 118.

Document 55:
ON THE DUTIES OF MAN (1848)
Giuseppe Mazzini

Giuseppe Mazzini, one of the leading proponents of the drive to unify Italy, used a combination of fiery nationalism and organizational technique to further the cause of Italian unification. Mazzini thought that nationalism was a divinely-ordained plan to best make use of the particular talents of various peoples. Geography, language, and customs defined nationalities, and any attempt to divide or to ignore the divine plan was doomed to eventual failure. One important distinction between Mazzini's romantic nationalism and the more chauvinistic nationalism espoused by many of his contemporaries is that Mazzini insisted that all nations have a unique contribution to make to civilization, and is superior to others only in the areas of its particular genius. The following selection eloquently states Mazzini's philosophy of nationalism and also contains his warnings not to confuse love of one's own country with intolerance toward another's country.

Your first duties—first as regards importance—are, as I have already told you, towards Humanity. You are men before you are either citizens or fathers. If you do not embrace the whole human family in your affection, if you do not bear witness to your belief in the Unity of that family, consequent upon the Unity of

God, and in that fraternity among the peoples which is destined to reduce that unity to action; if, wheresoever a fellow-creature suffers, or the dignity of human nature is violated by falsehood or tyranny—you are not ready, if able, to aid the unhappy, and do not feel called upon to combat, if able, for the redemption of the betrayed or oppressed—you violate your law of life, you comprehend not that Religion which will be the guide and blessing of the future.

But, you tell me, you cannot attempt united action, distinct and divided as you are in language, customs, tendencies, and capacity. The individual is too insignificant, and Humanity too vast. The mariner of Brittany prays to God as he puts to sea: Help me, my God! My boat is so small and thy ocean so wide! And this prayer is the true expression of the condition of each one of you, until you find the means of infinitely multiplying your forces and powers of action.

This means was provided for you by God when he gave you a country; when, even as a wise overseer of labour distributes the various branches of employment according to the different capacities of the workmen, he divided Humanity into distinct groups or nuclei upon the face of the earth, thus creating the germ of Nationalities. Evil governments have disfigured the divine design. Nevertheless you may still trace it, distinctly marked out—at least as far as Europe is concerned—by the course of the great rivers, the direction of the higher mountains, and other geographical conditions. They have disfigured it by their conquests, their greed, and their jealousy even of the righteous power of others; disfigured it so far that, if we except England and France—there is not perhaps a single country whose present boundaries correspond to that design.

These governments did not, and do not, recognize any country save their own families or dynasty, the egotism of caste. But the Divine design will infallibly be realized. Natural divisions, and the spontaneous, innate tendencies of the peoples, will take the place of the arbitrary divisions sanctioned by evil governments. The map of Europe will be redrawn. The countries of the Peoples, defined by the vote of free men, will arise upon the ruins of the countries of kings and privileged castes, and between these countries harmony and fraternity will exist. And the common work of Humanity, of general amelioration and the gradual discovery and application of its Law of life, being distributed according to local and general capacities, will be wrought out in peaceful and progressive development and advance. Then may each one of you, fortified by the power and the affection of many millions, all speaking the same language, gifted with the same tendencies, and educated by the same historical tradition, hope, even by your own single effort, to be able to benefit all Humanity.

O my brothers, love your Country! Our country is our Home, the house that God has given us, placing therein a numerous family that loves us, and whom we love; a family with whom we sympathize more readily, and whom we understand more quickly than we do others; and which from its being centred around a given spot, and from the homogeneous nature of its elements, is adapted to a special branch of activity. Our country is our common workshop, whence the products of our activity are sent forth for the benefit of the whole world; wherein the tools and implements of labour we can most usefully employ are gathered together: nor may we reject them without disobeying the plan of the Almighty, and diminishing our own strength.

In labouring for our own country on the right principle, we labour for Humanity. Our country is the fulcrum of the lever we have to wield for the common good. If we abandon that fulcrum, we run the risk of rendering ourselves useless not only to humanity but to our country itself. Before men can associate with the nations of which humanity is composed, they must have a National existence. There is no true association except among equals. It is only through our country that we can have a recognized collective existence.

Humanity is a vast army advancing to the conquest of lands unknown, against enemies both powerful and astute. The peoples are the different corps, the divisions of that army. Each of them has its post assigned to it, and its special operation to execute; and the common victory depends upon the exactitude with which those distinct operations shall be fulfilled. Disturb not the order of battle. Forsake not the banner given you by God. Wheresoever you may be, in the centre of whatsoever people circumstances may have placed you, be ever ready to combat for the liberty of that people should it be necessary, but combat in such wise that the blood you shed may reflect glory, not on yourselves alone, but on your country. Say not I, but we. Let each man among you strive to incarnate his country in himself. Let each man among you regard himself as a guarantee, responsible for his fellow-countrymen, and learn so to govern his actions as to cause his country to be loved and respected through him. Your country is the sign of the mission God has given you to fulfill towards Humanity. The faculties and forces of all her sons should be associated in the accomplishment of that mission. The true country is a community of free men and equals, bound together in fraternal concord to labour towards a common aim. You are bound to make it and to maintain it such. The country is not an aggregation, but an association. There is, therefore, no true country without an uniform right. There is no true country where the uniformity of that right is violated by the existence of castes, privilege, and inequality. Where the activity of a portion of the powers and faculties of the individual is either cancelled or dormant; where there is not a common Principle, recognized, accepted, and developed by all, there is no true nation, no People, but only a multitude, a fortuitous agglomeration of men whom circumstances have called together, and whom circumstances may again divide. In the name of the love you bear your country you must peacefully but untiringly combat the existence of privilege and inequality in the land that gave you life.

There is but one sole legitimate privilege, the privilege of Genius when it reveals itself united with virtue. But this is a privilege given by God, and when you acknowledge it and follow its inspiration, you do so freely, exercising your own reason and your own choice. Every privilege which demands submission from you in virtue of power, inheritance, or any other right than the Right common to all, is a usurpation and a tyranny which you are bound to resist and destroy.

Be your country your Temple. God at the summit; a people of equals at the base.

Accept no other formula, no other moral law, if you would not dishonour alike your country and yourselves. Let all secondary laws be but the gradual regulation of your existence by the progressive application of this supreme law. And in order that they may be such, it is necessary that all of you should aid in framing them. Laws framed only by a single fraction of the citizens, can never, in the very nature of things, be other than the mere expression of the thoughts, aspirations, and desires of that fraction; the representation, not of the Country, but of a third or fourth part, of a class or zone of the country.

The laws should be the expression of the universal aspiration and promote the universal good. They should be a pulsation of the heart of the nation. The entire nation should, either directly or indirectly, legislate.

By yielding up this mission into the hands of a few, you substitute the egotism of one class for the Country, which is the union of all classes.

Country is not a mere zone or territory. The true country is the Idea to which it gives birth; it is the Thought of love, the sense of communion which unites in one all the sons of that territory.

So long as a single one amongst your brothers has no vote to represent him in the development of the national life, so long as there is one left to vegetate in ignorance where others are educated, so long as a single man, able and willing to work, languishes in poverty through want of work to do, you have no country in the sense in which country ought to exist—the country of all and for all.

Education, labour, and the franchise, are the three main pillars of the nation. Rest not until you have built them strongly up with your own labour and exertions.

Never deny your sister nations. Be it yours to evolve the life of your country in loveliness and strength; free from all servile fears or skeptical doubts; maintaining as its basis the People; as its guide the consequences of the principles of its Religious Faith, logically and energetically applied; its strength, the united strength of all; its aim, the fulfillment of the mission given to it by God.

And so long as you are ready to die for Humanity, the life of your country will be immortal.

From Emilie A. Venturi, *Joseph Mazzini: A Memoir*, reprinted in *The Western Tradition*, edited by Eugen Weber, Lexington, Mass.: D.C. Heath & Co., 1990, 628–630.

SECTION III 1900–1945

The first half of the twentieth century was dominated by wars, revolutions, and their consequences. World War I unleashed the full fury of industrialized nations with armies. Old animosities and unfulfilled dreams kept the war going despite stalemate on the battlefield and domestic unrest. Some empires did not survive. Germany became a republic and the Austro-Hungarian Empire dissolved. The Russian Empire fell to revolution and the aspirations of its ethnic groups. The Bolshevik Revolution produced the first state headed by a Communist Party, which transformed Russsia and impacted politics throughout the West. Anti-communism became a regular part of political life in the West and was an important facet of the new fascist parties, which attracted many who were unhappy with the consequences of World War I.

National self-determination was the solution offered by the American president, Woodrow Wilson, to a world torn by the war. While the war was still being fought, he announced his Fourteen Points, which called for an association of nations to end the dangerous, unregulated, national state system. Wilson advocated an end to secret treaties, which he believed were responsible for World War I, as well as a reduction in arms, freedom of the seas and trade, a restoration of nations attacked and occupied, and consideration for the minority populations both within and outside Europe. He spoke for the free economic marketplace and democratic participation of peoples in their governance.

But the peace system could not devise acceptable boundaries nor financial payments that would be assumed without resistance. The Paris Peace Conference produced settlements, including the Versailles Treaty for Germany, whose provisions caused problems until the next world war. Wilson's ideas had to be compromised at many points. He had not reckoned with the British, French, Italian, and other allied leaders who had different agendas. Each victor wished to extract the maximum advantage from the victory and the temporary eclipse of Germany and her allies. The huge costs of the war were shunted onto the shoulders of the defeated powers; boundary changes favored the victors and their allies or potential allies.

Wilson placed his hopes in the League of Nations to solve the problems that the peace conference could not resolve. Often he compromised on one point or another, anticipating ultimate resolution in the new international organization. But the League contained a natural contradiction: it was to ensure the international order and protect it from change and, at the same time, it was to be the agent of peaceful change. Of course, success depended on the individual nations. Some wanted revisions of the peace treaties and others wished to retain the results of World War I forever.

Nonetheless, the Peace and the League represented steps forward in bringing some kind of order to the conditions that had produced World War I. The victorious nations acted in concert in attempting to resolve the outstanding issues. Attention was given to some minorities in order to give them self-determination, especially when these were peoples of the German, Ottoman or Austro-Hungarian Empire. Thus a new Poland appeared from Germany, Russia and Austria; the Baltic states of Estonia, Latvia and Lithuania from Russia; Czechoslovakia, Hungary, and enlarged Rumania and Serbia—which became Yugoslavia—from Austria. Bulgaria was also enlarged, and with the collapse of the Ottoman Empire, the national state of Turkey appeared.

Other minorities were to be protected by annual reports to the League of Nations. Thus Poland would answer to the international community for her treatment of the Germans now located in the new Polish state. A "mandate" system was created for colonial areas. For example, the German colonies distributed as booty were put into categories in accordance with their phase of economic and governmental development, and reports were to indicate how the new European administrators treated the subject peoples as they were moved toward eventual self-determination.

The division of the Ottoman Empire gave many Arab lands to the British and French, to the disappointment of many Arabs who had fought against the Turks in order to get independence. In all of these areas, boundaries continued to be drawn that ignored historical and ethnic factors and created problems for the future. The reporting system was disappointing. But another important international responsibility was asserted that took precedence over the rights of sovereign national states.

Attempts continued to limit the horrors of war and the dangers of excessive armaments. Naval conferences locked the great powers into limitations on the numbers of capital ships and submarines that each could have. Some ships above the agreed levels were destroyed. Germany, of course, was singled out for severe disarmament. In 1925, the Geneva Protocol outlawed the use of gases in warfare, although some major nations, notably the United States, did not sign it. With perhaps one or two exceptions, gases were not used again for military purpose until after World War II. The Kellogg-Briand Pact of 1929 outlawed aggressive war as an instrument of foreign policy for the nations which signed the treaty. Within a decade of the signing of the Kellogg-Briand Pact, World War II began in Europe; it was already being fought in Asia. The pact to outlaw war would be used in the International Military Tribunals after World War II to convict Germans and Japanese of violations of international agreements.

Within Western nations, the debates over human rights continued. The franchise was extended to women in most Western nations and to some colonial peoples. Various colonial peoples had already realized that the heady propaganda of national self-determination could be used against the Germans, Austrians and Turks in World War I, but was not tolerated when it was used against the Western nations which controlled the colonies. Disappointments bred future conflict and a search for other support for what would later be called "wars of national liberation." Military skills learned fighting for Britain and France during World War I were used against Britain or France in independence movements. The transfer to many colonies of technology and skills needed for civil and military administration occurred much more quickly than many in the West expected.

Great discussion continued about what governments should do for people. Socialist parties kept up the pressure for change. Here and there, democratic socialists came to power and had their moderate reforms accepted. Britain had two Labour governments in the 1920s; France had socialist-led governments in the crises of the 1930s. However, the specters of communism and socialism were often used in Western politics to stop moderate reforms. Thus a national health program would be labeled "socialized medicine," and it could be associated with conditions in the Soviet Union, in order to increase opposition to it. Pension rights remained weak and trade unions were crippled because of domestic opposition in the West to changes that were later labelled characteristics of a "welfare state." Despite the ideological vigor of such opposition, however, governments were forced to greater activity by the complexity of modern life.

The Great Depression of 1929 stopped a century of growth in Western economies and raised questions about the value of a free market economy. Governments were forced to act, however reluctantly, to deal with the human consequences of depression. Most governments acted inappropriately by cutting and reducing spending. Almost accidentally, spending to get out of depression occurred. John Maynard Keynes produced his theories of "pump priming" which allowed democratic governments with capitalist free market economies to act in crisis: when the economy was flat, governments could borrow and spend and when the economy became over-heated and inflation occurred, governments could tax and reduce the boom, paying back the earlier loans. Leaders would not have to stand paralyzed in the face of depressions.

The decades between World War I and World War II thus present a very mixed picture. In the West, some individuals were admitted into fuller membership in the system and governments accepted greater responsibility for ameliorating human needs. In England public housing was a product of Conservative government in the 1920s; in the United States, the fear of a powerful federal government was overcome by depression-era needs for public projects to create employment and government interference in the economy to help trade or agriculture. The Popular Front (a liberal-left coalition) government in France addressed the problem of a powerful privately-owned national bank and urged a 40 hour work week and two weeks of paid vacation; opposition to such measures overturned the government.

World War II brought massive government intervention into all segments of life, and governments grew to unprecedented size. The suffering of so many in the war caused many Western nations to resolve to do more for the citizenry after the war ended. Britain's Lord Beveridge submitted a report that outlined the post-war welfare state designed to protect individuals from the destitution caused by unemployment, illness, injury or old age. In France, from the underground movement, came a desire to improve the lives of all French people.

In America, however, the sentiments of President Roosevelt's "Freedom from Want and Fear" speech would be combatted by powerful interests that thought the Roosevelt reforms had gone far enough. By 1948, civil rights legislation and a national health program were defeated, and a national campaign was underway to erode the rights of trade unions. The Cold War provided a reason to spend money on projects other than domestic needs.

The Soviet experiment ended with the crushing dictatorship of Joseph Stalin who directed the single party to incredible acts of political repression and controls over his people. A centralized economy provided the framework for the forced industrialization of the Soviet Union.

Agriculture was collectivized and millions were displaced, reduced to hunger or were killed. Ethnic groups' hopes for autonomy or independence were ended in bloodshed. Political opponents within the party or in the various ethnic areas were treated as traitors and the labor camps exploded in numbers. The Great Purge erupted into a long campaign during the late 1930s, and a large number of "Old Bolshevik" leaders were removed from office; in all civil and military organizations and especially the Communist Party, crimes were admitted in ritualized show trials and harsh penalties were meted out. The list of innocent victims is still being assembled in the decade of the 1990s. Speculation continues as to Stalin's motives: was it his personality, fear of the growing fascist movement in Europe, fear of the West's opposition, fear of domestic opponents, fear that the revolution might end? The fear that communism might be exported to other nations terrified many in the West.

Fascism was surely one of the surprises of the era. Variously explained, it appears to have been a new movement, but one that involved traditional ideas or values reinvigorated by the disappointments of World War I. Nationalism spawned by imperialism and the war characterized most fascist movements. Military hierarchy, uniforms and dreams of glory dominated most of these movements. Women were the victims of fascists who prescribed the return to earlier attitudes. "Children, the church, and the kitchen" was a more vulgar German interpretation of National Socialist ideology concerning the place of women. The nation, the racial group and the community were given precedence over individuals. Individual rights were subordinated to the state. Anti-communism made fascism attractive to many. Racialism, reinforced with ultra-nationalism and anti-semitism in the German party, provided simplistic answers to profound problems and created scapegoats to blame for such problems.

Fascists derided democracy and exalted heroic individuals as the answer to leadership and political needs. Adolf Hitler refused to call his party a party. Rather, it was a "movement" that was temporarily forced to play by the rules of the German constitution, which Hitler and his followers despised. In Italy, Mussolini rallied those who could not forget the grandeur of war, the loss of the idealism or demands for national expansion. Factory owners contributed money when he attacked trade unions. The military secretly agreed with his nationalism and provided weapons and transportation. The Church in Italy was absorbed in a struggle against socialism, communism and secularism, and was slow in identifying the threats that fascists represented to human rights and the independence of cultural institutions. Similar interests in Spain coalesced behind Franco and supported his one-party dictatorship. In Hungary, Romania, and many other parts of Europe, similar parties and coalitions of interests were found between the two world wars.

Within Germany, democratic institutions were destroyed and the absolute rule of one party and one man led to assaults upon individual human rights that filled the jails and prisons and led to the erection of concentration camps. Step by step, the Jews of Germany lost their political and economic rights. With the outbreak of the war and the German conquests of Poland and Eastern Europe, great masses of European Jews fell into Hitler's hands. Jews were first herded into ghettoes and starved; then they were relocated into the new concentration camps which were designed to carry out the "final solution." Six million Jews were murdered, the victims of racialist thought carried to its logical, insane conclusion: that those murdered were inferior and could not be tolerated by those who felt themselves superior. Businessmen competed for the contracts to supply gas and to build crematoria. Tens of thousands of Germans and other Europeans worked at or near the camps or were somehow involved in the movement, death or burial of the victims. The German dictatorship allowed no discussion of or information about the Holocaust to appear.

No international institutions or arrangements stopped this drift to Holocaust. Eyes were averted, national sovereignty impeded action, and the war made for other priorities. When information was taken to the powers at war, it was disbelieved, ignored or downgraded. Some survivors lost their faith in a higher power or in their fellow human beings. Some concluded that only a national homeland could protect them from future holocausts and the demand for a national homeland took priority over all other claims. Israel was created, partially to compensate one of history's greatest injustices, the Holocaust. But the seeds of a new injustice were sown in soil of post-war Palestine, plowed by the boots of Arab and Jewish armies, where to this day Arab residents have little right of self-determination.

World War II lasted six long years in Europe and consumed an estimated 40 million lives. The Soviets alone claim losses of 20 million. Two-thirds of European Jews were destroyed. The war caused one of the greatest mass movements of humans in history. These results, in addition to the economic and environmental damages, called for great human efforts for the future.

Again there would be a call for an assembly of nations, the United Nations, to usher in an era of international community control of human affairs. Agreements looked beyond the defeat of Germany and Japan to the post-war era. Nations would cooperate in bringing war criminals to trial. Economic cooperation was proffered with American help and monetary funds, tariffs and trade agreements. The terrifying first use of nuclear weapons did not yet arouse the discussion that it would later: it was enough to deal with the victims of China, Russia, Poland, as well as Buchenwald and Auschwitz.

The horrors of World War II thus compelled strong responses to advance human rights. A discussion of human rights was of greatest importance as the extent of human death and suffering became known with the collapse of Germany and Japan, and as the Cold War turned attention and hostility towards the Soviet Union. In 1945, and in the future, there was a need to codify and enforce basic agreements on what constituted the rights of human beings in the twentieth century.

CHAPTER 8

International Affairs, World War and Individual Rights

Document 56:
HAGUE CONVENTION WITH RESPECT TO THE LAWS AND CUSTOMS OF WAR ON LAND (1899)

The Hague Convention was the major turn-of-the-century agreement on limiting the impact of war. A document of 1899, it was amended in 1907 and remains the primary international code on the treatment of military and civilian people in time of warfare. It regulates the treatment of prisoners of war, civilians, and the use of weapons, among other matters.

...Considering that, while seeking means to preserve peace and prevent armed conflicts among nations, it is likewise necessary to have regard to cases where an appeal to arms may be caused by events which their solicitude could not avert;

Animated by the desire to serve, even in this extreme hypothesis, the interests of humanity and the ever increasing requirements of civilization;

Thinking it important, with this object, to revise the laws and general customs of war, either with the view of defining them more precisely, or of laying down certain limits for the purpose of modifying their severity as far as possible;...

CHAPTER II—ON PRISONERS OF WAR

Article 4. Prisoners of war are in the power of the hostile Government, but not in that of the individuals or corps who captured them.

They must be humanely treated.

All their personal belongings, except arms, horses, and military papers remain their property....

Article 6. The State may utilize the labor of prisoners of war according to their rank and aptitude. Their tasks shall not be excessive, and shall have nothing to do with the military operations....

Article 7. The Government into whose hands prisoners of war have fallen is bound to maintain them.

Failing a special agreement between the belligerents, prisoners of war shall be treated as regards food, quarters, and clothing, on the same footing as the troops of the Government which has captured them.

Article 8. Prisoners of war shall be subject to the laws, regulations, and orders in force in the army of the State into whose hands they have fallen.

Any act of insubordination warrants the adoption, as regards them, of such measures of severity as may be necessary.

Escaped prisoners, recaptured before they have succeeded in rejoining their army, or before quitting the territory occupied by the army that captured them, are liable to disciplinary punishment.

Prisoners who, after succeeding in escaping are again taken prisoners, are not liable to any punishment for the previous flight.

Article 9. Every prisoner of war, if questioned, is bound to declare his true name and rank, and if he disregards this rule, he is liable to a curtailment of the advantages accorded to the prisoners of war of his class....

Article 13. Individuals who follow an army without directly belonging to it, such as newspaper correspondents and reporters, sutlers, contractors, who fall into the enemy's hands, and whom the latter think fit to detain, have a right to be treated as prisoners of war, provided they can produce a certificate from the military authorities of the army they were accompanying.

Article 14. A Bureau for information relative to prisoners of war is instituted, on the commencement of hostilities, in each of the belligerent States, and, when necessary, in the neutral countries on whose territory belligerents have been received. This Bureau is intended to answer all inquiries about prisoners of war, and is furnished by the various services concerned with all the necessary information to enable it to keep an individual return for each prisoner of war. It is kept informed of internments and changes, as well as of admissions into hospital and deaths.

It is also the duty of the Information Bureau to receive and collect all objects of personal use, valuables, letters, etc., found on the battlefields or left by prisoners who have died in hospital or ambulance, and to transmit them to those interested.

Article 15. Relief societies for prisoners of war, which are regularly constituted in accordance with the law of the country with the object of serving as the intermediary for charity, shall receive from the belligerents for themselves and their duly accredited agents every facility, within the bounds of military requirements and Administrative Regulations, for the effective accomplishment of their humane task. Delegates of these Societies may be admitted to the places of internment for the distribution of relief, as also to the halting places of repatriated prisoners, if furnished with a personal permit by the military authorities, and on giving an engagement in writing to comply with all their Regulations for order and police....

Article 18. Prisoners of war shall enjoy every latitude in the exercise of their religion, including attendance at their own church services, provided only they comply with the regulations for order and police issued by the military authorities....

Article 20. After the conclusion of peace, the repatriation of prisoners of war shall take place as speedily as possible.

Article 21. The obligations of belligerents with regard to the sick and wounded are governed by the Geneva Convention of the 22nd August, 1864, subject to any modifications which may be introduced into it.

Article 22. The right of belligerents to adopt means of injuring the enemy is not unlimited.

Article 23. Besides the prohibitions provided by special Conventions, it is especially prohibited:

(a) To employ poison or poisoned arms;

(b) To kill or wound treacherously individuals belonging to the hostile nation or army;

(c) To kill or wound an enemy who, having laid down arms, or having no longer means of defence, has surrendered at discretion;

(d) To declare that no quarter will be given;

(e) To employ arms, projectiles or material of a nature to cause superfluous injury;

(f) To make improper use of a flag of truce, the national flag, or military ensigns and the enemy's uniform, as well as the distinctive badges of the Geneva Convention;

(g) To destroy or seize the enemy's property, unless such destruction or seizure be imperatively demanded by the necessities of war.

Article 24. Ruses of war and the employment of methods necessary to obtain information about the enemy and the country, are considered *allowable*.

Article 25. The attack or bombardment of towns, villages, habitations or buildings which are not defended, is prohibited.

Article 26. The Commander of an attacking force, before commencing a bombardment, except in the case of an assault, should do all he can to warn the authorities.

Article 27. In sieges and bombardments all necessary steps should be taken to spare as far as possible edifices devoted to religion, art, science, and charity, hospitals, and places where the sick and wounded are collected, provided they are not used at the same time for military purposes.

The besieged should indicate these buildings or places by some particular and visible signs, which should previously be notified to the assailants.

Article 28. The pillage of a town or place, even when taken by assault, is prohibited.

Chapter II—On Spies

Article 29. An individual can only be considered a spy if, acting clandestinely, or on false pretences, he obtains or seeks to obtain information in the zone of operations of a belligerent, with the intention of communicating to the hostile party.

Thus, soldiers not in disguise who have penetrated into the zone of operations of hostile army to obtain information are not considered spies. Similarly, the following are not considered spies: soldiers or civilians, carrying out their mission openly, charged with the delivery of despatches destined either for their own army or for that of the enemy. To this class belong likewise individuals sent in balloons to deliver despatches, and generally to maintain communication between the various parts of an army or a territory.

Article 30. A spy taken in the act cannot be punished without previous trial....

Article 42. Territory is considered occupied when it is actually placed under the authority of the hostile army.

The occupation applies only to the territory where such authority is established, and in a position to assert itself.

Article 43. The authority of the legitimate power having actually passed into the hands of the occupant, the latter shall take all steps in his power to re-establish and insure, as far as possible, public order and safety, while respecting, unless absolutely prevented, the laws in force in the country.

Article 44. Any compulsion of the population of occupied territory to take part in military operations against its own country is prohibited.

Article 45. Any pressure on the population of occupied territory to take the oath to the hostile Power is prohibited.

Article 46. Family honors and rights, individual lives and private property, as well as religious convictions and liberty, must be respected.

Private property cannot be confiscated.

Article 47. Pillage is formally prohibited.

Article 48. If, in the territory occupied, the occupant collects the taxes, dues, and tolls imposed for the benefit of the State, he shall do it, as far as possible, in accordance with the rules in existence and the assessment in force, and will in consequence be bound to defray the expenses of the administration of the occupied territory on the same scale as that by which the legitimate Government was bound.

Article 49. If, besides the taxes mentioned in the preceding Article, the occupant levies other money taxes in the occupied territory, this can only be for military necessities or the administration of such territory.

Article 50. No general penalty, pecuniary or otherwise, can be inflicted on the population on account of the acts of individuals for which it cannot be regarded as collectively responsible....

Article 52. Neither requisitions in kind nor services can be demanded from communes or inhabitants except for the necessities of the army of occupation. They must be in proportion to the resources of the country, and of such a nature as not to involve the population in the obligation of taking part in military operations against their country.

These requisitions and services shall only be demanded on the authority of the Commander in the locality occupied.

The contributions in kind shall, as far as possible, be paid for in ready money; if not, their receipt shall be acknowledged.

Article 53. An army of occupation can only take possession of the cash, funds, and property liable to requisition belonging strictly to the State, depots of arms, means of transport, stores and supplies, and, generally, all movable property of the State which may be used for military operations.

Railway plants, land telegraphs, telephones, steamers, and other ships, apart from cases governed by maritime law, as well as depots of arms and, generally, all kinds of war materials, even though belonging to Companies or to private persons, are likewise material which may serve for military operations, but they must be restored at the conclusion of peace, and indemnities paid for them....

Article 55. The occupying State shall only be regarded as administrator and usufructuary of the public buildings, real property, forests, and agricultural works belonging to the hostile State, and situated in the occupied country. It must protect the capital of these properties, and administer it according to the rules of usufruct.

Article 56. The property of the communes, that of religious, charitable, and educational institutions, and those of arts and science, even when State property, shall be treated as private property.

All seizure of, and destruction, or intentional damage done to such institutions, to historical monuments, works of art or science, is prohibited, and should be made the subject of proceedings....

From Committee on Foreign Affairs, United States House of Representatives, *Human Rights Documents, A Compilation of Documents Pertaining to Human Rights*, Washington, D.C.: GPO, 1983, 305–324.

Document 57:
THOUGHTS FOR THE TIMES ON WAR AND DEATH (1915)
Sigmund Freud

The twentieth century has been a disturbing time in which to live, and Sigmund Freud, the founder of psychoanalysis, was one of its most important social critics. The individual, Freud argued, is forced, simply by belonging to a society with a moral code of behavior, to face constant conflicts between the instinctual, selfish needs of the self and demands imposed by society. In this conflict often lies the basis for neuroses. Freud saw no easy solution to this dilemma. He could not agree with some earlier thinkers such as Nietzsche, who claimed that the instinctual drives of individuals were supreme. Freud thought that not only must the pleasure principle be recognized, but that it must also be controlled. No hedonist, he asserted that the preservation of society demanded that selfish gratification must, albeit with difficulty, be subsumed to the common interest. Freud turned his attention to the subject of war in 1915. His most famous treatment of the subject, Civilization and its Discontents (1930), *is well-known, but Freud's views of war are admirably summed up in* Thoughts for the Times on War and Death (1915), *which is excerpted in the following passage.*

Swept as we are into the vortex of this wartime, our information one-sided, ourselves too near to focus the mighty transformations which have already taken place or are beginning to take place, and without a glimmering of the inchoate future, we are incapable of apprehending the significance of the thronging impressions, and know not what value to attach to the judgments we form. We are constrained to believe that never has any event been destructive of so much that is valuable in the common wealth of humanity, nor so misleading to many of the clearest intelligences, nor so debasing to the highest that we know. Science herself has lost her passionless impartiality; in their deep embitterment her servants seek for weapons from her with which to contribute towards the defeat of the enemy. The anthropologist is driven to declare the opponent inferior and degenerate; the psychiatrist to publish his diagnosis of the enemy's disease of mind or spirit. But probably our sense of these immediate evils is disproportionately strong, and we are not entitled to compare them with the evils of other times of which we have not undergone the experience.

The individual who is not himself a combatant—and so a wheel in the gigantic machinery of war—feels conscious of disorientation, and of an inhibition in his powers and activities. I believe that he will welcome any indication, however slight, which may enable him to find out what is wrong with himself at least. I propose to distinguish two among the most potent factors in the mental distress felt by noncombatants, against which it is such a heavy task to struggle, and to treat of them here....

When I speak of disillusionment, everyone at once knows what I mean. One need not be a sentimentalist; one may perceive the biological and psychological necessity of suffering in the economics of human life, and yet condemn war both in its means and in its aims, and devoutly look forward to the cessation of all wars. True, we have told ourselves that wars can never cease so long as nations live under such widely differing conditions, so long as the value of individual life is in each nation so variously computed, and so long as the animosities which divide them represent such powerful instinctual forces in the mind. And we were prepared to find that wars between the primitive and the civilized peoples, between those races whom a colour-line divides, nay, wars with and among the undeveloped nationalities of Europe or those whose culture has perished—that for a considerable period such wars would occupy mankind. But we permitted ourselves to have other hopes. We had expected the great ruling powers among the white nations upon whom the leadership of the human species has fallen, who were known to have cultivated world-wide interests, to whose creative powers were due our technical advances in the direction of dominating nature, as well as the artistic and scientific acquisitions of the mind—peoples such as these we had expected to succeed in discovering another way of settling misunderstandings and conflicts of interest. Within each of these nations there prevailed high standards of accepted custom for the individual, to which his manner of life was bound to conform if he desired a share in communal privileges. These ordinances, frequently too stringent, exacted a great deal from him, much self-restraint, much renunciation of instinctual gratification. He was especially forbidden to make use of the immense advantages to be gained by the practice of lying and deception in the competition of his fellow-men. The civilized state regarded these accepted standards as the basis of its existence; stern were its proceedings when an impious hand was laid upon them; frequent the pronouncement that to subject them even to examination by a critical intelligence was entirely impracticable. It could be assumed therefore, that the state itself would respect them, nor would contemplate undertaking any infringement of what it acknowledged as the basis of its own existence. To be sure, it was evident that within these civilized states were mingled remnants of certain other races who were universally unpopular and had therefore been only reluctantly, and even so not to the fullest extent, admitted to participation in the common task of civilization, for which they had shown themselves suitable enough. But the great nations themselves, it might have been supposed, had acquired so much comprehension of their common interests, and enough tolerance for the differences that existed between them, that 'foreigner' and 'enemy' could no longer, as still in antiquity, be regarded as synonymous....

Then the war in which we had refused to believe broke out, and brought—disillusionment. Not only was it more sanguinary and more destructive than any war of other days, because of the enormously increased perfection of weapons of attack and defence; but it is at least as cruel, as embittered and as implacable as any that has preceded it. It sets at naught all those restrictions known as International Law, which in peace-time the states had bound themselves to observe; it ignores the prerogatives of the wounded and the medical service, the distinction between civil and military sections of the population, the claims of private property. It tramples in blind fury on all that comes in its way, as though there were to be no future and no goodwill among men after it has passed. It rends all bonds of fellowship between the contending peoples, and threatens to leave such a legacy of embitterment as will make any renewal of such bonds impossible for a long time to come....

Nations are in a measure represented by the states which they have formed; these states, by the governments which administer them. The individual in any given nation has in this war a terrible opportunity to convince himself of what would occasionally strike him in peace-time—that the state has forbidden to the individual the practice of wrong-doing, not because it desired to abolish it, but because it desires to monopolize it, like salt and tobacco. The warring state permits itself every such misdeed, every such act of violence, as would disgrace the individual man. It practices not only the accepted stratagems, but also deliberate lying and deception against the enemy; and this, too, in a measure which appears to surpass the usage of former wars. The state exacts the utmost degree of obedience and sacrifice from its citizens, but at the same time treats them as children by maintaining an excess of secrecy, and a censorship of news and expressions of opinion that renders the spirits of those thus intellectually oppressed defenceless against every unfavourable turn of events and every sinister rumour. It absolves itself from the guarantees and contracts it had formed with other states, and makes unabashed confession of its rapacity and lust for power, which the private individual is then called upon to sanction in the name of patriotism.

Nor may it be objected that the state cannot refrain from wrong-doing, since that would place it at a disadvantage. It is no less disadvantageous, as a general rule, for the individual man to conform to the customs of morality and refrain from brutal arbitrary conduct; and the state but seldom proves able to indemnify him for the sacrifices it exacts. It cannot be a matter for astonishment, therefore, that this relaxation of all the moral ties between the greater units of mankind should have had a seducing influence on the morality of individuals; for our conscience is not the inflexible judge that ethical teachers are wont to declare it, but in its origin is 'dread of the community' and nothing else. When the community has no rebuke to make, there is an end of all suppression of the baser passions, and men perpetrate deeds of cruelty, fraud, treachery and barbarity so incompatible with their civilization that one would have held them to be impossible....

In criticism of this disillusionment, certain things must be said. Strictly speaking, it is not justified, for it consists in the destruction of—an illusion! We welcome illusions because they spare us emotional distress, and enable us instead to indulge in gratification. We must not then complain if now and again they come into conflict with some portion of reality, and are shattered against it.

Two things in this war have evoked our sense of disillusionment: the destitution shown in moral relations externally by the states which in their interior relations pose as the guardians of accepted moral usage, and the brutality in behaviour shown by individuals, whom, as partakers in the highest form of human civilization, one would not have credited with such a thing....

"Thoughts for the Times on War and Death," from *The Collected Works of Sigmund Freud*, Vol. IV. Reprinted by permission of Harper & Row Publishers.

Document 58:
DEFENCE OF THE REALM ACT (D.O.R.A.) (1915)

Britain was a model for the development of bills of rights and rules of law. However, under the stress of World War I, the Defence of the Realm Act, an act with vague language and arbitrary power assigned to law enforcement officials, was passed. Complaints would even be filed against individuals playing Beethoven—an obvious aid to the German war effort!

An Act to confer on His Majesty in Council power to make Regulations during the present War for the Defence of the Realm.

Be it enacted by the King's most Excellent Majesty by and with the advice and consent of the Lords Spiritual and Temporal, and Commons in this present Parliament assembled, and by the authority of the same as follows:

1. His Majesty in Council has power during the continuance of the present war to issue regulations as to the powers and duties of the Admiralty and Army Council, and of the members of His Majesty's forces, and other persons acting on His behalf, for securing the public safety and defence of the realm; and may by such regulations authorize the trial by courts martial and punishment of persons contravening any of the provisions of such regulations designed—

(a) to prevent persons communicating with the enemy or obtaining information for that purpose or any purpose calculated to jeopardize the success of the operations of any of His Majesty's forces or to assist the enemy; or

(b) to secure the safety of any means of communication, or of railways, docks or harbours; in a like manner as if such persons were subject to military law and had on active service committed an offence under section five of the Army Act.

Copyright © Arthur Marwick 1965. *The Deluge.* By permission of Little Brown and Company.

Document 59:
THE FOURTEEN POINTS (1918)
Woodrow Wilson

The Fourteen Points summarized some of the major political values of American and Western thought. Self-determination and greater democracy fill many of the points. Problems arose, however, because some Americans at home did not agree with Wilson. Germans felt betrayed because these points were violated at the peace conference after the war. America's allies rejected several of the points because they conflicted with their goals.

There is no confusion of counsel among the adversaries of the Central Powers, no uncertainty of principle, no vagueness of detail. The only secrecy of counsel, the only lack of fearless frankness, the only failure to make definite statement of the objects of the war, lies with Germany and her allies. The issues of life and death hang upon these definitions. No statesman who has the least conception of his responsibility ought for a moment to permit himself to continue this tragical and appalling outpouring of blood and treasure unless he is sure beyond a peradventure that the objects of the vital sacrifice are part and parcel of the very life of society and that the people for whom he speaks think them right and imperative as he does....

It will be our wish and purpose that the processes of peace, when they are begun, shall be absolutely open and that they shall involve and permit henceforth no secret understandings of any kind. The day of conquest and aggrandizement is gone by; so is also the day of secret covenants entered into in the interest of particular governments and likely at some unlooked-for moment to upset the peace of the world....This happy fact...makes it possible for every nation whose purposes are consistent with justice and the peace of the world to avow now or at any other time the objects it has in view....

We demand in this war...nothing peculiar to ourselves. It is that the world be made fit and safe to live in; and particularly that it be made safe for every peace-loving nation which, like our own, wishes to live its own life, determine its own institutions, be assured of justice and fair dealing by the other peoples of the world as against force and selfish aggression. All the peoples of the world are in effect partners in this interest, and for our own part we see very clearly that unless justice be done to others it will not be done to us. The program of the world's peace, therefore, is our program; and that program, the only possible program, as we see it, is this:

I. Open covenants of peace, openly arrived at, after which there shall be no private international understandings of any kind but diplomacy shall proceed always frankly and in the public view.

II. Absolute freedom of navigation upon the seas, outside territorial waters, alike in peace and in war, except as the seas may be closed in whole or in part by international action for the enforcement of international covenants.

III. The removal, so far as possible, of all economic barriers and the establishment of an equality of trade conditions among all the nations consenting to the peace and associating themselves for its maintenance.

IV. Adequate guarantees given and taken that national armaments will be reduced to the lowest point consistent with domestic safety.

V. A free, open-minded, and absolutely impartial adjustment of all colonial claims, based upon a strict observance of the principle that in determining all such questions of sovereignty the interests of the populations concerned must have equal weight with the equitable claims of the government whose title is to be determined.

VI. The evacuation of all Russian territory and such a settlement of all questions affecting Russia as will secure the best and freest cooperation of the other nations of the world in obtaining for her an unhampered and unembarrassed opportunity for the independent determination of her own political development and national policy and assure her of a sincere welcome into the society of free nations under institutions of her own choosing; and, more than a welcome, assistance also of every kind that she may need and may herself desire....

VII. Belgium, the whole world will agree, must be evacuated and restored, without any attempt to limit the sovereignty which she enjoys in common with all other free nations. No other single act will serve as this will serve to restore confidence among the nations in the laws which they have themselves set and determined for the government of their relations with one another. Without this healing act the whole structure and validity of international law is forever impaired.

VIII. All French territory should be freed and the invaded portions restored, and the wrong done to France by Prussia in 1871 in the matter of Alsace-Lorraine, which has unsettled the peace of the world for nearly fifty years, should be righted, in order that peace may once more be made secure in the interest of all.

IX. A readjustment of the frontiers of Italy should be effected along clearly recognizable lines of nationality.

X. The peoples of Austria-Hungary, whose place among the nations we wish to see safeguarded and assured, should be accorded the freest opportunity of autonomous development.

XI. Rumania, Serbia, and Montenegro should be evacuated; occupied territories restored; Serbia accorded free and secure access to the sea; and the relations of the several Balkan states to one another determined by friendly counsel along historically established lines of allegiance and nationality; and international guarantees of the political and economic independence and territorial integrity of the several Balkan states should be entered into.

XII. The Turkish portions of the present Ottoman Empire should be assured a secure sovereignty, but other nationalities which are now under Turkish rule should be assured an undoubted security of life and an absolutely unmolested opportunity of autonomous development, and the Dardanelles should be permanently opened as free passage to the ships and commerce of all nations under international guarantees.

XIII. An independent Polish state should be erected which should include the territories inhabited by indisputably Polish populations, which should be assured a free and secure access to the sea, and whose political and economic independence and territorial integrity should be guaranteed by international covenant.

XIV. A general association of nations must be formed under specific covenants for the purpose of affording mutual guarantees of political independence and territorial integrity to great and small states alike.

In regard to these essential rectifications of wrong and assertions of right we feel ourselves to be intimate partners of all the governments and peoples associated together against the Imperialists. We cannot be separated in interest or divided in purpose. We stand together until the end.

For such arrangements and covenants we are willing to fight and to continue to fight until they are achieved; but only because we wish the right to prevail and desire a just and stable peace such as can be secured only by removing the chief provocations to the war, which this program does remove. We have no jealousy of German greatness, and there is nothing in this program that impairs it. We grudge her no achievement or distinction of learning or of pacific enterprise such as have made her record very bright and very enviable. We do not wish to injure her or to block in any way her legitimate influence or power. We do not wish to fight her either with arms or with hostile arrangements of trade if she is willing to associate herself with us and the other peace-loving nations of the world in covenants of justice and law and fair dealing. We wish her only to accept a place of equality among the peoples of the world—the new world in which we now live—instead of a place of mastery.

Neither do we presume to suggest to her any alteration or modification of her institutions. But it is necessary, we must frankly say, and necessary as a preliminary to any intelligent dealings with her on our part, that we should know whom her spokesmen speak for when they speak to us, whether for the Reichstag majority or for the military party and the men whose creed is imperial domination.

From *Congressional Record—Senate, First Session of the Sixty-Sixty Congress of the United States of America, Vol. LVI*, Washington, D.C., GPO, 1918, 680–1.

Document 60:
THE COVENANT OF THE LEAGUE OF NATIONS (1919)
(Edition embodying Amendments in force, 1 February 1938)

The statesmen of the allied powers devised peace treaties at the end of of World War I and at the same time wrote a constitutional document for the League of Nations. The League was to represent a step forward in creating a community of nations which would institute an international rule of law. The Covenant outlines the major characteristics of the League. Note especially attitudes towards individual and collective rights, mechanisms for change and means to maintain the existing international order.

Article 8

1. The Members of the League recognise that the maintenance of peace requires the reduction of national armaments to the lowest point consistent with national safety, and the enforcement by common action of international obligations.

2. The Council, taking account of the geographical situation and circumstances of each State, shall formulate plans for such reduction for the consideration and action of the several Governments....

5. The Members of the League agree that the manufacture by private enterprise of munitions and implements of war is open to grave objections. The Council shall advise how the evil effects attendant upon such manufacture can be prevented, due regard being had to the necessities of those Members of the League which are not able to manufacture the munitions and implements of war necessary for their safety....

Article 10. The Members of the League undertake to respect and preserve, as against external aggression, the territorial integrity and existing political independence of all Members of the League. In case of any such aggression, or in case of any threat or danger of such aggression, the Council shall advise upon the means by which this obligation shall be fulfilled.

Article 11

1. Any war or threat of war, whether immediately affecting any of the Members of the League or not, is hereby declared a matter of concern to the whole League, and the League shall take any action that may be deemed wise and effectual to safeguard the peace of nations. In case any such emergency should arise, the Secretary-General shall, on the request of any Member of the League, forthwith summon a meeting of the Council.

2. It is also declared to be the friendly right of each Member of the League to bring to the attention of the Assembly or of the Council any circumstance whatever affecting international relations which threatens to disturb international peace or the good understanding between nations upon which peace depends.

Article 12

1. The Members of the League agree that, if there should arise between them any dispute likely to lead to a rupture, they will submit the matter either to arbitration or judicial settlement or to enquiry by the Council, and they agree in no case to resort to war until three months after the award by the arbitrators or the judicial decision, or the report by the Council....

Article 13

1. The Members of the League agree that, whenever any dispute shall arise between them which they recognise to be suitable for submission to arbitration or judicial settlement, and which cannot be satisfactorily settled by diplomacy, they will submit the whole subject-matter to arbitration or judicial settlement.

2. Disputes as to the interpretation of a Treaty, as to any question of international law, as to the existence of any fact which, if established, would constitute a breach of any international obligation, or as to the extent and nature of the reparation to be made for any such breach, are declared to be among those which are generally suitable for submission to arbitration or judicial settlement.

3. For the consideration of any such dispute, the Court to which the case is referred shall be the Permanent Court of International Justice, established in accordance with Article 14, or any tribunal agreed on by the parties to the dispute or stipulated in any Convention existing between them.

4. The Members of the League agree that they will carry out in full good faith any award or decision that may be rendered, and that they will not resort to war against a Member of the League which complies therewith. In the event of any failure to carry out such an award or decision, the Council shall propose what steps should be taken to give effect thereto.

Article 14. The Council shall formulate and submit to the Members of the League for adoption plans for the establishment of a Permanent Court of International Justice. The Court shall be competent to hear and determine any dispute of an international character which the parties thereto submit to it. The Court may also give an advisory opinion upon any dispute or question referred to it by the Council or by the Assembly.

Article 15

1. If there should arise between Members of the League any dispute likely to lead to a rupture, which is not submitted to arbitration or judicial settlement in accordance with Article 13, the Members of the League agree that they will submit the matter to the Council. Any party to the dispute may effect such submission by giving notice of the existence of the dispute to the Secretary-General, who will make all necessary arrangements for a full investigation and consideration thereof.

2. For this purpose the parties to the dispute will communicate to the Secretary-General, as promptly as possible, statements of their case with all the relevant facts and papers, and the Council may forthwith direct the publication thereof.

3. The Council shall endeavour to effect a settlement of the dispute, and, if such efforts are successful, a statement shall be made public giving such facts and explanations regarding the dispute and the terms of settlement thereof as the Council may deem appropriate.

4. If the dispute is not thus settled, the Council, either unanimously or by a majority vote, shall make and publish a report containing a statement of the facts of the dispute and the recommendations which are deemed just and proper in regard thereto.

5. Any Member of the League represented on the Council may make a public statement of the facts of the dispute and of its conclusions regarding the same.

6. If a report by the Council is unanimously agreed to by the members thereof, other than the representatives of one or more of the parties to the dispute, the Members of the League agree that they will not go to war with any party to the dispute which complies with the recommendations of the report.

7. If the Council fails to reach a report which is unanimously agreed to by the members thereof, other than the representatives of one or more of the parties to the dispute, the Members of the League reserve to themselves the right to take such action as they shall consider necessary for the maintenance of right and justice.

8. If the dispute between the parties is claimed by one of them, and is found by the Council to arise out of a matter which by international law is solely within the domestic jurisdiction of that party, the Council shall so report, and shall make no recommendation as to its settlement.

9. The Council may in any case under this Article refer the dispute to the Assembly. The dispute shall be so referred at the request of either party to the dispute provided that such request be made within fourteen days after the submission of the dispute to the Council.

10. In any case referred to the Assembly, all the provisions of this Article and of Article 12, relating to the action and powers of the Council, shall apply to the action and powers of the Assembly, if concurred in by the representatives of those Members of the League represented on the Council, and of a majority of the other Members of the League, exclusive in each case of the representatives of the parties to the dispute, shall have the same force as a report by the Council concurred in by all the members thereof other than the representatives of one or more of the parties to the dispute.

Article 16

1. Should any Member of the League resort to war in disregard of its Covenants under Articles 12, 13 or 15, it shall *ipso facto* be deemed to have committed an act of war against all other Members of the League, which hereby undertake immediately to subject it to the severance of all trade or financial relations, the prohibition of all intercourse between their nationals and the nationals of the Covenant-breaking State, and the prevention of all financial, commercial or personal intercourse between the nationals of the Covenant-breaking State and the nationals of any other State, whether a Member of the League or not.

2. It shall be the duty of the Council in such case to recommend to the several Governments concerned what effective military, naval or air force the Members of the League shall severally contribute to the armed forces to be used to protect the Covenant of the League.

3. The Members of the League agree, further, that they will mutually support one another in the financial and economic measures which are taken under this Article, in order to minimise the loss and inconvenience resulting from the above measures, and that they will mutually support one another in resisting any special measures aimed at one of their number by the Covenant-breaking State, and that they will take the necessary steps to afford passage through their territory to the forces of any of the Members of the League which are co-operating to protect the Covenants of the League.

4. Any Member of the League which has violated any Covenant of the League may be declared to be no longer a Member of the League by a vote of the Council concurred in by the representatives of all the other Members of the League represented thereon....

Article 22

1. To those colonies and territories, which as a consequence of the late war have ceased to be under the sovereignty of the States which formerly governed them, and which are inhabited by peoples not yet able to stand by themselves under the strenuous conditions of the modern world, there should be applied the principle that the well-being and development of such peoples form a sacred trust of civilisation, and that securities for the performance of this trust should be embodied in this Covenant.

2. The best method of giving practical effect to this principle is that the tutelage of such peoples should be entrusted to advanced nations who, by reason of their resources, their experience, or their geographical position, can best undertake this responsibility, and who are willing to accept it, and that this tutelage should be exercised by them as Mandatories on behalf of the League.

3. The character of the Mandate must differ according to the stage of the development of

the people, the geographical situation of the territory, its economic conditions and other similar circumstances.

4. Certain communities formerly belonging to the Turkish Empire have reached a stage of development where their existence as independent nations can be provisionally recognised subject to the rendering of administrative advice and assistance by a Mandatory until such time as they are able to stand alone. The wishes of these communities must be a principal consideration in the selection of the Mandatory.

5. Other peoples, especially those of Central Africa, are at such a stage that the Mandatory must be responsible for the administration of the territory under conditions which will guarantee freedom of conscience and religion, subject only to the maintenance of public order and morals, the prohibition of abuses such as the slave trade, the arms traffic and the liquor traffic, and the prevention of the establishment of fortifications or military and naval bases, and of military training of the natives for other than police purposes and the defence of territory, and will also secure equal opportunities for the trade and commerce of other Members of the League.

6. There are territories, such as South-West Africa and certain of the South Pacific Islands, which, owing to the sparseness of their population, or their small size, or their remoteness from the centres of civilisation, or their geographical contiguity to the territory of the Mandatory, and other circumstances, can be best administered under the laws of the Mandatory as integral portions of its territory, subject to the safeguards above mentioned in the interests of the indigenous population.

7. In every case of Mandate, the Mandatory shall render to the Council an annual report in reference to the territory committed to its charge....

Article 23. Subject to and in accordance with the provisions of international Conventions existing or hereafter to be agreed upon, the Members of the League—

(a) Will endeavour to secure and maintain fair and humane conditions of labour for men, women and children, both in their own countries and in all countries to which their commercial and industrial relations extend, and for that purpose will establish and maintain the necessary international organisations.

(b) Undertake to secure just treatment of the native inhabitants of territories under their control.

(c) Will entrust the League with the general supervision over the execution of agreements with regard to the traffic in women and children, and the traffic in opium and other dangerous drugs.

(d) Will entrust the League with the general supervision of the trade in arms and ammunition with the countries in which the control of this traffic is necessary in the common interest.

(e) Will make provision to secure and maintain freedom of communications and of transit and equitable treatment for the commerce of all Members of the League. In this connection, the special necessities of the regions devastated during the war of 1914–18 shall be borne in mind.

(f) Will endeavour to take steps in matters of international concern for the prevention and control of disease....

From *Congressional Record—Senate, First Session of the Sixty-Sixth Congress of the United States of America, Vol. XVIII*, Washington, D.C., GPO, 1919, 2340–2350.

Document 61:
ROUMANIAN MINORITY TREATY

The new or enlarged nations of Eastern Europe after World War I signed treaties that committed them to respect the rights of national or religous minorities in the new states. Each treaty was similar, with special articles covering the specific minorities within each nation. Below is the treaty for Romania. These treaties symbolize the responsibility of the international community for arrangements to protect minorities. The signatory powers were to report to the League on these minorities.

The United States of America, the British Empire, France, Italy, and Japan, the Principal Allied and Associated Powers, on the one hand; and Roumania, on the other hand; whereas under Treaties to which the Principal Allied and Associated Powers are parties large accessions of territory are being and will be made to the Kingdom of Roumania, and whereas Roumania desires of her own free will to give full guarantees of liberty and justice to all inhabitants both of the old Kingdom of Roumania and of the territory added thereto, to whatever race, language or religion they may belong...

Article 3....Roumania admits and declares to be Roumanian nationals *ipso facto* and without the requirement of any formality all persons habitually resident at the date of the coming into force of the present Treaty within the whole territory of Roumania, including the extensions made by the Treaties of Peace with Austria and Hungary, or any other extensions which may hereafter be made, if such persons are not at that date nationals of a foreign state other than Austria or Hungary.

Nevertheless, Austrian and Hungarian nationals who are over eighteen years of age will be entitled under the conditions contained in the said Treaties to opt for any other nationality which may be open to them. Option by a husband will cover his wife and option by parents will cover their children under eighteen years of age.

Persons who have exercised the above right to opt must within the succeeding twelve months transfer their place of residence to the State for which they have opted. They will be entitled to retain their immovable property in Roumanian territory. They may carry with them their movable property of every description. No export duties may be imposed upon them in connection with the removal of such property.

Article 4. Roumania admits and declares to be Roumanian nationals *ipso facto* and without the requirement of any formality persons of Austrian Hungarian nationality who were born in the territory transferred to Roumania by the Treaties of Peace with Austria and Hungary, or subsequently transferred to her, of parents habitually resident there, even if at the date of the coming into force of the present Treaty they are not themselves habitually resident there.

Nevertheless, within two years after the coming into force of the present Treaty, these persons may make a declaration before the competent Roumanian authorities in the country in which they are resident, stating that they abandon Roumanian nationality, and they will then cease to be considered as Roumanian nationals. In this connection a declaration by a husband will cover his wife, and a declaration by parents will cover their children under eighteen years of age.

Article 5. Roumania undertakes to put no hindrance in the way of the exercise of the right which the persons concerned have, under the Treaties concluded or to be concluded by the Allied and Associated Powers with Austria and Hungary, to choose whether or not they will acquire Roumanian nationality.

Article 6. All persons born in Roumanian territory who are not born nationals of another State shall *ipso facto* become Roumanian nationals.

Article 7. Roumania undertakes to recognize as Roumanian nationals *ipso facto* and without the requirement of any formality Jews inhabiting any Roumanian territory, who do not possess other nationality.

Article 8. All Roumanian nationals shall be equal before the law and shall enjoy the same civil and political rights without distinction as to race, language or religion.

Differences of religion, creed or confession shall not prejudice any Roumanian national in matters relating to the enjoyment of civil or political rights, as for instance admission to public employments, functions and honours, or the exercise of professions and industries.

No restriction shall be imposed on the free use by any Roumanian national of any language in private intercourse, in commerce, in religion, in the press or in public-actions of any kind, or at public meetings.

Notwithstanding any establishment by the Roumanian Government of an official language, adequate facilities shall be given to Roumanian nationals of non-Roumanian speech for the use of their language, either orally or in writing, before the courts.

Article 9. Roumanian nationals who belong to racial, religious or linguistic minorities shall enjoy the same treatment and security in law and in fact as the other Roumanian nationals. In particular they shall have an equal right to establish, manage and control at their own expense charitable, religious and social institutions, schools and other educational establishments, with the right to use their own language and to exercise their religion freely therein.

Article 10. Roumania will provide in the public educational system in towns and districts in which a considerable proportion of Roumanian nationals of other than Roumanian speech are resident adequate facilities for ensuring that in the primary schools the instruction shall be given to the children of such Roumanian nationals through the medium of their own language. This provision shall not prevent the Roumanian Government from making the teaching of the Roumanian language obligatory in the said schools.

In towns and districts where there is a considerable proportion of Roumanian nationals belonging to racial, religious or linguistic minorities, these minorities shall be assured an equitable share in the enjoyment and application of the sums which may be provided out of public funds under the State, municipal or other budget, for educational, religious or charitable purposes....

Article 12. Roumania agrees that the stipulations in the foregoing Articles, so far as they affect persons belonging to racial, religious or linguistic minorities, constitute obligations of international concern and shall be placed under the guarantee of the League of Nations. They shall not be modified without the assent of a majority of the Council of the League of Nations. The United States, the British Empire, France, Italy and Japan hereby agree not to withold their assent from any modification to these Articles which is in due form assented to by a majority of the Council of the League of Nations.

Roumania agrees that any Member of the Council of the League of Nations shall have the right to bring to the attention of the Council any infraction, or any danger of infraction, of any of these obligations, and that the Council may thereupon take such action and give such direction as it may deem proper and effective in the circumstances.

Roumania further agrees that any difference of opinion as to questions of law or fact arising out of these Articles between the Roumanian Government and any one of the Principal Allied and Associated Powers or any other Power, a Member of the Council of the League of Nations, shall be held to be a dispute of an international character under Article 14 of the Covenant of the League of Nations. Roumania hereby consents that any such dispute shall, if the other party thereto demands, be referred to the Permanent Court of International Justice. The decision of the Permanent Court shall be final and shall have the same force and effect as an award under Article 13 of the Covenant....

From *League of Nations—Treaty Series, Volume 5, Nos. 1, 2, 3 & 4, Publication of Treaties and International Agreements Registered with the Secretariat of the League of Nations*, Geneva: League of Nations, 1921, 337–347.

Document 62:
PROTOCOL FOR THE PROHIBITION OF THE USE IN WAR OF ASPHYXIATING, POISONOUS OR OTHER GASES, AND OF BACTERIOLOGICAL METHODS OF WARFARE (THE GENEVA PROTOCOL) 26 U.S.T. 575 (1925)

In 1925, major nations outlawed the use of gases in warfare. This was an important step in outlawing one of the most horrible weapons of World War I. With only one or two exceptions, gas was not used as a weapon against enemy troops again until well after World War II.

The Undersigned Plenipotentiaries, in the name of their respective Governments: whereas the use in war of asphyxiating, poisonous or other gasses, and of all analogous liquids, materials or devices, has been justly condemned by the general opinion of the civilised world; and whereas the prohibition of such use has been declared in Treaties to which the majority of Powers of the world are Parties; and to the end that this prohibition shall be universally accepted as a part of the International Law, binding alike the conscience and the practice of nations; DECLARE: that the High Contracting parties, so far as they are not already Parties to Treaties prohibiting such use, accept this prohibition, agree to extend this prohibition to the use of bacteriological methods of warfare and agree to be bound as between themselves according to the terms of this declaration.

The High Contracting Parties will exert every effort to induce other States to accede to the present Protocol. Such accession will be notified to the Government of the French Republic, and by the latter to all signatory and acceding Powers, and will take effect on the date of the notification by the Government of the French Republic.

The present Protocol, of which the French and English texts are both authentic, shall be ratified as soon as possible. It shall bear today's date.

The ratifications of the present Protocol shall be addressed to the Government of the French Republic, which will at once notify the deposit of such ratification to each of the signatory and acceding Powers.

The instruments of ratification of and accession to the present Protocol will remain deposited in the archives of the Government of the French Republic.

The present Protocol will come into force for each signatory Power as from the date of deposit of its ratification, and, from that moment, each Power will be bound as regards other Powers which have already deposited their ratifications....

From *League of Nations—Treaty Series, Volume 90, Publication of Treaties and International Agreements Registered with the Secretariat of the League of Nations*, Geneva: League of Nations, 1929, 66–69.

Document 63:
KELLOGG-BRIAND PACT (1929)

The Kellogg-Briand Pact asserts the international principle that war is not a permissible means for settling disputes. It also suggests that humankind has a right to peace. This treaty served as the basis for the famous war crimes trials in Germany and Japan after World War II.

Article 1. The high contracting parties solemnly declare in the names of their respective peoples that they condemn recourse to war for the solution of international controversies, and renounce it as an instrument of national policy in their relations with one another.

Article 2. The high contracting parties agree that the settlement or solution of all disputes or conflicts of whatever nature or of whatever origin they may be, which may arise among them, shall never be sought except by pacific means.

Article 3. The present treaty shall be ratified by the high contracting parties named in the preamble in accordance with their respective constitutional requirements, and shall take effect as between them as soon as all their several instruments of ratification shall have been deposited at Geneva.

This treaty shall, when it has come into effect as prescribed in the preceding paragraph, remain open as long as may be necessary for adherence by all the other powers of the world.

From *Congressional Record—Senate, Second Session of the Seventieth Congress of the United States of America, Volume LXX, Part 1*, Washington: GPO, 1929, 1062.

Document 64:
THE ANTI-FRENCH RESISTANCE (1921–26)
Nguyen Ai Quoc (Ho Chi Minh)

The rights of national self-determination expressed by the peoples of Europe in World War I, and, often recognized by the Paris Peace Conferences, were not extended to the dependent colonial peoples of Europe's empires. Here, Ho Chi Minh voices the demands of the Vietnamese around 1924.

When the Great War ended the Vietnamese people like other peoples were deceived by Wilson's "generous" declarations on the right of peoples to self-determination. A group of Vietnamese, which included myself, sent the following demands to the French Parliament and to all delegations to the Versailles Conference.

CLAIMS OF THE VIETNAMESE PEOPLE

Ever since the victory of the Allies, all the subjected peoples have entertained high hopes about an era of right and justice which should follow the formal and solemn pledges taken before the whole world by the various powers of the Entente in the struggle of Civilization against Barbarism.

While waiting for the realization of the principle of Nationalities through the effective recognition of the sacred right of the peoples to self-determination, the people of the former Empire of Annam, now French Indochina, proposed to the governments of the Entente in general and the French government in particular the following demands:

1. Amnesty for all Vietnamese political detainees;

2. Reform of the Indochinese judicial system by giving the Vietnamese the same judicial safeguards as to the Europeans and completely and definitively abolishing the special tribunals which are instruments of terror and oppression against the most honest part of the Vietnamese people;

3. Freedom of the press and freedom of opinion;

4. Freedom of association and freedom of assembly;

5. Freedom to emigrate and travel abroad;

6. Freedom of teaching and creation in all provinces of technical and vocational schools for natives;

7. Replacement of the regime of decrees by that of laws;

8. Presence in the French Parliament of a permanent delegation elected by the natives to keep it informed of their aspirations!...

To these demands we added a tribute to the peoples and to feelings of humanity.

However, after a time of waiting and study, we realized that the "Wilson doctrine" was but a big fraud. The liberation of the proletariat is the necessary condition for national liberation. Both these liberations can only come from Communism and world revolution.

From Ho Chi Minh, *Selected Writings (1920–1969)*, Hanoi: Foreign Languages Publishing House, 1973, 22–23.

Document 65:
APPEAL TO AMERICA (1931)
Mahatma Gandhi

Another voice for the colonial peoples of the world after World War I was that of Mahatma Gandhi. He had begun his career fighting for the rights of Indians who lived and worked in South Africa. In 1931, he tried to inform Americans about his people's claims for rights and self-determination. His strategy was to use peaceful "passive resistance" or "satyagraha" to force the British to give up India.

In my opinion, the Indian struggle [for freedom] bears in its consequences not only upon India [and England] but upon the whole world. It contains one-fifth of the human race. It represents one of the most ancient civilizations. It has traditions handed down from tens of thousands of years, some of which, to the astonishment of the world, remain intact. No doubt the ravages of time have affected the purity of that civilization as they have that of many other cultures and many institutions.

If India is to revive the glory of her ancient past, she can only do so when she attains her freedom. The reason for the struggle having drawn the attention of the world I know does not lie in the fact that we Indians are fighting for our liberty, but in the fact that the means adopted by us for attaining that liberty are unique and, as far as history shows us, have not been adopted by any other people of whom we have any record.

The means adopted are not violence, not bloodshed, not diplomacy as one understands it nowadays, but they are purely and simply truth and non-violence. No wonder that the attention of the world is directed toward this attempt to lead a successful bloodless revolution. Hitherto, nations have fought in the manner of the brute. They have wreaked vengeance upon those whom they have considered to be their enemies.

We find in searching national anthems adopted by great nations that they contain imprecation upon the so-called enemy. They have vowed destruction and have not hesitated to take the name of God and seek divine assistance for the destruction of the enemy. We in India have endeavored to reverse the process. We feel that the law that governs brute creation is not the law that should guide the human race. That law is inconsistent with human dignity.

I, personally, would wait, if need be, for ages rather than seek to attain the freedom of my country through bloody means. I feel in the innermost recesses of my heart, after a political experience extending over an unbroken period of close upon thirty-five years, that the world is sick unto death of blood-spilling. The world is seeking a way out, and I flatter myself with the belief that perhaps it will be the privilege of the ancient land of India to show the way out to the hungering world.

I have, therefore, no hesitation whatsoever in inviting all the great nations of the earth to give their hearty cooperation to India in her mighty struggle. It must be a sight worth contemplating and treasuring, that of millions of people giving themselves to suffering without retaliation in order that they might vindicate the dignity and honor of the nation.

I have called that suffering a process of self-purification. It is my certain conviction that no man loses his freedom except through his own weakness. I am painfully conscious of our own weaknesses. We represent in India all the principal religions of the earth, and it is a matter of deep humiliation to confess that we are a house divided against itself, that we Hindus and Mussalmans are flying at one another. It is a matter of still deeper humiliation to me that we Hindus regard several millions of our own kith and kin as too degraded even for our touch. I refer to the so-called "untouchables."

These are no small weaknesses in a nation struggling to be free. And hence you will find that in this struggle through self-purification we have assigned a foremost place to the removal of the curse of untouchability and the attainment of unity amongst all the different classes and communities of India representing the different creeds.

It is along the same lines that we seek to rid our land of the curse of drink. Happily for us, intoxicating drinks and drugs are confined to comparatively a very small number of people, largely factory hands and the like. Fortunately for us, the drink and drug curse is accepted as a curse. It is not considered to be the fashion of a man or a woman to drink or to take intoxicating drugs. All the same, it is an uphill fight that we are fighting to remove this evil from our midst.

For it is a matter of regret, deep regret, for me to have to say that the existing government has made of this evil a source of very large revenue, amounting to nearly twenty-five crores of rupees [about $85,000,000 in 1956]. But I am thankful to be able to say that the women of India have risen to the occasion in combatting it by peaceful means, that is, by fervent appeal to those who are given to the drink habit to give it up, and by an equally fervent appeal to the liquor dealers. A great impression has been created upon those who are addicted to these two evil habits.

I wish that it were possible for me to say that in this, at least, we are receiving the hearty cooperation of the rulers. If we could only have received that cooperation, [even] without any legislation, I dare say that we would have achieved this reform and banished intoxicating drink and drugs from our afflicted land.

There is a force which has a constructive effect and which has been put forth by the nation during this struggle. That is the great care for the semi-starved millions scattered throughout the 700,000 villages dotted over a surface of 1,900 miles long and 1,500 miles broad. It is a painful phenomenon that these simple villagers, through no fault of their own, have nearly six months in the year idleness upon their hands. The time was not very long ago when every village was self-sufficient in regard to the two primary human wants, food and clothing.

Unfortunately for us, the East India Company, by means which I would prefer not to describe, destroyed that supplementary village industry as well as the livelihood of millions of spinners who had become famous through the cunning of their deft fingers for drawing the finest thread, such as has never yet been drawn by any modern machinery. These village spinners found themselves one fine morning with their noble occupation gone. And from that day forward India has become progressively poor.

No matter what may be said to the contrary, it is a historical fact that before the advent of the East India Company, these villagers were not idle, and he who wants may see today that these villagers are idle. It, therefore, requires no great effort or learning to know that these villagers must starve if they cannot work for six months in the year.

May I not, then, on behalf of these semi-starved millions, appeal to the conscience of the world to come to the rescue of a people dying to regain its liberty?

From *The Gandhi Reader*, edited by Homer A. Jack, Bloomington: Indiana University Press, 1956, 262–266.

Document 66:
THE ATLANTIC CONFERENCE (1941)
Franklin Delano Roosevelt

In his meeting with the British Prime Minister two years after the beginning of World War II, the American President,

Franklin Delano Roosevelt, indicated the principles for which his people would fight. He asserts again many of the ideas of Wilson's Fourteen Points.

The President [Roosevelt] and the Prime Minister [Winston S. Churchill] have had several conferences. They have considered the dangers to world civilization arising from the policies of military domination by conquest upon which the Hitlerite government of Germany and other governments associated therewith have embarked, and have made clear the steps which their countries are respectively taking for their safety in the face of these dangers.

They have agreed upon the following joint declaration:

"...The President of the United States of America and the Prime Minister, Mr. Churchill, representing His Majesty's Government in the United Kingdom, being met together, deem it right to make known certain common principles in the national policies of their respective countries on which they base their hopes for a better future for the world.

First, their countries seek no aggrandizement, territorial or other;

Second, they desire to see no territorial changes that do not accord with the freely expressed wishes of the peoples concerned;

Third, they respect the right of all peoples to choose the form of government under which they will live; and they wish to see sovereign rights and self-government restored to those who have been forcibly deprived of them;

Fourth, they will endeavor, with due respect for their existing obligations, to further the enjoyment by all states, great or small, victor or vanquished, of access, on equal terms to the trade and to the raw materials of the world which are needed for their economic prosperity;

Fifth, they desire to bring about the fullest collaboration between all nations in the economic field with the object of securing, for all, improved labor standards, economic advancement, and social security;

Sixth, after the final destruction of the Nazi tyranny, they hope to see established a peace which will afford to all nations the means of dwelling in safety within their own boundaries, and which will afford assurance that all the men in all the lands may live out their lives in freedom from fear and want;

Seventh, such a peace should enable all men to traverse the high seas and oceans without hindrance;

Eighth, they believe that all of the nations of the world, for realistic as well as spiritual reasons, must come to the abandonment of the use of force. Since no future peace can be maintained if land, sea, or air armaments continue to be employed by nations which threaten, or may threaten, aggression outside of their frontiers, they believe, pending the establishment of a wider and permanent system of general security, that the disarmament of such nations is essential. They will likewise aid and encourage all other practicable measures which will lighten for peace-loving peoples the crushing burden of armaments...."

The Congress and the President having heretofore determined, through the Lend-Lease Act, on the national policy of American aid to the democracies which East and West are waging war against dictatorships, the military and naval conversations at these meetings made clear gains in furthering the effectiveness of this aid.

Furthermore, the Prime Minister and I are arranging for conferences with the Soviet Union to aid it in its defense against the attack made by the principal aggressor of the modern world—Germany.

Finally, the declaration of principles at this time presents a goal which is worthwhile for our type of civilization to seek. It is so clearcut that it is difficult to oppose in any major particular without automatically admitting a willingness to accept compromise with naziism; or to agree to a world peace which would give to nazi-ism domination over large numbers of conquered nations. Inevitably such a peace would be a gift to nazi-ism to take breath — armed breath— for a second war to extend their control over Europe and Asia, to the American Hemisphere itself.

From Franklin Delano Roosevelt, Message to Congress, August 21, 1941, 77th Congress, reprinted in *Peace and War. United States Foreign Policy 1931–1941*, Washington, D.C.: GPO, 1943, 718–719.

CHAPTER 9

Human Rights and Human Needs

Document 67:
THE FIGHT FOR THE VOTE MILITANT SUFFRAGISM IN ENGLAND (1914)

These articles from The Times *of London indicate the hostility to the goals and tactics of the suffragists, who resorted to demonstrations to attract attention to their demand for the right to vote. Some suffragists resorted to violence, which included attacks upon some works of art, the disruption of church services and the like. The general tone of these articles indicates how women were treated. Notice how casually the reporter treats rather severe attacks upon the women's right to have a political center. The language is replete with emotionally laden terms such as "militancy" and "anarchy".*

THE SUPPRESSION OF MILITANCY
Another Police Raid

The police yesterday made a further move in their action against the militant suffragists by raiding the temporary headquarters of the Women's Social and Political Union in Westminster. In future, it is understood, the militants will not be permitted to resume occupation of any premises that have once been seized.

NEW HEADQUARTERS RAIDED
BY POLICE
Search For Documents

A further step directed against the campaign of anarchy of the militant suffragists was taken yesterday, when a raid was made on the temporary headquarters of the Women's Social and Political Union, at 17, Tothill-street, Westminster.

Since the visit to Lincoln's Inn House, Kingsway, a fortnight ago, when a list of subscribers to the funds of the union was found, the police have been in possession of the offices, and the business has been conducted at Tothill-street. The success of the last raid has led to much great caution on that part of the union officials for no documents of an incriminating character were found, although the visit of the police took the staff completely by surprise.

The raid was effected without any disorder. Mrs. Hatfield, who was in charge of the office, and a number of girl clerks gave their names and were then told to leave the premises. No arrests were made, although the police were provided with warrants which are understood to have been for the arrest of certain militants released under the "Cat-and-Mouse" Act who have evaded capture. A score of detectives who have been specially engaged for some months in tracing the activities of suffragists examined all the correspondence and other documents and made an inventory of what they found. They then took possession of the premises.

We understand that the authorities will not vacate either the headquarters in Kingsway or the offices in Tothill-street. In future the headquarters of the Women's Social and Political Union will be subject to constant supervision and militant organizers will not be permitted to return to any premises that have been taken possession of by the police. Should the action of the police be challenged by civil process the Law Officers of the Crown are prepared to vindicate their attitude in the Courts.

POLITICAL NOTES
Mr. Lloyd George And The Women

Mr. Lloyd George made a short speech to the members of the Women's Liberal Federation in the Downing-street Gardens yesterday afternoon. He told them the Government were happy and then they intended to finish all their work. They intended to overcome whatever difficulties they had to combat. He had never known the Prime Minister more full of fight and determination. Finally, he wished all his women hearers had the vote, and declared that if they could persuade some members of their sex to have more wisdom they would soon get it.

From *The Times*, London, June 10, 1914, 8, columns 3 & 4.

Document 68:
BIRTH CONTROL—A PARENT'S PROBLEM OR WOMAN'S? (1920)
Margaret Sanger

Birth control was illegal in Western nations until well after World War II. Only the spread of venereal disease in the brothels behind the Western front induced the British and Allied forces to give instructions in the use of condoms during World War I. Thus many men were introduced to birth control devices. But organized resistance based primarily upon religious institutions continued through most of the twentieth century. Despite prohibitions, birth control devices and knowledge of their usage spread through Europe and the West after World War II. An American advocate of family planning, Margaret Sanger, explains her views in this reading. She was imprisoned for her opinions and operating a birth control clinic.

The problem of birth control has arisen directly from the effort of the feminine spirit to free itself from bondage. Woman herself has wrought that bondage through her reproductive powers and while enslaving herself has enslaved the world. The physical suffering to be relieved is chiefly woman's. Hers, too, is the love life that dies first under the blight of too prolific breeding. Within her is wrapped up the future of the race—it is hers to make or mar. All of these considerations point unmistakably to one fact—it is woman's duty as well as her privilege to lay hold of the means of freedom. Whatever men may do, she cannot escape the responsibility. For ages she has been deprived of the opportunity to meet this obligation. She is now emerging from her helplessness. Even as no one can share the suffering of the overburdened mother, so no one can do this work for her. Others may help, but she and she alone can free herself.

The basic freedom of the world is woman's freedom. A free race cannot be born of slave mothers. A woman enchained cannot choose but give a measure of that bondage to her sons and daughters. No woman can call herself free who does not own and control her body. No woman can call herself free until she can choose consciously whether she will or will not be a mother.

It does not greatly alter the case that some women call themselves free because they earn their own livings, while others profess freedom because they defy the conventions of sex relationship. She who earns her own living gains a sort of freedom that is not to be undervalued, but in quality and in quantity it is of little account beside the untrammeled choice of mating or not mating, of being a mother or not being a mother. She gains food and clothing and shelter, at least, without submitting to the charity of her companion, but the earning of her own living does not give her the development of her inner sex urge, far deeper and more powerful in its outworkings than any of these externals. In order to have that development, she must still meet and solve the problem of motherhood.

With the so-called "free" woman, she chooses a mate in defiance of convention, freedom is largely a question of character and audacity. If she does attain to an unrestricted choice of a mate, she is still in a position to be enslaved through her reproductive powers. Indeed, the pressure of law and custom upon the woman not legally married is likely to make her more of a slave than the woman fortunate enough to marry the man of her choice.

Look at it from any standpoint you will, suggest any solution you will, conventional or unconventional, sanctioned by law or in defiance of law, woman is in the same position, fundamentally, until she is able to determine for herself whether she will be a mother and to fix the number of her offspring. This unavoidable situation is alone enough to make birth control, first of all, a woman's problem. On the very face of the matter, voluntary motherhood is chiefly the concern of the woman.

It is persistently urged, however, that since sex expression is the act of two, the responsibility of controlling the results should not be placed upon woman alone. Is it fair, it is asked, to give her, instead of the man, the task of protecting herself when she is, perhaps, less rugged in physique than her mate, and has, at all events, the normal, periodic inconveniences of her sex?

We must examine this phase of her problem in two lights—that of the ideal, and of the conditions working toward the ideal. In an ideal society, no doubt, birth control would become the concern of the man as well as the woman. The hard, inescapable fact which we encounter to-day is that man has not only refused any such responsibility, but has individually and collectively sought to prevent woman from obtaining knowledge by which she could assume this responsibility for herself. She is still in the position of a dependent to-day because her mate has refused to consider her as an individual apart from his needs. She is still bound because she has in the past left the solution of the problem to him. Having left it to him, she finds that instead of rights, she has only such privileges as she has gained by petitioning, coaxing and cozening. Having left it to him, she is exploited, driven and enslaved to his desires.

While it is true that he suffers many evils as the consequence of this situation, she suffers vastly more. While it is true that he should be awakened to the cause of these evils, we know that they come home to her with crushing force every day. It is she who has the long burden of carrying, bearing and rearing the unwanted children....It is her heart that the sight of the deformed, the subnormal, the undernourished, the overworked child smites first and oftenest and hardest. It is *her* love life that dies first in the fear of undesired pregnancy. It is her opportunity for self expression that perishes first and most hopelessly because of it.

Conditions, rather than theories, facts, rather than dreams, govern the problem. They place it squarely upon the shoulders of woman. She has learned that whatever the moral responsibility of the man in this direction may be, he does not discharge it. She has learned that, lovable and considerate as the individual husband may be, she has nothing to expect from men in the mass, when they make laws and decree customs. She knows that regardless of what ought to be, the brutal, unavoidable fact is that she will never receive her freedom until she takes it for herself.

Having learned this much, she has yet something more to learn. Women are too much inclined to follow in the footsteps of men, to try to think as men think, to try to solve the general problems of life as men solve them. If after attaining their freedom, women accept conditions in the spheres of government, industry, art, morals and religion as they find them, they will be but taking a leaf out of man's book. The woman is not needed to do man's work. She is not needed to think man's thoughts. She need not fear that the masculine mind, almost universally dominant, will fail to take care of its own. Her mission is not to enhance the masculine spirit, but to express the feminine; hers is not to preserve a man-made world, but to create a human world by the infusion of the feminine element into all of its activities.

Woman must not accept; she must challenge. She must not be awed by that which has been built up around her; she must reverence that within her which struggles for expression. Her eyes must be less upon what is and more clearly upon what should be. She must listen only with a frankly questioning attitude to the dogmatized opinions of man-made society. When she chooses her new, free course of action, it must be in the light of her own opinion—of her own intuition. Only so can she give play to the feminine spirit. Only thus can she free her mate from the bondage which he wrought for himself when he wrought hers. Only thus can she restore to him that of which he robbed himself in restricting her. Only thus can she remake the world....

Woman must have her freedom—the fundamental freedom of choosing whether or not she shall be a mother and how many children she will have. Regardless of what man's attitude may be, that problem is hers—and before it can be his, it is hers alone.

She goes through the vale of death alone, each time a babe is born. As it is the right neither of man nor the state to coerce her into this ordeal, so it is her right to decide whether she will endure it. That right to decide imposes upon her the duty of clearing the way to knowledge by which she may make and carry out the decision.

Birth control is woman's problem. The quicker she accepts it as hers and hers alone, the quicker will society respect motherhood. The quicker, too, will the world be made a fit place for her children to live.

From Margaret Sanger, *Woman and the New Race* reprinted in *The Feminist Papers: From Adams to de Beauvoir*, edited by Alice S. Rossi, New York: Columbia University Press, 1973, 533–536. Reprinted by permission of Grant Sanger.

Document 69: CHILDREN'S WORK (1922)

Restriction of child labor in the United States followed Britain and Western Europe by nearly a century. This report resembles the findings of the Mine Commission in Britain in the 1830s. This reading describes the situation of child labor in American mines in the 1920s.

The life of the district revolves around the mines and for the boys more than for their fathers their place of employment was the mines. The canvass made by the Children's Bureau showed that for the district as a whole 90.4 per cent of the boys doing full-time work were in mining as compared with 78 per cent of their fathers....The fact that the breakers offered opportunities for profitable employment of young boys is the explanation of the large number of boys employed in connection with the mining of anthracite coal.... These breakers which tower above the town...are great barn-like structures filled with chutes, sliding belts, and great crushing and sorting machines. Around these machines a scaffolding was built on which the workers stand or sit. The coal is raised from the mine to the top of the breaker and dumped down the chute into a crushing machine, which breaks it into somewhat smaller lumps. These are carried along a moving belt or gravity incline on each side of which men and boys stand or sit picking out pieces of slate and any coal which has slate mixed with it....

Whatever the hazards and dangers of the breakers are, underground work is much more undesirable for young boys....Young boys were working daily underground at the time this investigation was made....Of the trapper boys, seventeen were only thirteen and three were only twelve years old when they began to do regular full-day duty at this work....

The boys who turned by hand the ventilating fans frequently worked on the dangerous robbing sections where the last remaining coal is being cut away from pillars and walls and where, in consequence, the roof sometimes falls in or the section is filled with a waste material known as slush. The men interviewed told of the nervous strain they experienced when they worked at robbing. Turning the fans for these workers was the first underground work for twelve boys....A few other boys were employed underground, as oilers and laborers doing a variety of work.

It is unnecessary to point out the dangers of underground work. Where electric cars are operated, where dynamiting is done, where supports give way and cave-ins and squeezes occur, and rock and coal fall, serious accidents and sudden death, more terrible to endure because of the victim's isolation and consequent distance from relief of any kind, are incidents of the occupation....

Accidents...occurred to boys in the breakers as well as underground....One boy told of a friend who had dropped a new cap in the rollers and how in trying to pull it out his arm was caught, crushed, and twisted....One boy told of the death of another while watching the dam beneath the breaker. He and some of the other breaker boys had helped to extricate the mutilated body from the wheels in which their companion was caught; he himself had held the bag into which the recovered parts of the dead body were put....

No compensation was paid forty-four boys who were incapacitated for a period of two weeks or more as the result of injuries received while they were employed in the mines, although the Pennsylvania compensation law entitled them to receive it. Of those who received compensation, eleven boys reported that they were paid in all less that $5; nine that they received from $5 to $10; twenty-three from $10 to $25; twelve received between $25 and $50; four between $50 and $75; five between $75 and $100; while three reported that they received $100 or more....

Public opinion had already prohibited underground work in Pennsylvania and in most other states, and the Federal Government had imposed a penalty in the form of a tax if children under sixteen were employed in or about a mine. The real problem here, as in many other parts of the country, was how to secure the enforcement of the child-labor laws that had been enacted.

From "Child Labor and the Welfare of Children in an Anthracite Coal-Mining District," in U.S. Children's Bureau, *Publication No. 106*, Washington, D.C.: GPO 1922, 15–16, 18–20, reprinted in *Readings in American History*, edited by Oscar Handlin, New York: Alfred A. Knopf, 1963, 569–570.

Document 70: REPORT ON THE SHARECROPPER DEMONSTRATIONS (1939)
Aubrey Williams

In 1939, Aubrey Williams reported to President Roosevelt on demonstrations by African American sharecroppers in

Mississippi. It details the plight of the workers, and in addition, relates their economic and social disadvantage to their lack of civil liberties as well. In this report, the workers' camps are called "concentration camps."

January 19, 1939

Dear Mr. President:

Here is my report summarizing facts and conclusions on major issues involved in the sharecropper demonstration in southeastern Missouri in January of 1939.

Causes: The primary cause is the feeling of the workers, sharecroppers, ex-sharecroppers, renters and day laborers all, that their economic condition is intolerable. They say they had just as well starve and freeze on the highways, or in their present concentration camps, as in their shacks. Their cotton picking money and sharecropping payoffs are all gone. After that, all that most of them have in prospect is 100 days work a year, at $1.00 a day—some of the farmers pay only seventy-five cents. As far as our man can learn, there is no credit available to them.

This condition has become increasingly serious in recent years, through the action of land-owners in switching from sharecropping and renting to operation of their land by day labor. The principal reason for this is to enable the land-owner to retain all of the AAA benefit money, which otherwise would go to the renter or in part to the sharecropper. In addition, many land-owners are reducing the amount of land given sharecroppers to operate, apparently in line with acreage reduction. In two cases interviewed, sharecroppers produced "wildcat cotton" and were deprived of any return, the land-owner explaining that the penalty tax took all the crop money.

Of the 102 family heads interviewed, some spoke of their hope that the government would set them up in cotton growing. The movement as yet has formulated no definite demand for a resettlement project, however. It is quite likely that the hope for such a project is responsible to a considerable extent for their action. Their determination to hold out against returning to their former status is indicated by the fact that about one-half of the 1200 persons on the highways went to the concentration camps off the highways when evacuated by State Highway Police, instead of returning to farm shacks as proposed by the land-owners and the authorities.

Southern Tenant Farmers Union activities may have had some part in organizing the protest, although the persons interviewed in many cases were apparently unacquainted with the organization.

The 102 histories demonstrate the falsity of the charge that the demonstrators were day laborers from Arkansas. Most of them are or have been in recent years, sharecroppers or renters in this section of Missouri.

As to the charge that wholesale eviction orders caused the protest, this is not literally true. State Highway Police said that only one legally served eviction order (in Mississippi County, Missouri) has been registered with the proper legal authorities. In substance, however, the charge is true. Our investigator was shown at least three notices, couched in legal language, in the concentration camp near Wyatt, Missouri. The 102 personal histories are full of statements, obviously truthful because of the circumstantial details given to the interviewer, that farmowners orally informed these folk that (1) he was switching from sharecropping to day labor basis, (2) that he wanted the house for a larger family, (3) that he would not be wanted next year. There are many variations, nearly all of which gave the worker to believe that there was nothing for him to do at that place.

It seems to me that the mere presence in the vicinity of the laForge cooperative colony, (Farm Security, 100 homesteads including 80 white and 20 black families) was a large factor in leading the workers to make their demonstration.

Civil Liberties: There appear to have been numerous violations of civil liberties. The action of the State Highway Police in escorting organizers of the Southern Tenant Farmers Union out of the state on January fourteenth is one. The forcible removal of the demonstrators from the public highways, in one instance by Sheriff Stanley of New Madrid County, and in the others by the State Highway Police, in State Highway Department trucks in all instances, is another. This was done under the pretext of the order by the State Public Health Commissioner that they were a menace to public health. In fact, their living conditions in the two concentration camps to which they were moved are as conducive to serious epidemic sickness, if not more so, than in their highway camps. The seizure of the campers' shotguns and a few rifles, necessary to enable them to add rabbits, squirrels, etc. to their diet, is another example. Sheriff Stanley reported this seizure, and our men there witnessed a part of it. One Negro was struck by two men in Sheriff Stanley's posse during the highway evacuation, being clubbed in the face and gashed by blows. In addition, there is an apparent guard, or at least a consciousness of compulsion for the demonstrators to remain at the two concentration camps, away from the highways. Several white men were present at the levee camp during most of January seventeenth, and a uniformed State Highway Policeman visited the camp and inquired what was our purpose in interviewing these people, although our man had previously called on Highway Police Captain Sheppard in Sikeston and explained his mission of information gathering. Captain Sheppard was frank in expressing hope and belief that the demonstrators would return to their previous farm existence in a few days. He commented that our man did not appear to be a southerner and might not understand what was necessary in "handling niggers."

Relief Possibilities: These people will not starve for a few weeks, and may continue indefinitely, as a few are getting $10 relief checks from the Farm Security Administration. The Farm Security Administration, however, is understaffed and slow to clear applications. The regional FSA man has informed the regional relief man in Sikeston that he is planning to do something definite soon to prevent difficulties. In addition, surplus commodities are being distributed at relief centers, such as New Madrid, ten or twelve miles away from the levee camp, to those who apply in person. A few of them have old automobiles and trucks. However, their egress for this purpose may be shut off by the unsympathetic whites in the neighborhood and by the land-owners. One member of the New Madrid County Advisory Committee on Relief has complained against the County Supervisor because of this issuance of food. No inquiry was made as to whether Farm Security Administration has any long range plan to provide for them.

Effect of the Interviews: Nearly all those interviewed indicated by their manner a rather child-like confidence that the federal government would act to relieve their condition. Many appeared to feel that giving their name and the other information would place them in a position for early aid.

One other item may be noted: Ryland, the Missouri director of the National Emergency Council, was reported in the Missouri press as having stated, after a visit to the highway camps, that he was investigating "subversive influences" in connection with the demonstration.

Press Attitude: Most of the news and headlines noted, as usual in such circumstances, were based on statements and activities of the authorities and land-owners. The St. Louis *Globe-Democrat* displayed active bias against the demonstrators in its reports, and the St. Louis *Post-Dispatch* did a full and complete job of reporting both sides and an accurate report of conditions as seen by our investigator.

Basic Remedy: This is a boil that has come to a head, indicating a wide-spread condition in the cotton region. It is probable that nothing less than a great resettlement campaign, involving both housing and land, could materially improve living conditions among these fold.

Sincerely,
Aubrey Williams, Administrator
National Youth Administration.

From *Black Workers, A Documentary History from Colonial Times to the Present*, edited by Philip S. Foner and Ronald L. Lewis, Philadelphia: Temple University Press, 1989, 504–507. © by Temple University Press. Reprinted by permission of Temple University Press.

Document 71:
WHY SHOULD WE MARCH (1942)
A. Philip Randolph

A. Philip Randolph organized the Brotherhood of Sleeping Car Porters, the strongest Black union, in 1925. During World War II, he organized the March on Washington Movement to demand open hirings in industries that received government contracts. In this document, he urges African-Americans to continue to fight against racism in the United States as they fight the Germans and Japanese abroad. He lists the demands that African-Americans need to be free in America.

Though I have found no Negroes who want to see the United Nations lose this war, I have found many who, before the war ends, want to see the stuffing knocked out of white supremacy and of empire over subject peoples. American Negroes, involved as we are in the general issues of the conflict, are confronted not with a choice but with the challenge both to win democracy for ourselves at home and to help win the war for democracy the world over.

There is no escape from the horns of this dilemma. There ought not to be escape. For if the war for democracy is not won abroad, the fight for democracy cannot be won at home. If this war cannot be won for the white peoples, it will not be won for the darker races.

Conversely, if freedom and equality are not vouchsafed the peoples of color, the war for democracy will not be won. Unless this double-barreled thesis is accepted and applied the darker races will never wholeheartedly fight for the victory of the United Nations. That is why those familiar with the thinking of the American Negro have sensed his lack of enthusiasm, whether among the educated or uneducated, rich or poor, professional or non-professional, religious or secular, rural or urban, north, south, east or west.

That is why questions are being raised by Negroes in church, labor union and fraternal society; in poolroom, barbershop, schoolroom, hospital, hairdressing parlor; on college campus, railroad, and bus. One can hear such questions asked as these: What have Negroes to fight for? What's the difference between Hitler and that "cracker" Talmadge of Georgia? Why has a man got to be Jim-Crowed to die for democracy? If you haven't got democracy yourself, how can you carry it to somebody else?

What are the reasons for this state of mind? The answer is: discrimination, segregation, Jim Crow. Witness the navy, the army, the air corps; and also government services at Washington. In many parts of the South, Negroes in Uncle Sam's uniform are being put upon, mobbed, sometimes even shot down by civilian and military police, and on occasion lynched. Vested political interests in race prejudice are so deeply entrenched that to them winning the war against Hitler is secondary to preventing Negroes from winning democracy for themselves. This is worth many divisions to Hitler and Hirohito. While labor, business, and farm are subjected to ceilings and floors and not allowed to carry on as usual, these interests trade in the dangerous business of race hate as usual.

When the defense program began and billions of the taxpayers' money were appropriated for guns, ships, tanks and bombs, Negroes presented themselves for work only to be given the cold shoulder. North as well as South, and despite their qualifications, Negroes were denied skilled employment. Not until their wrath and indignation took the form of a proposed protest march on Washington, scheduled for July 1, 1941, did things begin to move in the form of defense jobs for Negroes. The march was postponed by the timely issuance (June 25, 1941) of the famous Executive Order No. 8802 by President Roosevelt. But this order and the President's Committee on Fair Employment Practice, established thereunder, have as yet only scratched the surface by way of eliminating discriminations on account of race or color in war industry. Both management and labor unions in too many places and in too many ways are still drawing the color line.

It is to meet this situation squarely with direct action that the March on Washington Movement launched its present program of protest mass meetings. Twenty thousand were in attendance at Madison Square Garden, June 16; sixteen thousand in the Coliseum in Chicago, June 26; nine thousand in the City Auditorium of St. Louis, August 14. Meetings of such magnitude were unprecedented among Negroes. The vast throngs were drawn from all walks and levels of Negro life—businessmen, teachers, laundry workers, Pullman porters, waiters, and red caps; preachers, crapshooters, and social workers; jitterbugs, and Ph.D.'s. They came and sat in silence, thinking, applauding only when they considered the truth was told, when they felt strongly that something was going to be done about it.

The March on Washington Movement is essentially a movement of the people. It is all

Negro and pro-Negro, but not for that reason anti-white or anti-Semitic, or anti-Catholic, or anti-foreign, or anti-labor. Its major weapon is the non-violent demonstration of Negro mass power. Negro leadership has united back of its drive for jobs and justice. "Whether Negroes should march on Washington, and if so, when?" will be the focus of a forthcoming national conference. For the plan of a protest march has not been abandoned. Its purpose would be to demonstrate that American Negroes are in deadly earnest, and all out for their full rights. No power on earth can cause them today to abandon their fight to wipe out every vestige of second class citizenship and the dual standards that plague them.

A community is democratic only when the humblest and weakest person can enjoy the highest civil, economic, and social rights that the biggest and most powerful possess. To trample on these rights of both Negroes and poor whites is such a commonplace in the South that it takes readily to anti-social, anti-labor, anti-Semitic and anti-Catholic propaganda. It was because of laxness in enforcing the Weimar constitution in republican Germany that Nazism made headway. Oppression of the Negroes in the United States, like suppression of the Jews in Germany, may open the way for a fascist dictatorship.

By fighting for their rights now, American Negroes are helping to make America a moral and spiritual arsenal of democracy. Their fight against the poll tax, against lynch law, segregation, and Jim Crow, their fight for economic, political, and social equality, thus becomes part of the global war for freedom.

PROGRAM OF THE MARCH ON WASHINGTON MOVEMENT

1. We demand, in the interest of national unity, the abrogation of every law which makes a distinction in treatment between citizens based on religion, creed, color, or national origin. This means an end to Jim Crow in education, in housing, in transportation and in every other social, economic, and political privilege; and especially, we demand, in the capital of the nation, an end to all segregation in public places and in public institutions.

2. We demand legislation to enforce the Fifth and Fourteenth Amendments guaranteeing that no person shall be deprived of life, liberty or property without due process of law, so that the full weight of the national government may be used for the protection of life and thereby may end the disgrace of lynching.

3. We demand the enforcement of the Fourteenth and Fifteenth Amendments and the enactment of the Pepper Poll Tax bill so that all barriers in the exercise of the suffrage are eliminated.

4. We demand the abolition of segregation and discrimination in the army, navy, marine corps, air corps, and all other branches of national defense.

5. We demand an end to discrimination in jobs and job training. Further, we demand that the F.E.P.C. be made a permanent administration of the U.S. Government and that it be given power to enforce its decisions based on its findings.

6. We demand that federal funds be withheld from any agency which practices discrimination in the use of such funds.

7. We demand colored and minority group representation on all administrative agencies so that these groups may have recognition of their democratic right to participate in formulating policies.

8. We demand representation for the colored and minority racial groups on all missions, political and technical, which will be sent to the peace conference so that the interests of all people everywhere may be fully recognized and justly provided for in the post-war settlement.

From *Black Workers, A Documentary History from Colonial Times to the Present*, edited by Philip S. Foner and Ronald L. Lewis, Philadelphia: Temple University Press, 1989, 527–530. Copyright 1989 by Temple University Press. Reprinted by permission of Temple University Press.

Document 72:
"FOUR FREEDOMS" SPEECH (1941)
Franklin Delano Roosevelt

Franklin Delano Roosevelt held the office of president of the United States longer than any other person. He was forced to confront the Great Depression and World War II during his administrations. Roosevelt saw much suffering during the years of crisis that characterized his long period in office.

As president, Roosevelt came to the conclusion that the freedoms guaranteed to Americans in law tended to be stated in the negative, and stressed the things that could not be done to a person. He stressed the positive rights of persons, however, and recognized that abstract freedoms were only one type of freedom, and that another, practical type existed. These "other" freedoms included rights such as the freedom from want and freedom from hunger. The following selection is from Roosevelt's famous "Four Freedoms" speech, and illustrates his position concerning these basic needs of human beings. Every nation faces the problem of moving from government inactivity to government promotion of its people's well being. The United States remains one of the nations most resistant to the reforms we call those of the "welfare state," those that address health, pensions, unemployment insurance and the like.

The Nation takes great satisfaction and much strength from the things which have been done to make its people conscious of their individual stake in the preservation of democratic life in America. Those things have toughened the fiber of our people, have renewed their faith and strengthened their devotion to the institutions we make ready to protect.

Certainly this is no time to stop thinking about the social and economic problems which are the root cause of the social revolution which is today a supreme factor in the world.

There is nothing mysterious about the foundations of a healthy and strong democracy. The basic things expected by our people of their political and economic systems are simple. They are:

Equality of opportunity for youth and for others.

Jobs for those who can work.

Security for those who need it.

The ending of special privilege for the few.

The preservation of civil liberties for all.

The enjoyment of the fruits of scientific progress in a wider and constantly rising standard of living.

These are the simple and basic things that must never be lost sight of in the turmoil and unbelievable complexity of our modern world. The inner and abiding strength of our economic and political systems is dependent upon the degree to which they fulfill these expectations.

Many subjects connected with our social economy call for immediate improvement.

As examples:

We should bring more citizens under the coverage of old age pensions and unemployment insurance.

We should widen the opportunities for adequate medical care.

We should plan a better system by which persons deserving or needing gainful employment may obtain it.

I have called for personal sacrifice. I am assured of the willingness of almost all Americans to respond to that call.

A part of the sacrifice means the payment of more money in taxes. In my budget message I recommend that a greater portion of this great defense program be paid for from taxation than we are paying today. No person should try, or be allowed, to get rich out of this program; and the principle of tax payments in accordance with ability to pay should be constantly before our eyes to guide our legislation.

If the Congress maintains these principles, the voters, putting patriotism ahead of pocketbooks, will give you their applause.

In the future days, which we seek to make secure, we look forward to a world founded upon four essential human freedoms.

The first is freedom of speech and expression—everywhere in the world.

The second is freedom of every person to worship God in his own way—everywhere in the world.

The third is freedom from want—which, translated into world terms, means economic understandings which will secure to every nation a healthy peace time life for its inhabitants—everywhere in the world.

The fourth is freedom from fear—which, translated into world terms, means a worldwide reduction of armaments to such a point and in such a thorough fashion that no nation will be in a position to commit an act of physical aggression against any neighbor—anywhere in the world.

That is no vision of a distant millennium. It is a definite basis for a kind of world attainable in our own time and generation. That kind of world is the very antithesis of the so-called new order of tyranny which the dictators seek to create with the crash of a bomb.

To that new order we oppose the greater conception—the moral order. A good society is able to face schemes of world domination and foreign revolutions alike without fear.

Since the beginning of our American history we have been engaged in change—in a perpetual peaceful revolution—a revolution which goes on steadily, quietly adjusting itself to changing conditions—without the concentration camp or the quick-lime in the ditch. The world order which we seek is the cooperation of free countries, working together in a friendly, civilized society.

This Nation has placed its destiny in the hands and heads and hearts of its millions of free men and women; and its faith in freedom under the guidance of God. Freedom means the supremacy of human rights everywhere. Our support goes to those who struggle to gain those rights or keep them. Our strength is in our unity of purpose.

To that high concept there can be no end save victory.

From *Congressional Record—Senate, of the First Session of the Seventy-Seventh Congress, Volume 87*, Washington, D.C.: GPO, 1941, 44–47.

CHAPTER 10 The Soviet Challenge

Document 73:
PETITION TO THE TSAR (1905)
Father Gapon

A Russian Orthodox priest, Father Gapon, led a procession of workers to present a petition to Tsar Nicholas II. Troops opened fire and the massacre precipitated a revolution. This event symbolizes the difficulty of getting necessary changes to occur in an autocratic system far removed from people and their needs.

SIR—We, working men and inhabitants of St. Petersburg of various classes, our wives and our children and our helpless old parents, come to Thee, Sire, to seek for truth and defence. We have become beggars; we have been oppressed; we are burdened by toil beyond our powers; we are scoffed at; we are not recognized as human beings; we are treated as slaves who must suffer their bitter fate and who must keep silence. We suffered, but we are pushed farther into the den of beggary, lawlessness, and ignorance. We are choked by despotism and irresponsibilty, and we are breathless. We have no more power, Sire, the limit of patience has been reached. There has arrived for us that tremendous moment when death is better than the continuation of intolerable tortures. We have left off working, and we have declared to the masters that we shall not begin to work until they comply with our demands. We beg but little; we desire only that without which life is not life, but hard labour and eternal torture. The first request which we made was that our masters should discuss our needs with us; but this they refused, on the ground that no right to make this request is recognized by law. They also declared to be illegal our requests to diminish the working hours to eight hours daily, to agree with us about the prices for our work, to consider our misunderstandings with the inferior administration of the mills, so that the minimum daily wage should be one ruble per day, to abolish overtime work, to give us medical attention without insulting us, to arrange the workshops so that it might be possible to work there, and not find in them death from awful draughts and from rain and snow. All these requests appear to be, in the opinion of our masters and of the factory and mill administrations, illegal. Every one of our requests was a crime, and the desire to improve our condition was regarded by them as impertinence, and as offensive to them.

Sire, here are many thousands of us, and all are human beings only in appearance. In reality in us, as in all Russian people, there is not recognized any human right, not even the right of speaking, thinking, meeting, discussing our needs, taking measures for the improvement of our conditions. We have been enslaved, and enslaved under the auspices of Thy officials, with their assistance, and with their cooperation. Every one of us who dared to raise a voice in defence of working-class and popular interest is thrown into jail or is sent into banishment. For the possession of good hearts and sensitive souls we are punished as for crimes. Even to pity a beaten man—a man tortured and without rights—means to commit a heavy crime. All the people—working men as well as peasants—are handed over to the discretion of the officials of the Government, who are thieves of the property of the State—robbers who not only take no care of the interests of the people but who trample these interests under their feet. The Government officials have brought the country to complete destruction, have involved it in a detestable war, and have further and further led it to ruin. We working men have no voice in the expenditure of the enormous amounts raised from us in taxes. We do not know even where and for what is spent the money collected from a beggared people. The people are deprived of the possibility of expressing their desires, and they now demand that they be allowed to take part in the introduction of taxes and in the expenditure of them.

The working men are deprived of the possibility of organizing themselves in unions for the defence of their interests....

Russia is too great. Its necessities are too various and numerous for officials alone to rule it. National representation is indispensable. It is indispensable that people should assist and should rule themselves. To them only are known their real necessities. Do not reject their assistance, accept it, order immediately the convocation of representatives of the Russian land from all ranks, including representatives from the working men. Let there be capitalists as well as working men—offical and priest, doctor and teacher—let all, whatever they may be, elect their representatives. Let everyone be equal and free in the right of election, and for this purpose order that the elections for the Constitutional Assembly be carried on under the condition of universal, equal, and secret voting. This is the most capital of our requests. In it and upon it everything is based. This is the principal and only plaster for our painful wounds, without which our wounds will fester and bring us rapidly near to death. Yet one measure alone cannot heal our wounds. Other measures are also indispensable. Directly and openly as to a Father, we speak to Thee, Sire, about them in person, for all the toiling classes of Russia. The following are indispensable:

I. Measures against the ignorance and rightlessness of the Russian people:

1. The immediate release and return of all who have suffered for political and religious convictions, for strikes, and for national peasant disorders.

2. The immediate declaration of freedom and of the inviolability of the person—freedom of speech and press, freedom of meetings, and freedom of conscience in religion.

3. Universal and compulsory elementary education of the people at the charge of the State.

4. Responsibility of the Ministers before the people and guarantee that the Government will be law-abiding.

5. Equality before the law of all without exception.

6. Separation of the Church from the State.

II. Measures against the oppression of labour:

1. Abolition of the factory inspectorships.

2. Institution at factories and mills of permanent committees of elected workers, which, together with the administration (of the factories) would consider the complaints of individual workers. Discharge of working men should not take place otherwise than by resolution of this committee.

3. Freedom of organization of cooperative societies of consumers and of labour trade unions immediately.

4. Eight-hour working day and regulation of overtime working.

5. Freedom of the struggle of labour against capital immediately.

6. Normal wages immediately.

7. Participation of working-class representatives in the working out of project law upon workmen's State insurance immediately.

From *Readings in European History Since 1814*, edited by Jonathan F. Scott and Alexander Baltzley, New York: F.S. Crofts & Co., 1931, 345–346.

Document 74:
IMPERIALISM: THE HIGHEST STAGE OF CAPITALISM (1916)
V.I. Lenin

Vladimir I. Lenin, later to be revered in the Soviet Union as the leader of the revolution, was also a theorist of great importance to the development of twentieth-century Marxist thought. In his 1916 work, Imperialism: The Highest Stage of Capitalism, *he argues that imperialism is an inevitable stage of the capitalistic system. Capitalist competition and the monopolies caused by it had lowered profits at home, and so forced those who controlled surplus capital to reinvest it in foreign markets. If surplus capital were used in any other way, as, for instance, by raising wages of workers to increase the size of domestic markets, the result would be an even greater decrease in profits to capitalist owners. Thus, the capitalist system contained internal contradictions that forced it to turn to a policy of imperialism.*

We must now try to sum up and put together what has been said above on the subject of imperialism. Imperialism emerged as the development and direct continuation of the fundamental attributes of capitalism in general. But capitalism only became capitalist imperialism at a definite and very high stage of its development, when certain of its fundamental attributes began to be transformed into their opposites, when the features of a period of transition from capitalism to a higher social and economic system began to take shape and reveal themselves all along the line. Economically, the main thing in this process is the substitution of capitalist monopolies for capitalist free competition. Free competition is the fundamental attribute of capitalism, and of commodity production generally. Monopoly is exactly the opposite of free competition; but we have seen the latter being transformed into monopoly before our very eyes, creating large-scale industry and eliminating small industry, replacing large-scale industry by still larger-scale industry, finally leading to such a concentration of production and capital that monopoly has been and is the result: cartels, syndicates and trusts, and merging with them, the capital of a dozen or so banks manipulating thousands of millions. At the same time monopoly, which has grown out of free competition, does not abolish the latter, but exists over it and alongside of it, and thereby gives rise to a number of very acute, intense antagonisms, friction and conflicts. Monopoly is the transition from capitalism to a higher system. If it were necessary to give the briefest possible definition of imperialism we should have to say that imperialism is the monopoly stage of capitalism. Such a definition would include what is most important, for, on the one hand, finance capital is the bank capital of a few big monopolist banks, merged with the capital of the monopolist combines of manufacturers; and, on the other hand, the division of the world is the transition from a colonial policy which has extended without hindrance to territories unoccupied by any capitalist power, to a colonial policy of monopolistic possession of the territory of the world which has been completely divided up.

But very brief definitions, although convenient, for they sum up the main points, are nevertheless inadequate, because very important features of the phenomenon that has to be defined have to be especially deduced. And so, without forgetting the conditional and relative value of all definitions, we must give a definition of imperialism that will embrace the following five essential features:

1) The concentration of production and capital developed to such a high stage that it created monopolies which play a decisive role in economic life.

2) The merging of bank capital with industrial capital, and the creation, on the basis of this "finance capital," of a "financial oligarchy."

3) The export of capital, which has become extremely important, as distinguished from the export of commodities.

4) The formation of international capitalist monopolies which share the world among themselves.

5) The territorial division of the whole world among the greatest capitalist powers is completed.

Imperialism is capitalism in that stage of development in which the dominance of monopolies and finance capital has established itself; in which the export of capital has acquired pronounced importance; in which the division of the world among the international trusts has begun; in which the division of all of the territories of the globe among the greatest capitalist powers has been completed.

We shall see later that imperialism can and must be defined differently if consideration is to be given, not only to the basic, purely economic factors—to which the above definition is limited—but also to the historical place of this stage of capitalism in relation to capitalism in general, or to the relations between imperialism and the two main trends in the working class movement....

From V.I. Lenin, *Imperialism, The Highest Stage of Capitalism*, New York: International Publishers, 1939, 88–90.

Document 75:
DECLARATION OF THE RIGHTS OF THE RUSSIAN PEOPLES (1917)
Pravda

This statement of rights early in the Bolshevik Revolution indicates the great idealism of early communism in Russia. It lists the immediate gains of the Revolution.

The October Revolution of the workers and peasants has begun under the common banner of deliverance.

The peasants have been freed from the yoke of the great landed proprietors, for there is no more private property in land—it is abolished.

The soldiers and sailors have been freed from the power of autocratic generals; the generals henceforth will be elected and removable at pleasure. The workers have been freed from the caprices and the arbitrariness of the capitalists, for starting from today control will be established by the workers over the workshops and the factories.

There remain but the people of Russia, who have been forbearing, have bided their time under the yoke and the arbitrariness, and whom it is necessary immediately to enfranchise and liberate.

In the epoch of Czarism, the peoples of Russia were aroused against each other. The results of this policy are known: massacres and pogroms on one side, enslaving of people on the other.

There can be no return to this shameful policy. Today it must be replaced by a voluntary and honest policy of union of the peoples of Russia.

In the epoch of imperialism, after the February revolution, when power passed into the hands of the Cadet bourgeoisie, the policy of incitation was replaced by a dastardly policy of distrust of the peoples of Russia, a policy of chicanery and provocation covering itself by the words of "liberty" and of "equality" of peoples. The results of this policy are known: increase of the antagonism between nationalities, lack of mutual confidence.

This unworthy policy of lies and mistrust, of chicanery and provocation must be definitely ended. It must be replaced today by an open and honest policy, leading to a complete mutual confidence of the peoples of Russia.

It is only thanks to such a confidence that the honest and solid union of all the peoples of Russia can be formed.

It is only thanks to such a union that the workers and peasants of Russia can be welded into a revolutionary force capable of defending itself against every attack on the part of the imperialist and annexationist bourgeoisie.

Starting on this principle, the first congress of soviets, in the month of June of this year, proclaimed the right of the peoples of Russia to self-determination.

The second congress of soviets in the month of October last confirmed this right in a more decisive and more precise fashion.

Executing the will of these soviets, the council of the people's commissaries has resolved to be guided in the question of nationalities by the following principles:

1. the equality and sovereignty of the peoples of Russia.

2. The right of the peoples of Russia to dispose of their own fate, even to separation and the establishment of an independent state.

3. Aboliton of all privileges and limitations, national or religious.

4. Free development of national minorities and ethnographic groups inhabiting Russian territory.

Decrees will be prepared immediately after the creation of a commission on nationalities. In the name of the Russian Republic,

The People's Commissary for Nationalities,
IOUSSIF DJOUGACHVILI STALIN
The President of the Council of the People' Commissaries,
V. ULIANOV

From *Readings in European History since 1814*, edited by Jonathan F. Scott and Alexander Baltzley, New York: F.S. Crofts & Co., 1931, 581–583.

Document 76:
THE FIVE-YEAR PLAN (1933)
Joseph Stalin

Joseph Stalin's first Five-Year Plan was carried out between 1928–1932. It was an attempt to modernize Soviet agriculture and industry so that it could compete with the capitalist countries. The plan enforced a radical reorganization of Russian society and caused such widespread disaffection that Stalin had to stop short of full implementation, a fact that he never publicly admitted.

THE FUNDAMENTAL TASK OF THE FIVE-YEAR PLAN AND THE PATH OF ITS FULFILLMENT

We now come to the question of the Five-Year Plan as such.

What is the Five-Year Plan?

What was the fundamental task of the Five-Year Plan?

The fundamental task of the Five-Year Plan was to transfer our country, with its backward, and in part medieval, technique, to the lines of new, modern technique.

The fundamental task of the Five-Year Plan was to convert the U.S.S.R. from an agrarian and weak country, dependent upon the caprices of the capitalist countries, into an industrial and powerful country, fully self-reliant and independent of the caprices of world capitalism.

The fundamental task of the Five-Year Plan was, in converting the U.S.S.R. into an industrial country, fully to eliminate the capitalist elements, to widen the front of socialist forms of economy, and to create the economic base for the abolition of classes in the U.S.S.R., for the construction of socialist society.

The fundamental task of the Five-Year Plan was to create such an industry in our country as would be able to re-equip and reorganize, not only the whole of industry, but also transport and agriculture—on the basis of socialism.

The fundamental task of the Five-Year Plan was to transfer small and scattered agriculture to the lines of large-scale collective farming, so as to ensure the economic base for socialism in the rural districts and thus to eliminate the possibility of the restoration of capitalism in the U.S.S.R.

Finally, the task of the Five-Year Plan was to create in the country all the necessary technical and economic prerequisites for increasing to the utmost the defensive capacity of the country, to enable it to organize determined resistance to any and every attempt at military intervention from outside, to any and every attempt at military attack from without.

What dictated this fundamental task of the Five-Year Plan; what were the grounds for it?

The necessity of putting an end to the technical and economic backwardness of the Soviet Union, which doomed it to an unenviable existence; the necessity of creating in the country such prerequisites as would enable it not only to overtake but in time to outstrip, economically and technically, the advanced capitalist countries....

The Five-Year Plan in the sphere of agriculture was a Five-Year Plan of collectivization. What did the party proceed from in carrying out collectivization?

The party proceeded from the fact that in order to consolidate the dictatorship of the proletariat and to build up socialist society it was necessary, in addition to industrialization, to pass from small, individual peasant farming to large-scale collective agriculture equipped with tractors and modern agricultural machinery, as the only firm basis for the Soviet power in the rural districts.

The party proceeded from the fact that without collectivization it would be impossible to lead our country onto the highroad of building the economic foundations of socialism, impossible to free the vast masses of the laboring peasantry from poverty and ignorance....

In this connection, the object of the Five-Year Plan in the sphere of agricultural was to unite the scattered and small individual peasant farms, which lacked the opportunity of utilizing tractors and modern agricultural machinery, into large collective farms, equipped with all the modern implements of highly developed agriculture, and to cover unoccupied land with model state farms.

The object of the Five-Year Plan in the sphere of agriculture was to convert the U.S.S.R. from a small-peasant and backward country into a large-scale agriculture organized on the basis of collective labor and providing maximum output for the market.

What has the party achieved in carrying out the program of the Five-Year Plan in four years in the sphere of agriculture? Has it fulfilled this program, or has it failed?

The party has succeeded, in a matter of three years, in organizing more than 200,000 collective farms and about 5,000 state farms specializing mainly in grain growing and livestock raising, and at the same time it has succeeded, in the course of four years, in enlarging the crop area by 21,000,000 hectares.

The party has succeeded in getting more than 60 per cent of the peasant farms, which account for more than 70 per cent of land cultivated by peasants, to unite into collective farms, which means that we have *fulfilled* the Five-Year Plan *threefold*.

The party has succeeded in creating the possibility of obtaining, not 500,000,000 to 600,000,000 poods [1 pood = 36 pounds] of marketable grain, which was the amount purchased in the period when individual peasant farming predominated, but 1,200,000,000 to 1,4000,000,000 poods of grain annually.

The party has succeeded in routing the kulaks as a class, although they have not yet been dealt the final blow; the laboring peasants have been emancipated from kulak bondage and exploitation, and a firm economic basis for the Soviet government, the basis of collective farming, has been established in the countryside.

The party has succeeded in converting the U.S.S.R. from a land of small peasant farming into a land where agriculture is run on the largest scale in the world.

Such, in general terms, are the results of the Five-Year Plan in four years in the sphere of agriculture.

Now you may judge for yourselves what all the talk of the bourgeois press about the "collapse" of collectivization, about the "failure" of the Five-Year Plan in the sphere of agriculture is worth after all this?

From Joseph Stalin, *Selected Writings*, New York: International Publishers, 1942, 242, 252–254.

Document 77:
ARTICLE 58 OF THE CRIMINAL CODE OF THE R.S.F.S.R. (1934)

This document is from the Russian Republic—the largest state within the Soviet Federation. It is from the criminal code and gives a broad definition of "counter-revolutionary crimes" so that it could be applied in many different circumstances. This permitted the police enormous powers and allowed the misconduct that characterizes the activities of the secret police, particularly in the "Great Purges."

Special Section, Chapter I
1. Counter-Revolutionary Crimes

Art. 58(i). Any act designed to overthrow, undermine or weaken the authority of the workers' and peasants' Soviets and the workers' and peasants' government of the Union of Soviet Socialist Republics, and of the Union and Autonomous Republics, elected by the Soviets on the basis of the Constitution of the U.S.S.R. and the Constitutions of the Union Republics or designed to undermine or weaken the external security of the U.S.S.R. and of the basic economic, political and national achievements of the proletarian revolution, is deemed to be a counter-revolutionary act.

In view of the international solidarity of the interests of all the toilers, such acts are also regarded as counter-revolutionary when they are directed against any other Workers' State, even though not forming part of the U.S.S.R.

Art. 58(i.a.). Treason against the homeland, i.e. acts committed by citizens of the U.S.S.R. to the detriment of the military strength of the U.S.S.R., its State independence, or the inviolability of its territory, such as: espionage, betrayal of a military or State secret, desertion to the enemy, flight abroad by land or air are punishable: by the supreme measure of criminal punishment—death by shooting and the confiscation of all property; in extenuating circumstances—by deprivation of liberty for a period of ten years and the confiscation of all property....

Art. 58(i.c.). In the event of flight abroad by land or air of a member of the armed forces, the adult members of his family, if they in any way assisted the preparation or the commission of this act of treason, or even if they knew of it but failed to report it to the authorities, are to be punished: by deprivation of liberty for a period of from five to ten years and confiscation of all property.

The remaining adult members of the traitor's family, and those living with him or dependent on him at the time of the commission of the crime are liable to deprivation of their electoral rights and to exile to the remote areas of Siberia for a period of five years....

Art. 58(ii). Armed insurrection or incursion of armed bands into Soviet territory, with counter-revolutionary aims, the seizure of power at the centre or in the provinces with the same aims and, in particular, with the aim of forcibly separating from the U.S.S.R or from a separate Union Republic any part of its territory or of violating treaties concluded between the U.S.S.R. and foreign States, entail: the supreme measure of social defence—death by shooting, or declaration as an enemy of the labouring masses, and the confiscation of property and deprivation of citizenship of the Union Republic and thereby of the U.S.S.R., and banishment beyond the frontiers of the U.S.S.R. for ever; in extenuating circumstances a reduction of sentence is permitted to deprivation of liberty for a period of not less than three years and the confiscation of all or part of the property.

Art. 58(iii). Maintenance of relations for counter-revolutionary purposes with foreign States or with individual representatives of those

States and also assistance, rendered by any means whatsoever, to a foreign State at war with the U.S.S.R. or engaged in fighting the U.S.S.R. by means of intervention or blockade entail: measures of social defence as indicated in Art. 58(ii) of the present Code.

Art. 58(iv). The rendering of assistance, by any means whatsoever, to that section of the international bourgeoisie, which, not recognizing the equal rights of the communist system which is coming to replace the capitalist system, is endeavouring to overthrow it, and also to public groups and organizations, under the influence of or directly organized by that bourgeoisie in conducting activities hostile to the U.S.S.R.: deprivation of liberty for a period of not less than three years and confiscation of all or part of his property; to be increased in especially grave circumstances to the supreme measure of social defence—death by shooting, or declaration as an enemy of the toiling masses, coupled with deprivation of citizenship of the Union Republic and thereby of citizenship of the U.S.S.R., and banishment for ever beyond the frontiers of the U.S.S.R., and the confiscation of property....

Art. 58(x). Propaganda or agitation containing an appeal to overthrow, undermine or weaken the Soviet regime, or to commit individual counter-revolutionary crimes and also the distribution, the preparation, or the conservation of literature of this nature, entails: deprivation of liberty for a period of not less than six months. Similar actions undertaken under conditions of mass unrest or involving the exploitation of the religious or national prejudices of the masses, or under conditions of war, or in localities placed under martial law are punishable by: measures of social defence, indicated in Article 58(ii) of the present Code.

Art. 58(xi). Any type of organizational activity, directed towards the preparation or the commission of crimes provided for in the present chapter, and also participation in an organization formed for the preparation or the commission of one of the crimes provided for in this chapter, is punishable by: the measures of social defence, indicated in the relevant articles of the present chapter.

Art. 58(xii). Failure to report reliable knowledge of preparation for, or commission of counter-revolutionary crime entails: deprivation of liberty for a period of not less than six months.

Art. 58(xiii). Actions or active struggle directed against the working class and the revolutionary movement, if committed by those in a responsible or secret (agent's) post under the Tsarist regime, under counter-revolutionary Governments during the Civil War, are punishable by: the measures of social defence indicated in Art. 58(ii) of the present Code.

Art. 58(xiv). Counter-revolutionary sabotage, i.e., deliberate nonfulfillment by anyone of duties laid down or the wilfully careless execution of those duties with a view to weakening the authority of the government, the functioning of the State apparatus, entails: deprivation of liberty for a period of not less than one year, with confiscation of all or part of his property; to be increased in especially grave circumstances, to the supreme measure of social defence—death by shooting with confiscation of property.

From Robert Conquest, *The Great Terror, Stalin's Purge of the Thirties*, New York: Macmillan, 1973, Appendix G, 741–746.

Document 78:
THE GREAT PURGE TRIAL (1938)
The Trial of Nikolai Ivanovich Bukharin

In the late 1930s, Stalin introduced the "Great Purges"—a time when many of the most respected leaders of the party, state and military were accused of treason and counter-revolutionary acts. They were paraded before tribunals where they made improbable confessions. Witnesses and victims reported that they had been brutally treated or tortured. This transcription is from the public trial of one of the original Bolshevik revolutionaries, Bukharin.

Evening Session, March 12, 1938

Bukharin: Citizen President and Citizens Judges, I fully agree with Citizen the Procurator regarding the significance of the trial, at which were exposed our dastardly crimes, the crimes committed by the "bloc of Rights and Troskyites," one of whose leaders I was, and for all the activities of which I bear responsibility.

This trial, which is the concluding one of a series of trials has exposed all the crimes and the treasonable activities, it has exposed the historical significance and the roots of our struggle against the Party and the Soviet government.

I have been in prison for over a year, and I therefore do not know what is going on in the world. But, judging from those fragments of real life that sometimes reached me by chance, I see, feel and understand that the interests which we so criminally betrayed are entering a new phase of gigantic development, are now appearing in the international arena as a great and mighty factor of the international proletarian phase.

We, the accused, are sitting on the other side of the barrier, and this barrier separates us from you, Citizens Judges. We found ourselves in the accursed ranks of the counter-revolution, became traitors to the Socialist fatherland.

At the very beginning of the trial, in answer to the question of Citizen the President, whether I pleaded guilty, I replied by a confession.

In answer to the question of Citizen the President whether I confirmed the testimony I had given, I replied that I confirmed it fully and entirely.

When, at the end of the preliminary investigation, I was summoned for interrogation to the State Prosecutor, who controlled the sum total of the materials of the investigation, he summarized them as follows:

Question: Were you a member of the centre of the counter-revolutionary organization of the Rights? I answered: Yes, I admit it.

Second question: Do you admit that the centre of the anti-Soviet organization, of which you are a member, engaged in counter-revolutionary activities and set itself the aim of violently overthrowing the leadership of the Party and the government? I answered: Yes, I admit it.

Third question: Do you admit that this centre engaged in terrorist activities, organized kulak uprisings and prepared for White-guard Kulak uprisings against members of the Political Bureau, against the leadership of the Party and the Soviet power? I answered: It is true.

Fourth question: Do you admit that you are guilty of treasonable activities, as expressed in preparations for a conspiracy aiming at a coup d'etat? I answered: Yes, that is also true.

In Court I admitted and still admit my guilt in respect to the crimes which I committed and of which I was accused by Citizen the State Prosecutor at the end of the Court investigation and on the basis of the materials of the investigation in the possession of the Procurator. I declared also in Court, and I stress and repeat it now, that I regard myself politically responsible for the sum total of the crimes committed by the "bloc of Rights and Trotskyites."

I have merited the most severe punishment, and I agree with Citizen the Procurator, who several times repeated that I stand on the threshold of my hour of death.

Nevertheless, I consider that I have the right to refute certain charges which were brought: a) in the printed indictment, b) during the Court investigation, and c) in the speech for the Prosecution made by Citizen the Procurator of the U.S.S.R.

I consider it necessary to mention that during my interrogation by Citizen the State Prosecutor, the latter declared in a very categorical form that I, as one of the accused, must not admit more than I had admitted and that I must not invent facts that have never happened, and he demanded that this statement of his should be placed on the records.

I once more repeat that I admit that I am guilty of treason to the Socialist fatherland, the most heinous of possible crimes, of the organization of kulak uprisings, of preparations for terrorist acts and of belonging to an underground, anti-Soviet organization. I further admit that I am guilty of organizing a conspiracy for a "palace coup." And this, incidentally, proves the incorrectness of all those passages in the speech for the prosecution made by Citizen the State Prosecutor, where he makes out that I adopted the pose of a pure theoretician, the pose of a philosopher, and so on. These are profoundly practical matters. I said, and I now repeat, that I was a leader and not a cog in the counter-revolutionary affairs. It follows from this, as will be clear to everybody, that there were many specific things which I could not have known, and which I actually did not know, but that this does not relieve me of responsibility.

I admit that I am responsible both politically and legally for the defeatist orientation, for it did dominate in the "bloc of Rights and Trotskyites," although I affirm:

a) that personally I did not hold this position;

b) that the phrase about opening the front was not uttered by me, but was an echo of my conversation with Tomsky;

c) that if Rykov heard this phrase for the first time from me, then, I repeat, it was an echo of my conversation with Tomsky.

But I consider myself responsible for a grave and monstrous crime against the Socialist fatherland and the whole international proletariat. I further consider myself responsible both politically and legally for wrecking activities, although I personally do not remember having given directions about wrecking activities. I did not talk about this. I once spoke positively on this subject to Grinko. Even in my testimony I mentioned that I had once told Radek that I considered this method of struggle as not very expedient. Yet Citizen the State Prosecutor makes me out to be a leader of the wrecking activities.

Citizen the Procurator explained in the speech for the prosecution that the members of a gang of brigands might commit robberies in different places, but that they would nevertheless be responsible for each other. That is true, but in order to be a gang the members of the gang of brigands must know each other and be in more or less close contact with each other. Yet I first learnt the name of Sharangovich from the Indictment, and I first saw him here in Court. It was here that I first learnt about the existence of Maximov, I have never been acquainted with Pletnev, I have never been acquainted with Kazakov, I have never spoken about counter-revolutionary matters with Rakovsky, I have never spoken on this subject with Rosengoltz, I have never spoken about it to Zelensky, I have never in my life spoken to Bulanov, and so on. Incidentally, even the Procurator did not ask me a single question about these people.

The "block of Rights and Trotskyites" is first and foremost a bloc of Rights and Trotskyites. How then, generally, could it include Levin, for example, who stated here in court that to this day he does not know what a Menshevik is? How could it include Pletnev, Kazakov and others?

Consequently, the accused in this dock are not a group. They are confederates in a conspiracy along various lines, but they are not a group in the strict and legal sense of the word. All the accused were connected in one way or another with the "bloc of Rights and Troskyites," some of them were also connected with intelligence services, but that is all. This, however, provides no grounds of asserting that this group is the "bloc of Rights and Troskyites."

Secondly, the "block of Rights and Trotskyites," which actually did exist and which was smashed by the organs of the People's Commissariate of Internal Affairs, arose historically. It did really exist until it was smashed by the organs of the People's Commissariat of Internal Affairs. It arose historically. I have testified that I first spoke to Kamenev as far back as 1928, during the Sixth Congress of the Comintern, which I at that time directed.

How then can it be asserted that the bloc was organized on the instructions of fascist intelligence services? Why, this was in 1929! By the way, at that time I narrowly missed death at the hands of an agent of the Polish "Defensiva," a fact very well known to everybody who stood close to the Party leadership.

Thirdly, I categorically deny that I was connected with foreign intelligence services, that they were my masters and that I acted in accordance with their wishes.

Citizen the Procurator asserts that I was one of the major organizers of espionage, on a par with Rykov. What are the proofs? The testimony of Sharangovich, of whose existence I had not even heard until I read the indictment.

From *The Great Purge Trial*, edited by Robert C. Tucker and Stephen F. Cohen, New York: Grosset & Dunlap, 1965, 656–659.

CHAPTER 11

The Fascist Assault on Human Rights

Document 79:
MEIN KAMPF (1925)
Adolf Hitler

Adolph Hitler was born in Austria, served in the German Army in World War I and became a member of a tiny party which he expanded into the German National Socialist Party. He was sentenced to prison for attempting to overthrow the democratic republic after World War I. In prison, he wrote Mein Kampf. *In these paragraphs he discusses the racial state he hoped to create. In the succeeding text he reveals his deep hatred of Jews and points to the eventual solution—extermination.*

The folkish state must make up for what everyone else today has neglected in this field. It must set race in the center of all life. It must take care to keep it pure. It must declare the child to be the most precious treasure of the people. It must see to it that only the healthy beget children; that there is only one disgrace: despite one's own sickness and deficiencies, to bring children into the world, and one highest honor: to renounce doing so. And conversely it must be considered reprehensible: to withhold healthy children from the nation. Here the state must act as the guardian of a millenial future in the face of which the wishes and the selfishness of the individual must appear as nothing and submit. It must put the most modern medical means in the service of this knowledge. It must declare unfit for propagation all who are in any way visibly sick or who have inherited a disease and can therefore pass it on, and put this into actual practice. Conversely, it must take care that the fertility of the healthy woman is not limited by the financial irresponsibility of a state regime which turns the blessing of children into a curse for the parents. It must put an end to that lazy, nay criminal, indifference with which the social premises for a fecund family are treated today, and must instead feel itself to be the highest guardian of this most precious blessing of a people. Its concern belongs more to the child than to the adult.

Those who are physically and mentally unhealthy and unworthy must not perpetuate their suffering in the body of their children. In this the folkish state must perform the most gigantic educational task. And some day this will seem to be a greater deed than the most victorious wars of our present bourgeois era. By education it must teach the individual that it is no disgrace, but only a misfortune deserving of pity, to be sick and weakly, but that it is a crime and hence at the same time a disgrace to dishonor one's misfortune by one's own egotism in burdening innocent creatures with it; that by comparison it bespeaks a nobility of highest idealism and the most admirable humanity if the innocently sick, renouncing a child of his own, bestows his love and tenderness upon a poor, unknown young scion of his own nationality, who with his health promises to become some day a powerful member of a powerful community. And in this educational work the state must perform the purely intellectual complement of its practical activity. It must act in this sense without regard to understanding or lack of understanding, approval or disapproval....

Once, as I was strolling through the Inner City, I suddenly encountered an apparition in a black caftan and black hair locks. Is this a Jew? was my first thought.

For, to be sure, they had not looked like that in Linz. I observed the man furtively and cautiously, but the longer I stared at this foreign face, scrutinizing feature for feature, the more my first question assumed a new form:

Is this a German?

As always in such cases, I now began to try to relieve my doubts by books. For a few hellers I bought the first anti-Semitic pamphlets of my life. Unfortunately, they all proceeded from the supposition that in principle the reader knew or even understood the Jewish question to a certain degree. Besides, the tone for the most part was such that doubts again arose in me, due in part to the dull and amazingly unscientific arguments favoring the thesis.

I relapsed for weeks at a time, once even for months.

The whole thing seemed to me so monstrous, the accusations so boundless, that, tormented by the fear of doing injustice, I again became anxious and uncertain.

Yet I could no longer very well doubt that the objects of my study were not Germans of a special religion, but a people in themselves; for since I had begun to concern myself with this question and to take cognizance of the Jews, Vienna appeared to me in a different light than before. Wherever I went, I began to see Jews, and the more I saw, the more sharply they became distinguished in my eyes from the rest of humanity. Particularly the Inner City and the districts north of the Danube Canal swarmed with a people which even outwardly had lost all resemblance to Germans.

And whatever doubts I may still have nourished were finally dispelled by the attitude of a portion of the Jews themselves.

Among them there was a great movement, quite extensive in Vienna, which came out sharply in confirmation of the national character of the Jews: this was the *Zionists*.

It looked, to be sure, as though only a part of the Jews approved this viewpoint, while the great majority condemned and inwardly rejected such a formulation. But when examined more closely, this appearance dissolved itself into an unsavory vapor of pretexts advanced for mere reasons of expedience, not to say lies. For the so-called liberal Jews did not reject the Zionists as non-Jews, but only as Jews with an impractical, perhaps even dangerous, way of publicly avowing their Jewishness.

Intrinsically they remained unalterably of one piece.

In a short time this apparent struggle between Zionistic and liberal Jews disgusted me; for it was false through and through, founded on lies and scarcely in keeping with the moral elevation and purity always claimed by this people.

The cleanliness of this people, moral and otherwise, I must say, is a point in itself. By their very exterior you could tell that these were no lovers of water, and, to your distress, you often knew it with your eyes closed. Later I often grew sick to my stomach from the smell of these caftan-wearers. Added to this, there was their unclean dress and their generally unheroic appearance.

All this could scarcely be called very attractive; but it became positively repulsive when, in addition to their physical uncleanliness, you discovered the moral stains on this "chosen people."

In a short time I was made more thoughtful than ever by my slowly rising insight into the type of activity carried on by the Jews in certain fields.

Was there any form of filth or profligacy, particularly in cultural life, without at least one Jew involved in it?

If you cut even cautiously into such an abscess, you found, like a maggot in a rotting body, often dazzled by the sudden light—a kike!

From Adolf Hitler, *Mein Kampf*, translated by Ralph Manheim, Boston: Houghton Mifflin Co., 1943. © 1943 and © renewed 1971 by Houghton Mifflin Co. Reprinted by permission of Houghton Mifflin Co.

Document 80:
THE POLITICAL AND SOCIAL DOCTRINE OF FASCISM (1935)
Benito Mussolini

Mussolini founded the Fascist Party of Italy at the end of World War I. In 1922 he was put into power, despite his lacking anything near a majority in the Italian Parliament. Through violence and intimidation and the collusion of important interests in the state, economy, military, and royal family, he turned Italy into a dictatorship. In this selection he defines Fascism. Note the place of the individual and human rights in this doctrine.

...Fascism was not the nursing of a doctrine worked out beforehand with detailed elaboration; it was born of the need for action and it was itself from the beginning practical rather than theoretical; it was not merely another political party but, even in the first two years, in opposition to all political parties as such, and itself a living movement. The name which I then gave to the organization fixed its character. And yet, if one were to re-read, in the now dusty columns of that date, the report of the meeting in which the *Fasci Italiana di combattimento* were constituted, one would there find no ordered expression of doctrine, but a series of aphorisms, anticipations, and aspirations which, when refined by time from the original ore, were destined after some years to develop into an ordered series of doctrinal concepts, forming the Fascist political doctrine—different from all others either of the past or the present day....

And above all, Fascism, the more it considers and observes the future and the development of humanity quite apart from political considerations of the moment, believes neither in the possibility nor the utility of perpetual peace. It thus repudiates the doctrine of Pacifism—born of a renunciation of the struggle and an act of cowardice in the face of sacrifice. War alone brings up to its highest tension all human energy and puts the stamp of nobility upon the peoples who have the courage to meet it. All other trials are substitutes, which never really put men into the position where they have to make the great decision—the alternative of life or death. Thus a doctrine which is founded upon this harmful postulate of peace is hostile to Fascism. And thus hostile to the spirit of Fascism, though accepted for what use they can be in dealing with particular political situations, are all the international leagues and societies which, as history will show, can be scattered to the winds when once strong national feeling is aroused by any motive—sentimental, ideal or practical....

...Fascism, now and always, believes in holiness and heroism; that is to say, in actions influenced by no economic motive, direct or indirect. And if the economic conception of history be denied, according to which theory men are no more than puppets, carried to and fro by the waves of chance, while the real directing forces are quite out of their control, it follows that the existence of an unchangeable and unchanging class-war is also denied—the natural progeny of the economic conception of history. And above all Fascism denies that class-war can be the preponderant force in the transformation of society. These two fundamental concepts of Socialism being thus refuted, nothing is left of it but the sentimental aspiration—as old as humanity itself—towards a social convention in which the sorrows and sufferings of the humblest shall be alleviated. But here again Fascism repudiates the conception of "economic" happiness, to be realized by Socialism and, as it were, at a given moment in economic evolution to assure everyone the maximum of well-being. Fascism denies the materialist conception of happiness as a possibility, and abandons it to its inventors, the economists of the first half of the nineteenth century: that is to say, Fascism denies the validity of the equation, well-being—happiness, which would reduce men to the level of animals, caring for one thing only—to be fat and well-fed—and would thus degrade humanity to a purely physical existence.

After Socialism, Fascism combats the whole complex system of democratic ideology, and repudiates it, whether in its theoretical premises or in its practical application. Fascism denies that the majority, by the simple fact that it is a majority, can direct human society; it denies that numbers alone can govern by means of a periodical consultation, and it affirms the immutable, beneficial, and fruitful inequality of mankind, which can never be permanently leveled through the mere operation of a mechanical process such as universal suffrage. The democratic regime may be defined as from time to time giving the people the illusion of sovereignty, while the real effective sovereignty lies in the hands of other concealed and irresponsible forces. Democracy is a regime nominally without a king, but it is ruled by many kings—more absolute, tyrannical, and ruinous than one sole king, even though a tyrant. This explains why Fascism, having first in 1922 (for reasons of expediency) assumed an attitude tending towards republicanism, renounced this point of view before the march to Rome; being convinced that the question of political form is not today of prime importance, and after having studied the examples of monarchies and republics past and present reached the conclusion that monarchy or republicanism are not to be judged, as it were, by an absolute standard; but that they represent forms in which the evolution—political, historical, traditional, or psychological—or a particular country has expressed itself....

Fascism has taken up an attitude of complete opposition to the doctrines of Liberalism, both in the political field and the field of economics. There should be no undue exaggeration (simply with the objects of immediate success in controversy) of the importance of Liberalism in the last century, nor should what was but one among many theories which appeared in that period be put forward as a religion for humanity for all time, present and to come. Liberalism only flourished for half a century....

In 1929, at the first five-yearly assembly of the Fascist regime, I said: For us Fascists, the State is not merely a guardian, preoccupied solely with the duty of assuring the personal safety of the citizens; nor is it an organization with purely material aims, such as to guarantee a certain level of well-being and peaceful conditions of life; for a mere council of administration would be sufficient to realize such objects. Nor is it a purely political creation, divorced from all contact with the complex material reality which makes up the life of the individual and the life of the people as a whole. The State, as conceived of and as created by Fascism, is a spiritual and moral fact in itself, since its political, juridical, and economic organization of the nation is a concrete thing: and such an organization must be in its origins and development a manifestation of the spirit. The State is the guarantor of security both internal and external, but it is also the custodian and transmitter of the spirit of the people, as it has grown up through the centuries in language, in customs, and in faith. And the State is not only a living reality of the present, it is also linked with the past and above all with the future, and thus transcending the brief limits of individual life, it represents the immanent spirit of the nation. The forms in which States express themselves may change, but the necessity for such forms is eternal. It is the State which educates its citizens in civic virtue, gives them a consciousness of their mission and welds them into unity; harmonizing their various interests through justice, and transmitting to future generations the mental conquests of science, of art, of law and the solidarity of humanity. It leads men from primitive tribal life to that highest expression of human power of its members who have died for its existence and in obedience to its laws, it holds up the memory of the leaders who have increased its territory and the geniuses who have illumined it with glory as an example to be followed by future generations. When the conception of the State declines, and disunifying and centrifugal tendencies prevail, whether of individuals or of particular groups, the nations where such phenomena appear are in their decline.

From 1929 until today, evolution, both political and economic, has everywhere gone to prove the validity of these doctrinal premises....

For Fascism, the growth of empire, that is to say the expansion of the nation, is an essential manifestation of vitality, and its opposite a sign of decadence. Peoples which are rising, or rising again after a period of decadence, are always imperialist; any renunciation is a sign of decay and of death. Fascism is the doctrine best adapted to represent the tendencies and the aspirations of a people, like the people of Italy, who are rising again after many centuries of abasement and foreign servitude. But empire demands discipline, the coordination of all forces and a deeply felt sense of duty and sacrifice: this fact explains many aspects of the practical working of the regime, the character of many forces in the State, and the necessarily severe measures which must be taken against those who would oppose this spontaneous and inevitable movement of Italy in the twentieth century, and would oppose it by recalling the outworn ideology of the nineteenth century—repudiated wheresoever there has been the courage to undertake great experiments of social and political transformation: for never before has the nation stood more in need of authority, of direction, and of order. If every age has its own characteristic doctrine, there are a thousand signs which point to Fascism as the characteristic doctrine of our time. For if a doctrine must be a living thing, this is proved by the fact that Fascism has created a living faith; and that this faith is very powerful in the minds of men, is demonstrated by those who have suffered and died for it.

Fascism has henceforth in the world the universality of all those doctrines which, in realizing themselves, have represented a stage in the history of the human spirit.

From Benito Mussolini, "The Political and Social Doctrine of Fascism", published in *International Conciliation*, No. 306, January 1935, 5–17. Reprinted by permission of Carnegie Endowment for International Peace.

Document 81:
THE COMMON INTEREST BEFORE SELF-INTEREST: NAZI VALUES

Below are several famous statements or policies of leaders of Nazi Germany.

Goebbels, the propaganda minister, subordinates the individual to the Nazi-stated needs of Germany. He also defines what a true Nazi is. In a devastating document, a German professor of physics gives a scandalous description of "German physics" which he says is different from "Jewish physics."

THE COMMON INTEREST BEFORE SELF-INTEREST (1926)
Joseph Goebbels

What is the first commandment of every National Socialist?
Love Germany more than anything, and your fellow Germans more than yourself!
What is the aim of the National Socialist idea of liberty?
To create the national community of all honestly creative Germans!
What is the content of that national community?
Freedom and bread for every German!
Who is a fellow German, a racial comrade?
Every honestly creative German is, provided his blood, his customs, his culture are German, and provided he speaks the German tongue!
What is the basic economic principle with which National Socialism wishes to replace the present economic warfare of all against all?
The Common Interest Before Self-Interest!

THE TRUE NATIONAL SOCIALIST (1944)
Joseph Goebbels

What does it mean to be a National Socialist?
To be a National Socialist means nothing but: Fight, Faith, Work, Sacrifice!
What do we National Socialists want for ourselves?
Nothing!
What do we National Socialists want for the creative German people?
Freedom!
What ties us National Socialists together, in this fight for Germany's freedom, within and without our borders?
The awareness of belonging to a community of fate, a community imbued with a spirit of radical innovation, a community whose members shall be companions, one to the other, in good times and in bad.
What is the National Socialist password to freedom:
God helps those who help themselves!!!

GERMAN PHYSICS (1935)
Philipp Lenard (Professor of Physics, Heidelberg University)

"...German physics?" people will ask. I might have said Aryan physics, too, or physics of Nordic man, physics of the truth-seekers and the reality-illuminators, physics of those who are the founders of natural science. "Science is and remains international!" people will want to object. But the objection proceeds from erroneous assumptions. In reality, science—like anything else created by man—is conditioned by blood and race. An illusion of internationality can be created by the fallacy of concluding that because the results of science are universally valid, its origins must be equally universal. Or else the illusion will be due to a failure to realize that people in other countries who pursued science in a manner identical or similar to that of the German people, could do so only because (and to the extent that) they, too, are or were of a predominantly Nordic racial mixture. People of different racial mixtures have different ways of pursuing science.

Of course no nation so much as began research in the natural sciences unless it based it on the nourishing soil of the achievements already supplied by Aryans. The stranger at first joined in, and imitated, many things; it takes a fairly long development to reveal his peculiar racial characteristics. Considering the literature now available, it might already be possible to talk of a physics of the Japanese; in the past, there was a physics of the Arabs. A physics of the negroes is unknown; however, a peculiar physics of the Jews has been spreading far and wide. Until now, it has not been very much recognized as such, mainly because of the custom of categorizing a literature according to the language in which it is written. Jews are everywhere, and people who today still defend the international quality of science mean, probably quite unconsciously, Jewish science. That science, so much is true, can indeed be found wherever Jews are, and is the same everywhere.

It is important to take a brief look at the "physics" of the Jewish people, because it is the antithesis of German physics, and because it is only by contrasting the two that the nature of German physics will truly be illuminated for many. As with everything Jewish, it has only been recently that an unprejudiced inquiry into Jewish physics could take place. For a long time, Jewish physics had developed reluctantly and surreptitiously. With the end of the war, however, when the Jews came to dominate Germany and to set its fashions, it suddenly, and with all its racial peculiarities intact, burst forth like a flood. Soon, it also found zealous defenders among authors of non-Jewish, or at least not wholly Jewish blood. To characterize it briefly, it would be fairest and best to recall the activities of its probably most outstanding representative, the presumably pure-blooded Jew A. Einstein. His "relativity theories" were meant to reshape and dominate the whole science of physics but when faced with reality, they lost all shred of validity. Nor can one assume that they were ever intended to be true. The Jew is remarkably lacking in a feeling for truth, for a more than surface recognition of that reality which will exist no matter what men's thought processes might be. In this, he represents the opposite of the—concerned and boundless—will to truth of the Aryan researcher....

From *The Nazi Years, A Documentary History*, edited by Joachim Remak, New York: Simon & Schuster, 1969, 39–40, 59–60.

Document 82:
THE NUREMBERG LAWS (1935)

After establishing the dictatorship in Germany, Hitler dismissed Jews from public affairs and removed their civil and economic rights—a series of acts that included special laws for Jews called the Nuremberg Laws. Note the collapse of Western traditions of human rights that these laws represent.

Law for the Protection of German Blood and German Honor (September 1935)
Entirely convinced that the purity of German blood is essential to the further existence of the German people, and inspired by the uncompromising determination to safeguard the future of the German nation, the Reichstag has unanimously resolved upon the following law, which is promulgated herewith:

Section 1. Marriages between Jews and citizens of German or kindred blood are forbidden. Marriages concluded in defiance of this law are void, even if, for the purpose of evading this law, they were concluded abroad.

Proceedings for annulment may be initiated only by the Public Prosecutor.

Section 2. Sexual relations outside marriage between Jews and nationals of German or kindred blood are forbidden.

Section 3. Jews will not be permitted to employ female citizens of German or kindred blood as domestic servants.

Section 4. Jews are forbidden to display the Reich and national flag or the national colours.

On the other hand they are permitted to display the Jewish colours. The exercise of this right is protected by the State.

Section 5. A person who acts contrary to the prohibition of Section 1 will be punished with hard labour.

A person who acts contrary to the prohibition of Section 2 will be punished with imprisonment or with hard labour.

A person who acts contrary to the provisions of Sections 3 or 4 will be punished with imprisonment up to a year and with a fine, or with one of these penalties.

From Office of United States Chief of Counsel for Prosecution of Axis Criminality, *Nazi Conspiracy and Aggression, Volume IV*, Washington, D.C.: GPO, 1946, 1415–1419.

Document 83:
THE POISONOUS MUSHROOM (Der Giftpilz) (1938)
Ernst Heimer

This odious piece indicates the depth to which literature and the arts sank in serving the racist ideas of the Nazi Third Reich. This was intended for the youth of Germany and was used after the war in the Nuremberg Trials as evidence of Nazi racial doctrine.

"It is almost noon," he said, "now we want to summarize what we have learned in this lesson. What did we discuss?"

All children raise their hands. The teacher calls to Karl Scholz, a little boy on the first bench. "We talked about how to recognize a Jew."

"Good! Now tell us about it!"

Little Karl takes the pointer, goes to the black board and points to the sketches.

"One usually recognizes a Jew by his nose. The Jewish nose is crooked at the end. it looks like the figure 6. Therefore it is called the 'Jewish Six'. Many non-Jews have crooked noses too. But their noses are bent, not at the end but further up. Such a nose is called a hook nose or eagle's beak. It has nothing to do with a Jewish nose."

"Right!" says the teacher. "But the Jew is recognized not only by his nose...." The boy continues. The Jew is also recognized by his lips. His lips are usually thick. Often the lower lip hangs down. That is called "sloppy". And the Jew is also recognized by his eyes. His eyelids are usually thicker and more fleshy than ours. The look of the Jew is lurking and sharp. Then the teacher goes to the desk and turns over the black board, on its back is a verse. The children recite it in chorus:

> From a Jew's countenance—
> the evil devil talks to us.
> The devil, who in every land—
> is known as evil plague.
> If we shall be free of the Jew—
> and again will be happy and glad.
> Then the youth must struggle with us—
> to subdue the Jew devil.

Inge sits in the reception room of the Jew doctor. She has to wait a long time. She looks through the journals that are on the table. But she is almost too nervous to read even a few sentences. Again and again she remembers the talk with her mother. And again and again her mind reflects on the warnings of her leader of the BDM [League of German Girls]: "A German must not consult a Jew doctor! And particularly not a German girl! Many a girl that went to a Jew doctor to be cured, found disease and disgrace!"

When Inge had entered the waiting room, she experienced an extraordinary incident. From the doctor's consulting room she could hear the sound of crying. She heard the voice of a young girl: "Doctor, doctor leave me alone!"

Then she heard the scornful laughing of a man. And then all of a sudden it became absolutely silent. Inge had listened breathlessly.

"What may be the meaning of all this?" she asked herself and her heart was pounding. And again she thought of the warning of her leader in the BDM.

Inge was already waiting for an hour. Again she takes the journals in an endeavor to read. Then the door opens. Inge looks up. The Jew appears. She screams. In terror she drops the paper. Frightened she jumps up. Her eyes stare into the face of the Jewish doctor. And this face is the face of the devil. In the middle of this devil's face is a huge crooked nose. Behind the spectacles two criminal eyes. And the thick lips are grinning. A grinning that expresses: "Now I got you at last, you little German girl!"

And then the Jew approaches her. His fleshy fingers stretch out after her. But now Inge has her wits. Before the Jew can grab hold of her, she hits the fat face of the Jew doctor with her hand. Then one jump to the door. Breathlessly Inge runs down the stairs. Breathlessly she escapes the Jew house....

From Office of United States Chief of Counsel for Prosecution of Axis Criminality, *Nazi Conspiracy and Aggression, Volume IV*, Washington, D.C.: GPO, 1946, 358–359.

Document 84: UNNECESSARY SENTIMENT (1943)
Heinrich Himmler

In the middle of World War II, German troops had occupied great parts of Europe. In this speech, Himmler reveals his government's attitudes toward the peoples controlled by the Nazis. Obviously international agreements and Western concepts of human rights were not to be observed.

In 1941 the Fuehrer attacked Russia. That was, as we can well see now, shortly,—perhaps three to six months—before Stalin prepared to embark on his great penetration into Central and Western Europe. I can give a picture of this first year in a few words. The attacking forces cut their way through. The Russian Army was herded together in great pockets, ground down, taken prisoner. At that time we did not value the mass of humanity as we value it today, as raw material, as labour. What after all, thinking in terms of generations, is not to be regretted, but is now deplorable by reason of the loss of labour, is that the prisoners died in tens and hundreds of thousands of exhaustion and hunger.

It is basically wrong for us to infuse all our inoffensive soul and spirit, our good-nature, and our idealism into foreign peoples. This is true since the time of Herder who clearly wrote "Voices of the Nations" [Stimmen der Voelker], in a state of drunkenness, thereby bringing on us, who come after him, such immeasurable sorrow and misery. This is true for instance, of the Czechs and the Slovenes to whom we gave their consciousness of nationality. They were just not capable of it themselves; we had to discover it for them.

One basic principle must be the absolute rule for the SS man: we must be honest, decent, loyal, and comradely to members of our own blood and to nobody else. What happens to a Russian, to a Czech does not interest me in the slightest. What the nations can offer in the way of good blood of our type, we will take, if necessary by kidnapping their children and raising them here with us. Whether nations live in prosperity or starve to death [verrecken—to die—used of cattle] interests me only in so far as we need them as slaves for our Kultur; otherwise, it is of no interest to me. Whether 10,000 Russian females fall down from exhaustion while digging an anti-tank ditch interests me only in so far as the anti-tank ditch for Germany is finished. We shall never be rough and heartless when it is not necessary, that is clear. We Germans, who are the only people in the world who have a decent attitude towards animals, will also assume a decent attitude towards these human animals. But it is a crime against our own blood to worry about them and give them ideals, thus causing our sons and grandsons to have a more difficult time with them. When somebody comes to me and says, "I cannot dig the anti-tank ditch with women and children, it is inhuman, for it would kill them," then I have to say, "You are a murderer of your own blood because if the anti-tank ditch is not dug, German soldiers will die, and they are sons of German mothers. They are our own blood." That is what I want to instill into the SS and what I believe have instilled into them as one of the most sacred laws of the future. Our concern, our duty is our people and our blood. It is for them that we must provide and plan, work and fight, nothing else. We can be indifferent to everything else. I wish the SS to adopt this attitude to the problem of all else. I wish the SS to adopt this attitude to the problem of all foreign, non-Germanic peoples, especially Russians. All else is vain, fraud against our own nation and an obstacle to the early winning of the war.

From Office of United States Chief of Counsel for Prosecution of Axis Criminality, *Nazi Conspiracy and Aggression, Volume IV*, Washington, D.C.: GPO, 1946, 558–559.

Document 85:
FIRST NIGHT IN AUSCHWITZ (1943)
Elie Wiesel

Elie Wiesel survived the Holocaust and in this selection describes the dehumanizing experience of a young man entering Auschwitz, the concentration camp in which the greatest number of Jews were murdered.

...Never shall I forget that night, the first night in camp, which has turned my life into one long night, seven times cursed and seven times sealed. Never shall I forget that smoke. Never shall I forget the little faces of the children, whose bodies I saw turned into wreaths of smoke beneath a silent blue sky.

Never shall I forget those flames which consumed my faith forever.

Never shall I forget that nocturnal silence which deprived me, for all eternity, of the desire to live. Never shall I forget those moments which murdered my God and my soul and turned my dreams to dust. Never shall I forget these things, even if I am condemned to live as long as God Himself. Never.

The barracks we had been made to go into was very long. In the roof were some blue-tinged skylights. The ante-chamber of Hell must look like this. So many crazed men, so many cries, so much bestial brutality.

There were dozens of prisoners to receive us, truncheons in their hands, striking out anywhere, at anyone, without reason. Orders:

"Strip! Fast! *Los*! Keep only your belts and shoes in your hands...."

We had to throw our clothes at one end of the barracks. There was already a great heap there. New suits and old, torn coats, rags. For us, this was the true equality: nakedness. Shivering with the cold.

Some SS officers moved about in the room, looking for strong men. If they were so keen on strength, perhaps one should try and pass oneself off as sturdy? My father thought the reverse. It was better not to draw attention to oneself. Our fate would then be the same as the others. (Later, we were to learn that he was right. Those who were selected that day were enlisted in the *Sonder-Kommando*, the unit which worked in the crematories. Bela Katz—son of a big tradesman from our town—had arrived at Birkenau with the first transport, a week before us. When he heard of our arrival, he managed to get word to us that, having been chosen for his strength, he had himself put his father's body into the crematory oven.)

Blows continued to rain down.

"To the barber!"

Belt and shoes in hand, I let myself be dragged off to the barbers. They took our hair off with clippers, and shaved off all the hair on our bodies. The same thought buzzed all the time in my head—not to be separated from my father.

Freed from the hands of the barbers, we began to wander in the crowd, meeting friends and acquaintances. These meetings filled us with joy—yes, joy—"Thank God! You're still alive!"

But others were crying. They used all their remaining strength in weeping. Why had they let themselves be brought here? Why couldn't they have died in their beds? Sobs choked their voices.

Suddenly, someone threw his arms round my neck in an embrace: Yechiel, brother of the rabbi of Sighet. He was sobbing bitterly. I thought he was weeping with joy at still being alive.

"Don't cry, Yechiel," I said. "Don't waste your tears...."

"Not cry? We're on the threshold of death.... Soon we shall have crossed over....Don't you understand? How could I not cry?"

Through the blue-tinged skylights I could see the darkness gradually fading. I had ceased to feel fear. And then I was overcome by an inhuman weariness.

Those absent no longer touched even the surface of our memories. We still spoke of them—"Who knows what may have become of them?"—but we had little concern for their fate. We were incapable of thinking of anything at all. Our senses were blunted; everything was blurred as in a fog. It was no longer possible to grasp anything. The instincts of self-preservation, of self-defense, of pride, had all deserted us. In one ultimate moment of lucidity it seemed to me that we were damned souls wandering in the half-world, souls condemned to wander through space till the generations of man came to an end, seeking their redemption, seeking oblivion—without hope of finding it....

I glanced at my father. How he had changed! His eyes had grown dim. I would have liked to speak to him, but I did not know what to say.

The night was gone. The morning star was shining in the sky. I too had become a completely different person. The student of the Talmud, the child that I was, had been consumed in the flames. There remained only a shape that looked like me. A dark flame had entered into my soul and devoured it.

So much had happened within such a few hours that I had lost all sense of time. When had we left our houses? And the ghetto? And the train? Was it only a week? One night—*one single night*?

How long had we been standing like this in the icy wind? An hour? Simply an hour? Sixty minutes?

Surely it was a dream....

From Elie Wiesel, *Night*. Translation copyright © 1960 by MacGibbon & Kee. Renewal copyright © 1988 by The Collins Publishing Group. Reprinted by permission of Hill and Wang, a division of Farrar, Straus and Giroux, Inc.

SECTION IV 1945–PRESENT

World War II exacted a terrible cost in human lives and liberties. Perhaps forty million people died and possibly a similar number were forced to leave their homes. The victors in the West were determined to set a new course in international affairs. A new order with a human rights doctrine at its core emerged momentarily in a rush of actions after 1945. Although the Cold War and events in both the East and the West paralyzed the new order, the ideals survived as progressive norms for international behavior. These norms occasionally have had a salutary effect on international behavior even during the era of Soviet-American confrontation. And with the waning of that era, the prospect of a second and more lasting birth of a new world order seems at least possible.

Four major characteristics distinguish international society after World War II from international society before the war. The first is the emergence of a host of significant international structures and organizations. The United Nations was the first and is still the most important of these. Its scope of concern spans virtually all global matters. It is the parent organization of many subsidiary entities dealing with economics, security, environment, communications, human rights and other concerns. It has been a sponsor of a multitude of treaties including major ones on human rights, a number of which are found in the following chapters. Regional organizations and subject-specific organizations such as the European Community, the Organization for African Unity, NATO, etc., have also taken their place on the world stage, sometimes fulfilling important roles. The emergence of such organizations and the formulation of important international conventions on a multitude of issues reflect the diminishing centrality of the state in international affairs. Prior to the twentieth century, sovereignty was a rather absolutist notion and the state was all. In today's international order, the state is still significant, but other entities are important as well.

A second major characteristic of the world since 1945 has been the Cold War. Such East-West tension has to some degree put limits on the impact of the growth of international organizations discussed above. Worldwide efforts on a range of issues, including human rights, were frequently frustrated by the politics of Cold War competition. The nuclear balance of terror undermined the realization of a collective right to peace, just as Soviet-American competition undermined the successful functioning of the United Nations Security Council. Human rights violations occurred in both camps. And they were minimized or publicized depending on which side they were committed. Soviet propaganda blared about racial discrimination in the West, particularly in the United States, and also pointed out economic injustices that existed in the Western democracies. All the while, the Soviets ignored repression at home and invaded countries on its periphery when those countries showed rebelliousness toward their satellite status. With equal hypocrisy, the West trumpeted its disapproval of Soviet repression while being less than perfect in domestic human rights enforcement and being highly imperfect in supporting governmental brutality in Argentina, Chile, Pakistan and elsewhere. Perhaps, with the Cold War at an end, the temptation to subjugate human rights to narrowly beneficial needs of national security will diminish.

The third major reality of the post-war world is decolonization. This phenomena is a concrete expression of the collective human right to self-determination. Much of today's scene is a product of this phenomenon. The colonial powers often resisted independence movements and responded with violence to the legitimate desires for self-determination unleashed by forces in World War II and unintentionally aided by the rhetoric of the West. In economic matters, colonial powers paid little attention to the needs of subject peoples and gave even less regard to their future development. Natural wealth in Africa, Asia and elsewhere was bought cheaply by Western companies whose disproportionate share in those former colonies' wealth continues to this day. Subsistence agriculture had been changed into raising cash crops desired by the European or world markets. Colonial powers played off one group against another. Boundaries were drawn without reference to ethnic, tribal or religious realities. The seeds were sown for terrible future problems. Unhappily, the final decolonization process has been so incomplete or imperfect, so late and so costly, that the Third World seems dominated by debt, deprivation, and dictatorship.

Whether human rights can be truly universalized or whether they remain normatively central only in the countries of the North is an unanswered question. Masses plagued by poverty throughout the underdeveloped world have legitimate grievances ignored by the industrialized democracies. These grievances are easily played upon by messianic tyrants. In 1990 such a concert of hate was orchestrated by Saddam Hussein in Iraq. One might question whether human rights norms in the developing world are more undercut by indigenous problems of tribalism and fundamentalism or by the inattention of the wealthy states to the suffering of others. Some see a danger in the possibility that the decolonization that removed the sahib may be replaced with a recolonization by the multi-national corporate executive.

For suppressed nations, self-determination often precedes democratic governance and assured civil liberties. This is seen in history from Irish support for the dictatorial James II in resistance to the Glorious Revolution to the attraction of Arab masses to leaders like Gamal Nasser and Saddam Hussein.

The fourth major characteristic of global society since World War II is the emergence of human rights itself as a concern in international relations. Prior to the war, there was some discussion periodically in international fora regarding rights of minorities, but there was nothing like the worldwide body of law that has emerged today prescribing treatment of humans by other humans. Today, discrimination, child labor, inadequate housing, etc. are no longer matters of mere domestic concern, they are matters for all the world. The civil rights movement begun in the 1950s in the United States shared mutual inspiration with the international human rights movement, then in its early stages worldwide. Concern for how brutal military dictators have treated their citizens in Cambodia, Turkey, Argentina, Uganda and elsewhere has led to international intervention ranging from mere investigation to actual humanitarian invasion in at least two instances (Bangladesh and Uganda). The cloak of domestic jurisdiction has been lifted and modern human rights is a concern for all, wherever the abuse of such rights is found.

The documents that follow reflect the characteristics of Post-War society described above. The Nuremburg trials and the founding of the United Nations were the watershed events at the conclusion of the Second World War that firmly implanted mandatory human rights norms into the international landscape. The Universal Declaration of Human Rights and the two United Nations Human Rights Covenants articulate those norms with institutionalized authority. The aspirations of emerging colonialized peoples are reflected in the statements of Kenyatta, Gandhi, Ho Chi Minh and Tutu, spanning a generation of decolonization. And Martin Luther King's loving manifesto for justice and tolerance represents a kind of domestic decolonization in America. Events within national borders have become inextricably linked to events across national borders as rights to liberty, equality and well-being have become internationalized. The promises of such rights are far from being realized, but women and men of all races and nationalities affirm the reality of humanity's obligation to itself to keep these promises.

CHAPTER 12

Post-War Internationalization of Human Rights

Document 86:
CRIMES COMING WITHIN THE JURISDICTION OF THE INTERNATIONAL MILITARY TRIBUNAL (NUREMBERG) (1945)

The Nuremberg Trials were a major event in the development of international law generally and Human Rights doctrine in particular. The trial of Nazi war criminals entrenched a number of crucial principles of world law and morality. It is illegal for a nation to wage aggressive war against its neighbors; it is illegal for a nation to enslave and murder innocent masses of people, either outside or within its own borders; and persons who commit such crimes may be held individually responsible and punished accordingly.

II. Jurisdiction and General Principles

Article 6. The Tribunal established by the Agreement referred to in Article 1 hereof for the trial and punishment of the major war criminals of the European Axis countries shall have the power to try and punish persons who, acting in the interests of the European Axis countries, whether as individuals or as members of organizations, committed any of the following crimes.

The following acts, or any of them, are crimes coming within the jurisdiction of the Tribunal for which there shall be individual responsibility:

(a) *Crimes Against the Peace* [ed. note: italics are the editors' for the purpose of emphasis]: namely, planning, preparation, in initiation or waging of a war of aggression, or a war in violation of international treaties, agreements or assurances, or participation in a common plan or conspiracy for the accomplishment of any of the foregoing;

(b) *War Crimes*: namely, violations of the laws or customs of war. Such violations shall include, but not be limited to, murder, ill-treatment or deportation to slave labor or for any other purpose of civilian population of or in occupied territory, murder or ill-treatment of prisoners of war or persons on the seas, killing of hostages, plunder of public or private property, wanton destruction of cities, towns or villages, or devastation not justified by military necessity;

(c) *Crimes Against Humanity*: namely, murder, extermination, enslavement, deportation, and other inhumane acts committed against *any civilian population*, before or during the war; or persecutions on political, racial or religious grounds in execution of or in connection with any crime within the jurisdiction of the Tribunal, whether or not in violation of domestic law of the country where perpetrated.

Leaders, organizers, instigators and accomplices participating in the formulation or execution of a common plan or conspiracy to commit any of the foregoing crimes are responsible for all acts performed by any persons in execution of such plan.

From International Military Tribunal, *Trial of the Major War Criminals before the International Military Tribunal*, 42 volumes [Blue Series], Volume 1, Nuremberg, Germany, 1949, 8–16.

Document 87:
CHARTER OF THE UNITED NATIONS (1945)

The Charter of the United Nations was a blueprint for a new world order when it was drafted in 1945. Its practical impact has been limited by the Cold War and only now may its vision again come into prominence. As seen in this short excerpt, one of the United Nations' primary purposes is the promotion of human rights through international law and institutions.

We the peoples of the United Nations determined to save succeeding generations from the scourge of war, which twice in our lifetime has brought untold sorrow to mankind, and to reaffirm faith in fundamental human rights, in the dignity and worth of the human person, in the equal rights of men and women and of nations large and small, and to establish conditions under which justice and respect for the obligations arising from treaties and other sources of international law can be maintained, and to promote social progress and better standards of life in larger freedom, and for these ends to practice tolerance and live together in peace with one another as good neighbors, and to unite our strength to maintain international peace and security, and to ensure, by the acceptance of principles and the institution of methods, that armed force shall not be used, save in the common interest, and to employ international machinery for the promotion of the economic and social advancement of all peoples have resolved to combine our efforts to accomplish these aims.

Accordingly, our respective Governments, through representatives assembled in the city of San Francisco, who have exhibited their full powers found to be in good and due form, have agreed to the present Charter of the United Nations and do hereby establish an international organization to be known as the United Nations.

Article 1. The purposes of the United Nations are:

1. To maintain international peace and security, and to that end: to take effective collective measures for the prevention and removal of threats to the peace, and for the suppression of acts of aggression or other breaches of the peace, and to bring about by peaceful means, and in conformity with the principles of justice and international law, adjustment or settlement of international disputes or situations which might lead to a breach of the peace;

2. To develop friendly relations among nations based on respect for the principle of equal rights and self-determination of peoples, and to take other appropriate measures to strengthen universal peace;

3. To achieve international cooperation in solving international problems of an economic, social, cultural, or humanitarian character, and in promoting and encouraging respect for human rights and for fundamental freedoms for all without distinction as to race, sex, language, or religion; and

4. To be a center for harmonizing the actions of nations in the attainment of these common ends.

Article 2. The Organization and its Members in pursuit of the Purposes stated in Article 1, shall act in accordance with the following Principles.

1. The Organization is based on the principle of the sovereign equality of all its Members.

2. All Members, in order to ensure to all of them the rights and benefits resulting from membership, shall fulfil in good faith the obligations assumed by them in accordance with the present Charter.

3. All Members shall settle their international disputes by peaceful means in such a manner that international peace and security, and justice are not endangered.

4. All Members shall refrain in their international relations from the threat or use of force against the territorial integrity or political independence of any state, or in any other manner inconsistent with the Purposes of the United Nations.

5. All Members shall give the United Nations every assistance in any action it takes in accordance with the present Charter, and shall refrain from giving assistance to any state against which the United Nations is taking preventive or enforcement action.

6. The Organization shall ensure that states which are not Members of the United Nations are in accordance with these Principles so far as may be necessary for the maintenance of international peace and security.

7. Nothing contained in the present Charter shall authorize the United Nations to intervene in matters which are essentially within the domestic jurisdiction of any state or shall require the Members to submit such matters to settlement under the present Charter; but this principle shall not prejudice the application of enforcement measures under Chapter VII....

Article 11.

1. The General Assembly may consider the general principles of cooperation in the maintenance of international peace and security, including the principles governing disarmament and the regulation of armaments, and may make recommendations with regard to such principles to the Members or to the Security Council or to both.

2. The General Assembly may discuss any questions relating to the maintenance of international peace and security brought before it by a state which is not a Member of the United Nations in accordance with Article 35, paragraph 2, and except as provided in Article 12, may make recommendations with regard to any

such question to the state or states concerned or to the Security Council or to both. Any such question on which action is necessary shall be referred to the Security Council by the General Assembly either before or after discussion.

3. The General Assembly may call the attention of the Security Council to situations which are likely to endanger international peace and security....

Article 55. With a view to the creation of conditions of stability and well-being which are necessary for peaceful and friendly relations among nations based on respect for the principle of equal rights and self-determination of peoples, the United Nations shall promote:

  a. higher standards of living, full employment, and conditions of economic and social progress and development.

  b. solutions of international economic, social, health, and related problems; and international cultural and educational cooperation; and

  c. universal respect for, and observance of, human rights and fundamental freedoms for all without distinction as to race, sex, language, or religion.

Article 56. All members pledge themselves to take joint and separate action in cooperation with the Organization for the achievement of the purposes set forth in Article 55....

Article 62

1. The Economic and Social Council may make or initiate studies and reports with respect to international economic, social, cultural, educational, health, and related matters and may make recommendations with respect to any such matters to the General Assembly, to the Members of the United Nations, and to the specialized agencies concerned.

2. It may make recommendations for the purpose of promoting respect for, and observance of, human rights and fundamental freedoms for all.

3. It may prepare draft conventions for submission to the General Assembly, with respect to matters falling within its competence.

4. It may call, in accordance with the rules prescribed by the United Nations, international conferences on matters falling within its competence....

Article 76. The basic objectives of the trusteeship system, in accordance with the Purposes of the United Nations laid down in Article 1 of the present Charter shall be:

  a. to further international peace and security;

  b. to promote the political, economic, social, and educational advancement of the inhabitants of the trust territories, and their progressive development towards self-government or independence as may be appropriate to the particular circumstances of each territory and its peoples and the freely expressed wishes of the peoples concerned, and as may be provided by the terms of each trusteeship agreement;

  c. to encourage respect for human rights and for fundamental freedoms for all without distinction as to race, sex, language, or religion, and to encourage recognition of the interdependence of the peoples of the world; and

  d. to ensure equal treatment in social, economic, and commercial matters for all Members of the United Nations and their nationals, and also equal treatment for the latter in the administration of justice, without prejudice to the attainment of the foregoing objectives and subject to the provisions of Article 80....

From *Charter of the United Nations, Commentary and Documents*, edited by Leland M. Goodrich Evard Hambro and Anne Patricia Simons, third and revised edition, NY: Columbia University Press, 1969, 2.

Document 88:
CONVENTION ON THE PREVENTION AND PUNISHMENT OF THE CRIME OF GENOCIDE (1948)

Genocide is probably the ultimate international crime, denying the primary human right—life—to entire ethnic groups. The Holocaust of the Jews, Gypsies and others during World War II prompted this convention. Tragically, genocide had occurred before the World War II Holocaust, and it has happened since.

Approved and proposed for signature and ratification or accession by General Assembly resolution 260 A (III) of 9 December 1948

Entry into force: 12 January 1951, in accordance with article XIII

The Contracting Parties, having considered the declaration made by the General Assembly of the United Nations in its resolution 96 (I)

dated 11 December 1946 that genocide is a crime under international law, contrary to the spirit and aims of the United Nations and condemned by the civilized world, recognizing that at all periods of history genocide has inflicted great losses on humanity, and being convinced that, in order to liberate mankind from such an odious scourge, international co-operation is required, hereby agree as hereinafter provided:

Article I. The Contracting Parties confirm that genocide, whether committed in time of peace or time of war, is a crime under international law which they undertake to prevent and to punish.

Article II. In the present Convention, genocide means any of the following acts committed with intent to destroy, in whole or in part, a national, ethnical, racial or religious group, as such:

(a) Killing members of the group;

(b) Causing serious bodily or mental harm to members of the group;

(c) Deliberately inflicting on the group conditions of life calculated to bring about its physical destruction in whole or in part;

(d) Imposing measures intended to prevent births within the group;

(e) Forcibly transferring children of the group to another group.

Article III. The following acts shall be punishable:

(a) Genocide;

(b) Conspiracy to commit genocide;

(c) Direct and public incitement to commit genocide;

(d) Attempt to commit genocide;

(e) Complicity in genocide.

Article IV. Persons committing genocide or any of the other acts enumerated in article III shall be punished, whether they are constitutionally responsible rulers, public officials or private individuals.

Article V. The Contracting Parties undertake to enact, in accordance with their respective Constitutions, the necessary legislation to give effect to the provisions of the present Convention and, in particular, to provide effective penalties for persons guilty of genocide or any of the other acts enumerated in article III.

Article VI. Persons charged with genocide or any of the other acts enumerated in article III shall be tried by a competent tribunal of the State in the territory of which the act was committed, or by such international penal tribunal as may have jurisdiction with respect to those Contracting Parties which shall have accepted its jurisdiction.

Article VII. Genocide and the other acts enumerated in article III shall not be considered as political crimes for the purpose of extradition.

The Contracting Parties pledge themselves in such cases to grant extradition in accordance with their laws and treaties in force.

Article VIII. Any Contracting Party may call upon the competent organs of the United Nations to take such action under the Charter of the United Nations as they consider appropriate for the prevention and suppression of acts of genocide or any of the other acts enumerated in article III.

Article IX. Disputes between the Contracting Parties relating to the interpretation, application or fulfillment of the present Convention, including those relating to the responsibility of a State for genocide or for any of the other acts enumerated in article III, shall be submitted to the International Court of Justice at the request of any of the parties to the dispute.

Article X. The present Convention, of which the Chinese, English, French, Russian and Spanish texts are equally authentic, shall bear the date of 9 December 1948....

From U.S. House of Representatives Committee on Foreign Affairs, *Human Rights Documents, A Compilation of Documents Pertaining to Human Rights*, Washington, D.C.: GPO, 1983, 105–108.

Document 89:
UNIVERSAL DECLARATION OF HUMAN RIGHTS (1948)

International statespersons and human rights activists promoted an "International Bill of Rights" to be adopted under the auspices of the United Nations in the late 1940s. It was to include a Declaration of Human Rights and a more detailed treaty elaborating such rights. In 1948, the United Nations General Assembly took the first step by adopting nearly unanimously, with some Soviet bloc abstentions, the Universal Declaration of Human Rights. However, a General Assembly resolution is not, by itself, binding law. The second step of negotiating a binding multi-nation treaty codifying all major human rights was more difficult. In fact, the treaty was split into two covenants, one dealing with civil and political rights and one with economic, social and cultural ones.

The negotiations were difficult, especially regarding the economic rights treaty, with Western nations somewhat uncomfortable with promises of entitlements that had socialist undertones. The Conventions were not even opened for signatures until 1966, almost two decades after an international bill of rights was first conceived, evidence of the complexity of the negotiation and drafting. Today, however, by their high status and wide acceptance, the Conventions, together with the Universal Declaration of Human Rights, represent customary norms of international human rights.

At this point, the United States is the only major democracy which has not ratified these Conventions.

Adopted and Proclaimed by General Assembly Resolution 217 A (III) of 10 December 1948

Preamble

WHEREAS recognition of the inherent dignity and of the equal and inalienable rights of all members of the human family is the foundation of freedom, justice and peace in the world, whereas disregard and contempt for human rights have resulted in barbarous acts which have outraged the conscience of mankind, and the advent of a world in which human beings shall enjoy freedom of speech and belief and freedom from fear and want has been proclaimed as the highest aspiration of the common people, whereas it is essential, if man is not to be compelled to have recourse, as a last resort, to rebellion against tyranny and oppression, that human rights should be protected by the rule of law, whereas it is essential to promote the development of friendly relations between nations, whereas the peoples of the United Nations have in the Charter reaffirmed their faith in fundamental human rights, in the dignity and worth of the human person and in the equal rights of men and women and have determined to promote social progress and better standards of life in larger freedom, whereas Member States have pledged themselves to achieve, in co-operation with the United Nations, the promotion of universal respect for and observance of human rights and fundamental freedoms, whereas a common understanding of these rights and freedoms is of the greatest importance for the full realization of this pledge, now therefore, the General Assembly proclaims this Universal Declaration of Human Rights as a common standard of achievement for all peoples and all nations, to the end that every individual and every organ of society, keeping this Declaration constantly in mind, shall strive by teaching and education to promote respect for these rights and freedoms and by progressive measures, national and international, to secure their universal and effective recognition and observance, both among the peoples of Member States themselves and among the peoples of territories under their jurisdiction.

Article 1. All human beings are born free and equal in dignity and rights. They are endowed with reason and conscience and should act towards one another in a spirit of brotherhood.

Article 2. Everyone is entitled to all the rights and freedoms set forth in this Declaration, without distinction of any kind, such as race, colour, sex, language, religion, political or other opinion, national or social origin, property, birth or other status.

Furthermore, no distinction shall be made on the basis of the political, jurisdictional or international status of the country or territory to which a person belongs, whether it be independent, trust, non-self-governing or under any other limitation of sovereignty.

Article 3. Everyone has the right to life, liberty and security of person.

Article 4. No one shall be held in slavery or servitude; slavery and the slave trade shall be prohibited in all their forms.

Article 5. No one shall be subjected to torture or to cruel, inhuman or degrading treatment or punishment.

Article 6. Everyone has the right to recognition everywhere as a person before the law.

Article 7. All are equal before the law and are entitled without any discrimination to equal protection of the law. All are entitled to equal protection against any discrimination in violation of this Declaration and against any incitement to such discrimination.

Article 8. Everyone has the right to an effective remedy by the competent national tribunals for acts violating the fundamental rights granted him by the constitution or by law.

Article 9. No one shall be subjected to arbitrary arrest, detention or exile.

Article 10. Everyone is entitled in full equality to a fair and public hearing by an independent and impartial tribunal, in the determination of his rights and obligations and of any criminal charge against him.

Article 11

1. Everyone charged with a penal offence has the right to be presumed innocent until proved guilty according to law in a public trial at which he has had all the guarantees necessary for his defence.

2. No one shall be held guilty of any penal offence on account of any act or omission which did not constitute a penal offence, under national or international law, at the time when it was committed. Nor shall a heavier penalty be imposed than the one that was applicable at the time the penal offence was committed.

Article 12. No one shall be subjected to arbitrary interference with his privacy, family, home or correspondence, nor to attacks upon his honour and reputation. Everyone has the right to the protection of the law against such interference or attacks.

Article 13

1. Everyone has the right to freedom of movement and residence within the borders of each State.

2. Everyone has the right to leave any country, including his own, and to return to his country.

Article 14

1. Everyone has the right to seek and to enjoy in other countries asylum from persecution.

2. This right may not be invoked in the case of prosecutions genuinely arising from non-political crimes or from acts contrary to the purposes and principles of the United Nations.

Article 15

1. Everyone has the right to a nationality.

2. No one shall be arbitrarily deprived of his nationality nor denied the right to change his nationality.

Article 16

1. Men and women of full age, without any limitation due to race, nationality or religion, have the right to marry and to found a family. They are entitled to equal rights as to marriage, during marriage and its dissolution.

2. Marriage shall be entered into only with the free and full consent of the intending spouses.

3. The family is the natural and fundamental group unit of society and is entitled to protection by society and the State.

Article 17

1. Everyone has the right to own property alone as well as in association with others.

2. No one shall be arbitrarily deprived of his property.

Article 18. Everyone has the right to freedom of thought, conscience and religion; this right includes freedom to change his religion or belief, and freedom, either alone or in community with others and in public or private, to manifest his religion or belief in teaching, practice, worship and observance.

Article 19. Everyone has the right to freedom of opinion and expression; this right includes freedom to hold opinions without interference and to seek, receive and impart information and ideas through any media and regardless of frontiers.

Article 20

1. Everyone has the right to freedom of peaceful assembly and association.

2. No one may be compelled to belong to an association.

Article 21

1. Everyone has the right to take part in the government of his country, directly or through freely chosen representatives.

2. Everyone has the right of equal access to public service in his country.

3. The will of the people shall be the basis of the authority of government; this will shall be expressed in periodic and genuine elections which shall be by universal and equal suffrage and shall be held by secret vote or by equivalent free voting procedures.

Article 22. Everyone, as a member of society, has the right to social security and is entitled to realization, through national effort and international co-operation and in accordance with the organization and resources of each State, of the economic, social and cultural rights indispensable for his dignity and the free development of his personality.

Article 23

1. Everyone has the right to work, to free choice of employment, to just and favourable conditions of work and to protection against unemployment.

2. Everyone, without any discrimination, has the right to equal pay for equal work.

3. Everyone who works has the right to just and favourable remuneration ensuring for himself and his family an existence worthy of human dignity, and supplemented, if necessary, by other means of social protection.

4. Everyone has the right to form and to join trade unions for the protection of his interests.

Article 24. Everyone has the right to rest and leisure, including reasonable limitation of working hours and periodic holidays with pay.

Article 25

1. Everyone has the right to a standard of living adequate for the health and well-being of himself and of his family, including food, clothing, housing and medical care and necessary social services, and the right to security in the event of unemployment, sickness, disability, widowhood, old age or other lack of livelihood in circumstances beyond his control.

2. Motherhood and childhood are entitled to special care and assistance. All children, whether born in or out of wedlock, shall enjoy the same social protection.

Article 26

1. Everyone has the right to education. Education shall be free, at least in the elementary and fundamental states. Elementary education shall be compulsory. Technical and professional education shall be made generally available and higher education shall be equally accessible to all on the basis of merit.

2. Education shall be directed to the full development of the human personality and to the strengthening of respect for human rights and fundamental freedoms. It shall promote understanding, tolerance and friendship among all nations, racial or religious groups, and shall further the activities of the United Nations for the maintenance of peace.

3. Parents have a prior right to choose the kind of education that shall be given to their children.

Article 27

1. Everyone has the right freely to participate in the cultural life of the community, to enjoy the arts and to share in scientific advancement and its benefits.

2. Everyone has the right to the protection of the moral and material interests resulting from any scientific, literary or artistic production of which he is the author.

Article 28. Everyone is entitled to a social and international order in which the rights and freedoms set forth in this Declaration can be fully realized.

Article 29

1. Everyone has duties to the community in which alone the free and full development of his personality is possible.

2. In the exercise of his rights and freedoms, everyone shall be subject only to such limitations as are determined by law solely for the purpose of securing due recognition and respect for the rights and freedoms of others and of meeting the just requirement of morality, public order and the general welfare in a democratic society.

3. These rights and freedoms may in no case be exercised contrary to the purposes and principles of the United Nations.

Article 30. Nothing in this Declaration may be interpreted as implying for any State, group or person any right to engage in any activity or to perform any act aimed at the destruction of any of the rights and freedoms set forth herein.

From U.S. House of Representatives Committee on Foreign Affairs, *Human Rights Documents, A Compilation of Documents Pertaining to Human Rights*, Washington, D.C.: GPO, 1983, 63–68.

Document 90: THE GENEVA CONVENTION OF 1949

There are four Geneva Conventions of 1949 dealing with the law governing human conduct in warfare (or "humanitarian law"). They are successors to the Geneva conventions of 1924. These treaties are among the most widely subscribed to of all international conventions. The overwhelming bulk of the world's nations, including virtually all major states, are parties. They are so widely accepted that the bulk of their provisions should now be regarded as customary international law. Treaty 1 governs the treatment of the wounded on land, Treaty 2 governs the treatment of the wounded at sea, Treaty 3 governs the treatment of prisoners and Treaty 4 governs the treatment of civilians. While principally dealing with international warfare, common provision 3 sets at least minimum standards of humane behavior for civil wars.

CONVENTION (I) FOR THE AMELIORATION OF THE CONDITION OF THE WOUNDED AND SICK IN ARMED FORCES IN THE FIELD—SIGNED AT GENEVA, 12 AUGUST 1949; U.S. SENATE RATIFIED JULY 6, 1955

Article 1. The High Contracting Parties undertake to respect and to ensure respect for the present Convention in all circumstances.

Article 2. In addition to the provisions which shall be implemented in peacetime, the present Convention shall apply to all cases of declared war or of any other armed conflict which may arise between two or more of the High Contracting Parties, even if the state of war is not recognized by one of them.

The Convention shall also apply to all cases of partial or total occupation of the territory of a High Contracting Party, even if the said occupation meets with no armed resistance.

Although one of the Powers in conflict may not be a party to the present Convention, the Powers who are parties thereto shall remain bound by it in their mutual relations. They shall furthermore be bound by the Convention in relation to the said Power, if the latter accepts and applies the provisions thereof.

Article 3. In the case of armed conflict not of an international charter occurring in the territory of one of the High Contracting Parties, each Party to the conflict shall be bound to apply, as a minimum, the following provisions:

(1) Persons taking no active part in the hostilities, including members of armed forces who have laid down their arms and those placed *hors de combat* by sickness, wounds, detention, or any other cause, shall in all circumstances be treated humanely, without any adverse distinction founded on race, colour, religion or faith, sex, birth or wealth, or any other similar criteria.

To this end, the following acts are and shall remain prohibited at any time and in any place whatsoever with respect to the above-mentioned persons:

(a) violence to life and person, in particular murder of all kinds, mutilation, cruel treatment and torture;

(b) taking of hostages;

(c) outrages upon personal dignity, in particular humiliating and degrading treatment;

(d) the passing of sentences and the carrying out of executions without previous judgment pronounced by a regularly constituted court, affording all the judicial guarantees which are recognized as indispensable by civilized peoples.

(2) The wounded and sick shall be collected and cared for.

An impartial humanitarian body, such as the International Committee of the Red Cross, may offer its services to the Parties to the conflict....

Article 12. Members of the armed forces and other persons mentioned in the following Article, who are wounded or sick, shall be respected and protected in all circumstances.

They shall be treated humanely and cared for by the Party to the conflict in whose power they may be, without any adverse distinction founded on sex, race, nationality, religion, political opinions, or any other similar criteria. Any attempts upon their lives, or violence to their persons, shall be strictly prohibited; in particular, they shall not be murdered or exterminated, subjected to torture or to biological experiments; they shall not wilfully be left without medical assistance and care, nor shall conditions exposing them to contagion or infection be created.

Only urgent medical reasons will authorize priority in the order of treatment to be administered.

Women shall be treated with all consideration due to their sex.

The Party to the conflict which is compelled to abandon wounded or sick to the enemy shall, as far as military considerations permit, leave with them a part of its medical personnel and material to assist in their care.

Article 13. The present Convention shall apply to the wounded and sick belonging to the following categories:

(1) Members of the armed forces of a Party to the conflict, as well as members of militias or volunteer corps forming part of such armed forces.

(2) Members of other militias and members of other volunteer corps, including those of organized resistance movements, belonging to a Party to the conflict and operating in or outside their own territory, even if this territory is occupied, provided that such militias or volunteer corps, including such organized resistance movements, fulfill the following conditions:

(a) that of being commanded by a person responsible for his subordinates;

(b) that of having a fixed distinctive sign recognizable at a distance;

(c) that of carrying arms openly;

(d) that of conducting their operations in accordance with the laws and customs of war.

(3) Members of regular armed forces who profess allegiance to a Government or an authority not recognized by the Detaining Power.

(4) Persons who accompany the armed forces without actually being members thereof, such as civil members of military aircraft crews, war correspondents, supply contractors, members of labour units or of services responsible for the welfare of the armed forces, provided that they have received authorization from the armed forces which they accompany.

(5) Members of crews, including masters, pilots and apprentices, of the merchant marine and the crews of civil aircraft of the Parties to the conflict, who do not benefit by more favourable treatment under any other provisions in international law.

(6) Inhabitants of a non-occupied territory, who on the approach of the enemy, spontaneously take up arms to resist the invading forces, without having had time to form themselves into regular armed units, provided they carry arms openly and respect the laws and customs of war.

Article 14. Subject to the provisions of Article 12, the wounded and sick of a belligerent who fall into enemy hands shall be prisoners of war, and the provisions of international law concerning prisoners of war shall apply to them.

Article 15. At all times, and particularly after an engagement, Parties to the conflict shall, without delay, take all possible measures to search for and collect the wounded and sick, to protect them against pillage and ill-treatment, to insure their adequate care, and to search for the dead and prevent their being despoiled.

Whenever circumstances permit, an armistice or a suspension of fire shall be arranged or local arrangements made, to permit the removal, exchange and transport of the wounded left on the battlefield.

Likewise, local arrangements may be concluded between Parties to the conflict for the removal or exchange of wounded and sick from a besieged or encircled area, and for the passage of medical and religious personnel and equipment on their way to that area.

Article 16. Parties to the conflict shall record as soon as possible, in respect of each wounded, sick or dead person of the adverse Party falling into their hands, any particulars which may assist in his identification.

These records should if possible include:

(a) designation of the Power on which he depends;

(b) army, regimental, personal or serial number;

(c) surname;

(d) first name or names;

(e) date of birth;

(f) any other particulars on his identity card or disc;

(g) date and place of capture or death;

(h) particulars concerning wounds or illness, or cause of death.

As soon as possible the above mentioned information shall be forwarded to the Information Bureau described in Article 122 of the Geneva Convention relative to the Treatment of Prisoners of War of 12 August 1949, which shall transmit this information to the Power on which these persons depend through the intermediary of the Protecting Power and of the Central Prisoners of War Agency.

Parties to the conflict shall prepare and forward to each other through the same bureau, certificates of death or duly authenticated lists of the dead. They shall likewise collect and forward through the same bureau one half of a double identity disc, last wills or other documents of importance to the next of kin, money and in general all articles of an intrinsic or sentimental value, which are found on the dead.

These articles, together with unidentified articles, shall be sent in sealed packets, accompanied by statements giving all particulars necessary for the identification of the deceased owners, as well as by a complete list of the contents of the parcel.

Article 17. Parties to the conflict shall insure that burial or cremation of the dead, carried out individually as far as circumstances permit, is preceded by a careful examination, if possible by a medical examination, of the bodies, with a view to confirming death, establishing identity and enabling a report to be made. One half of the double identity disc, or the identity disc itself if it is a single disc, should remain on the body.

Bodies shall not be cremated except for imperative reasons of hygiene or for motives based on the religion of the deceased. In case of cremation, the circumstances and reasons for cremation shall be stated in detail in the death certificate or on the authenticated list of the dead.

They shall further insure that the dead are honourably interred, if possible according to the rites of the religion to which they belonged, that their graves are respected, grouped if possible according to the nationality of the deceased, properly maintained and marked so that they may always be found. For this purpose, they shall organize at the commencement of hostilities an Official Graves Registration Service, to allow subsequent exhumations and to insure the identification of bodies, whatever the site of the graves, and the possible transportation to the home country. These provisions shall likewise apply to the ashes, which shall be kept by the Graves Registration Service until proper disposal thereof in accordance with the wishes of the home country.

As soon as circumstances permit, and at latest at the end of hostilities, these Services shall exchange, through the information Bureau mentioned in the second paragraph of Article 16, lists showing the exact location and markings of the graves, together with particulars of the dead interred therein.

Article 18. The military authorities may appeal to the charity of the inhabitants voluntarily to collect and care for, under their direction, the wounded and sick, granting persons who have responded to this appeal the necessary protection and facilities. Should the adverse Party take or retake control of the area, he shall likewise grant these persons the same protection and the same facilities.

The military authorities shall permit the inhabitants and relief societies, even in invaded or occupied areas, spontaneously to collect and care for wounded or sick of whatever nationality. The civilian population shall respect these wounded and sick, and in particular abstain from offering them violence.

No one may ever be molested or convicted for having nursed the wounded or sick.

The provisions of the present Article do not relieve the occupying Power of its obligation to give both physical and moral care to the wounded and sick.

Article 19. Fixed establishments and mobile medical units of the Medical Service may in no circumstances be attacked, but shall at all times be respected and protected by the Parties to the conflict. Should they fall into the hands of the adverse Party, their personnel shall be free to pursue their duties, as long as the capturing Power has not itself insured the necessary care of the wounded and sick found in such establishments and units.

The responsible authorities shall insure that the said medical establishments and units are, as far as possible, situated in such a manner that attacks against military objectives cannot imperil their safety.

Article 20. Hospital ships entitled to the protection of the Geneva Convention for the Amelioration of the Condition of Wounded, Sick and Shipwrecked Members of Armed Forces at Sea of 12 August 1949, shall not be attacked from the land.

Article 21. The protection to which fixed establishments and mobile medical units of the Medical Service are entitled shall not cease unless they are used to commit, outside their humanitarian duties, acts harmful to the enemy. Protection may, however, cease only after a due warning has been given, naming, in all appropriate cases, a reasonable time limit, and after such warning has remained unheeded.

Article 22. The following conditions shall not be considered as depriving a medical unit or establishment of the protection guaranteed by Article 19:

(1) That the personnel of the unit or establishment are armed, and that they use the arms in their own defence, or in that of the wounded and sick in their charge.

(2) That in the absence of armed orderlies, the unit or establishment is protected by a picket or by sentries or by an escort.

(3) That small arms and ammunition taken from the wounded and sick and not yet handed to the proper service, are found in the unit or establishment.

(4) That personnel and material of the veterinary service are found in the unit or establishment, without forming an integral part thereof.

(5) That the humanitarian activities of medical units and establishments or of their personnel extend to the care of civilian wounded or sick.

Article 23. In times of peace the High Contracting Parties and, after the outbreak of hostilities the Parties thereto, may establish in their own territory and, if the need arises, in occupied areas, hospital zones and localities so organized as to protect the wounded and sick from the effects of war, as well as the personnel entrusted with the organization and administration of these zones and localities and with the care of persons therein assembled.

Upon the outbreak and during the course of hostilities, the Parties concerned may conclude agreements on mutual recognition of the hospital zones and localities they have created. They may for this purpose implement the provisions of the Draft Agreement annexed to the present Convention, with such amendments as they may consider necessary.

The protecting Powers and the International Committee of the Red Cross are invited to lend their good offices in order to facilitate the institution and recognition of these hospital zones and localities.

Article 24. Medical personnel exclusively engaged in the search for, or the collection, transport or treatment of the wounded or sick, or in the prevention of disease, staff exclusively engaged in the administration of medical units and establishments, as well as chaplains attached to the armed forces, shall be respected and protected in all circumstances.

Article 25. Members of the armed forces specially trained for employment, should the need arise, as hospital orderlies, nurses or auxiliary stretcher-bearers, in the search for or the collection, transport or treatment of the wounded and sick shall likewise be respected and protected if they are carrying out these duties at the time when they come into contact with the enemy or fall into his hands.

Article 26. The staff of National Red Cross societies and that of other Voluntary Aid Societies, duly recognized and authorized by their Governments, who may be employed on the same duties as the personnel named in Article 24, are placed on the same footing as the personnel named in the said Article, provided that the staff of such societies are subject to military laws and regulations....

CONVENTION (II) FOR THE AMELIORATION OF THE CONDITION OF THE WOUNDED, SICK AND SHIPWRECKED MEMBERS OF ARMED FORCES AT SEA—SIGNED AT GENEVA, 12 AUGUST 1949; U.S. SENATE RATIFIED JULY 6, 1955 [ed. note: Convention II is, for the intents of this volume, virtually identical to Convention I and has been omitted for that reason.]

CONVENTION (III) RELATIVE TO THE TREATMENT OF PRISONERS OF WAR—SIGNED AT GENEVA, 12 AUGUST 1949; U.S. SENATE RATIFIED JULY 6, 1955 [ed. note: see Convention I for common articles]

...Article 13. Prisoners of war must at all times be humanely treated. Any unlawful act or omission by the Detaining Power causing death or seriously endangering the health of a prisoner of war in its custody is prohibited and will be regarded as a serious breach of the present Convention. In particular, no prisoner of war may be subjected to physical mutilation or to medical or scientific experiments of any kind which are not justified by the medical, dental or hospital treatment of the prisoner concerned and carried out in his interest.

Likewise, prisoners of war must at all times be protected, particularly against acts of violence or intimidation and against insults and public curiosity.

Measures of reprisal against prisoners of war are prohibited.

Article 14. Prisoners of war shall retain the full civil capacity which they enjoyed at the time of their capture. The Detaining Power may not restrict the exercise, either within or without its own territory, of the rights such capacity confers except in so far as the captivity requires....

Article 17. Every prisoner of war, when questioned on the subject, is bound to give only his surname, first names and rank, date of birth, and army, regimental, personnel or serial number, or failing this, equivalent information.

If he wilfully infringes this rule, he may render himself liable to a restriction of the privileges accorded to his rank or status.

Each Party to a conflict is required to furnish the persons under its jurisdiction who are liable to become prisoners of war, with an identity card showing the owner's surname, first names, rank, army, regimental, personal or serial number or equivalent information, and date of birth. The identity card may, furthermore, bear the signature or the fingerprints, or both, of the owner, and may bear, as well, any other information the Party to the conflict may wish to add concerning persons belonging to its armed forces. As far as possible the card shall measure 6.5x10 cm. and shall be issued in duplicate. The identity card shall be shown by the prisoner of war upon demand, but may in no case be taken away form him.

No physical or mental torture, nor any form of coercion may be inflicted on prisoners of war to secure from them information of any kind whatever. Prisoners of war who refuse to answer may not be threatened, insulted, or exposed to any unpleasant or disadvantageous treatment of any kind.

Prisoners of war who, owing to their physical or mental condition, are unable to state their identity shall be handed over to the medical service. The identity of such prisoners shall be established by all possible means, subject to the provisions of the preceding paragraph.

The questioning of prisoners of war shall be carried out in a language which they understand....

Article 19. Prisoners of war shall be evacuated, as soon as possible after capture, to camps situated in an area far enough from the combat zone for them to be out of danger.

Only those prisoners of war who, owing to wounds or sickness, would run greater risks by being evacuated than by remaining where they are, may be temporarily kept back in a danger zone.

Prisoners of war shall not be unnecessarily exposed to danger while awaiting evacuation from a fighting zone.

Article 20. The evacuation of prisoners of war shall always be effected humanely and in conditions similar to those for the forces of the Detaining Power in their changes of station.

The Detaining Power shall supply prisoners of war who are being evacuated with sufficient food and potable water, and with the necessary clothing and medical attention. The Detaining Power shall take all suitable precautions to ensure their safety during evacuation, and shall establish as soon as possible a list of the prisoners of war who are evacuated...

Article 21. The Detaining Power may subject prisoners of war to internment. It may impose on them the obligation of not leaving, beyond certain limits, the camp where they are interned, or if the said camp is fenced in, of not going outside its perimeter. Subject to the provisions of the present Convention relative to penal and disciplinary sanctions, prisoners of war may not be held in close confinement except where necessary to safeguard their health and then only during the continuation of the circumstances which make such confinement necessary....

Article 23. No prisoner of war may at any time be sent to, or detained in areas where he may be exposed to the fire of the combat zone, nor may his presence be used to render certain points or areas immune from military operations.

Prisoners of war shall have shelters against air bombardment and other hazards of war, to the same extent as the local civilian population. With the exception of those engaged in the protection of their quarters against the aforesaid hazards, they may enter such shelters as soon as possible after the giving of the alarm. Any other protective measure taken in favour of the population shall also apply to them.

Detaining Powers shall give the powers concerned, through the intermediary of the Protecting Powers, all useful information regarding the geographical location of prisoner of war camps.

Whenever military considerations permit, prisoner of war camps shall be indicated in the day-time by the letters PW or PG, placed so as to be clearly visible from the air. The Powers concerned may, however, agree upon any other system of marking. Only prisoner of war camps shall be marked as such....

Article 26. The basic daily food rations shall be sufficient in quantity, quality and variety to keep prisoners of war in good health and to prevent loss of weight or the development of nutritional deficiencies....

Adequate premises shall be provided for messing.

Collective disciplinary measures affecting food are prohibited.

Article 27. Clothing, underwear and footwear shall be supplied to prisoners of war in sufficient quantities by the Detaining Power, which shall make allowance for the climate of the region where the prisoners are detained. Uniforms of enemy armed forces captured by the Detaining Power should, if suitable for the climate, be made available to clothe prisoners of war.

The regular replacement and repair of the above articles shall be assured by the Detaining Power. In addition, prisoners of war who work shall receive appropriate clothing, wherever the nature of the work demands....

Chapter III—Hygiene and Medical Attention

Article 29. The Detaining Power shall be bound to take all sanitary measures necessary to ensure the cleanliness and healthfulness of camps, and to prevent epidemics....

Article 39. Every prisoner of war camp shall be put under the immediate authority of a responsible commissioned officer belonging to the regular armed forces of the Detaining Power. Such officer shall have in his possession a copy of the present Convention; he shall ensure that its provisions are known to the camp staff and the guard and shall be responsible, under the direction of his government, for its application....

Article 42. The use of weapons against prisoners of war, especially against those who are escaping or attempting to escape, shall constitute an extreme measure, which shall always be preceded by warnings appropriate to the circumstances....

Article 84. A prisoner of war shall be tried only by a military court, unless the existing laws of the Detaining Power expressly permit the civil courts to try a member of the armed forces of the Detaining Power in respect of the particular offense alleged to have been committed by the prisoner of war.

In no circumstances whatever shall a prisoner of war be tried by a court of any kind which does not offer the essential guarantees of independence and impartiality as generally recognized, and, in particular, the procedure of which does not afford the accused the rights and means of defense provided for in Article 105.

Article 85. Prisoners of war prosecuted under the laws of the Detaining Power for acts committed prior to capture shall retain, even if convicted, the benefits of the present Convention.

Article 86. No prisoner of war may be punished more than once for the same act or on the same charge....

Collective punishment for individual acts, corporal punishments, imprisonment in premises without daylight and, in general, any form of torture or cruelty, are forbidden....

Article 91. The escape of a prisoner of war shall be deemed to have succeeded when

(1) he has joined the armed forces of the Power on which he depends, or those of an allied Power;

(2) he has left the territory under the control of the Detaining Power, or of an ally of the said Power;

(3) he has joined a ship flying the flag of the Power on which he depends or of an allied Power, in the territorial waters of the Detaining Power, the said ship not being under the control of the last named Power.

Prisoners of war who have made good their escape in the sense of this Article and who are recaptured, shall not be liable to any punishment in respect of their previous escape.

Article 92. A prisoner of war who attempts to escape and is recaptured before having made good his escape in the sense of Article 91 shall be liable only to a disciplinary punishment in respect of this act, even if it is a repeated offence.

A prisoner of war who is recaptured shall be handed over without delay to the competent military authority....

Article 99. No prisoner of war may be tried or sentenced for an act which is not forbidden by the law of the Detaining Power or by International Law in force at the time the said act was committed.

No moral or physical coercion may be exerted on a prisoner of war in order to induce him to admit himself guilty of the act of which he is accused.

No prisoner of war may be convicted without having had an opportunity to present his defence and the assistance of a qualified advocate or counsel....

Article 105. The prisoner of war shall be entitled to assistance by one of his prisoner comrades, to defence by a qualified advocate or counsel of his own choice, to the calling of witnesses and, if he deems necessary, to the services of a competent interpreter. He shall be advised of these rights by the Detaining Power in due time before the trial.

Failing a choice by the prisoner of war, the Protecting Power shall find him an advocate or counsel, and shall have at least one week at its disposal for the purpose. The Detaining Power shall deliver to the said Power, on request, a list of persons qualified to present the defence. Failing a choice of an advocate or counsel by the prisoner of war or the Protecting Power, the Detaining Power shall appoint a competent advocate or counsel to conduct the defence....

CONVENTION (IV) RELATIVE TO THE PROTECTION OF CIVILIAN PERSONS IN TIME OF WAR—SIGNED AT GENEVA, 12 AUGUST 1949; RATIFIED BY U.S. SENATE JULY 6, 1955 [ed. note: see Convention I for common articles]

...Article 4. Persons protected by the Convention are those who, at a given moment and in any manner whatsoever, find themselves, in case of a conflict or occupation, in the hands of a Party to the conflict or Occupying Power of which they are not nationals....

Article 13. The provisions of Part II cover the whole of the populations of the countries in conflict, without any adverse distinction based, in particular, on race, nationality, religion or political opinion, and are intended to alleviate the sufferings caused by war.

Article 14. In time of peace the High Contracting Parties and, after the outbreak of hostilities, the Parties thereto, may establish in their own territory and, if the need arises, in occupied areas, hospital and safety zones and localities so organized as to protect from the effects of war, wounded, sick and aged persons, children under fifteen, expectant mothers and mothers of children under seven....

Article 16. The wounded and sick, as well as the infirm, and expectant mothers, shall be the object of particular protection and respect.

As far as military considerations allow, each Party to the conflict shall facilitate the steps taken to search for the killed and wounded, to assist the shipwrecked and other persons exposed to grave danger, and to protect them against pillage and ill-treatment....

Article 19. The protection to which civilian hospitals are entitled shall not cease unless they are used to commit, outside their humanitarian duties, acts harmful to the enemy. Protection may, however, cease only after due warning has been given, naming, in all appropriate cases, a reasonable time limit and after such warning has remained unheeded.

The fact that sick or wounded members of the armed forces are nursed in these hospitals, or the presence of small arms and ammunition taken from such combatants which have not yet been handed to the proper service, shall not be considered to be acts harmful to the enemy.

Article 20. Persons regularly and solely engaged in the operation and administration of civilian hospitals, including the personnel engaged int he search for, removal and transporting of and caring for wounded and sick civilians, the infirm and maternity cases shall be respected and protected....

Article 24. The Parties to the conflict shall take the necessary measures to ensure that children under fifteen, who are orphaned or are separated from their families as a result of the war, are not left to their own resources, and that their maintenance, the exercise of their religion and their education are facilitated in all circumstances. Their education shall, as far as possible, be entrusted to persons of a similar cultural tradition....

Article 27. Protected persons are entitled, in all circumstances, to respect for their persons, their honour, their family rights, their religious convictions and practices, and their manners and customs. They shall at all times be humanely treated, and shall be protected especially against all acts of violence or threats thereof and against insults and public curiosity.

Women shall be especially protected against any attack on their honour, in particular against rape, enforced prostitution, or any form of indecent assault.

Without prejudice to the provisions relating to the state of health, age and sex, all protected persons shall be treated with the same consideration by the Party to the conflict in whose power they are, without any adverse distinction based, in particular, on race, religion or political opinion.

However, the Parties to this conflict may take such measures of control and security in regard to protected persons as may be necessary as a result of the war.

Article 28. The presence of a protected person may not be used to render certain points or areas immune from military operations.

Article 29. The Party to the conflict in whose hands protected persons may be, is responsible for the treatment accorded to them by its agents, irrespective of any individual responsibility which may be incurred....

Article 47. Protected persons who are in occupied territory shall not be deprived, in any case or in any manner whatsoever, of the benefits of the present Convention by any change introduced, as the result of the occupation of a territory, into the institutions or government of the said territory, nor by any agreement concluded between the authorities of the occupied territories and the Occupying Power, nor by any annexation by the latter of the whole or part of the occupied territory....

Article 49. Individual or mass forcible transfers, as well as deportations of protected persons from occupied territory to the territory of the Occupying Power or that of any other country, occupied or not, are prohibited, regardless of their motive.

Nevertheless, the Occupying Power may undertake total or partial evacuation of a given area if the security of the population or imperative military reasons so demand. Such evacuations may not involve the displacement of protected persons outside the bounds of the occupied territory except when for material reasons it is impossible to avoid such displacement. Persons thus evacuated shall be transferred back to their homes as soon as hostilities in the area of question have ceased....

The Occupying Power shall not detain protected persons in an area particularly exposed to the danger of war unless the security of the population or imperative military reasons so demand.

The Occupying Power shall not deport or transfer parts of its own civilian population into the territory it occupies.

Article 50. The Occupying Power shall, with the cooperation of the national and local authorities, facilitate the proper working of all institutions devoted to the care and education of children.

The Occupying Power shall take all necessary steps to facilitate the identification of children and the registration of their parentage. It may not, in any case, change their personal status, nor enlist them in formations or organizations subordinate to it....

Article 51. The Occupying Power may not compel protected persons to serve in its armed or auxiliary forces. No pressure or propaganda which aims at securing voluntary enlistment is permitted.

The Occupying Power may not compel protected persons to work unless they are over eighteen years of age, and then only on work which is necessary either for the needs of the army of occupation, or for the public utility services, or for the feeding, sheltering, clothing, transportation or health of the population of the occupied country. Protected persons may not be compelled to undertake any work which would involve them in the obligation of taking part in military operations. The Occupying Power may not compel protected persons to employ forcible means to ensure the security of the installations where they are performing compulsory labour....

In no case shall requisition of labour lead to a mobilization of workers in an organization of a military or semi-military character....

Article 53. Any destruction by the Occupying Power of real or personal property belonging individually or collectively to private persons, or to the State, or to other public authorities, or to social or cooperative organizations, is prohibited, except where such destruction is rendered absolutely necessary by military operations.

Article 54. The Occupying Power may not alter the status of public officials or judges in the occupied territories, or in any way apply sanctions to or take any measures of coercion or discrimination against them, should they abstain from fulfilling their functions for reasons of conscience....

Article 55. To the fullest extent of the means available to it, the Occupying Power has the duty of ensuring the food and medical supplies of the population; it should, in particular, bring in the necessary foodstuffs, medical stores and other articles if the resources of the occupied territory are inadequate.

The Occupying Power may not requisition foodstuffs, articles or medical supplies available in the occupied territory, except for use by the occupation forces and administration personnel, and then only if the requirements of the civilian population have been taken into account. Subject to the provisions of other international Conventions, the Occupying Power shall make arrangements to ensure that fair value is paid for any requisitioned goods....

Article 56. To the fullest extent of the means available to it, the Occupying Power has the duty of ensuring and maintaining, with the cooperation of national and local authorities, the medical and hospital establishments and services, public health and hygiene in the occupied territory, with particular reference to the adoption and application of the prophylactic and preventive measures necessary to combat the spread of contagious diseases and epidemics. Medical personnel of all categories shall be allowed to carry out their duties....

Article 57. The Occupying Power may requisition civilian hospitals only temporarily and only in cases of urgent necessity for the care of military wounded and sick, and then on condition that suitable arrangements are made in due time for the care and treatment of the patients and for the needs of the civilian population for hospital accommodation.

The material and stores of civilian hospitals cannot be requisitioned so long as they are necessary for the needs of the civilian population.

Article 58. The Occupying Power shall permit ministers of religion to give spiritual assistance to the members of their religious communities....

Article 64. The penal laws of the occupied territory shall remain in force, with the exception that they may be repealed or suspended by the Occupying Power in cases where they constitute a threat to its security or an obstacle to the application of the present Convention. Subject to the latter consideration and to the necessity for ensuring the effective administration of justice, the tribunals of the occupied territory shall continue to function in respect of all offences covered by the said laws....

Article 70. Protected persons shall not be arrested, prosecuted or convicted by the Occupying Power for acts committed or for opinions expressed before the occupation, or during a temporary interruption thereof, with the exception of breaches of the laws and customs of war.

Nationals of the Occupying Power who, before the outbreak of hostilities, have sought refuge in the territory of the occupied State, shall not be arrested, prosecuted, convicted or deported from the occupied territory, except for offences committed after the outbreak of hostilities, or for offences under common law committed before the outbreak of hostilities which, according to the law of the occupied State, would have justified extradition in time of peace.

Article 71. No sentence shall be pronounced by the competent courts of the Occupying Power except after a regular trial....

Article 78. If the Occupying Power considers it necessary, for imperative reasons of security, to take safety measures concerning protected persons, it may, at the most, subject them to assigned residence or to internment....

Article 80. Internees shall retain their full civil capacity and shall exercise such attendant rights as may be compatible with their status....

Article 82. The Detaining Power shall, as far as possible, accommodate the internees according to their nationality, language and customs. Internees who are nationals of the same country shall not be separated merely because they have different languages....

From 6 U.S.T. 3114, T.I.A.S. No. 3362, 75 U.N.T.S. 31.

Document 91:
UNITED NATIONS COVENANT ON CIVIL AND POLITICAL RIGHTS (1966)

Adopted and opened for signature, ratification and accession by General

Assembly resolution 2200 A (XXI) of 16 December 1966. [ed. note: signed by United State Oct. 5, 1977; ratified by the United States 1992]

Entry into force: 23 March 1976....
PART I. Article 1
1. All peoples have the right of self-determination. By virtue of that right they freely determine their political status and freely pursue their economic, social and cultural development.
2. All peoples may, for their own ends, freely dispose of their natural wealth and resources without prejudice to any obligations arising out of international economic co-operation, based upon the principle of mutual benefit, and international law. In no case may a people be deprived of its own means of subsistence.
3. The States Parties to the present Covenant, including those having responsibility for the administration of Non-Self-Governing and Trust Territories, shall promote the realization of the right of self-determination, and shall respect that right, in conformity with the provisions of the Charter of the United Nations.
PART II. Article 2
1. Each State Party to the present Covenant undertakes to respect and to ensure to all individuals within its territory and subject to its jurisdiction the rights recognized in the present Covenant, without distinction of any kind, such as race, colour, sex, language, religion, political or other opinion, national or social origin, property, birth or other status.
2. Where not already provided for by existing legislative or other measures, each State Party to the present Covenant undertakes to take the necessary steps, in accordance with its constitutional processes and with the provisions of the present Covenant, to adopt such legislative or other measures as may be necessary to give effect to the rights recognized in the present Covenant.
3. Each State Party to the present Covenant undertakes:
(a) to ensure that any person whose rights or freedoms as herein recognized are violated shall have an effective remedy, notwithstanding that the violation has been committed by persons acting in an official capacity;
(b) to ensure that any person claiming such a remedy shall have his right thereto determined by competent judicial, administrative or legislative authorities, or by any other competent authority provided for by the legal system of the State, and to develop the possibilities of judicial remedy;
(c) to ensure that the competent authorities shall enforce such remedies when granted.
Article 3. The States Parties to the present Covenant undertake to ensure the equal right of men and women to the enjoyment of all civil and political rights set forth in the present Covenant.
Article 4
1. In time of public emergency which threatens the life of the nation and the existence of which is officially proclaimed, the States parties to the present Covenant may take measures derogating from their obligations under the present Covenant to the extent strictly required by the exigencies of the situation, provided that such measures are not inconsistent with their other obligations under international law and do not involve discrimination solely on the ground of race, colour, sex, language, religion or social origin.
2. No derogation from articles 6, 7, 8 (paragraphs 1 and 2), 11, 15, 16 and 18 may be made under this provision.
3. Any State Party to the present Covenant availing itself of the right of derogation shall immediately inform the other States Parties to the present Covenant, through the intermediary of the Secretary-General of the United Nations, of the provisions from which it has derogated and of the reasons by which it was actuated. A further communication shall be made, through the same intermediary, on the date on which it terminates such derogation.
Article 5
1. Nothing in the present Covenant may be interpreted as implying for any State, group or person any right to engage in any activity or perform any act aimed at the destruction of any of the rights and freedoms recognized herein or at their limitation to a greater extent than is provided for in the present Covenant.
2. There shall be no restriction upon or derogation from any of the fundamental human rights recognized or existing in any State Party to the present Covenant pursuant to law, con-

ventions, regulations or custom on the pretext that the present Covenant does not recognize such rights or that it recognizes them to a lesser extent.

PART III. Article 6

1. Every human being has the inherent right to life. This right shall be protected by law. No one shall be arbitrarily deprived of his life.

2. In countries which have not abolished the death penalty, sentence of death may be imposed only for the most serious crimes in accordance with the law in force at the time of the commission of the crime and not contrary to the provisions of the present Covenant and to the Convention on the Prevention of the Crime of Genocide. This penalty can only be carried out pursuant to a final judgement rendered by a competent court.

3. When deprivation of life constitutes the crime of genocide, it is understood that nothing in this article shall authorize any State Party to the present Covenant to derogate in any way from any obligation assumed under the provisions of the Convention on the Prevention and Punishment of the Crime of Genocide.

4. Anyone sentenced to death shall have the right to seek pardon or commutation of the sentence. Amnesty, pardon or commutation of the sentence of death may be granted in all cases.

5. Sentence of death shall not be imposed for crimes committed by persons below eighteen years of age and shall not be carried out on pregnant women.

6. Nothing in this article shall be invoked to delay or to prevent the abolition of capital punishment by any State Party to the present Covenant.

Article 7. No one shall be subjected to torture or to cruel, inhuman or degrading treatment or punishment. In particular, no one shall be subjected without his free consent to medical or scientific experimentation.

Article 8

1. No one shall be held in slavery; slavery and the slave-trade in all their forms shall be prohibited.

2. No one shall be held in servitude.

3. (a) No one shall be required to perform forced or compulsory labour.

(b) Paragraph 3(a) shall not be held to preclude, in countries where imprisonment with hard labour may be imposed as a punishment for a crime, the performance of hard labour in pursuance of a sentence of such punishment by a competent court;

(c) For the purpose of this paragraph the term "forced or compulsory labour" shall not include:

(i) Any work or service, not referred to in subparagraph (b), normally required of a person who is under detention in consequence of a lawful order of a court, or of a person during conditional release from such detention;

(ii) Any service of a military character and, in countries where conscientious objection is recognized, any national service required by law of conscientious objectors;

(iii) Any service exacted in cases of emergency or calamity threatening the life or well-being of the community;

(iv) Any work or service which forms part of normal civil obligations.

Article 9

1. Everyone has the right to liberty and security of person. No one shall be subjected to arbitrary arrest or detention. No one shall be deprived of his liberty except on such grounds and in accordance with such procedure as are established by law.

2. Anyone who is arrested shall be informed, at the time of arrest, of the reasons for his arrest and shall be promptly informed of any charges against him.

3. Anyone arrested or detained on a criminal charge shall be brought promptly before a judge or other officer authorized by law to exercise judicial power and shall be entitled to trial within a reasonable time or to release. It shall not be the general rule that persons awaiting trial shall be detained in custody, but release may be subject to guarantees to appear for trial, at any other stage of the judicial proceedings, and should occasion arise, for execution of the judgement.

4. Anyone who is deprived of his liberty by arrest of detention shall be entitled to take proceedings before a court, in order that that court may decide without delay on the lawfulness of his detention and order his release if the detention is not lawful.

5. Anyone who has been the victim of unlawful arrest or detention shall have an enforceable right to compensation.

Article 10

1. All persons deprived of their liberty shall be treated with humanity and with respect for the inherent dignity of the human person.

2. (a) Accused persons shall, save in exceptional circumstances be segregated from convicted persons and shall be subject to separate treatment appropriate to their status as unconvicted persons;

(b) Accused juvenile persons shall be separated from adults and brought as speedily as possible for adjudication.

3. The penitentiary system shall comprise treatment of prisoners the essential aim of which shall be their reformation and social rehabilitation. Juvenile offenders shall be segregated from adults and be accorded treatment appropriate to their age and legal status.

Article 11. No one shall be imprisoned merely on the ground of inability to fulfil a contractual obligation.

Article 12

1. Everyone lawfully within the territory of a State shall, within that territory, have the right to liberty of movement and freedom to choose his residence.

2. Everyone shall be free to leave any country, including his own.

3. The above-mentioned rights shall not be subject to any restrictions except those which are provided by law, are necessary to protect national security, public order, public health or morals or the rights and freedoms of others, and are consistent with the other rights recognized in the present Covenant.

4. No one shall be arbitrarily deprived of the right to enter his own country.

Article 13. An alien lawfully in the territory of a State Party to the present Covenant may be expelled therefrom only in pursuance of a decision reached in accordance with law and shall, except where compelling reasons of national security otherwise require, be allowed to submit the reasons against his expulsion and to have his case reviewed by, and be represented for the purpose before, the competent authority or a person or persons especially designated by the competent authority.

Article 14

1. All persons shall be equal before the courts and tribunals. In the determination of any criminal charge against him, or of his rights and obligations in a suit at law, everyone shall be entitled to a fair and public hearing by a competent, independent and impartial tribunal established by law. The Press and the public may be excluded from all or part of a trial for reasons of morals, public order or national security in a democratic society, or when the interest of the private lives of the parties so requires, or to the extent strictly necessary in the opinion of the court in special circumstances where publicity would prejudice the interests of justice; but any judgement rendered in a criminal case or in a suit at law shall be made public except where the interest of juvenile persons otherwise requires or the proceedings concern matrimonial disputes or the guardianship of children.

2. Everyone charged with a criminal offence shall have the right to be presumed innocent until proved guilty according to law.

3. In the determination of any criminal charge against him, everyone shall be entitled to the following minimum guarantees, in full equality:

(a) to be informed promptly and in detail in a language which he understands of the nature and cause of the charge against him.

(b) to have adequate time and facilities for the preparation of his defence and to communicate with counsel of his own choosing;

(c) to be tried without undue delay;

(d) to be tried in his presence, and to defend himself in person or through legal assistance of his own choosing; to be informed, if he does not have legal assistance, of this right; and to have legal assistance assigned to him, in any case where the interests of justice so require, and without payment by him in any such case if he does not have sufficient means to pay for it;

(e) to examine, or have examined, the witnesses against him and to obtain the attendance and examination of witnesses on his behalf under the same conditions as witnesses against him;

(f) to have the free assistance of an interpreter if he cannot understand or speak the language used in court;

(g) not to be compelled to testify against himself or confess guilt.

4. In the case of juvenile persons, the procedure shall be such as will take account of their

age and the desirability of promoting their rehabilitation.

5. Everyone convicted of a crime shall have the right to this conviction and sentence being reviewed by a higher tribunal according to law.

6. When a person has by a final decision been convicted of a criminal offence and when subsequently his conviction has been reversed or he has been pardoned on the ground that a new or newly discovered fact shows conclusively that there has been a miscarriage of justice, the person who has suffered punishment as a result of such conviction shall be compensated according to law unless it is proved that the non-disclosure of the unknown fact in time is wholly or partly attributable to him.

7. No one shall be liable to be tried or punished again for an offence for which he has already been finally convicted or acquitted in accordance with the law and penal procedure of each country.

Article 15

1. No one shall be held guilty of any criminal offense on account of any act or omission which did not constitute a criminal offence under national or international law, at the time when it was committed. Nor shall a heavier penalty be imposed than the one that was applicable at the time when the criminal offence was committed. If, subsequent to the commission of the offence, provision is made by law for the imposition of the lighter penalty, the offender shall benefit thereby.

2. Nothing in this article shall prejudice the trial and punishment of any person for any act or omission which, at the time when it was committed, was criminal according to the general principles of law recognized by the community of nations.

Article 16. Everyone shall have the right to recognition everywhere as a person before the law.

Article 17

1. No one shall be subjected to arbitrary or unlawful interference with his privacy, family, home or correspondence, or to unlawful attacks on his honour and reputation.

2. Everyone has the right to the protection of the law against such interference or attacks.

Article 18

1. Everyone shall have the right to freedom of thought, conscience and religion. This right shall include freedom to have or to adopt a religion or belief of his choice, and freedom, either individually or in community with others and in public or private, to manifest his religion or belief in worship, observance, practice and teaching.

2. No one shall be subject to coercion which would impair his freedom to have or to adopt a religion or belief of his choice.

3. Freedom to manifest one's religion or beliefs may be subject only to such limitations as are prescribed by law and are necessary to protect public safety, order, health, or morals or the fundamental rights and freedoms of others.

4. The States Parties to the present Covenant undertake to have respect for the liberty of parents and, when applicable, legal guardians to ensure the religious and moral education of their children in conformity with their own convictions.

Article 19

1. Everyone shall have the right to hold opinions without interference.

2. Everyone shall have the right to freedom of expression; this right shall include freedom to seek, receive and impart information and ideas of all kinds, regardless of frontiers, either orally, in writing or in print, in the form of art, or through any other media of his choice.

3. The exercise of the rights provided for in paragraph 2 of this article carries with it special duties and responsibilities. It may therefore be subject to certain restrictions, but these shall only be such as are provided by law and are necessary:

(a) For respect of the rights or reputations of others;

(b) For the protection of national security or public order, or of public health or morals.

Article 20

1. Any propaganda for war shall be prohibited by law.

2. Any advocacy of national, racial or religious hatred that constitutes incitement to discrimination, hostility or violence shall be prohibited by law.

Article 21. The right of peaceful assembly shall be recognized. No restrictions may be placed on the exercise of this right other than those imposed in conformity with the law and which are necessary in a democratic society in the interests of national security or public safety, public order, the protection of public health or morals or the protection of the rights and freedoms of others.

Article 22

1. Everyone shall have the right to freedom of association with others, including the right to form and join trade unions for the protection of his interests.

2. No restrictions may be placed on the exercise of this right other than those which are prescribed by law and which are necessary in a democratic society in the interests of national security or public safety, public order, the protection of public health or morals or the protection of the rights and freedoms of others. This article shall not prevent the imposition of lawful restrictions on members of the armed forces and of the police in their exercise of this right.

3. Nothing in this article shall authorize States Parties to the International Labour Organisation Convention of 1948 concerning Freedom of Association and Protection of the Right to Organize to take legislative measures which would prejudice, or to apply the law in such a manner as to prejudice the guarantees provided for in that Convention.

Article 23

1. The family is the natural and fundamental group unit of society and is entitled to protection by society and the State.

2. The right of men and women of marriageable age to marry and to found a family shall be recognized.

3. No marriage shall be entered into without the free and full consent of the intending spouses.

4. States Parties to the present Covenant shall take appropriate steps to ensure equality of rights and responsibilities of spouses as to marriage, during marriage and at its dissolution. In the case of dissolution, provision shall be made for the necessary protection of any children.

Article 24

1. Every child shall have, without any discrimination as to race, colour, sex, language, religion, national or social origin, property or birth, the right to such measures of protection as are required by his status as a minor, on the part of his family, society and the State.

2. Every child shall be registered immediately after birth and shall have a name.

3. Every child has the right to acquire nationality.

Article 25. Every citizen shall have the right and the opportunity, without any of the distinctions mentioned in article 2 and without unreasonable restrictions:

(a) to take part in the conduct of public affairs, directly or through freely chosen representatives;

(b) to vote and to be elected at genuine periodic elections which shall be by universal and equal suffrage and shall be held by secret ballot, guaranteeing the free expression of the will of the electors;

(c) to have access, on general terms of equality, to public service in his country.

Article 26. All persons are equal before the law and are entitled without any discrimination to the equal protection of the law. In this respect, the law shall prohibit any discrimination and guarantee to all persons equal and effective protection against discrimination on any ground such as race, colour, sex, language, religion, political or other opinion, national or social origin, property, birth or other status.

Article 27. In those States in which ethnic, religious or linguistic minorities exist, persons belonging to such minorities shall not be denied the right, in community with the other members of their group, to enjoy their own culture, to profess and practice their own religion, or to use their own language.

PART IV. Article 28

1. There shall be established a Human Rights Committee (hereafter referred to in the present Covenant as the Committee). It shall consist of eighteen members and shall carry out the functions hereinafter provided.

2. The Committee shall be composed of nationals of the States Parties to the present Covenant who shall be person of high moral character and recognized competence in the field of human rights, consideration being given to the usefulness of the participation of some persons having legal experience.

3. The members of the Committee shall be elected and shall serve in their personal capacity....

From U.S. House of Representatives Committee of Foreign Affairs, *Human Rights Documents, A Compilation of Documents Pertaining to Human Rights*, Washington, D.C.: GPO, 79–88.

Document 92:
OPTIONAL PROTOCOL TO THE U.N. COVENANT ON CIVIL AND POLITICAL RIGHTS (1966)

Adopted and opened for signature, ratification and accession by General Assembly resolution 2200 A (XXI) of 16 December 1966.

Entry into force: 23 March 1976, in accordance with article 9.

The States Parties to the present protocol considering that in order further to achieve the purposes of the Covenant on Civil and Political Rights (hereinafter referred to as the Covenant) and the implementation of its provisions it would be appropriate to enable the Human Rights Committee set up in part IV of the Covenant (hereinafter referred to as the Committee) to receive and consider, as provided in the present Protocol, communication from individuals claiming to be victims of violations of any of the rights set forth in the Covenant have agreed as follows:

Article 1. A State Party to the Covenant that becomes a party to the present Protocol recognizes the competence of the Committee to receive and consider communications from individuals subject to its jurisdiction who claim to be victims of a violation by that State Party of any of the rights set forth in the Covenant. No communication shall be received by the Committee if it concerns a State Party to the Covenant which is not a party to the present protocol.

Article 2. Subject to the provisions of article 1, individuals who claim that any of their rights enumerated in the Covenant have been violated and who have exhausted all available domestic remedies may submit a written communication to the Committee for consideration.

Article 3. The Committee shall consider inadmissible any communication under the present Protocol which is anonymous, or which it considers to be an abuse of the right of submission of such communications or to be incompatible with the provision of the Covenant.

Article 4

1. Subject to the provisions of article 3, the Committee shall bring any communication submitted to it under the present Protocol to the attention of the State Party to the present Protocol alleged to be violating any provision of the Covenant.

2. Within six months, the receiving State shall submit to the Committee written explanations or statements clarifying the matter and the remedy, if any, that may have been taken by that State.

Article 5

1. The Committee shall consider communications received under the Protocol in the light of all written information made available to it by the individual and by the State Party concerned.

2. The Committee shall not consider any communication from an individual unless it has ascertained that:

(a) The same matter is not being examined under another procedure of international investigation or settlement;

(b) The individual has exhausted all available domestic remedies. This shall not be the rule where the application of the remedies is unreasonably prolonged.

3. The Committee shall hold closed meetings when examining communication under the present Protocol.

4. The Committee shall forward its views to the State Party concerned and to the individual....

From U.S. House of Representatives Committee on Foreign Affairs, *Human Rights Documents, A Compilation of Documents Pertaining to Human Rights*, Washington, D.C.: GPO, 1983, 96–97.

Document 93:
UNITED NATIONS COVENANT ON ECONOMIC, SOCIAL AND CULTURAL RIGHTS (1966)

Adopted and opened for signature, ratification and accession by General Assembly resolution 2200 A (XXI) of 16 December 1966

Entry into force: 3 January 1976, in accordance with article 17....

Part II. Article 2

1. Each State Party to the present Covenant undertakes to take steps, individually and through international assistance and co-opera-

tion, especially economic and technical, to the maximum of its available resources, with a view to achieving progressively the full realization of the rights recognized in the present Covenant by all appropriate means, including particularly the adoption of legislative measures.

2. The States Parties to the present Covenant undertake to guarantee that the rights enunciated in the present Covenant will be exercised without discrimination of any kind as to race, colour, sex, language, religion, political or other opinion, national or social origin, property, birth or other status.

3. Developing countries, with due regard to human rights and their national economy, may determine to what extent they would guarantee the economic rights recognized in the present Covenant to non-nationals.

Article 3. The States Parties to the present Covenant undertake to ensure the equal right of men and women to the enjoyment of all economic, social and cultural rights set forth in the present Covenant.

Article 4. The States Parties to the present Covenant recognize that, in the enjoyment of those rights provided by the State in conformity with the present Covenant, the State may subject such rights only to such limitations as are determined by law only in so far as they may be compatible with the nature of these rights and solely for the purpose of promoting the general welfare in a democratic society.

Article 5

1. Nothing in the present Covenant may be interpreted as implying for any State, group or person any right to engage in any activity or to perform any act aimed at the destruction of any of the rights or freedoms recognized herein, or at their limitation to a greater extent than is provided for in the present Covenant.

2. No restriction upon or derogation from any of the fundamental human rights recognized or existing in any country in virtue of law, conventions, regulations or custom shall be admitted on the pretext that the present Covenant does not recognize such rights or that it recognizes them to a lesser extent.

Part III. Article 6

1. The States Parties to the present Covenant recognize the right to work, which includes the right of everyone to the opportunity to gain his living by work which he freely chooses or accepts, and will take appropriate steps to safeguard this right.

2. The steps to be taken by a State Party to the present Covenant to achieve the full realization of this right shall include technical and vocational guidance and training programmes, policies and techniques to achieve steady economic, social and cultural development and full and productive employment under conditions safeguarding fundamental political and economic freedoms to the individual.

Article 7. The States Parties to the present Covenant recognize the right of everyone to the enjoyment of just and favourable conditions of work which ensure, in particular:

(a) Remuneration which provides all workers, as a minimum, with:

(i) Fair wages and equal remuneration for work of equal value without distinction of any kind, in particular women being guaranteed conditions of work not inferior to those enjoyed by men, with equal pay for equal work;

(ii) A decent living for themselves and their families in accordance with the provisions of the present Covenant;

(b) Safe and healthy working conditions;

(c) Equal opportunity for everyone to be promoted in his employment to an appropriate higher level, subject to no considerations other than those of seniority and competence;

(d) Rest, leisure and reasonable limitation of working hours and periodic holidays with pay, as well as remuneration for public holidays.

Article 8

1. The States Parties to the present Covenant undertake to ensure:

(a) The right of everyone to form trade unions and join the trade union of his choice, subject only to the rules of the organization concerned, for the promotion and protection of his economic and social interests. No restrictions may be placed on the exercise of this right other than those prescribed by law and which are necessary in a democratic society in the interests of national security or public order or for the protection of the rights and freedoms of others;

(b) The right of trade unions to establish national federations or confederations and the right of the latter to form or join international trade-union organizations;

(c) The right of trade unions to function freely subject to no limitations other than those prescribed by law and which are necessary in a democratic society in the interests of national security or public order or for the protection of the rights and freedoms of others;

(d) The right to strike, provided that it is exercised in conformity with the laws of the particular country.

2. This article shall not prevent the imposition of lawful restrictions on the exercise of these rights by members of the armed forces or of the police of the administration of the State.

3. Nothing in this article shall authorize States Parties to the International Labour Organization Convention of 1948 concerning Freedom of Association and Protection of the Right to Organize to take legislative measures which would prejudice, or apply the law in such a manner as would prejudice, the guarantees provided for in that Convention.

Article 9. The States Parties to the present Covenant recognize the right of everyone to social security, including social insurance.

Article 10. The States Parties to the present Covenant recognize that:

1. The widest possible protection and assistance should be accorded to the family, which is the natural and fundamental group unit of society, particularly for its establishment and while it is responsible for the care and education of dependent children. Marriage must be entered into with the free consent of the intending spouses.

2. Special protection should be accorded to mothers during a reasonable period before and after childbirth. During such period working mothers should be accorded paid leave or leave with adequate social security benefits.

3. Special measures of protection and assistance should be taken on behalf of all children and young persons without any discrimination for reasons of parentage or other conditions. Children and young persons should be protected from economic and social exploitation. Their employment in work harmful to their morals or health or dangerous to life or likely to hamper their normal development should be punishable by law. States should also set age limits before which the paid employment of child labour should be prohibited and punishable by law.

Article 11

1. The States Parties to the present Covenant recognize the right of everyone to an adequate standard of living for himself and his family, including adequate food, clothing and housing, and to the continuous improvement of living conditions. The States Parties will take appropriate steps to ensure the realization of this right recognizing to this effect the essential importance of international co-operation based on free consent.

2. The States Parties to the present Covenant, recognizing the fundamental right of everyone to be free from hunger, shall take individually and through international co-operation, the measures, including specific programmes, which are needed:

(a) To improve methods of production, conservation and distribution of food by making full use of technical and scientific knowledge, by disseminating knowledge of the principles of nutrition and by developing or reforming agrarian systems in such a way as to achieve the most efficient development and utilization of natural resources;

(b) Taking into account the problems of food-importing and food-exporting countries, to ensure an equitable distribution of world food supplies in relation to need.

Article 12

1. The States Parties to the present Covenant recognize the right of everyone to the enjoyment of the highest attainable standard of physical and mental health.

2. The steps to be taken by the States Parties to the present Covenant to achieve the full realization of this right shall include those necessary for:

(a) The provision for the reduction of the stillbirthrate and of infant mortality and for the healthy development of the child;

(b) The improvement of all aspects of environmental and industrial hygiene;

(c) The prevention, treatment and control of epidemic, endemic, occupational and other diseases;

(d) The creation of conditions which would assure to all medical service and medical attention in the event of sickness.

Article 13

1. The States Parties to the present Covenant recognize the right of everyone to education. They agree that education shall be directed to the full development of the human personality and the sense of its dignity, and shall strengthen the respect for human rights and fundamental freedoms. They further agree that education shall enable all persons to participate effectively in a free society, promote understanding, tolerance and friendship among all nations and all racial, ethnic or religious groups, and further the activities of the United Nations for the maintenance of peace.

2. The States Parties to the present Covenant recognize that, with a view to achieving the full realization of this right:

(a) Primary education shall be compulsory and available free to all;

(b) Secondary education in its different forms, including technical and vocational secondary education, shall be made generally available and accessible to all by every appropriate means, and in particular by the progressive introduction of free education;

(c) Higher education shall be made equally accessible to all, on the basis of capacity, by every appropriate means, and in particular by the progressive introduction of free education;

(d) Fundamental education shall be encouraged or intensified as far as possible for those persons who have not received or completed the whole period of their primary education;

(e) The development of a system of schools at all levels shall be actively pursued, an adequate fellowship system shall be established, and the material conditions of teaching staff shall be continuously improved.

3. The States Parties to the present Covenant undertake to have respect for the liberty of parents and, when applicable, legal guardians to choose for their children schools, other than those established by the public authorities, which conform to such minimum educational standards as may be laid down or approved by the State and to ensure the religious and moral education of their children in conformity with their own convictions.

4. No part of this article shall be construed so as to interfere with the liberty of individuals and bodies to establish and direct educational institutions, subject always to the observance of the principles set forth in paragraph 1 of this article and to the requirement that the education given in such institutions shall conform to such minimum standards as may be laid down by the State.

Article 14. Each State Party to the present Covenant which, at the time of becoming a Party, has not been able to secure in it metropolitan territory or other territories under its jurisdiction compulsory primary education, free of charge, undertakes, within two years, to work out and adopt a detailed plan of action for the progressive implementation, within a reasonable number of years, to be fixed in the plan, of the principle of compulsory education free of charge for all.

Article 15

1. The States Parties to the present Covenant recognize the right of everyone:

(a) To take part in cultural life;

(b) To enjoy the benefits of scientific progress and its applications;

(c) To benefit from the protection of the moral and material interests resulting from any scientific, literary or artistic production of which he is the author.

2. The steps to be taken by the States Parties to the present Covenant to achieve the full realization of this right shall include those necessary for the conservation, the development and the diffusion of science and culture.

3. The States Parties to the present Covenant undertake to respect the freedom indispensable for scientific research and creative activity.

4. The States Parties to the present Covenant recognize the benefits to be derived from the encouragement and development of international contacts and co-operation in the scientific and cultural fields.

Part IV. Article 16

1. The States Parties to the present Covenant undertake to submit in conformity with this part of the Covenant reports on the measures which they have adopted and the progress made in achieving the observance of the rights recognized herein.

2.(a) All reports shall be submitted to the Secretary-General of the United Nations, who shall transmit copies to the Economic and Social Council for consideration in accordance with the provisions of the present Covenant;

(b) The Secretary-General of the United Nations shall also transmit to the specialized agencies copies of the reports, or any relevant parts therefrom, from States Parties to the present Covenant which are also members of these specialized agencies in so far as these reports or parts therefrom, relate to any matters which fall within the responsibilities of the said agencies in accordance with their constitutional instruments.

Article 17

1. The States parties to the present Covenant shall furnish their reports in stages, in accordance with a programme to be established by the Economic and Social Council within one year of the entry into force of the present Covenant after consultation with the States Parties and the specialized agencies concerned.

2. Reports may indicate factors and difficulties affecting the degree of fulfillment of obligations under the present Covenant.

3. Where relevant information has previously been furnished to the United Nations or to any specialized agency by any State Party to the present Covenant, it will not be necessary to reproduce that information, but a precise reference to the information so furnished will suffice.

Article 18. Pursuant to its responsibilities under the Charter of the United Nations in the field of human rights and fundamental freedoms, the Economic and Social Council may make arrangements with the specialized agencies in respect of their reporting to it on the progress made in achieving the observance of the provisions of the present Covenant falling within the scope of their activities. These reports may include particulars of decisions and recommendations on such implementation adopted by their competent organs.

Article 19. The Economic and Social Council may transmit to the Commission on Human Rights for study and general recommendation or, as appropriate, for information the reports concerning human rights submitted by States in accordance with articles 16 and 17, and those concerning human rights submitted by the specialized agencies in accordance with article 18.

Article 20. The States Parties to the present Covenant and the specialized agencies concerned may submit comments to the Economic and Social Council on any general recommendation under article 19 or reference to such general recommendation in any report of the Commission on Human Rights or any documentation referred to therein.

Article 21. The Economic and Social Council may submit from time to time to the General Assembly reports with recommendations of a general nature and a summary of the information received from the States Parties to the present Covenant and the specialized agencies on the measures taken and the progress made in achieving general observance of the rights recognized in the present Covenant.

Article 22. The Economic and Social Council may bring to the attention of other organs of the United Nations, their subsidiary organs and specialized agencies concerned with furnishing technical assistance any matters arising out of the reports referred to in this part of the present Covenant which may assist such bodies in deciding, each within its field of competence, on the advisability of international measures likely to contribute to the effective progressive implementation of the present Covenant.

Article 23. The States Parties to the present Covenant agree that international action for the achievement of the rights recognized in the present Covenant includes such methods as the conclusion of conventions, the adoption of recommendations, the furnishing of technical assistance and the holding of regional meetings and technical meetings for the purpose of consultation and study organized in conjunction with the Government concerned....

From U.S. House of Representatives Committee on Foreign Affairs, *Human Rights Documents, A Compilation of Documents Pertaining to Human Rights*, Washington, D.C.: GPO, 1983, 69–78.

Document 94:
EUROPEAN CONVENTION ON HUMAN RIGHTS (1953)

There exist a number of regional agreements and institutions that promote human rights. The most successful system has been the European one. Virtually all of the democracies of Europe, except the emerging ones in the formerly Soviet East, participate in the Council of Europe, under the auspices the European Commission on Human

Rights, and the European Court of Human Rights enforces the guarantees of the following regional agreement.

Signed November 4, 1950; entry into force September 3, 1953

Section 1—Convention for the Protection of Human Rights and Fundamental Freedoms and Its Five Protocols

The Governments signatory hereto, being Members of the Council of Europe, Considering the Universal Declaration of Human Rights proclaimed by the General Assembly of the United Nations on 10th December 1948; considering that this Declaration aims at securing the universal and effective recognition and observance of the Rights therein declared; considering that the aim of the Council of Europe is the achievement of greater unity between its Members and that one of the methods by which that aim is to be pursued is the maintenance and further realisation of Human Rights and Fundamental Freedoms; reaffirming their profound belief in those Fundamental Freedoms which are the foundation of justice and peace in the world and are best maintained on the one hand by an effective political democracy and on the other by a common understanding and observance of the Human Rights upon which they depend; being resolved, as the Governments of European countries which are likeminded and have a common heritage of political traditions, ideals, freedom and the rule of law, to take the first steps for the collective enforcement of certain of the Rights stated in the Universal Declaration; have agreed as follows:

Article 1. The High Contracting Parties shall secure to everyone within their jurisdiction the rights and freedoms defined in Section 1 of this Convention.

Section 1. Article 2

1. Everyone's right to life shall be protected by law. No one shall be deprived of his life intentionally save in the execution of a sentence of a court following his conviction of a crime for which this penalty is provided by law.

2. Deprivation of life shall not be regarded as inflicted in contravention of this Article when it results from the use of force which is no more than absolutely necessary:

(a) in defence of any person from unlawful violence;

(b) in order to effect a lawful arrest or to prevent the escape of a person lawfully detained;

(c) in action lawfully taken for the purpose of quelling a riot or an insurrection.

Article 3

No one shall be subjected to torture or to inhuman or degrading treatment or punishment.

Article 4

1. No one shall be held in slavery or servitude.

2. No one shall be required to perform forced or compulsory labour....

Article 5

1. Everyone has the right to liberty and security of person. No one shall be deprived of his liberty save in the following cases and in accordance with a procedure prescribed by law:

(a) the lawful detention of a person after conviction by a competent court;

(b) the lawful arrest or detention of a person effected for non-compliance with the lawful order of a court or in order to secure the fulfillment of any obligation prescribed by law;

(c) the lawful arrest or detention of a person effected for the purpose of bringing him before the competent legal authority on reasonable suspicion of having committed an offence or when it is reasonably considered necessary to prevent his committing an offence or fleeing after having done so;

(d) the detention of a minor by lawful order for the purpose of educational supervision or his lawful detention for the purpose of bringing him before the competent legal authority;

(e) the lawful detention of persons for the prevention of the spreading of infectious diseases, of persons of unsound mind, alcoholics or drug addicts or vagrants;

(f) the lawful arrest or detention of person to prevent his effecting an unauthorized entry into the country or of a person against whom action is being taken with a view to deportation or extradition.

2. Everyone who is arrested shall be informed promptly, in a language which he understands, of the reasons for his arrest and of any charge against him.

3. Everyone arrested or detained in accordance with the provisions of paragraph I(c) of

this Article shall be brought promptly before a judge or other officer authorised by law to exercise judicial power and shall be entitled to trial within a reasonable time or release pending trial. Release may be conditioned by guarantees to appear for trial.

4. Everyone who is deprived of his liberty by arrest or detention shall be entitled to take proceedings by which the lawfulness of his detention shall be decided speedily by a court and his release ordered if the detention is not lawful.

5. Everyone who has been the victim of arrest or detention in contravention of the provisions of this Article shall have an enforceable right to compensation.

Article 6

1. In the determination of his civil rights and obligations or of any criminal charge against him, everyone is entitled to a fair and public hearing within a reasonable time by an independent and impartial tribunal established by law. Judgment shall be pronounced publicly but the press and public may be excluded from all or part of the trial in the interests of morals, public order or national security in a democratic society, where the interests of juveniles or the protection of the private life of the parties so require, or to the extent strictly necessary in the opinion of the court in special circumstances where publicity would prejudice the interests of justice.

2. Everyone charged with a criminal offence shall be presumed innocent until proved guilty according to law.

3. Everyone charged with a criminal offence has the following minimum rights:

(a) to be informed promptly, in a language which he understands and in detail, of the nature and cause of the accusation against him;

(b) to have adequate time and facilities for the preparation of his defence;

(c) to defend himself in person or through legal assistance of his own choosing or, if he has not sufficient means to pay for legal assistance, to be given it free when the interests of justice so require;

(d) to examine or have examined witnesses against him and to obtain the attendance and examination of witnesses on his behalf under the same conditions as witnesses against him;

(e) to have the free assistance of an interpreter if he cannot understand or speak the language used in court.

Article 7

1. No one shall be held guilty of any criminal offence on account of any act or omission which did not constitute a criminal offence under national or international law at the time when it was committed. Nor shall a heavier penalty be imposed than the one that was applicable at the time the criminal offence was committed.

2. This article shall not prejudice the trial and punishment of any person for any act or omission which, at the time when it was committed, was criminal according to the general principles of law recognized by civilized nations.

Article 8

1. Everyone has the right to respect for his private and family life, his home and his correspondence.

2. There shall be no interference by a public authority with the exercise of this right except such as is in accordance with the law and is necessary in a democratic society in the interests of national security, public safety or the economic well-being of the country, for the prevention of disorder or crime, for the protection of health or morals, or for the protection of the rights and freedoms of others.

Article 9

1. Everyone has the right to freedom of thought, conscience and religion; this right includes freedom to change his religion or belief and freedom, either alone or in community with others and in public or private, to manifest his religion or belief, in worship, teaching, practice and observance.

2. Freedom to manifest one's religion or beliefs shall be subject only to such limitations as are prescribed by law and are necessary in a democratic society in the interests of public safety, for the protection of public order, health or morals, or for the protection of the rights and freedoms of others.

Article 10

1. Everyone has the right to freedom of expression. This right shall include freedom to hold opinions and to receive and impart information and ideas without interference by public authority and regardless of frontiers. This

article shall not prevent States from requiring the licensing of broadcasting, television or cinema enterprises.

2. The exercise of these freedoms, since it carries with it duties and responsibilities, may be subject to such formalities, conditions, restrictions or penalties as are prescribed by law and are necessary in a democratic society, in the interests of national security, territorial integrity of public safety, for the prevention of disorder or crime, for the protection of health or morals, for the protection of the reputation or rights of others, for preventing the disclosure of information received in confidence, or for maintaining the authority and impartiality of the judiciary.

Article 11

1. Everyone has the right to freedom of peaceful assembly and to freedom of association with others, including the right to form and to join trade unions for the protection of his interests.

2. No restrictions shall be placed on the exercise of these rights other than such as are prescribed by law and are necessary in a democratic society in the interests of national security or public safety, for the prevention of disorder or crime, for the protection of health or morals or for the protection of the rights and freedoms of others. This article shall not prevent the imposition of lawful restrictions on the exercise of these rights by members of the armed forces, of the police or of the administration of the State.

Article 12. Men and women of marriageable age have the right to marry and to found a family, according to the national laws governing the exercise of this right.

Article 13. Everyone whose rights and freedoms as set forth in this Convention are violated shall have an effective remedy before a national authority notwithstanding that the violation has been committed by persons acting in an official capacity.

Article 14. The enjoyment of the rights and freedoms set forth in this Convention shall be secured without discrimination on any ground such as sex, race, colour, language, religion, political or other opinion, national or social origin, association with a national minority, property, birth or other status.

Article 15

1. In time of war or other public emergency threatening the life of the nation any High Contracting Party may take measures derogating from its obligations under this Convention to the extent strictly required by the exigencies of the situation, provided that such measures are not inconsistent, with its other obligations under international law.

2. No derogation from article 2, except in respect of deaths resulting from lawful acts of war, or from articles 3, 4 (paragraph 1) and 7 shall be made under this provision.

3. Any High Contracting Party availing itself of this right of derogation shall keep the Secretary-General of the Council of Europe fully informed of the measures which it has taken and the reasons therefor. It shall also inform the Secretary-General of the Council of Europe when such measures have ceased to operate and the provisions of the Convention are again being fully executed.

From U.S. House of Representatives Committee on Foreign Affairs, *Human Rights Documents, A Compilation of Documents Pertaining to Human Rights*, Washington, D.C.: GPO, 1983, 191–204.

Document 95:
INTERNATIONAL CONVENTION ON THE ELIMINATION OF ALL FORMS OF RACIAL DISCRIMINATION (1965)

The elimination of racial discrimination has been a major human rights theme throughout the world in the last half of this century. From revulsion at Hitler's racist genocidal campaign against the Jews in the 1940s to world-wide support for the civil rights campaign of African-Americans in the 1950s and 1960s to universal condemnation of South African apartheid, consensus has developed among humanity that pernicious theories and practices based on notions of racial superiority are intolerable and dangerous.

The following multi-national treaty is evidence of this consensus. Again, the United States is among the few major nations that have not yet ratified it.

Adopted and opened for signature and ratification by General Assembly resolution 2106 A (XX) of 21 December 1965

Entry into force: 4 January 1969, in accordance with article 19. (U.S. signed on September 28, 1966; Submitted to U.S. Senate February 23, 1978; Action by U.S. Senate pending)

Part I. Article 1

1. In this Convention, the term "racial discrimination" shall mean any distinction, exclusion, restriction or preference based on race, colour, descent, or national or ethnic origin which has the purpose or effect of nullifying or impairing the recognition, enjoyment or exercise, on an equal footing, of human rights and fundamental freedoms in the political, economic, social, cultural or any other field of public life.

2. This Convention shall not apply to distinctions, exclusions, restrictions or preferences made by a State Party to this Convention between citizens and noncitizens.

3. Nothing in this Convention may be interpreted as affecting in any way the legal provisions of States Parties concerning nationality, citizenship or naturalization, provided that such provisions do not discriminate against any particular nationality.

4. Special measures taken for the sole purpose of securing adequate advancement of certain racial or ethnic groups or individuals requiring such protection as may be necessary in order to ensure such groups or individuals equal enjoyment or exercise of human rights and fundamental freedoms shall not be deemed racial discrimination, provided, however, that such measures do not, as a consequence, lead to the maintenance of separate rights for different racial groups and that they shall not be continued after the objectives for which they were taken have been achieved.

Article 2

1. States Parties condemn racial discrimination and undertake to pursue by all appropriate means and without delay a policy of eliminating racial discrimination in all its forms and promoting understanding among all races, and, to this end:

(a) Each State Party undertakes to engage in no act or practice of racial discrimination against persons, groups of persons or institutions and to ensure that all public authorities and public institutions, national and local, shall act in conformity with this obligation;

(b) Each State Party undertakes not to sponsor, defend or support racial discrimination by any persons or organizations;

(c) Each State Party shall take effective measures to review governmental, national and local policies, and to amend, rescind or nullify any laws and regulations which have the effect of creating or perpetuating racial discrimination wherever it exists;

(d) Each State Party shall prohibit and bring to an end, by all appropriate means, including legislation as required by circumstances, racial discrimination by any persons, group or organization;

(e) Each State Party undertakes to encourage, where appropriate, integrationist multiracial organizations and movements and other means of eliminating barriers between races, and to discourage anything which tends to strengthen racial division.

2. States Parties shall, when the circumstances so warrant, take, in the social, economic, cultural and other fields, special and concrete measures to ensure the adequate development and protection of certain racial groups of individuals belonging to them, for the purpose of guaranteeing them the full and equal enjoyment of human rights and fundamental freedoms. These measures shall in no case entail as a consequence the maintenance of unequal or separate rights for different racial groups after the objectives for which they were taken have been achieved.

Article 3. States Parties particularly condemn racial segregation and apartheid and undertake to prevent, prohibit and eradicate all practices of this nature in territories under their jurisdiction.

Article 4. States Parties condemn all propaganda and all organizations which are based on ideas or theories of superiority of one race or group of persons of one colour or ethnic origin, or which attempt to justify or promote racial hatred and discrimination in any form, and undertake to adopt immediate and positive measures designed to eradicate all incitement to, or act of, such discrimination and, to this end, with due regard to the principles embodied in the Universal Declaration of Human Rights and the rights expressly set forth in article 5 of this Convention, *inter alia*.

(a) Shall declare an offence punishable by law all dissemination of ideas based on racial superiority or hatred, incitement to racial discrimination, as well as all acts of violence or incitement to such act against any race or group of persons of another colour or ethnic origin, and also the provision of any assistance to racist activities, including the financing thereof;

(b) Shall declare illegal and prohibit organizations and also organized and all other propaganda activities which promote and incite racial discrimination, and shall recognize participation in such organizations or activities as an offence punishable by law;

(c) Shall not permit public authorities of public institutions, national or local, to promote or incite racial discrimination.

Article 5. In compliance with the fundamental obligations laid down in article 2 of this Convention, State Parties undertake to prohibit and to eliminate racial discrimination in all its forms and to guarantee the right of everyone, without distinction as to race, colour, or national or ethnic origin, to equality before the law, notably in the enjoyment of the following rights:

(a) The right to equal treatment before the tribunals and all other organs administering justice;

(b) The right to security of person and protection by the State against violence or bodily harm, whether inflicted by government officials or by any individual group or institution;

(c) Political rights, in particular the rights to participate in universal and equal suffrage, to take part in the Government as well as in the conduct of public affairs at any level and to have equal access to public service;

(d) Other civil rights, in particular:

(i) The right to freedom of movement and residence within the border of the State;

(ii) The right to leave any country, including one's own, and to return to one's country;

(iii) The right to nationality;

(iv) The right to marriage and choice of spouse;

(v) The right to own property alone as well as in association with others;

(vi) The right to inherit;

(vii) The right to freedom of thought, conscience and religion;

(viii) The right to freedom of opinion and expression;

(ix) The right to freedom of peaceful assembly and association;

(e) Economic, social and cultural rights, in particular:

(i) The rights to work, to free choice of employment, to just and favourable conditions of work, to protection against unemployment, to equal pay for equal work, to just and favourable remuneration;

(ii) The right to form and join trade unions;

(iii) The right to housing;

(iv) The right to public health, medical care, social security and social services;

(v) The right to education and training;

(vi) The right to equal participation in cultural activities;

(f) The right to access to any place or service intended for use by the general public, such as transport, hotels, restaurants, cafs, theatres and parks.

Article 6. States Parties shall assure to everyone within their jurisdiction effective protection and remedies, through the competent national tribunals and other State institutions, against any acts of racial discrimination which violate his human rights and fundamental freedoms contrary to this Convention, as well as the right to seek from such tribunals just and adequate reparation or satisfaction for any damage suffered as a result of such discrimination.

Article 7. States Parties undertake to adopt immediate and effective measures, particularly in the fields of teaching, education, culture and information, with a view to combating prejudices which lead to racial discrimination and to promoting understanding, tolerance and friendship among nations and racial or ethnical groups, as well as to propagating the purposes and principles of the Charter of the United Nations, the Universal Declaration of Human Rights, the United Nations Declaration on the Elimination of All Forms of Racial Discrimination and this Convention.

Part II. Article 8

1. There shall be established a Committee on the Elimination of Racial Discrimination (hereinafter referred to as the Committee) consisting of eighteen experts of high moral standing and acknowledged impartiality elected by States

Parties from among their nationals, who shall serve in their personal capacity, consideration being given to equitable geographical distribution and to the representation of the different forms of civilization as well as of the principal legal systems.

2. The members of the Committee shall be elected by secret ballot from a list of persons nominated by the States Parties. Each State Party may nominate one person from among its own nationals....

Article 9

1. States Parties undertake to submit to the Secretary-General of the United Nations, for consideration by the Committee, a report on the legislative, judicial, administrative or other measures which they have adopted and which give effect to the provisions of this Convention: (a) within one year after the entry into force of the Convention for the State concerned; and (b) thereafter every two years and whenever the Committee so requests. The Committee may request further information from the States Parties.

2. The Committee shall report annually, through the Secretary-General, to the General Assembly of the United Nations on its activities and may make suggestions and general recommendations based on the examination of the reports and information received from the States Parties. Such suggestions and general recommendations shall be reported to the General Assembly together with comments, if any, from States Parties....

From U.S. House of Representatives Committee on Foreign Affairs, *Human Rights Documents, A Compilation of Documents Pertaining to Human Rights*, Washington: D.C.: GPO, 1983, 109–114.

Document 96:
CONVENTION AGAINST TORTURE AND OTHER CRUEL, INHUMAN OR DEGRADING TREATMENT OR PUNISHMENT (1984)

Because of the massive misuse of power by governments in many nations, this convention states an international policy against torture. Torture remains a major problem in the world today. Often governments are reluctant to protest such practices because of politics or strategic considerations. Private organizations are often the most vigilant observers of governmental misconduct.

Part I, Article 1

1. For the purposes of this Convention, the term "torture" means any act by which severe pain or suffering, whether physical or mental, is intentionally inflicted on a person for such purposes as obtaining from him or a third person information or a confession, punishing him for an act he or a third person has committed or is suspected of or for any reason based on discrimination of any kind, when such pain or suffering is inflicted by or at the instigation of or with the consent or acquiescence of a public official or other person acting in an official capacity. It does not include pain or suffering arising only from, inherent in or incidental to lawful sanctions.

2. This article is without prejudice to any international instrument or national legislation which does or may contain provisions of wider application.

Article 2

1. Each State Party shall take effective legislative, administrative, judicial or other measures to prevent acts of torture in any territory under its jurisdiction.

2. No exceptional circumstances whatsoever, whether a state of war or a threat of war, internal political instability or any other public emergency, may be invoked as a justification of torture.

Article 3

1. No State Party shall expel, return ("refouler") or extradite a person to another State where there are substantial grounds for believing that he would be in danger of being subjected to torture.

2. For the purpose of determining whether there are such grounds, the competent authorities shall take into account all relevant considerations including, where applicable, the existence in the State concerned of a consistent pattern of gross, flagrant or mass violations of human rights.

Article 4

1. Each State Party shall ensure that all acts of torture are offenses under its criminal law. The same shall apply to an attempt to commit

torture and to an act by any person which constitutes complicity or participation in torture.

2. Each State Party shall make these offenses punishable by appropriate penalties which take into account their grave nature.

Article 5

1. Each State Party shall take such measures as may be necessary to establish its jurisdiction over the offenses referred to in article 4 in the following cases:

   a. When the offenses are committed in any territory under its jurisdiction or on board a ship or aircraft registered in that State;

   b. When the alleged offender is a national of that State;

   c. When the victim is a national of that State if that State considers it appropriate.

2. Each State Party shall likewise take such measures as may be necessary to establish its jurisdiction over such offenses in cases where the alleged offender is present in any territory under its jurisdiction and it does not extradite him pursuant to article 8 to any of the States mentioned in paragraph 1 of this article.

3. This Convention does not exclude any criminal jurisdiction exercised in accordance with internal law.

Article 6

1. Upon being satisfied, after an examination of information available to it, that the circumstances so warrant, any State Party in whose territory a person alleged to have committed any offenses referred to in article 4 is present shall take him into custody or take other legal measures to ensure his presence. The custody and other legal measures shall be as provided in the law of that State but may be continued only for such time as is necessary to enable any criminal or extradition proceedings to be instituted.

2. Such State shall immediately make a preliminary inquiry into the facts.

3. Any person in custody pursuant to paragraph 1 of this article shall be assisted in communicating immediately with the nearest appropriate representative of the State of which he is a national, or, if he is a stateless person, with the representative of the State where he usually resides.

4. When a State, pursuant to this article, has taken a person into custody, it shall immediately notify the States referred to in article 5, paragraph 1, of the fact that such person is in custody and of the circumstances which warrant his detention. The State which makes the preliminary inquiry contemplated in paragraph 2 of this article shall promptly report its findings to the said States and shall indicate whether it intends to exercise jurisdiction.

Article 7

1. The State Party in the territory under whose jurisdiction a person alleged to have committed any offense referred to in article 4 is found shall in the cases contemplated in article 5, if it does not extradite him, submit the case to its competent authorities for the purpose of prosecution.

2. These authorities shall make their decision in the same manner as in the case of any ordinary offense of a serious nature under the law of that State. In the cases referred to in article 5, paragraph 2, the standards of evidence required for prosecution and conviction shall in no way be less stringent than those which apply in the cases referred to in article 5, paragraph 1.

3. Any person regarding whom proceedings are brought in connection with any of the offenses referred to in article 4 shall be guaranteed fair treatment at all stages in the proceedings.

Article 8

1. The offenses referred to in article 4 shall be deemed to be included as extraditable offenses in any extradition treaty existing between States Parties. States Parties undertake to include such offenses as extraditable offenses in every extradition treaty to be concluded between them.

2. If a State Party which makes extradition conditional on the existence of a treaty receives a request for extradition from another State Party with which it has no extradition treaty, it may consider this Convention as the legal basis for extradition in respect of such offenses. Extradition shall be subject to the other conditions provided by the law of the requested State.

3. States Parties which do not make extradition conditional on the existence of a treaty shall recognize such offenses as extraditable offenses between themselves subject to the conditions provided by the law of the requested State.

4. Such offenses shall be treated, for the purpose of extradition between States Parties, as if they had been committed not only in the place in which they occurred but also in the territories of the States required to establish their jurisdiction in accordance with article 5, paragraph 1.

Article 9

1. States Parties shall afford one another the greatest measure of assistance in connection with criminal proceedings brought in respect of any of the offenses referred to in article 4, including the supply of all evidence at their disposal necessary for the proceedings.

2. States Parties shall carry out their obligations under paragraph 1 of this article in conformity with any treaties on mutual judicial assistance that may exist between them.

Article 10

1. Each State Party shall ensure that education and information regarding the prohibition against torture are fully included in the training of law enforcement personnel, civil or military, medical personnel, public officials and other persons who may be involved in the custody, interrogation or treatment of any individual subjected to any form of arrest, detention or imprisonment.

2. Each State party shall include this prohibition in the rules or instructions issued in regard to the duties and functions of any such persons.

Article 11. Each State Party shall keep under systematic review interrogation rules, instructions, methods and practices as well as arrangements for the custody and treatment of persons subjected to any form of arrest, detention or imprisonment in any territory under its jurisdiction, with a view to preventing any cases of torture.

Article 12. Each State Party shall ensure that its competent authorities proceed to a prompt and impartial investigation, wherever there is reasonable ground to believe that an act of torture has been committed in any territory under its jurisdiction.

Article 13. Each State Party shall ensure that any individual who alleges he has been subjected to torture in any territory under its jurisdiction has the right to complain to, and to have his case promptly and impartially examined by, its competent authorities. Steps shall be taken to ensure that the complainant and witnesses are protected against all ill-treatment or intimidation as a consequence of his complaint or any evidence given.

Article 14

1. Each State Party shall ensure in its legal system that the victim of an act of torture obtains redress and has an enforceable right to fair and adequate compensation, including the means for as full rehabilitation as possible. In the event of the death of the victim as a result of an act of torture, his dependents shall be entitled to compensation.

2. Nothing in this article shall affect any right of the victim or other persons to compensation which may exist under national law.

Article 15. Each State Party shall ensure that any statement which is established to have been made as a result of torture shall not be invoked as evidence in any proceedings, except against a person accused of torture as evidence that the statement was made.

Article 16

1. Each State Party shall undertake to prevent in any territory under its jurisdiction other acts of cruel, inhuman or degrading treatment or punishment which do not amount to torture as defined in article 1, when such acts are committed by or at the instigation of or with the consent or acquiescence of a public official or other person acting in an official capacity. In particular, the obligations contained in articles 10, 11, 12 and 13 shall apply with the substitution for references to torture or references to other forms of cruel, inhuman or degrading treatment or punishment.

From Resolution of the General Assembly of the United Nations A-Res-39–46, December 10, 1984. See *The Report of the Committee Against Torture*, microform, New York: United Nations, 1988.

CHAPTER 13

National Challenges and Challenges to Nationalism

Document 97:
FOR ALL MANKIND (1945)
Leon Blum

Leon Blum, a socialist, was Premier of France in the 1930s and was put in prison by the National Socialists when Germany conquered France in World War II. Blum published the following in 1945 and writes of nationalism and the need for humankind to get beyond national states and the mistakes of the past.

I fully realize that to look forward in this way to an international society ruling the world of tomorrow is to arouse not only the facile skepticism of those who, at bottom, are only over-credulous (and who can therefore be left out of account), but also the perfectly honorable and legitimate feeling that we call patriotism. Patriotic feeling, always more acute and sensitive after a defeat, becomes, by the same fact of defeat, more touchy and more jealous. I can hear the objections that will be put forward: "What! France has not yet arisen from her ruins, her wounds are not yet healed, and you talk about Europe and the world! You invoke all over again the humanitarian softheartedness from which we have suffered so much in the past, and that at a time when our sense of patriotic duty should be our one clear-cut, imperative, and exclusive preoccupation. No! France first, France above all! France's only chance of salvation lies in the egoistic devotion of all her children."

It is true that in our country's misfortune we become more deeply and clearly conscious of the love we all bear her, even though at other times it may go unrecognized within us. It is true that the history of recent years ought to have taught us how to preserve all the natural dignity and vigor of the patriotic feeling. And yet I believe that when I try to show that the Europe and the world of tomorrow must be organized within a larger framework than that of the nation if they are not once again to revert to chaos and war, I have said nothing that need offend, injure, or lessen patriotic feeling. I am not suggesting that patriotism must go, that it must give way, as if it were an old-fashioned instinct belonging to a past age and no longer corresponding to the aspirations of the modern mind. Nor do I think that it must be absorbed—which, in effect, means dissipated—in a more general and, if you like, more noble sentiment, such as faith in human solidarity, love of humanity. Love of country is eternal. It is on the same plane as love of family, love of one's native town or village, of all the fundamental realities that in our heart of hearts we hold nearest and dearest. But I am quite sure that there is nothing incompatible between patriotism and humanism—or, if you like, between national and international loyalties. Love of a nation and love of the human race, as one great man once said, can co-exist in the same conscience as naturally as patriotism and love of family, or as patriotism and religious belief.

From Leon Blum, *For All Mankind*, translated by W. Pickles, New York: The Viking Press, 1946, 163–164.

Document 98:
IDEAS THAT HAVE HARMED MANKIND (1950)
Bertrand Russell

Bertrand Russell was one of the founders of the antimetaphysical philosophy of Logical Positivism. This school of philosophy reduces philosophical speculation to the search for meaningful answers to solve problems. He was an active spokesperson against nuclear testing and a powerful supporter of disarmament. Russell won the Nobel Prize for Literaure in 1950, the year the following essay was published.

The misfortunes of human beings may be divided into two classes: First, those inflicted by the nonhuman environment, and, second, those inflicted by other people. As mankind have progressed in knowledge and technique, the second class has become a continually increasing percentage of the total. In old times, famine, for example, was due to natural causes, and, although people did their best to combat it, large numbers of them died of starvation. At the present moment large parts of the world are faced with the threat of famine, but although natural causes have contributed to the situation, the principal causes are human. For six years the civilized nations of the world devoted all their best energies to killing each other, and they find it difficult suddenly to switch over to keeping each other alive. Having destroyed harvests, dismantled agricultural machinery, and disorganized shipping, they find it no easy matter to relieve the shortage of crops in one place by means of a superabundance in another, as would easily be done if the economic system were in normal working order. As this illustration shows, it is now man that is man's worst enemy. Nature, it is true, still sees to it that we are mortal, but with the progress in medicine it will become more and more common for people to live until they have had their fill of life. We are supposed to wish to live forever and to look forward to the unending joys of heaven, of which, by miracle, the monotony will never grow stale. But in fact, if you question any candid person who is no longer young, he is very likely to tell you that, having tasted life in this world, he has no wish to begin again as a "new boy" in another. For the future, therefore, it may be taken that much the most important evils that mankind have to consider are those which they inflict upon each other through stupidity or malevolence or both.

I think that the evils that men inflict on each other, and by reflection upon themselves, have their main source in evil passions rather than in ideas or beliefs. But ideas and principles that do harm are, as a rule, though not always, cloaks for evil passions. In Lisbon when heretics were publicly burned, it sometimes happened that one of them, by a particularly edifying recantation, would be granted the boon of being strangled before being put into the flames. This would make the spectators so furious that the authorities had great difficulty in preventing them from lynching the penitent and burning him on their own account. The spectacle of the writhing torments of the victims was, in fact, one of the principal pleasures to which the populace looked forward to enliven a somewhat drab existence. I cannot doubt that this pleasure greatly contributed to the general belief that the burning of heretics was a righteous act. The same sort of thing applies to war. People who are vigorous and brutal often find war enjoyable, provided that it is a victorious war and that there is not too much interference with rape and plunder....

The world at the present day stands in need of two kinds of things. On the one hand, organization—political organization for the elimination of wars, economic organization to enable men to work productively, especially in the countries that have been devastated by war, educational organization to generate a sane internationalism. On the other hand it needs certain moral qualities—the qualities which have been advocated by moralists for many ages, but hitherto with little success. The qualities most needed are charity and tolerance, not some form of fanatical faith such as is offered to us by the various rampant isms. I think these two aims, the organizational and the ethical, are closely interwoven; given either the other would soon follow. But, in effect, if the world is to move in the right direction it will have to move simultaneously in both respects. There will have to be a gradual lessening of the evil passions which are the natural aftermath of war, and a gradual increase of the organizations by means of which mankind can bring each other mutual help. There will have to be a realization at once intellectual and moral that we are all one family, and that the happiness of no one branch of this family can be built securely upon the ruin of another. At the present time, moral defects stand in the way of clear thinking, and muddled thinking encourages moral defects. Perhaps, though I scarcely dare to hope it, the hydrogen bomb will terrify mankind into sanity and tolerance. If this should happen we shall have reason to bless its inventors.

From Bertrand Russell, "Ideas That Have Harmed Mankind," in *Unpopular Essays*, New York: Simon and Schuster, 1950, 146–165.

Document 99:
REPORT ON THE TRIPARTITE CONFERENCE OF BERLIN (THE POTSDAM PROTOCOL) (1945)

The behavior of Germany has been judged the prime cause of World War II in Europe; unlike the case of World War I, most agree with this idea of German responsibility. Hitler's government exterminated six million Jews and caused the deaths of over twenty million other people in the war. The Great Powers, the United States, the Soviet Union and Great Britain were forced to agree on what should be done to Germany after the war ended. A great part of Post-World War II history is affected by the decisions in this Potsdam Agreement. Note especially the concern for individual rights and responsibilities.

2 August 1945

I. On 17 July 1945, the President of the United States of America Harry S. Truman, the Chairman of the Council of People's Commissars of the Union of Soviet Socialist Republics, Generalissimo J.V. Stalin, and the Prime Minister of Great Britain, together with Mr. Clement R. Attlee, met in the Tripartite Conference of Berlin....

III. Germany. The Allied armies are in occupation of the whole of Germany and the German people have begun to atone for the terrible crimes committed under the leadership of those whom, in the hour of their success, they openly approved and blindly obeyed.

Agreement has been reached at this Conference on the political and economic principles of a coordinated Allied policy toward defeated Germany during the period of Allied control.

The purpose of this agreement is to carry out the Crimea declaration on Germany. German militarism and Nazism will be extirpated and the Allies will take in agreement together, now and in the future, the other measures necessary to assure that Germany never again will threaten her neighbors or the peace of the world.

It is not the intention of the Allies to destroy or enslave the German people. It is the intention of the Allies that the German people be given the opportunity to prepare for the eventual reconstruction of their life on a democratic and peaceful basis. If their own efforts are steadily directed to this end, it will be possible for them in due course to take their place among the free and peaceful people of the world.

The text of the agreement is as follows:

The political and economic principles to govern the treatment of Germany in the initial control period.

A. Political Principles

1. In accordance with the Agreement on Control Machinery in Germany, supreme authority in Germany is exercised, on instructions from their respective Governments, by the Commanders-in-Chief of the armed forces of the United States of America, the United Kingdom, the Union of Soviet Socialist Republics, and the French Republic, each in his own zone of occupation, and also jointly, in matters affecting Germany as a whole, in their capacity as members of the Control Council.

2. So far as is practicable, there shall be uniformity of treatment of the German population throughout Germany.

3. The purposes of the occupation of Germany by which the Control Council shall be guided are:

(i) The complete disarmament and demilitarization of Germany and the elimination or control of all German industry that could be used for military production. To these ends:

(a) All German land, naval and air forces, the SS, SA, SD and Gestapo, with all their organizations, staffs and institutions, including the General Staff, the Officers' Corps, Reserve Corps, military schools, war veterans' organizations and all other military and quasi-military organizations, together with all clubs and associations which serve to keep alive the military tradition in Germany, shall be completely and finally abolished in such manner as permanently to prevent the revival or reorganization of German militarism and Nazism.

(b) All arms, ammunition and implements of war and all specialized facilities for their production shall be held at the disposal of the Allies or destroyed. The maintenance and production of all aircraft and all arms, ammunition and implements of war shall be prevented.

(ii) To convince the German people that they have suffered a total military defeat and that they cannot escape responsibility for what they have brought upon themselves, since their own ruthless warfare and the fanatical Nazi resistance have destroyed the German economy and made chaos and suffering inevitable.

(iii) To destroy the National Socialist Party and its affiliated and supervised organizations, to dissolve all Nazi institutions, to ensure that they are not revived in any form, and to prevent all Nazi and militarist activity or propaganda.

(iv) To prepare for the eventual reconstruction of German political life on a democratic basis and for eventual peaceful cooperation in international life by Germany.

4. All Nazi laws which provided the basis of the Hitler regime or established discrimination on grounds of race, creed, or political opinion shall be abolished. No such discriminations, whether legal, administrative or otherwise, shall be tolerated.

5. War criminals and those who have participated in planning or carrying out Nazi enterprises involving or resulting in atrocities or war crimes shall be arrested and brought to judgment. Nazi leaders, influential Nazi supporters and high officials of Nazi organizations and institutions and any other persons dangerous to the occupation or its objectives shall be arrested and interned.

6. All members of the Nazi Party who have been more than nominal participants in its activities and [all other persons hostile to Allied purposes shall] be removed from public and semi-public office, and from positions of responsibility in important private undertakings. Such persons shall be replaced by persons who, by their political and moral qualities, are deemed capable of assisting in developing genuine democratic institutions in Germany.

7. German education shall be so controlled as to completely eliminate Nazi and militarist doctrines and to make possible the successful development of democratic ideas.

8. The judicial system will be reorganized in accordance with the principles of democracy, of justice under law, and of equal rights for all citizens without distinction of race, nationality or religion.

9. The administration of affairs in Germany should be directed towards the decentralization of the political structure and the development of local responsibility. To this end—

(i) local self-government shall be restored throughout Germany on democratic principles and in particular through elective councils as rapidly as is consistent with military security and the purposes of military occupation;

(ii) all democratic political parties with rights of assembly and of public discussion shall be allowed and encouraged throughout Germany;

(iii) representative and elective principles shall be introduced into regional, provincial and state (Land) administration as rapidly as may be justified by the successful application of these principles in local self government;

(iv) for the time being no central German government shall be established. Notwithstanding this, however, certain essential German administrative departments, headed by State Secretaries, shall be established, particularly in the fields of finance, transport, communications, foreign trade and industry. Such departments will act under the direction of the Control Council.

10. Subject to the necessity for maintaining military security, freedoms of speech, press and religion shall be permitted and religious institutions shall be respected. Subject likewise to the maintenance of military security, the formation of free trade unions shall be permitted.

B. Economic Principles

11. In order to eliminate Germany's war potential, the production of arms, ammunition and implements of war as well as all types of aircraft and sea-going ships shall be prohibited and prevented. Production of metals, chemicals, machinery and other items that are directly necessary to a war economy, shall be rigidly controlled and restricted to Germany's approved post-war peacetime needs to meet the objectives stated in paragraph 15. Productive capacity not needed for permitted production shall be removed in accordance with the reparations plan recommended by the Allied Commission on reparations and approved by the Governments concerned or if not removed shall be destroyed.

12. At the earliest practicable date, the German economy shall be decentralized for the purpose of eliminating the present excessive concentration of economic powers as exemplified in particular by cartels, syndicates, trusts and other monopolistic arrangements.

13. In organizing the German economy, primary emphasis shall be given to the development of agriculture and peaceful domestic industries.

14. During the period of occupation Germany shall be treated as a single economic unit....

IV. Reparations from Germany

In accordance with the Crimea decision that Germany be compelled to compensate to the greatest possible extent for the loss and suffering that she has caused to the United Nations and for which the German people cannot escape responsibility, the following agreement on reparations was reached...

VII. War criminals

The three Governments have taken note of the discussions which have been proceeding in recent weeks in London between British, United States, Soviet and French representatives with a view to reaching agreement on the methods of trial of those major war criminals whose crimes under the Moscow Declaration of October 1943 have no particular geographical localization. The three Governments reaffirm their intention to bring those criminals to swift and sure justice. They hope that the negotiations in London will result in speedy agreement being reached for this purpose, and they regard it as a matter of great importance that the trial of those major criminals should begin at the earliest possible date. The first list of defendants will be published by 1 September....

XIII. Orderly Transfers of German Populations

The Conference reached the following agreement on the removal of Germans from Poland, Czechoslovakia and Hungary:—

The three Governments, having considered the question in all its aspects, recognize that the transfer to Germany of German populations or elements thereof, remaining in Poland, Czechoslovakia and Hungary, will have to be undertaken. They agree that any transfers that take place should be effected in an orderly and humane way....

Approved:

J.V. Stalin

Harry S. Truman

C.R. Attlee

From U.S. Department of State, *Foreign Relations of the United States, The Conference of Berlin, (The Potsdam Conference), Volume II,* Washington: GPO, 1960, 1499–1513.

Document 100:
CIVIL RIGHTS ACT OF 1964

The Civil Rights Act of 1964 *provided the necessary federal laws to ensure voting rights, access to public places and employment opportunities. It established the Commission on Civil Rights. It set in motion the changes that were needed since Lincoln's* Emancipation Proclamation.

Title I—Voting Rights

To enforce the constitutional right to vote, to confer jurisdiction upon the district courts of the United States to provide injunctive relief against discrimination in public accommodations, to authorize the Attorney General to institute suits to protect constitutional rights in public facilities and public education, to extend the Commission on Civil Rights, to prevent discrimination in federally assisted programs, to establish a Commission on Equal Employment Opportunity, and for other purposes.

Title I—Voting Rights

Sec. 101. Section 2004 of the Revised Statutes (42 U.S.C. 1971), as amended by section 131 of the Civil Rights Act of 1957 (71 Stat. 637), and as further amended by section 601 of the Civil Rights Act of 1960 (74 Stat. 90), is further amended as follows:

(a) Insert "1" after "(a)" in subsection (a) and add at the end of subsection (a) the following new paragraphs:

"(2) No person acting under color of law shall—

"(A) in determining whether any individual is qualified under State law or laws to vote in any Federal election, apply any standard, practice, or procedure different from the standards, practices, or procedures applied under such law or laws to other individuals within the same county, parish, or similar political subdivision who have been found by State officials to be qualified to vote;

"(B) deny the right of any individual to vote in any Federal election because of an error or omission on any record or paper relating to any application, registration, or other act requisite to voting, if such error or omission is not material in determining whether such individual is qualified under State law to vote in such election; or

"(C) employ any literacy test as a qualification for voting in any Federal election unless (i) such test is administered to each individual and is conducted wholly in writing, and (ii) a certified copy of the test and of the answers given by the individual is furnished to him within twenty-five days of the submission of his request made within the period of time during which records and papers are required to be retained and preserved pursuant to title III of the Civil Rights Act of 1960 (42 U.S.C. 1974–74e;

74 Stat. 88): *Provided, however*, that the Attorney General may enter into agreements with appropriate State or local authorities that preparation, conduct, and maintenance of such tests in accordance with the provisions of applicable State or local law, including such special provisions as are necessary in the preparation, conduct, and maintenance of such tests for persons who are blind or otherwise physically handicapped, meet the purposes of this subparagraph and constitute compliance therewith. . . .

Title II—Injunctive Relief Against Discrimination In Places Of Public Accommodation

Sec. 201. (A) All persons shall be entitled to full and equal enjoyment of the goods, services, facilities, privileges, advantages, and accommodations of any place of public accommodation, as defined in this section, without discrimination or segregation on the ground of race, color, religion, or national origin.

(b) Each of the following establishments which serves the public is a place of public accommodation within the meaning of this title if its operations affect commerce, or if discrimination or segregation by it is supported by State action:

(1) any inn, hotel, motel, or other establishment which provides lodging to transient guests, other than an establishment located within a building which contains not more than five rooms for rent or hire and which is actually occupied by the proprietor of such establishment as his residence;

(2) any restaurant, cafeteria, lunchroom, lunch counter, soda fountain, or other facility principally engaged in selling food for consumption on the premises, including, but not limited to, any such facility located on the premises of any retail establishment; or any gasoline station;

(3) any motion picture house, theater, concert hall, sports arena, stadium or other place of exhibition or entertainment; and

(4) any establishment (A)(i) which is physically located within the premises of any establishment otherwise covered by this subsection, or (ii) within the premises of which is physically located any such covered establishment, and (B) which holds itself out as serving patrons of such covered establishment. . . .

Title III—Desegregation Of Public Facilities

Sec. 301. (a) Whenever the Attorney General receives a complaint in writing signed by an individual to the effect that he is being deprived of or threatened with the loss of his right to the equal protection of the laws, on account of his race, color, religion, or national origin, by being denied equal utilization of any public facility which is owned, operated, or managed by or on behalf of any State or subdivision thereof, other than a public school or public college as defined in section 401 of title IV hereof and the Attorney General believes the complaint is meritorious and certifies that the signer or signers of such complaint are unable, in his judgment, to initiate and maintain appropriate legal proceedings for relief and that the institution of an action will materially further the orderly progress of desegregation in public facilities, the Attorney General is authorized to institute for or in the name of the United States a civil action in any appropriate district court of the United States against such parties and for such relief as may be appropriate, and such court shall have and shall exercise jurisdiction of proceedings instituted pursuant to this section. The Attorney General may implead as defendants such additional parties as are or become necessary to the grant of effective relief hereunder.

(b) The Attorney General may deem a person or persons unable to initiate and maintain appropriate legal proceedings within the meaning of subsection (a) of this section when such person or persons are unable, either directly or through other interested persons or organizations, to bear the expense of the litigation or to obtain effective legal representation; or whenever he is satisfied that the institution of such litigation would jeopardize the personal safety, employment, or economic standing of such person or persons, their families, or their property. . . .

Title IV—Desegregation
Definitions

Sec. 401. As used in this title—

(a) "Commissioner" means the Commissioner of Education.

(b) "Desegregation" means the assignment of students to public schools and within such schools without regard to their race, color, religion, or national origin, but "desegregation" shall not mean the assignment of students to public schools in order to overcome racial imbalance.

(c) "Public School" means any elementary or secondary educational institution, and "public college" means any institution of higher education or any technical or vocational school above the secondary school level, provided that such public school or public college is operated by a State, subdivision of a State, or governmental agency within a State, or operated wholly or predominantly from or through the use of governmental funds or property, or funds or property derived from a governmental source.

(d) "School board" means any agency or agencies which administer a system of one or more public schools and any other agency which is responsible for the assignment of students to or within such system.

Survey And Report Of Educational Opportunities

Sec. 402. The Commissioner shall conduct a survey and make a report to the President and the Congress, within two years of the enactment of this title, concerning the lack of availability of equal educational opportunities for individuals by reason of race, color, religion, or national origin in public educational institutions at all levels in the United States, its territories and possessions, and the District of Columbia....

Title V—Commission on Civil Rights....

"Duties Of The Commission

"Sec. 104. (a) The Commission shall—

"(1) investigate allegations in writing under oath or affirmation that certain citizens of the United States are being deprived of their right to vote and have that vote counted by reason of their color, race, religion, or national origin; which writing under oath or affirmation, shall set forth the facts upon which such belief or beliefs are based;

"(2) study and collect information concerning legal developments constituting a denial of equal protection of the laws under the Constitution because of race, color, religion or national origin or in the administration of justice;

"(3) appraise the laws and policies of the Federal Government with respect to denials of equal protection of the laws under the Constitution because of race, color, religion or national origin or in the administration of justice;

"(4) serve as a national clearinghouse for information in respect to denials of equal protection of the laws because of race, color, religion or national origin, including but not limited to the fields of voting, education, housing, employment, the use of public facilities, and transportation, or in the administration of justice;

"(5) investigate allegations, made in writing and under oath or affirmation, that citizens of the United States are unlawfully being accorded or denied the right to vote, or to have their votes properly counted, in any election of presidential electors, Members of the United States Senate, or of the House of Representatives, as a result of any patterns or practice of fraud or discrimination in the conduct of such election; and

"(6) Nothing in this or any other Act shall be construed as authorizing the Commission, its Advisory Committees, or any person under its supervision or control to inquire into or investigate any membership practices or internal operations of any fraternal organization, any college or university fraternity or sorority, any private club or any religious organization...."

Title VI—Nondiscrimination in Federally Assisted Programs

Sec. 601. No person in the United States shall, on the ground of race, color, or national origin, be excluded from participation in, be denied the benefits of, or be subjected to discrimination under any program or activity receiving Federal financial assistance.

Sec. 602. Each Federal department and agency which is empowered to extend Federal financial assistance to any program or activity, by way of grant, loan, or contract other than a contract of insurance or guaranty, is authorized and directed to effectuate the provisions of section 601 with respect to such program or activity by issuing rules, regulations, or orders of general applicability which shall be consistent with achievement of the objectives of the statute authorizing the financial assistance in connection with which the action is taken. No such rule, regulation, or order shall become effective unless and until approved by the President....

Title VII—Equal Employment Opportunity

Discrimination Because Of Race, Color, Religion, Sex, Or National Origin

Sec. 703. (a) It shall be an unlawful employment practice for an employer—

(1) to fail or refuse to hire or to discharge any individual, or otherwise to discriminate against any individual with respect to his compensation, terms, conditions, or privileges of employment, because of such individual's race, color, religion, sex, or national origin; or

(2) to limit, segregate, or classify his employees in any way which would deprive or tend to deprive any individual of employment opportunities or otherwise adversely affect his status as an employee, because of such individual's race, color, religion, sex, or national origin.

(b) It shall be an unlawful employment practice for an employment agency to fail or refuse to refer for employment, or otherwise to discriminate against, any individual because of his race, color, religion, sex, or national origin, or to classify or refer for employment any individual on the basis of his race, color, religion, sex, or national origin.

(c) It shall be an unlawful employment practice for a labor organization—

(1) to exclude or to expel from its membership, or otherwise to discriminate against, any individual because of his race, color, religion, sex, or national origin;

(2) to limit, segregate, or classify its membership, or to classify or fail or refuse to refer for employment any individual, in any way which would deprive or tend to deprive any individual of employment opportunities, or would limit such employment opportunities or otherwise adversely affect his status as an employee or as an applicant for employment, because of such individual's race, color, religion, sex, or national origin; or

(3) to cause or attempt to cause an employer to discriminate against an individual in violation of this section....

Equal Employment Opportunity Commission
Sec. 705. (a) There is hereby created a Commission to be known as the Equal Employment Opportunity Commission, which shall be composed of five members, not more than three of whom shall be members of the same political party, who shall be appointed by the President by and with the advice and consent of the Senate....

Title VII—Registration And Voting Statistics
Sec. 801. The Secretary of Commerce shall promptly conduct a survey to compile registration and voting statistics in such geographic areas as may be recommended by the Commission on Civil Rights. Such a survey and compilation shall, to the extent recommended by the Commission on Civil Rights, only include a count of persons of voting age by race, color, and national origin, and determination of the extent to which such persons are registered to vote, and have voted in any statewide primary or general election in which the Members of the United States House of Representatives are nominated or elected, since January 1, 1960....

From Committee on the Judiciary, House of Representatives, *Civil Rights Acts of 1957, 1960, 1964, 1968 and Voting Rights Act of 1965*, Washington, D.C.: GPO, 1969, 15–46.

Document 101:
PASTORAL LETTER ON WAR AND PEACE (1983)
U.S. Catholic Bishops

In 1983, American Catholic Bishops issued this statement on the "just war"—a war that Catholics might support. War can be acceptable to American Roman Catholics if it meets the criteria listed in the statement.

The Just-War Criteria
...(80) The moral theory of the "just-war" or "limited-war" doctrine begins with the presumption which binds all Christians: We should do no harm to our neighbors; how we treat our enemy is the key test of whether we love our neighbor; and the possibility of taking even one human life is a prospect we should consider in fear and trembling. How is it possible to move from these presumptions to the idea of a justifiable use of lethal force?

(81) Historically and theologically the clearest answer to the question is found in St. Augustine. Augustine was impressed by the fact and the consequences of sin in history—the "not yet" dimension of the kingdom. In his view war was both the result of sin and a tragic remedy for sin in the life of political societies. War arose from disordered ambitions, but it could also be used in some cases at least to restrain evil and protect the innocent. The classic case which illustrated his view was the use of lethal force to prevent aggression against

innocent victims. Faced with the fact of attack on the innocent, the presumption that we do no harm even to our enemy yielded to the command of love understood as the need to restrain an enemy who would injure the innocent.

(82) The just-war argument has taken several forms in the history of Catholic theology, but this Augustinian insight is its central premise. In the 20th century, papal teaching has used the logic of Augustine and Aquinas to articulate a right of self-defense for states in a decentralized international order and to state the criteria for exercising that right. The essential position was stated by Vatican II: "As long as the danger of war persists and there is no international authority with the necessary competence and power, governments cannot be denied the right of lawful self-defense, once all peace efforts have failed."....

(84) The determination of *when* conditions exist which allow the resort to force in spite of the strong presumption against it is made in light of *jus ad bellum* criteria. The determination of *how* even a justified resort to force must be conducted is made in light of the *jus in bello* criteria. We shall briefly explore the meaning of both.

(85) *Just ad Bellum*: Why and when recourse to war is permissible.

(86) a. Just Cause: War is permissible only to confront "a real and certain danger," i.e., to protect innocent life, to preserve conditions necessary for decent human existence and to secure basic human rights. As both Pope Pius XII and Pope John XXIII made clear, if war of retribution was ever justifiable, the risks of modern war negate such a claim today....

(87) b. Competent Authority: In the Catholic tradition the right to use force has always been joined to the common good; war must be declared by those with responsibility for public order, not by private groups or individuals....

(92) c. Comparative Justice: Questions concerning the means of waging war today, particularly in view of the destructive potential of weapons, have tended to override questions concerning the comparative justice of the positions of respective adversaries or enemies. In essence: Which side is sufficiently "right" in a dispute, and are the values at stake critical enough to override the presumption against war? The question in its most basic form is this:

Do the rights and values involved justify killing? For whatever the means used, war by definition involves violence, destruction, suffering and death....

(95) d. Right Intention: Right intention is related to just cause—war can be legitimately intended only for the reasons set forth above as a just cause. During the conflict, right intention means pursuit of peace and reconciliation, including avoiding unnecessarily destructive acts or imposing unreasonable conditions (e.g., unconditional surrender).

(95) e. Last Resort: For resort to war to be justified all peaceful alternatives must have been exhausted. There are formidable problems in this requirement. No international organization currently in existence has exercised sufficient internationally recognized authority to be able either to mediate effectively in most cases or to prevent conflict by the intervention of U.N. or other peacekeeping forces. Furthermore, there is a tendency for nations or peoples which perceive conflict between or among other nations as advantageous to themselves to attempt to prevent a peaceful settlement rather than advance it....

(98) f. Probability of Success: This is a difficult criterion to apply, but its purpose is to prevent irrational resort to force or hopeless resistance when the outcome of either will clearly be disproportionate or futile. The determination includes a recognition that at times defense of key values, even against great odds, may be a "proportionate" witness....

(99) g. Proportionality: In terms of the *jus ad bellum* criteria, proportionality means that the damage to be inflicted and the costs incurred by war must be proportionate to the good expected by taking up arms. Nor should judgments concerning proportionality be limited to the temporal order without regard to a spiritual dimension in terms of "damage," "cost" and "the good expected." In today's interdependent world even a local conflict can affect people everywhere; this is particularly the case when the nuclear powers are involved. Hence a nation cannot justly go to war today without considering the effect of its action on others and the international community.

Jus in Bello

Even when the stringent conditions which justify resort to war are met, the conduct of the war (i.e., strategy, tactics and individual actions) remains subject to continuous scrutiny in light of two principles which have special significance today precisely because of the destructive capability of modern technological warfare. These principles are proportionality and discrimination. In discussing them here we shall apply them to the question of *jus ad bellum* as well as *jus in bello*; for today it becomes increasingly difficult to make a decision to use any kind of armed force, however limited initially in intention and in the destructive power of the weapons employed, without facing at least the possibility of escalation to broader, or even total, war and to the use of weapons of horrendous destructive potential....

(103) Response to aggression must not exceed the nature of the aggression. To destroy civilization as we know it by waging a "total war" as today it *could* be waged would be a monstrously disproportionate response to aggression on the part of any nation.

(104) Moreover, the lives of innocent persons may never be taken directly, regardless of the purpose alleged for doing so. To wage truly "total" war is by definition to take huge numbers of innocent lives. Just response to aggression must be discriminate; it must be directed against unjust aggressors, not against innocent people caught up in a war not of their making....

When confronting choices among specific military options, the question asked by proportionality is: Once we take into account not only the military advantages that will be achieved by using this means, but also all the harms reasonably expected to follow from using it, can its use still be justified? We know, of course, that no end can justify means evil in themselves, such as the executing of hostages or the targeting of non-combatants. Nonetheless, even if the means adopted is not evil in itself, it is necessary to take into account the probable harms that will result from using it and the justice of accepting those harms....

In terms of the arms race, if the *real* end in view is legitimate defense against unjust aggression and the means to this end are not evil in themselves, we must still examine the question of proportionality concerning attendant evils....Do the exorbitant costs, the general climate of insecurity generated, the possibility of accidental detonation of highly destructive weapons, the danger of error and miscalculation that could provoke retaliation and war—do such evils or others attendant upon and indirectly deriving from the arms race make the arms race itself a disproportionate response to aggression? Pope John Paul II is very clear in his insistence that the exercise of the right and duty of a people to protect their existence and freedom is contingent on the use of proportionate means....

(107) Finally, another set of questions concerns the interpretation of the principle of discrimination. The principle prohibits directly intended attacks on non-combatants and non-military targets. It raises a series of questions about the term "international," the category of "non-combatant" and the meaning of "military"....

These two principles in all their complexity must be applied to the range of weapons—conventional, nuclear, biological and chemical—with which nations are armed today....

(141) c. *The Use of Nuclear Weapons*: Establishing moral guidelines in the nuclear debate means addressing first the question of the use of nuclear weapons....

(147) 1. *Counterpopulation Warfare*: Under no circumstances may nuclear weapons or other instruments of mass slaughter be used for the purpose of destroying population centers or other predominantly civilian targets....

(148) Retaliatory action, whether nuclear or conventional, which would indiscriminately take many wholly innocent lives, lives of people who are in no way responsible for feckless actions of their government, must also be condemned. This condemnation, in our judgment, applies even to retaliatory use of weapons striking enemy cities after our own have already been struck. No Christian can rightfully carry out orders or policies deliberately aimed at killing non-combatants....

(150) 2. *The Initiation of Nuclear War*: We do not perceive any situation in which the deliberate initiation of nuclear warfare on however restricted a scale can be morally justified. Non-nuclear attacks by another state must be resisted by other than nuclear means. Therefore, a serious moral obligation exists to develop non-nuclear defensive strategies as rapidly as possible....

(152) Whether under conditions of war in Europe, parts of Asia or the Middle East, or the exchange of strategic weapons directly between the United States and the Soviet Union, the difficulties of limiting the use of nuclear weapons are immense. A number of expert witnesses advise us that the commanders operating under conditions of battle probably would not be able to exercise strict contol; the number of weapons used would rapidly increase, the targets would be expanded beyond the military and the level of civilian casualties would rise enormously. No one can be certain that this escalation would not occur even in the face of political efforts to keep such an exchange "limited." The chances of keeping use limited seem remote, and the consequences of escalation to mass destruction would be appalling. Former public officials have testified that it is improbable that any nuclear war could actually be kept limited. Their testimony and the consequences involved in this problem lead us to conclude that the danger of escalation is so great that it would be morally unjustifiable to initiate nuclear war in any form. The danger is rooted not only in the technology of our weapons systems, but in the weakness and sinfulness of human communities. We find the moral responsibility of beginning nuclear war not justified by rational political objectives....

(154) At the same time we recognize the responsibility the United States has had and continues to have in assisting allied nations in their defense against either a conventional or a nuclear attack. Especially in the European theater, the deterrence of a *nuclear* attack may require nuclear weapons for a time, even though their possession and deployment must be subject to rigid restrictions.

(155) The need to defend against a conventional attack in Europe imposes the political and moral burden of developing adequate, alternative modes of defense to present reliance on nuclear weapons....

(175) The moral duty today is to prevent nuclear war from ever occurring and to protect and preserve those key values of justice, freedom and independence which are necessary for personal dignity and national integrity....

(178) Targeting doctrine raises significant moral questions because it is a significant determinant of what would occur if nuclear weapons were ever to be used. Although we acknowledge the need for deterrent, not all forms of deterrence are morally acceptable. There are moral limits to deterrence policy as well as to policy regarding use. Specifically, it is not morally acceptable to intend to kill the innocent as part of a strategy of deterring nuclear war. The question of whether U.S. policy involves an intention to strike civilian centers has been one of our factual concerns.

(180) These statements do not address or resolve another very troublesome moral problem, namely, an attack on military targets or militarily significant industrial targets could involve "indirect" (i.e., unintended) but massive civilian casualties.... The number of civilians who would necessarily be killed by such strikes is horrendous. This problem is unavoidable because of the way modern military facilities and production centers are so thoroughly interspersed with civilian living and working areas. It is aggravated if one side deliberately positions military targets in the midst of a civilian population.

In our consultations, administration officials readily admitted that while they hoped any nuclear exchange could be kept limited, they were prepared to retaliate in a massive way if necessary. They also agreed that once any substantial numbers of weapons were used, the civilian casualty levels would quickly become truly catastrophic and that even with attacks limited to "military" targets the number of deaths in a substantial exchange would be almost indistinguishable from what might occur if civilian centers had been deliberately and directly struck....

(184) A second issue of concern to us is the relationship of deterrence doctrine to war-fighting capabilities is to enhance the credibility of the deterrent, particularly the strategy of extended deterrence. But the development of such capabilities raises other strategic and moral questions. The relationship of war-fighting capabilities and targeting doctrine exemplifies the difficult choices in this area of policy. Targeting civilian populations would violate the principle of discrimination—one of the central moral principles of a Christian ethic of war. But "counterforce targeting," while preferable from the perspective of protecting civilians, is often joined with a declaratory policy which

conveys the notion that nuclear war is subject to precise rational and moral limits.... Furthermore, a purely counter-force strategy may seem to threaten the viability of other nations' retaliatory forces, making deterrence unstable in a crisis and war more likely....

Excerpts from *The Challenge of Peace*, 1983, United States Catholic Conference, Washington, D.C. Reprinted with permission.

Document 102: ISRAEL'S PROCLAMATION OF INDEPENDENCE (1948)

The British divided their Middle Eastern possessions after World War II and the new state of Israel was subsequently created. The United Nations organization recognized Israel and war began between the citizens of the new state and Arabs, particularly Palestinians, who felt betrayed and dispossessed. Israel's declaration of independence repeats the history of the search for a national state.

The Land of Israel was the birthplace of the Jewish people. Here their spiritual, religious and national identity was formed, here they achieved independence and created a culture of national and universal significance. Here they wrote and gave the Bible to the world.

Exiled from the Land of Israel the Jewish people remained faithful to it in all the countries of their dispersion, never ceasing to pray and hope for their return and the restoration of their national freedom.

Impelled by this historic association, Jews strove throughout the centuries to go back to the land of their fathers and regain their statehood. In recent decades they returned in their masses. They reclaimed the wilderness, revived their language, built cities and villages, established a vigorous and ever-growing community, with its own economic and cultural life. They sought peace yet were prepared to defend themselves. They brought the blessings of progress to all inhabitants of the country and looked forward to sovereign independence.

In the year 1897 the First Zionist Congress, inspired by Theodor Herzl's vision of the Jewish state, proclaimed the right of the Jewish people to national revival in their own country.

This right was acknowledged by the Balfour Declaration of November 2, 1917, and reaffirmed by the Mandate of the League of Nations, which gave explicit international recognition to the historic connection of the Jewish people with Palestine and their right to reconstitute their National Home.

The recent holocaust, which engulfed millions of Jews in Europe, proved anew the need to solve the problem of the homelessness and lack of independence of the Jewish people by means of the re-establishment of the Jewish State, which would open the gates to all Jews and endow the Jewish people with equality of status among the family of nations.

The survivors of the disastrous slaughter in Europe and also Jews from other lands, have not desisted from their efforts to reach Eretz-Yisreal, in face of difficulties, obstacles and perils; and have not ceased to urge their right to a life of dignity, freedom and honest toil in their ancestral land.

In the second World War the Jewish people in Palestine made their full contribution to the struggle of the freedom-loving nations against the Nazi evil. The sacrifices of their soldiers and their war effort gained them the right to rank with the nations which founded the United Nations.

On November 29, 1946, the General Assembly of the United Nations adopted a Resolution requiring the establishment of a Jewish State in Palestine. The General Assembly called upon the inhabitants of the country to take all the necessary steps on their part to put the plan into effect. This recognition by the United Nations of the right of the Jewish people to establish their independent State was unassailable.

It is the natural right of the Jewish people to lead, as do all other nations, an independent existence in its sovereign State.

Accordingly, we, the members of the National Council, representing the Jewish people in Palestine and the World Zionist Movement, are met together in solemn assembly today, the day of termination of the British Mandate for Palestine, and by virtue of the natural and historic right of the Jewish people and of the Resolution of the General Assembly of the United Nations:

We hereby proclaim the establishment of the Jewish State in Palestine, to be called: Medinat Yisreal (The State of Israel).

We hereby declare that, as from the termination of the Mandate at midnight, May 14–15, 1948, and pending the setting up of the duly elected bodies of the State in accordance with a Constitution, to be drawn up by the Constituent Assembly not later than October 1, 1948, the National Council shall act as the Provisional State Council and that the National Administration shall constitute the Provisional Government of the Jewish State, which shall be known as Israel.

The State of Israel will be open to the immigration of Jews from all countries of their dispersion; will promote the development of the country for the benefit of all its inhabitants; will be based on the principles of liberty, justice and peace as conceived by the Prophets of Israel; will uphold the full social and political equality of all its citizens, without distinction of religion, race or sex; will guarantee freedom of religion, conscience, education and culture, will safeguard the Holy Places of all religions; and will loyally uphold the principles of the United Nations Charter.

The State of Israel will be ready to cooperate with the organs and representatives of the United Nations in the implementation of the Resolution of the Assembly of November 19, 1947, and will take steps to bring about the Economic Union over the whole of Palestine.

We appeal to the United Nations to assist the Jewish people in the building of its State and to admit Israel into the family of nations.

In the midst of wanton aggression, we yet call upon the Arab inhabitants of the State of Israel to preserve the ways of peace and play their part in the development of the state, on the basis of full and equal citizenship and due representation in all its bodies and institutions—provisional and permanent.

We extend our hand in peace and neighbourliness to all the neighbouring states and their peoples, and invite them to cooperate with the independent Jewish nation for the common good of all. The State of Israel is prepared to make its contribution in the progress of the Middle East as a whole.

Our call goes out to the Jewish people all over the world to rally to our side in the task of immigration and development and to stand by us in the great struggle for the fulfillment of the dream of generations for the redemption of Israel.

With trust in the Rock of Israel, we set our hand to this Declaration, at this Session of the Provisional State Council, on the soil of the Homeland, in the city of Tel Aviv, on this Sabbath eve, the fifth of Iyar, 5708, the Fourteenth of May, 1948....

From *The Israel-Arab Reader, A Documentary History of the Middle East Crisis*, edited by Walter Laqueur, New York, Citadel Press, 1968, 125–128.

Document 103: DECLARATION OF THE PALESTINIAN STATE (1988)

Because of the failure of significant international discussion of the national self-determination of Palestinians, the major internationally-recognized representation of Palestinians, the Palestinian National Council declared the establishment of an independent Palestine at a meeting in Algiers on November 15, 1988. This statement reflects the history of the Palestinian quest for national self-determination.

Palestine, the land of the three monotheistic faiths, is where the Palestinian Arab people was born, on which it grew, developed and excelled. The Palestinian people was never separated from or diminished in its integral bonds with Palestine. Thus the Palestinian Arab people ensured for itself an everlasting union between itself, its land and its history....

Despite the historical injustice inflicted on the Palestinian Arab people resulting in their dispersion and depriving them of their right to self-determination, following upon U.N. General Assembly Resolution 181 (1947), which partitioned Palestine into two states, one Arab, one Jewish, yet it is this Resolution that still provides those conditions of international legitimacy that ensure the right of the Palestinian Arab people to sovereignty.

By stages, the occupation of Palestine and parts of other Arab territories by Israeli forces, the willed dispossession and expulsion from their ancestral homes of the majority of Palestine's civilian inhabitants, was achieved by organized terror; those Palestinians who remained, as a vestige subjugated in its homeland, were persecuted and forced to endure the destruction of their national life.

Thus were principles of international legitimacy violated. Thus were the Charter of the United Nations and its Resolutions disfigured, for they had recognized the Palestinian Arab people's national rights, including the right of Return, the right to independence, the right to sovereignty over territory and homeland.

...[F]rom out of the long years of trial in evermounting struggle, the Palestinian political identity emerged further consolidated and confirmed. And the collective Palestinian national will forged for itself a political embodiment, the Palestine Liberation Organization, its sole, legitimate representative recognized by the world community as a whole.... And so Palestinian resistance was clarified and raised into the forefront of Arab and world awareness, as the struggle of the Palestinian Arab people achieved unique prominence among the world's liberation movements in the modern era.

The massive national uprising, the intifada, now intensifying in cumulative scope and power on occupied Palestinian territories, as well as the unflinching resistance of the refugee camps outside the homeland, have elevated awareness of the Palestinian truth and right into still higher realms of comprehension and actuality. Now at last the curtain has been dropped around a whole epoch of prevarication and negation. The intifada has set siege to the mind of official Israel, which has for too long relied exclusively upon myth and terror to deny Palestinian existence altogether. Because of the intifada and its revolutionary irreversible impulse, the history of Palestine has therefore arrived at a decisive juncture.

Whereas the Palestinian people reaffirms most definitively its inalienable rights in the land of its patrimony:

Now by virtue of natural, historical and legal rights, and the sacrifices of successive generations who gave of themselves in defense of freedom and independence of their homeland;

In pursuance of Resolutions adopted by Arab Summit Conferences and relying on the authority bestowed by international legitimacy as embodied in the Resolutions of the United Nations Organizations since 1947;

And in exercise by the Palestinian Arab people of its rights to self-determination, political independence and sovereignty over its territory,

The Palestine National Council, in the name of God, and in the name of the Palestinian Arab people, hereby proclaims the establishment of the State of Palestine on our Palestinian territory with its capital Jerusalem (Al-Quds Ash-Sharif).

The State of Palestine is the state of Palestinians wherever they may be. The state is for them to enjoy in it their collective national and cultural identity, theirs to pursue in it a complete equality of rights. In it will be safeguarded their political and religious convictions and their human dignity by means of a parliamentary democratic system of governance, itself based on freedom of expression and the freedom to form parties. The rights of minorities will duly be respected by the majority, as minorities must abide by decisions of the majority. Governance will be based on principles of social justice, equality and non-discrimination in public rights of men or women, on grounds of race, religion, color or sex, under the aegis of a constitution which ensures the rule of law and an independent judiciary. Thus shall these principles allow no departure from Palestine's age-old spiritual and civilizational heritage of tolerance and religious coexistence.

The State of Palestine is an Arab state, an integral and indivisible part of the Arab nation, at one with that nation in heritage and civilization, with it also in its aspiration for liberation, progress, democracy and unity. The State of Palestine affirms its obligation to abide by the Charter of the League of Arab States, whereby the coordination of the Arab states with each other shall be strengthened. It calls upon Arab compatriots to consolidate and enhance the emergence in reality of our state, to mobilize potential, and to intensify efforts whose goal is to end Israeli occupation.

The State of Palestine proclaims its commitment to the principles and purposes of the United Nations, and to the Universal Declaration of Human Rights. It proclaims its commitment to the principles and purposes of the

United Nations, and to the Universal Declaration of Human Rights.

It further announces itself to be a peace-loving State, in adherence to the principles of peaceful co-existence.... In the context of its struggle for peace in the land of Love and Peace, the State of Palestine calls upon the United Nations to bear special responsibility for the Palestinian Arab people and its homeland. It calls upon all peace- and freedom-loving peoples and states to assist it in the attainment of its objectives, to provide it with security, to alleviate the tragedy of its people, and to help it terminate Israel's occupation of the Palestinian territories.

The State of Palestine herewith declares that it believes in the settlement of regional and international disputes by peaceful means, in accordance with the U.N. Charter and resolutions. Without prejudice to its natural right to defend its territorial integrity and independence, it therefore rejects the threat or use of force, violence and terrorism against the territorial integrity of other states. Therefore, on this day unlike all others, November 15, 1988, as we stand at the threshold of a new dawn, in all honor and modesty we humbly bow to the sacred spirits of our fallen ones, Palestinian and Arab, by the purity of whose sacrifice for the homeland our sky has been illuminated and our Land given life....

Therefore, we call upon our great people to rally to the banner of Palestine, to cherish and defend it, so that it may forever be the symbol of our freedom and dignity in that homeland, which is a homeland for the free, now and always.

From *The Middle East*, Seventh edition, Washington, D.C.: Congressional Quarterly, Inc., 1990, 310.

Document 104:
STATEMENT ON ISRAEL AND TERRORISM (1988)
Yasir Arafat

At a press conference in Geneva, on 14 December 1988, Yasir Arafat, the leader of the Palestinian Liberation Organization, accepted the right of Israel to exist and renounced terrorism. These were dramatic changes in Arafat's traditional stance.

Let me highlight my views before you. Our desire for peace is a strategy and not an interim tactic. We are bent on peace come what may, come what may.

Our statehood provides salvation to the Palestinians and peace to both Palestinians and Israelis.

Self-determination means survival for the Palestinians and our survival does not destroy the survival of the Israelis as their rulers claim.

Yesterday in my speech I made reference to United Nations Resolution 181 as the basis for Palestinian independence. I also made reference to our acceptance of Resolution 242 and 338 as the basis for negotiations with Israel within the framework of the international conference. These three resolutions were endorsed by our Palestine National Council session in Algiers.

In my speech also yesterday, it was clear that we mean our people's rights to freedom and national independence, according to Resolution 181, and the right of all parties concerned in the Middle East conflict to exist in peace and security, and, as I have mentioned, including the state of Palestine, Israel and other neighbors, according to Resolution 242 and 338.

As for terrorism, I renounced it yesterday in no uncertain terms, and yet, I repeat for the record. I repeat for the record that we totally and absolutely renounce all forms of terrorism, including individual, group and state terrorism.

Between Geneva and Algiers, we have made our position crystal clear. Any more talk such as "The Palestinians should give more"—you remember this slogan?—or "It is not enough" or "The Palestinians are engaging in propaganda games, and public-relations exercises" will be damaging and counterproductive.

Enough is enough. Enough is enough. Enough is enough. All remaining matters should be discussed around the table and within the international conference.

Let it be absolutely clear that neither Arafat, nor any for that matter, can stop the intifada, the uprising. The intifada will come to an end only when practical and tangible steps have been taken towards the achievement of our national aims and establishment of our independent Palestinian state.

In this context, I expect the E.E.C. [European Economic Community] to play a more effective role in promoting peace in our region. They have a political responsibility, they have a moral responsibility, and they can deal with it.

Finally, I declare before you and I ask you to kindly quote me on that: We want peace. We want peace. We are committed to peace. We are committed to peace. We want to live in our Palestinian state, and let live. Thank you.

From *The Middle East*, seventh edition, Washington, D.C.: Congressional Quarterly, Inc., 1990, 311.

Document 105:
DECLARATION OF INDEPENDENCE OF THE DEMOCRATIC REPUBLIC OF VIETNAM (1945)
Ho Chi Minh (Nguyen Ai Quoc)

In 1945 Ho Chi Minh declared the independence of the Democratic Republic of Vietnam. Vietnam had been the French colony of Indochina. In 1942 the Japanese occupied Vietnam, at first allowing the French to continue to rule under Japanese guidance and then, in 1945, by themselves. With the end of the war, the French returned to claim their property. Ho Chi Minh felt that the Vietnamese had earned their independence through resisting the Japanese. The French need to retain Vietnam as a colony led to almost 30 years of war in Indochina.

"All men are created equal. They are endowed by their Creator with certain unalienable Rights; among these are Life, Liberty and the pursuit of Happiness."

This immortal statement appeared in the Declaration of Independence of the United States of America in 1776. In a broader sense, it means: All the peoples on the earth are equal from birth, all the peoples have a right to live and to be happy and free.

The Declaration of the Rights of Man and the Citizen, made at the time of the French Revolution, in 1791, also states: "All men are born free and with equal rights, and must always remain free and have equal rights."

Those are undeniable truths.

Nevertheless, for more than eighty years, the French imperialists, abusing the standard of Liberty, Equality and Fraternity, have violated our Fatherland and oppressed our fellow-citizens. They have acted contrary to the ideals of humanity and justice.

Politically, they have deprived our people of every democratic liberty.

They have enforced inhuman laws; they have set up three different political regimes in the North, the Centre and the South of Viet Nam in order to wreck our country's oneness and prevent our people from being united.

They have built more prisons than schools. They have mercilessly massacred our patriots. They have drowned our uprisings in seas of blood.

They have fettered public opinion and practised obscurantism.

They have weakened our race with opium and alchohol.

In the field of economics, they have sucked us dry, driven our people to destitution and devastated our land.

They have robbed us of our rice fields, our mines, our forests and our natural resources. They have monopolized the issue of bank-notes and the import and export trade.

They have invented numerous unjustifiable taxes and reduced our people, especially our peasantry, to extreme poverty.

They have made it impossible for our national bourgeousie to prosper; they have mercilessly exploited the workers.

In the autumn of 1942, when the Japanese fascists invaded Indochina to establish new bases against the Allies, the French colonialists went down on their bended knees and opened the doors of our country to welcome the Japanese in.

Thus, from that date, our people were subjected to the double yoke of the French and the Japanese. Their sufferings and miseries increased. The result was that towards the end of last year and beginning of this year, from Quang Tri province to the North, more than two million of our fellow-citizens died from starvation.

On the 9th of March this year, the French troops were disarmed by the Japanese. The French colonialists either fled or surrendered, showing that not only were they incapable of "protecting" us, but that, in a period of five years, they had twice sold our country to the Japanese.

Before the 9th of March, how often the Viet Minh had urged the French to ally themselves with it against the Japanese! But instead of agreeing to this proposal, the French colonialists only intensified their terrorist activites against the Viet Minh. After their defeat and before fleeing, they massacred the political prisoners detained at Yen Bai and Cao Bang.

In spite of all this, our fellow-citizens have always manifested a lenient and humane attitude towards the French. After the Japanese putsch of March 9, 1945, the Viet Minh helped many Frenchmen to cross the frontier, rescued others from Japanese jails and protected French lives and property. In fact, since the autumn of 1940, our country had ceased to be a French colony and had become a Japanese possession.

When the Japanese surrendered to the Allies, our entire people rose to gain power and founded the Democratic Republic of Viet Nam.

The truth is that we have wrested our independence from the Japanese, not from the French.

The French have fled, the Japanese have capitulated, Emperor Bao Dai has abdicated. Our people have broken the chains which have fettered them for nearly a century and have won independence for Viet Nam. At the same time they have overthrown the centuries-old monarchic regime and established a democratic republican regime.

We, the Provisional Government of the new Viet Nam, representing the entire Vietnamese people, hereby declare that from now on we break off all relations of a colonial character with France; cancel all treaties signed by France on Viet Nam, and abolish all privileges by France in our country.

The entire Vietnamese people are of one mind in the determination to oppose all wicked schemes by the French colonialists.

We are convinced that the Allies which at the Teheran and San Francisco Conferences upheld the principle of equality among the nations cannot fail to recognize the right of the Vietnamese people to independence.

A people who have courageously opposed French enslavement for more than eighty years, a people who have resolutely sided with the Allies against the fascists during these last years, such a people must be free, such a people must be independent.

For these reasons, we, the Provisional Government of the Democratic Republic of Viet Nam, solemnly make this declaration to the world.

Viet Nam has the right to enjoy freedom and independence and in fact has become a free and independent country. The entire Vietnamese people are determined to mobilize all their physical and mental strength, to sacrifice their lives and property in order to safeguard their freedom and independence.

From Ho Chi Minh, *Selected Writings,* Hanoi: Foreign Languages Publishing House, 1973, 53–56.

CHAPTER 14 Contemporary Problems Of Human Rights

Document 106:
MYTH AND REALITY (1952)
Simone de Beauvoir

Simone de Beauvoir was a leading intellectual force for the feminist movement. Her work, The Second Sex, *published in 1952, gave a thoughtful analysis of the process by which males have managed to create an image of female "types." Women were forced to fit these preordained images of femininity, at the expense of their freedom to be complete flesh and blood individuals. Males condemned themselves to remain in ignorance concerning females because they were unable to move past the stereotypes of goddess or prostitute.*

The myth of woman plays a considerable part in literature; but what is its importance in daily life? To what extent does it affect the customs and conduct of individuals? In replying to this question it will be necessary to state precisely the relations this myth bears to reality.

There are different kinds of myths. This one, the myth of woman, sublimating an immutable aspect of the human condition—namely, the "division" of humanity into two classes of individuals—is a static myth. It projects into the realm of Platonic ideas a reality that is directly experienced or is conceptualized on a basis of experience; in place of fact, value, significance, knowledge, empirical law, it substitutes a transcendental Idea, timeless, unchangeable, necessary. This idea is indisputable because it is beyond the given: it is endowed with absolute truth. Thus, as against the dispersed, contingent, and multiple existences of actual women, mythical thought opposes the Eternal Feminine, unique and changeless. If the definition provided for this concept is contradicted by the behavior of flesh-and-blood women, it is the latter who are wrong: we are told not that Femininity is a false entity, but that the women concerned are not feminine. The contrary facts of experience are impotent against the myth. In a way, however, its source is in experience. Thus it is quite true that woman is other than man, and this alternative is directly felt in desire, the embrace, love; but the real relation is one of reciprocity; as such it gives rise to authentic drama. Through eroticism, love, friendship, and their alternatives, deception, hate, rivalry, the relation is a struggle between conscious beings each of whom wishes to be essential, it is the mutual recognition of free beings who confirm one another's freedom, it is the vague transition from aversion to participation. To pose Woman is to pose the absolute Other, without reciprocity, denying against all experience that she is a subject, a fellow human being.

In actuality, of course, women appear under various aspects; but each of the myths built up around the subject of woman is intended to sum her up *in toto*; each aspires to be unique. In consequence, a number of incompatible myths exist, and men tarry musing before the strange incoherences manifested by the idea of Femininity. As every woman has a share in a majority of these archetypes—each of which lays claim to containing the sole Truth of woman—men of today also are moved again in the presence of their female companions to an astonishment like that of the old sophists who failed to understand how man could be blond and dark at the same time! Transition toward the absolute was indicated long ago in social phenomena: relations are easily congealed in classes, functions in types, just as relations, to the childish mentality, are fixed in things. Patriarchal society, for example, being centered upon the conservation of the patrimony, implies necessarily, along with those who own and transmit wealth, the existence of men and women who take property away from its owners and put it into circulation. The men—adventurers, swindlers, thieves, speculators—are generally repudiated by the group; the women, employing their erotic attraction, can induce young men and even fathers of families to scatter their patrimonies, without ceasing to be within the law. Some of these women appropriate their victims' fortunes or obtain legacies by using undue influence; this role being regarded as evil, those who play it are called "bad women." But the fact is that quite to the contrary they are able to appear in some other setting—at home with their fathers, brothers, husbands, or lovers—as guardian angels; and the courtesan who "plucks" rich financiers is, for painters and writers, a generous patroness. It is easy to understand in actual experience the ambiguous personality of Aspasia or Mme de Pompadour. But if woman is depicted as the Praying Mantis, the Mandrake, the Demon, then it is most confusing to find in woman also the Muse, the Goddess Mother, Beatrice.

As group symbols and social types are generally defined by means of antonyms in pairs, ambivalence will seem to be an intrinsic quality of the Eternal Feminine. The saintly mother has for correlative the cruel stepmother, the angelic young girl has the perverse virgin; thus it will be said sometimes that Mother equals Life, sometimes that Mother equals Death, that every virgin is pure spirit or flesh dedicated to the devil.

Evidently it is not reality that dictates to society or to individuals their choice between the two opposed basic categories; in every period, in each case, society and the individual decide in accordance with their needs. Very often they project into the myth adopted the institutions and values to which they adhere. Thus the paternalism that claims woman for hearth and home defines her as sentiment, inwardness, immanence. In fact every existent is at once immanence and transcendence; when one offers the existent no aim, or prevents him from attaining any, or robs him of his victory, then his transcendence falls vainly into the past— that is to say, falls back into immanence. This is the lot assigned to woman in the patriarchate; but it is in no way a vocation, any more than slavery is the vocation of the slave. The development of this mythology is to be clearly seen in August Comte. To identify Woman with Altruism is to guarantee to man absolute rights in her devotion, it is to impose on women a categorical imperative.

From Simone de Beauvoir, *The Second Sex*, translated by H.M. Parshley. Copyright © 1952 and renewed 1980 by Alfred A. Knopf.

Document 107:
EQUAL RIGHTS AMENDMENT (1972)

This is the Equal Rights Amendment that has been discussed for three generations. Its supporters say that it will abolish unfair legal discrimination against women without robbing them of necessary legal protection.

Section 1. Equality of rights under the law shall not be denied or abridged by the United States or by any State on account of sex. This article shall not impair, however, the validity of any law of the United States or any state which exempts women from compulsory military service or which is reasonably designed to promote the health, safety, privacy, education, or economic welfare of women, or to enable them to perform their duties as homemakers or mothers.

Sec. 2 The Congress and the several States shall have power, within their respective jurisdictions, to enforce this article by appropriate legislation.

Sec. 3. This amendment shall take effect two years after the date of ratification."

From Catharine Stimpson, ed., in conjunction with the Congressional Information Service, *Women and the "Equal Rights", Senate Subcommittee Hearings on the Constitutional Amendment*, 91st Congress, New York: R.R. Bowker Co., 1972, 5.

Document 108:
Roe v. Wade (1973)

Roe v. Wade was a landmark decision of the United States Supreme Court which established the right of a woman to discontinue a pregnancy. This has stirred one of the most contentious debates in United States history and neither side can compromise their differences. The right to privacy—the control of one's body—conflicts with others' views on the primacy of life— whatever the stage of fetal development.

Mr. Justice Blackmun delivered the opinion of the Court:....

It perhaps is not generally appreciated that the restrictive criminal abortion laws in effect in a majority of the States today are of relatively recent vintage. Those laws, generally proscribing abortion or its attempt at any time during pregnancy except when necessary to preserve the pregnant woman's life, are not of ancient or even of common law origin. Instead, they derive from statutory changes effected, for the most part, in the latter half of the 19th century.

1. *Ancient attitudes*. These are not capable of precise determination. We are told that at the time of the Persian Empire abortifacients

were known and that criminal abortions were severely punished. We are also told, however, that abortion was practiced in Greek times as well as in the Roman Era, and that "it was resorted to without scruple."...Greek and Roman law afforded little protection to the unborn....Ancient religion did not bar abortion.

2. *The Hippocratic Oath.* What then of the famous Oath that has stood so long as the ethical guide of the medical profession and that bears the name of the Greek who has been described as the Father of Medicine.... The Oath varies somewhat according to the particular translation, but in any translation the content is clear: "I will give no deadly medicine to anyone if asked, nor suggest any such counsel; and in like manner I will not give to a woman a pessary to produce abortion."...

....[T]he Oath [however] originated in a group representing only a small segment of Greek opinion and...it certainly was not accepted by all ancient physicians....[M]edical writings down to Galen (130–200 A.D.) "give evidence of the violation of almost every one of its injunctions." But with the end of antiquity a decided change took place. Resistance against suicide and against abortion became common. The Oath came to be popular. The emerging teachings of Christianity were in agreement with the Pythagorean ethic. The Oath "became the nucleus of all medical ethics" and "was applauded as the embodiment of truth."...

This, it seems to us, is a satisfactory and acceptable explanation of the Hippocratic Oath's apparent rigidity. It enables us to understand, in historical context, a long accepted and revered statement of medical ethics.

3. *The Common Law.* It is undisputed that at the common law, abortion performed *before* "quickening"—the first recognizable movement of the fetus *in utero*, appearing usually from the 16th to the 18th week of pregnancy—was not an indictable offense. The absence of a common law crime for pre-quickening abortion appears to have developed from a confluence of earlier philosophical, theological, and civil and canon law concepts of when life begins. These disciplines variously approached the question in terms of the point at which the embryo or fetus became "formed" or recognizably human, or in terms of when a "person" came into being, that is, infused with a "soul" or "animated." A loose consensus evolved in early English law that these events occurred at some point between conception and live birth.... There was agreement that prior to this point the fetus was to be regarded as part of the mother and its destruction, therefore, was not homicide.... The significance of quickening was echoed by later common law scholars and found its way into the received common law in this country.

Whether abortion of a *quick* fetus was a felony at common law, or even a lesser crime, is still disputed.... [I]t now appears doubtful that abortion was ever firmly established as a common law crime even with respect to the destruction of a quick fetus.

4. *The English statutory law.* England's first criminal abortion statute, came in 1803....

Recently Parliament enacted a new abortion law. This is the Abortion Act of 1967. The Act permits...a physician, to terminate a pregnancy where he is of the good faith opinion that the abortion "is immediately necessary to save the life or to prevent grave permanent injury to the physical or mental health of the pregnant woman."

5. *The American law.* In this country the law in effect in all but a few States until mid-19th century was the pre-existing English common law.... In 1828 New York enacted legislation that, in two respects, was to serve as a model for early anti-abortion statutes. First, while barring destruction of an unquickened fetus as well as a quick fetus, it made the former only a misdemeanor, but the latter second-degree manslaughter. Second, it incorporated a concept of therapeutic abortion by providing that an abortion was excused if it "shall have been necessary to preserve the life of such mother, or shall have been advised by two physicians to be necessary for such purpose." By 1840, when Texas had received the common law, only eight American States had statutes dealing with abortion. It was not until after the War Between the States that legislation began generally to replace the common law. Most of these initial statutes dealt severely with abortion after quickening but were lenient with it before quickening. Most punished attempts equally with completed abortions. While many statutes included the exception for an abortion thought

by one or more physicians to be necessary to save the mother's life, that provision soon disappeared and the typical law required that the procedure actually be necessary for that purpose.

Gradually, in the middle and late 19th century the quickening distinction disappeared from the statutory law of most States and the degree of the offense and the penalties were increased. By the end of the 1950's, a large majority of the States banned abortion, however and whenever performed, unless done to save or preserve the life of the mother.... Three other States permitted abortions that were not "unlawfully" performed or that were not "without lawful justification." In the past several years, however, a trend toward liberalization of abortion statutes has resulted in adoption, by about one-third of the States, of less stringent laws....

It is thus apparent that at common law, at the time of the adoption of our Constitution, and throughout the major portion of the 19th century, abortion was viewed with less disfavor than under most American statutes currently in effect. Phrasing it another way, a woman enjoyed a substantially broader right to terminate a pregnancy than she does in most States today. At least with respect to the early stage of pregnancy, and very possibly without such a limitation, the opportunity to make this choice was present in this country well into the 19th century. Even later, the law continued for some time to treat less punitively an abortion procured in early pregnancy....

Parties challenging state abortion laws have sharply disputed in some courts the contention that a purpose of these laws, when enacted, was to protect prenatal life. Pointing to the absence of legislative history to support the contention, they claim that most state laws were designed solely to protect the woman. Because medical advances have lessened this concern, at least with respect to abortions in early pregnancy, they argue that with respect to such abortions the laws can no longer be justified by any state interest....

The Constitution does not explicitly mention any right of privacy. In a line of decision, however, going back perhaps as far as *Union Pacific R. Co. v. Botsford*, 141 U.S. 250, 251 (1891), the Court has recognized that a right of personal privacy, or a guarantee of certain areas or zones of privacy, does exist under the Constitution. In varying contexts the Court or individual Justices have indeed found at least the roots of that right in the First Amendment, *Stanley v. Georgia*, 394 U.S. 557, 564 (1969); in the Fourth and Fifth Amendments, *Terry v. Ohio*, 392 U.S. 1, 8–9 (1968), *Katz v. United States*, 389 U.S. 347, 350 (1967)....; in the penumbras of the Bill of Rights, *Griswold v. Connecticut*, 381 U.S. 479, 484–485 (1965); in the Ninth Amendment, *id.*, at 486 (Goldberg, J., concurring); or in the concept of liberty guaranteed by the first section of the Fourteenth Amendment, see *Meyer v. Nebraska*, 262 U.S. 390, 399 (1923). These decisions make it clear that only personal rights that can be deemed "fundamental" or "implicit" in the "concept of ordered liberty," are included in this guarantee of personal privacy. They also make it clear that the right has some extension to activities relating to marriage, *Loving v. Virginia*, 388 U.S. 1, 12 (1967); procreation, *Skinner v. Oklahoma*, 316 U.S. 535, 541–542 (1942); contraception, *Eisenstadt v. Baird*, 405 U.S. 438, 453–454 (1972); family relationships, *Prince v. Massachusetts*, 321 U.S. 158, 166 (1944); and child rearing and education, *Pierce v. Society of Sisters*, 268 U.S. 510, 535 (1925), *Meyer v. Nebraska, supra.*

This right of privacy, whether it be founded in the Fourteenth Amendment's concept of personal liberty and restrictions upon state action, as we feel it is, or, as the District Court determined, in the Ninth Amendment's reservation of rights to the people, is broad enough to encompass a woman's decision whether or not to terminate her pregnancy. The detriment that the State would impose upon the pregnant woman by denying this choice altogether is apparent. Specific and direct harm medically diagnosable even in early pregnancy may be involved. Maternity, or additional offspring, may force upon the woman a distressful life and future. Psychological harm may be imminent. Mental and physical health may be taxed by child care. There is also the distress, for all concerned, associated with the unwanted child, and there is the problem of bringing a child into a family already unable, psychologically and otherwise, to care for it. In other cases, as in this one, the additional difficulties and continuing stigma of unwed motherhood may be involved. All these are factors the woman and her responsible physician necessarily will consider in consultation.

On the basis of elements such as these, appellants and some *amici* argue that the woman's right is absolute and that she is entitled to terminate her pregnancy at whatever time, in whatever way, and for whatever reason she alone chooses. With this we do not agree. Appellants' arguments that Texas either has no valid interest at all in regulating the abortion decision, or no interest strong enough to support any limitation upon the woman's sole determination, is unpersuasive. The Court's decisions recognizing a right of privacy also acknowledge that some state regulation in areas protected by that right is appropriate. As noted above, a state may properly assert important interests in safeguarding health, in maintaining medical standards, and in protecting potential life. At some point in pregnancy, these respective interests become sufficiently compelling to sustain regulation of the factors that govern the abortion decision. The privacy right involved, therefore, cannot be said to be absolute. In fact, it is not clear to us that the claim asserted by some *amici* that one has an unlimited right to do with one's body as one pleases bears a close relationship to the right of privacy previously articulated in the Court's decisions. The Court has refused to recognize an unlimited right of this kind in the past. *Jacobson v. Massachusetts*, 197 U.S. 11 (1905) (vaccination); *Buck v. Bell*, 274 U.S. 200 (1927) (sterilization).

We therefore conclude that the right of personal privacy includes the abortion decision, but that this right is not unqualified and must be considered against important state interest in regulation....

The appellee and certain *amici* argue that the fetus is a "person" within the language and meaning of the Fourteenth Amendment....

The Constitution does not define "person" in so many words.... [T]he use of the word is such that it has application only postnatally....

All this, together with our observation, *supra*, that throughout the major portion of the 19th century prevailing legal abortion practices were far freer than they are today, persuades us that the word "person," as used in the Fourteenth Amendment, does not include the unborn....

The pregnant woman cannot be isolated in her privacy. She carries an embryo and, later, a fetus.... The situation therefore is inherently different from marital intimacy, or bedroom possession of obscene material, or marriage, or procreation, or education.... As we have intimated above, it is reasonable and appropriate for a State to decide that at some point in time another interest, that of health of the mother or that of potential human life, becomes significantly involved. The woman's privacy is no longer sole and any right of privacy she possesses must be measured accordingly.

Texas urges that, apart from the Fourteenth Amendment, life begins at conception and is present throughout pregnancy, and that, therefore, the State has a compelling interest in protecting that life from and after conception. We need not resolve the difficult question of when life begins. When those trained in the respective disciplines of medicine, philosophy, and theology are unable to arrive at any consensus, the judiciary, at this point in the development of man's knowledge, is not in a position to speculate as to the answer.

It should be sufficient to note briefly the wide divergence of thinking on this most sensitive and difficult question. There has always been strong support for the view that life does not begin until live birth. This was the belief of the Stoics. It appears to be a predominant, though not the unanimous, attitude of the Jewish faith. It may be taken to represent also the position of a large segment of the Protestant community, insofar as that can be ascertained; organized groups that have taken a formal position on the abortion issue have generally regarded abortion as a matter for the conscience of the individual and her family. As we have noted, the common law found greater significance in quickening. Physicians and their scientific colleagues have regarded that event with less interest and have tended to focus either upon conception or upon live birth or upon the interim point at which the fetus becomes "viable," that is, potentially able to live outside the mother's womb, albeit with artificial aid. Viability is usually placed at about seven months (28 weeks) but may occur earlier, even at 24 weeks....

In areas other than criminal abortion the law has been reluctant to endorse any theory that life, as we recognize it, begins before live birth or to accord legal rights to the unborn except in narrowly defined situations and except when the rights are contingent upon live birth....

In view of all this, we do not agree that, by adopting one theory of life, Texas may override the rights of the pregnant woman that are at stake....

With respect to the State's important and legitimate interest in the health of the mother, the "compelling" point, in the light of present medical knowledge, is at approximately the end of the first trimester. This is so because of the now established medical fact...that until the end of the first trimester mortality in abortion is less than mortality in normal childbirth. It follows that, from and after this point, a State may regulate the abortion procedure to the extent that the regulation reasonably relates to the preservation and protection of maternal health....

This means, on the other hand, that, for the period of pregnancy prior to this "compelling" point, the attending physician, in consultation with his patient, is free to determine, without regulation by the State, that in his medical judgment the patient's pregnancy should be terminated. If that decision is reached, the judgment may be effectuated by an abortion free of interference by the State.

With respect to the State's important and legitimate interest in potential life, the "compelling" point is at viability. This is so because the fetus then presumably has the capability of meaningful life outside the mother's womb. State regulation protective of fetal life after viability thus has both logical and biological justifications. If the State is interested in protecting fetal life after viability, it may go so far as to proscribe abortion during that period except when it is necessary to preserve the life or health of the mother....

To summarize and to repeat:

1. A state criminal abortion statute of the current Texas type, that excepts from criminality only a *life saving* procedure on behalf of the mother, without regard to pregnancy state and without recognition of the other interests involved, is violative of the Due Process Clause of the Fourteenth Amendment.

(a) For the stage prior to approximately the end of the first trimester, the abortion decision and its effectuation must be left to the medical judgment of the pregnant woman's attending physician.

(b) For the stage subsequent to approximately the end of the first trimester, the State, in promoting its interest in the health of the mother, may, if it chooses, regulate the abortion procedure in ways that are reasonably related to maternal health.

(c) For the stage subsequent to viability, the State in promoting its interest in the potentiality of human life may, if it chooses, regulate, and even proscribe, abortion except where it is necessary, in appropriate medical judgment, for the preservation of the life or health of the mother.

2. The state may define the term "physician,"...to mean only a physician currently licensed by the State, and may proscribe any abortion by a person who is not a physician as so defined....

This holding, we feel, is consistent with the relative weights of the respective interests involved, with the lessons and examples of medical and legal history, with the lenity of the common law, and with the demands of the profound problems of the present day. The decision leaves the State free to place increasing restrictions on abortion as the period of pregnancy lengthens, so long as those restrictions are tailored to the recognized state interests. The decision vindicates the right of the physician to administer medical treatment according to his professional judgment up to the points where important state interests provide compelling justifications for intervention. Up to those points, the abortion decision in all its aspects is inherently, and primarily, a medical decision, and basic responsibility for it must rest with the physician. If an individual practitioner abuses the privilege of exercising proper medical judgment, the usual remedies, judicial and intra-professional, are available....

It is so ordered.

Mr. Chief Justice Burger, concurring: [omitted]

Mr. Justice Douglas, concurring: [omitted]

Mr. Justice Stewart, concurring: [omitted]

Mr. Justice Rehnquist, dissenting:....

I have difficulty in concluding, as the court does, that the right of "privacy" is involved in this case. Texas by the statute here challenged bars the performance of a medical abortion by a licensed physician on a plaintiff such as Roe. A transaction resulting in an operation such as this is not "private" in the ordinary usage of that word. Nor is the "privacy" which the Court finds here even a distant relative of the freedom from searches and seizures protected by the Fourth Amendment to the Constitution which the Court has referred to as embodying a right to privacy.... [T]he adoption of the compelling state interest standard will inevitably require this Court to examine the legislative policies and pass on the wisdom of these policies in the very process of deciding whether a particular state interest put forward may or may not be "compelling." The decision here to break the term of pregnancy into three distinct terms and to outline the permissible restrictions the State may impose in each one, for example, partakes more of judicial legislation than it does of a determination of the intent of the drafters of the Fourteenth Amendment.

The fact that a majority of the States, reflecting after all the majority sentiment in those States, have had restrictions on abortions for at least a century seems to me as strong an indication there is that the asserted right to an abortion is not "so rooted in the traditions and conscience of our people as to be ranked as fundamental." Even today, when society's views on abortion are changing, the very existence of the debate is evidence that the "right" to an abortion is not so universally accepted as the appellants would have us believe.

To reach its result the Court necessarily has had to find within the scope of the Fourteenth Amendment a right that was apparently completely unknown to the drafters of the Amendment....

Mr. Justice White, with whom Mr. Justice Rehnquist joins, dissenting:

At the heart of the controversy in these cases are those recurring pregnancies that pose no danger whatsoever to the life or health of the mother but are nevertheless unwanted for any one or more of a variety of reasons—convenience, family planning, economics, dislike of children, the embarrassment of illegitimacy, etc. The common claim before us is that for any one of such reasons, or for no reason at all, and without asserting or claiming any threat to life or health, any woman is entitled to an abortion at her request if she is able to find a medical advisor willing to undertake the procedure.

The Court for the most part sustains this position:

During the period prior to the time the fetus becomes viable, the Constitution of the United States values the convenience, whim or caprice of the putative mother more than the life or potential life of the fetus; the Constitution, therefore, guarantees the right to an abortion as against any state law or policy seeking to protect the fetus from an abortion not prompted by more compelling reasons of the mother.

With all due respect, I dissent. I find nothing in the language or history of the Constitution to support the Court's judgment. The Court simply fashions and announces a new constitutional right for pregnant mothers and, with scarcely any reason or authority for its action, invests that right with sufficient substance to override most existing state abortion statutes. The upshot is that the people and the legislatures of the 50 States are constitutionally disentitled to weigh the relative importance of the continued existence and development of the fetus on the one hand against a spectrum of possible impacts on the mother on the other hand. As an exercise of raw judicial power, the Court perhaps has authority to do what it does today; but in my view its judgment is an improvident and extravagant exercise of the power of judicial review which the Constitution extends to this Court.... In a sensitive area such as this, involving as it does issues over which reasonable men may easily and heatedly differ, I cannot accept the Court's exercise of its clear power of choice by interposing a constitutional barrier to state efforts to protect human life and by investing mothers and doctors with the constitutionally protected right to exterminate it. This issue, for the most part, should be left with the people and to the political processes the people have devised to govern their affairs....

From Sheldon Goldman, *Constitutional Law, Cases and Essays*, New York: Harper & Row, Publishers, 1987, 232–237.

Document 109:
TORTURING CHILDREN (1976)
Alicia B. Morales de Galamba

The military dictatorship in Argentina used its power to murder opponents of the regime or those with ideas that it condemned as communist or treasonous. The victims included social workers, journalists, trade unionists, professors, students, anyone who helped the poor and many professionals. About 12,000 people simply "disappeared" and have not been seen or heard of since. After the Falkland Islands War, the military-controlled government fell. The democratic government that took its place authorized an investigation that revealed the next two stories and many thousands of others like them. Only a few of those responsible for the torturing and the deaths were brought to justice. The total number of victims is still unknown. Since World War II similar campaigns have occurred in Chile, El Salvador, Peru, Nicaragua and Panama.

We lived in Mendoza with my children, Paula Natalia and Mauricio, aged one and a half years and two months respectively. A friend, Maria Luisa Sènchez de Vargas lived with us, together with her two children, Josefina, aged five, and Soledad, aged one and a half. On 12 June 1976 at 11 p.m. Maria Luisa and I were in the kitchen when we heard knocking, and a troop of people burst in. Before we had time to think what was going on, or become aware of the situation, they beat us and blindfolded us. The din and the sound of voices woke the children up, and they began to cry desperately. The men turned the house upside down, breaking anything that was in their way, asking me again and again about my husband. Every so often they clicked the safety catches of their guns, as if they were about to shoot. The terror was palpable and we could not breathe. It was a terror that grew alongside the shouts of the children, which became more and more frenzied. Maria Luisa and I took them in our arms in an attempt to calm them down. About twenty or thirty minutes had passed when they forced us out of the house and made us all get into a car, perhaps a Ford Falcon, and took us to a place that we later learnt was the D2, that's to say the Police Headquarters in Mendoza. They put us in an empty room, and for several hours they kept Mauricio, my son aged two months. I felt that the world was falling to pieces, I did not want to live. I did not even cry. Lying on the floor, I rolled myself up into a ball like a foetus. After many hours they returned Mauricio, and slowly but surely I recovered. For two days the four children stayed with us. Josefina and Paula could not stand being cooped up. They cried and beat at the door, begging to be released. At one moment one of the warders took Josefina out of the room alone. It was a new torment. We did not know what they were going to do to her. When they returned with her, after two hours, Josefina said she had been taken to a bus terminal to 'recognize' people. A short time after, they took all four children away and gave them to their respective grandparents. Then they separated Maria Luisa and me, though we both stayed in the D2 building. One day one of the prison warders told me they were going to bring Maria Luisa back to my cell. I was happy at the thought of seeing her again, though I feared for her. Maria Luisa had become a different person, the pain had aged her. She told me in tears that thanks to some prostitutes she had managed to see her husband José Vargas, in the first few days after being separated from me. He was also being held in the prison. Now he is on the list of the disappeared. At this meeting, José told his wife that their daughter Josefina had been present during one of the torture sessions. They had made her witness her father's sufferings so that he would talk. I calculated that this happened between 12 and 14 June when they took Josefina from the cell. But the story of Maria Luisa does not end there. What I heard later was so terrible that even today I feel as I did then, that of all the crises a person can live through there can be none worse than this. A few days before, she told me, they had taken her to her parents' house in San Juan. "I really believed that it was to give pleasure to my old parents, to show them that I was alive and to allow me to renew contact with the children. But no, they took me to a funeral. And do you know whose funeral it was? It was that of my eldest child, my Josefina." When Maria Luisa asked her father, Dr. Sánchez Sarmiento, a lawyer in the federal courts, how such a thing had happened, he said that a few days after the child came home, she opened the drawer of a cupboard, took out a gun belonging to her grandfather, and shot herself.

From *Nunca Más; The Report of the Argentine National Commission on the Disappeared*, New York: Farrar Straus Giroux, 1986, 307–308.

Document 110:
TORTURE AND KIDNAPPING (1978)
Norberto Liwsky

As I was inserting the key in the lock I realized what was happening, because the door was pulled inwards violently and I stumbled forward.

I jumped back, trying to escape. Two shots (one in each leg) stopped me. However, I still put up a struggle, and for several minutes resisted, being handcuffed and hooded, as best I could. At the same time, I was shouting at the top of my lungs that I was being kidnapped, begging my neighbours to tell my family, and to try to stop them taking me away.

Finally, exhausted and blindfolded, I was told by the person who apparently was in command that my wife and two daughters had already been captured and 'disappeared.'

They had to drag me out, since I couldn't walk because of the wounds in my legs. As were leaving the building, I saw a car with a flashing red light in the street. By the sound of the voices and commands, and the slamming of car doors, interspersed with shouts from my neighbours, I presumed that this was a police car.

After several minutes of heated argument, the police car left. The others then took me out of the building and threw me on to the floor of a car, possibly a Ford Falcon, and set off.

They hauled me out of the car in the same way, carrying me between four of them. We crossed four or five metres of what by the sound of it was a graveled yard, then they threw me on to a table. They tied me by my hands and feet to its four corners.

The first voice I heard after being tied up was of someone who said he was a doctor. He told me the wounds on my legs were bleeding badly, so I should not try to resist in any way.

Then I heard another voice. This one said he was the 'Colonel.' He told me they knew I was not involved with terrorism or the guerrillas, but that they were going to torture me because I opposed the regime, because: 'I hadn't understood that in Argentina there was no room for any opposition to the Process of National Reorganization.' He then added: 'You're going to pay dearly for it...the poor won't have any goody-goodies to look after them any more!'

Everything happened very quickly. From the moment they took me out of the car to the beginning of the first electric shock session took less time than I am taking to tell it. For days they applied electric shocks to my gums, nipples, genitals, abdomen and ears. Unintentionally, I managed to annoy them, because, I don't know why, although the shocks made me scream, jerk and shudder, they could not make me pass out.

They then began to beat me systematically and rhythmically with wooden sticks on my back, the backs of my thighs, my calves and the soles of my feet. At first the pain was dreadful. Then it became unbearable. Eventually I lost all feeling in the part of my body being beaten. The agonizing pain returned a short while after they finished hitting me. It was made still worse when they tore off my shirt, which had stuck to the wounds, in order to take me off for a fresh electric shock session. This continued for several days, alternating the two tortures. Sometimes they did both at the same time.

Such a combination of tortures can be fatal because, whereas electric shock produces muscular contractions, beating causes the muscle to relax (as a form of protection). Sometimes this can bring on heart failure.

In between torture sessions they left me hanging by my arms from hooks fixed in the wall of the cell where they had thrown me.

Sometimes they put me on the torture table and stretched me out, tying my hands and feet to a machine which I can't describe since I never saw it, but which gave me the feeling that they were going to tear part of my body off.

At one point when I was face-down on the torture table, they lifted my head then removed my blindfold to show me a blood-stained rag. They asked me if I recognized it and, without waiting for a reply impossible anyway because it was unrecognizable, and my eyesight was very badly affected they told me it was a pair of my wife's knickers. No other explanation was given, so that I would suffer all the more...then they blindfolded me again and carried on with their beating.

Ten days after I entered this 'pit,' they brought my wife, Hilda Nora Ereñu, to my cell. I could scarcely see her, but she seemed in a pitiful state. They only left us together for two or three minutes, with one of the torturers present. When they took her away again, I thought (I later learned that both of us had thought the same) that this would be the last time we saw each other. That it was the end for both of us. Despite the fact that I was told she had been set free with some other people, the next news I had of her was after I had been put into official custody at the Gregario de Laferrére police station, and she came at the first visiting time with my daughters.

On two or three occasions they also burnt me with a metal instrument. I didn't see this either, but I had the impression that they were pressing something hard into me. Not like a cigarette, which gets squashed, but something more like a red-hot nail.

One day they put me face-down on the torture table, tied me up (as always), and calmly began to strip the skin from the soles of my feet. I imagine, though I didn't see it because I was blindfolded, that they were doing it with a razor blade or a scalpel. I could feel them pulling as if they were trying to separate the skin at the edge of the wound with a pair of pincers. I passed out. From then on, strangely enough, I was able to faint very easily. As for example on the occasion when, showing me more bloodstained rags, they said these were my daughters' knickers, and asked me whether I wanted them to be tortured with me or separately.

I began to feel that I was living alongside death. When I wasn't being tortured I had hallucinations about death sometimes when I was awake, at other times while sleeping.

When they came to fetch me for a torture session, they would kick the door open and shout at me, flailing out at everything in their way. That is how I knew what was going to happen even before they reached me. I lived in a state of suspense waiting for the moment when they would come to fetch me.

The most vivid and terrifying memory I have of all that time was of always living with death. I felt it was impossible to think. I desperately tried to summon up a thought in order to convince myself I wasn't dead. That I wasn't mad. At the same time, I wished with all my heart that they would kill me as soon as possible.

There was a constant struggle in my mind. On the one hand: 'I must remain lucid and get my ideas straight again;' on the other: 'Let them finish me off once and for all.' I had the sensation of sliding towards nothingness down a huge slippery tube where I could get no grip. I felt that just one clear thought would be something solid for me to hold on to and prevent my fall into the void. My memory of that time is at once so concrete and so personal and private that the image I have of it is of an intestine existing both inside and outside my own body.

In the midst of all this terror, I'm not sure when, they took me off to the 'operating theatre.' There they tied me up and began to torture my testicles. I don't know if they did this by hand or with a machine. I'd never experienced such pain. It was as though they were pulling out all my insides from my throat and brain downwards. As though my throat, brain, stomach and testicles were linked by a nylon thread which they were pulling on, while at the same time crushing everything. My only wish was for them to succeed in pulling all my insides out so that I would be completely empty. Then I passed out.

Without knowing how or when, I regained consciousness and they were tugging at me again. I fainted a second time.

At that moment, fifteen or eighteen days after my abduction, I began to have kidney problems, difficulties with passing water. Three-and-a-half months later, when I was a prisoner in Villa Devoto prison, the doctors from the International Red Cross diagnosed acute renal failure of a traumatic origin, which could be traced to the beatings I had undergone.

After being held for twenty-five days in complete isolation, I was thrown into a cell with another person. This was a friend of mine, a colleague from the dispensary, Dr. Francisco García Fernández.

I was in very bad shape. It was Fernández who gave me the first minimal medical attention, because in all that time I had been unable to think of cleaning or looking after myself.

It was only several days later that, by moving the blindfold slightly, I could see all they had done to me. Before that it had been impossible, not because I didn't try to remove the blindfold, but because my eyesight had been so poor.

It was then for the first time that I saw the state of my testicles...I remembered that as a medical student I saw, in the famous Houssay textbook, a photograph of a man who, because of the enormous size of his testicles, wheeled them along in a wheelbarrow! Mine were of similar dimensions, and were coloured a deep black and blue.

Another day they took me out of my cell and, despite my swollen testicles, placed me face-down again. They tied me up and raped me slowly and deliberately by introducing a metal object into my anus. They then passed an electric current through the object. I cannot describe how everything inside me felt as though it were on fire....

After that, the torture eased. They only gave me beatings two or three times a week. Now they used their hands and feet rather than metal or wooden instruments.

Thanks to this new, relatively mild policy, I began to recover physically. I had lost more than 25 kilos and was suffering from the kidney complaint I've already mentioned....

[Dr. Liwsky also described the psychological torture that the "disappeareds" had to endure.]

...The normal attitude of the torturers and guards towards us was to consider us less than slaves. We were objects. And useless, troublesome objects at that. They would say: 'You're dirt.' 'Since we "disappeared" you, you're nothing.' 'Anyway, nobody remembers you.' 'You don't exist.' 'If anyone were looking for you (which they aren't), do you imagine they'd look for you here?' 'We are everything for you.' 'We are justice.' 'We are God.'

Phrases like these, repeated endlessly. By all of them. All the time, and often accompanied by a slap, trip, punch or kick. Or they would drench our cell, mattress and clothes at two in the morning in winter....

From *Nunca Más; The Report of the Argentine National Commission on the Disappeared*, New York: Farrar Straus Giroux, 1986, 21–26.

Document 111:
THE LAST SERMON (1980)
Archbishop Oscar Romero

Archbishop Oscar Romero was assassinated, probably by a secret agent of the El Salvadoran Army, in 1980. He was killed because he believed that the message of Christ for humankind included economic and social reforms which were missing in a country like El Salvador. Special interests, particularly the great landlords, allied with the dominant government party and the Army, opposed land reform and other changes.

Let no one be offended because we use the divine words read at our mass to shed light on the social, political and economic situation of our people. Not to do so would be unchristian. Christ desires to unite himself with humanity, so that the light he brings from God might become life for nations and individuals.

I know many are shocked by this preaching and want to accuse us of forsaking the gospel for politics. But I reject this accusation. I am trying to bring to life the message of the Second Vatican Council and the meetings at Medellin and Puebla. The documents from these meetings should not just be studied theoretically. They should be brought to life and translated into the real struggle to preach the gospel as it should be for our people. Each week I go about the country listening to the cries of the people, their pain from so much crime, and the ignominy of so much violence. Each week I ask the Lord to give me the right words to console, to denounce, to call for repentance. And even though I may be a voice crying in the desert, I know that the church is making the effort to fulfill its mission....

Every country lives its own "exodus"; today El Salvador is living its own exodus. Today we are passing to our liberation through a desert strewn with bodies and where anguish and pain are devastating us. Many suffer the temptation of those who walked with Moses and wanted to turn back and did not work together. It is the same old story. God, however, wants to save the people by making a new history....

History will not fail; God sustains it. That is why I say that insofar as historical projects attempt to reflect the eternal plan of God, to that extent they reflect the kingdom of God. This attempt is the work of the church. Because of this, the church, the people of God in history, is not attached to any one social system, to any political organization, to any party. The church does not identify herself with any of those forces because she is the eternal pilgrim of history and is indicating at every historical moment what reflects the kingdom of God and what does not reflect the kingdom of God. She is the servant of the kingdom of God.

The great task of Christians must be to absorb the spirit of God's kingdom and, with souls filled with the kingdom of God, to work on the projects of history. It's fine to be organized in popular groups; it's all right to form political parties; it's all right to take part in the government. It's fine as long as you are a christian who carries the reflection of the kingdom of God and tries to establish it where you are working, and as long as you are not being used to further worldly ambitions. This is the great duty of the people of today. My dear Christians, I have always told you, and I will repeat, that the true liberators of our people must come from us Christians, from the people of God. Any historical plan that's not based on what we spoke of in the first point the dignity of the human being, the love of God, the kingdom of Christ among people will be a fleeting project. Your project, however, will grow in stability the more it reflects the eternal design of God. It will be a solution of the common good of the people every time, if it meets the needs of the people.... Now I invite you to look at things through the eyes of the church, which is trying to be the kingdom of God on earth and so often must illuminate the realities of our national situation.

We have lived through a tremendously tragic week. I could not give you the facts before, but a week ago last Saturday, on 15 March, one of the largest and most distressing military operations was carried out in the countryside. The villages affected were La Laguna, Plan de Ocotes and El Rosario. The operation brought tragedy: a lot of ranches were burned, there was looting, and inevitably people were killed. In La Laguna, the attackers killed a married couple, Ernest Navas and Audelia Mejía de Navas, their little children, Martin and Hilda, thirteen and seven years old, and eleven more peasants.

Others deaths have been reported, but we do not know the names of the dead. In Plan de Ocotes, two children and four peasants were killed, including two women. In El Rosario, three more peasants were killed. That was last Saturday.

Last Sunday, the following were assassinated in Arcatao by four members of ORDEN: peasants Marcelino Serrano, Vincente Ayala, twenty-four years old, and his son, Freddy. That same day, Fernando Hernández Navarro, a peasant, was assassinated in Galera de Jutiapa, when he fled from the military.

Last Monday, 17 March, was a tremendously violent day. Bombs exploded in the capital as well as in the interior of the country. The damage was very substantial at the headquarters of the Ministry of Agriculture. The campus of the national university was under armed siege from dawn until 7 p.m. Throughout the day, constant bursts of machine-gun fire were heard in the university area. The archbishop's office intervened to protect people who found themselves caught inside.

On the Hacienda Colima, eighteen persons died, at least fifteen of whom were peasants. The administrator and the grocer of the ranch also died. The armed forces confirmed that there was a confrontation. A film of the events appeared on TV, and many analyzed interesting aspects of the situation.

At least fifty people died in serious incidents that day: in the capital, seven persons died in events at the Colonia Santa Lucía; on the outskirts of Tecnillantas, five people died; and in the area of the rubbish dump, after their evacuation of the site by the military, were found the bodies of four workers who had been captured in that action.

Sixteen peasants died in the village of Montepeque, thirty-eight kilometers along the road to Suchitoto. That same day, two students at the University of Central America were captured in Tecnillantas: Mario Nelson and Miquel Alberto Rodríguez Velado, who were brothers. The first one, after four days of illegal detention, was handed over to the courts. Not so his brother, who was wounded and is still held in illegal detention. Legal Aid is intervening on his behalf.

Amnesty International issued a press release in which it described the repression of the peasants, especially in the area of Chalatenango. The week's events confirm this report in spite of the fact the government denies it. As I entered the church, I was given a cable that says, "Amnesty International confirmed today that in El Salvador human rights are violated to extremes that have not been seen in other countries." That is what Patricio Fuentes (spokesman for the urgent action section for Central America in Swedish Amnesty International) said at a press conference in Managua, Nicaragua.

Fuentes confirmed that, during two weeks of investigations he carried out in El Salvador, he was able to establish that there had been eighty-three political assassinations between 10 and 14 March. He pointed out that Amnesty International recently condemned the government of El Salvador, alleging that it was responsible for six hundred political assassinations. The Salvadorean government defended itself against the charges, arguing that Amnesty International based its condemnation on unproved assumptions.

Fuentes said that Amnesty had established that in El Salvador human rights are violated to a worse degree than the repression in Chile after the coupe d'état. The Salvadorean government also said that the six hundred dead were the result of armed confrontations between army troops and guerrillas. Fuentes said that during his stay in El Salvador, he could see that the victims had been tortured before their deaths and mutilated afterward.

The spokesman of Amnesty International said that the victims' bodies characteristically appeared with the thumbs tied behind their backs. Corrosive liquids had been applied to the corpses to prevent identification of the victims by their relatives and to prevent international condemnation, the spokesman added. Nevertheless, the bodies were exhumed and the dead have been identified. Fuentes said that the repression carried out by the Salvadorean army was aimed at breaking the popular organizations through the assassination of their leaders in both town and country.

According to the spokesman of Amnesty International, at least three thousand five hundred peasants have fled from their homes to the capital to escape persecution. "We have complete lists in London and Sweden of young children and women who have been assassinated for being organized," Fuentes stated....

I would like to make a special appeal to the men of the army, and specifically to the ranks of the National Guard, the police and the military. Brothers, you come from our own people. You are killing your own brother peasants when any human order to kill must be subordinate to the law of God which says, "Thou shalt not kill." No soldier is obliged to obey an order contrary to the law of God. No one has to obey an immoral law. It is high time you recovered your consciences and obeyed your consciences rather than a sinful order. The church, the defender of the rights of God, of the law of God, of human dignity, of the person, cannot remain silent before such an abomination. We want the government to face the fact that reforms are valueless if they are to be carried out at the cost of so much blood. In the name of God, in the name of this suffering people whose cries rise to heaven more loudly each day, I implore you, I beg you, I order you in the name of God: stop the repression.

The church preaches your liberation just as we have studied it in the holy Bible today. It is a liberation that has, above all else, respect for the dignity of the person, hope for humanity's common good, and the transcendence that looks before all to God and only from God derives its hope and its strength.

From a recording of Archbishop Oscar Romero's last sermon as transcribed in *Sojourner*, 12 May 1980, 13–16.

Document 112:
Salvador's Grievous Loss (1993)
Mark O. Hatfield

The United Nations released a report on El Salvador in 1993 which discloses United States knowledge and support of terror in El Salvador against the leftist revolutionaries in the 1980s. Denials by the U.S. government are proved false. El Salvador is another example of a politically and socially divided nation that erupted into a civil war with forces on both sides receiving foreign assistance in the Cold War era. A recent settlement was facilitated by the heads of

Central American governments, led especially by Costa Rica's Oscar Ariás, who received a Nobel Peace Prize for his efforts. Senator Mark O. Hatfield of Oregon was at odds with his Republican presidents over policy in El Salvador during the 1980s, and in this article states that his worst fears have been substantiated by the report of the United Nation's Truth Commission.

A Spanish Jesuit once remarked, "It is harder to tell the truth than to hide it." An important component of the United Nations-sponsored peace agreement for El Salvador was fulfilled March 15 [1993] when the three-member Commission on the Truth issued its report on what it called "some of the worst and most widespread violations of human rights in El Salvador." To nobody's suprise, the UN Commission found that the overwhelming majority of the cases studied, involving some 18,000 victims, were linked to the Salvadoran military.

In the wake of the Commissions's report, those who tried for more than 10 years to hide the truth about the record of the Salvadoran military now want to bury it by granting amnesty to the accused. By ignoring the crying need for justice in the human rights abuse cases investigated by the Truth Commission, El Salvador's political leadership may cause permanent damage to the reconciliation effort.

It is time to stop rewarding the brutal and corrupt. Twelve years and $6 billion in United States aid later, it is time to learn and understand the truth. Those who spread tyranny and death throughout El Salvador for 10 years should not be protected under the umbrella of peace. The Salvadoran National Assembly seeks to do this with its passage of legislation providing general amnesty for those who are named by the Commission on the Truth. Rubén Zamora, the vice president of the Assembly, walked out on the vote, proclaiming that "justice must come before forgiving and forgetting."

The stakes are high for US foreign policy. The members of the Truth Commission, Belisario Betancur, former Colombian president; Reinaldo Figueredo Planchart, former foreign minister of Venezuela; and Thomas Buergenthal, professor of law at George Washington University, have boldly and bravely identified by name the military leadership responsible for atrocities such as the assassination of Archbishop Oscar Arnulfo Romero, the killing of four American churchwomen, and the murder of six Jesuits, their cook, and her daughter. The Truth Commission has confirmed what many of us have believed for a long time: The US was bankrolling the Salvador military at a time when it was killing with impunity.

Those who continue to justify the role of the US in the Salvadoran civil war take several lines of defense. Many involved in Latin American policy through the 1980s claim ignorance of what was happening around them. Others skip over the bloody history preferring to argue that the cost of not being involved would have been greater. We cannot accept either excuse in light of the truth. For a decade the US was willing to allow its policy to be shaped by the dictum that the "ends justify the means." This misguided policy must be abandoned.

The civil war in El Salvador brought no gains or freedom to the Salvadoran people. It brought only destruction of the country and death to tens of thousands of men, women, and children. This was obvious even eight years ago, when the Congressional Arms Control and Foreign Policy Caucus, which I have twice chaired, initiated its first report on US involvement in El Salvador. In 1985 we issued a report from the Caucus detailing the effect of US assistance on El Salvador's economy and living standards. We concluded that US aid programs were not helping end the war. Instead, we found that the US was perpetuating the conflict. Our report argued that it was futile to pursue a military solution to a civil conflict that had its roots in poverty and deprivation.

In the frenzy of the Central American "red scare," the Caucus report fell on deaf ears. During the mid-1980s, only a handful of us argued against involvement in El Salvador or Nicaragua. Neither Congress nor the administration was willing to shut off the pipeline of support to the crippled Salvadoran government and the corrupt Salvadoran military.

The shameful truth of the military's involvement in the killings did not sink in until the brutal killing of six Jesuits and their assistants. From the beginning it was suspected that the attack was a military operation. Yet the early discovery of the military's involvement in these murders was played down.

As always, there was a desire to avoid staring at the facts. But we in the Caucus could no longer avert our eyes to the truth. The Caucus issued its third report on El Salvador just six months after the Jesuits died, and once again the subject was the military leadership.

In 1990, we evaluated the Salvadoran high command and the record of documented human-rights abuses carried out by their troops. The findings indicated that 14 of the 15 officers in El Salvador's primary commands rose to their positions despite documented abuses and in none of the more than 50 violent cases listed in the reports was justice served. No officer was brought to trial.

In 1991 Congress began withholding some military aid to El Salvador. But just last year the US government continued to argue against the complete withdrawal of our support from the Salvadoran military, lest the commanders decide to walk away from the peace accords drafted under the guidance of the UN.

There have been more than 75,000 victims fo the Salvadoran conflict. We can only hope that justice will not be the final victim. The US should press the Salvadoran government to reconsider the national Assembly's vote to provide general amnesty to those identified by the Truth Commission, and there should be a full public accounting of our own government's knowledge of the record of abuses committed by the Salvadoran military while it was accepting US aid.

From Mark O. Hatfield, "Salvador's Grievous Loss," in *The Christian Science Monitor*, March 31, 1993, 19.

Document 113:
I HAVE A DREAM (1963)
Martin Luther King, Jr.

This is one of the most famous speeches in American history. At the height of the civil rights campaigns, a mass demonstration occurred in Washington, D.C. Only after the death of President John F. Kennedy did a Civil Rights Act, which ensured voting rights for African Americans, pass in the United States Congress.

I am happy to join with you today in what will go down in history as the greatest demonstration for freedom in the history of our nation.

Five score years ago, a great American, in whose symbolic shadow we stand today, signed the Emancipation Proclamation. This momentous decree came as a great beacon light of hope to millions of Negro slaves who had been seared in the flames of withering injustice. It came as a joyous daybreak to end the long night of their captivity.

But one hundred years later, the Negro still is not free; one hundred years later, the life of the Negro is still sadly crippled by the manacles of segregation and the chains of discrimination; one hundred years later, the Negro lives on a lonely island of poverty in the midst of a vast ocean of material prosperity; one hundred years later, the Negro is still languishing in the corners of American society and finds himself in exile in his own land.

So we've come here today to dramatize a shameful condition. In a sense we've come to our nation's capital to cash a check. When the architects of our republic wrote the magnificent words of the Constitution and the Declaration of Independence, they were signing a promissory note to which every American was to fall heir. This note was the promise that all men, yes, black men as well as white men, would be guaranteed the unalienable rights of life, liberty, and the pursuit of happiness.

It is obvious today that America has defaulted on this promissory note in so far as her citizens of color are concerned. Instead of honoring this sacred obligation, America has given the Negro people a bad check; a check which has come back marked "insufficient funds." We refuse to believe that there are insufficient funds in the great vaults of opportunity of this nation. And so we've come to cash this check, a check that will give us upon demand the riches of freedom and the security of justice.

We have also come to this hallowed spot to remind America of the fierce urgency of now. This is no time to engage in the luxury of cooling off or to take the tranquilizing drug of gradualism. Now is the time to make real the promises of democracy; now is the time to rise from the dark and desolate valley of segregation to the sunlit path of racial justice; now is the time to lift our nation from the quicksands of racial injustice to the solid rock of brotherhood; now is the time to make justice a reality for all God's children. It would be fatal for the nation to overlook the urgency of the moment. This sweltering summer of the Negro's legitimate discontent will not pass until there is an invigorating autumn of freedom and equality.

Nineteen sixty-three is not an end, but a beginning. And those who hope that the Negro needed to blow off steam and will now be content, will have a rude awakening if the nation returns to business as usual. There will be neither rest nor tranquility in America until the Negro is granted his citizenship rights. The whirlwinds of the revolt will continue to shake the foundations of our nation until the bright day of justice emerges.

But there is something that I must say to my people, who stand on the warm threshold which leads into the palace of justice. In the process of gaining our rightful place, we must not be guilty of wrongful deeds. Let us not seek to satisfy our thirst for freedom by drinking from the cup of bitterness and hatred. We must forever conduct our struggle on the high plain of dignity and discipline. We must not allow our creative protest to generate into physical violence. Again and again we must rise to the majestic heights of meeting physical force with soul force; and the marvelous new militancy, which has engulfed the Negro community, must not lead us to a distrust of all white people. For many of our white brothers, as evidenced by their presence here today, have come to realize that their destiny is tied up with our destiny. And they have come to realize that their freedom is inextricably bound to our freedom. We cannot walk alone. And as we talk, we must make the pledge that we shall always march ahead. We cannot turn back.

There are those who are asking the devotees of Civil Rights, "When will you be satisfied?" We can never be satisfied as long as the Negro is the victim of the unspeakable horrors of police brutality; we can never be satisfied as long as our bodies, heavy with the fatigue of travel, cannot gain lodging in the motels of the highways and the hotels of the cities; we cannot be satisfied as long as the Negro's basic mobility is from a smaller ghetto to a larger one; we can never be satisfied as long as our children are stripped of their selfhood and robbed of their dignity by signs stating "For Whites Only;" we cannot be satisfied as long as the Negro in Mississippi cannot vote and a Negro in New York believes he has nothing for which to vote. No! No, we are not satisfied, and we will not be satisfied until "justice rolls down like waters and righteousness like a mighty stream."

I am not unmindful that some of you have come here out of great trials and tribulations. Some of you have come fresh from narrow jail cells. Some of you have come from areas where your quest for freedom left you battered by the storms of persecution and staggered by the winds of police brutality. You have been the veterans of creative suffering. Continue to work with the faith that unearned suffering is redemptive. Go back to Mississippi. Go back to Alabama. Go back to South Carolina. Go back to Georgia. Go back to Louisiana. Go back to the slums and ghettos of our Northern cities, knowing that somehow this situation can and will be changed. Let us not wallow in the valley of despair.

I say to you today, my friends, so even though we face the difficulties of today and tomorrow, I still have a dream. It is a dream deeply rooted in the American dream. I have a dream that one day this nation will rise up and live out the true meaning of its creed. "We hold these truths to be self-evident, that all men are created equal." I have a dream that one day on the red hills of Georgia, sons of former slaves and the sons of former slave owners will be able to sit down together at the table of brotherhood. I have a dream that one day even the state of Mississippi, a state sweltering with the heat of injustice, sweltering with the heat of oppression, will be transformed into an oasis of freedom and justice. I have a dream that my four little children will one day live in a nation where they will not be judged by the color of their skin, but by the content of their character.

I have a dream today!

I have a dream that one day down in Alabama with its vicious racists, with its Governor having his lips dripping with the words of interposition and nullificationone day right there in Alabama, little black boys and black girls will be able to join hands with little white boys and white girls as sisters and brothers.

I have a dream today!

This is our hope. This is the faith that I go back to the South with. With this faith we shall be able to transform the jangling discords of our nation into a beautiful symphony of brotherhood. With this faith we will be able to work together, to pray together, to struggle together, to go to jail together, to stand up for freedom together, knowing that we will be free one day. And this will be the day. This will be the day when all of God's children will be able to sing with new meaning, "My country 'tis of thee, sweet land of liberty, of thee I sing. Land where my fathers died, land of the pilgrim's pride, from every mountain side, let freedom ring." And if America is to be a great nation, this must become true.

So let freedom ring from the prodigious hilltops of New Hampshire; let freedom ring from the mighty mountains of New York; let freedom ring from the heightening Alleghenies of Pennsylvania; let freedom ring from the snow-capped Rockies of Colorado; let freedom ring from the curvaceous slopes of California. But not only that. Let freedom ring from Stone Mountain of Georgia; let freedom ring from Lookout Mountain of Tennessee; let freedom ring from every hill and molehill of Mississippi. From every mountainside, let freedom ring.

And when this happens, and when we allow freedom to ring, when we let it ring from every village and every hamlet, from every state and every city, we will be able to speed up that day when all God's children, black men and white men, Jews and gentiles, Protestants and Catholics, will be able to join hands and sing in the words of the old Negro spiritual: "Free at last. Free at last. Thank God Almighty, we are free at last."

Reprinted by arrangement with The Heirs to the Estate of Martin Luther King, Jr., % Joan Daves Agency as agent for the proprietors. Copyright © 1963 by the Estate of Martin Luther King, Jr. Copyright renewed 1991 by Corretta Scott King.

Document 114:
LETTER FROM BIRMINGHAM JAIL (1963)
Martin Luther King, Jr.

Jailed for his support of the economic demands of workers in Birmingham, Alabama, Martin Luther King, Jr., penned this letter to his fellow clergymen, explaining the need for social and economic reforms.

My Dear Fellow Clergymen:

While confined here in the Birmingham city jail, I came across your recent statement calling my present activities "unwise and untimely." Seldom do I pause to answer criticism of my work and ideas. If I sought to answer all the criticisms that cross my deck, my secretaries would have little time for anything other than such correspondence in the course of the day, and I would have no time for constructive work. But since I feel that you are men of genuine good will and that your criticisms are sincerely set forth, I want to try to answer your statement in what I hope will be patient and reasonable terms....

I am in Birmingham because injustice is here. Just as the prophets of the eighth century B.C. left their villages and carried their "thus saith the Lord" far beyond the boundaries of their home towns, and just as the Apostle Paul left his village of Tarsus and carried the gospel of Jesus Christ to the far corners of the Greco-Roman world, so am I compelled to carry the gospel of freedom beyond my own home town....

You deplore the demonstrations taking place in Birmingham. But your statement, I am sorry to say, fails to express a similar concern for the conditions that brought about the demonstrations. I am sure that none of you would want to rest content with the superficial kind of social analysis that deals merely with effects and does not grapple with underlying causes. It is unfortunate that demonstrations are taking place in Birmingham, but it is even more unfortunate that the city's white power structure left the Negro community with no alternative.

In any nonviolent campaign there are four basic steps: collection of the facts to determine whether injustices exist; negotiation; self-purification; and direct action. We have gone through all these steps in Birmingham. There can be no gainsaying the fact that racial injustice engulfs this community. Birmingham is probably the most thoroughly segregated city in the United States. Its ugly record of brutality is widely known. Negroes have experienced grossly unjust treatment in the courts. There have been more unsolved bombings of Negro homes and churches in Birmingham than in any other city in the nation. These are the hard, brutal facts of the case. On the basis of these conditions, Negro leaders sought to negotiate with the city fathers. But the latter consistently refused to engage in good-faith negotiation.

Then, last September, came the opportunity to talk with leaders of Birmingham's economic community. In the course of the negotiations, certain promises were made by the merchants for example, to remove the stores' humiliating racial signs. On the basis of these promises, the Reverend Fred Shuttlesworth and the leaders of the Alabama Christian Movement for Human Rights agreed to a moratorium on all demonstrations. As the weeks and months went by, we realized that we were the victims of a broken promise. A few signs, briefly removed, returned; the others remained.

As in so many past experiences, our hopes had been blasted, and the shadow of deep disappointment settled upon us. We had no alternative except to prepare for direct action, whereby we would present our very bodies as a means of laying our case before the conscience of the local and the national community. Mindful of the difficulties involved, we decided to undertake a process of self-purification. We began a series of workshops on nonviolence and we repeatedly asked ourselves: "Are you able to accept blows without retaliation?" "Are you able to endure the ordeal of jail?" We decided to schedule our direct-action program for the Easter season, realizing that except for Christmas, this is the main shopping period of the year. Knowing that a strong economic-withdrawal program would be the by-product of direct action, we felt that this would be the best time to bring pressure to bear on the merchants for the needed change.

Then it occurred to us that Birmingham's mayoral election was coming up in March, and we speedily decided to postpone action until after election day. When we discovered that the Commissioner of Public Safety, Eugene "Bull" Connor, had piled up enough votes to be in the run-off, we decided again to postpone action until the day after the run-off so that the demonstrations could not be used to cloud the issues. Like many others, we waited to see Mr. Connor defeated, and to this end we endured postponement after postponement. Having aided in this community need, we felt that our direct-action program could be delayed no longer.

You may well ask, "Why direct action? Why sit-ins, marches, and so forth? Isn't negotiation a better path?" You are quite right in calling for negotiation. Indeed, this is the very purpose of direct action. Nonviolent direct action seems to create such a crisis and foster such a tension that a community which has constantly refused to negotiate is forced to confront the issue. It seeks to so dramatize the issue that it can no longer be ignored. My citing the creation of tension as part of the work of the nonviolent-resister may sound rather shocking. But I must confess that I am not afraid of the word "tension." I have earnestly opposed violent tension, but there is a type of constructive, nonviolent tension which is necessary for growth....

The purpose of our direct-action program is to create a situation so crisis-packed that it will inevitably open the door to negotiation. I therefore concur with you in your call for negotiation. Too long has our beloved Southland been bogged down in a tragic effort to live in monologue rather than dialogue....

We know through painful experience that freedom is never voluntarily given by the oppressor; it must be demanded by the oppressed. Frankly, I have yet to engage in a direct-action campaign that was "well timed" in view of those who have not suffered unduly from the disease of segregation. For years now I have heard the word "Wait!" It rings in the ear of every Negro with piercing familiarity. This "Wait" has almost always meant "Never." We must come to see, with one of our distinguished jurists, that "justice too long delayed is justice denied."

We have waited for more than 340 years for our constitutional and God given rights. The nations of Asia and Africa are moving with jet-like speed toward gaining political independence, but we still creep at horse-and-buggy pace toward gaining a cup of coffee at a lunch counter. Perhaps it is easy for those who have never felt the stinging darts of segregation to say, "Wait." But when you have seen vicious mobs lynch your mothers and fathers at will and drown your sisters and brothers at whim; when you have seen hate-filled policemen curse, kick, and even kill your black brothers and sisters; when you see the vast majority of your twenty million Negro brothers smothering in an airtight cage of poverty in the midst of an affluent society, when you suddenly find your tongue twisted and your speech stammering as you seek to explain to your six-year-old daughter why she can't go to the public amusement park that has just been advertised on television, and see tears welling up in her eyes when she is told that Funtown is closed to colored children, and see ominous clouds of inferiority beginning to form in her little mental sky, and see her beginning to distort her personality by developing an unconscious bitterness toward white people; when you have to concoct an answer for a five-year-old son who is asking, "Daddy, why do white people treat colored people so mean?;" when you take a cross-country drive and find it necessary to sleep night after night in the uncomfortable corners of your automobile because no motel will accept you; when you are humiliated day in and day out by nagging signs reading "white" and "colored;" when your first name becomes "nigger," your middle name becomes "boy" (however old you are) and your last name becomes "John" and your wife and mother are never given the respected title "Mrs.;" when you are harried by day and haunted by night by the fact that you are a Negro, living constantly at tiptoe stance, never quite knowing what to expect next, and are plagued with inner fears and outer resentments; when you are forever fighting a degenerating sense of "nobodiness" then you will understand why we find it difficult to wait. There comes a time when the cup of endurance runs over, and men are no longer willing to be plunged into the abyss of despair. I hope, sirs, you can understand our legitimate and unavoidable impatience.

You express a great deal of anxiety over our willingness to break laws. This is certainly a legitimate concern. Since we so diligently urge people to obey the Supreme Court's decision of 1954 outlawing segregation in public schools, at first glance it may seem rather paradoxical for us consciously to break laws. One may well ask: "How can you advocate breaking some laws and obeying others?" The answer lies in the fact that there are two types of laws: just and unjust. I would be the first to advocate obeying just laws. One has not only a legal but a moral responsibility to obey just laws. Conversely, one has a moral responsibility to disobey unjust laws. I would agree with St. Augustine that "an unjust law is no law at all."

Now, what is the difference between the two? How does one determine whether a law is just or unjust? A just law is a man-made code that squares with the moral law or the law of God. An unjust law is a code that is out of harmony with the moral law. To put it in the terms of St. Thomas Aquinas: An unjust law is a human law that is not rooted in eternal law and natural law. Any law that uplifts human personality is just. Any law that degrades human personality is unjust. All segregation statutes are unjust because segregation distorts the soul and damages the personality. it gives the segregator a false sense of superiority and the segregated a false sense of inferiority.... Hence segregation is not only politically, economically, and sociologically unsound, it is morally wrong and sinful.... Thus it is that I can urge men to obey the 1954 decision of the Supreme Court, for it is morally right; and can urge them to disobey segregation ordinances, for they are morally wrong.

Let us consider a more concrete example of just and unjust laws. An unjust law is a code that a numerical or power majority group compels a minority group to obey but does not make binding on itself. This is *difference* made legal. By the same token, a just law is a code that a majority compels a minority to follow and that it is willing to follow itself. This is *sameness* made legal.

Let me give another explanation. A law is unjust if it is inflicted on a minority that, as a result of being denied the right to vote, had no part in enacting or devising the law. Who can say that the legislature of Alabama which set up that state's segregation laws was democratically elected? Throughout Alabama all sorts of devious methods are used to prevent Negroes from becoming registered voters, and there are some counties in which, even though Negroes constitute a majority of the population, not a single Negro is registered. Can any law enacted under such circumstances be considered democratically structured?

Sometimes a law is just on its face and unjust in its application. For instance, I have been arrested on a charge of parading without a permit. Now, there is nothing wrong in having an ordinance which requires a permit for a parade.

But such an ordinance becomes unjust when it is used to maintain segregation and to deny citizens the First-Amendment privilege of peaceful assembly and protest.

I hope you are able to see the distinction I am trying to point out. In no sense do I advocate evading or defying the law, as would the rabid segregationist. That would lead to anarchy. One who breaks an unjust law must do so openly, lovingly, and with a willingness to accept the penalty. I submit that an individual who breaks a law that conscience tells him is unjust, and who willingly accepts the penalty of imprisonment in order to arouse the conscience of the community over its injustice, is in reality expressing the highest respect for law.

Of course, there is nothing new about this kind of civil disobedience....

We should never forget that everything Adolf Hitler did in Germany was "legal" and everything the Hungarian freedom fighters did in Hungary was "illegal." It was "illegal" to aid and comfort a Jew in Hitler's Germany. Even so, I am sure that, had I lived in Germany at the time, I would have aided and comforted my Jewish brothers. If today I lived in a Communist country where certain principles dear to the Christian faith are suppressed, I would openly advocate disobeying that country's anti-religious laws.

I must make two honest confessions to you, my Christian and Jewish brothers. First, I must confess that over the past few years I have been gravely disappointed with the white moderate. I have almost reached the regrettable conclusion that the Negro's great stumbling block in his stride toward freedom is not the White Citizen's Councilor or the Ku Klux Klanner, but the white moderate, who is more devoted to "order" than to justice; who prefers a negative peace which is the absence of tension to a positive peace which is the presence of justice; who constantly says, "I agree with you in the goal you seek, but I cannot agree with your methods of direct action;" who paternalistically believes he can set the timetable for another man's freedom; who lives by a mythical concept of time and who constantly advises the Negro to wait for a "more convenient season." Shallow understanding from people of good will is more frustrating than absolute misunderstanding from people of ill will. Lukewarm acceptance is much more bewildering than outright rejection.

I had hoped that the white moderate would understand that law and order exist for the purpose of establishing justice and that when they fail in this purpose they become the dangerously structured dams that block the flow of social progress. I had hoped that the white moderate would understand that the present tension in the South is a necessary phase of the transition from an obnoxious negative peace, in which the Negro passively accepted his unjust plight, to a substantive and positive peace, in which all men will respect the dignity and worth of human personality. Actually, we who engage in nonviolent direct action are not the creators of tension. We merely bring to the surface the hidden tension that is already alive. We bring it out in the open, where it can be seen and dealt with. Like a boil that can never be cured so long as it is covered up but must be opened with all its ugliness to the natural medicines of air and light, injustice must be exposed, with all the tension its exposure creates, to the light of human conscience and the air of national opinion, before it can be cured.

In your statement you assert our actions, even though peaceful, must be condemned because they precipitate violence. But is this a logical assertion? Isn't this like condemning a robbed man because his possession of money precipitated the evil act of robbery? Isn't this like condemning Socrates because his unswerving commitment to truth and his philosophical inquiries precipitated the act by the misguided populace in which they made him drink hemlock? Isn't this like condemning Jesus because his unique God-consciousness and never-ceasing devotion to God's will precipitated the evil act of crucifixion? We must come to see that, as the federal courts have consistently affirmed, it is wrong to urge an individual to cease his efforts to gain his basic constitutional rights because the quest may precipitate violence. Society must protect the robbed and punish the robber.

I had also hoped that the white moderate would reject the myth concerning time in relation to the struggle for freedom. I have just received a letter from a white brother in Texas. He writes: "All Christians know that the colored people will receive equal rights eventually, but it is possible that you are in too great a religious hurry. It has taken Christianity almost two thousand years to accomplish what it has. The teachings of Christ take time to come to earth." Such an attitude stems from a tragic misconception of time, from the strangely irrational notion that there is something in the very flow of time that will inevitably cure all ills. Actually, time itself is neutral; it can be used either destructively or constructively. More and more I feel that the people of ill will have used time much more effectively than have the people of good will. We will have to repent in this generation not merely for the hateful words and actions of the bad people, but for the appalling silence of the good people. Human progress never rolls in on wheels of inevitability; it comes through the tireless efforts of men willing to be co-workers with God, and without this hard work, time itself becomes an ally of the forces of stagnation. We must use time creatively, in the knowledge that the time is always ripe to do right. Now is the time to make real the promise of democracy and transform our pending national elegy into a creative psalm of brotherhood. Now is the time to lift our national policy from the quicksand of racial injustice to the solid rock of human dignity.

You speak of our activity in Birmingham as extreme. At first I was rather disappointed that fellow clergymen would see my nonviolent efforts as those of an extremist. I began thinking about the fact that I stand in the middle of two opposing forces in the Negro community. One is a force of complacency, made up in part of Negroes who, as a result of long years of oppression, are so drained of self-respect and a sense of "somebodiness" that they have adjusted to segregation; and in part of a few middle-class Negroes who, because of a degree of academic and economic security and because in some ways they profit by segregation, have become insensitive to the problems of the masses. The other force is one of bitterness and hatred, and it comes perilously close to advocating violence. It is expressed in the various black nationalist groups that are springing up across the nation.... Nourished by the Negro's frustration over the continued existence of racial discrimination, this movement is made up of people who have lost faith in America, who have absolutely repudiated Chrisitanity, and who have concluded that the white man is an incorrigible "devil."

I have tried to stand between these two forces, saying that we need emulate neither the "do-nothingism" of the complacent nor the hatred and despair of the black nationalist. For there is the more excellent way of love and nonviolent protest. I am grateful to God that, through the influence of the Negro church, the way of nonviolence became an integral part of our struggle.

If this philosophy had not emerged, by now many streets of the South would, I am convinced, be flowing with blood. And I am further convinced that if our white brothers dismiss us as "rabble-rousers" and "outside agitators" those of us who employ nonviolent direct action, and if they refuse to support our nonviolent efforts, millions of Negroes will, out of frustration and despair, seek solace and security in black-nationalist ideologies a development that would inevitably lead to a frightening racial nightmare.

Oppressed people cannot remain oppressed forever. The yearning for freedom eventually manifests itself, and that is what has happened to the American Negro. Something within has reminded him of his birthright of freedom, and something without has reminded him that it can be gained. Consciously or unconsciously, he has been caught up by the *Zeitgeist*, and with his black brothers of Africa and his brown and yellow brothers of Asia, South America, and the Caribbean, the United States Negro is moving with a sense of great urgency toward the promised land of racial justice. If one recognizes this vital urge that has engulfed the Negro community, one should readily understand why public demonstrations are taking place. The Negro has many pent-up resentments and latent frustrations, and he must release them. So let him march; let him make prayer pilgrimages to the city hall; let him go on freedom rides and try to understand why he must do so. If his repressed emotions are not released in nonviolent ways, they will seek expression through violence; this is not a threat but a fact of history. So I have not said to my people, "Get rid of your discontent." Rather, I have tried to say that this normal and healthy discontent can be channeled into the creative outlet of nonviolent direct action. And now this approach is being termed extremist.

But though I was initially disappointed at being categorized as an extremist, as I continued to think about the matter I gradually gained a measure of satisfaction from the label. Was not Jesus an extremist for love: "Love your enemies, bless them that curse you, do good to them that hate you, and pray for them which despitefully use you, and persecute you.". . . [S]o the question is not whether we will be extremists, but what kind of extremists we will be. Will we be extremists for hate or for love? Will we be extremists for the preservation of injustice or for the extension of justice?...

I had hoped that the white moderate would see this need. Perhaps I was too optimistic; perhaps I expected too much. I suppose I should have realized that few members of the oppressor race can understand the deep groans and passionate yearnings of the oppressed race, and still fewer have the vision to see that injustice must be rooted out by strong, persistent, and determined action....

I have no fear about the outcome of our struggle in Birmingham, even if our motives are at present misunderstood. We will reach the goal of freedom in Birmingham and all over the nation, because the goal of America is freedom. Abused and scorned though we may be, our destiny is tied up with America's destiny. Before the pilgrims landed at Plymouth, we were here. For more than two centuries our forebears labored in this country without wages; they made cotton king; they built the homes of their masters while suffering gross injustice and shameful humiliation and yet out of a bottomless vitality they continued to thrive and develop. If the inexpressible cruelties of slavery could not stop us, the opposition we now face will surely fail. We will win our freedom because the sacred heritage of our nation and the eternal will of God are embodied in our echoing demands.

Before closing I feel impelled to mention one other point in your statement that has troubled me profoundly. You warmly commended the Birmingham police force for keeping "order" and "preventing violence." I doubt that you would have so warmly commended the police force if you had seen its dogs sinking their teeth into unarmed, nonviolent Negroes. I doubt that you would so quickly commend the policemen if you were to observe their ugly and inhumane treatment of Negroes here in the city jail; if you were to watch them punch and curse old Negro women and young Negro girls; if you were to see them slap and kick old Negro men and young boys; if you were to observe them, as they did on two occasions, refuse to give us food because we wanted to sing our grace together. I cannot join you in your praise of the Birmingham police department.

It is true that the police have exercised a degree of discipline in handling the demonstrators. In this sense they have conducted themselves rather "nonviolently" in public. But for what purpose? To preserve the evil system of segregation. Over the past few years I have consistently preached that nonviolence demands that the means we use must be as pure as the ends we seek. I have tried to make clear that it is wrong to use immoral means to attain moral ends. But now I must affirm that it is just as wrong, or perhaps even more so, to use moral means to preserve immoral ends. Perhaps Mr. Connor and his policemen have been rather nonviolent in public, as was Chief Pritchett in Albany, Georgia, but they have used the moral means of nonviolence to maintain the immoral end of racial injustice. As T.S. Eliot has said, "The last temptation is the greatest treason. To do the right deed for the wrong reason."

I wish you had commended the Negro sit-inners and demonstrators of Birmingham for their sublime courage, their willingness to suffer, and their amazing discipline in the midst of great provocation. One day the South will recognize its real heroes. They will be the James Merediths, with the noble sense of purpose than enables them to face jeering and hostile mobs, and with the agonizing loneliness that characterizes the life of the pioneer. They will be old, oppressed, battered Negro women, symbolized in a seventy-two-year old woman in Montgomery, Alabama, who rose up with a sense of dignity and with her people decided not to ride segregated buses, and who responded with ungrammatical profundity to one who inquired about her weariness: "My feets is tired, but my soul is at rest." They will be the young high school and college students, the young ministers of the gospel and a host of their elders,

courageously and nonviolently sitting in at lunch counters and willingly going to jail for conscience sake. One day the South will know that when these disinherited children of God sat down at lunch counters, they were in reality standing up for what is best in the American dream and for the most sacred values in our Judaeo-Christian heritage, thereby bringing our nation back to those great wells of democracy which were dug deep by the founding fathers in their formulation of the Constitution and the Declaration of Independence....
Yours in the Cause of Peace and Brotherhood
Martin Luther King, Jr.

Reprinted by arrangement with The Heirs to the Estate of Martin Luther King, Jr., % Joan Daves Agency as agent for the proprietors. Copyright © 1963 by the Estate of Martin Luther King, Jr. Copyright renewed 1991 by Corretta Scott King.

Document 115:
NOBEL LECTURE ON ACCEPTANCE OF THE NOBEL PEACE PRIZE (1984)
Bishop Desmond Mpilo Tutu

Bishop Tutu received the Nobel Peace Prize for his efforts to convince South Africans and others to change that nation's dictatorship of a minority that ruled through apartheid. This speech reveals the plight of South African Blacks who have been deprived of almost all basic human rights and opportunities.

Before I left South Africa, a land I love passionately, we had an emergency meeting of the Executive Committee of the South African Council of Churches with the leaders of our member churches. We called the meeting because of the deepening crisis in our land, which has claimed nearly 200 lives this year alone. We visited some of the troublespots on the Witwatersrand. I went with the others to the East Rand. We visited the home of an old lady. She told us that she looked after her grandson and the children of neighbors while their parents were at work. One day the police chased some pupils who had been boycotting classes, but they disappeared between the township houses. The police drove down the old lady's street. She was sitting at the back of the house in her kitchen, whilst her charges were playing in the front of the house in the yard. Her daughter rushed into the house, calling out to her to come quickly. The old lady dashed out of the kitchen into the living room. Her grandson had fallen just inside the door, dead. He had been shot in the back by the police. He was 6 years old. A few weeks later, a white mother, trying to register her black servant for work, drove through a black township. Black rioters stoned her car and killed her baby of a few months old, the first white casualty of the current unrest in South Africa. Such deaths are two too many. These are part of the high cost of apartheid.

Every day in a squatter camp near Cape Town, called K.T.C., the authorities have been demolishing flimsy plastic shelters which black mothers have erected because they were taking their marriage vows seriously. They have been reduced to sitting on soaking mattresses, with their household effects strewn round their feet, and whimpering babies on their laps, in the cold Cape winter rain. Every day the authorities have carried out these callous demolitions. What heinous crime have these women committed, to be hounded like criminals in this manner? All they have wanted is to be with their husbands, the fathers of their children. Everywhere else in the world they would be highly commended, but in South Africa, a land which claims to be Christian, and which boasts a public holiday called Family Day, these gallant women are treated so inhumanely, and yet all they want is to have a decent and stable family life. Unfortunately, in the land of their birth, it is a criminal offence for them to live happily with their husbands and fathers of their children. Black family life is thus being undermined, not accidentally, but by deliberate Government policy. It is part of the price human beings, God's children are called to pay for apartheid. An unacceptable price.

I come from a beautiful land, richly endowed by God with wonderful natural resources, wide expanses, rolling mountains, singing birds, bright shining stars out of blue skies, with radiant sunshine, golden sunshine. There is enough of the good things that come from God's bounty, there is enough for everyone, but apartheid has confirmed some in their selfishness, causing them to grasp greedily a disproportionate share, the lion's share, because of their power. They have taken 87% of the land, though being only about 20% of our population. The rest have had to make do with the remaining 13%. Apartheid has decreed the politics of exclusion. 73% of the population is excluded from any meaningful participation in the political decision-making processes of the land of their birth. The new constitution, making provision for three chambers, for whites, coloureds, and Indians, mentions blacks only once, and thereafter ignores them completely. Thus this new constitution, lauded in parts of the West as a step in the right direction, entrenches racism and ethnicity. The constitutional committees are composed in the ratio of 4 whites to 2 coloureds to 1 Indian. Zero black. Two plus one can never equal, let alone be more than, four. Hence this constitution perpetuates by law and entrenches white minority rule. Blacks are expected to exercise their political ambitions in unviable, poverty-stricken, arid, bantustan homelands, ghettoes of misery, inexhaustible reservoirs of cheap black labour, bantustans into which South Africa is being balkanized. Blacks are systematically being stripped of their South African citizenship and being turned into aliens in the land of their birth. This is apartheid's Final Solution, just as Nazism had its final solution for the Jews in Hitler's Aryan madness. The South African government is smart. Aliens can claim very few rights, least of all political rights.

In pursuance of apartheid's ideological racist dream, over 3,000,000 of God's children have been uprooted from their homes, which have been demolished, whilst they have been dumped in the bantustan homeland resettlement camps. I say dumped advisedly: only things or rubbish are dumped, not human beings. Apartheid has, however, ensured that God's children, just because they are black, should be treated as if they were things, and not as of infinite value as being created in the image of God. These dumping grounds are far from where work and food can be procured easily. Children starve, suffer from the often irreversible consequences of malnutrition—this happens to them not accidentally, but by deliberate Government policy. They starve in a land that could be the bread basket of Africa, a land that normally is a net exporter of food.

The father leaves his family in the bantustan homeland, there eking out a miserable existence, whilst he, if he is lucky, goes to the so-called white man's town as a migrant, to live an unnatural life in a single sex hostel for 11 months there, being prey to drunkenness, prostitution and worse. This migratory labour policy is declared Government policy, and has been condemned, even by the white Dutch Reform Church, not noted for being quick to criticise the Government, as a cancer in our society. This cancer, eating away at the vitals of black family life, is deliberate Government policy. It is part of the cost of apartheid, exorbitant in terms of human suffering.

Apartheid has spawned discriminatory education, such as Bantu education, education for serfdom, ensuring that the Government spends only about one-tenth on one black child per annum for education what it spends on a white child. It is education that is decidedly separate and unequal. It is to be wantonly wasteful of human resources, because so many of God's children are prevented, by deliberate Government policy, from attaining their fullest potential. South Africa is paying a heavy price already for this iniquitous policy because there is a desperate shortage of skilled manpower, a direct result of the short-sighted schemes of the racist regime. It is a moral universe that we inhabit, and good and right and equity matter in the universe of the God we worship. And so, in this matter, the South African Government and its supporters are being properly hoisted with their own petard.

Apartheid is upheld by a phalanx of iniquitous laws, such as the Population Registration Act, which decrees that all South Africans must be classified ethnically, and duly registered according to these race categories. Many times, in the same family one child has been classified *white* whilst another with a slightly darker hue, has been classified *coloured*, with all the horrible consequences for the latter of being shut out from membership of a greatly privileged caste. There have, as a result, been several child suicides. This is too high a price to pay for racial purity, for it is doubtful whether an end, however desirable, can justify such a means. There are laws, such as the Prohibition of Mixed Marriages Act, which regard marriages between a white and a person of another race as illegal. Race becomes an impediment to a valid marriage. Two persons who have fallen in love are prevented by race from consummating their love in the marriage bond. Something beautiful is made to be sordid and ugly. The Immorality Act decrees that fornication and adultery are illegal if they happen between a white and one of another race. The police are reduced to the level of peeping Toms to catch couples red-handed. Many whites have committed suicide rather than face the disastrous consequences that follow in the train of just being charged under this law. The cost is too great and intolerable.

Such an evil system, totally indefensible by normally acceptable methods, relies on a whole phalanx of draconian laws such as the security legislation which is almost peculiar to South Africa. There are the laws which permit the indefinite detention of persons whom the Minister of Law and Order has decided are a threat to the security of the State. They are detained at his pleasure, in solitary confinement, without access to their family, their own doctor, or a lawyer. That is severe punishment when the evidence apparently available to the Minister has not been tested in open court—perhaps it could stand up to such rigorous scrutiny, perhaps not; we are never to know. It is a far too convenient device for a repressive regime, and the minister would have to be extra special not to succumb to the temptation to circumvent the awkward process of testing his evidence in an open court; and thus he lets his power under the law to be open to the abuse where he is both judge and prosecutor. Many, too many, have died mysteriously in detention. All this is too costly in terms of human lives. The minister is able, too, to place people under banning orders without being subjected to the annoyance of the checks and balances of due process. A banned person for 3 or 5 years becomes a non-person, who cannot be quoted during the period of her banning order. She cannot attend a gathering, which means more than one other person. Two persons talking to a banned person are a gathering! She cannot attend the wedding or funeral of even her own child without special permission. She must be at home from 6.00 P.M. of one day to 6.00 A.M. of the next and on all public holidays, and from 6.00 P.M. Fridays until 6.00 A.M. on Mondays for three years. She cannot go on holiday outside the magisterial area to which she has been confined. She cannot go to the cinema, nor to a picnic. That is severe punishment, inflicted without the evidence allegedly justifying it being made available to the banned person, nor having it scrutinized in a court of law. It is serious erosion and violation of basic human rights, of which blacks have precious few in the land of their birth. They do not enjoy the rights of freedom of movement and association. They do not enjoy freedom of security of tenure, the right to participate in the making of decisions that affect their lives. In short, this land, richly endowed in so many ways, is sadly lacking in justice.

Once a Zambian and a South African, it is said, were talking. The Zambian then boasted about their Minister of Naval Affairs. The South African asked, "But you have no navy, no access to the sea. How then can you have a Minister of Naval Affairs?" The Zambian retorted, "Well, in South Africa you have a Minister of Justice, don't you?"

It is against this system that our people have sought to protest peacefully since 1912 at least, with the founding of the African National Congress. They have used the conventional methods of peaceful protest—petitions, demonstrations, deputations, and even a passive resistance campaign. A tribute to our people's commitment to peaceful change is the fact that the only South Africans to win the Nobel Peace Prize are both black. Our people are peace-loving to a fault. The response of the authorities has been an escalating intransigence and violence, the violence of police dogs, tear gas, detention without trial, exile, and even death. Our people protested peacefully against the Pass Laws in 1960, and 69 of them were killed on March 21, 1960, at Sharpeville, many shot in the back running away. Our children protested against inferior education, singing songs and displaying placards and marchings peacefully. Many in 1976, on June 16th and subsequent times, were killed or imprisoned. Over 500 people died in that uprising. Many children went into exile. The whereabouts of many are unknown to their parents. At present, to protest that self-same discriminatory education, and the exclusion of blacks from the new constitutional dispensation, the sham local black government, rising unemployment, increased rents and General Sales Tax, our people have boycotted and demonstrated. They have staged a successful 2-day stay away. Over 150 people have been killed. It is far too high a price to pay. There has been little revulsion or outrage at this wanton destruction of human life in the West. In parenthesis, can somebody please explain to me something that has puzzled me. When a priest goes missing and is subsequently found dead, the media in the West carry his story in a very extensive coverage. I am glad that the death of one person can cause so much concern. But in the self-same week when this priest was found dead, the South African police kill 24 blacks who had been participating in the protest, and 6,000 blacks are sacked for being similarly involved, and you are lucky to get that much coverage. Are we being told something I do not want to believe, that we blacks are expendable and that blood is thicker than water, that when it comes to the crunch, you cannot trust whites, that they will club together against us? I don't want to believe that is the message being conveyed to us.

Be that as it may, we see before us a land bereft of much justice, and therefore without peace and security. Unrest is endemic, and will remain an unchanging feature of the South African scene until apartheid, the root cause of it all, is finally dismantled. At this time the Army is being quartered on the civilian population. There is a civil war being waged. South Africans are on either side. When the ANC and PAC where banned in 1960, they declared that they had no option but to carry out the armed struggle. We in the South African Council of Churches have said that we are opposed to all forms of violence—that of a repressive and unjust system, and that of those who seek to overthrow that system. However, we have added that we understand those who say that they have had to adopt what is a last resort for them. Violence is not being introduced into the South African situation *de novo* from outside by those who are called terrorists or freedom fighters, depending on whether you are oppressed or an oppressor. The South African situation is violent already, and the primary violence is that of apartheid, the violence of forced population removals, of inferior education, of detention without trial, of the migratory labour systems, etc.

There is war on the border of our country. South Africa faces fellow South African. South African soldiers are fighting against Namibians who oppose illegal occupation of their country by South AFrica, which has sought to extend its repressive systems of apartheid, unjust and exploitative.

There is no peace in Southern Africa. There is no peace because there is no justice. There can be no real peace and security until there is first justice enjoyed by all the inhabitants of that beautiful land. The Bible knows nothing about peace without justice, for that would be crying "peace, peace, where there is no peace." God's Shalom, peace, involves inevitable righteousness, justice, wholeness, fullness of life, participation in decision making, goodness, laughter, joy, compassion, sharing and reconciliation.

I have spoken extensively about South Africa, first because it is the land I know best, but because it is also a microcosm of the world and an example of what is to be found in other lands in differing degree—where there is injustice, invariably peace becomes a casualty. In El Salvador, in Nicaragua, elsewhere in Latin America, there have been repressive regimes which have aroused opposition in those countries. Fellow citizens are pitted against one another, sometimes attracting the unhelpful attention and interest of outside powers, who want to extend their spheres of influence. We see this in the Middle East, in Korea, in the Philippines, in Kampuchea, in Vietnam, in Ulster, in Afghanistan, in Mozambique, in Angola, in Zimbabwe, behind the Iron Curtain.

Because there is global insecurity, nations are engaged in a mad arms race, spending billions of dollars wastefully on instruments of destruction, when millions are starving. And yet, just a fraction of what is expended so obscenely on defence budgets would make the difference in enabling God's children to fill their stomachs, be educated, and given the chance to lead fulfilled and happy lives. We have the capacity to feed ourselves several times over, but we are daily haunted by the spectacle of the gaunt dregs of humanity shuffling along in endless queues, with bowls to collect what the charity of the world has provided, too little too late. When will we learn, when will the people of the world get up and say, Enough is enough. God created us for fellowship. God created us so that we should form the human family, existing together because we were made for one another. We are not made for an exclusive self-sufficiency but for interdependence, and we break the law of our being at our peril. When will we learn that an escalated arms race merely escalates global insecurity? We are now much closer to a nuclear holocaust than when our technology and our spending were less.

Unless we work assiduously so that all of God's children, our brothers and sisters, members of our one human family, all will enjoy the basic human rights, the right to a fulfilled life, the right of movement, the freedom to be fully human, within a humanity measured by nothing less than the humanity of Jesus Christ Himself, then we are on the road inexorably to self-destruction, we are not far from global suicide; and yet it could be so different.

When will we learn that human beings are of infinite value because they have been created in the image of God, and that it is blasphemy to treat them as if they were less than this and to do so ultimately recoils on those who do this? In dehumanising others, they are themselves dehumanised. Perhaps oppression dehumanises the oppressor as much, if not more than, the oppressed. They need each other to become truly free, to become human. We can be human only in fellowship, in community, in *koinonia*, in peace.

Let us work to be peacemakers, those given a wonderful share in Our Lord's ministry of reconciliation. If we want peace, so we have been told, let us work for justice. Let us beat our swords into ploughshares.

God calls us to be fellow workers with Him, so that we can extend His Kingdom of shalom, of justice, of goodness, of compassion, of caring, of sharing, of laughter, joy and reconciliation, so that the kingdoms of this world will become the Kingdom of our God and of His Christ, and He shall reign forever and ever. Amen. Then there will be fulfillment of the wonderful vision in the Revelation of St. John the Divine (Rev 7:9ff):

"9. After this I beheld, and lo, a great multitude, which no man could number of all nations and kindreds and people and tongues, stood before the throne and before the Lamb, clothed with white robes, and palms in their hands.

10. And cried with a loud voice, saying, 'Salvation to our God, who sitteth upon the throne, and unto the Lamb.'

11. And all the angels stood round about the throne, and about the elders and the four beasts, and fell before the throne on their faces, and worshipped God.

12. Saying, 'Amen; Blessing and glory and wisdom and thanksgiving and honour and power and might, be unto our God forever and ever. Amen.'"

From Desmond Tutu, *The Nobel Peace Prize Lecture*, Statements- Occasional Papers of the Phelps-Stokes Fund, Number 1, November 1986. 31–39.

Document 116:
APARTHEID HAS NO FUTURE, AFRICA IS OURS (1990)
Nelson Mandela

Nelson Mandela was imprisoned for 27 years in South Africa because he disagreed with the white minority that controlled his nation. Released only in 1990, he gave this speech which condemns the segregation called Apartheid. Under Apartheid, the vast majority of South Aricans, who are not white, are restricted in almost every area of existance. Increasing unrest and the effectiveness of an international boycott moved the South African authorities to begin a dialogue with the representatives of the majority of the people and to undertake changes.

Amandla! Amandla! i-Afrika, mayibuye! My friends, comrades and fellow South Africans, I greet you all in the name of peace, democracy and freedom for all. I stand here before you not as a prophet but as a humble servant of you, the people.

Your tireless and heroic sacrifices have made it possible for me to be here today. I therefore place the remaining years of my life in your hands.

On this day of my release, I extend my sincere and warmest gratitude to the millions of my compatriots and those in every corner of the globe who have campaigned tirelessly for my release....

Today the majority of South Africans, black and white, recognize that apartheid has no future. It has to be ended by our own decisive mass actions in order to build peace and security. The mass campaigns of defiance and other actions of our organizations and people can only culminate in the establishment of democracy.

The apartheid destruction on our subcontinent is incalculable. The fabric of family life of millions of my people has been shattered. Millions are homeless and unemployed.

Our economy—our economy lies in ruins and our people are embroiled in political strife. Our resort to the armed struggle in 1960 with the formation of the military wing of A.N.C., Umkonto We Sizwe, was a purely defensive action against the violence of apartheid.

The factors which necessitated the armed struggle still exist today. We have no option but to continue. We express the hope that a climate conducive to a negotiated settlement would be created soon so that there may no longer be the need for the armed struggle.

I am a loyal and disciplined member of the African National Congress. I am, therefore, in full agreement with all of its objectives, strategies and tactics.

The need to unite the people of our country is as important a task now as it always has been. No individual leader is able to take all these enormous tasks on his own. It is our task as leaders to place our views before our organization and to allow the democratic structures to decide on the way forward.

On the question of democratic practice, I feel duty bound to make the point that a leader of the movement is a person who has been democratically elected at a national conference. This is a principle which must be upheld without any exceptions.

Today, I wish to report to you that my talks with the Government have been aimed at normalizing the political situation in the country. We have not as yet begun discussing the basic demands of the struggle.

I wish to stress that I myself had at no time entered into negotiations about the future of our country, except to insist on a meeting between the A.N.C. and the Government.

Mr. de Klerk has gone further than any other Nationalist president in taking real steps to normalize the situation. However, there are further steps as outlined in the Harare Declaration that have to be met before negotiations on the basic demands of our people can begin.

I reiterate our call for *inter alia* the immediate ending of the state of emergency and the freeing of all, and not only some, political prisoners.

Only such a normalized situation which allows for free political activity can allow us to consult our people in order to obtain a mandate. The people need to be consulted on who will negotiate and on the content of such negotiations.

Negotiations cannot take place—negotiations cannot take up a place above the heads or behind the backs of our people. It is our belief that the future of our country can only be determined by a body which is democratically elected on a nonracial basis.

Negotiations on the dismantling of apartheid will have to address the overwhelming demand of our people for a democratic nonracial and unitary South Africa. There must be an end to white monopoly on political power.

And a fundamental restructuring of our political and economic systems to insure that the inequalitieis of apartheid are addressed and our society thoroughly democratized.

It must be added that Mr. de Klerk himself is a man of integrity who is acutely aware of the dangers of a public figure not honoring his undertakings. But as an organization, we base our policy and strategy on the harsh reality we are faced with, and this reality is that we are still suffering under the policies of the Nationalist Government.

Our struggle has reached a decisive moment. We call on our people to seize this moment so that the process toward democracy is rapid and uninterrupted. We have waited too long for our freedom. We can no longer wait. Now is the time to intensify the struggle on all fronts.

To relax our efforts now would be a mistake which generations to come will not be able to forgive. The sight of freedom looming on the horizon should encourage us to redouble our efforts. It is only through disciplined mass action that our victory can be assured.

We call on our white compatriots to join us in the shaping of a new South Africa. The freedom movement is the political home for you, too. We call on the international community to continue the campaign to isolate the apartheid regime.

To lift sanctions now would be to run the risk of aborting the process toward the complete eradication of apartheid. Our march to freedom is irreversible. We must not allow fear to stand in our way.

Universal suffrage on a common voters roll in a united democratic and nonracial South Africa is the only way to peace and racial harmony.

In conclusion, I wish to go to my own words during my trial in 1964. They are as true today as they were then. I wrote: I have fought against white domination. I have cherished the idea of a democratic and free society in which all persons live together in harmony and with equal opportunities.

It is an ideal which I hope to live for and to achieve. But if needs be, it is an ideal for which I am prepared to die.

My friends, I have no words of eloquence to offer today except to say that the remaining days of my life are in your hands.

I hope you will disperse with discipline. And not a single one of you should do anything which will make other people say that we can't control our own people.

From Nelson Mandela, "Apartheid Has No Future, Africa is Ours," *Vital Speeches of the Day*, Volume LVI, No. 10, March 1, 1990, 295–297.

Document 117:
INDEPENDENCE DAY ADDRESS (1963)
Jomo Kenyatta

Jomo Kenyatta was a leading figure in the struggle for Kenyan Independence, and after freedom from colonial rule had been attained, he was the first leader of the new republic. This speech, given in 1963, stresses the aims of the newly-created internal government of Kenya.

It is with great pride and pleasure that I receive these constitutional instruments today as the embodiment of Kenya's freedom. This is the greatest day in Kenya's history, and the happiest day of my life.

Our march to freedom has been long and difficult. There have been times of despair, when only the burning conviction of the rightness of our cause has sustained us. Today, the tragedies and misunderstandings of the past are behind us. Today, we start on the great adventure of building the Kenya nation.

As we start on this great task, it is right that we who are assembled at this historic ceremony here today, and all the people of Kenya, should remember and pay tribute to those people of all races, tribes and colours who—over the years—have made their contribution to Kenya's rich heritage: administrators, farmers, missionaries, traders and others, and above all the people of Kenya themselves. All have laboured to make this fair land of Kenya the thriving country it is today. It behoves each one of us to vow that, in the days ahead, we shall be worthy of our great inheritance.

Your Royal Highness, your presence here today as the personal representative of Her Majesty the Queen is for us a great honour, and one which gives the highest pleasure to all the people of Kenya. We thank Her Majesty for her message of good wishes, and would request you, Sir, to convey to the Queen the warm greetings of all our people.

We welcome also today Her Majesty's Secretary of State for Commonwealth Relations, who has been so closely concerned with us in the final stages of our march to Independence. With Britain, which has watched over our destinies for so long, we now enter a new relationship. The close ties which have bound our two countries are not severed today. Rather, they will now grow in strength as we work together as two sovereign nations within the Commonwealth, that unique association of free and independent States to whose counsels we look forward to making our contribution.

To all our honoured guests, I extend—on behalf of the people of Kenya—a warm and fraternal welcome to our country on this great occasion. Your presence here today brings added pleasure to our rejoicings.

Today is rightly a day of great rejoicing. But it must also be a day of dedication. Freedom is a right, and without it the dignity of man is violated. But freedom by itself is not enough. At home, we have a duty to ensure that all our citizens are delivered from the afflictions of poverty, ignorance and disease, otherwise freedom for many of our people will be neither complete nor meaningful. We shall count as our friends, and welcome as fellow-citizens, every man, woman and child in Kenya—regardless of race, tribe, colour or creed—who is ready to help us in this great task of advancing the social well-being of all our people.

Freedom also means that we are now a member of the international community, and that we have a duty to work for the peace of the world. Abroad, we shall count as our friends all those who strive for peace.

My friends, we are now an independent nation, and our destiny is henceforward in our own hands. I call on every Kenyan to join me today in this great adventure of nation building. In the spirit of 'harambee', let us all work together so to mould our country that it will set an example to the world in progress, toleration and high endeavour.

From Jomo Kenyatta, Speech given on Uhuru Day, December 12, 1963, from *Harambee! The Prime Minister of Kenya's Speeches 1963–1964*, Nairobi: Oxford University Press, 1964, 15–16.

Document 118:
MULTI-PARTY DEBATE: KENYA NEEDS A STRONG OPPOSITION (1990)

In new nations, self-determination consumes the attention of leaders until the nation is fully established. Often these new nations are ruled in autocratic ways because there has been no tradition of democratic rule and great problems remain from the past because of the nature of colonial rule. Artificial boundaries, economic dependency, unresolved historical hostilities, all militate against peaceful democratic processes. In some cases, new nations have democratic institutions at the beginning but these are overthrown for autocratic institutions, typically with a one party system. Individual liberties are thus ended or relegated to a future stage of development. Kenya fought for its independence from Britain after World War II only to succumb to many violations of human rights in the recent past.

This article appeared in the Nairobi Law Monthly *and the authors risked a great deal in calling for democratic political rights in Kenya, with the right to oppose the government in power. Several of the lawyers who signed this article are in exile; several have been arrested and detained on occassion. The problem is unhappily a general one, as recent events in Eastern Europe as well as in Latin America have shown.*

We, the undersigned, citizens of this country, and Advocates of the High Court of Kenya, who have sworn to defend the constitution of Kenya and the Rule of Law, are concerned that the Law Society in breach of its statutory duties under Section 4 of the Law Society Act (cap. 18) *inter alia* to protect and assist the public of Kenya in all matters touching, ancillary or incidental to the law, and to assist the government in all matters relating to law and the administration of justice, has not either in the past nor during the current debate on mono-party and multi-party systems, drawn to the attention of the public, the great dangers that the mono-party system poses both in theory and in fact to the liberty of the citizen, Rule of Law and Democracy.

Kenyans will recall that until 1963, Kenya was ruled by an unrepresentative, authoritarian, colonial apartheid regime. The majority of the members of colonial parliament (Legco) were appointees of the Governor. The judges were civil servants who could be dismissed at will by the Governor, because they had no security of tenure. Civil servants could also be dismissed at any time because they held their offices at the pleasure of the Governor. The Government was paternalistic and was not accountable to the people. It was by law an unlimited government, not founded on the doctrine of separation of powers. Its philosophical assumption was that there was no need to control the power of the Government or to consult the people because the government knew all the problems of the people and their solutions. The people of Kenya, it was said were not mature enough to know what was good for them. The implementation of this arrogant and paternalistic philosophy, contrary to the wishes of the majority of Kenyans, led to much human suffering and loss of life. To rid themselves of that totalitarian system, Kenyans launched a bitter struggle for independence which culminated in the armed conflict in the 1950's. This armed conflict created in every heart a yearning for real freedom and peace. Kenyans of all ethnic and racial origins earnestly searched for a constitutional framework which would bring about the longed for peace and guarantee its continued enjoyment. The search was not an easy one, it was long and arduous. It required great patience, tolerance and compromise between the various contending parties.

The final product was the independence constitution of 1963, which was intended to safeguard continued peace in Kenya by abolishing once and for all the injustices and oppression institutionalized by the colonial regime, and by guarding against their recurrence as a result of human frailty. Unlike the colonial government, the government of independent Kenya was to be a limited government based on the consent of the governed through free, fair and regular elections at which competing programmes and individuals would offer themselves for elections. The independence constitution did not prescribe any particular political ideology or political party as the official or the ruling party or ideology. Kenyans reserved their right to choose or adopt whatever political ideology or party that would meet their needs. Unlike the colonial paternalistic ideology which treated all Kenyan Africans as children, the independence constitution asserted the maturity and autonomy of every Kenyan, and his right to self-determination and clearly spelt out a no-go area for the government which is set out in Chapter 5 of its Constitution.

The Constitution left every Kenyan free to hold any political opinions and to form or join any political parties that might further his political beliefs. Section 82 of the Constitution prohibits discrimination [against] of any Kenyan on grounds of his political opinions. Section 80 of the Constitution protect[s] the freedom of every Kenyan to form or join any political party. Originally KANU itself was formed by a group of Kenyans to advocate this right. All other political parties at the time recognised this. Since Section 3 of the Constitution makes the Constitution the highest institution in Kenya, no Kenyan or group of Kenyans can lawfully take away, or exercise on behalf of others, these inherent fundamental human rights.

As a result of their bitter colonial and other human experience, the constitutional makers displayed great distrust of unlimited governmental power.... They wrote into the constitution an elaborate system of checks and balances chief of which were:

1. Semi-federal structure of government: the government was to be shared between a federal government and regional government (Majimbo).

2. Government power was divided between three organs: the legislature, the executive and the judiciary: each would check and balance the authority of the other to avoid totalitarianism. The judiciary would act as a fair and independent arbitrator of disputes not only between the three organs but between any of the organs and individual Kenyans. Access to High Court on these crucial areas was unrestricted.

3. The Legislature was made of two houses: House of Representatives, and the Senate. The Senate had to approve legislation passed by House of Representatives. The Senate had to approve legislation passed by House of Representatives.

4. There was a Bill of Rights specifying areas which the government could not interfere with in the individual's life.

5. The Bill of Rights was to be enforced by an independent judiciary, which was insulated from legislative and executive influence by guaranteeing it a high degree of tenure, and by an independent body of lawyers also insulated from political pressures of the day.

6. The civil service was insulated from political influence by establishment of an independent Public Service Commission, with a high degree of tenure. With its independence from Executive and legislative influence of Public Service Commission could oversee and conduct a fair and free election.

7. Senior civil servants such as Attorney General and Auditor-General were given security of tenure to ensure governmental accountability, and independence of action.

8. A multi-party system of government was recognised under Section 80 of the Constitution to guarantee the voice of minorities against the tyranny of a majority.

Since independence, the KANU government has dismantled these safeguards and sought to build an all-powerful Executive with total control which was being avoided at independence. KANU has arrogated to itself the role of banning other political parties and preventing registration of others.

1. The federal system and the bicameral legislature were abolished through constitutional amendments between 1964 and 1966.

2. In 1966 the Constitution was amended to make provision for detention without trial.

3. In 1982 the Constitution was amended to make Kenya a one party state followed a few years later by other amendments to remove tenure of the offices of the Attorney General and members of the Public Service Commission.

4. In 1988 the Constitution was amended to remove the tenure of Judges of the High Court and Court of Appeal, and that of the Auditor and Controller-General.

The cumulative effect of all these amendments was to dramatically change the basic structure of the constitutional framework agreed at independence as the means of ensuring continued peace and liberty. These changes were not preceded by adequate or sufficient consultation with Kenyans. The amendments resulted in an over-concentration of power in the Presidency and great weakening of the other organs, contrary to the letter and spirit of the original independence constitution. The doctrine of the supremacy of the party which is controlled by the President, has supplanted the doctrine of separation of powers and the supremacy of the Constitution on which our independence was based. The Rule of Law, fundamental freedoms and democracy have been debased.

The Rule of Law, fundamental freedoms and democracy have been seriously undermined because of these institutional assaults, which could not have occurred if there was a strong and effective opposition.

The Law Society has failed the nation by not sufficiently canvassing against these fundamental errors. The Law Society which is the champion of civil rights, and the Rule of Law should champion the right of every Kenyan to political participation. WE believe that Kenya needs a strong and effective opposition, to keep the government on its toes, and to keep it awake to the rights, freedoms and aspirations of the people.

We have issued this statement because we are patriotic Kenyans committed to the principles upon where this nation was founded. We are no puppets of anybody.

The above statement was signed by the following advocates of the High Court of Kenya:

Paul Muite, Martha Wangari Njoka, Gervase B.K. Akhaabi, Rumba Kinuthia, Mbiou Mbawki, Peter Nganga, Mbugiwa, Ngugi Muhindi, Beatrice Riunga, Otieno Kajwang', S.M. Ruhi, S.K. Ndungi, S.W. Murage, Kiraitu Murungi, John M. Khaminwa, Nganga Thiongo, David Ireri and Gibson Kambu Kuria.

From *The Nairobi Law Monthly*, No. 23, April/May, 1990. Kaibi, Ltd., P.O. Box 53234, Nairobi, Kenya. 4th Floor, Tumaini House, Nkrumah Ave., Tel. 728978/330480.

Document 119:
FAMINE IN SOMALIA: AMID THE DEAD IN SOMALI TOWN, TEARS OF LIFE (1992)
Jane Perlez

This article illustrates the problems that beset Africa in its continuing search to provide human rights to those who reside there.

Baidoa, Somalia—The almost naked body of a small boy was wheeled into an outdoor center for the starving on a rickety wheelbarrow in the late-afternoon chill and placed under a tree with others lined up ready for burial.

But when Anita Ennis touched the motionless form, with the thin, bare legs caked in dirt, he opened his eyes. Two tears crept down his sunken cheeks.

"Nothing else, he was not able to talk," said Miss Ennis, a nurse who had already seen 12 children die in this center Sunday, despite intravenous drips and liquid food administered by a team of 30 workers organized in the last several weeks by her relief agency, Irish Concern.

She coaxed the boy, too weak to move, to open his lips for some oral rehydration salts, and after a few sips, he lifted his wisp of a hand.

"We gave him some milk and he immediately responded," Miss Ennis said. "He said his name was Mohammed and he'd come to town this morning. He said his mother died a few weeks ago, his father a few months ago.

"He said his father used to give him honey and could we give him some honey?"

Instead, Miss Ennis who runs the center in this bush town 150 miles (240 kilometers) northwest of the Somali capital, Mogadishu, offered milk, water and the only resting place she had—the ground in a drafty hut. Mohammed lay in the corner on an empty bag, covered by a cardboard box, its corner battened by a stone against the wind.

"This is Mohammed," she said, propping him up with a gentle arm and introducing the 14-year-old to some visitors, including a senior official of the United Nations World Food Program, Trevor Page, who came with the first UN airlift to Baidoa on Sunday.

"Is it any wonder we have a death rate as high as today when all we can offer is a used milk-powder bag to lie on and a used biscuit box to cover?" she said as she knelt to help the shivering child take some more water.

"He's frozen," she said, "Trevor, what about some blankets?"

Baidoa is perhaps the grimmest place in Somalia, where a combination of clan-based fighting and drought have brought mass starvation. No one can be precise about figures, but the International Committee of the Red Cross estimates that about 7,000 people died of hunger in Baidoa alone during late June and July. Tens of thousands have died elsewhere in the country, according to the Red Cross.

Irish Concern and the Red Cross have been struggling to stem the tragedy here. In the last three weeks the Irish group has opened four centers with four feedings a day for the 8,300 neediest, most of them starving or ill children.

The Red Cross, which has been airlifting food here for a month, serves a portion of rice and beans once a day to 25,000 people at more than 20 kitchens. The food and milk that Miss Ennis is providing is intended to be supplemental, but there has not been very much to supplement. Mr. Page said the UN airlift would continue.

The town is expected to be a main benefactor of the American airlift, which is to ferry food to outlying districts in Somalia.

So far, the continuing violence, the looting of food that is flown and trucked in, and the extent of the hunger makes improvement hard to discern.

Miss Ennis said she believed that there had been some progress—only three or four deaths daily in each of her four centers in the last week or so—until Sunday. It was cold for Somalia—50 degrees Fahrenheit or 10 degrees centigrade—and the wind made it feel colder still, aggravating the effects of illness and hunger.

"Today was a particularly bad day," she said, showing a visitor around the roofless, gutted one-story buildings that had once been a tuberculosis treatment center.

In a small building that still had a roof, three small bodies lay, partially covered in the frayed rugs the children had died in, waiting for burial the next morning.

"Often they don't have any clothes and get buried in biscuit boxes," Miss Ennis said.

Mohammed was one of the strongest—or perhaps just lucky, caught in the nick of time.

Miss Ennis said a 14-year-old girl, the last survivor of three children, had been sick for some time and asked her mother to take her to the center Sunday morning for some cereal.

"We put her on an intravenous tube, but a few hours later she was dead. That's it—no kids left."

From *The International Herald-Tribune*, August 18, 1992, 1.

Document 120:
AFRICAN CHARTER ON HUMAN AND PEOPLES' RIGHTS (1981)

The African Charter on Human and People's Rights grants and reaffirms to all citizens of the African Continent the basic rights described in the United Nations Charter. As in many other regions of the world, it can be difficult to enforce basic human rights. With increasing famine in drought stricken areas and decades-long civil wars in many African countries, the rights of many Africans, especially children, are almost completely ignored.

Preamble: The African States members of the Organization of African Unity, parties to the present convention entitled "African Charter on Human and Peoples' Rights"; recalling Decision 115 (XVI) of the Assembly of Heads of State and Government at its Sixteenth Ordinary Session held in Monrovia, Liberia, from 17 to 20 July 1979 on the preparation of "a preliminary draft on an African Charter on Human and Peoples' Rights providing *inter alia* for the establishment of bodies to promote and protect human and peoples' rights"; considering the Charter of the Organization of African Unity, which stipulates that "freedom, equality, justice and legitimate aspirations of the African peoples"; reaffirming the pledge they solemnly made in Article 2 of the said Charter to eradicate all forms of colonialism from Africa, to co-ordinate and intensify their co-operation and efforts to achieve a better life for the peoples' of Africa and to promote international co-operation having due regard to the Charter of the United Nations and the Universal Declaration of Human Rights; taking into consideration the virtues of their historical tradition and the values of African civilization which should inspire and characterize their reflection on the concept of human and peoples' rights; recognizing on the one hand that fundamental human rights stem from the attributes of human beings, which justifies their international protection and on the other hand that the reality and respect of peoples' rights should necessarily guarantee human rights;   considering that the enjoyment of rights and freedoms also implies the performance of duties on the part of everyone; convinced that it is henceforth essential to pay a particular attention to the right to development and that civil and political rights cannot be dissociated from economic, social and cultural rights in their conception as well as universality and that the satisfaction of economic, social and cultural rights is a guarantee for the enjoyment of civil and political rights; conscious of their duty to achieve the total liberation of Africa, the peoples of which are still struggling for their dignity and genuine independence, and undertaking to eliminate colonialism, neo-colonialism apartheid, zionism and to dismantle aggressive foreign military bases and all forms of discrimination, language, religion or political opinions; reaffirming their adherence to the principles of human and peoples' rights and freedoms contained in the declarations, conventions and other instruments adopted by the Organization of African Unity, the Movement of Non-Aligned Countries and the United Nations; firmly convinced of their duty to promote and protect human and peoples' rights and freedoms taking into account the importance traditionally attached to these rights and freedoms in Africa; have agreed as follows:

Part 1—RIGHTS AND DUTIES
Chapter 1—Human and Peoples' Rights

Article 1. The Member States of the Organization of African Unity parties to the present Charter shall recognize the rights, duties and freedoms enshrined in this Charter and shall undertake to adopt legislative or other measures to give effect to them.

Article 2. Every individual shall be entitled to the enjoyment of the rights and freedoms recognized and guaranteed in the present Charter without distinction of any kind such as race, ethnic group, colour, sex, language, religion, political or any other opinion, national and social origin, fortune, bith or other status.

Article 3

1. Every individual shall be equal before the law.

2. Every individual shall be entitled to equal protection of the law.

Article 4. Human beings are inviolable. Every human being shall be entitled to respect for his life and the integrity of his person. No one may be arbitrarily deprived of this right.

Article 5. Every individual shall have the right to the respect of the dignity inherent in a human being and to the recognition of his legal status. All forms of exploitation and degradation of man particularly slavery, slave trade, torture, cruel, inhuman or degrading punishment and treatment shall be prohibited.

Article 6. Every individual shall have the right to liberty and to the security of his person. No one may be deprived of his freedom except for reasons and conditions previously laid down by law. In particular, no one may be arbitrarily arrested or detained.

Article 7

1. Every individual shall have the right to have his cause heard. This comprises:

a. The right to an appeal to competent national organs against acts of violating his fundamental rights as recognized and guaranteed by conventions, laws, regulations and customs in force;

b. The right to be presumed innocent until proved guilty by a competent court or tribunal;

c. The right to defence, including the right to be defended by counsel of his choice;

d. The right to be tried within a reasonable time by an impartial court or tribunal.

2. No one may be condemned for an act or omission which did not constitute a legally punishable offence at the time it was committed. No penalty may be inflicted for an offence for which no provision was made at the time it was committed. Punishment is personal and can be imposed only on the offender.

Article 8. Freedom of conscience, the profession and free practice of religion shall be guaranteed. No one may, subject to law and order, be submitted to measures restricting the exercise of these freedoms.

Article 9

1. Every individual shall have the right to receive information.

2. Every individual shall have the right to express and disseminate his opinions within the law.

Article 10

1. Every individual shall have the right to free association provided that he abides by the law.

2. Subject to the obligation of solidarity provided for in Article 29 no one may be compelled to join an association.

Article 11. Every individual shall have the right to assemble freely with others. The exercise of this right shall be subject only to necessary restrictions provided for by law in particular those enacted in the interest of national security, the safety, health, ethics and rights and freedoms of others.

Article 12

1. Every individual shall have the right to freedom of movement and residence within the borders of a State provided he abides by the law.

2. Every individual shall have the right to leave any country including his own, and to return to his country. This right may only be subject to restrictions, provided for by law for the protection of national security, law and order, public health or morality.

3. Every individual shall have the right, when persecuted, to seek and obtain asylum in other countries in accordance with law of those countries and international conventions.

4. A non-national legally admitted in a territory of a State Party to the present Charter, may only be expelled from it by virtue of a decision taken in accordance with the law.

5. The mass expulsion of non-nationals shall be prohibited. Mass expulsion shall be that which is aimed at national, racial, ethnic or religious groups.

Article 13

1. Every citizen shall have the right to participate freely in the government of his country, either directly or through freely chosen representatives in accordance with the provisions of the law.

2. Every citizen shall have the right of equal access to the public service of his country.

3. Every individual shall have the right of access to public property and services in strict equality of all persons before the law.

Article 14. The right to property shall be guaranteed. It may only be encroached upon in the interest of public need or in the general interest of the community and in accordance with the provisions of appropriate laws.

Article 15. Every individual shall have the right to work under equitable and satisfactory conditions, and shall receive equal pay for equal work.

Article 16

1. Every individual shall have the right to enjoy the best attainable state of physical and mental health.

2. States Parties to the present Charter shall take the necessary measures to protect the health of their people and to ensure that they receive medical attention when they are sick.

Article 17

1. Every individual shall have the right to education.

2. Every individual may freely take part in the cultural life of the community.

3. The promotion and protection of morals and traditional values recognized by the community shall be the duty of the State.

Article 18

1. The family shall be the natural unit and basis of society. It shall be protected by the State which shall take care of its physical health and morals.

2. The State shall have the duty to assist the family which is the custodian of morals and traditional values recognized by the community.

3. The State shall ensure the elimination of every discrimination against women and also ensure the protection of the rights of the

woman and the child as stipulated in international declarations and conventions.

4. The aged and the disabled shall also have the right to special measures of protection in keeping with their physical or moral needs.

Article 19. All peoples shall be equal; they shall enjoy the same respect and shall have the same rights. Nothing shall justify the domination of a people by another.

Article 20

1. All peoples shall have the right to existence. They shall have the unquestionable and inalienable right to self-determination. They shall freely determine their political status and shall pursue their economic and social development according to the policy they have freely chosen.

2. Colonized or oppressed peoples shall have the right to free themselves from the bonds of domination by resorting to any means recognized by the international community.

3. All peoples shall have the right to the assistance of the States Parties to the present Charter in their liberation struggle against foreign domination, be it political, economic or cultural.

Article 21

1. All peoples shall freely dispose of their wealth and natural resources. This right shall be exercised in the exclusive interest of the people. In no case shall a people be deprived of it.

2. In case of spoliation the dispossessed people shall have the right to the lawful recovery of its property as well as to an adequate compensation.

3. The free disposal of wealth and natural resources shall be exercised without prejudice to the obligation of promoting international economic co-operation based on mutual respect, equitable exchange and the principles of international law.

4. States parties to the present Charter shall individually and collectively exercise the right to free disposal of their wealth and natural resources with a view to strengthening African unity and solidarity.

5. States parties to the present Charter shall undertake to eliminate all forms of foreign economic exploitation particularly that practised by international monopolies so as to enable their peoples to fully benefit from the advantages derived from their national resources.

Article 22

1. All peoples shall have the right to their economic, social and cultural development with due regard to their freedom and identity and in the equal enjoyment of the common heritage of mankind.

2. States shall have the duty, individually or collectively to ensure the exercise of the right to development.

Article 23

1. All peoples shall have the right to national and international peace and security. The principles of solidarity and friendly relations implicitly affirmed by the Charter of the United Nations and reaffirmed by that of the Organization of African Unity shall govern relations between States.

2. For the purpose of strengthening peace, solidarity and friendly relations, States parties to the present Charter shall ensure that:

a. any individual enjoying the right of asylum under Article 12 of the present Charter shall not engage in subversive activities against his country of origin or any other State party to the present Charter.

b. their territories shall not be used as bases for subversive or terrorist activities against the people of any other State party to the present Charter.

Article 24. All peoples shall have the right to a general satisfactory environment favourable to their development.

Article 25. States parties to the present Charter shall have the duty to promote and ensure through teaching, education and publication, the respect of the rights and freedoms contained in the present Charter and to see to it that these freedoms and rights as well as corresponding obligations and duties are understood.

Article 26. States parties to the present Charter shall have the duty to guarantee the independence of the Courts and shall allow the establishment and improvement of appropriate national institutions entrusted with the promotion and protection of the rights and freedoms guaranteed by the present Charter.

Chapter II—Duties

Article 27

1. Every individual shall have duties towards his family and society, the State and other

legally recognised communities and the international community.

2. The rights and freedoms of each individual shall be exercised with due regard to the rights of others, collective security, morality and common interest.

Article 28. Every individual shall have the duty to respect and consider his fellow beings without discrimination, and to maintain relations aimed at promoting, safeguarding and reinforcing mutual respect and tolerance.

Article 29. The individual shall also have the duty:

1. To preserve the harmonious development of the family and to work for the cohesion and respect of the family; to respect his parents at all times, to maintain them in case of need;

2. To serve his national community by placing his physical and intellectual abilities at its service;

3. Not to compromise the security of the State whose national or resident he is;

4. To preserve and strengthen social and national solidarity, particularly when the latter is threatened;

5. To preserve and strengthen the national independence and the territorial integrity of his country and to contribute to its defence in accordance with the law;

6. To work to the best of his abilities and competence, and to pay taxes imposed by law in the interest of the society;

7. To preserve and strengthen positive African cultural values in his relations with other members of the society, in the spirit of tolerance, dialogue and consultation and, in general, to contribute to the promotion of the moral well being of society;

8. To contribute to the best of his abilities, at all times and at all levels, to the promotion and achievement of African unity.

PART II—MEASURES OF SAFEGUARD
Chapter 1—Establishment and organisation of the African Commission on Human and Peoples' Rights

Article 30. An African Commission on Human and Peoples' Rights, hereinafter called "the Commission," shall be established within the Organization of African Unity to promote human and peoples' rights and ensure their protection in Africa....

Chapter II—Mandate of the Commission

The functions of the Commission shall be:

1. To promote Human and Peoples' Rights and in particular:

a. To collect documents, undertake studies and researches on African problems in the field of human and peoples' rights, organize seminars, symposia and conferences, disseminate information, encourage national and local institutions concerned with human and peoples' rights, and should the case arise, give its views, or make recommendations to Governments.

b. To formulate and lay down principles and rules aimed at solving legal problems relating to human and peoples' rights and fundamental freedoms upon which African Governments may base their legislation.

c. To co-operate with other African and international institutions concerned with the promotion and protection of human and peoples' rights.

2. Ensure the protection of human and peoples' rights under conditions laid down by the present Charter.

3. Interpret all the provisions of the present Charter at the request of a State Party, an institution of the OAU or an African Organization recognized by the OAU.

4. Perform any other tasks which may be entrusted to it by the Assembly of Heads of State and Government.

From 1OAU Doc. CAB/LEG/67/3 rev. 5, 21 I.L.M. 58 (1982)

Document 121:
KHRUSHCHEV'S SECRET SPEECH (1956)
Nikita Khrushchev

In a dramatic speech in 1956, Nikita Khrushchev denounced Stalin, who had emerged as the Soviet leader after Lenin, consolidated his power and ruled dictatorially until his death in 1953. This speech was in Western hands within days of its being given and the United States Department of State published the following note and the speech itself.

The Department of State has recently obtained from a confidential source a copy of a document which purports to be a version of the speech of Party First Secretary N.S. Khrushchev at a session of the XXth Party Congress of the Communist Party of the Soviet Union on February 25, 1956. This session was limited in attendance to the delegates from the USSR.

The document is being released in response to many inquiries. This version is understood to have been prepared for the guidance of the party leadership of a Communist Party outside of the USSR. The Department of State does not vouch for the authenticity of the document and in releasing it intends that the document speak for itself.

TEXT OF KHRUSHCHEV'S SPEECH:

Comrades! In the report of the Central Committee of the Party at the XXth Congress, in a number of speeches by delegates to the Congress, as also formerly during the plenary CC/CPSU sessions, quite a lot has been said about the cult of the individual and about its harmful consequences. After Stalin's death the Central Committee of the Party began to implement a policy of explaining concisely and consistently that it is impermissible and foreign to the spirit of Marxism-Leninism to elevate one person, to transform him into a superman possessing supernatural characteristics akin to those of a god. Such a man supposedly knows everything, sees everything, thinks for everyone, can do anything, is infallible in his behavior.

Such a belief about a man, and specifically about Stalin, was culativated among us for many years.

The objective of the present report is not a thorough evaluation of Stalin's life and activity. Concerning Stalin's merits, an entirely sufficient number of books, pamphlets and studies had already been written in his lifetime. The role of Stalin in the preparation and execution of the Socialist Revolution, in the Civil War, and in the fight for the construction of Socialism in our country is universally known. Everyone knows this well. At the present we are concerned with a question which has immense importance for the Party now and for the future—(we are concerned) with how the cult of the person of Stalin has been gradually growing, the cult exceedingly serious and causing grave perversions of Party principles, of Party democracy, of revolutionary legality.

Because of the fact that not all as yet realize fully the practical consequences resulting form the cult of the individual, the great harm caused by the violation of the principle of collective direction of the Party and because of the accumulation of immense and limitless power in the hands of one person—the Central Committee of the Party considers it absolutely necessary to make the material pertaining to this matter available to the XXth Congress of the Communist Part of the Soviet Union....

The great modesty of the genius of the revolution, Vladimir Ilyich Lenin is known. Lenin had always stressed the role of the people as the creator of history, the directing and organizational role of the party as a living and creative organism, and also the role of the Central Committee.

Marxism does not negate the role of the leaders and organizers of the masses, Lenin at the same time mercilessly stigmatized every manifestation of the cult of the individual, inexorably combated the foreign-to-Marxism views about a "hero" and a "crowd" and countered all efforts to oppose a "hero" to the masses and to the people.

Lenin taught that the Party's strength depends on its indissoluble unity with the masses, on the fact that behind the Party follow the people -workers, peasants and intelligentsia. "Only he will win and retain the power," said Lenin, "who believes in the people, who submerges himself in the fountain of the living creativeness of the people."

Lenin spoke with pride about the Bolshevik Communist Party as the leader and teacher of the people; he called for the presentation of all the most important questions before the opinion of knowledgeable workers, before the opinion of their Party; he said: "We believe in it, we see in it the wisdom, the honor, and the conscience of our epoch."...

We must affirm that the Party had fought a serious fight against the Trotskyites, rightists and bourgeois nationalists, and that it disarmed ideologically all the enemies of Leninism. This ideological fight was carried on successfully as a result of which the Party became strengthened and tempered. Here Stalin played a positive role.

The Party led a great political ideological struggle against those in its own ranks who proposed anti-Leninist theses, who represented a political line hostile to the Party and to the cause of Socialism. This was a stubborn and a difficult fight but a necessary one, because the political line of both the Trotskyite-Zinovievite bloc and of the Bukharinites led actually toward the restoration of capitalism and capitulation to the world bourgeoisie. Let us consider for a moment what would have happened if in 1928–1929 the political line of right deviation had prevailed among us, or orientation toward "cotton-dress industrialization," or toward the kulak, etc. We would not now have a powerful heavy industry, we would not have the Kolkhozes, we would find ourselves disarmed and weak in a capitalist encirclement....

It was precisely during this period (1935–1937–1938) that the practice of mass repression through the government apparatus was born, first against the enemies of Leninism—Trotskyites, Zinovievites, Bukharinites, long since politically defeated by the Party, and subsequently also against many honest Communists, against those Party cadres who had borne the heavy load of the Civil War and the first and most difficult years of industrialization and collectivization, who actively fought against the Trotskyites and the rightists of the Leninist Party line.

Stalin originated the concept "enemy of the people." This term automatically rendered it unnecessary that the ideological errors of a man or men engaged in a controversy be proven; this term made possible the usage of the most cruel repression, violating all norms of revolutionary legality, against anyone who in any way disagreed with Stalin, against those who were only suspected of hostile intent, against those who had bad reputations. This concept, "enemy of the people," actually eliminated the possibility of any kind of ideological fight or the making of one's views known on this or that issue, even those of a practical character. In the main, and in actuality, the only proof of guilt used, against all norms of current legal science, was the "confession" of the accused himself; and, as subsequent probing proved, "confessions" were acquired through physical pressures against the accused.

This led to glaring violations of revolutionary legality, and to the fact that many entirely innocent persons, who in the past had defended the Party line, became victims.

We must assert that in regard to those persons who in their time had opposed the Party line, there were often no sufficient serious reasons for their physical annihilation. The formula, "enemy of the people" was specifically introduced for the purpose of physically annihilating such individuals.

It is a fact that many persons, who were later annihilated as enemies of the Party and people had worked with Lenin during his life. Some of these persons had made errors during Lenin's life, but, despite this, Lenin benefited by their work, he corrected them and he did everything possible to retain them in the ranks of the Party; he induced them to follow him....

Arbitrary behavior by one person encouraged and permitted arbitrariness in others. Mass arrests and deportations of many thousands of people, execution without trial and without normal investigation created conditions of insecurity, fear and even desperation....

Lenin used severe methods only in the most necessary cases, when the exploiting classes were still in existence and were vigorously opposing the revolution, when the struggle for survival was decidedly assuming the sharpest forms, even including a civil war.

Stalin, on the other hand, used extreme methods and mass repressions at a time when the revolution was already victorious, when the Soviet state was strengthened, when the exploiting classes were already liquidated and Socialist relations were rooted solidly in all phases of national economy, when our Party was politically consolidated and had strengthened itself both numerically and ideologically. It is clear that here Stalin showed in a whole series of cases his intolerance, his brutality and his abuse of power. Instead of proving his political correctness and mobilizing the masses, he often chose the path of repression and physical annihilation, not only against actual enemies, but also against individuals who had not committed any crimes against the Party and the Soviet government. Here we see no wisdom but only a demonstration of the brutal force which had once so alarmed V.I. Lenin.

Lately, especially after the unmasking of the Beriya gang, the Central Committee looked into a series of matters fabricated by this gang. This revealed a very ugly picture of brutal willfulness connected with the incorrect behavior of Stalin. As facts prove, Stalin, using his unlimited power, allowed himself many abuses, acting in the name of the Central Committee, not asking for the opinion of the Committee members nor even of the members of the Central Committee's Political Bureau; often he did not inform them about his personal decisions concerning very important Party and government matters....

The Commission has become acquainted with a large quantity of materials in the NKVD archives and with other documents and has established many facts pertaining to the fabrication of cases against Communists, to false accusations, to glaring abuses of Socialist legality—which resulted in the death of innocent people. It became apparent that many resulted in the death of innocent people. It became apparent that many Party, Soviet and economic activists, who were branded in 1937–1938 as "enemies," were actually never enemies, spies, wreckers, etc., but were always honest Communists; they were only so stigmatized and often, no longer able to bear barbaric tortures, they charged themselves (at the order of the investigative judges—falsifiers) with all kinds of grave and unlikely crimes. The Commission has presented to the Central Committee Presidium lengthy and documented materials pertaining to mass repressions against the delegates to the XVIIth Party Congress and against members of the Central Committee elected at that Congress. These materials have been studied by the Presidium of the Central Committee.

It was determined that of the 139 members and candidates of the Party's Central Committee who were elected at the XVIIth Congress, 98 persons, i.e., 70 percent, were arrested and shot (mostly in 1937–1938)....

The same fate met not only the Central Committee members but also the majority of the delegates to the XVIIth party Congress. Of 1966 delegates with either voting or advisory rights, 1108 persons were arrested on charges of anti-revolutionary crimes, i.e., decidedly more than a majority. This very fact show how absurd, wild and contrary to common sense were the charges of counter-revolutionary crimes made out, as we now see, against a majority of participants at the XVIIth Party Congress....

After the criminal murder of S.M. Kirov, mass repressions and brutal acts of violation of socialist legality began. On the evening of 1 December 1934 on Stalin's initiative (without the approval of the Political Bureau—which was passed two days later, casually) the secretary of the Presidium of the Central Executive Committee, Yenukidze, signed the following directive.

"I. Investigative agencies are directed to speed up the cases of those accused of the preparation or execution of acts of terror.

"II. Judicial organs are directed not to hold up the execution of death sentences pertaining to crimes of this category in order to consider the possibility of pardon, because the Presidium of the Central Executive Committee USSR does not consider as possible the receiving of petitions of this sort.

"III. The organs of the Commissariat of Internal Affairs are directed to execute the death sentences against criminals of the above-mentioned category immediately after the passage of sentences."

This directive became the basis for mass acts of abuse against Socialist legality. During many of the fabricated court cases the accused were charged with "the preparation" of terroristic acts; this deprived them of any possibility that their cases might be re-examined, even when they stated before the court that their "confessions" were secured by force, and when, in a convincing manner, they disproved the accusations against them....

An example of vile provocation, of odious falsification and of criminal violation of revolutionary legality is the case of the former candidate for the Central Committee Political Bureau, one of the most eminent workers of the Party and of the Soviet government, Comrade Eikhe, who was a Party member since 1905.

Comrade Eikhe was arrested on 29 April 1938 on the basis of slanderous materials, without the sanction of the Prosecutor of the USSR, which was finally received 15 months after the arrest.

Investigation of Eikhe's case was made in a manner which most brutally violated Soviet legality and was accompanied by willfulness and falsification.

Eikhe was forced under torture to sign ahead of time a protocol of his confession prepared by the investigative judges, in which he and several other eminent Party workers were accused of anti-Soviet activity.

On 1 October 1939 Eikhe sent his declaration to Stalin in which he categorically denied his guilt and asked for an examination of his case. In the declaration he wrote:

"There is no more bitter misery than to sit in the jail of a government for which I have always fought."

A second declaration of Eikhe has been preserved which he sent to Stalin on 27 October 1939; in it he cited facts very convincingly and countered the slanderous accusations made against him, arguing that this provocatory accusation was on the one hand the work of real Trotskyites whose arrests he had sanctioned as First Secretary of the West Siberian Krai Party Committee and who conspired in order to take revenge on him, and, on the other hand, the result of the base falsification of materials by the investigative judges.

Eikhe wrote in his declaration: "...On 25 October of this year I was informed that the investigation in my case has been concluded and I was given access to the materials of this investigation. Had I been guilty of only one-hundredth of the crimes with which I am charged, I would not have dared to send you this pre-execution declaration; however, I have not been guilty of even one of the things with which I am charged and my heart is clean of even the shadow of baseness. I have never in my life told you a word of falsehood and now, finding my two feet in the grave, I am also not lying. My whole case is a typical example of provocation, slander and violation of the elementary basis of revolutionary legality....

"The confessions which were made part of my file are not only absurd but contain some slander toward the Central Committee of the All-Union Communist Party (Bolsheviks) and toward the Council of People's Commissars because correct resolutions of the Central Committee of the All-Union Communist Party (Bolsheviks) and of the Council of People's Commissars which was not made on my initiative and without my participation are presented as hostile acts of counter-revolutionary organizations made at my suggestion....

"I am now alluding to the most disgraceful part of my life and to my really grave guilt against the Party and against you. This is my confession of counter-revolutionary activity.... The case is as follows: not being able to suffer the tortures to which I was submitted by Ushakov and Nikolayev—and especially by the first one—who utilized the knowledge that my broken ribs have not properly mended and have caused me great pain—I have been forced to accuse myself and others.

"The majority of my confession has been suggested or dictated by Ushakov, and the remainder is my reconstruction of NKVD materials from western Siberia for which I assumed all responsibility. If some part of the story which Ushakov fabricated and which I signed did not properly hang together, I was forced to sign another variation. The same thing was done to Rukhimovich, who was at first designated as a member of the reserve net and whose name later was removed without telling me anything about it; the same was also done with the leader of the reserve net, supposedly created by Bukharin in 1935. At first I wrote my name in, and then I was instructed to insert Mezhlauk. There were other similar incidents.

"...I am asking and begging you that you again examine my case and this not for the purpose of sparing me but in order to unmask the vile provocation which like a snake wound itself around many persons in a great degree due to my meanness and criminal slander. I have never betrayed you or the Party. I know that I perish because of vile and mean work of the enemies of the Party and of the people, who fabricated the provocation against me."

It would appear that such an important declaration was worth an examination by the Central Committee. This, however, was not done and the declaration was transmitted to Beriya while the terrible maltreatment of the Political Bureau candidate, Comrade Eikhe, continued.

On 2 February 1940 Eikhe was brought before the court. Here he did not confess any guilt and said as follows:

"In all the so-called confessions of mine there is not one letter written by me with the exception of my signatures under the protocols which were forced from me. I have made my confession under pressure from the investigative judge who from the time of my arrest tormented me. After that I began to write all this nonsense.... The most important thing for me is to tell the court, the Party and Stalin that I am not guilty. I have never been guilty of any conspiracy. I will die believing in the truth of Party policy as I have believed in it during my whole life."

On 4 February Eikhe was shot. It has been definitely established now that Eikhe's case was fabricated; he has been posthumously rehabilitated.

Mass arrests of Party, Soviet, economic and military workers caused tremendous harm to our country and to the cause of Socialist advancement.

Mass repressions had a negative influence on the moral-political condition of the Party, created a situation of uncertainty, contributed to the spreading of unhealthy suspicion, and sowed distrust among Communists. All sorts of slanderers and careerists were active....

All this brought about the situation which existed at the beginning of the war and which was the great threat to our Fatherland.

It would be incorrect to forget that after the first severe disaster and defeats at the front Stalin thought that this was the end. In one of the speeches in those days he said: "All that which Lenin created we have been forever."

After this Stalin for a long time actually did not direct the military operations and ceased to do anything whatever. He returned to active leadership only when some members of the Political Bureau visited him and told him that it was necessary to take certain steps immediately in order to improve the situation at the front.

Therefore, the threatening danger which hung over our Fatherland in the first period of the war was largely due to the faulty methods of directing the nation and the Party by Stalin himself.

However, we speak not only about the moment when the war began, which led to serious disorganization of our army and brought us severe losses. Even after the war began, the nervousness and hysteria which Stalin demonstrated, interfering with actual military operations, caused our army serious damage.

Stalin was very far from an understanding of the real situation which was developing at the front. This was natural because during the whole Patriotic War he never visited any section of the front or any liberated city except for one short ride on the Mozhaisk Highway during a stabilized situation at the front. To this incident were dedicated many literary works full of fantasies of all sorts and so many paintings. Simultaneously, Stalin was interfering with operations and issuing orders which did not take into consideration the real situation at a given section of the front and which could not help but result in huge personnel losses....

The magnificent and heroic deeds of hundreds of millions of people of the East and of the West during the fight against the threat of Fascist subjugation which loomed before us will live centuries and millennia in the memory of thankful humanity.

The main role and the main credit for the victorious ending of the war belongs to our Communist Party, to the Armed forces of the Soviet Union, and to the tens of millions of Soviet people raised by the Party.

Comrades, let us reach for some other facts. The Soviet Union is justly considered as a model of a multi-national State because we have in practice assured the equality and friendship of all nations which live in our great Fatherland.

All the more monstrous are the acts whose initiator was Stalin and which are rude violations of the basic Leninist principles of the nationality policy of the Soviet State. We refer to the mass deportations from their native places of whole nations, together with all Communists and Komsomols without any exception; this deportation action was not dictated by any military considerations.

Thus, already at the end of 1943, when there occurred a permanent breakthrough at the fronts of the Great Patriotic War benefiting the Soviet Union a decision was taken and executed concerning the deportation of all the Karachai from the lands on which they lived. In the same period, at the end of December 1943, the same lot befell the whole population of the Autonomous Kalmyk Republic. In March 1944 all the Chechen and Ingush peoples were deported and the Chechen-Ingush Autonomous Republic was liquidated. In April 1944, all Balkars were deported to faraway places from the territory of the Kabardyno-Balkar Autonomous Republic and the Republic itself was renamed the Autonomous Kabardynian Republic. The Ukrainians avoided meeting this fate only because there were too many of them and there was no place to which to deport them. Otherwise, he would have deported them also....

Comrades: We must abolish the cult of the individual decisively, once and for all; we must draw the proper conclusions concerning both ideological-theoretical and practical work.

It is necessary for this purpose:

First, in a Bolshevik manner to condemn and to eradicate the cult of the individual as alien to Marxism-Leninism and not consonant with the principles of Party leadership and the norms of Party life, and to fight inexorably all attempts at bringing back this practice in one form or another....

From Department of State note from *The Anti-Stalin Campaign and International Communism, A selection of Documents*, edited by the Russian Institute, Columbia University Press, NY: Columbia University Press, 1956, 2. Text of Khrushchev's speech from *The Anatomy of Terror, Khrushchev; Revelations About Stalin's Regime*, Washington, D.C., Public Affairs Press, 1956, 19–71.

Document 122:
PEACE, PROGRESS, AND HUMAN RIGHTS: THE NOBEL PRIZE LECTURE (1975)
Andrei Sakharov

Andrei Sakharov was a physicist who worked on the Soviet development of nuclear weapons. He became convinced that the Soviet system would not survive if it did not permit intellectual freedom and all civil rights for Soviet citizens. He and his wife became human rights advocates and were jailed and exiled for years. He was presented the Nobel Peace Prize and his lecture reveals his views on the needs for change to ensure peace and human rights. He died in late 1989 as fundamental reforms began in the Soviet Union.

Citation for the 1975 Nobel Peace Prize Award

The Nobel Committee of the Norwegian Parliament has awarded Nobel's peace prize for 1975 to Andrei Sakharov.

Sakharov's personal and fearless effort in the cause of peace among mankind serves as a mighty inspiration to all true endeavors to promote peace. Uncompromisingly and forcefully, Sakharov has fought not only against the abuse of power and violations of human dignity in all its forms, but he has with equal vigor fought for the ideal of a state founded on the principle of justice for all.

In a convincing fashion Sakharov has emphasized that the individual rights of man can serve as the only sure foundation for a genuine and long-lasting system of international cooperation. In this manner he has succeeded very effectively, and under trying conditions, in reinforcing respect for such values as all true friends of peace are anxious to support.

Andrei Dmitrivich Sakharov has addressed his message of peace and justice to all peoples of the world. For him it is a fundamental principle that wold peace can have no lasting value, unless it is founded on respect for the individual human being in society. This respect has found expression in several international declarations; for example, the UN declaration on the rights of man. Sakharov has demanded that the national authorities of each country must live up to the commitments they have undertaken in signing these declarations.

In the various agreements signed this year by 35 states at the security conference in Helsinki, it was again emphasized that this respect for human dignity was an obligation undertaken by the states themselves. In the agreement the parties acknowledge that respect for human rights and fundamental freedoms is an important factor in the cause of peace, justice, and well-being which is essential to ensure the development of friendly relations and cooperation not only among themselves but among all the countries of the world.

In more forceful terms than others, Andrei Sakharov has warned us against not taking this seriously, and he has placed himself in the vanguard of the efforts to make the ideals expressed in this paragraph of the Helsinki agreement a living reality.

Andrei Sakharov is a firm believer in the brotherhood of man, in genuine coexistence, as the only way to save mankind. It was precisely by means of encouraging fraternization between all peoples, based on truth and sincerity, that Alfred Nobel envisaged the possibilities of creating a safer future for all mankind. When states violate the fundamental precepts of human rights, they are also, in Sakharov's view, undermining the work to promote confidence across national borders.

Sakharov has warned against the dangers connected with a bogus detente based on wishful thinking and illusions. As a nuclear physicist he has, with his special insight and sense of responsibility, been able to speak out against the dangers inherent in the armaments race between the states. His aims are demilitarization, democratization of society in all countries and a more rapid pace of social progress.

Sakharov's love of truth and strong belief in the inviolability of the human being, his fight against violence and brutality, his courageous defense of the freedom of the spirit, his unselfishness and strong humanitarian convictions have turned him into the spokesman for the conscience of mankind, which the world so sorely needs today.

SAKHAROV'S ACCEPTANCE SPEECH

Peace, progress, human rights—these three goals are indissolubly linked: it is impossible to achieve one of them if the others are ignored. This idea provides the main theme of my lecture.

I am deeply grateful that this great and significant award, the Nobel Peace Prize, has been given to me, and that I have the opportunity of addressing you here today. I was particularly gratified at the Committee's citation which stresses the defense of human rights as the only sure basis for genuine and lasting international cooperation. This idea is very important to me; I am convinced that international trust, mutual understanding, disarmament, and international security are inconceivable without an open society with freedom of information, freedom of conscience, the right to publish, and the right to travel and choose the country in which one wishes to live. I am also convinced that freedom of conscience, together with other civic rights, provides both the basis for scientific progress and a guarantee against its misuse to harm mankind, as well as the basis for economic and social progress, which in turn is a political guarantee making the effective defense of social rights possible. At the same time I should like to defend the thesis of the original and decisive significance of civic and political rights in shaping the destiny of mankind. This view differs essentially from the usual Marxist theory, as well as from technocratic opinions, according to which only material factors and social and economic conditions are of decisive importance. (But in saying this, of course, I have no intention of denying the importance of people's material welfare.)

I should like to express all these theses in my lecture, and in particular to dwell on a number of specific problems affecting the violation of human rights. A solution of these problems is imperative, and the time at our disposal is short.

This is the reason why I have called my lecture "Peace, Progress, and Human Rights." There is, naturally, a conscious parallel with the title of my 1968 article "Thoughts on Progress, Peaceful Coexistence, and Intellectual Freedom," with which my lecture, both in its contents and its implications, has very close affinities.

There is a great deal to suggest that mankind, at the threshold of the second half of the twentieth century, entered a particularly decisive and critical historical era.

Nuclear missiles exist capable in principle of annihilating the whole of mankind; this is the greatest danger threatening our age. Thanks to economic, industrial, and scientific advances, so-called "conventional" arms have likewise grown incomparably more dangerous, not to mention chemical and bacteriological instruments of war.

There is no doubt that industrial and technological progress is the most important factor in overcoming poverty, famine, and disease. But this progress leads at the same time to ominous changes in the environment in which we live and to the exhaustion of our natural resources. Thus, mankind faces grave ecological dangers.

Rapid changes in traditional forms of life have resulted in an unchecked demographic explosion which is particularly noticeable in the developing countries of the Third World. The growth in population has already created exceptionally complicated economic, social, and psychological problems and will in the future inevitably pose still more serious problems. In many countries, particularly in Asia, Africa, and Latin America, the lack of food will be an overriding factor in the lives of many hundreds of millions of people, who from the moment of birth are condemned to a wretched existence on the starvation level. Moreover, future prospects are menacing, and in the opinion of many specialists, tragic, despite the undoubted success of the "green revolution."

But even in the developed countries, people face serious problems. These include the pressure resulting from excessive urbanization, all the changes that disrupt the community's social and psychological stability, the incessant pursuit of fashion and trends, overproduction, the frantic, furious tempo of life, the increase in nervous and mental disorders, the growing number of people deprived of contact with nature and of normal human lives, the dissolution of the family and the loss of simple human pleasures, the decay of the community's moral and ethical principles, and the loss of faith in the purpose of life. Against this background there is a whole host of ugly phenomena: an increase in crime, in alcoholism, in drug addiction, in terrorism, and so forth. The imminent exhaustion of the world's resources, the threat of overpopulation, the constant and deep-rooted international, political, and social problems are making a more and more forceful impact on the developed countries too, and will deprive—or at any rate threaten to deprive a great many people who are accustomed to abundance, affluence, and creature comforts.

However, in the pattern of problems facing the world today a more decisive and important role is played by the global political polarization of mankind, which is divided into the so-called First World (conventionally called the Western world), the Second (socialist), and the Third (the developing countries). Two powerful socialist states, in fact, have become mutually hostile totalitarian empires, in which a single party and the state exercise immoderate power in all spheres of life. They possess an enormous potential for expansion, striving to increase their influence to cover large areas of the globe. One of these states—the Chinese People's Republic—has reached only a relatively modest stage of economic development, whereas the other—the Soviet Union—by exploiting its unique natural resources, and by taxing to the utmost the powers of its inhabitants and their ability to suffer continued privation, has built up a tremendous war potential and a relatively high—though one sided—economic development. But in the Soviet Union, too, the people's standard of living is low, and civic rights are more restricted than in less socialist countries. Highly complicated global problems also affect the Third World, where relative economic stagnation goes hand in hand with growing international political activity.

Moreover, this polarization further reinforces the serious dangers of nuclear annihilation, famine, pollution of the environment, exhaustion of resources, overpopulation, and dehumanization.

If we consider this complex of urgent problems and contradictions, the first point that must be made is that any attempt to reduce the tempos of scientific and technological progress, to reverse the process of urbanization, to call for isolationism, patriarchal ways of life, and a renaissance based on ancient national traditions, would be unrealistic. Progress is indispensable and to halt it would lead to the decline and fall of our civilization.

Not long ago we were unfamiliar with artificial fertilizers, mechanized farming, chemical pesticides, and intensive agricultural methods. There are voices calling for a return to more traditional and possibly less dangerous forms of agriculture. But can this be accomplished in a world in which hundreds of millions of people are suffering from hunger? On the contrary, there is no doubt that we need increasingly intensive methods of farming, and we must spread modern methods all over the world, including the developing countries.

We cannot reject the idea of a spreading use of the results of medical research or the extension of research in all its branches, including bacteriology and virology, neurophysiology, human genetics, and gene surgery, no matter what potential dangers lurk in their abuse and the undesirable social consequences of this research. This also applies to research in the creation of artificial intelligence systems, research involving behavior, and the establishment of a unified system of global communication, systems for selecting and storing information, and so forth. It is quite clear that in the hands of irresponsible bureaucratic authorities operating secretly, all this research may prove exceptionally dangerous, but at the same time it may prove extremely important and necessary to mankind, if it is carried out under public supervision and discussion and socio-scientific analysis. We cannot reject wider application of artificial materials, synthetic food, or the modernization of every aspect of life; we cannot obstruct growing automation and industrial expansion, irrespective of the social problems these may involve.

We cannot condemn the construction of bigger nuclear power stations or research into nuclear physics, since energetics is one of the bases of our civilization. In this connection I should like to remind you that twenty-five years ago I and my teacher, the winner of the Nobel Prize for Physics, Igor Yevgenevich Tamm, laid the basis for nuclear research in our country. This research has achieved tremendous scope, extending into the most varied directions, from the classical method for magnetic heat insulation to those for the use of lasers.

We cannot cease interplanetary and intergalactic space research, including the attempts to intercept signals from civilizations outside our own earth. The chance that such experiments will prove successful is probably small, but precisely for this reason the results may well be tremendous.

I have mentioned only a few examples. In actual fact all important aspects of progress are closely interwoven; none of them can be discarded without the risk of destroying the entire structure of our civilization. Progress is indivisible. But intellectual factors play a special role in the mechanism of progress. Underestimating these factors is particularly widespread in the socialist countries, probably due to the populist-ideological dogmas of official philosophy, and may well result in distortion of the path of progress or even its cessation and stagnation.

Progress is possible and innocuous only when it is subject to the control of reason. The important problems involving environmental protection exemplify the role of public opinion, the open society, and freedom of conscience. The partial liberalization in our country after the death of Stalin made it possible to engage in public debate on this problem during the early 1960s. But an effective solution demands increased tightening of social and international control. The military application of scientific results and controlled disarmament are an equally critical area, in which international confidence depends on public opinion and an open society. The example I gave involving the manipulation of mass psychology is already highly topical, even though it may appear farfetched.

Freedom of conscience, the existence of an informed public opinion, a pluralistic system of education, freedom of the press, and access to other sources of information—all these are in very short supply in the socialist countries. This situation is a result of the economic, political, and ideological monism which is characteristic of these nations. At the same time these conditions are a vital necessity, not only to avoid all witting or unwitting abuse of progress, but also to strengthen it.

An effective system of education and a creative sense of heredity from one generation to another are possible only in an atmosphere of intellectual freedom. Conversely, intellectual bondage, the power and conformism of a pitiful bureaucracy, acts from the very start as a blight on humanistic fields of knowledge, literature and art and results eventually in a general intellectual decline, the bureaucratization and formalization of the entire system of education, the decline of scientific research, the thwarting of all incentive to creative work, stagnation, and dissolution.

In the polarized world the totalitarian states, thanks to détente, today may indulge in a special form of intellectual parasitism. And it seems that if the inner changes that we all consider necessary do not take place, those nations will soon be forced to adopt an approach of this kind. If this happens, the danger of an explosion in the world situation will merely increase. Cooperation between the Western states, the socialist nations, and the developing countries is a vital necessity for peace, and it involves exchanges of scientific achievements, technology, trade, and mutual economic aid, particularly where food is concerned. But this cooperation must be based on mutual trust between open societies, or—to put it another way—with an open mind, on the basis of genuine equality and not on the basis of the democratic countries' fear of their totalitarian neighbors. If that were the case, cooperation would merely involve an attempt at ingratiating oneself with a formidable neighbor. But such a policy would merely postpone the evil day, soon to arrive anyway and, then, ten times worse. This is simply another version of Munich. Détente can only be assured if from the very outset it goes hand in hand with continuous openness on the part of all countries, an aroused sense of public opinion, free exchange of information, and absolute respect in all countries for civic and political rights. In short: in addition to détente in the material sphere, with disarmament and trade, détente should take place in the intellectual and ideological sphere. President Giscard d'Estang of France expressed himself in an admirable fashion during his visit to Moscow. Indeed, it was worth enduring criticism from shortsighted pragmatists among his countrymen to support such an important principle.

Before dealing with the problem of disarmament I should like to take this opportunity to remind you of some of my proposals of a general nature. First and foremost is the idea of setting up an international consultative committee for questions related to disarmament, human rights, and the protection of the environment, under the aegis of the United Nations. In my opinion a committee of this kind should have the right to exact replies from all governments to its inquiries and recommendations. The committee could become an important working body in securing international discussion and information on the most important problems affecting the future of mankind. I hope this idea will receive support and be discussed.

I should also emphasize that I consider it particularly important for United Nations armed forces to be used more generally for the purpose of restricting armed conflicts between states and ethnic groups. I have a high regard for the United Nations role, and I consider the institution to be one of mankind's most important hopes for a better future. Recent years have proved difficult and critical for this organization. I have written on this subject in *My Country and the World*, but after it was published, a deplorable event took place: the General Assembly adopted—without any real debate—a resolution declaring Zionism a form of racism and racial discrimination. Zionism is the ideology of a national rebirth of the Jewish people after two thousand years of diaspora, and it is not directed against any other people. The adoption of a resolution of this kind has damaged the prestige of the United Nations. But despite such motions, which are frequently the result of an insufficient sense of responsibility among leaders of some of the UN's younger members, I believe nevertheless that the organization may sooner or later be in a position to play a worthy role in the life of mankind, in accordance with its Charter's aims.

Let me now address one of the central questions of the present age, the problem of disarmament. I have described in detail just what my position is in *My Country and the World*. It is imperative to promote confidence between nations, and carry out measures of control with the aid of international inspection groups. This is only possible if détente is extended to the ideological sphere, and it presupposes greater openness in public life. I have stressed the need for international agreements to limit arms supplies to other states, special agreements to halt production of new weapons systems, treaties banning secret rearmament, the elimination of strategically unbalancing factors, and in particular a ban on multi-warhead nuclear missiles.

What would be the ideal international agreement on disarmament on the technical plane?

I believe that prior to such an agreement we must have an official declaration—though not necessarily public in the initial stages—on the extent of military potential (ranging from the number of nuclear warheads to forecast figures on the number of personnel liable for military service), with, for example, an indication of areas of "potential confrontation." The first step would be to ensure that for every single strategic area and for all sorts of military strength an adjustment would be made to iron out the superiority of one party to the agreement in relation to the other. (Naturally this is the kind of pattern that would be liable to some adjustment.) This would in the first place obviate the possibility of an agreement in one strategic area (Europe, for instance) being utilized to strengthen military positions in another area (e.g., the Soviet-Chinese border). In the second place, potential imbalances arising from the difficulty of equating different weapons systems would be excluded. (It would, for example, be difficult to say how many batteries of the ABM type would correspond to a cruiser, and so on.)

The next step in disarmament would entail proportional and simultaneous de-escalation for all countries and in all strategic areas. Such a formula for "balanced" two-stage disarmament would ensure continuous security for all countries, an interrelated equilibrium between armed forces in areas where there is a potential danger of confrontation, while at the same time providing a radical solution to the economic and social problems that have arisen as a result of militarization. In the course of time a great many experts and politicians have put forward similar views, but hitherto these have not had significant impact. However, now that humanity is faced with a real threat of annihilation in the holocaust of nuclear explosion, I hope that we will not hesitate to take this step. Radical and balanced disarmament is in effect both necessary and possible, constituting an integral part of a manifold and complicated process for the solution of the menacing and urgent problems facing the world. The new phase in international relations which has been called détente, and which appears to have culminated with the Helsinki Conference, does in principle open up certain possibilities for a move in this direction.

The Final Act signed at the Helsinki Conference is particularly noteworthy because for the first time official expression was given to an approach which appears to be the only possible one for a solution of international security problems. This document contains far-reaching declarations on the relationship between international security and preservation of human rights, freedom of information, and freedom of movement. These rights are guaranteed by solemn obligations entered into by the participating nations. Obviously we cannot speak here of a guaranteed result, but we can speak of fresh possibilities that can only be realized as a result of long-term planned activities, in which the participating nations, and especially the democracies, maintain a unified and consistent attitude.

Regarding the problem of human rights, I should like to speak mainly of my own country. During the months since the Helsinki Conference there has been no real improvement in this direction. In fact there have been attempts on the part of hard-liners to "give the screw another turn," in international exchange of information, the freedom to choose the country in which one wishes to live, travel abroad for studies, work, or health reasons, as well as ordinary tourist travel. To illustrate my assertion, I should like to give you a few examples—chosen at random and without any attempt to provide a complete picture.

You all know, even better than I do, that children from Denmark can get on their bicycles and cycle off to the Adriatic. No one would ever suggest that they were "teenage spies." But Soviet children are not allowed to do this! I am sure you are familiar with analogous examples.

The UN General Assembly, influenced by the socialist states, has imposed restrictions on the use of satellites for international TV transmissions. Now that the Helsinki Conference has taken place, there is every reason to deal afresh with this problem. For millions of Soviet citizens this is an important and interesting matter.

In the Soviet Union there is a severe shortage of artificial limbs and similar aids for invalids. But no Soviet invalid, even though he may have received formal invitation from a foreign organization, is allowed to travel abroad in response to such an invitation.

Soviet newsstands rarely offer non-Communist newspapers, and it is not possible to buy every issue of Communist periodicals. Even informative magazines like *Amerika* are in very short supply. They are on sale only at a small number of newsstands and are immediately snapped up by eager buyers.

Any person wishing to emigrate from the Soviet Union must have a formal invitation from a close relative. For many this is an insoluble problem—for 300,000 Germans, for example, who wish to go to West Germany. (The emigration quota for Germans is 5,000 a year which means that one might be forced to wait sixty years!) The situation for those who wish to be reunited with relatives in Socialist countries is particularly tragic. There is no one to plead their case, and in such circumstances the arbitrary behavior of the authorities knows no bonds.

The freedom to travel and the freedom to choose where one wishes to work and live are still violated in the case of millions of collective-farm workers, and in the situation of hundreds of thousands of Crimean Tatars, who thirty years ago were cruelly and brutally deported from the Crimea and who to this day have been denied the right to return to their homeland.

The Helsinki Accord confirms the principle of freedom of conscience. However, a relentless struggle will have to be carried on if the provisions of this agreement are to be realized in practice. In the Soviet Union today many thousands of people are both judicially and extrajudicially persecuted for their convictions: for their religious faith and their desire to bring up their children in a religious spirit, or for reading and disseminating—often only to a few acquaintances—literature of which the state disapproves, but which from the standpoint of ordinary democratic practice is absolutely legitimate. On the moral plane, there is particular gravity in the persecution of persons who have defended other victims of unjust treatment, who have worked to publish and, in particular, to distribute information regarding both the persecution and trials of persons with deviant opinions and the conditions in places of imprisonment.

It is unbearable to consider that at the very moment we are gathered together in this hall on this festive occasion hundreds and thousands of prisoners of conscience are suffering from undernourishment, as the result of year-long hunger, of an almost total lack of proteins and vitamins in their diet, of a shortage of medicines (there is a ban on the sending of vitamins and medicines to inmates), and of overexertion. They shiver from cold, damp, and exhaustion in ill-lit dungeons, where they are forced to wage a ceaseless struggle for their human dignity and to maintain their convictions against the "indoctrination machine," in fact against the destruction of their souls. The special nature of the concentration-camp system is carefully concealed. The sufferings a handful have undergone, because they exposed the terrible conditions, provide the best proof of the truth of their allegations and accusations. Our concept of human dignity demands and immediate change in this system for all imprisoned persons, no matter how guilty they may be. But what about the sufferings of the innocent? Worst of all is the hell that exists in the special psychiatric clinics in Dnepropetrovsk, Sytchevka, Blagoveshchensk, Kazan, Chernyakhovsk, Orel, Leningrad, Tashkent....

There is no time for me today to describe in detail particular trials, or the fates of particular persons. There is a wealth of literature on this subject: may I draw your attention to the publications of Khronika Press in New York, which specializes in reprints of the Soviet *samisdat* periodical *The Chronicle of Current Events* and issues similar bulletins of current information. I should like to mention the names of some of the internees I know. I would ask you to remember that all prisoners of conscience and all political prisoners in my country share with me the honor of the Nobel Prize. Here are some of the names that are known to me:

Plyushch, Bukovsky, Gluzman, Moroz, Maria Semyonova, Nadezhda Svitlichnaya, Stefania Shabatura, Irina Stasiv-Kalinets, Irina Senik, Nijole Sadunaite, Anait Karapetian, Osipov, Kronid Lyubarsky, Shumuk, Vins, Rumachik, Khaustov, Superfin, Paulaitis, Simutis, Karavanskiy, Valery Marchenko, Shukhevich, Pavlenkov, Chernoglaz, Abankin, Suslenskiy, Meshener, Svitlichny, Safronov, Rode, Shakirov, Heifetz, Afanasiev, Ma-Khun, Butman, Lukianenko, Ogurtsov, Sergienko, Antoniuk, Lupynos, Ruban, Plakhotnyuk, Kovgar, Belov, Igrunov, Soldatov, Myattik, Kiirend, Jushkevich, Zdorovy, Tovmasian, Shakhverdian, Zagrobian, Airikian, Markosian, Arshakian, Mirauskas, Stus, Sverstiuk, Kandyba, Ubozhko, Romanyuk, Vorobyov, Gel, Pronyuk, Gladko, Malchevsky, Grazhis, Prishliak, Sapeliak, Kalinets, Suprei, Valdman, Demidov, Bernitchuk, Shovkovy, Gorbachov, Berchov, Turik, Zhukauskas, Bolonkin, Lsovoi, Petrov, Chekalin, Gorodetsky, Chornovil, Balakhonov, Bondar, Kalinichencko, Kolomin, Plumpa, Jaugelis, Fedoseyev, Osadchy, Budulak-Sharigin, Makarenko, Malkin, Shtern, Lazar Lyubarsky, Feldman, Roitburd, Shkolnik, Murzhendo, Fyodorov, Dymshits, Kuznetsov, Mendelevich, Altman, Penson, Knokh, Vulf Zalmanson, Izrail Zalmanson, and many, many others. Among those unjustly exiled are Anatoly Marchenko, Nashpits, and Tsitlyonok.

Mustafa Dzhemilev, Kovalev, and Tverdokhlebov are awaiting trial. There is no time to mention all the prisoners I know of, and there are many more whom I do not know, or of whom I have insufficient knowledge. But their names are all implicit in what I have to say, and I should like those whose names I have not announced to forgive me. Every single name, mentioned as well as unmentioned, represents a hard and heroic destiny, years of suffering, years of struggling for human dignity.

A final solution to persecutions can be based on international agreement—amnesty for political prisoners, for prisoners of conscience in prisons, internment camps, and psychiatric clinics as set forth in a UN General Assembly resolution. This proposal involves no intervention in the internal affairs of any country. It would apply to every state on the same basis—to the Soviet Union, to Indonesia, to Chile, to the Republic of South Africa, to Spain, to Brazil, and to every other country. Since the protection of human rights has been proclaimed in the United Nations Declaration of Human Rights, there can be no reason to call this issue a matter of purely internal or domestic concern. In order to achieve this goal, no efforts can be too great, however long the road may seem. And that the road is long was clearly shown during the recent session of the United Nations, in the course of which the United States moved a proposal for political amnesty, only to withdraw it after attempts had been made by a number of countries to expand the scope of the amnesty. I much regret what took place. A problem cannot be removed from circulation. I am profoundly convinced that it would be better to liberate a certain number of people—even though they might be guilty of some offense or other—than to keep thousands of innocent people locked up or exposed to torture.

Without losing sight of an overall solution of this kind, we must fight against injustice and the violation of human rights for every individual person separately. Much of our future depends on this.

In struggling to defend human rights we ought, I am convinced, first and foremost to protect the innocent victims of regimes installed in various countries, without demanding the destruction or total condemnation of these regimes. We need reform, not revolution. We need a flexible, pluralist, tolerant society, which selectively and experimentally can foster a free, undogmatic use of the experiences of all kinds of social systems. What is détente? What is rapprochement? We are concerned not with words, but with a willingness to create a better and more decent society, a better world order.

Thousands of years ago human tribes suffered great privations in the struggle to survive. It was then important not only to be able to handle a club, but also to possess the ability to think intelligently, to take care of the knowledge and experience garnered by the tribe, and to develop the links that would provide cooperation with other tribes. Today the human race is faced with a similar test. In infinite space many civilizations are bound to exist, among them societies that may be wiser and more "successful" than ours. I support the cosmological hypothesis which states that the development of the universe is repeated in its basic characteristics an infinite number of times. Further, other civilizations, including more "successful" ones, should exist an infinite number of times on the "preceding" and "following" pages of the Book of the Universe. Yet we should not minimize our sacred endeavors in this world, where, like faint glimmers in the dark, we have emerged for a moment from the nothingness of dark unconsciousness into material existence. We must make good the demands of reason and create a life worthy of ourselves and of the goals we only dimly perceive.

Note: The Nobel Lecture was read in Oslo, December 11, 1975, not by Sakharov, but by his wife, Elena Bonner. Sakharov had applied on October 20 for an exit visa to attend the award ceremony and deliver his speech, but his request was refused, according to an official's published statement, "for reasons of security, because A. Sakharov is the possessor of exceptionally important state and military secrets."

Bowing to the inevitable, Sakharov wrote the Nobel Committee of the Norwegian Parliament, designating his wife—who was then in Italy for treatment of advancing glaucoma—to be his official representative. "Over the past years," he wrote, "to a considerable degree her selfless support and help, sometimes her initiative, and our mutual understanding have made possible the public activity of which you have honored me so highly."

Instead of flying to Oslo, Sakharov and a group of friends, including two whom he had wanted to invite as his guests to the Nobel ceremonies, went to Vilnius, the postwar capital of Lithuania, for the trial of a close and respected colleague in the human rights movement, the biologist Sergei Kovalev.

From Andrei Dmitrivich Sakharov, *Alarm and Hope.* Copyright © 1978 by Alfred A. Knopf, Inc. Reprinted by permission.

Document 123:
A FREE PRESS IN THE SOVIET UNION (1988)
Mikhail S. Gorbachev

Mikhail S. Gorbachev came to power in the Soviet Union in 1984, and had to deal with many crucial issues in the Soviet Union, including the 1986 nuclear disaster at Chernobyl, the war in Afghanistan, internal nationalist movements, and the consequences of his policies of glastnost *and* perestroika. *The new policy of "openness" is evident in the exchange of free dialogue reproduced below, where Gorbachev argues the usefulness of a free press in a one-party system.*

[Gorbachev.—]In the past, the mass news media was a monopoly controlled by certain people, and we know where that led. Now we see that another group of people wants to use a press monopoly on the sly as a nationwide rostrum. We want a pluralism of opinions. Therefore, we must make it possible for different viewpoints to be expressed; then the entire spectrum of attitudes and problems will become clearer, and on this basis a solution will emerge.

M.A. Ulyanov.—We have two monopolies now. One is at the local level—

M.S. Gorbachev.—That's just it: We don't need to replace one monopoly with another, one half-truth with another half-truth. We need the whole truth as we need life itself, we need to know it and restructure it on socialist principles, on the principles of our morality, and not to suit another monopoly group. In general, during the period in which we are setting our line as to how we will live in the future, we should be thinking not about what chair someone is going to wind up in tomorrow, we should be thinking about the country, about the fate of the country. Then we will find the truth. (Applause.)

The difference between the local press and the central press consists of two factors. On the one hand, the local press embarked more slowly on the path of restructuring and has still not fully developed the potential of openness and democracy. This is true. On the other hand, it has avoided some bad things that the central press has sometimes presented to us. A person can be insulted in our newspapers and magazines. Is this really permissible in a socialist society? The conference must speak out resolutely on this point, but at the same time openness and criticism must be preserved as forms for the permanent existence of an active exchange of opinions in the country. Without this, we will not be able to accomplish the tasks facing us. In my opinion, you and I have no difference in views, Mikhail Aleksandrovich.

M.A. Ulyanov.—May I ask you a question, Mikhail Sergeyevich?

M.S. Gorbachev.—Please do.

M.S. Ulyanov.—Are you in favor of having there actually be no mistakes and having no one be insulted, and therefore of belittling the press, or, on the contrary, are you in favor of elevating the role of the press, as I understood you to say, even if we make mistakes? In this struggle, there may be mistakes—

M.S. Gorbachev.—Mikhail Aleksandrovich, since we are saying that the primary lesson of the past is that the people were excluded from the process of working out and adopting decisions, today we must include people in these matters through political democracy, the press and public organizations. At the same time, we cannot allow the press—this rostrum of all the people—to become the special department of some new group. In the past there was one group, now there is another. That is the issue here. A distinction must be drawn. (Prolonged applause.)

I do not see any difference of opinion here, and I even welcome the fact that you began this discussion, because you have given me the opportunity to take part in it. There should be complete clarity on this point. If someone is touched by a critical article in the press and he feels discomfort about it, but the article was right—well then, he should swallow the criticism, go to people and explain why things are the way they are, and think about how to rectify the situation. Then our Party will live. Under the one-party system, we will have the sort of democracy that has never been dreamed of by any of those people abroad who present themselves as a model of democracy or wish to do so. And there are many of them in the world now.

M.A. Ulyanov.—It is perfectly right that the press is a mighty weapon, that it must be used skillfully and in the interests of the people and the Party.

M.S. Gorbachev.—Correct. (Applause.)

M.A. Ulyanov.—But it is also a weapon that can punish. This is also true.

From M.A. Ulyanov, "Pluralistic Press Works for Democracy in One-Party System," originally in *Pravda* and *Izvestia*, June 30, 7–8. Condensed text in *The Current Digest of the Soviet Press XL* (1988), 8.

Document 124:
A STATE OF EMERGENCY: ALL POWER TRANSFERRED TO THE STATE COMMITTEE (1991)
Gennadi Yanayev

Gennadi Yanayev, Vice-President of the USSR led a coup d'état against Mikhail Gorbachev in August 1991. Document 124 is Yanayev's speech to the Heads of State and Government of the Soviet Republics informing them of the coup and Document 125 is a justification of the coup in the name of "law and order."

At the instruction of the Soviet leadership I hereby notify you that a state of emergency is introduced in individual localities of the Union of Soviet Socialist Republics for a period of six months from August 19, 1991, in keeping with the Constitution and laws of the U.S.S.R.

All power in the country is transferred for this period to the State Committee for the State of Emergency in the U.S.S.R.

The measures that are being adopted are temporary. They in no way mean renunciation of the course toward profound reforms in all spheres of life of the state and society.

These are forced measures, dictated by the vital need to save the economy from ruin and the country from hunger to prevent the escalation of the threat of a large-scale civil conflict with unpredictable consequences for the peoples of the U.S.S.R. and the entire international community.

The most important objective of the state of emergency is to secure conditions that would guarantee each citizen's personal safety and the safety of his or her property.

It is envisaged to liquidate anticonstitutional, ungovernable and essentially criminal military formations spreading moral and physical terror in several regions of the U.S.S.R. and serving as a catalyst for disintegration processes.

The entire range of measures adopted is directed at the earliest stabilization of the situation in the U.S.S.R., the normalization of social and economic life, the implementation of necessary transformations, and the creation of conditions for the country's all-round development.

Any other way would lead to enhanced confrontation and violence, to the innumerable suffering of our peoples and the creation of a dangerous focus of tension from the viewpoint of international security.

The temporary emergency measures by no means affect international commitments assumed by the Soviet Union under existing treaties and agreements.

The U.S.S.R. is prepared to develop further its relations with all states on the basis of universally recognized principles of good-neighborliness, equality, mutual benefit, and noninterference in internal affairs of each other.

We are convinced that our current difficulties are transitory in character and the Soviet Union's contribution to preserving peace and consolidating international security will remain substantial.

The leadership of the U.S.S.R. hopes that the temporary emergency measures will find proper understanding on the part of the peoples and governments, and the United Nations Organization.

From *Vital Speeches of the Day*, Volume LVII, No. 23, September 15, 1991, 706.

Document 125:
THE GRAVEST CRISIS: TO RESTORE LAW AND ORDER (1991)
Gennadi Yanayev

Ladies and Gentlemen, dear friends, comrades, as I am sure you know from the media reports, due to the inability to continue in office, and under article 127.7 of the U.S.S.R. Constitution, of the U.S.S.R. president, the Vice President has taken office of the U.S.S.R. president.

I'm addressing you, Mister—you, ladies and gentlemen, at a crucial moment for the Soviet Union and for the entire international community who took a path and have gone a long way toward reform, and now the Soviet Union has faced a deep crisis which can call into question further reform and bring major upheavals in the international scene.

It is not secret to anyone that a drastic drop in production, which is not being compensated by alternative economic structures, posing a real threat to further development and survival of the U.S.S.R. nations. The situation has gone out of control in the U.S.S.R. and we are facing a situation of multi-rule.

This is a cause of popular discontent. We're also facing a threat of disintegration, a breakup of a single economic space, a single space of civil liberties, single defense, and a single foreign policy.

A normal life under these circumstances is impossible. In many regions of the U.S.S.R., due to interethnic rivalry, there is a bloodshed, and the breakup of the Soviet Union would entail the gravest internal and international repercussions.

Under the circumstances, we have no other alternative but to take resolute action in order to stop the country from sliding down to a disaster.

As I am sure you know, in order to provide an effective government under the state of emergency, it has been decided to set up a State Committee for the State of Emergency in the U.S.S.R., which will consist of Mr. Baklanov, first deputy chairman of the Defense Council; Mr. Kryuchkov, Chairman of the K.G.B.; Mr. Pavlov, Soviet Prime Minister; Mr. Pugo, who is Minister of the Interior; Mr. Starodubtsev, chairman of the U.S.S.R. Peasants Council; Mr. Tizyakov, president of the Transport and Communications Association; Mr. Yazov, Soviet Defense Minister; and Gennadi Yanayev, Acting President of the U.S.S.R.

Today I would like to say the following. The State Committee on the State of Emergency in the U.S.S.R. is well aware of the gravest crisis which we're going through, and it is determined to take full responsibility and to adopt urgent measures to get the country out of the crisis. We pledge to insure a nationwide discussion of the draft union treaty, and every citizen of the U.S.S.R. will have the opportunity to assess this document at his leisure and make a decision that will shape the future of our multinational homeland.

We are determined without further delay to restore law and order, stop the bloodshed, and to wage relentless war on the criminal underworld and to root out this social scourge. We will rid our cities of crime and will prevent further pilfering.

We stand for genuine democratic reforms, for a consistent reform policy toward a social renewal and economic prosperity which will enable our country to adopt the place it deserves in the world community of nations.

But the development of the country must not be built on the falling living standards. Without departing from the human rights principles, we will emphasize the protection of rights of those individuals who are most at disadvantage and suffer most from inflation, economic disintegration, crime and corruption. We will develop an economic diversification, we will uphold free enterprise and create all the conditions for the development of production and the services sector. Our top priority is food and housing.

We will mobilize all the forces to meet these most urgent needs of the people. We call on the peasants, the workers and the working intelligentsia—in other words, all Soviet people, to re-establish labor discipline and to uphold production in order to continue forward. On this will depend the future of our children and grandchildren and the future of our homeland.

We are a peaceful nation and we will strictly adhere to the obligations we have assumed. We have no claims on anyone at all. We want to live in peace and harmony with everyone, but we state that nobody, but nobody, can infringe on our sovereignty, independence and territorial integrity, and any attempt to dictate terms to our country, whoever they come from, will be stopped.

Our multi-national country has lived for generations in pride for its homeland. We have never been ashamed of our patriotic feelings, and we think it justified that the younger generation be raised in that spirit.

To do nothing at this crucial period means to take a grave responsibility for tragic, really unpredictable circumstances. Anyone who wants to live and work in peace, who does not accept the bloodshed, who wants to see his homeland in prosperity must take the only right choice. We call on all genuine patriots, all people of good will to put an end to this turbulent time. We call on all the citizens of U.S.S.R. to fulfill their responsibility and to provide the necessary support to the State Emergency Committee to get the country out of the crisis.

All constructive proposals from individuals and work collectives will be considered with gratitude as their manifestation of patriotism and a desire to re-establish multinational friendship for the revival of our homeland. I thank you.

From *Vital Speeches of the Day*, Volume LVII, NO. 23, September 15, 1991, 707.

Document 126:
A BOLD FACED AND UNPRECEDENTED COUP D'ETAT (1991)
Boris N. Yeltsin

Boris N. Yeltsin, President of the Russian Republic, the largest state within the former USSR, defied the leaders of the Coup in Moscow and rallied his people to face down the tanks sent to the Russian parliamentary building. The following speech by Yeltsin was delivered before the Russian Parliament soon after he had stood on a tank defending the movement towards democratization on August 21, 1991.

Distinguished people, deputies. Russia and the country, as a whole, are living through a dramatic period in its history, or perhaps this is a tragic period. In the history of our country there have been several attempts to stage a coup, at a time when it would have seemed that democracy was on the rise, and gathering momentum. The right-wing forces have tried several times to stage a coup d'etat.

You would recall that the first time it was at the beginning of the year, but at that time they were scared by the statements made by the Minister of Foreign Affairs, Eduard Shevardnadze, which created a situation when public opinion in Russia, in the country, and in the world scared them.

The second time it took place at a time when virtually the same people, i.e., Kryuchkov, Yazov, tried to demand special powers for themselves, and the removal of the President from his post.

And that was the second attempt that failed, and the Supreme Soviet of the U.S.S.R. did not support that attempt, and finally, the third attempt, which did prove to be successful, took place just a short time ago. It was when the President was on vacation, but now he is incommunicado in the Crimea, and this is an unconstitutional coup d'etat. It has succeeded. It is unconstitutional because there have been no statements made by the President of the country, either in writing, or oral statements on the television, on the radio. There has been no medical examination, either by Soviet doctors or international experts, stating that he was unable to perform his functions.

According to the information that is available to us, and this is information provided by Gorbachev's doctor on the 19th, after which he was removed from his post, Gorbachev had been in good health, suffering from a minor back pain which could not affect his ability to work or speak.

This is a bold-faced and unprecedented coup d'etat in a situation where democracy is on the rise, and you see that the people taking part in the coup are on the right. They couldn't find at least a few people, so-called quasi democrats, to join them, although they did attempt to find such people, but the people they approached refused to cooperate with them.

They refused to take part in this unconstitutional plot. Now this is what we have done.

Firstly, during the first hours in the morning of the 19th, we issued a statement to the people of Russia which was signed by myself, Comrade Silayev and Khasbulatov.

Although the mass media of the Russian Federation has been placed under a virtual blackout, we have set up a radio station right in this building, and we've talked to people on the phone, and we have succeeded in broadcasting that statement and the subsequent decrees of the President of the Russian Federation to other regions of the country.

These are some of the measures that we have taken.

Decree No. 59 proclaimed that the committee was unconstitutional. We have set up Russia's Committee for Defense. We have published a decree stating that the troops of the K.G.B. and the Ministry of the Interior, as well as the army, are placed under the jurisdiction of the President of the Russian Federation, in the absence of the Commander in Chief of the armed forces, and taking into account the fact that the Minister of Defense is a criminal, that meant that we have to assume the responsibility for the armed forces on the territory of the Russian Federation.

Then we published a decree which set up a group headed by top ranking officials of the Russian Federation. The group was dispatched to the heartland of Russia and it started work. That was designed to set up an additional center of power if an attempt were made to seize the building and to remove the leadership of the Russian Federation from power.

In that event the group would have assumed authority.

As regards the actions of Yanayev, Pavlov, and others, there was a decree on the armed forces. The President of the Russian Federation has assumed the authority over the armed forces. The Tulskaya and Kantinuyevskaya Divisions, airborne troops, have gone over to the side of the Russian Federation, and they are acting on orders of the President of the Russian Federation.

What are the reasons for the failure of the attempts to intern the leadership of the Russian Federation? The President, the chairman of the Council of Ministers, and the acting chairman of the Supreme Soviet of the Russian Federation. The reasons for that are that the Tulskaya Division, instead of seizing the building of the Russian Federation Parliament, protected the building of the Russian Parliament from attack.

We are grateful to the men of the division and General Lebedev, although he is obviously under stress, but by a decree of the President of the Russian Federation, I have assumed the responsibility for that, and I have assumed the responsibility for any actions taken by the law enforcement agencies and the troops acting on my orders.

I have also signed a decree on the operation of enterprises on the territory of the Russian Federation, a decree on the economic sovereignty of the Russian Federation. Let me elaborate on this.

Taking into account that the union treaty was to be signed on the 20th, we had an agreement with the President of the union, that on the 21st and the 22d we would sign a decree transferring the property and the enterprises on the territory of the Russian Federation to the jurisdiction of the Russian Federation. We wanted to place those enterprises under the jurisdiction of the Russian Federation.

But now that the union treaty was not signed yesterday, because of the actions taken by the unconstitutional group of rebels, and since the President is virtually incommunicado, I have signed a decree providing for the economic sovereignty of the Russian Federation, stating that all property on the territory of the Russian Federation is placed under the jurisdiction of the Russian Federation.

In light of the curfew imposed in Moscow and Leningrad, I have removed the commanders of the Moscow and Leningrad military districts, and I have appointed different persons who act on orders of appropriate authorities and I have also appointed the Minister for Defense of the Russian Federation, Colonel General Kobets.

I have also signed several appeals. I have already said that I have signed an appeal to the citizens of Russia and the people of Moscow. I have sent an address to President Bush. I have signed an appeal to servicemen, and to the citizens of Russia, to Patriarch Aleksy II, the Patriarch of all Russia. The first address was delivered by hand, by Vice President Rutskoy, and the Patriarch has supported us at this difficult period of time, and he said that the believers will support us at this difficult time.

As Khasbulatov said earlier, we have formulated an ultimatum consisting of 10 points. We talked with Lukyanov about this ultimatum, but we cannot trust Lukyanov when he says that he did not know about the imminent coup. We cannot trust him.

Also I have authorized troops to take the building of Parliament under the protection of troops, because there were plans to launch an attack on the building of Parliament, and it is only our decisive action and the actions of the people of Moscow who staged an all-day vigil at the building, we were inside the building and the people of Moscow were outside the building in the rain, and that was the major factor which helped to stop tanks and armored personnel carriers which tried to storm the building and in turn the members of the Russian government.

Yes, I think the people of Moscow deserve praise for their resolute actions.

Also, the Minister for Foreign Affairs of the Russian Federation, Kozyrev has been dispatched to the United Nations organization in order to inform both Secretary General Pérez de Cuéllar, and the international community about the unconstitutional events unfolding in this country and the actions of the government of the Russian Federation.

Over the past few hours I had telephone conversations with President Bush, President Mitterrand, Prime Minister Major, President of Czechoslovakia Havel, President of Bulgaria Zhelev, Mrs. Thatcher, and leaders of the union republics.

Let me be quite frank, and say that both Bush and Mitterand and others said in no uncertain terms that they condemned the unconstitutional coup d'etat and the actions of the group, and that they do not recognize any decisions they have taken, and they support the actions of the Russian leadership and they will take measures so that the international community supports our actions and makes its position clear.

Also, I called on them in order for them to demand, first, to establish communication with the President of the U.S.S.R., because the President is held incommunicado in the Crimea. The access to him has been blocked by the troops of the Ministry of the Interior, the K.G.B., and the naval vessels operating in the area, and the troops, security troops of the K.G.B., three circles of troops, and there is no access to the President here. There have been two attempts to get through to him but they have failed.

Silayev talked with Kryuchkov on the telephone, and the conversation has shown that they are trying to justify their actions, saying that they have been acting constitutionally, that Gorbachev is unable to perform his functions, but this is not true.

During the night, finally, Kryuchkov lifted the blockade around the Parliament building, and abandoned plans to seize the building.

I suggested, and he agreed, to go with me to Foros and to bring President Gorbachev back to Moscow, but I need your permission in order to do that.

Well, this is what I have been telling the President as well. Kryuchkov is due to appear at this session at 13 hours, and you will be able to ask him in person about the situation.

As regards the flight to the Crimea, I believe this is the only way of clarifying this situation. Given appropriate guarantees by Kryuchkov—well, let me say again, that I'm ready to go, but the decision is in your hands.

So this is the situation as of now. The leadership of the Russian Federation, the President and the leadership of the Supreme Soviet, and the Council of Ministers have been acting energetically, there is no panic, there is no despair, and we do hope that the days of the junta are numbered, and they must be removed from power. This committee must be dissolved, and the eight members of the committee should be brought to justice.

From *Vital Speeches of the Day*, Volume LVII, No. 23, September 15, 1991, 709–711.

CHAPTER 15 New Problems and New Rights

As we enter a period called the "post-Cold War era," more attention can be given to human problems that were obscured by our great concern with the East-West crisis after 1945. Often scholars of human rights speak of generations of human rights. The first, as we have seen, were political in nature and often required governments *not to act* in limiting rights. The second generation of social and economic rights required governments *to act* to reach new goals of well-being or opportunities. The same is true of the "third generation." These include attention to the environment, to minorities of various kinds within national states and collective or "group" rights.

Document 127:
KEEPING OUR BALANCE IN THE 90'S: WOMEN AT WORK, WOMEN AT HOME (1990)
Rosalyn Wiggins Berne

In the following speech, Rosalyn Wiggins Berne reflects on the change in women's lives of the last thirty years and the difficult juggling act that many women have as they try to fulfill their roles as a career woman, mother and manager of a home.

I happened to mention to our new baby sitter that I would be speaking to you this evening. After explaining the topic she looked puzzled, and so I turned the discussion and asked if her own mother worked outside of the home while they were growing up. She paused, and replied, "Well, I guess so. In those days. we didn't have no running water so she was hulling water from down at the well. And we heated in the stove, so she was carrying wood up to the house. She had all the washing, and tending to the chickens and garden and all, so I guess you could say she always worked." Our baby sitter is 40 years old. "Those days" for her were not so long ago. I realized after listening to her that my words to you this evening will not apply to all women. The subject addresses the lives of women who have a choice. And while in theory we all have choice, some of us have virtually none.

My reflections this evening are the result of a fairly extensive review of recent literature on the subject, interviews I conducted with twenty women, and my own personal and professional experiences.

In 1954 Ann Morrow Lindberg wrote *Gifts From the Sea*, in which she said,

"What a circus act we women perform every day of our lives. It puts the trapeze artist to shame. Look at s. We run a tight rope daily, balancing a pile of books on the head. Baby carriage, parasol, kitchen chair, still under control. Steady now! This is not the life of simplicity, but the life of multiplicity that the wise men warn us of. It leads not to unification but to fragmentation. It does not bring grace, it destroys the soul. And this is not true only of my life, I am forced to conclude; it is the life of millions of women in America. I stress American, because today, the American woman more than any other has the privilege of choosing such a life."

Thirty-five years ago, when these words were printed, the world was an entirely different place. The roles of men and women were clearly defined. And while there were certainly women pioneers forging their way into the professions, most women knew without a doubt that their primary responsibility lay with the family. If they needed for financial reasons to earn wages outside of the home, they did so. The primary focus, however, was not on our personal development but rather on the woman's commitment within the home. Well-to-do women who ventured forth in pursuit of careers, were not taken seriously, but considered a novelty; kind of cute. In those days, women were encouraged to marry so that they would be cared for, and to marry well meant finding a husband who made it so one did not have to work. Middle income women who did work did so out of economic need, risking the stigma that their husbands were not succeeding well enough to afford for them to stay at home. But, whether we worked for pleasure or necessity, women still, first and foremost, were mothers and wives. That was a time when childbirth meant a return to the home from our jobs and in most cases, we stayed at home with our young at least until they were school aged. Women worked conscientiously out of personal and societal obligation to sustain their responsibilities to the family and community. It was within that environment that Lindberg wrote of the fragmentation and multiplicity of a woman's life. Imagine what she might say if she were writing today.

Today, when on a weekday, I walk my son to the neighborhood playground, where we find empty swings, quiet benches, and solitude. Thirty-five years ago, that same park would have been filled with the sound of playing children, crying babies, and chatting women whose discussions would have lent support to one another for the lives they were living. Not today. Today, most children play in day care centers, or in the backyards of baby sitters' homes.

Life now is significantly different from the days when our mothers pushed strollers to the park. As far as I can tell, it is a much more complicated world, especially for American women. Not only have we got a pile of books on our head dealing with family and home, but both arms are filled as well dealing with our careers. Today, over 80 percent of wage earning women are also mothers, and managers of the home. Whether this lifestyle is chosen out of economic necessity, economic preference, or out of a desire for career advancement and intellectual fulfillment, the choices have been made. And with these choices, we have inherited difficult and burdensome consequences.

Consider the following statistics:

The number of working women with children under age 1 increased 70 percent during the past decade. Seventy-three percent of employed women are of child-bearing age, and women with children under 6 are the fastest growing segment of the workforce. The number of divorced, widowed, or separated working women with children under 18 years of age increased 76 percent between 1971 and 1982. In 1984, 11 million men and 6 million women were the only wage earners of their families. Among all American families, nearly 1 out of 5 is maintained by a woman, with 1/3 of them having incomes below the poverty line. Today, fewer than 9.9 percent of U.S. households consist of a man working outside the home and a woman at home taking care of the household and children.

This is the reality, but it is also a reality that women have greater opportunities than ever before for achieving economic and professional success. The opportunities are greater to define our roles as individuals and women. We have much more freedom of choice in career, mate, offspring, and lifestyle. Thirty-five years ago, it would have been difficult and in many cases impossible for our mothers to become MBA's; M.D.'s; C.P.A.'s; clergy; electricians; computer technicians; dentists and newscasters.

However, the privilege of choice is bitter sweet. Because, with choice, comes the natural obligation and desire to choose. Although our choices have brought us freedom, they have also brought us hectic, fragmented, complex lives. The problem isn't hard work. Hard work is not new to women. On the contrary, in many ways life was much harder in the past. The stress we bear today is a different beast from the pain we carried in the past. Today's burden is more mental than it is physical; it is more a matter of unclear role definition; guilt; lack of support and the emotional stress inherent in a life of mulitiple, conflicting responsibilities.

In the past, only very few women had, and exercised, the choices open to us today. Now, more women are equal or major wage earners in the household. As the cost of living soars, two incomes per family are required to sustain the quality of life given us by our parents, so there is pressure on women to earn a living as well as to be a homemaker. Today, the breadth and complexity of a woman's role expands far beyond what our parents would have imagined as they began their adult lives, 30, 40 and 50 years ago.

The concern is not about having choices. In fact, most women if asked would say they are grateful to the women of the past whose sweat and devotion and tears have created the opportunities we relish today. Most of us enthusiastically embrace the opportunities that exist. Technology has given us time our grandmothers never had. The problem is that we have filled that time in the exercise of our new found options, and are attempting to handle husbands, children, commmunity work, shopping, laundry, house repairs, cooking, political leadership, PTA *and* careers. Careers in which women demand to be treated equal with men, which has meant working the same 50 and 60 hour weeks that men put in at the office in order to succeed at the level that men do. As women today we drive cars and tractors and ships and shopping carts. We wear overalls and tailored suits and aprons and maternity clothes.

We carry brief cases and shopping bags and chain saws and bricks and vacuum cleaners and calculators and ledgers and babies.

Thirty-five years ago, Anne Morrow Lindberg wrote:

"To be a woman is to have interest and duties, raying out in all directions, from the central mother-core, like spokes from the hub of a wheel. The pattern of our lives is essentially circular. We must be open to all points of the compass, husband, children, friends, home, community; stretched out, exposed, sensitive like a spider's web to each breeze that comes. How difficult for us, then, to achieve a balance in the midst of these contradictory tensions; and yet, how necessary for the proper functioning of our lives."

This she wrote a generation ago in a changing and yet traditional society. Today, however, we function in the midst of radical social change, in a transition of rapidly shifting roles, responsibilities and expectations. Expectations from others and expectations self imposed. Women's diverse interests and aspirations have few, if any natural limits...which is a dream many mothers worked for their daughters to realize. But that dream also has elements of a nightmare for a number of reasons. For one, we are functioning amidst change, in a social-economic structure which is not yet adapted to embrace the roles we are attempting to assume. It is a nightmare because many employed mothers feel like they are going at it alone. Far more adapted to the working world than it is to working women who are mothers, most of us function with very little understanding from our employers, who have never before been asked to share any interest or responsibility in the family or in our dual responsibilities to work and home. Far more adapted to the working world than men are to the world of child care and home management, women may have to accept that most men simply are not inclined to do as much as we do in upkeep of the home. Dual career couples and single mothers in the work force face the difficult task of finding child care and then often worry about the quality of care that we do arrange. Many of us have the added responsibility of caring for our aging parents. Employed women are in need of more flexible work options and yet want to excel in the work force. How many of us are there still fighting for equal pay and comparable worth? While adjusting to the changes, and carrying the myriad of responsibilities, many women are beginning to ask whether what we are attempting is even possible. Possible at least, without the major sacrifices which seem to accompany the choice to pursue this lifestyle.

Eighty percent of the women in the work force are mothers and spouses who have chosen, for whatever reason, to assume multiple and competing roles. While this choice makes for a stressful, imbalanced life, the benefits are apparent. Women are experiencing greater economic gains, greater independence, and the enhanced sense of self-worth which comes from making valuable contributions in the work force. But something is wrong. Each of the twenty-two women I spoke with and nearly all of the literature on the subject I reviewed, indicated a deep and prevalent discontent with trying to do it all.

Perhaps what we need to do as individuals and as couples is to think realistically beyond the benefits about what these decisions mean in sacrifices. We should ask ourselves, for example, honestly, do we in some way sacrifice our children's well being when we choose full-time demanding careers? One local resident thinks so and expressed his concerns recently in a newspaper editorial. He writes...

"I firmly believe that many of the problems we are now experiencing with our children stem from the fact that we as a society no longer value motherhood. To be a mother and to stay at home at least for the first four years of your child's early development has taken on a stigma that labels women, especially college age women as something less than a whole person. Our priorities in this country have shifted so that now we place more value on earning large sums of money or on self-centered goals related to career-advancement. No longer do we value as our greatest asset the one thing that can truly bring us happiness—our children. The concept of people sacrificing today for the tomorrow of their children has become quaint and out of date. Who in today's world would suggest that women reassume the lifetime role of homemaker. But unless women, and men, at all economic levels of society become more willing to participate regularly in the development of their children, even if it means personal sacrifice, nothing the government can do will succeed in solving our long term slide into a third rate country."

Could he be correct? It is certainly a concern most employed mothers have, conscious or unconscious. It's no wonder so many of us struggle to find a sense of balance when so much seems to be riding on our decisions. But what of the other side? The side which asks why must it be the woman who gives up the option to pursue a career?

Having children almost necessarily means a woman will sacrifice some degree of career success. Most women have found re-entry into the work force to be very difficult after an extended maternity/child rearing leave. And executive women with children truly forgo the ultimate reach for the top of the corporate ladder. Though 90 percent of male executives have children, only 35 percent of their female counterparts are parents. In a 1986 survey of the 413 women that the largest U.S. companies identified as corporate officers, the typical woman was a 44-year-old white protestant who was married, childless and spent fewer than 10 hours a week on homemaking tasks. These women believed that motherhood must be forgone to succeed.

Do we sacrifice healthy relationships with our husbands? Perhaps not. One recent study revealed that the highest level of marital satisfaction is found among dual career couples. On the other hand, husbands of fully employed mothers may feel an extra burden as well. They too come home to a household of chores waiting to be done. It is more work for both husband and wife at the end of a dual-career work day.

Whether the compromise is child-rearing, marriage, career, or simply self-nurturing and preservation, sacrifice is unavoidable. At home mothers have shared with me that given current social patterns, it is emotionally difficult to feel fully valued and personally fulfilled while homemaking full time. Fully employed mothers have shared that it is simply unrealistic, in today's culture, to think that we can excel in a work force that rewards excessive time commitments, and at the end of the day, to be energetic and enthusiastic for their children; cheerful and loving for their husbands.

The scenario of the perfect career, wife, and mother is a brutal myth. It is the myth of Clare Huxtible. Wife on the popular TV Cosby show, Clare Huxtible—a successful lawyer, who returns home at the end of a day in court to a beautiful, clean, orderly house, to greet happy, well adjusted, smiling children. She is a devoted and loving wife with an adoring supportive husband. Clare Huxtible; woman with a beautiful physique, a radiant smile, and a demeanor always relaxed and in control. There she is, greeting us every Thursday night at 8:00—the epitome of perfect grace; representing the perfect balance so many of us desperately aspire to achieve. The reality is, she does not, and cannot exist.

Any one who has pursued this path knows—something has to give, and does. The reality is that good day care is costly, and very difficult to find. The reality is that ambitious full-time employed mothers are ahead of society at large which has yet to adapt to their presence in the work force. As long as this is the case, most women are going to feel pain and frustration. We will wonder why our employers don't understand that sick babies have to stay home with someone, and that someone is us; we are going to question why it is so difficult to find a good paying part-time job, comparable to our skills and abilities; and we're going to wonder why we feel a constant sense of falling short; in effect *why we're trying to do it at all*. In fact, a recent and increasingly common trend is that employed women who are mothers are leaving the work place, and returning to traditional family roles—a trend which has its own sacrifices and rewards.

Women in the work force, mothers at home, women doing both, husbands, fathers, employers, and legislators...are all in transition—slowly responding to rapidly changing roles, expectations, and responsibilities of both women and men. Most men are having to rely on the role model provided by their own fathers who functioned in an entirely different world. But, these role models can no longer be relied upon, so men also are forging through new, untreaded territory.

An interesting article appeared in the *Chicago Tribune* which was captioned "Men Dragging Feet on Helping Working Wives in the Home." The article opens

"There she is, Ms. America. Dressed for success. Briefcase in one hand, preschooler clutching the other. On the fast track at work. Super mom at home. The woman who has it all, 1990's model. What she also has is most of the housework and child care—and a husband who is far more skilled at evading his fair share than she is at cajoling or bargaining or gently persuading him to do it."

The writer proceeds to say that men's underlying feelings about taking responsibility at home have changed much less than women's feelings have changed about forging some kind of identity at work.

Employing organizations are also using dated models; models based on the right to work ethic, where devotion to the job comes first, and family is cared for by someone else whose responsibility it is to do just that. But demographics are beginning to force the issue, and employers are having to look hard at the growing work force of women. For it's now a widely understood projection that by the year 2000, 61 percent of new entrants to the work force will be women. This means that change is inevitable. Tax breaks for employers who offer family leaves, job-sharing, part-time work and flexible hours may be necessary costs for doing business.

Society lags as well. I believe we need to revalue homemaking and child care so that women and men who choose this role will have sufficient social support, and so employed men will be more comfortable assuming sharing previously "female" roles. Marriage needs to evolve so that work-sharing couples can become role models of the future. Perhaps we also need to ask whether we can raise our children with values of equitable responsibility within the home and the work place. Wouldn't it be helpful if we taught our sons to cook, and clean, and change the diapers with a sense of satisfaction and esteem? Shouldn't we also teach our daughters to stop apologizing for self imposed failures and to stop nurturing unrealistic standards of success and self imposed guilt? Guilt about being out there while someone else cares for our children. Guilt about dusty window sills. Guilt about being too fatigued at the end of the day to give "quality time" to our husbands and children.

How can women find balance in the 90's? Personally, I do not think it is possible as long as we choose to assume multiple and conflicting, socially unsupported roles. What we can do is what women have always done: to bend, adjust, persist and respond to the demands of each individual moment, then pause briefly for rejuvenation.

Can we have it all? Yes. If we can be satisfied with giving less than 100 percent, or even 85 percent to everything we do. If we can live with the sense that nothing receives our full and devoted attention. If we can compromise our standards and expectations.

There was a time, not so long ago, that I aspired to have it all, and worked very hard in pursuit of it. Let me take a few minutes, by way of summary, to share with you a bit about my personal quest for balance and perfection.

In October of 1989, 6 months pregnant, I left my position as Director of Admissions at the Darden Graduate School of Business Administration to assume the position of Assistant Vice President of Administration for the University of Virginia. At the time, I was also a part-time Ph.D. student in Ethics. I don't know whether it was ego or just pure foolishness, but I was truly convinced that I could be mother to a newborn, graduate student and spouse, and do all three well. I worked very hard at this vision. I took four weeks maternity leave, returning energetically back to work. And then one day, the day care center teachers walked six children, including my son Ari, up to the Rotunda where my office was located. I nursed Ari, and then handed him back to the care provider. As they walked away—my baby, five other children and two adults—tears began to stream from my eyes, and then an overwhelming sense of grief welled up inside of me. I realized that I had fallen in love with our son, and that someone else, someone I didn't even know, was raising him. All at once, my goals, dreams, and values came crashing in on one another, and I began to doubt the decisions I had made. After two weeks of painful soul searching and discussions with my husband, it was clear to me that I should find a way to spend more time with Ari. Luckily, my former employer, an ardent supporter of professional working mothers, hired me back into a flexible position which supports my professional, scholarly and maternal needs.

The decision to leave a full-time, lucrative, fairly responsible position, in exchange for a life of mothering and low-keyed work was absolutely the right decision for me. But it might not have been for another woman. It is an individual choice, and in my opinion, it is not inherently, morally, a right or wrong choice, just a choice. But mine, and those of countless other women today, was not a choice without pain and some sorrow over the sacrifices made. Who knows what the ramifications are for my future career. But for now, I gladly take the smaller paycheck, and the lesser status for many wonderful hours at home with the family, and a saner, more balanced daily life.

Lindberg concluded her book by saying, "we cannot have all the beautiful shells from the sea." Perhaps this is the reality for women in the 90's.

From Rosalyn Wiggins Berne, "Keeping Our Balance in the 90s: Women at Work, Women at Home," *Vital Speeches of the Day*, Volume LVII, No. 2, November 1, 1990, 55–58.

Document 128:
THE RECOMMENDATIONS OF THE NATIONAL COMMISSION ON CHILDREN (1991)
Senator John D. Rockefeller IV

Senator Jay Rockefeller of West Virginia has been a strong proponent of increased services for children in the United States. An early backer of a national health program, he became a presidential candidate in 1992. In this speech, he summarizes the findings of the National Commission on Children on what needs to be done for America's children.

Good morning. Today I have the privilege of presenting the findings and recommendations of the National Commission on Children. With me at the podium are three commissioners: Berry Brazelton, Professor of Pediatrics at Harvard University; Marian Wright Edelman, President and Founder of the Children's Defense Fund; and Wade Horn, Commissioner of the Administration for Children, Youth, and Families in the Bush Administration. Also with us are William Woodside, Chairman of Sky Chefs, Inc. and Chairman of the Commission's Corporate Advisory Board, and Chri Hayes, the Commission's Executive Dirctor. Other members of the Commission are also present this morning.

Our report is an historic achievement. In a 32 to 0 vote, individuals with very different personal, professional, and political viewpoints have reached unanimous agreement on a bold blueprint for strengthening America's families and improving the health and well-being of the nation's children.

Are there differences among us? Yes, of course. Thoughtful and honest people will always differ on complex issues. But we are unanimous in our concern for America's children and families, and we share the same goals. We *all* want a nation where *every* family is strong and stable—where *no* child is touched by poverty and avoidable illness—where *every* child enters school ready to learn and *every* school provides an excellent education—and where *every* child is prepared for the privileges and responsibilities of parenthood, citizenship, and employment. So I am proud to declare our consensus on a course of action for the nation. This is a stunning achievement and a great victory for America's children and their families.

Over the past two and a half years, the National Commission on Children conducted an ambitious assessment of the current status and future prospects of America's children and families. We travelled the nation to investigate issues that touch the heart of our national well-being. We met the parents and children behind the statistics that are so widely studied and reported in the press. We struggled long and hard, through many months of intensive deliberations, to translate what we saw and heard into a bold yet realistic policy agenda to guide this nation through the 1990s.

What did we find? Not surprisingly, many children grow up healthy and happy, in strong, stable families. But far too many—of all races, in all income groups, and in all parts of the country—do not.

—Too many lack the time and attention of parents and other important adults. One in four children grows up with just one parent, almost always a mother. Absent fathers are the greatest disappearing act of the century. They simply are not there for their children—not physically, not emotionally, and not financially. Unfortunately, living with both parents is no guarantee either. We encountered mothers and fathers in two-parent families who are too stressed and drained to give their children the love and attention they need.

—Too many children—one in five—grow up in poverty, without the health care, adequate nutrition, and early childhood experiences necessary to succeed in school and in life. Poverty is hard enough on adults, but it's devastating for children. It robs many young people of health, hope, and opportunity.

—Too many youngsters—half a million—drop out of school each year. Those who do graduate often lack the basic skills to get a job or go to college. Half a million bear babies while they are still children themselves. More than half have tried illegal drugs by the time they leave high school. More than half consume alcohol on a regular basis. And more teenage boys die of gunshot wounds than of all natural causes combined.

These problems don't affect *every* child in America directly. But they place *every* child—and every one of us—in jeopardy. Our future as a democratic nation, a world leader, and an economic power depends as much on youngsters who are poor, ill educated, or alienated from the mainstream as on those who are more advantaged.

Americans claim to love children, but these are often empty words. The National Commission on Children has gone beyond rhetoric to craft a comprehensive plan that calls upon all Americans to step forward and do what is necessary to save our children, strengthen their families, and secure our future as a gret nation.

Several important themes are at the heart of our proposals:

First, all children need strong and stable families. The best way to help children is to help their families. Individually and collectively, our recommendations are aimed at strengthening families and enabling parents to do a good job of raising their children.

Second, all children have essential needs—for food, health care, and education—for hope and opportunities that lend meaning to life. These basic ingredients go together. We can't scrimp on any of them. So our recommendations address the needs of the whole child, at every stage of development from before birth through adolescence.

Third, as a nation we need to invest early in healthy children and strong families. We need to prevent problems before they occur instead of waiting—as we often do—until they are too mammoth to ignore. It's foolish and shortsighted to pay for intensive care but not prenatal care—for special education but not Head Start—for foster care but not family support—for prisons but not education and job opportunities. The Commission's recommendations focus on policies, practices, and personal behavior to *prevent* problems that harm children, weaken their families, and mortgage America's future.

Finally, meeting the needs of children and families is everybody's business. Solutions are within our reach, but they require leadership and sustained action by all of us, whether we are raising children or not—by employers and community organizations, and yes, by government at all levels. Make no mistake. What this nation needs are more child and family-centered values *and* better public and private sector policies to support *all* children, strengthen *all* families, and help those in special need.

Having said this, let me now introduce our recommendations. I will highlight several this morning and refer you to the Commission's report and other materials in your packets for more complete information.

First, children are the big economic losers of the last decade. They are the poorest Americans and have been since the mid-1970s. Poverty takes a terrible toll on children, yet our welfare system makes it difficult for low-income families to earn their way out of poverty. Middle-class families are hurting as well. Wages have stagnated over the past two decades, while the costs of housing, feeding, and clothing children, purchasing health care, and paying college tuition have skyrocketed. At the same time, the tax burden on working families with children nearly doubled. It's no wonder so many middle-class families can no longer make ends meet on just one paycheck.

To reduce childhood poverty and relieve the pressure on middle-class families, we propose a comprehensive income security package based on fundamental American values of work, family, and independance.

At its center is a $1,000 refundable child tax credit to replace the current personal exemption for children—a tax cut for families raising children. For middle-income families, this credit is worth three times the amount of the present exemption. For low-income families, it provides help without the stigma of welfare. For *all* families, it says that we think the job of raising children is important and valuable.

Second, working poor families have been playing by the rules for years and have the least to show for it. I know, because many of these families live in my state of West Virginia. This Commission thinks hard work should be rewarded. We strongly support the recent expansion of the Earned Income Tax Credit to make work pay and encourage low-income parents to get jobs and stay in the labor force.

Third, one parent should not be expected to bear the burden of two. All parents are responsible for supporting their children, whether they live with them or not. We recommend much tougher child support enforcement, because absent fathers have had a free ride long enough. In those instances where absent parents cannot pay child support, we propose a government-insured benefit for their children. This is a radical departure from present practice, so we first recommend a national demonstration which, if successful, should immediately be implemented nationwide.

Fourth, parents who are willing and able to work sometimes need a helping hand. For those moving from welfare to work, we recommend job training, child care, continued health insurance benefits, and other provisions of the Family Support Act. For those who have difficulty entering the job market on their own, we encourage states and communities to provide employment opportunities.

Full implementation of the Commission's income security package will make *all* families raising children economically better off. Middle-class families will keep more of what they earn. And the combination of a minimum wage job, the Earned Income Tax Credit, the refundable child tax credit, and guaranteed child support will lift most low-income families out of poverty—in a way that rewards work and encourages personal responsibility. Welfare could once again become the transitional program it was intended to be, helping families through periods of economic hardship rather than supporting them indefinitely and inadequately. Families who work hard and play by the rules will no longer lose out—and their children will be the biggest winners of all....The Commission's recommendations will improve the economic well-being of all families with children and will significantly reduce the population of children growing up in poverty.

Our second set of recommendations addresses the health needs of America's children. Here, we did not reach consensus. We *all* agree that every child deserves the chance to be born healthy and to grow up healthy, but we disagree on the best means to achieve this goal. I will summarize the recommendations endorsed by all but nine of the 34 commissioners....

Speaking for the majority, we believe first and foremost that parents are responsible for protecting their children's health by protecting their own health and being models for healthful behavior. Parents must do everything in their power to provide a safe home environment, and seek essential health services for their children.

But we also know that America's health care system is in shambles. More than 8 million children and 430,000 pregnant women in this country have no access to health care. Most live in families with at least one full-time worker, but they have no health insurance and cannot affort their medical bills. For families of children with chronic illnesses and disabilities, the problems are often devastating. Many are denied insurance coverage at any cost, threatening their families with financial ruin. These are travesties that cannot continue.

We recommend universal health insurance coverage for all children and pregnant women, provided jointly by the federal government and employers. We would require all employers to provide insurance for employees who are pregnant and for employee's children or pregnant spouses. Alternatively, employers could contribute to a public health insurance program for children and pregnant women who do not receive insurance coverage through the workplace. We also call for a basic level of medical care with a strong emphasis on prevention. And we insist on tough provisions to contain costs and improve the quality of care. In particular, we urge adoption of Medicare's increasingly effective payment system for doctors and hospitals.

In many cities and rural communities, the absence of health care providers, clinics, and hospitals makes it impossible for families—

even those with insurance—to obtain medical services. To reach these underserved areas and populations, the majority of commissioners calls for a long-overdue expansion of WIC, the Maternal and Child Health Block Grant, Community and Migrant Health Centers, and the National Health Service Corps.

We also took a long, hard look at education. Despite a decade of education reform, America remains a nation at risk. U.S. students still lag behind their foreign counterparts in math, science, and reading. There are too many dropouts and too many graduates who can't function in the workplace or in a college classroom.

As a first step, all children must start school ready to learn. Good health is a prerequisite to school success. We believe the health proposals offered by the majority of commissioners will protect children's health during their formative years. In addition, communities must ensure that high-quality child care and early childhood programs are available to all children who need them. And all income-eligible children at risk of early school failure must be able to participate in Head Start.

To reach the education goals set by the President and the Governors—and we absolutely must reach them—schools need to adopt several fundamental reforms. They need a more challenging curriculum, more school-based management, more participation by parents, more skill teachers and principals, and more equitable financing across school districts. As part of an overall package of reforms, we call for school choice policies within the public school system.

Let me turn now to the shameful circumstances facing abused and neglected children. Every year thousands of American children are removed from their families and placed in the protective custody of the states. Many bounce from one foster home or insitution to another for years on end. Through no fault of their own, they are effectively denied a permanent home and family. Foster care, intended to protect children who are abused and neglected by their parents, is too often an equally cruel form of abuse and neglect by the states. This is intolerable, and it must not continue.

The number of children in foster care has exploded in recent years, and will continue to grow if we don't act now to reverse the tide of broken homes and troubled families. We must relieve the pressures and stresses that push families at all income levels to the breaking point. We must also change federal funding incentives. Right now, it's cheaper for states to place children in foster care than to provide the supports and services that can keep many families safely together.

It's time to turn the child welfare system on its head, so that assistance is available to families *early*—before tragedies occur. This means family support and early intervention to strengthen families and avoid problems down the road. It means family preservation—intensive in-home services to salvage families on the brink of crisis. And it means more and better care for those children who must be removed from their homes and placed in foster care.

The value society places on families and the way it supports their needs have a great deal to do with how children fare. More and more mothers *and* fathers are struggling to balance work and family responsibilities. Therefore, we recommend that government and all private sector employers establish family-oriented policies and practices, including family and medical leave, flexible scheduling, and career sequencing. That's good business, it's good public policy, and it's good parenting. The substantial majority of commissioners would go even further to recommend that the federal government require employers to provide the option of a job-protected leave at the time of childbirth, adoption and family and medical emergencies. A minority of commissioners opposes such a mandate and instead prefers to rely on the voluntary efforts of employers.

How much will this ambitious set of proposals cost? In the first year, the federal share will be $52 to $56 billion in new spending. Because the federal government cannot and should not bear full responsibility, we also call upon state and local governments, employers, and the voluntary community to contribute their share. Every sector of society benefits when families are strong and stable, and when children grow into healthy, literate, and productive adults. Therefore, every sector must bear some financial responsibility.

It's not easy to call for more government spending in the face of a looming federal deficit. But we have to face reality. In the end, we're going to pay one way or the other. There are no cheap, quick, or easy fixes. I for one would rather pay for Head Start than for prisons. I'll also take prenatal care over intensive care any day. And work sounds a lot better to me than welfare.

To finance these proposals, the Commission has held steadfastly to a "pay as you go" approach. Even though the refundable tax credit will surely fuel the economy and generate offsetting revenues, we have suggested options for funding the full federal costs of our recommendations.... [W]e offer seven alternative financing packages that in varying combinations include new revenue sources and possible reallocations of current federal spending. In suggesting these options we are determined that families raising children should not bear the primary burden of paying the bill.

Much of what this Commission saw and heard about children and their families was painful and sobering. Our shared experiences brought this very diverse group of individuals much closer together. Today, we share with you a vision of a nation where no child is poor, hungry, uneducated, or unloved—where raising children is a valued undertaking—and where children are at the center of their families, and families are at the center of our social policies.

For millions of American children and families, the hour is already late. But if the Persian Gulf experience taught us anything, it's that a unified nation can accomplish great things. Today, we call on all Americans to move beyond rhetoric—to replace partisan bickering with thoughtful action—and to accomplish great things for *all* the nation's children....

From John D. Rockefeller, IV, "The Recommendations of the National Commission on Children," *Vital Speeches of the Day*, Volume LVII, No. 19, 588–590.

Document 129:
THE SECOND EPIDEMIC—VIOLENCE AGAINST LESBIANS AND GAY MEN (1990)
Kevin T. Berrill

Our concept of human rights has evolved steadily over the past few centuries, as the documents in this book prove. One group fighting for their rights is the gay and lesbian community. In April, 1990, the Hate Crime Statistics Act was signed into law. This act will provide evidence of the results of fear and hatred and therefore discrimination, that exists for gay people.

After years of silence, anti-gay violence is beginning to receive attention and response. As I watched President Bush sign the Hate Crime Statistics Act on April 23, 1990, I felt pride and relief knowing that crimes of hate against lesbian and gay people, as well as members of other minority communities, will at least be acknowledged. The Hate Crime Statistics Act requires the federal government to collect statistics on crime based on race, religion, sexual orientation, and ethnicity. The inclusion of "sexual orientation" in this new law was the result of years of organizing, lobbying, and coalition building. Despite, or perhaps because of, the devastation of AIDS and the growing attacks from the political and religious Right, there has been an explosion of lesbian and gay activism in recent years. The slogan of the 1987 March on Washington for Lesbian and Gay Rights, one of the largest civil rights marches in U.S. History, summed up best where we stand: "For Love and For Life, We're Not Going Back!" Back to the closet, that is. Whatever legal, social, political gains we have made occurred because lesbian women and gay men stepped out of the isolation, suffocation, and self-hatred of the closet to unapologetically acknowledge their identity. Some call this "flaunting" our sexuality, but we call it survival. Given the pervasiveness of anti-gay prejudice, it is impossible for us to remain hidden and still maintain a positive sense of identity and community. Only by being visible can gay people build a movement and organize for equality.

But visibility has its price. In coming out and in speaking out, we have become more of a target to those who hate and want to harm us. Although much media attention has focused on the impact of AIDS on the gay community, there is a second epidemic: an epidemic of hatred and violence that is sweeping this country. Indeed, there is considerable evidence to show that AIDS has fanned the flames of anti-gay prejudice and negatively affected the social climate in which anti-gay violence occurs. Examples of the "second epidemic" include:

—In May, 1988, a lone assailant stalked and shot two lesbians hiking in the hills of Pennsylvania, killing one of the women and shooting the second.

—In November, 1989, in Springfield (MO), amid a controversy over a local production of a play about AIDS, the home of a gay activist was destroyed by arson.

—In April, 1989, in Portland (OR), several skinheads dismembered a dog and placed the dog's head on a gay man's front porch.

—In May, 1989, at the University of Akron (OH), several male students verbally abused a lesbian activist and smashed eggs in her face.

—In January, 1990, a Staten Island (NY) gay man was verbally abused by two assailants and stabbed to death.

These incidents are not isolated. Numerous studies have shown anti-gay violence to be a widespread and critical problem. For example, in a study conducted in 1989 for the San Francisco Examiner by Teichner Associates, an independent polling firm, 7% of lesbians and gay men surveyed nationwide (N=400) reported having been physically attacked at least once during the past year because of their sexual orientation. According to a study sponsored by the U.S. Department of Justice, "the most frequent victims of hate violence today are Blacks, Hispanics, Southeast Asians, Jews, gays and lesbians. Homosexuals are probably the most frequent victims." Clearly, there is a large and growing body of information showing that anti-gay violence is a problem at least as serious as other crimes motivated by bigotry.

Anti-gay violence occurs in a variety of settings including schools and colleges, prisons and jails, the workplace, and even in the home. Although most perpetrators are not affiliated with organized hate groups, anti-gay violence by such groups, especially neo-Nazi skinheads, appears to be growing. According to the Klanwatch Project of the Southern Poverty Law Center, gays along with Blacks and Jews were the most frequent victims of skinhead attacks in 1989. Recent examples of anti-gay activity by hate groups include the execution-style murders of three men in North Carolina perceived to be homosexual, the firebombing of a church based in the gay community, and the national dissemination of anti-gay propaganda via computer bulletin boards.

While most victims of ethnoviolence decline to report the incident to authorities, victims of anti-gay violence are especially reluctant to step forward. This reluctance is justified. Lacking civil rights protection, lesbian and gay victims risk loss of jobs, housing and other rights by reporting anti-gay crimes. As with victims of rape, they are often blamed for attacks against them and frequently encounter indifference, hostility, and censure from the criminal justice system.

Despite widespread victimization of lesbians and gay men, only a handful of laws aimed at combatting hate violence addresses violence based on sexual orientation. Crimes based on gender, disability, and other social categories are also frequently ignored. Moreover, only a few school-based programs aimed at countering prejudice include mention of homophobia and anti-gay violence.

Such silence is not benign or even neutral. To condemn some forms of violence while ignoring others creates an unacceptable hierarchy of oppression. This shifts the focus of hatred to those who are the least protected and therefore the most vulnerable. If there is one lesson that we should have learned by now, it is that people who hate do not discriminate. Neither should people of conscience.

From "The Second Epidemic, Violence Against Lesbians and Gay Men," in *Forum*, Vol. 5, No. 2, June 1990, 1–2.

Document 130:
GOD IS NOT A HOMOPHOBE (1993)
James A. Michener

As the arguments over whether gays should be accorded the protection of law to ensure that they receive the same civil rights as other citizens, the Bible, *and specifically the Book of Leviticus, has frequently been invoked as the reason gays should not be given legal protection. In this article, James Michener decries the selective use of the Bible to prove a point.*

In the debate over gays in the military, which entered its second phase yesterday as the Senate Armed Services Committee convened hearings on the issue, many have argued that the Bible has strict and clear edicts against homosexuality. The extreme expression of this belief was succinctly stated by Sgt. Maj. S.H. Mellinger in the January issue of the Marine Corps Gazette: "The Bible has a very clear and specific message toward homosexuals 'those that practice such things are worthy of death.'"

He is correct. In Leviticus 20:13, it says: "If a man also lie with mankind, as he lieth with a woman, both of them have committed an abomination: they shall surely be put to death; their blood shall be upon them."

But one must read all of Leviticus to understand the condition of the ancient Hebrews when this harsh judgment was being promulgated. They lived in a rude, brutal, almost uncivilized place where abominations abounded. To read the list of the things the Jews were enjoined to stop doing is to realize that God had to be unusually strict with such an undisciplined mob. Women who had sexual intercourse with animals were to be put to death. "And if a man take a wife and her mother, it is wickedness: they shall be burnt with fire, both he and they." A father who had sex with his daughter-in-law "shall be put to death." On and on goes the litany of common abuses that the Jews must henceforth forgo.

Two other verses from the same chapter of Leviticus bring into question the relevance of these edicts today. Verse 9 warns: "For every one that curseth his father or his mother shall be surely put to death." Would we be willing to require the death sentence for boys who in a fit of rage oppose their parents? How many of us would have been guilty of that act at some point in our upbringing?

Just as perplexing is Verse 10: "And the man that committeth adultery with another man's wife...the adulterer and the adulteress shall surely be put to death." Can you imagine the holocaust that would ensue if that law were enforced today?

The Old Testament condemnation of homosexuality must be seen as one law among many intended to bring order in human relationships. Because the Jewish community was in deplorable disarray, harsh measures were required. As order was installed, the extreme penalties advocated in Leviticus were relaxed in the civilized nations that followed.

But not in all societies. When I was in Jalalabad, Afghanistan, in the 1950's, I watched as a woman accused of adultery was dragged to the marketplace, covered with a flimsy white woolen shroud, tied to a stake and stoned to death, in accordance with Muslim law. As blood stains began to appear on the cloth, the watchers cheered.

In the crowd, though, watching and cheering, were many pairs of young men, obviously in love with each other and holding hands. For in this mountainous land where contact with women was almost impossible outside of family-arranged marriages, male homosexuality was common, and apparently accepted by the general public.

Western society, reacting in its own way, has advanced far beyond the primitive days of Leviticus. We do not kill young people who oppose their parents or execute adulterers.

So when zealots remind us that the Bible says male homosexuals should be put to death rather than be admitted to the armed forces, it is proper to reply: "You are correct that Leviticus says that. But it also has an enormous number of edicts, which have had to be modified as we became civilized."

From James A. Michener, "God Is Not A Homophobe," in *The New York Times*, March 30, 1993.

Document 131:
THE RIGHTS OF THE ENVIRONMENT (1976–1991),xm

One of the most important of the "third generation" rights to have emerged in the last few decades is the right of people to a clean environment. Not only is this right found in numerous environmental statutes and treaties, but it is enshrined as a fundamental concern in numerous modern constitutions. A few excerpts below:

CONSTITUTION OF THE REPUBLIC OF BULGARIA (Established by the Grand National Assembly on 12 July, 1991)

...Article 15. The Republic of Bulgaria shall ensure the protection and reproduction of the environment, the conservation of living Nature in all its variety, and the sensible utilization of the country's natural and other resources....

Article 55. Citizens shall have the right to a healthy and favourable environment corresponding to the established standards and norms. They shall protect the environment....

From *State Gazette* No. 56, 13 July 1991

CONSTITUTION OF TURKEY (1982)

....Article 56

(1) Everyone has the right to live in a healthy, balanced environment.

(2) It is the duty of the State and the citizens to improve the natural environment, and to prevent environmental pollution....

From *2 Constitutions of Nations, Asia, Australia, and Oceania 1591, 1605* (Peaslee ed., 4th ed. 1985).

CONSTITUTION OF SPAIN (December 29, 1979)

....Chapter III, Article 45

(1) Everyone has the right to enjoy an environment suitable for the development of the person as well as the duty to preserve it.

(2) The public authorities shall concern themselves with the rational use of all natural resources for the purpose of protecting and improving the quality of life and protecting and restoring the environment, supporting themselves on an indispensable collective solidarity.

(3) For those who violate the provisions of the foregoing paragraph, penal or administrative sanctions, as applicable, shall be established and they shall be obliged to repair the damage caused....

From the Spanish constitution, art. 45, translated in *16 Constitutions of the Countries of the World, Spain 52* (Albert P. Blaustein & Gisbert H. Flanz eds., 1990).

CONSTITUTION OF THE NETHERLANDS (as amended in 1983)

....Article 21. It shall be the concern of the authorities to keep the country habitable and to protect and improve the environment.

From *11 Constitutions of the Countries of the World, The Netherlands 10* (Albert P. Blaustein & Gisbert H. Flanz eds., 1990).

CONSTITUTION OF THE FEDERATIVE REPUBLIC OF BRAZIL (1988)

....Article 255. Everyone is entitled to an ecologically balanced environment, which is an asset of everyday use to the common man and essential to a healthy quality of life; this imposes a duty on the government and the community to protect and preserve it for the present and future generations.

(1) In order to assure that this right is effectively available, it is incumbent on the government to:

(I) Preserve and restore essential ecological processes and arrange for the ecological management of species and ecosystems;

(II) Preserve the diversity and integrity of the genetic patrimony of Brazil and oversee the entities that are engaged in research and manipulation of genetic material;

(III) Define, in all the units of the Federation, the geographical spaces and components thereof that are to be specially protected, these may be changed or deleted only by law, and any use that compromises the integrity of the features which justify protection of such areas is prohibited;

(IV) Require, pursuant to law, that an environmental impact study be made prior to the installation of a project or activity that may potentially cause significant harm to the environment, and that the results of such study be publicized;

(V) Control the production, marketing, and use of techniques, methods, and substances that pose a risk to life, the quality of life, and the environment;

(VI) Promote environmental education at all levels of instruction and help to increase public awareness of the need to preserve the environment;

(VII) Protect the flora and fauna; practices that place their ecological function at risk, lead to the extinction of species, or submit animals to cruel treatment are hereby prohibited;

Paragraph 2. Anyone who exploits mineral resources is obliged to restore the damaged environment by such technical means as may be required by the appropriate public agency, pursuant to law.

Paragraph 3. Behaviors and activities deemed injurious in the environment shall subject the violators, whether individuals or legal entitites, to criminal and administrative penalties, apart from the obligation to repair the damages caused.

Paragraph 4. The Brazilian Amazonian forest, the Atlantic jungle, the Serra do Mar mountain range, the Mato Grosso Pantanal [swamp], and the Coastal Zone are part of the national patrimony and are to be utilized, pursuant to law, under terms and conditions that assure the preservation of the environment; this also applies to the use of the natural resources.

Paragraph 5. Lands vacated or taken over by the States through adjudication and needed in order to protect the natural ecosystems may not be made available for any purpose.

Paragraph 6. The location of power plants that employ a nuclear reactor must be defined in federal law; no such facility may be installed until such determination has been made.

From *3 Constitutions of the Countries of the World, Federative Republic of Brazil 65–66* (Albert P. Blaustein & Gisbert H. Flanz, eds., 1990).

Document 132:
AMERICANS WITH DISABILITIES ACT (1990)

In 1990, the Americans With Disabilities Act (ADA) was passed became enforceable in July of 1992. The ADA was written to ensure that disabled Americans can have equal access to public buildings and privately owned businesses. It also provides equal access to public transportation and a means to lessen the discrimination that the disabled have traditionally met when seeking employment.

Section 2. Findings and Purposes.

(a) Findings. The Congress finds that

(1) some 43,000,000 Americans have one or more physical or mental disabilities, and this number is increasing as the population as a whole is growing older;

(2) historically, society has tended to isolate and segregate individuals with disabilities, and, despite some improvements, such forms of discrimination against individuals with disabilities continue to be a serious and pervasive social problem;

(3) discrimination against individuals with disabilities persists in such critical areas as employment, housing, public accommodations, education, transportation, communications, recreation, institutionalization, health services, voting, and access to public services;

(4) unlike individuals who have experienced discrimination on the basis of race, color, sex, national origin, religion, or age, individuals who have experienced discrimination on the basis of disability have often had no legal recourse to redress such discrimination;

(5) individuals with disabilities continually encounter various forms of discrimination, including outright intentional exclusion, the discriminatory effects of architectural, transportation, and communication barriers, overprotective rules and policies, failure to make modifications to existing facilities and practices, exclusionary qualification standards and criteria, segregation, and relegation to lesser services, programs, activities, benefits, jobs, or other opportunities;

(6) census data, national polls, and other studies have documented that people with disabilities, as a group, occupy an inferior status in our society, and are severely disadvantaged socially, vocationally, economically, and educationally;

(7) individuals with disabilities are a discrete and insular minority who have been faced with restrictions and limitations, subjected to a history of purposeful unequal treatment, and relegated to a position of political powerlessness in our society, based on characteristics that are beyond the control of such individuals and resulting form stereotypic assumptions not truly indicative of the individual ability of such individuals to participate in, and contribute to, society;

(8) the Nation's proper goals regarding individuals with disabilities are to assure equality of opportunity, full participation, independent living, and economic self-sufficiency for such individuals; and

(9) the continuing existence of unfair and unnecessary discrimination and prejudice denies people with disabilities the opportunity to compete on an equal basis and to pursue those opportunities for which our free society is justifiably famous, and costs the United States billions of dollars in unnecessary

expenses resulting from dependency and nonproductivity.

(b) Purpose. It is the purpose of this Act

(1) to provide a clear and comprehensive national mandate for the elimination of discrimination against individuals with disabilities;

(2) to provide clear, strong, consistent, enforceable standards addressing discrimination against individuals with disabilities;

(3) to ensure that the Federal Government plays a central role in enforcing the standards established in this Act on behalf of individuals with disabilities; and

(4) to invoke the sweep of congressional authority, including the power to enforce the fourteenth amendment and to regulate commerce, in order to address the major areas of discrimination faced day-to-day by people with disabilities....

Title I—Employment

Section 102. Discrimination.

(a) General Rule. No covered entity shall discriminate against a qualified individual with a disability because of the disability of such individual in regard to job application procedures, the hiring, advancement, or discharge of employees, employee compensation, job training, and other terms, conditions, and privileges of employment.

(b) Construction. As used in subsection (a), the term "discriminate" includes

(1) limiting, segregating, or classifying a job applicant or employee in a way that adversely affects the opportunities or status of such applicant or employee because of the disability of such applicant or employee;

(2) participating in a contractual or other arrangement or relationship that has the effect of subjecting a covered entity's qualified applicant or employee with a disability to the discrimination prohibited by this title (such relationship includes a relationship with an employment or referral agency, labor union, an organization providing fringe benefits to an employee of the covered entity, or an organization providing training and apprenticeship programs);

(3) utilizing standards, criteria, or methods of administration

(A) that have the effect of discrimination on the basis of disability; or

(B) that perpetuate the discrimination of others who are subject to common administrative control;

(4) excluding or otherwise denying equal jobs or benefits to a qualified individual because of the known disability of an individual with whom the qualified individual is known to have a relationship or association;

(5)(A) not making reasonable accommodations to the known physical or mental limitations of an otherwise qualified individual with a disability who is an applicant or employee, unless such covered entity can demonstrate that the accommodation would impose an undue hardship on the operation of the business of such covered entity; or

(B) denying employment opportunities to a job applicant or employee who is an otherwise qualified individual with a disability, if such denial is based on the need of such covered entity to make reasonable accommodation to the physical or mental impairments of the employee or applicant;

(6) using qualification standards, employment tests or other selection criteria that screen out or tend to screen out an individual with a disability or a class of individuals with disabilities unless the standard, test or other selection criteria, as used by the covered entity, is shown to be job-related for the position in question and is consistent with business necessity; and

(7) failing to select and administer tests concerning employment in the most effective manner to ensure that, when such test is administered to a job applicant or employee who has a disability that impairs sensory, manual, or speaking skills, such test results accurately reflect the skills, aptitude, or whatever other factor of such applicant or employee that such tests purports to measure, rather than reflecting the impaired sensory, manual, or speaking skills of such employee or applicant (except where such skills are the factors that the test purports to measure).

(c) Medical Examinations and Inquiries

(1) In general. The prohibition against discrimination as referred to in subsection (a) shall include medical examinations and inquiries....

Title II—Public Services

Section 201. (1) Public Entity. The term "public entity" means

(A) any state or local government;

(B) any department, agency, special purpose district, or other instrumentality of a State or States or local government; and

(C) the National Railroad Passenger Corporation [AMTRAK], and any commuter authority.

Subtitle A. Section 202. Discrimination. Subject to the provisions of this title, no qualified individual with a disability shall, by reason of such disability, be excluded from participation in or be denied the benefits of the services, programs, or activities of a public entity, or be subjected to discrimination by any such entity....[ed. note: these sections of the ADA pertain to accessible public transportation]

Title III—Public Accommodations and Services Operated by Private Entities

Section 301. (7) Public Accommodation. The following private entities are considered public accommodations for purposes of this title, if the operations of such entities affect commerce

(A) an inn, hotel, motel, or other place of lodging;...

(B) a restaurant, bar, or other establishment serving food or drink;

(C) a motion picture house, theater, concert hall, stadium, or other place of exhibition or entertainment;

(D) an auditorium, convention center, lecture hall, or other place of public gathering;

(E) a bakery, grocery store, clothing store, hardware store, shopping center, or other sales or rental establishment;

(F) a laundromat, dry-cleaner, bank, barber shop, beauty shop, travel service, shoe repair service, funeral parlor, gas station, office of an accountant or lawyer, pharmacy, insurance office, professional office of a health care provider, hospital, or other service establishment;

(G) a terminal, depot, or other station used for specified public transportation;

(H) a museum, library, gallery, or other place of public display or collection;

(I) a park, zoo, amusement park, or other place of recreation;

(J) a nursery, elementary, secondary, undergraduate, or postgraduate private school, or other place of education;

(K) a day care center, senior citizen center, homeless shelter, food bank, adoption agency, or other social service center establishment; and

(L) a gymnasium, health spa, bowling alley, golf course, or other place of exercise or recreation....

Section 302. Prohibition of Discrimination by Public Accommodations.

(a) General Rule. No individual shall be discriminated against on the basis of disability in the full and equal enjoyment of the goods, services, facilities, privileges, advantages, or accommodations of any place of public accommodation by any person who owns, leases (or leases to), or operates a place of public accommodation....

(2) Specific Prohibitions.

(A) Discrimination. For purposes of subsection (a), discrimination includes

(i) the imposition or application of eligibility criteria that screen out or tend to screen out an individual with a disability or any class of individuals with disabilities from fully and equally enjoying any goods, services, facilities, privileges, advantages, or accommodations, unless such criteria can be shown to be necessary for the provision of the goods services, facilities, privileges, advantages, or accommodations being offered;

(ii) a failure to make reasonable modifications in policies, practices, or procedures, when such modifications are necessary to afford such goods, services, facilities, privileges, advantages, or accommodations to individuals with disabilities, unless the entity can demonstrate that making such modifications would fundamentally alter the nature of such goods, services, facilities, privileges, advantages, or accommodations;

(iii) a failure to take such steps as may be necessary to ensure that no individual with a disability is excluded, denied services, segregated or otherwise treated differently than other individuals because of the absence of auxiliary aids and services, unless the entity can demonstrate that taking such steps would fundamentally alter the nature of the good, service, facility, privelege, advantage, or accommodation being offered or would result in an undue burden;

(iv) a failure to remove architectural barriers, and communication barriers that are structural in nature, in existing facilities, and transportation barriers in existing vehicles and rail passenger cars used by an establishment for transporting individuals..., where such removal is readily achievable; and

(v) where an entity can demonstrate that the removal of a barrier under clause (iv) is not readily achievable, a failure to make such goods, services, facilities, privileges, advantages, or accommodations available through alternative methods if such methods are readily achievable....

Section 303. New Construction and Alterations in Public Accommodations and Commercial Facilities.

(a) Application of term. Except as provided in subsection (b), as applied to public accommodations and commercial facilities, discrimination for purposes of section 302(a) includes

(1) a failure to design and construct facilities for first occupancy later than 30 months after the date of enactment of this Act that are readily accessible to and usable by individuals with disabilities, except where an entity can demonstrate that it is structurally impracticable to meet the requirements of such subsection in accordance with standards set forth or incorporated by reference in regulations issued under this title; and

(2) with respect to a facility or part thereof that is altered by, on behalf of, or for the use of an establishment in a manner that affects or could affect the usability of the facility or part thereof, a failure to make alterations in such a manner that, to the maximum extent feasible, the altered portions of the facility are readily accessible to and usable by individuals with disabilities, including individuals who use wheelchairs. Where the entity is undertaking an alteration that affects or could affect usability of or access to an area of the facility containing a primary function, the entity shall also make the alterations in such a manner that, to the maximum extent feasible, the path of travel to the altered area and the bathrooms, telephones, and drinking fountains serving the altered area, are readily accessible to and usable by individuals with disabilities where such alterations to the path of travel or the bathrooms, telephones, and drinking fountains serving the altered area are not disproportionate to the overall alterations in terms of cost and scope....

Section 304. Prohibition of Discrimination in Specified Public Transportation Services Provided by Private Entities.

(a) General Rule. No individual shall be discriminated against on the basis of disability in the full and equal enjoyment of specified public transportaiton services provided by a private entity that is primarily engaged in the business of transporting people and whose operations affect commerce....

Section 307. Exemptions for Private Clubs and Religious Organizations. The provisions of this title shall not apply to private clubs or establishments exempted from coverage under title II of the Civil Rights Act of 1964 (42 U.S.C. 2000-a(e)) or to religious organizations or entities controlled by religious organizations, including places of worship....

From *Americans With Disabilities Act of 1990* (Public Law 101–336) As Signed by President George Bush on July 26, 1990.

Document 133: MANIFESTO OF CHARTER 77 (1977)

The following manifesto first appeared in Western Europe in early January 1977. Within a few days Charter 77—as its anonymous authors called the document and the movement responsible for its appearance—had been translated into most major languages and had received attention throughout the world. Charter 77 soon became well known within Czechoslovakia as a result of Western radio broadcasts. Charter 77 indicts the government for violations of human rights provisions in the nation's 1960 Constitution and in various treaties and covenants of which Czechoslovakia is a signatory. The translation presented here appeared in The Times *of London on January 7, 1977, bearing a notation that it was an "authorized" translation. The notation indicated neither who had made nor who had authorized the translation.*

In the Czechoslovak Register of Laws No. 120 of October 13, 1976, texts were published of the International Covenant on Civil and Political Rights, and of the International Covenant on Economic, Social and Cultural Rights, which were signed on behalf of our republic in 1968, reiterated at Helsinki in 1975 and came into force in our country on March 23, 1976. From that date our citizens have enjoyed the rights, and our state the duties, ensuing from them.

The human rights and freedoms underwritten by these covenants constitute features of civilized life for which many progressive movements have striven throughout history and whose codification could greatly assist humane developments in our society.

We accordingly welcome the Czechoslovak Socialist Republic's accession to those agreements.

Their publication, however, serves as a powerful reminder of the extent to which basic human rights in our country exist, regretably, on paper alone.

The right to freedom of expression, for example, guaranteed by Article 19 of the first-mentioned covenant, is in our case purely illusory. Tens of thousands of our citizens are prevented from working in their own fields for the sole reason that they hold views differing from official ones, and are discriminated against and harassed in all kinds of ways by the authorities and public organizations. Deprived as they are of any means to defend themselves, they become victims of a virtual apartheid.

Hundreds of thousands of other citizens are denied that "freedom from fear" mentioned in the preamble to the first covenant, being condemned to the constant risk of unemployment of other penalties if they voice their own opinions.

In violation of Article 13 of the second-mentioned covenant, guaranteeing everyone the right to education, countless young people are prevented from studying because of their own views or even their parents'. Innumerable citizens live in fear of their own, or their children's right to education being withdrawn if they should ever speak up in accordance with their convictions.

Any exercise of the right to "seek, receive and impart information and ideas of all kinds, regardless of frontiers, either orally, in writing or in print" or "in the form of art" specified in Article 19, Clause 2 of the first covenant is followed by extra-judicial and even judicial sanctions, often in the form of criminal charges, as in the recent trial of young musicians.

Freedom of public expression is inhibited by the centralized control of all the communication media and of publishing and cultural institutions. No philosophical, political or scientific view or artistic activity that departs ever so slightly from the narrow bounds of official ideology or aesthetics is allowed to be published; no open criticism can be made of abnormal social phenomena; no public defense is possible against false and insulting charges made in official propaganda—the legal protection against "attacks on honor and reputation" clearly guaranteed by Article 17 of the first covenant is in practice non-existent: false accusations cannot be rebutted, and any attempt to secure compensation or correction through the courts is futile; no open debate is allowed in the domain of thought and art.

Many scholars, writers, artists and others are penalized for having legally published or expressed, years ago, opinions which are condemned by those who hold political power today.

Freedom of religious confession, emphatically guaranteed by Article 18 of the first covenant, is continually curtailed by arbitrary official action; by interference with the activity of churchmen, who are constantly threatened by the refusal of the state to permit them the exercise of their functions, or by the withdrawal of such permission; by financial or other transactions against those who express their religious faith in word or action; by constraints on religious training and so forth.

One instrument for the curtailment or in many cases complete elimination of many civic rights is the system by which all national institutions and organizations are in effect subject to political directives from the machinery of the ruling party and to decisions made by powerful individuals.

The constitution of the republic, its laws and legal norms do not regulate the form or content, the issuing or application of such decisions; they are often only given out verbally, unknown to the public at large and beyond its powers to check; their originators are responsible to no one but themselves and their own hierarchy; yet they have a decisive impact on the decision-making and executive organs of government, justice, trade unions, interest groups and all other organizations, of the other political parties, enterprises, factories, insitutions, offices and so on, for whom these instructions have precedence even before the law.

Where organizations or individuals, in the interpretation of their rights and duties, come into conflict with such directives, they cannot have recourse to any non-party authority, since none such exists. This constitutes, of course, a serious limitation of the right ensuing from Articles 21 and 22 of the first-mentioned covenant, which provides for freedom of association and forbids any restriction on its exercise, from Article 25 on the right to take part in the conduct of public affairs, and from Article 26 stipulating equal protection by the law without discrimination.

This state of affairs likewise prevents workers and others from exercising the unrestricted right to establish trade unions and other organizations to protect their economic and social interests, and from freely enjoying the right to strike provided for in Clause 1 of Article 8 in the second-mentioned covenant.

Further civic rights, including the explicit prohibition of "arbitrary interference with privacy, family, home or correspondence" (Article 17 of the first covenant), are seriously vitiated by the various forms of interference in the private life of citizens exercised by the Ministry of the Interior, for example by bugging telephones and houses, opening mail, following personal movements, searching homes, setting up networks of neighborhood informers (often recruited by illicit threats or promises) and in other ways.

The ministry frequently interferes in employers' decisions, instigates acts of discrimination by authorities and organizations, brings weight to bear on the organs of justice and even orchestrates propaganda campaigns in the media. This activity is governed by no law and, being clandestine, affords the citizen no chance to defend himself.

In cases of prosecution on political grounds the investigative and judicial organs violate the rights of those charged and those defending them, as guaranteed by Article 14 of the first covenant and indeed by Czechoslovak law. The prison treatment of those sentenced in such cases is an affront to their human dignity and a menace to their health, being aimed at breaking their morale.

Clause 2, Article 12 of the first covenant, guaranteeing every citizen the right to leave the country, is consistently violated, or under the pretense of "defense of national security" is subjected to various unjustifiable conditions (Clause 3). The granting of entry visas to foreigners is also treated arbitrarily, and many are unable to visit Czechoslovakia merely because of professional or personal contacts with those of our citizens who are subject to discrimination.

Some of our people—either in private, at their places of work or by the only feasible public channel, the foreign media—have drawn attention to the systematic violation of human rights and democratic freedoms and demanded amends in specific cases. But their pleas have remained largely ignored or been made grounds for police investigation.

Responsibility for the maintenance of civic rights in our country naturally devolves in the first place on the political and state authorities. Yet not only on them: everyone bears his share of responsibility for the conditions that prevail and accordingly also for the observance of legally enshrined agreements, binding upon all individuals as well as upon governments.

It is this sens of co-responsibility, our belief in the importance of its conscious public acceptance and the general need to give it new and more effective expression that led us to the idea of creating Charter 77, whose inception we today publicly announce.

Charter 77 is a loose, informal and open association of people of various shades of opinion, faiths and professions united by the will to strive individually and collectively for the respecting of civic and human rights in our own country and throughout the world—rights accorded to all men by the two mentioned international covenants, by the Final Act of the Helsinki conference and by numerous other international documents opposing war, violence and social or spiritual oppression, and which are comprehensively laid down in the UN Universal Charter of Human Rights.

Charter 77 springs from a background of friendship and solidarity among people who share our concern for those ideals that have inspired, and continue to inspire, their lives and their work.

Charter 77 is not an organization; it has no rules, permanent bodies or formal membership. It embraces everyone who agrees with its ideas and participates in its work. It does not form the basis for any oppositional political activity.

Like many similar citizen initiatives in various countries, West and East, it seeks to promote the general public interest.

It does not aim, then, to set out its own platform of political or social reform or change, but within its own field of impact to conduct a constructive dialogue with the political and state authorities, particularly by drawing attention to individual cases where human and civic rights are violated, to document such grievances and suggest remedies, to make proposals of a more general character calculated to reinforce such rights and machinery for protecting them, to act as an intermediary in situations of conflict which may lead to violations of rights, and so forth.

By its symbolic name Charter 77 denotes that it has come into being at the start of a year proclaimed as Political Prsoners' Year—a year in which a conference in Belgrade is due to review the implementation of the obligations assumed at Helsinki.

As signatories, we hereby authorize Professor Dr. Jan Patocka, Dr. Vaclav Havel and Professor Dr. Jiri Hajek to act as the spokesmen for the Charter. These spokesmen are endowed with full authority to represent it vis-a-vis state and other bodies, and the public at home and abroad, and their signatures attest to the authenticity of documents issued by the Charter. They will have us and others who join us as their colleagues taking part in any needful negotiations, shouldering particular tasks and sharing every responsibility.

We believe that Charter 77 will help all citizens of Czechoslovakia to work and live as free human beings.

From *Czechoslovakia, A Country Study*, Washington, D.C.: GPO (DA Pam 550–155), 357–361.

Document 134:
INTELLECTUAL DISSENT (1985)
Fang Lizhi

Fang Lizhi, the leading intellectual dissident in China, sought protection in the United States Embassy after the June 1989 massacre in Tiananmen Square. As a critic of the Chinese system, it was no longer safe for him to remain at large in his own country, where he was outlawed and probably would meet a harsh fate. Fang has been known as a public speaker, and the following remarks are taken from an address he delivered in 1985.

As intellectuals, we are obligated to work for the improvement of society. . . .

One reason for this situation [the fact that China has yet to produce work worthy of consideration for a Nobel prize] is our social environment. Many of us who have been to foreign countries to study or work agree that we can perform much more efficiently and productively abroad than in China. . . . Foreigners are no more intelligent than we Chinese.

Intellectuals in the West differ from us in that they not only have a great deal of specialized knowledge, but they are also concerned about their larger society. If they were not, they wouldn't even be qualified to call themselves intellectuals. But in China, with its poorly developed scientific culture, intellectuals do not exert significant influence on society. This is a sign of backwardness. . . .

There is a social malaise in our country today, and the primary reason for it is the poor example set by the Party members. Unethical behavior by Party leaders is especially to blame. . . . Some of us dare not speak out. But if we all spoke out, there would be nothing to be afraid of. This is surely one important cause of our lack of idealism and discipline.

Another cause is that over the years our propaganda about communism has been seriously flawed. In my view this propaganda's greatest problem has been that it has had far too narrow an interpretation—not only too narrow but too shallow. I, too, am a member of the Communist Party, but my dreams are not so narrow. They are of a more open society, where differences are allowed. Room must be made for the great variety of excellence that has found expression in human civilization. Our narrow propaganda seems to imply that nothing that came before us has any merit whatsoever. This is the most worthless and destructive form of propaganda. Propaganda can be used to praise Communist heroes, but it should not be used to tear down other heroes.

We Communist Party members should be open to different ways of thinking. We should be open to different cultures and willing to adopt the elements of those cultures that are clearly superior. A great diversity of thought should be allowed in colleges and universities. For if all thought is narrow and simplistic, creativity will die. At present, there are certainly some people in power who still insist on dictating to others according to their own narrow principles. They always wave the flag of Marxism when they speak. But what they are spouting is not Marxism.

From Orville Schell, *Discos and Democracy*, quoted by Bill Gifford, "Fang of the Revolution," *Village Voice*, 20 June 1989, 27.

Document 135:
POLAND—SOLIDARITY AND FREEDOM (1989)
Lech Walesa

Lech Walesa emerged as the leader of a free trade union in Poland in 1980. He remains today a leading figure in Polish politics. This speech was given to the a joint session of the United States Congress during his visit in 1989. He spoke of Polish goals and Polish needs. Later he was elected to lead the Polish government.

Mr. Speaker, Mr. President, members of the Cabinet, distinguished Members of the House and Senate, ladies and gentlemen, "We the people...." With these words I wish to begin my address. I do not need to remind anyone here where these words come from. And I do not need to explain that I, an electrician from Gdansk, am also entitled to invoke them.

"We the people...."

I stand before you as the third foreign non-head-of-state invited to address the joint Houses of Congress of the United States. The Congress, which for many people in the world, oppressed and stripped of their rights, is a beacon of freedom and a bulwark of human rights. And here I stand before you, to speak to America in the name of my nation. To speak to citizens fo the country and the continent whose threshold is guarded by the famous Statue of Liberty. It is for me an honor so great, a moment so solemn, that I can find nothing to compare it with.

The people in Poland link the name of the United States with freedom and democracy, with generosity and high-mindedness, with human friendship and friendly humanity. I realize that not everywhere in the world is America so perceived. I speak of her image in Poland....

The world remembers the wonderful principle of the American democracy: "government of the people, by the people, for the people."

I too remember these words; I, a shipyard worker from Gdansk, who has devoted his entire life—along with other members of the Solidarity movement—to the service of this idea: "government of the people, by the people, for the people." Against privilege and monopoly, against violations of the law, against the trampling of human dignity, against contempt and injustice....

Ladies and gentlemen, here is the fundamental, most important fact I want to tell you about. I want to tell you that the social movement bearing the beautiful name of Solidarity, born of the Polish Nation, is an effective movement. After many years of struggle it bore fruit which is there for all to see. It pointed to a direction and a way of action which are today affecting the lives of millions of people speaking different languages. It has swayed monopolies, overturning some altogether. It has opened up entirely new horizons.

And this struggle was conducted without resorting to violence of any kind—a point that cannot be stressed too much. We were being locked up in prison, deprived of our jobs, beaten and sometimes killed. And we did not so much as strike a single person. We did not destroy anything. We did not smash a single windowpane. But we were stubborn, very stubborn, ready to suffer, to make sacrifices. We knew what we wanted and our power prevailed in the end.

The movement called Solidarity received massive support and scored victories because at all times and in all matters it opted for the better more human, and more dignified solution, standing against brutality and hate. It was a consistent movement, stubborn, never giving up. And that is why after all these hard years, marked by so many tragic moments, Solidarity is today succeeding and showing the way to millions of people in Poland and other countries.

Ladies and Gentlemen, it was 10 years ago, in August 1980, that there began in the Gdansk shipyard the famous strike which led to the emergence of the first independent trade union in Communist countries, which soon became a vast social movement supported by the Polish Nation.... In those days, at the beginning, many warnings, admonitions, and even condemnations were reaching us from many parts of the world. "What are those Poles up to?" we hear, "They are mad, they are jeopardizing world peace and European stability. They ought to stay quiet and not get on anybody's nerves."

We gathered from those voices that the other nations have the right to live incomfort and well-being, they have the right to democracy and freedom, and it is only the Poles who should give up these rights so as not to disturb the peace of others....

Looking at what is happening around us today we may state positively that the Polish road of struggle for human rights, struggle without violence, the Polish stubbornness and firmness in the quest for pluralism and democracy show many people today, and even nations, how to avoid the greatest dangers. If there is something threatening European stability today, it certainly is not Poland. Poland's drive toward profound transformations, transformations achieved through peaceful means, through evolution, negotiated with all the parties concerned, makes it possible to avoid the worst pitfalls, and may be held up as a model for many other regions. And as we know, changes elsewhere are not so peaceful.

Peacefully and prudently, with their eyes open to dangers, but not giving up what is right and necessary, the Poles gradually paved the way for historic transformations. We are joined along this way, albeit to various extents, by others: Hungarians and Russians, the Ukrainians and people of the Baltic Republics, Armenians and Georgians, and, in recent days, the East Germans. We wish them luck and rejoice at each success they achieve. We are certain that others will also take our road, since there is no other choice.

So I ask now. Is there any sensible man understanding the world around him who could now say that it would be better if the Poles kept quiet because what they are doing is jeopardizing world peace? Couldn't we rather say that Poles are doing more to preserve and consolidate peace than many of their frightened advisers? Could we not say that stability and peace face greater threats from countries which have not yet brought themselves to carry out long-ranging and comprehensive reforms, which do their utmost to preserve the old and disgraced ways of government, contrary to the wishes of their societies?

Things are different in Poland. And I must say that our task is viewed with understanding by our eastern neighbors and their leader, Mikhail Gorbachev. This understanding lays foundations for new relations between Poland and the U.S.S.R. much better than before. These improved mutual relations will also contribute to stabilization and peace in Europe, removing useless tensions. Poles have had a long and difficult history, and no one wants peaceful coexistence and friendship with all nations and countries—and particularly with the Soviet Union—more than we do. We believe that it is only now the right and favorable conditions for such coexistence and friendship are emerging.

Poland is making an important contribution to a better future for Europe, to a European reconciliation—also to the vastly important Polish-German reconciliation - to overcoming of old divisions and to strengthening of human rights on our continent. But it does not come easily for Poland....

The Poles have traveled a long way. It would be worthwhile for all those commenting on Poland, often criticizing Poland, to bear in mind that whatever Poland has achieved she achieved through her own effort, through her own stubbornness, her own relentlessness. Everything was achieved thanks to the unflinching faith in our nation in human dignity and in what is described as the values of Western culture and civilization.

Our nation knows well the price of all this.

Ladies and gentlemen, for the past 50 years the Polish nation has been engaged in a difficult and exhausting battle. First to preserve its very biological existence, later to save its national identity. In both instances Polish determination won the day. Today Poland is rejoining the family of democratic and pluralistic countries, returning to the tradition of religious and European values.

For the first time in half a century Poland has a non-Communist and independent government, supported by the nation.

But on our path there looms a serious obstacle, a grave danger. Our long subjection to a political system incompatible with national traditions, to a system of economy incompatible with rationality and common sense, coupled with the stifling of independent thought and disregard for national interests—all this has led the Polish economy to ruin, to the verge of utter catastrophe. The first government in 50 years elected by the people and serving the people has inherited from the previous rulers of the country a burden of an economy organized in a manner preventing it from satisfying even the basid needs of the people.

The economy we inherited after almost five decades of Communist rule is in need of thorough overhaul. This will require patience and great sacrifice. This will require time and means. The present condition of the Polish economy is not due to chance, and is not a specifically Polish predicament. All the countries of the Eastern bloc are bankrupt. The Communist economy has failed in every part of the world. One result of this is the exodus of the citizens of those countries, by land and by sea, by boat and by plane, swimming and walking across borders. This is a mass-scale phenomenon, well known in Europe, Asia and Central America.

But Poland entered its new road and will never be turned back. The sense of our work and struggle in Poland lies in our creating situations and prospects that would hold Poles back from seeking a place for themselves abroad, that would encourage them to seek meaning in their work and a hope for a better future in their own country, their own home....

Pope John Paul II once said:

"Freedom is not just something to have and to use, it is something to be fought for. One must use freedom to build with it personal life as well as the life of the nation."

I think this weighty thought can equally well be applied to Poland and America.

I wish all of you to know and to keep in mind that the ideals which underlie this glorious American Republic and which are still alive here, are also living in faraway Poland. And although for many long years efforts were made to cut Poland off from these ideals, Poland held her ground and is now reaching for the freedom to which she is justly entitled. Together with Poland, other nations of Eastern Europe are following this path. The wall that was separating people from freedom has never collapsed. And I hope that the nations of the world will never let it be rebuilt.

From Lech Walesa, "Poland—Solidarity and Freedom," *Vital Speeches of the Day*, Volume LVI, No. 5, Dec. 15, 1989, 132–135.

Document 136:
HOW THE WALL WAS CRACKED—A SPECIAL REPORT: PARTY COUP TURNED THE EAST GERMAN TIDE (1989
Based on reporting by Craig R. Whitney, David Binder and Serge Schmemann and written by Mr. Whitney

From shortly after the end of World War II, the Soviet Union directed the installation of client regimes throughout Eastern Europe. Typically these were states dominated by the Communist Party despite the existence of other parties. In the German Democratic Republic (East Germany), the Socialist Unity Party was among the most obsequious of Eastern European satellites. But the forces unleashed by Mikhail Gorbachev's "perestroika" and "glasnost" led to demonstrations throughout Eastern Europe in favor of democracy and the end of the authoritarian systems. Gorbachev also decided during the crisis year 1989 that he would no longer pay the costs of keeping the Eastern European Bloc as it had been.

Changes occurred at a rapid pace throughout Eastern Europe in 1989. In the following article from the New York Times, *seasoned American reporters provided readers with a dramatic account of how a threatened crack-down of demonstrators in East Germany led to the loosening of Erich Honecker's hold on the party and the nation. When force was not used to keep the regime in power—and force was not offered by the Soviets, events rushed East Germany toward free elections and the chance to reunify with their fellow Germans in the west.*

East Berlin, Nov. 17—The turning point came on October 7, after the Communist Party leader,

Erich Honecker, ordered security forces to be prepared to open fire on demonstrators in Leipzig—a "Chinese solution" to the rising tide of dissent in East German.

But violence and killing were averted when Egon Krenz, then Politburo member in charge of security, flew to Leipzig on October 9 and canceled Mr. Honecker's order, allowing the protesters to march unmolested. Mr. Krenz became the new party chief on October 18.

What could have become a bloodbath as terrible as China's June crackdown instead became a peaceful revolution that is changing the face of East Germany and Eastern Europe. Within ten days, Mr. Honecker had resigned under pressure and the Communist Party was pledging profound changes. Within a month, the Berlin wall was broken.

Although this sequence of events would tend to bolster the image of Mr. Krenz, it is supported by the accounts of several members of the East German party, most of whom do not owe their current positions to Mr. Krenz.

They said Mr. Krenz reversed the order to shoot because he feared that hundreds of dead and wounded would be a fatal blow to the East German party's standing at home and abroad....

On October 7, with Mikhail S. Gorbachev in East Berlin, crowds took to the streets of the capital, chanting "Gorby! Gorby!" and "We want to stay!" With many foreign reporters looking on, the police waded into the throngs, and their actions were recorded and immediately played back to the rest of East Germany on West German television.

More violence followed on Sunday, and by Monday, October 9, the suspense was tangible. A weekly Monday peace service, held in the Nikolai Church in Leipzig, had in recent weeks become the launching point for broad protests, and after the weekend clashes, huge crowds were expected at the church.

According to Manfred Gerlach, the leader of the small Liberal Democratic Party, and others, a huge force of soldiers, policemen and secret police agents was assembled in Leipzig and issued with live ammunition. Their order was to shoot if necessary, and the order had reportedly been signed by Mr. Honecker himself.

"There was a written order form Honecker for a Chinese solution," said Markus Wolf, the retired head of East Germany's spy agencies, who has emerged as a leading advocate of reform. "It could have been worse than Beijing."

But by then many in the Politburo had come to the decision that Mr. Honecker must go, and that the situation was explosive. In Leipzig, Kurt Masur, the director of the Gewandhaus musical theater, and some local party officials opened urgent discussions on averting a clash.

Finally, Mr. Krenz and Wolfgang Herger, the Central Committee department chief under him, flew to Leipzig's Schkeuditz Airport. They drove into the city to meet with local Communist officials at the home of Mr. Masur.

"I was in Leipzig," Mr. Krenz later said. "I helped there to see to it that these things were solved politically."

When tens of thousands took to the streets of Leipzig that night, the police did not interfere. The "revolution from below" was under way.

The frustration that erupted in October had been long in gathering. Mikhail S. Gorbachev, the Soviet President, had set loose yearnings for change throughout Eastern Europe, but in East Germany the old loyalists around Mr. Honecker sat entrenched in their isolated villas on Lake Wandlitz, refusing to acknowledge any reason to change.

The words perestroika and glasnost could not be uttered over the airwaves or printed in the East German press, either in Russian or German, and Soviet publications were banned.

East Berlin continued to flaunt its rigidity. Local elections on May 7 were plainly rigged. After the massacre in Tiananmen Square in Beijing on June 4, Mr. Krenz sent a message to the authorities in China congratulating them on their firmness....

Mr. Honecker [after an operation] was back at work, and his attention was on the celebrations planned for October 7, the fortieth anniversary of the German Democratic Republic. Mr. Gorbachev was to lead a retinue of Communist leaders to East Berlin....

Mr. Gorbachev seemed intent, publicly at least, not to inflame the opposition. But it did not take much. It was enough that he said that East Germany had to decide its own future to signal to many that Soviet troops would not interfere. When he said that those who did not change with the times would see life punishing them, the comment was seen as a direct reference to Mr. Honecker. Wherever he went, the crowds chanted "Gorby! Gorby!" Mieczyslaw Rakowski, the Polish Communist Party leader, sat next to Mr. Gorbachev on the reviewing stand at the October 7 military parade. He later said with some irony that when he heard the chants he remarked to Mr. Gorbachev, "It looks as if they want you to liberate them again."

The Soviet leader was more direct when he met in private with the East German Politburo. An East German diplomat said Mr. Gorbachev did not try to prescribe what the East Germans should do. "He made it very clear that the spectacle of thousands of people running away from the country and of violence being the only way to keep them in was not helping him in his own difficult situation," he said.

According to a wide range of party insiders, Mr. Honecker was incapable of grasping the situation. He reacted with stubborn insistence that he was on the right course and would brook no leniency. He told a Chinese visitor that any attempt to change his course was "nothing more than Don Quixote's futile running against the steadily turning sails of a windmill."

On Saturday night, October 7, as Mr. Gorbachev was leaving for Moscow, tens of thousands of East Berliners moved from the anniversary celebrations to Alexanderplatz, the vast square at the heart of the city. Bearing candles and torches, they began chanting slogans demanding change.

The East German police, armed with riot sticks, chased them out of the square and north into the heavily populated and dilapidated Prenzlauer Berg section, a hotbed of the growing New Forum opposition group. Hundreds were beaten and jailed. The scene was played out again on Sunday night in the same area of East Berlin, as well as in Leipzig and Dresden.

Mr. Krenz, at 52 the youngest member of the Politburo, was hardly a predictable architect of change. He had followed Mr. Honecker's path from the Communist youth league to take charge of security and youth affairs, and his statements had given no sign that he was anything but a hard-liner.

But he was considered sharp, and he was young. And it was he who took the fateful step on October 9 to avert violence in Leipzig.

Back in East Berlin, the Politburo gathered for its regular Tuesday meeting. Nobody knew how Mr. Honecker or his ideological allies would react to the unilateral order by Mr. Krenz barring the Leipzig crackdown.

It was Erich Mielke, the tough 82-year-old security chief, who told Mr. Honecker, "Erich, we can't beat up hundreds of thousands of people."

But the 77-year-old Communist leader would not be swayed. Earlier in the day, three members of the Central Committee had handed Mr. Honecker a report on the unrest among the country's youth and its causes, with a request for a special session of the leadership to deal with it. Mr. Honecker flew into a rage, calling the report "the greatest attack on the party leadership in 40 years."

Now Kurt Hager, the 77-year-old chief ideologist, raised his voice. The young people were right, he said. The mood on the streets was more defiant than he had ever seen it. Gunter Schabowski, the respected party secretary for East Berlin, concurred.

Only two members firmly took Mr. Honecker's side: Gunter Mittag, the 63-year-old Economics Minister, who had dominated East German planning since the era of Walter Ulbricht, the first Communist Party chief, and Joachim Hermann, the 61-year-old secretary for propaganda.

Others wavered or kept silent. With the Politburo deadlocked, the secretaries of East Germany's 15 districts, including Hans Modrow, the party chief for Dresden who had a reputation as a reformer favored by favored by Moscow, were called in for an unusual expanded meeting of the leadership. The meeting went late into the night of October 10 and continued on October 11.

"The district leaders said that the grassroots wouldn't stand for things to continue the way they were," a Central Committee member said.

The leaders began discussing a conciliatory statement to the nation. According to several accounts, Mr. Honecker resisted this too, fuming instead about his betrayal by Hungary.

Over his objection, the statement was issued October 11, declaring that the Politburo was ready "to discuss all basic questions of our society," and acknowledging that those who had fled may have had valid reasons.

From that day, the press suddenly became more open, with panel discussions on major public complaints. The small "parties," traditionally subservient to the Communists, suddenly gained a voice of their own, and Mr. Gerlach, the Liberal Party chairman, even suggested in his party paper that the "leading role" of the party should be reconsidered.

The Politburo met again on October 17. By now it was clear to most of the other seventeen Politburo members that Mr. Honecker no longer understood what was happening. One Communist official said Mr. Honecker had been so infuriated by Mr. Gerlach's statement and considered taking action against him.

This time, several Central Committee members said, only Mr. Mittag and Mr. Hermann still supported Mr. Honecker. Some officials said Mr. Mittag was holding out in the hope of securing the party leadership for himself, after having filled in for the ailing Mr. Honecker through the summer.

An important defector was Mr. Hager. "Without Hager, nothing would have gone through in the Politburo," a party official said.

Finally, Willi Stoph, the 75-year-old Prime Minister, told Mr. Honecker that the time had come for him to resign, a Central Committee member said.

That was the decisive push. On the next day, October 18, Mr. Honecker announced to the Central Committee that he was resigning for reasons of health, and the Politburo moved that Mr. Mittag and Mr. Hermann be ousted. Mr. Krenz was the new party chief, head of state and Defense Council chairman.

The meeting was brief. Mr. Krenz read a speech promising an "earnest political dialogue," and then urged the Central Committee to quickly close its proceedings so he could go on nationwide television.

Mr. Krenz immediately set about trying to establish himself, within the party and outside, as the leader of real change. "We see the seriousness of the situation," he said. "But we also sense and recognize the major opportunity we have opened for ourselves to define policies in dialogue with our citizens."

The pace quickened. Mr. Krenz and other Politburo members met people in factories and in the streets. On October 17, the Government announced that it would restore free travel through Czechoslovakia, for people wanting to go to West Germany. On November 1, Mr. Krenz flew to Moscow to meet Mr. Gorbachev and endorsed a version of perestroika—economic and social restructuring—in East Germany.

Still, demonstrations swelled. Huge crowds marched in Leipzig, East Berlin, Dresden and other major cities, and thousands of East Germans perhaps seeing this as their last chance to flee resumed their efforts to get into the West German Embassy in Prague.

Finally, on November 4, Mr. Krenz announced that East Germans who wanted to settle in West Germany could travel freely through Czechoslovakia. More than 10,000 a day began quickly surging across the border into the West.

That same day, more than a half million East Germans demonstrated for democracy in the largest protest that East Berlin or East Germany had ever seen. The crisis was not over.

Hoping to slow the exodus, the Government hastily drafted a law on travel that said East German citizens would be free to go abroad, but for only 30 days a year and after applying at police offices. The bill was promptly denounced, and in a sign of the rebellious mood, the Legal and Constitutional Committee of the normally docile Parliament dismissed it as unacceptable.

The pace of change gathered speed. On November 7, the entire Council of Ministers resigned and called on Parliament to choose a new government. The Central Committee convened on November 8, and this time the entire Politburo resigned, to be replaced by a smaller group, still headed by Mr. Krenz, with five new members. Among them was Mr. Modrow, the party leader from Dresden, who would soon become the next Prime Minister.

Thousands of Communist Party members demonstrated outside, demanding a party congress to install an entirely new leadership.

On November 9, a Thursday, the Central Committee continued to sweep the ranks of the leadership. Four new members of the top leadership were swept out after their regional party organizations had rejected them.

Mr. Mittag came under intense criticism and was expelled from the Central Committee for "the most egregious violations of internal party democracy and of party and state discipline, as well as damaging the reputation of the party."

In the evening, Gunter Schabowski came to brief reporters. Toward the end of the session, he announced that a new travel law had been drafted, giving East Germans the right to leave the country through any border crossings. The Berlin wall, already circumvented, was beginning to crumble.

The measures had been drafted by the Politburo, officials later said. It was still fresh, and the details were not immediately clear, although it later became evident that citizens did have to obtain exit visas from local police stations before going across. But when Mr. Schabowski was asked directly if East Germans could freely go West, his answer was yes.

Soon after, a young East German couple went to the Invalident strasse crossing to test the announcement. To their amazement, the guards, who had hear Mr. Schabowski and had no instructions, let them cross. After 28 years, 2 months, 27 days and, the deaths of 80 killed trying to cross it, the wall was open. The astonishing event was reported on West German television, and within an hour tens of thousands were streaming into West Berlin for one of the most extraordinary reunions ever held. Over the weekend two million visited the West, bought chocolates and for the most part, returned home to East Germany. Only a few thousand remained.

Not even the Soviet Government, one of the four World War II Allied powers who hold occupation rights in Berlin, was told of what the East Germans were doing, an East German Government official said....

From *The Collapse of Communism*, edited by Bernard Gwertzman and Michael T. Kaufman, NY: Times Books, 1990, 216–222.

Document 137:
SOCIAL REFORMS IN RUSSIA: A PLEA TO PASS THE FREEDOM SUPPORT ACT (1992)
Boris N. Yeltsin

In 1992, Boris Yeltsin addressed a joint session of the United States Congress. In his speech, Yeltsin described the attempted coup that had only recently taken place in Russia and emphasized that a democratized Russia would make the world a much safer place. The primary goal of Yeltsin's address was to secure financial assistance from the United States.

Please don't count the applause against the time that I have been alloted for speaking. Mr. Speaker, Mr. President, Members of Congress, ladies and gentlemen, it is indeed a great honor for me to address the Congress of the great land of freedom as the first ever, in over 1,000 years of history of Russia, popularly elected President, as a citizen of a great country, which has made its choice in favor of liberty and democracy.

For many years our two nations were the two poles, the two opposites. They wanted to make us implacable enemies. That affected the destinies of the world in a most tragic way.

The world was shaken by the storms of confrontation. It was close to exploding, close to perishing beyond salvation.

That evil scenario is becoming a thing of the past. Reason begins to triumph over madness. We have left behind the period when America and Russia looked at each other through gunsights, ready to pull the trigger at any time.

Despite what we saw in the well-known American film, "The Day After," it can be said today, tomorrow will be a day of peace, a day less of fear, and more of hope for the happines of our children.

The world can sigh in relief. The idol of communism, which spread everywhere social strife, animosity, and unparalleled brutality which instilled fear in humanity, has collapsed, never to rise again.

I am here to assure you, we shall not let it rise again in our land.

I am proud that the people of Russia have found strength to shake off the crushing burden of the totalitarian system. I am proud that I am addressing you on behalf of the great people whose dignity is restored. I admire ordinary Russian people whose dignity is restored. I admire ordinary Russian men and women, who, in spite of severe trials, have preserved their intellectual integrity and are enduring tremendous hardships for the sake of the revival of their country.

Russia has made its final choice in favor of a civilized way of life, common sense, and universal human heritage. I am convinced that our people will reach that goal.

There is no people on this Earth who could be harmed by the air of freedom. There are no exceptions to that rule.

Liberty sets the mind free, fosters independence, and unorthodox thinking and ideas. But it does not offer instant prosperity or happiness and wealth to everyone.

This is something that politicians in particular must keep in mind. Even the most benevolent intentions will inevitably be abandoned and committed to oblivion if they are not translated into everyday efforts. Our experience of the recent years has conclusively borne that out.

Liberty will not be fooled. There can be no coexistence between democracy and a totalitarian state system. There can be no coexistence between market economy and power to control everything and everyone. There can be no coexistence between a civic society which is pluralist by definition and Communist intolerance to dissent.

The experience of the past decades has taught us, communism has no human face. Freedom and communism are incompatible.

You will recall August 1991, when for 3 days, Russia was under the dark cloud of dictatorship. I addressed the Muscovites who were defending the White House of Russia. I addressed all the people of Russia. I addressed them standing on top of the tank, whose crew had disobeyed criminal orders.

I will be candid with you—at that moment I feared, but I had no fear for myself. I feared for the future of democracy in Russia and throughout the world, because I was aware what could happen if we failed to win.

Citizens of Russia upheld their freedom and did not allow the continuation of the 75 years of nightmare.

From this high rostrum, I want to express our sincere thanks and gratitude to President Bush and to the American people for their invaluable moral support for the just cause of the people of Russia.

Last year citizens of Russia passed another difficult test of maturity. We chose to forgo vengeance and the intoxicating craving for summary justice over the fallen colossus known under the name of the CPSU.

There was no replay of history. The Communist Party Citadel next to the Kremlin, the "Communist Bastille," was not destroyed. There was not a hint of violence against Communists in Russia. People simply brushed off the venomous dust of the past and went about their business. There were no lynch law trials in Russia. The doings of the Communist Party over many years have been referred to the Constitutional Court of the Russian Federation. I am confident that its verdict will be fair.

Russia has seen for itself that any delay in strengthening the foundations of freedom and democracy can throw the society far back. For us, the ominous lesson of the past is relevant today as never before. it was precisely in a devastated country with an economy in near paralysis that bolshevism succeeded in building a totalitarian regime, creating a gigantic war machine and an insatiable military-industrial complex.

This must not be allowed to happen again. That is why economic and political reforms are the primary task for Russia today.

We are facing the challenges that no one has ever faced before at any one time. We must carry through unprecedented reforms in the economy that over the last seven decades has been stripped of all market infrastructure; lay the foundations for democracy and restore the rule of law in a country that for scores of years was poisoned with social strife and political oppression; and guarantee domestic social, and political stability, as well as maintenance of civil peace.

We have no right to fail in this most difficult endeavor, for there will be no second try, as in sports. Our predecessors have used them all up. The reforms must succeed.

I am given strength by the support of the majority of the citizens of Russia. The people of Russia are aware that there is no alternative to reform, and that this is very important.

My job, as everybody else's in Russia, is not an easy one, but in everything I do I have the reliable and invaluable support of my wife and of my entire large family.

Today I am telling you what I tell you my fellow countrymen: I will not go back on the reforms, and it is practically impossible to topple Yeltsin in Russia. I am in good health and I will not say "Uncle" before I make the reforms irreversible.

We realize our great responsibility for the success of our changes, not only toward the people of Russia, but also toward the citizens of America and of the entire world. Today the freedom of America is being upheld in Russia.

Should the reforms fail, it will cost hundreds of billions to offset that failure.

Yesterday we concluded an unprecedented agreement on cutting down strategic offensive arsenals. They will be reduced radically in two phases. Not by 30 or 40 percent as negotiated previously over 15 years. They will be slashed to less than one-third of today's strength, from 21,000 nuclear warheads on both sides down to 6,000 or 7,000 by the year 2000. And it has taken us only 5 months to negotiate. And I fervently hope that George Bush and myself will be there in the year 2000 to preside over that.

We have simply no right to miss this unique opportunity. All the more so that nuclear arms and the future of the Russian reforms are designed to make impossible any restoration of the totalitarian dictatorship in Russia are dramatically interrelated. I am here to say that we have the firm determination and the political will to move forward. We have proved that by what we have done. It is Russia that has put an end to the imperial policies and was the first to recognize the independence of the Baltic Republics

Russia is a founding member of the Commonwealth of Independent States which has averted uncontrolled disintegration of the former empire and the threat of a general interethnic blood bath.

Russia has granted tangible powers to its autonomous republics. Their Treaty of Federation has been signed and our Nation has escaped the fate of the Soviet Union. Russia has preserved its unity.

It was Russia that has substantially slowed down the flywheel of militarization and is doing all it can to stop it altogether.

I am formally announcing that without waiting for the treaty to be signed, we have begun taking off alert the heavy SS-18 missiles targeted on the United States of America, and the Defense Minister of Russia is here in this room to confirm that.

Russia has brought its policies toward a number of countries in line with its solemn declarations of the recent years. We have stopped arms deliveries to Afghanistan, where the senseless military adventure has taken thousands of Russian and hundreds of thousands of Afghan lives. With external props removed, the puppet regime collapsed.

We have corrected the well-known imbalances in relations with Cuba. At present that country is one of our Latin American partners. Our commerce with Cuba is based on universally accepted principles and world prices.

It is Russia that once and for all has done away with double standards in foreign policy. We are firmly resolved not to lie any more, either to our negotiating partners, or to the Russian, or American, or any other people. There will be no more lies, ever.

The same applies to biological weapon experiments and the facts that have been revealed about American prisoners of war, the KAL-007 flight, and many other things. That list could be continued.

The archives of the KGB and the Communist Party Central Committee are being opened. Moreover, we are inviting the cooperation of the United States and other nations to investigate these dark pages.

I promise you that each and every document in each and every archive will be examined in order to investigate the fate of every American unaccounted for. As President of Russia, I assure you that even if one American has been detained in my country and can still be found, I will find him. I will get him back to his family.

I thank you for the applause. I see everybody rise. Some of you who have just risen here to applaud me have also written in the press that until Yeltsin gets things done and gets all of the job done, there should be no Freedom Support Act passing through the Congress.

Well, I don't really quite understand you, ladies and gentlemen. This matter has been investigated and is being investigated. Yeltsin has already opened the archives and is inviting you to join us in investigating the fate of each and every unaccounted for American.

So now you are telling me, first do the job, and then we shall support you in passing that act. I don't quite understand you.

We have made tangible moves to make contacts between Russian and foreign business communities much easier. Under recent legislation, foreign nations who privatize a facility or a building in Russia are given property rights to the plot of land on which they are located.

Legislation on bankruptcy has been recently enacted.

Mandatory sale of foreign currency to the state at an artificially low rate of exchange has been ended. We are ready to bring our legal practice as much as possible in line with world standards, of course on the basis of symmetry with each country.

We are inviting the private sector of the United States to invest in the unique and untapped Russian market. And I am saying, do not be late.

Now that the period of global confrontation is behind us, I call upon you to take a fresh look at the current policy of the United States toward Russia and also to take a fresh look at the longer term prospects of our relations. Russia is a different country today. Sometimes the obsolete standards brought into being by a different era are artificially imposed on new realities. True, that equally applies to us. Let us together, therefore, master the art of reconciling our differences on the basis of partnership, which is the most efficient and democratic way. This would come naturally both for the Russians and the Americans.

If this is done, many of the problems which are now impeding mutually advantageous cooperation between Russia and the United States will become irrelevant. And I mean legislative frameworks, too.

It will not be a wasteful endeavor; on the contrary, it will promote a more efficient solution of your problems, as well as of ours, and, of course, it will create new jobs in Russia, as well as in the United States.

History is giving us a chance to fulfill President Wilson's dream; namely, to make the world safe for democracy.

More than 30 years ago, President Kennedy addressed these words to humanity:

"My fellow citizens of the world, ask not what American can do for you, but what together we can do for the freedom of man."

I believe that his inspired call for working together toward a democratic world is addressed above all to our two peoples, to the people of America and to the people of Russia.

Partnership and friendship of our two largest democracies in strengthening democracy is indeed a great goal.

Joining the world community, we wish to preserve our identity, our own image and history, promote culture, and strengthen moral standards of our people.

We find relevant the warning of the great Russian philosopher Berdyaev, who said, "To negate Russia in the name of humankind is to rob humankind."

At the same time, Russia does not aspire to change the world in its own image. It is the fundamental principle of the new Russia to be generous and to share experience, moral values, and emotional warmth, rather than to impose and coerce.

It is the tradition of the Russian people to repay kindness with kindness. This is the bedrock of the Russian lifestyle, the underlying truths revealed by the great Russian culture.

Free and democratic Russia will remain committed to this tenet.

Today free and democratic Russia is extending its hand of friendship to the people of America. Acting on the will of the people of Russia, I am inviting you, and through you the people of the United States, to join us in partnership in the quest for freedom and justice in the 21st century.

The Russian-American dialog has gone through many a dramatic moment, but the peoples of Russia and America have never gone to war against each other. Even in the darkest period, our affinity prevailed over our hatred.

In this context I would like to recall something that took place 50 years ago. The unprecedented world war was raging. Russia, which was bleeding white, and all our people were looking forward to the opening of the second front. And it was opened, first and foremost thanks to the active stand taken by President Roosevelt and by the entire American people.

Sometimes I think that if today, like during that war, a second, but peaceful front, could be opened to promote democratic market reforms, their success would be guaranteed earlier.

The passing by Congress of the Freedom Support Act could become the first step in that direction. Today, legislation promoting reforms is much more important than appropriations of funds. May I express the hope that the United States Congress, as the staunch advocate of freedom, will remain faithful to its strategic cause on this occasion as well.

Members of Congress, every man is a man of his own time. No exception is ever made for anyone, whether an ordinary citizen or the President. Much experience has been gained, many things have been reassessed.

I would like now to conclude my statement with the words from a song by Irving Berlin, an American of Russian descent:

"God bless America,"
to which I will add, "and Russia."

From *Vital Speeches of the Day*, Volume LVII, No. 23, 709–711.

Document 138:
HAITI: HUMAN RIGHTS VIOLATIONS IN THE MONTH OF FEBRUARY (1992)

The democratically elected president of Haiti, Aristide, was ousted by a dictatorship which has brutalized Haitians in the past years. United States' policy has vacillated, due to the fear of many many Americans that Haitian refugees will enter the United States competing for scarce jobs and services. Race and public attitudes toward AIDS has fueled opposition to granting asylum to Haitians. The Lawyers' Committee for Human Rights, a private American group of attorneys, has taken issue with American policy and outlined their case in this document of massive abuses of human rights that should compel the U.S. to open its borders to Haitian victims.

During the month of February the Platform received reports from all over the country describing the return of the feared rural police known as "section chiefs." While the Haitian armed forces may have only 7,000 men in uniform, the number of people actually serving in the security forces is much higher. The section chiefs have returned after having been dismissed by President Aristide. These officers are part of the Haitian army and report directly to their district military commanders. Haiti has 535 rural sections each ruled by a section chief. Many section chiefs hire numerous "assistants;" the Lawyers Committee has received reliable reports of section chiefs with 50 or even 100 assistants. Section chiefs and their private armies control every aspect of their subjects' lives: they arrest, imprison, try, torture and in some cases kill.

The Platform's report for February describes this total domination by the military and its allies, noting that:

"an 'institutionalization' of the repression has occurred, in particular in the rural areas. We have regularly received from numerous rural zones reports of human rights violations committed by section chiefs (arbitrary arrests, beatings, extortion and robbery). In certain cases section chiefs who had been fired by Aristide are responsible.... It is impossible to report all the facts which we have received but these confirm the existence of an extremely tense climate throughout the countryside."

The February report details the extortion and fear imposed by the section chiefs and their deputies: a favorite tactic is to accuse someone of being an Aristide supporter and then demanding money from the accused to avoid an arrest or a beating. The report also notes that the military's control over each section of the country via the section chiefs plays a crucial role in inhibiting any kind of support for Aristide.

The areas of the country suffering the most intense repression, according to the report are the Artibonite Valley, the Central Plateau region and the Northwest...

—on February 10, Ilès Bastien was arrested in the village of Darbonne near Léogane. The section chief beat him 100 times with his baton and Bastien had to be hospitalized. When questioned, the section chief said he had hit Bastien only 25 times;...

—Section chief Jean Marie Voltaire burned down 121 houses in Borgne after local residents refused to pay an illegal tax he tried to impose after resuming his post at the end of January. 57 soldiers and 157 armed "assistants" participated in this attack;

—two foreign journalists, Alan Tomlinson of the BBC and NPR and Nathaniel Sheppard of the *Chicago Tribune*, were arrested on February 13 by section chief Yvon Dieudonné in Sainvil after they had investigated the wholesale burning of houses in Borgne. Section chief Jean Voltaire soon appeared and claimed that he should have custody of the two journalists since they had been in his jurisdiction. After several hours of discussion, Voltaire and Dieudonné agreed to kill the journalists, but not before severely beating their Haitian interpreters....

From a summary in English of the report of human rights violations in February 1992 by a group of human rights organizations in Haiti provided by The Lawyers Committee for Human Rights, Michael H. Posner, Executive Director.

Document 139:
A WOUND TO THE SOUL (1993)
Amnesty International

"Ethnic cleansing" is a new term in Europe which describes the attempt to be rid of an ethnic or religious or linguistic group in an area another groups attempts to dominate. There have been many historical incidents of peoples being driven from their homes, including the Jews from medieval England and Spain, Protestants or Catholics in the Reformation era, Armenians in the old Ottoman Turkish Empire, and Volga Germans in the Soviet Union. Today, Croats, Bosnian Muslims, and Serbs have taken tens of thousands of lives in "ethnic cleansing" operations in the former Yugoslavia. Similar mixtures of people are at war with each other in the successor states to the former U.S.S.R. This represents an enormous human rights problem in many other parts of the world.

In 1991 the town of Bosanski Petrovac, in the northwest corner of Bosnia-Herzogovina, had approximately 15,000 citizens. The majority of the population was Serbian, about 20 percent was listed in the official census as Muslim with a smattering of Croats and other nationalities. By September 1992 most of the Muslims had left the town, either by force or on their own following months of intimidation.

One man (we will identify only as AH for his own protection) kept a diary of events in this small town from April 1992, shortly after Bosnia Herzegovina's independence was recognized internationally, until September 1992. His diary provides a graphic and disturbing portrait of what happens to neighbors in a small town when hatred comes to dwell among them.

A DIARY OF DESPAIR

In May the town's Muslims begin losing their jobs. Later in the month roadblocks are set up around town and—while initially most people are allowed to pass freely—soon Muslims are being prevented from leaving town, especially young men of military age. By June it becomes difficult for Muslims to buy food and other items from Serbian-run stores.

Early July. Two Muslim Mosques in town are destroyed with explosives. The first Muslim houses are set on fire. Unofficially ethnic cleansing has begun.

(*July 7: the diary of AH concludes with these words*) "A Wound to the Soul."

In the next weeks civilian Muslim men of military age are required by Serbian authorities to do forced labor.

(*July 15: from the diary of AH*) "Great fear reigns among Muslims, anxiety about what will happen. Terror, fear."

On August 8, four members of a Muslim family are murdered in their own homes. By mid-September, 14 Muslims have been killed in a series of separate incidents. But this is only the beginning.

September 20. A four day onslaught begins against the town's Muslims. In the next four days, 30 Muslims are deliberately killed and others injured in Bosanski Petrovac. It is unclear what unleashed the Serbian anger, although many attribute the killings to military reverses at the fron where 17 Serbian soldiers have been killed in action.

Eyewitnesses report seeing a white Volkswagen full of soldiers driving around the town indiscriminately shooting with automatic weapons.

(*September 21: from the diary of AH*) "The coming night is uncertain. One awaits with fear and trepidation. The Muslims are utterly terrified, conscious that they are surrounded and left to the mercy of those whom no one can pacify. The time is ideal for murder, plunder, rape. How much hatred is among these nations who were only recently neighbors and friends."

On the morning of September 24 a police car equipped with a loud speaker drives through town calling on Muslims to gather at a local hotel so they can leave Bosanski Petrovac. A convoy of 12 buses and eight trucks is organized by the Serbian authorities. The municipal leaders reportedly refuse to allow Muslims to leave unless they sign documents transferring their property to the authorities or to individual Serbs.

(*September 24: from the diary of AH*) "The day starts calmer with the announcement of the departure of the Muslims. People are exhilarated and happy to escape this hell; the day and night pass relatively peacefully...

Despite assurances of safe passage out of Serbian controlled territory and the presence of Serbian bus and truck drivers, the convoy is fired on shortly after leaving Bosanski Petrovac. Three Muslims die and nine are injured—the youngest survivor a six-year-old girl who had been shot in the back. At nightfall the battered convoy finally reaches the front lines at a place called Smet on Vlasic Mountain. The buses and trucks are unloaded and the passengers, including those injured in the shooting, are forced to walk at night through Serbian lines and down a steep road towards the Muslim-Croat positions and the town of Travnik.

(*September 25: from the diary of AH*) "Thousands of Muslims leave their houses, abandoning their age-old hearth, fleeing from terror and fear. The river of men, women, children, elderly people, eyes brimming with tears, paralyzed by fear, started off into the unknown towards Travnik."

Except for a few remaining people too old to travel or some women married to Serbian men, the town of Bosanski Petrovac is now "cleansed" of Muslim influences. The Mosques are in ruins, Muslim property either destroyed or distributed to their former neighbors.

From *Amnesty Action*, published by Amnesty International USA, Spring 1993, 3.

Document 140:
WOMEN UNDER THE GUN (1993)
Amnesty International

It is one of the oldest and most common forms of degradation visited upon women when armed men are given license to enforce their will at gunpoint. And in the ruptured republics that once comprised Yugoslavia, the rule of law has long been supplanted by the rule of guns.

Whatever ethnic, religious or political differences may divide them, all women share a common fear in Bosnia-Herzegovina today. Rape.

In November an Amnesty International fact-finding mission returned from the Balkans with confirmation that rape has become an all too common feature of the ugly civil conflict raging there—with all sides engaging in the practice.

"Sexual abuse has been widespread and sometimes systematic," says Amnesty. "It seems to fit into the pattern of ethnic repression which has tragically characterized this war. In fact, women have sometimes been taken captive by soldiers specifically to be raped."...

"While forces from all sides in the conflict have raped women, and women from all backgrounds have become victims, Muslim women, in particular, have been the chief victims at the hands of Serbian armed factions," says Amnesty.

Amnesty International believes that the rape and sexual abuse of women by Serbian forces throughout Bosnia Herzegovina has been carried out in an organized and systematic way, with the deliberate detention of women for sexual assault part of a wider pattern of terrorism and intimidation against the Muslim and Croat communities. The intimidation is apparently intended to force Muslims to flee or to leave compliantly when evicted from their homes.

"Whether rape has been explicitly singled out by political and military leaders as a weapon against their opponents remains open to question," says Amnesty. "What is clear is that so far effective measures have rarely, if ever, been taken against such abuses and that, in practice, local political and military officers must have had knowledge of and generally condoned it."

While many women have been randomly raped by soldiers simply passing through town, others have been picked up and taken to detention centers and hotels (now used as military brothels) where they have been repeatedly raped by soldiers.

In one case, a 17-year-old Muslim girl told a doctor that Serbian soldiers took her and other women from her village to some huts in the woods nearby. She said that they held her there for three months along with 23 other women. She was among 12 women who were repeatedly raped in front of the other women. When the other women tried to intervene, she said they were beaten by the soldiers.

Stories like hers are now beginning to be substantiated by Serbian soldiers who have themselves taken part in the abuse. A 21-year-old Bosnian Serb soldier, captured by Bosnian Government forces in 1992, confessed to and said he witnessed a number of gross human rights abuses.

The young soldier told a correspondent of the *New York Times* in November that he had personally been involved in the rape and murder of eight women in or around a small motel in Vogosca, north of Sarajevo. The soldier said a military commander controlling the premises had, in fact, encouraged the soldiers to "take the women" and not return them.

But, it is not only Muslim women who are being targetted. A 28-year-old Serbian nurse from Brcko told a Belgrade newspaper that she had been detained, raped and beaten by Croatian forces in Slavonski Brod. The woman said she was returning from a visit to Germany when she was stopped by Croat police near Sisak in Croatia in January 1992. She was ordered off the bus with three other women, all of Serbian nationality.

The nurse reported she was taken to a detention camp in an oil refinery at Slavonski Brod on the border with Bosnia-Herzegovina. She said she was repeatedly raped as were the other women held there. She was pregnant by the time she was transferred to another detention center in a school in Odzak. The woman ultimately bought her way out of captivity with foreign currency she had hidden in her clothing....

From *Amnesty Action*, published by Amnesty International USA, Spring 1993, 1.

Document 141:
ETHNIC CLEANSING (1992)
Russel Watson with Margaret Garrard Warner and Douglas Waller, Rod Nordland and Karen Breslau

After the collapse of communism and a loss of central control in many former East Bloc nations, ancient ethnic tensions have again surfaced. In a number of countries, particularly Yugoslavia, these ethnic rivalries have become open warfare.

The following article describes some of evergrowing episodes of atrocities committed in the Serbian-Bosnian war.

Most of the horror stories were impossible to confirm and came from hurt, frightened people. In the north Bosnian town of Trnopolje, it was said, Serbian irregulars rounded up 100 prisoners for a move from one detention camp to another. Along the way, they pulled about 30 men out of the column and shot them. At a makeshift camp in Prijedor, the family of one starving prisoner tried to bring him a food parcel. The guards took the food and beat the prisoner in front of his relatives. In Doboj, the Serbian irregulars sprayed insecticide on loaves of bread and fed them to Muslim boys, who became violently ill. Near Tuzla in eastern Bosnia, a distraught eyewitness saw three Muslim girls who were stripped to the waist and chained to a fence "for all to use." After three days of rape, the witness said, they were doused with gasoline and set on fire. Doctors reported that other Muslim and Croatian girls had been held for months as sex slaves, and when they became visibly pregnant, they were set free to "have Serbian babies."

The atrocities apparently started last spring, when Serbian forces began the "ethnic cleansing" of newly independent Bosnia and Herzegovina. The Serbs drove more than 1 million Muslims and Croats from their homes, torturing and killing some of them, abusing and terrorizing the rest. Some Muslims and Croats struck back with atrocities of their own. Now the grim results are finally showing up on television screens and the front pages of newspapers. Pictures sear the conscience of the world: a wailing baby beside a bullet-punctured window, the emaciated bodies of prisoners in the camps, an old woman shot down at her grandchild's funeral. The struggle in what used to be Yugoslavia turns out to be not just a civil war but a ruthless campaign by members of one ethnic group to "purify" the land by driving out others. Suddenly the response of the outside world so far—a lot of hand-wringing and a few relief supplies for one besieged city, Sarajevo—looks pathetically inadequate....

It's been going on for a long time. The Balkans are scarred by the fault lines of history. Orthodox Christian Serbs face off against Roman Catholic Croats on roughly the same terrain where the Turkish invasion of Europe reached its highwater mark, leaving behind a residue of Islamic Slavs. Religion and nationality make the Balkans more a flash point than a melting pot. The unstable region provided the spark that set off World War I and produced some of the worst atrocities of World War II when Croats backed the Nazis and Serbs became communist guerrillas. Today, after a long truce imposed by dictatorship, ambitious politicians still play on ethnic hatreds.

The present crisis was aggravated by miscalculations in Washington and Europe. Lawrence Eagleburger, the deputy secretary of state, admits that he misread Slobodan Milosevic, the thuggish leader of the Serbian Republic, the biggest remaining component of Yugoslavia. "I knew him when he was a banker," says Eagleburger, who served as the U.S. ambassador to Belgrade from 1977 to 1981. "I though him fairly sensible for a Marxist economist...Where I misjudged him in those early days was in not realizing that on the political side, he was clearly a Serbian nationalists of the worst sort." Although Washington tried last year to keep Yugoslavia from breaking up precipitously, Eagleburger says that by early 1990 he recognized that the country was heading for a tragedy in which Milosevic would play a major role. "I have said for two years that this man was intent on building a Greater Serbia," says Eagleburger. "But the question then and now is, how do you stop him? I didn't then, and I still don't, see how you do that."

The Europeans had no answers, either. Some of them took sides. "For their own reasons, the Germans have a good deal of sympathy for the Croats, and the French and Russians feel some sympathy for the Serbs," says an official at the British Foreign Office. "Our own view," he adds, "is that while the Serbs have been the greatest destabilizing force, none of the parties has clean hands." When Slovenia and Croatia became the first republics to declare their independence last year, the Germans pressed for nearly diplomatic recognition of the new countries, hastening Yugoslavia's descent into chaos. Last winter, Bosnia's Muslim and Croatian majority voted to secede from Serbian-dominated Yugoslavia. When Bosnian Serbs began their "ethnic cleansing" campaign, backed by Milosevic's regime, the French at first resisted sanctions against Serbia, until Baker shamed them into it....

Many Europeans think it may be impossible for all of the displaced Muslims, Croats and Serbs to return to their homes in Bosnia. The only permanent solution, they say, is to carve the republic into ethnic cantons. *The Economist* recently called for "the least inequitable redrawing of boundaries that is compatible with resettling the maximum number of refugees." But partition would reward aggression and validate "ethnic cleansing" by allowing the Serbs to retain control over much of the territory they have seized in recent months. It would leave many Muslims permanently dispossessed, making them the Palestinians of the Balkans. U.S. officials expect a confrontation with the Europeans on this issue. "For the civilized Western world to accept the principle of cantonization at this stage," says a senior American, "is to ask it to happen everywhere else in the former East bloc where one country decides it wants a hunk of its neighbor's territory."

For now, Washington will concentrate more on diplomacy than on military action. "The closest thing we have to a game plan is to try to get the shooting stopped then work on a political solution," says the senior offical. The process will continue this week in various U.N. forums and later this month at an international conference in London. If the outside world cannot figure out some way to stop the fighting, clean up the detention camps and feed the starving, the struggle in Bosnia could inspire other ethnic struggles—elsewhere in Yugoslavia, in divided East European nations and in the former Soviet Union, where dozens of resentful nationalities are jostling for position. Once again, the volatile Balkans could provide the spark for conflicts engulfing millions of Europeans.

From *Newsweek*, August 17, 1992, 16–20.